THE
FIERY TRIAL

◼

Other Books by Eric Foner

Free Soil, Free Labor, Free Men: The Ideology of the Republican Party before the Civil War (1970)

America's Black Past: A Reader in Afro-American History (editor, 1970)

Nat Turner (editor, 1971)

Tom Paine and Revolutionary America (1976)

Politics and Ideology in the Age of the Civil War (1980)

Nothing but Freedom: Emancipation and Its Legacy (1983)

Reconstruction: America's Unfinished Revolution, 1863–1877 (1988)

A Short History of Reconstruction (1990)

A House Divided: America in the Age of Lincoln
(with Olivia Mahoney, 1990)

The New American History (editor, 1990; rev. ed. 1997)

The Reader's Companion to American History (editor, with
John A. Garraty, 1991)

*Freedom's Lawmakers: A Directory of Black Officeholders during
Reconstruction* (editor, 1993; rev. ed. 1996)

Thomas Paine: Collected Writings (editor, 1995)

America's Reconstruction: People and Politics after the Civil War
(with Olivia Mahoney, 1995)

The Story of American Freedom (1998)

Who Owns History? Rethinking the Past in a Changing World (2002)

Give Me Liberty! An American History (2004; rev. eds. 2007, 2010)

Voices of Freedom: A Documentary History (editor, 2004;
rev. eds. 2007, 2010)

Forever Free: The Story of Emancipation and Reconstruction (2005)

Herbert Aptheker on Race and Democracy: A Reader
(editor, with Manning Marable, 2006)

Our Lincoln: New Perspectives on Lincoln and His World
(editor, 2008)

THE FIERY TRIAL

■ ■ ■

*Abraham Lincoln
and American Slavery*

■ ■ ■

Eric Foner

W · W · Norton & Company   New York   London

For information about permission to reproduce selections from this book,
write to Permissions, W. W. Norton & Company, Inc.,
500 Fifth Avenue, New York, NY 10110

For information about special discounts for bulk purchases, please contact
W. W. Norton Special Sales at specialsales@wwnorton.com or 800-233-4830

Manufacturing by RR Donnelley Harrisonburg
Book design by Margaret M. Wagner
Production manager: Julia Druskin

Library of Congress Cataloging-in-Publication Data

Foner, Eric.
The fiery trial : Abraham Lincoln and American slavery / Eric Foner. — 1st ed.
p. cm.
Includes bibliographical references and index.
ISBN 978-0-393-06618-0 (hardcover)
1. Lincoln, Abraham, 1809–1865—Views on slavery.
2. Slaves—Emancipation—United States. I. Title.
E457.2.F66 2010
973.7092—dc22

2010023425

W. W. Norton & Company, Inc.
500 Fifth Avenue, New York, N.Y. 10110
www.wwnorton.com

W. W. Norton & Company Ltd.
Castle House, 75/76 Wells Street, London W1T 3QT

2 3 4 5 6 7 8 9 0

To Henry Foner

Contents

■

List of Maps and Illustrations

◼

Fellow-citizens, we cannot escape history. We of this Congress and this administration, will be remembered in spite of ourselves. . . . The fiery trial through which we pass, will light us down, in honor or dishonor, to the latest generation.

ABRAHAM LINCOLN, *December 1, 1862*

Preface

∎

Ever since his death a century and a half ago, Abraham Lincoln has provided a lens through which we Americans examine ourselves. As an icon embodying the society's core values and myths—self-made man, frontier hero, liberator of the slaves—he exerts a unique hold on our historical imagination. Lincoln has been described as a consummate moralist and a shrewd political operator, a lifelong foe of slavery and an inveterate racist. Politicians from conservatives to communists, civil rights activists to segregationists, and members of almost every Protestant denomination as well as nonbelievers, have claimed him as their own. As early as 1870, the *Memorial Lincoln Bibliography* listing books, eulogies, sermons, and ephemera ran to 175 pages.[1] Today the Lincoln literature comprises many thousands of works. In the last decade, his psychology, marriage, law career, political practices, literary style, racial attitudes, and every one of his major speeches have been subjected to minute examination. There are even books about the myths and hoaxes surrounding Lincoln.

In a way we have found it too easy to understand Lincoln. We think we know him, because in looking at Lincoln we are really discovering ourselves. Hence, he seems perennially relevant; he is always our contemporary. And, of course, issues of Lincoln's era such as the enduring legacy of slavery, the nature of presidential leadership, the relationship between morality and politics, and the definition of American nationality and citizenship remain as urgent today as when he lived. In his own time, however, people found Lincoln in many ways enigmatic. A self-controlled, intensely private man, he seldom disclosed his innermost thoughts, even to close friends. David Davis, who knew Lincoln well, described him as "the most reticent, secretive man I ever saw or expect to see." Lincoln could be gregarious and outgoing, but he did not reveal himself to others. "No man can tell by any conversation with the president (and he is very free in *talk*) whether he means what he says, or designs only to extract ideas," wrote one government employee who spoke with Lincoln frequently during the Civil War.[2]

Lincoln jotted down notes and private musings on public issues, but he kept no diary and wrote few personal letters. Records of the law cases in which Lincoln participated have recently become available in digital form, but *The Collected Works of Abraham Lincoln* runs to a mere eight volumes plus two thin supplements and consists mostly of speeches and wartime directives. By contrast, the *Papers of Thomas Jefferson* consists of forty volumes to date and has only reached the first year of Jefferson's presidency. To fill in the gaps in the historical record, many writers rely on recollections of Lincoln's words related long after they were spoken and often of dubious reliability. Once Lincoln died, of course, such memories were filtered through his apotheosis as the Great Emancipator. For this reason, I have preferred in the chapters that follow to cite Lincoln's words as recalled by others only if they were recorded at the time they were spoken. Later recollections are clearly identified as such.[3]

In some ways, the private Lincoln will forever remain elusive; to plumb his thoughts we must rely on his actions and his public letters and addresses. Fortunately, Lincoln not only had a command of the English language matched, among presidents, only by Jefferson but also was a deliberate and meticulous writer who chose his words with extreme care.[4] Like any politician, he said things for strategic reasons. Moreover, his views changed over time. Yet at each point in his career his public statements revealed a consistency that allows us to take him at his word.

This book traces the evolution of Lincoln's ideas and policies about slavery from his early life through his career in the Illinois legislature in the 1830s, his term in Congress in the 1840s, his emergence as a leader of the new Republican party in the 1850s, and his presidency during the Civil War. It is intended to be both less and more than another biography. The chronology of Lincoln's life has been traced in numerous works from the brief to the multivolume, and there is no need to tell the story again. (Those who wish to consult a chronology focusing on Lincoln, slavery, and emancipation will find one at the end of this book.) Many aspects of his career, including his marriage and law practice and the military course of the Civil War over which he presided, do not appear here except to the extent that they illuminate his relationship with slavery. But what follows is also more than a biography because my aim is to situate Lincoln within what Charles Sumner, the most outspoken foe of slavery in the U.S. Senate, called the "antislavery enterprise." This social and political movement encompassed a wide variety of outlooks and practices. At one extreme, it included abolitionists who worked outside the party system and advocated an immediate end to slavery and the incorporation of the freed slaves as equal members of society. It also included those who adhered to what Sumner called "strictly constitutional endeavors,"[5] including steps to prevent the westward expansion of slavery and, in some cases, plans for gradual emancipation with monetary compensation to slaveowners and the "colonization" of the freedpeople outside the United States. At various times, Lincoln occupied different places on this spectrum.

Too much recent work on Lincoln is self-referential; it explains his ideas and actions primarily in terms of his own character, psychology, legal training, or a political philosophy that remained constant throughout his life. My intent is to return Lincoln to his historical setting, tracing the evolution of his ideas in the context of the broad antislavery impulse and the unprecedented crisis the United States confronted during his adult life. Of course, the events and decisions discussed in this book appear in numerous biographies of Lincoln and histories of the Civil War. But I believe that casting a bright, concentrated light on Lincoln and the politics of slavery—with politics defined in the broadest sense, not simply as elections and office-holding but the shaping of opinion within the extended public sphere—can illuminate his life and his era in new ways. Given the size of the Lincoln literature, differences of interpretation exist on almost every issue discussed in this book. However, I have generally chosen to tell the story as I see it without engaging in debates with other historians, which would result in a much longer, and extremely tedious, narrative.

Like other presidents, Lincoln had to reach accommodations with a Congress whose members believed they had a role to play in shaping public policy. As a shrewd and experienced party leader both before and during his presidency, he had to be sensitive to all strands of political opinion. I am particularly interested, however, in Lincoln's complex relationship with abolitionists, who strove to awaken the nation to the moral imperative of confronting the problem of slavery, and Radical Republicans, who represented the abolitionist sensibility within the political system. Too often, Lincoln is presented as a singular model of prudence and pragmatism while other critics of slavery are relegated to the fringe, caricatured as self-righteous fanatics with no sense of practical politics.[6] I believe that this displays a misunderstanding of how politics operates in a democratic society.

Lincoln was strongly antislavery, but he was not an abolitionist or a Radical Republican and never claimed to be one. He made a sharp distinction between his frequently reiterated personal wish that "all men everywhere could be free"[7] and his official duties as a legislator, congressman, and president in a legal and constitutional system that recognized the South's right to property in slaves. Even after issuing the Emancipation Proclamation he continued to declare his preference for gradual abolition. While his racial views changed during the Civil War, he never became a principled egalitarian in the manner of abolitionists such as Frederick Douglass and Wendell Phillips or Radical Republicans like Charles Sumner.

In locating Lincoln within the broad spectrum of antislavery thought, I have paid close attention to his writings and speeches, delineating not only what he said but also what he did not say. Unlike Radicals, for example, Lincoln rarely spoke of the physical brutality of slavery. Unlike conservatives in the Republican party, he forthrightly condemned slavery on moral as well as political and economic grounds. Lincoln consistently sought to locate the lowest common denominator of antislavery sentiment, the bases of agreement within the antislavery public. But Lincoln was well aware of the abolitionists' significance in creating public sentiment hostile to slavery. Despite their many differences on goals and tactics, he came to see himself as engaged, with them, in a common antislavery cause.

Lincoln, many recent scholars have argued, acted within the narrow limits of the possible, as established by northern public opinion. Public opinion, however, is never static; the interactions of enlightened political leaders, engaged social movements, and day-to-day experiences (such as the flight of slaves to Union lines or the encounters Union soldiers had with slavery) can change the nature of public debate and, in so doing, the boundaries of what is, in fact, practical. As the *Chicago Tribune* noted at the end of the Civil War, in crisis situations beliefs once "pronounced impractical radicalism" suddenly become "practical statesmanship." In his celebrated 1919 essay, "The Profession and Vocation of Politics," Max Weber defended the social utility of the politician's calling and identified three qualities required for success: devotion to a cause; a sense of responsibility; and judgment, or being attuned to the consequences of one's actions. These usefully define Lincoln's own qualities as a politician. Yet Weber concluded by noting the symbiotic relationship between political action and moral agitation. "What is possible," he wrote, "would not have been achieved, if, in this world, people had not repeatedly reached for the impossible."[8]

Abolitionists and Radicals play an important part in this book not because Lincoln was an abolitionist but because their agitation helped to establish the context within which politicians like Lincoln operated. On issue after issue in the 1850s and during the Civil War—the necessity of northern political unity to halt the expansion of slavery; opposition to compromise on this question during the secession crisis; emancipation in the District of Columbia; general emancipation under the Constitution's war power; the arming of black soldiers; amending the Constitution to abolish slavery; extending the right to vote to at least some blacks—Lincoln came to occupy positions first staked out by abolitionists and Radical Republicans.

In approaching the subject of Lincoln's views and policies regarding slavery and race, we should first bear in mind that the hallmark of Lincoln's greatness was his capacity for growth. It is fruitless to identify a single quotation, speech, or letter as the real or quintessential Lincoln. At the time of his death, he occupied a very different position with regard to slavery and the place of blacks in American society than earlier in his life. To be sure, the idea of Lincoln's "growth" has itself become a cliché. The current "consensus view" of Lincoln, one historian recently noted, is of a man who "never seems to stop growing."[9] This view is preferable to seeing Lincoln as born with a pen in his hand ready to sign the Emancipation Proclamation or as entering the White House with a fixed determination to preside over the end of slavery and waiting for the northern public to catch up with him. (It is also preferable to another approach, in which Lincoln is seen as a man with no deep convictions of his own, whose shifting policies and outlook arose entirely from forces outside his control.) The problem is that we tend too often to read Lincoln's growth backward, as an unproblematic trajectory toward a predetermined end.

This enables scholars to ignore or downplay aspects of Lincoln's beliefs with which they are uncomfortable—his long association with the idea of colonization, for example—while fastening on that which is most admirable at each stage of his career, especially his deep hatred of slavery. But I think there is value in tracing Lincoln's growth, as it were, forward, as it unfolded, with sideways and even backward steps along the way and with the future always unknown.

Much of Lincoln's career can fruitfully be seen as a search for a reconciliation of means and ends, an attempt to identify a viable mode of antislavery action in a political and constitutional system that erected seemingly impregnable barriers to effective steps toward abolition. For most of his career, Lincoln had no real idea how to rid the United States of slavery, although he announced many times his desire to see it end. But in this he was no different from virtually every other antislavery American of his era. No one before the war anticipated its outbreak or what Lincoln, in his second inaugural, would call its "astounding" result, the emancipation of the slaves. As late as 1858, the *Chicago Tribune*, a strong voice of antislavery radicalism, stated flatly that "no man living" would witness the death of American slavery.[10]

I admire Lincoln very much. But simply to anoint him as "a model of greatness for succeeding generations to follow"[11] or to see the task of the scholar as mounting a defense of Lincoln against his critics, then and now, does both Lincoln and the influences on him a disservice. If Lincoln achieved greatness, he grew into it. Not every individual possesses the capacity for growth; some, like Lincoln's successor as president, Andrew Johnson, seem to shrink, not grow, in the face of crisis. But to rise to the occasion requires not only an inner compass but also a willingness to listen to criticism, to seek out new ideas. Lincoln's career was a process of moral and political education and deepening antislavery conviction. He started out as a local politician in central Illinois, became a statewide public figure, and finally a national or at least a northern statesman. As his stage expanded, so did his experience. He came into contact with new people, new ideas, and a totally unprecedented situation, and was able to make the most of these encounters. He had to take into account the actions of groups with which he had previously had virtually no contact. Most notable among these groups were the slaves themselves, who seized the opportunity offered by the Civil War to strike for their freedom and who overwhelmingly rejected Lincoln's hope that many of them would agree to emigrate to some other country. Their actions forced the questions of slavery and the future place of blacks in American society onto the wartime agenda.

My aim then is to take Lincoln whole, incorporating his strengths and shortcomings, his insights and misjudgments. I want to show Lincoln in motion, tracking the development of his ideas and beliefs, his political abilities and strategies, as they engaged the issues of slavery and emancipation, the most critical in our nation's history.

THE
FIERY TRIAL

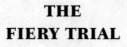

I

"I Am Naturally Anti-Slavery": Young Abraham Lincoln and Slavery

■

"**I** AM NATURALLY ANTI-SLAVERY. If slavery is not wrong, nothing is wrong. I can not remember when I did not so think, and feel." There is no reason to doubt the sincerity of Abraham Lincoln's emphatic declaration, written in April 1864, three years into the American Civil War. But as with so much of his early life, the origins of his thoughts and feelings about slavery remain shrouded in mystery.[1] Lincoln grew up in a world in which slavery was a living presence and where both deeply entrenched racism and various kinds of antislavery sentiment flourished. Until well into his life, he had only sporadic contact with black people, slave or free. In later years, he said almost nothing about his early encounters with slavery, slaves, and free African-Americans. Nonetheless, as he emerged in the 1830s as a prominent Illinois politician, the cumulative experiences of his early life led Lincoln to identify himself as an occasional critic of slavery. His early encounters with and responses to slavery were the starting point from which Lincoln's mature ideas and actions would later evolve.

I

ABRAHAM LINCOLN was born in 1809 in a one-room Kentucky log cabin. When he was seven, his family moved across the Ohio River to southwestern Indiana, where Lincoln spent the remainder of his childhood. In 1830, when Lincoln was twenty-one years old and about to strike out on his own, his father moved the family to central Illinois. Here Lincoln lived until he assumed the presidency in 1861.

At the time of Lincoln's birth and for most of the antebellum era, about one-fifth of Kentucky's population consisted of slaves. Outside a few counties, however, Kentucky slaveholders were primarily small farmers and urban dwellers, not plantation owners. Substantial parts of the state lay outside the full grip of slave society, "tolerating slavery, but not dominated by it." Kentucky formed part of the Border South, the northernmost belt of slave states that would play so crucial a role in the early years of the Civil War. Hardin County, where the Lincolns lived, lay south of the Ohio River in west-central Kentucky. In 1811 its population of around 7,500 included over 1,000 slaves, most of whom labored either on small farms or on the Ohio River. Kentucky at this time was an important crossroads of the domestic slave trade. The Lincolns' farm on Knob Creek lay not far from the road connecting Louisville and Nashville, along which settlers, peddlers, and groups of shackled slaves regularly passed.[2]

As an offshoot of Virginia, Kentucky recognized slavery from the earliest days of white settlement. The state's first constitution, written in 1792, prohibited the legislature from enacting laws for emancipation without the consent of the owners and full monetary compensation. In 1799, when a convention met to draft a new constitution (the first one being widely regarded as insufficiently democratic), a spirited debate over slavery took place. The young Henry Clay, just starting out on a career that would make him one of the nation's most prominent statesmen (and Lincoln's political idol), published a moving appeal asking white Kentuckians, "enthusiasts as they are for liberty," to consider the fate of "fellow beings, deprived of all rights that make life desirable." He urged the convention to adopt a plan of gradual emancipation. Clay's plea failed, but antislavery delegates did succeed in putting into the constitution a clause barring the introduction of slaves into the state for sale, although this soon became a dead letter. On one point, however, white Kentuckians, including emancipationists, agreed: they did not desire a free black population. In 1808, the year before Lincoln's birth, the legislature prohibited the migration of free blacks into Kentucky. When Lincoln was a boy, the state's population of 410,000 included only 1,700 free persons of color, 28 of whom lived in Hardin County.[3]

By the early nineteenth century, emancipationist sentiment had waned, but in some parts of Kentucky, including Hardin, disputes about slavery continued. The first place to look for early influences on Lincoln is his own family. Some of Lincoln's relatives owned slaves—his father's uncle, Isaac, had forty-three when he died in 1834. But Lincoln's parents exhibited an aversion to the institution. The South Fork Baptist Church to which they belonged divided over slavery around the time of Lincoln's birth; the antislavery group formed its own congregation, which his parents joined. However, as strict Calvinist predestinarians who believed that one's actions had no bearing on eventual salvation, which had already been determined by God, Lincoln's parents were not prone to become involved in reform movements that aimed at bettering conditions in this world.[4]

In a brief autobiography written in 1860, Lincoln recounted that his father moved the family to Indiana "partly on account of slavery." His main reason, however, Lincoln quickly added, was "land titles." Land surveys in Kentucky were notoriously unreliable and landownership often precarious. To purchase land in Kentucky, according to a visitor in the 1790s, was to buy a lawsuit. During Lincoln's boyhood, his father Thomas Lincoln owned three farms but lost two of them because of faulty titles. In Indiana, however, thanks to the federal land ordinances of the 1780s, the national government surveyed land prior to settlement and then sold it through the General Land Office, providing secure titles. When the War of 1812 destroyed Indians' power in much of the Old Northwest, their land, appropriated by the United States, became available for sale. Thousands of settlers from the Border South, among them Lincoln's family, moved across the Ohio River to occupy farms. "Kentucky," the saying went, "took Indiana without firing a shot."[5]

In Indiana and Illinois, where Lincoln lived from ages seven to fifty-one, the Northwest Ordinance of 1787 had prohibited slavery. Throughout the pre–Civil War decades, intrepid slaves tried to make their way across the Ohio River in search of liberty. Nonetheless, the Ohio did not mark a hard and fast dividing line between North and South, slavery and freedom. For many years it was far easier for people and goods to travel between Kentucky and southern Indiana and Illinois than to the northern parts of these states. Slave-catchers, too, frequently crossed the river, searching for fugitives.

Before the War of 1812, the Old Northwest was a kind of borderland, a meeting-ground of Native Americans and various people of English, French, and American descent where geographical and cultural boundaries remained unstable. The defeat of the British and their ally Tecumseh, who had tried to organize pan-Indian resistance to American rule, erased any doubt over who would henceforth control the region. But a new borderland quickly emerged. When Lincoln lived there, the southern counties of Indiana and Illinois formed part of a large area that encompassed the lower parts of the free states and the northernmost slave states. This region retained much of the cultural flavor of the Upper South. Its food, speech, settlement patterns, architecture, family ties, and economic relations had much more in common with Kentucky and Tennessee than with the northern counties of their own states, soon to be settled by New Englanders. The large concentration of people of southern ancestry made Indiana and Illinois key battlegrounds in northern politics as the slavery controversy developed. Here, a distinctive politics of moderation developed. On the eve of the Civil War, a writer in far-off Maine described the southern Northwest as "a sort of belt or break-water between the extremes of the North and South."[6]

In the decade before the Civil War, the population exploded in northern Illinois. But because they had been settled first, the southern counties long shaped the state's public life. Of the first seven governors, six had been born in a slave state. In 1848, more members of the Illinois legislature and constitutional convention hailed from Kentucky than from any other state. As late as 1858, during his campaign for the U.S. Senate, Lincoln made a point of affirming his geographical roots to voters in southern Illinois: "I was raised just a little east of here. I am a part of this people." By then, however, the southern counties had been eclipsed politically and economically by northern Illinois.[7]

Many pioneer settlers in Indiana and Illinois, like the Lincoln family, carried with them an aversion to slavery. Richard Yates, the Kentucky-born Civil War governor of Illinois, spoke of his view of slavery in words much like Lincoln's: "The earliest impressions of my boyhood were that the institution of slavery was a grievous wrong." Peter Cartwright, a Methodist preacher and political leader whom Lincoln defeated for Congress in 1846, later wrote that he emigrated from Tennessee in 1824 to "get entirely clear of the evil of slavery." Such men viewed slavery less as a moral problem than as an institution that degraded white labor, created an unequal distribution of wealth and power, and made it impossible for nonslaveholding farmers to advance.[8]

Since the eighteenth century, slavery had existed in the region. And despite the Northwest Ordinance, its death was long in coming. In Indiana, the territorial governor William Henry Harrison, the son of a Virginia planter, led an unsuccessful drive to have Congress suspend its ban on slavery, arguing that only in this way could the area's future economic growth be ensured. But antislavery settlers, organized as the Popular party and claiming to defend the interests of small farmers against "Virginia aristocrats," won control of the territorial legislature and foiled Harrison's plans. When Indiana drafted a constitution in 1816, the year the Lincoln family moved into the state, it prohibited slavery.[9]

Even though slavery was theoretically illegal in Illinois under the Northwest Ordinance, Ninian Edwards, the territorial governor between 1809 and 1816 (whose son became Lincoln's brother-in-law), advertised for sale twenty-two slaves, along with "a full blooded horse" and "a very large English bull." The Illinois constitution of 1818 prohibited slaves from being "hereafter . . . introduced" but did not declare free those already living in the state. As late as 1840, the census counted 331 slaves in Illinois. Illinois allowed slaveowners to sign supposedly voluntary indentures with black laborers brought in from other states, effectively keeping them in bondage. For many years, newspapers carried notices for the buying and selling of these "servants."[10]

In 1818, the Virginian Edward Coles brought his slaves to Illinois, freed them, and settled each family on 160 acres of land. Coles was elected governor of Illinois in 1822 and fought a determined battle against efforts to amend the state constitution to introduce slavery. After an electoral campaign in 1824, in which debate centered on the relative benefits of free and slave labor and charges that proslavery forces wished to substitute aristocracy for democracy, the voters of Illinois turned down a proposal for a new constitutional convention. Lincoln was not yet a resident of the state. But one thing that he concluded from this history was that direct political action against slavery, not simply an unfavorable soil or climate, had been necessary to keep the institution out of the Old Northwest.[11]

Hostility to slavery did not preclude deep prejudices against blacks. The early settlers wanted Indiana and Illinois to be free of any black presence. John Woods, an English farmer who settled in Illinois, wrote in 1819 of his neighbors: "Though now living in a free state, they retain many of the prejudices they imbibed in infancy, and still hold negroes in the utmost contempt." Like Kentucky, Indiana and Illinois did everything they could to discourage the growth of a free black population. The con-

stitutions under which they entered the Union offered liberal voting rights
to whites but barred blacks from suffrage. Laws in both states prohibited
blacks from marrying whites or testifying in court against them, and made
it a crime to harbor a fugitive slave or servant or to bring black persons into
the state with the intent of freeing them, as Governor Coles had done.
The public schools excluded black children.[12]

Before the Civil War, Illinois was notorious for its harsh Black Laws,
"repugnant to our political institutions," said Governor Coles, who tried
unsuccessfully to have the legislature modify them. One law declared
that young apprentices must be taught reading, writing, and arithmetic
"except when such apprentice is a negro or mulatto." Another required
any black person who entered Illinois to post a $1,000 bond. "In conse-
quence of these salutary arrangements," a periodical devoted to attracting
investment and immigration to the state proudly declared, Illinois "has
not become a retreat for runaway slaves, or free negroes." Later, the 1848
constitutional convention authorized a referendum on a provision empow-
ering the legislature to bar all free black persons from entering the state. It
received 70 percent of the vote, and five years later the lawmakers enacted
a "Negro exclusion" law. Although the legislature eventually restricted the
use of indentures, in the 1830s and 1840s it remained legal to bring blacks
under the age of fifteen into Illinois as servants and then to sell them.
"Illinois," declared the abolitionist weekly *The Liberator* in 1840, "is, to all
intents and purposes, a slaveholding state."[13]

The historical record contains very little information about Lincoln's
early encounters with slavery or black persons. As a young child in Kentucky, he may have seen groups of chained slaves pass near his house
on their way to the Lower South. He could not have had much direct
contact with blacks in Indiana. In 1830, on the eve of the family's departure for Illinois, the census reported no slaves and only fourteen free
blacks in Spencer County, where the Lincolns lived. When he settled in
Sangamon County, Illinois, the population of around 12,000 included only
thirty-eight blacks. When Lincoln moved to Springfield in 1837, the town's
eighty-six blacks comprised less than 5 percent of its residents.[14]

Lincoln's first real encounter with slavery—the heart of the institution, rather than its periphery—came on two journeys down the Ohio and
Mississippi rivers in 1828 and 1831, when he helped transport farm goods
for sale in New Orleans. Lincoln and his companions made the south-
bound voyage by flatboat and returned north by steamboat (although on

the second occasion, Lincoln walked home from St. Louis). Their trip exemplified how the market revolution of the early nineteenth century was simultaneously consolidating the national economy and heightening the division between slave and free societies. In the North, the building of canals and the advent of steamboats and, later, railroads set in motion economic changes that created an integrated economy of commercial farms and growing urban and industrial centers. In the South, the market revolution, coupled with the military defeat and subsequent removal of the Native American population, made possible the westward expansion of the slave system and the rise of the great Cotton Kingdom of the Gulf states. Southern society reproduced itself as it moved westward, remaining slave-based and almost entirely agricultural, even as the North witnessed the emergence of a diversified, modernizing economy.[15] Eventually, the clash between societies based on slave and free labor would come to dominate American life and shape the mature Lincoln's political career.

This, however, lay far in the future when Lincoln made his two trips. The first began at the end of December 1828 when James Gentry, an Indiana storekeeper, hired the nineteen-year-old Lincoln to join Gentry's son Allen in shipping a cargo of corn, oats, beans, and meat to New Orleans. The second trip, which started in April 1831, took place after Denton Offutt, an Illinois merchant, hired a crew including Lincoln, John Hanks (Lincoln's mother's cousin), and John D. Johnston (Lincoln's stepbrother) to accompany him to New Orleans. These trips were among thousands that followed a similar route during this period, when the Old Northwest shipped its surplus farm produce downriver to be sold in New Orleans and then consumed on slave plantations or transported by sea to the Northeast or Europe.[16]

What did Lincoln see on these journeys, which covered over 2,000 miles round-trip? The Ohio and Mississippi rivers were alive with vessels of all kinds. Lincoln could not have avoided contact with slaves, who worked on the huge cotton and sugar plantations that lined the Mississippi and on docks and steamboats. There were also bands of black robbers who preyed on shipping. One night as their flatboat lay tied up at the riverbank, one such group attacked Gentry and Lincoln. The incident left a vivid impression; in his brief autobiographical sketch written in 1860, the only black persons Lincoln mentioned were the "seven negroes" who tried to "kill and rob" him. He and Gentry, Lincoln recalled, succeeded "in driving the negroes from the boat."[17]

These trips must have been eye-opening for the young Lincoln. New Orleans, where he spent an undetermined amount of time in 1829 and a full month in mid-1831, was by far the largest city he had ever seen, with a population of some 50,000, including nearly 17,000 slaves and 12,000 free blacks. The diverse residents also included Creoles (descendants of French and Spanish colonial settlers), European immigrants, and Americans from every state. The French observer of American democracy Alexis de Tocqueville, who spent New Year's Day of 1832 in New Orleans, six months after Lincoln's second visit, took note of the city's beautiful architecture, the "faces with every shade of color," and what he deemed the "incredible laxity of morals" of the inhabitants. Every Sunday, the city's vibrant black culture was on display at Congo Square, where slaves gathered for dancing, music-making, and other pastimes. The free black population included many propertied skilled artisans. The city's back streets held numerous grog shops where slaves, free blacks, and whites mingled freely.[18]

Situated at the mouth of the Mississippi River, New Orleans was, after New York City, the country's second busiest port, the major export center for the staple crops of the Mississippi Valley. In 1828, vessels from throughout the Atlantic world arrived there, including some 750 steamboats and over 1,000 flatboats. New Orleans was also a major center of the domestic slave trade. Slave pens were scattered throughout the business district, newspapers carried daily advertisements for slave sales, and slave auctions took place not only at the central slave market—a major tourist attraction—but also at numerous other places, including the luxurious St. Charles Hotel. It would have been almost impossible to spend time in New Orleans and not witness the buying and selling of slaves.[19]

John Hanks later claimed that on the second trip to New Orleans, "we saw negroes chained, maltreated, whipped and scourged. Lincoln saw it. His heart bled. . . . I can say knowingly that it was on this trip that he formed his opinions of slavery." But, according to Lincoln's recollection in 1860, Hanks left the crew in St. Louis and did not accompany the others to New Orleans. After Lincoln's death, Hanks and Lincoln's law partner William Herndon recounted that in later life, Lincoln did speak about these journeys and about the New Orleans slave market.[20] The impact of these visits on Lincoln's views of slavery, however, must remain a matter of speculation. His account of being assaulted by thieves is his only surviving reference to these two journeys. But the sight of slaves being bought and sold powerfully affected many a visitor to the South. Lincoln's friend Orville H. Browning, an Illinois politician who had also been born in Kentucky, described his reaction to a slave sale in a diary entry in 1854:

> Saw a negro sold at public auction in the court-house yard. . . . Although I am not sensible in any change in my views upon the abstract question of slavery, many of its features, that are no longer familiar, make a much more vivid impression of wrong than they did before I lived away from the influence of the institution.[21]

Lincoln had more to say about a subsequent encounter with slavery, which took place on an 1841 boat trip to St. Louis with his close friend Joshua Speed. The trip followed a visit to Farmington, the Speed family plantation near Louisville, where his hosts assigned a house slave to wait on their guest. Recovering from a period of depression after the temporary breakup of his relationship with Mary Todd, Lincoln remained for a month at Farmington. In September, he and Speed took a steamboat down the Ohio River to St. Louis, from where Lincoln returned to Springfield, Illinois, by stagecoach. On the ship, Lincoln observed a group of slaves being transported from Kentucky to a farm farther south. In 1855, Lincoln would vividly recall this episode in a letter to Speed:

> You may remember, as I well do, that . . . there were, on board, ten or a dozen slaves, shackled together with irons. That sight was a continual torment to me; and I see something like it every time I touch the Ohio, or any other slave-border. . . . You ought . . . to appreciate how much the great body of the Northern people do crucify their feelings, in order to maintain their loyalty to the constitution and the Union.[22]

Lincoln's oft-quoted letter, addressed to a good friend who by 1855 differed substantially with him about slavery, has been described as a "cry from the heart." Lincoln's response in 1841, when he encountered the chained slaves, was quite different. Then, he sent a vivid description of what he had seen to Mary Speed, Joshua's half sister:

> A fine example was presented on board the boat for contemplating the effect of condition upon human happiness. . . . [The slaves] were

chained six and six together. A small iron clevis was around the left wrist of each, and this was fastened to the main chain by a shorter one at a convenient distance from the others; so that the negroes were strung together precisely like so many fish upon a trot-line. In this condition they were being separated forever from the scenes of their childhood, their friends, their fathers and mothers, and brothers and sisters, and many of them, from their wives and children, and going into perpetual slavery where the lash of the master is proverbially more ruthless and unrelenting than any other where; and yet amid all these distressing circumstances, as we would think of them, they were the most cheerful and apparently happy creatures on board. . . . How true it is that God . . . renders the worst of human conditions tolerable, while He permits the best, to be nothing better than tolerable.[23]

Clearly, the chained slaves fascinated Lincoln, and he observed closely their method of confinement and their behavior. This letter is one of very few at any point in his life in which Lincoln muses on cruel punishments and the uprooting and separation of families—the concrete reality to which black men, women, and children were subjected. One cannot read the letter without a sense of revulsion at what the slaves experienced. Yet whether he did not wish to offend an owner of slaves, or his melancholy at the time affected his thinking, or his own views on slavery had not yet matured, Lincoln's account was oddly dispassionate. He did not describe the scene, as he would in 1855, as a violation of rights, a way of illustrating a political outlook, or an affront to his feelings, but as an interesting illustration of how human beings have the capacity to remain cheerful even in the most dire circumstances.

Until they drifted apart in the 1850s over the slavery question, Lincoln's relationship with the Speeds illustrated the close connection his circle of friends in Springfield had with slavery. His early political mentor and first law partner, John Todd Stuart, represented traders in indentured servants and slaves. Most important, when he married Stuart's cousin Mary Todd in 1842, Lincoln became part of a significant slaveholding family. His wife grew up in Lexington, Kentucky, in the heart of bluegrass country, the focal point of slaveholding in the state and a major slave-trading center. One of Mary's uncles bought and sold slaves. A prominent businessman, lawyer, and well-connected political figure, Mary's father, Robert S. Todd, was a longtime member of the Kentucky legislature and an associate of Henry Clay.[24]

Robert S. Todd's first wife died in 1825. He soon remarried and four of his daughters, including Mary, eventually moved to Springfield as young women, in part because of difficulties with their stepmother. Mary's uncle, Dr. John Todd, also took up residence in Springfield and owned five slaves there in 1830. Mary's eldest sister Elizabeth married Ninian Edwards, who served in the legislature with Lincoln and was the son of the governor with the same name who had bought and sold slaves in territorial days. The Edwards family owned one of the six slaves still living in Springfield in 1840, in addition to black indentured servants. Yet Robert S. Todd, a follower of Clay, was one of the Kentucky slaveholders who disliked slavery and hoped to see it gradually abolished in the state. His daughter Mary, who had a strong interest in politics, seems to have imbibed his point of view. Robert S. Todd died in 1849 while running for reelection to the state senate. His opponent had castigated him as the "emancipation candidate."[25]

The Todds were a proud, self-important family whose pretensions Lincoln frequently ridiculed. "One 'd' was good enough for God," he quipped, "but not the Todds." Nonetheless, Lincoln remained extremely close to his wife's family. When the death of Robert S. Todd unleashed a bitter squabble over his estate, Lincoln became involved in the ensuing litigation. (His wife ended up losing money as a result of the eventual court decisions.) During the Civil War, as the *New York World* observed, referring to the Todds, Lincoln "appointed his whole family to government posts."[26]

On several occasions, Lincoln came into contact with slavery on visits to his in-laws' home in Lexington. With his wife and two young sons, he spent nearly a month there in 1847 on his way to taking up a seat in Congress. They enjoyed another extended stay in 1849, and Lincoln visited Lexington again while handling lawsuits in 1850, 1852, and 1853. The city's newspapers were filled with advertisements seeking the recovery of runaways and offering slaves for sale. It is unknown whether Lincoln witnessed a slave auction during any of these visits. If so, he never mentioned it.[27]

Thus, before his emergence in the 1850s as an antislavery politician, Lincoln lived in Kentucky, Indiana, and Illinois, all of which had histories of slavery and severe laws effectively denying black persons the rights of citizenship. All three, in fact, at one time or another prohibited free blacks from entering their territory.[28] Lincoln had seen the small-scale slavery of

Kentucky and the plantations and slave markets of the Mississippi Valley. He had married into a family of slaveholders.

From an early age, Lincoln demonstrated an independent cast of mind. He diverged in many ways from the boisterous and sometimes violent frontier culture in which he grew up. He did not drink, hunt, or chew tobacco, tried to avoid physical altercations, never joined a church, and early in life embarked on a program of self-improvement, bent on escaping the constraining circumstances of his youth.[29] Despite his penchant for thinking for himself, however, for most of his life Lincoln shared many of the racial prejudices so deeply rooted in the border region in which he grew up.

Yet Lincoln, had he desired, could have easily moved back to Kentucky like his friend Joshua Speed and, with the support of his prominent father-in-law, established himself as a member of Lexington's slaveowning high society. He chose not to do so. "Every American," Tocqueville observed, "is eaten up with longing to rise."[30] Lincoln was even more ambitious than most of his contemporaries. But to him, success meant advancement in a society based on free labor, not slave.

II

As LINCOLN grew to adulthood, the institution of slavery underwent a profound transformation. By the 1830s, when he entered Illinois politics, war, revolution, slave rebellion, and the spread of Enlightenment ideas concerning human freedom had combined to reduce significantly the geographical scope of slavery in the Western Hemisphere. In the United States, the combination of a revolutionary ideology centered on liberty and the disruptions caused by the War of Independence threw the future of slavery into doubt. Between 1777, when Vermont adopted a constitution prohibiting slavery, and 1804, when New Jersey acted, every northern state enacted measures to abolish the institution. These were the first legal steps toward emancipation in the New World. The 1790s witnessed the slave revolution on the rich French sugar island of Saint-Domingue, which destroyed slavery and established the nation of Haiti. Wars for independence in Spanish Latin America soon followed, producing new nations that embarked on the process of emancipation. In 1833, Parliament outlawed slavery throughout the British Empire. Although it persisted in Brazil, Cuba, and Puerto Rico, by the mid-nineteenth century slavery had become the South's "peculiar institution"—that is, the institution that set the region apart from the rest of the nation and, increasingly, the rest of the world.

With a few exceptions, the end of slavery came through gradual emancipation accompanied by some kind of recognition of the owners' legal right to property in slaves. In the United States, court decisions in Massachusetts and New Hampshire in the 1780s declared slavery incompatible with new state constitutions that affirmed mankind's natural right to liberty. But the abolition laws of the other northern states freed no living slave. Rather, slave children born after a specified date would work for the mother's owner as indentured servants until well into adulthood (age twenty-eight, for example, in Pennsylvania, far longer than what was customary for white indentured servants), and only then would become free. Most Latin American nations also allowed slaveholders to retain ownership of existing slaves, as well as the labor of their children for a number of years. These laws, in effect, required slaves to compensate their owners for their freedom by years of unpaid labor. As one official wrote, they "respected the past and corrected only the future."

In some cases, owners received direct cash payments as well. In the British Empire, Parliament in 1833 mandated almost immediate emancipation, with a seven-year transitional period of "apprenticeship" that produced so much conflict between former masters and former slaves that complete freedom was decreed in 1838. The law appropriated twenty million pounds to compensate the owners. Even Haiti, where slavery died amid a violent revolution, agreed in 1824 to pay a large indemnity to former slaveowners in exchange for French recognition of its independence, a financial burden the new nation could ill afford. No one proposed to compensate slaves for their years of unrequited toil. The experience of emancipation in the North and other parts of the hemisphere strongly affected subsequent debates over slavery and influenced Lincoln's own ideas about how to abolish the institution. Even after issuing the Emancipation Proclamation, he reiterated that he would be glad to see the southern states return to the Union and enact "the most approved plans of gradual emancipation."[31]

The end of slavery in the North did not imply political or social equality for blacks. Race, long one of many forms of legal and social inequality among colonial Americans, now emerged as a justification for the existence of slavery in a land of liberty. How else could the condition of blacks be explained other than by innate inferiority? Northern blacks who became free endured severe discrimination. At first, the northern states allowed black men to vote if they could meet existing property qualifications. But beginning with Ohio in 1803, every state that entered the Union, with the single exception of Maine in 1821, restricted the suffrage to whites. Between 1818 and 1837, moreover, Connecticut, New York, and Pennsylvania limited black voting rights or eliminated them altogether. With the federal government under the control of southerners (of the sixteen presidential elections between 1788 and 1848, all but four placed a slaveholder in the White House), free blacks were denied basic rights. The Naturalization Act of 1790 barred black immigrants from ever becoming citizens; the Militia Act of 1792, which established ground rules for a central responsibility of citizenship, limited service to whites. In 1853, Frederick Douglass, who had escaped from slavery as a young man and gone on to become one of the most prominent lecturers and newspaper editors in the abolitionist movement, described the condition of his people, free as well as slave, as "anomalous, unequal, and extraordinary. . . . Aliens we are in our native land."[32]

The U.S. Constitution contained several protections for slavery, notably the fugitive slave clause, which required the return of runaways, and the three-fifths clause, which gave the slave states increased representation in Congress and added electoral votes by counting part of their disenfranchised slave population. Nonetheless, many of the nation's founders hoped that slavery might eventually die out. Instead, with the opening of fertile land in the Deep South and the spectacular growth of world demand for cotton, the key raw material of the early industrial revolution, American slavery received a new lease on life. As the nation expanded westward, so did slavery. Cotton became by far the most important American export, an indispensable source of the foreign earnings that enabled the country to import manufactured goods.

The free states shared in the profits of slavery. As Lincoln experienced on his journeys to New Orleans, the slave states provided a crucial market for the produce of free western farmers. On the strength of its control of the transatlantic trade in cotton, New York City rose to commercial dominance. Even the abolition of the slave trade from Africa in 1808, a year before Lincoln's birth, did not slow slavery's growth. A flourishing domestic slave trade replaced the importation of slaves. By the eve of the Civil War, the slave population in the United States had reached nearly four million. The economic value of these men, women, and children when considered as property exceeded the combined worth of all the banks, railroads, and factories in the United States. In geographical extent, population, and the institution's economic importance, the South was home to the most powerful slave system the modern world has known.[33]

Nevertheless, abolition in the North drew a geographical line across the country. The Mason-Dixon Line, a boundary between Pennsylvania and Maryland drawn by a colonial-era surveyor, became a dividing line between freedom and slavery. Although the antislavery impulse inspired by the struggle for independence waned in the early nineteenth century, slavery remained a divisive political issue, and plans for abolition continued to be discussed. Between 1790 and 1830, dozens of proposals for gradual, compensated emancipation came before Congress.[34]

Increasingly, supporters of emancipation coupled their proposals with "colonization"—the removal of the black population from the United States. Until around 1830, most organized antislavery activism, at least among white Americans, took place under this rubric. In this respect, the United States was truly exceptional. As *Harper's Weekly* later pointed out, nowhere else in the Western Hemisphere was it seriously proposed "to extirpate the slaves after emancipation." Absurd as the idea of colonization may appear in retrospect, it seemed quite realistic to its advocates. Many large groups had been expelled from their homelands in modern times—for example, Spanish Muslims and Jews after 1492 and Acadians during the Seven Years' War. Virtually the entire Indian population east of the Mississippi River had been removed to the West by 1840. In an era of nation-building, colonization formed part of a long debate about what kind of nation the United States was to be. It allowed its advocates to imagine a society freed—gradually, peacefully, and without sectional conflict—from both slavery and the unwanted presence of blacks. At mid-century, the prospect of colonizing American slaves probably seemed more credible than immediate abolition.[35]

Colonization was hardly a fringe movement. "Almost every respectable man," as Frederick Douglass observed, supported it. Thomas Jefferson and Henry Clay, the statesmen most revered by Lincoln, favored colonization. Jefferson remained committed to the idea to his dying day. In 1824, he proposed that the federal government purchase and deport "the increase of each year" (that is, children) so that the slave population would age and eventually disappear. Critics, Jefferson admitted, might object on humanitarian grounds to "the separation of infants from their mothers." But this, he insisted, would be "straining at a gnat."[36]

The first emancipation—the gradual abolition of slavery in the North—contained no provision for colonization. It seems to have been assumed that the former slaves would somehow be absorbed into society. But the rapid growth of the free black population in the early republic spurred believers in a white America to action. Founded in 1816, just as slavery was becoming established in the Cotton Kingdom, the American Colonization Society at first directed its efforts toward removing blacks already free. But the long-term goal of many members was to abolish slavery. Planters and political leaders from the Upper South dominated the American Colonization Society. Few were more adamant about linking colonization with abolition than Henry Clay.[37]

Despite representing a slave state, and in the face of the spread of proslavery ideology during the 1830s, Clay never retreated from his conviction that slavery was "a great evil." He continued to look forward to the day "distant, very distant, perhaps" when not a single slave remained in the United States. Clay saw slavery as the greatest threat to the Union to whose preservation he was passionately devoted. He remained equally certain that "abolition is impossible, unless it be accompanied by colonization." Clay hoped that abolition would transform Kentucky into a modern, diversified economy modeled on the free-labor North. Slavery, he believed, was why his state lagged behind neighboring Ohio in manufacturing and general prosperity. Clay succeeded James Madison as president of the American Colonization Society in 1836 and served until his own death sixteen years later. He manumitted ten of his slaves during his lifetime and in his will offered freedom and transportation to Africa to the future children of his female slaves when they reached adulthood. The presentation of colonization as an adjunct of abolition by Clay and other northern and Upper South advocates helps explain why hostility to the idea became more and more intense in the Lower South.[38]

Many northern Whigs, observed the Indiana politician Schuyler Colfax, regarded Clay with "great reverence, almost adoration." Lincoln was no exception. In 1832, he cast his first vote for president for Clay and later referred to him as "my beau ideal of a statesman." During the Lincoln-Douglas debates of 1858, Lincoln referred to Clay no fewer than forty-one times. Clay's outlook on slavery—condemnation of the institution and affirmation of the blacks' humanity coupled with the conviction that emancipation could only come gradually and should be linked with colonization—strongly affected Lincoln's. More than once during the 1850s when speaking about slavery and race, Lincoln quoted or paraphrased Clay. "I can express all my views on the slavery question," he once said, "by quotations from Henry Clay."[39]

Some African-Americans shared the perspective of the colonization movement. Almost every printed report of the American Colonization Society included testimonials from blacks who either had gone to Africa or were anxious to do so. Throughout the nineteenth century, however, most black Americans rejected both voluntary emigration and government-sponsored efforts to encourage or coerce them to leave the country. In asserting their own Americanness, free blacks articulated a vision of American society as a land of birthright citizenship and equality before the law, where rights did not depend on color, ancestry, or racial designation. They denied colonizationists' arguments that racism was immutable, that a nation must be racially homogeneous, and that color formed an insurmountable barrier to equality. Through the attack on colonization, the modern idea of equality as something that knows no racial boundaries was born.[40]

The black mobilization against colonization formed one of the key catalysts for the rise of a new, militant abolitionism in the late 1820s and 1830s. Compared to previous antislavery organizations that promoted gradual emancipation, compensation, and colonization, abolitionism was different: immediatist, interracial, rejecting payment to slaveholders for their slaves, and committed to making the United States a biracial nation. The abolitionist movement arose as the joining of two impulses—black anti-colonization and white evangelicism and perfectionism. In his influential 1832 pamphlet, *Thoughts on African Colonization*, the white abolitionist William Lloyd Garrison explained that his experience with the vibrant black communities of Baltimore and Boston inspired his conversion from colonization to abolition and racial equality. The most potent objection to colonization, he wrote, was that it "is directly and irreconcilably opposed to the wishes of our colored population as a body." White abolitionists of the 1830s, most of whom, like Garrison, had previously been sympathetic to colonization, now denounced the American Colonization Society for intensifying racial prejudice in America. The New York merchant and religious reformer Lewis Tappan, another former colonizationist who embraced immediate abolitionism, called on Henry Clay to recognize the society's ineffectiveness. "Slavery is rapidly increasing," he wrote to Clay in 1835. "Colonization has not, nor will it . . . diminish slavery. What is to be done? I answer, emancipate." Clearly annoyed, Clay responded that northerners had no right to speak about slavery in the South.[41]

In 1795, the Virginia critic of slavery St. George Tucker inquired of the Massachusetts clergyman and historian Jeremy Belknap how his state had abolished slavery. Belknap replied, "Slavery hath been abolished here by public opinion." Understanding the importance of public sentiment, abolitionists pioneered the practice of radical agitation in a democracy. They did not put forward a detailed plan of emancipation. Rather, their aim, explained Wendell Phillips, perhaps the movement's greatest orator, was "to alter public opinion," to bring about a moral transformation whereby white Americans recognized the humanity and equal rights of blacks. By changing public discourse, by redefining the politically "possible," the abolitionist movement affected far more Americans than actually joined its ranks.[42]

Abolitionists seized on the weapons available to them—petitions, lectures, and the newly invented steam press, which made possible the mass production of pamphlets, newspapers, and broadsides—to challenge the conspiracy of silence that increasingly barred discussion of slavery from the national public sphere.[43] The movement appealed simultaneously to the hearts and minds of Americans, excoriating slaveowners and exposing the brutal reality of slavery—whippings, separation of families, and so on—while also condemning slavery for destroying "the influence which our otherwise free and republican institutions are justly entitled to in the world." Abolitionists pioneered the argument that the founders were explicitly or implicitly antislavery and expected the institution's demise. They tried to appropriate the Declaration of Independence for their cause, interpreting the Declaration (as Lincoln would later do) as a condemnation of slavery. The words of Jefferson's preamble affirming the equality of man graced the front page of every issue of Zebina Eastman's abolitionist newspaper, the *Western Citizen*, published in Chicago beginning in 1842. Abolitionists also argued for the superiority of free labor to slave, and insisted that slavery illegitimately denied slaves the fruits of their labor. Many critics of slavery, including Lincoln, who never thought of themselves as abolitionists, came to articulate ideas and themes that had first appeared in abolitionist writings.[44]

Where abolitionists diverged most profoundly from their contemporaries, including less radical critics of slavery, lay in their views concerning a post-slavery America. The crusade against slavery, wrote Angelina Grimké, the daughter of a South Carolina slaveholder who became an outspoken abolitionist and feminist, was the nation's preeminent "school in which *human rights* are . . . investigated." Abolitionists played a crucial role in giving new meaning to ideas such as personal liberty, political community, and the rights that attached to American citizenship. They insisted on the "Americanness" of slaves and free blacks, a position summarized in the title of Lydia Maria Child's popular treatise of 1833, *An Appeal in Favor of That Class of Americans Called Africans.* Child's text insisted that blacks were compatriots, not foreigners; they should no more be considered Africans than white Englishmen. The abolitionist idea of egalitarian birthright citizenship, later enshrined in the Constitution by the Fourteenth Amendment, was a radical departure from the traditions and practices of American life.[45]

The first racially integrated social movement in American history, abolitionism was also the first to insist on the inextricable connection between the struggles against slavery and racism. "While the word 'white' is on the statute-book of Massachusetts," declared the abolitionist editor Edmund Quincy, "Massachusetts is a slave state." Abolitionists challenged both southern slavery and the racial proscription that confined free blacks to second-class status throughout the nation. In the ideas of a national citizenship and of equal rights for all Americans, abolitionists glimpsed the possibility, which came to fruition during the Civil War, that the national state might become the guarantor of freedom and equality rather than its enemy.[46]

Initially, the federal government and many private citizens responded to the crusade against slavery by attempting to suppress it. The House of Representatives in 1836 adopted the notorious gag rule, prohibiting the consideration of abolitionist petitions. Throughout the 1830s, northern mobs (well over a hundred by one count) broke up meetings of abolitionists and destroyed their printing presses. Nonetheless, between the formation of the American Anti-Slavery Society in 1833 and the end of the decade, somewhere between 200,000 and 300,000 northerners joined local groups dedicated to the abolition of slavery and equal rights for black Americans.[47]

As abolitionism spread, a chasm opened between the movement and the American Colonization Society. Colonizationists often included the most prominent members of local communities. They not only found abolitionists' ideas unacceptable, but resented their efforts to organize ordinary citizens outside existing channels of authority. Colonizationists instigated and participated in the anti-abolitionist riots that swept the North in the mid-1830s. Among numerous supporters of colonization who viewed the abolitionists as "exerting the most unhappy influence" was Henry Clay, who feared that the emergence of abolitionism had set back hopes for ending slavery by "half a century." White southerners, he warned in 1839, would never accept the creation of a large class of free blacks who enjoyed equal rights. Therefore, if abolitionist views became widespread in the North, the inevitable result would be a bloody civil war.[48]

While no longer the main embodiment of white antislavery sentiment, colonization survived as part of the broad spectrum of ideas relating to slavery and abolition. This was particularly true in Illinois, where, until the mid-1830s, what antislavery sentiment existed took the form of colonizationism. The founding meeting of the Illinois Colonization Society, in 1830, attracted both genuine foes of slavery and those primarily concerned with ridding the state of free blacks. Among those present was former governor Edward Coles, who, as noted earlier, had emancipated his own slaves, brought them to Illinois, and fought for repeal of the state's Black Laws. By 1830, Coles had concluded that blacks could never enjoy full freedom in the United States. Also present was Cyrus Edwards, the uncle by marriage of Mary Todd's sister Elizabeth. Edwards dwelled on the "dangerous and baleful influence" of free blacks and insisted that freeing the South's slaves and allowing them to remain in the country was impossible. In 1833, a local colonization society was organized in Springfield, with numerous leading citizens as officers, including John Todd Stuart, who would soon become Lincoln's first law partner. Several other close associates of Lincoln, including the lawyers and Whig political leaders David Davis and Orville H. Browning, as well as Charles Dresser, the Episcopal minister who officiated at Lincoln's wedding, were also long-time advocates of colonization. Whigs "antagonistical to abolitionism," as one newspaper put it, dominated colonization ranks in Illinois.[49]

During the first two decades of Lincoln's political career, abolitionism proved far weaker in Illinois than in other northern states. In 1837, the *Liberator* reported that of the 607 local antislavery societies in the United States, only 3 were located in Illinois. Nonetheless, during the mid-1830s abolitionist ideas did begin to circulate in the northern and central parts of the state, thanks to the *Observer*, a newspaper published by the Maine-born Presbyterian minister Elijah P. Lovejoy first in St. Louis and then, after a mob destroyed his press, just across the Mississippi River in Alton, Illinois. Lovejoy's expulsion from St. Louis followed the killing of a constable by Francis McIntosh, a free black riverboat worker from Pittsburgh. Irate residents of the city subsequently lynched McIntosh. They blamed Lovejoy for spreading the ideas that allegedly caused McIntosh to commit the murder and for protesting the crime against him.[50]

In October 1837, Lovejoy and his brother Owen, a Congregationalist minister, called a meeting in Alton to organize the Illinois Anti-Slavery Society. On the appointed day, eighty-six delegates assembled. Only four hailed from Sangamon County, where Lincoln lived. The state attorney general, Usher F. Linder, organized a mob that packed the meeting and adopted resolutions condemning the idea of emancipation. The next day the town's mayor brought constables to break up another mob led by Linder and allowed the gathering to proceed.[51]

The Declaration of Sentiments of the Illinois Anti-Slavery Society began with a discussion of "the foundation of human rights." Since God had created every person with an "immortal soul," it proclaimed, all were entitled to "equality of fundamental rights." The document condemned slavery as a "subversion of the laws of God" and a violation of every human right, including education, family life, personal chastity, protection against injury, and individual self-determination. It called for immediate abolition by the southern states and the elevation of free blacks to "an equality with the whites." Opposition to the Illinois Black Laws quickly emerged as a central tenet of abolitionism in the state. In 1840, one group of abolitionists published a pamphlet claiming that these laws violated the comity clause of the U.S. Constitution, which required each state to accord citizens of other states the same rights as their own.[52]

With abolitionists widely stigmatized as advocates of racial equality who threatened to disrupt the Union, identifying with the cause required considerable courage. This became starkly evident on November 7, 1837, less than two weeks after the organization of the Anti-Slavery Society, when Elijah P. Lovejoy was murdered by a mob while defending his printing press in Alton. Owen Lovejoy vowed to dedicate himself to the cause now "sprinkled with my brother's blood"; he would go on to a long career as an abolitionist, member of Congress, and bridge between the Radical Republicans and Lincoln during the Civil War. Otherwise, so deep was the hostility to abolitionism in Illinois that Elijah P. Lovejoy's death evoked little reaction. In Springfield, a public meeting denounced the abolitionists as "dangerous members of society." In other northern states, however, dozens of newspapers, few of them sympathetic to the abolitionist movement, condemned the murder as a flagrant assault on freedom of the press. Lovejoy's death persuaded many northerners that slavery posed a threat to the liberties of white Americans as well as blacks.[53]

For several years after the murder it remained difficult to hold abolitionist gatherings in many parts of Illinois. In 1843, a mob armed with clubs prevented fifteen abolitionists from convening a public meeting in Bloomington. In the same year, a large crowd disrupted an abolitionist assembly in Peoria. Two years later, the governor appointed one of the mob's leaders, Norman H. Purple, to the state supreme court. Outside a few counties in northern Illinois settled by New Englanders, abolitionism remained weak well into the 1840s. This was certainly the case in Springfield, where Lincoln lived beginning in 1837. A correspondent of the *Liberator* reported in 1843 that of the city's clergymen, only two, including the lone black minister, had "the moral courage" to speak against slavery. "This is a bitter pro-slavery . . . community," he noted, adding that what was true of Springfield was equally true of "the entire middle and southern portions of this state."[54]

III

NOT SURPRISINGLY, Lincoln repeatedly denied any association with abolitionism. Yet he did not remain indifferent to the clash between colonizationists and abolitionists, or to the mob violence swirling around him. Questions arising from these events rarely came before the Illinois legislature during Lincoln's tenure there from 1834 to 1842. When they did, however, Lincoln proved willing, at some political risk, to set himself apart from his colleagues in both parties. The occasion arose in January 1837, after Joseph Duncan, the state's Democratic governor, informed the legislature that a number of southern states had asked their northern fellow countrymen to condemn abolitionists and take action against them. The Illinois legislature appointed a committee to consider the governor's message. Its chair, Orville H. Browning, a Whig state senator and close friend of Lincoln's (they lived in the same boardinghouse in Vandalia, then the state capital), presented a report and three resolutions.[55]

As southerners had requested, the report condemned the abolitionists, although it hardly offered a ringing defense of slavery. Even though it defended the constitutional right to own slaves, Browning's report was essentially a justification of colonization, which is presumably why the American Colonization Society published it in its monthly periodical, the *African Repository*. Browning's main complaint against the abolitionists was that their agitation had undermined the colonizationists' efforts to liberate "that unfortunate race of our fellow men" from "thraldom" and return them "to their own benighted land." On the other hand, the three resolutions offered strong support for owners of slaves. The first condemned "the formation of abolition societies, and of the doctrines promulgated by them." The second affirmed the legislators' "deep regard and affection" for southern slaveholders, declared the right of property in slaves "sacred to the slave-holding states by the Federal Constitution," and insisted that slavery could not be abolished there without state approval. The third condemned the idea of abolition in the District of Columbia—which abolitionists were demanding in petitions to Congress—without the consent of the District's white citizens. When the resolutions came before the Illinois House of Representatives, Lincoln moved to amend the one opposing abolition in the nation's capital by adding the words "unless the people of the said District petition for the same." His attempt failed, and the House adopted the resolutions, 77 to 6. The Senate then concurred, 18 to 0. Thus, only six members of the legislature voted no. One was Lincoln.[56]

Six weeks later, with the House about to adjourn, Lincoln and fellow Whig Dan Stone presented a "protest"—an explanation for their votes to be published in the legislative proceedings. "They believe," Lincoln and Stone wrote,

> that the institution of slavery is founded on both injustice and bad policy; but that the promulgation of abolition doctrines tends rather to increase than to abate its evils. They believe that the Congress of the United States has no power, under the constitution, to interfere with the institution of slavery in the different States. They believe that the Congress of the United States has the power, under the constitution, to abolish slavery in the District of Columbia; but that that power ought not to be exercised unless at the request of the people of said District. The difference between these opinions and those contained in the said resolutions, is their reason for entering this protest.[57]

Lincoln's "protest" differed from the resolutions primarily in its strong language against slavery and in omitting the description of slaveholders' property rights as "sacred." It foreshadowed Lincoln's public stance in the 1850s: slavery was unjust; northerners had an obligation to respect the constitutional compromises that protected the institution; the national government had the power to act against slavery in the District of Columbia; and Lincoln was not an abolitionist. In his 1860 autobiographical sketch, Lincoln wrote that the protest "briefly defined his position on the slavery question; and so far as it goes, it was then the same that it is now." He instructed John L. Scripps to include the text in the campaign biography of Lincoln that Scripps was writing. During the secession crisis, a member of Congress from Missouri cited Lincoln's words from 1837 as evidence that his intentions regarding slavery could not be trusted.[58]

Hardly a ringing condemnation of slavery, the protest did display genuine political courage. As Scripps pointed out in the *Chicago Press and Tribune* in 1860, the document's "intrinsic ideas" were less important than "the time they were avowed," well before "the conscience of the nation" had awakened to the evil of slavery. When Lincoln criticized slavery as unwise and unjust, abolitionism could not have been weaker or more unpopular in Illinois. The state Anti-Slavery Society had yet to be founded. Indeed, Browning explained that his committee did not recommend action against abolitionist activity because it was "not aware" of any in the state. Certainly, Lincoln could not have anticipated any political benefit from his course. Quite the contrary. The rules required that to be printed, any such protest had to be signed by two members. Lincoln canvassed the other five dissenters, but the four intending to run for reelection declined to join him. Only Stone, a Vermont-born lawyer who had recently been appointed to a judgeship and thus would not have to face the voters, agreed to sign.[59]

A year after his vote on the legislative resolutions, Lincoln again took the opportunity to speak about slavery, although in somewhat oblique fashion. The occasion was "The Perpetuation of Our Political Institutions," a speech he delivered before the Young Men's Lyceum of Springfield, one of thousands of local societies for political self-education and debate frequented by up-and-coming young men in Jacksonian America. Lincoln's subject was citizenship in a democratic republic and threats to American institutions. In keeping with the exceptionalist vision of nationhood so common in postrevolutionary America, he proclaimed that the founders had put in place a political system more conducive to liberty than any in history. His generation's duty was to preserve this "political edifice" and bequeath it to the future. The greatest danger to its continued existence lay within: "If destruction be our lot, we must ourselves be its author and finisher."

Where would this destruction originate? Lincoln pointed to "the increasing disregard for law" evident in a rising tide of mob violence. (He did not exaggerate: literally hundreds of riots of one kind or another took place in the United States in the 1830s, many of them reported in the Illinois press.) Americans, Lincoln warned, had fallen victim to "wild and furious passions, in lieu of the sober judgment of the courts." If respect for the rule of law disintegrated, the stage would be set for the emergence of an ambitious tyrant, a "towering genius" who would seek to gain a place in history even greater than the founders by "emancipating slaves or enslaving free men." The remedy was for Americans to rededicate themselves to the rule of "cold, calculating, unimpassioned reason" and make respect for the rule of law their "political religion."[60]

The Lyceum speech has provided fodder for all sorts of psychological speculations. Was he (or, as has been suggested, Stephen A. Douglas, his rival even then) the future tyrant who would refashion the political system created by the founders and in so doing surpass them in historical importance? Was his description of a battle between reason and passion a reflection of his own mood swings?[61] Certainly, in describing American democracy as a still-unfinished experiment in "liberty and equal rights" and identifying the core question facing the country as "the capability of a people to govern themselves" in the face of lawlessness, Lincoln anticipated themes of his later writings, including the first inaugural and Gettysburg Address. His presentation of the choice facing a future tyrant as "emancipating slaves or enslaving free men" suggested that even this early in his career, Lincoln recognized slavery as the crucial question the founders had failed to resolve and the greatest threat to the survival of the republic.

Condemnations of lawlessness were far from unusual in public orations of the 1830s.[62] What distinguished the Lyceum speech was that Lincoln indirectly but clearly placed the blame on slavery. Lincoln emphasized that no part of the country could claim exemption from mobs: "They spring up among the pleasure hunting masters of southern slaves, and the order loving citizens" of the North (a revealing contrast in a speech arguing that unruly passions constituted the greatest danger to American liberty). Yet speaking only three months after Elijah P. Lovejoy died in Alton at the hands of a mob, Lincoln condemned the "vicious portion of the population" who, among other things, "throw printing presses into rivers [and] shoot editors." No one in the audience could misunderstand the reference to the tragedy seventy miles west of Springfield; some, perhaps, realized that those Lincoln condemned as "vicious" included a number of Alton's most prominent citizens.

Lincoln directly addressed two acts of mob violence in the Lyceum speech, both of which took place in slave states. One was the case of the "mulatto man . . . McIntosh" (identified, unlike Lovejoy, by name), whose lynching in St. Louis in 1836 had led the abolitionist editor to move his newspaper to Alton. Lincoln described McIntosh's ordeal—he was "chained to a tree, and actually burned to death; and all within a single hour from the time he had been a freeman"—with details he may have learned from the extensive coverage in Lovejoy's newspaper. Lincoln also dwelled on the lynching in Mississippi of "negroes, suspected of conspiring to raise an insurrection" along with whites allegedly in league with them. "Dead men," he concluded in a stark, evocative image, "were seen literally dangling from the boughs of trees . . . in numbers almost sufficient, to rival the native Spanish moss." Given the pervasiveness of mob violence in the 1830s, Lincoln did not have to choose black victims to illustrate his point. His subtext was that slavery created a social environment that encouraged lawlessness.[63]

A few moments later, Lincoln explicitly turned to mob violence in relation to abolitionism:

> There is no grievance that is a fit object of redress by mob law. In any case that arises, as for instance, the promulgation of abolitionism, one of two positions is necessarily true; that is, the thing is right within itself, and therefore deserves the protection of all law and all good citizens; or, it is wrong, and therefore proper to be prohibited by legal enactments; and in neither case, is the interposition of mob law, either necessary, justifiable, or excusable.

Lincoln's affirmation of the state's right to prohibit the dissemination of "wrong" opinion may well surprise the modern reader. But it was hardly unusual at the time. Several southern states had enacted laws banning abolitionist agitation. A number of northern politicians, including New York's governor, William L. Marcy, had proposed legislation to criminalize speech that might incite insurrection in other states (a measure clearly aimed at the abolitionists). To be sure, the very attempts to suppress abolitionism had made many northerners sensitive to the crucial impor- tance of the right to dissent. Nonetheless, it would take many years before a jurisprudence defending this right superceded the venerable common law tradition that government enjoyed the power to punish speech and writing with a "bad tendency." (Until the twentieth century, the First Amendment applied only to the federal government and had no bear- ing on state laws that limited free speech.) Lincoln's comment certainly distinguished him from the abolitionists and their supporters. But his main point was not the legitimacy of laws suppressing opinion but the illegitimacy of mob actions against the abolitionists. At a time when most politicians condemned abolitionism as the greatest threat to the republic (an argument that President Martin Van Buren had made in his inaugural address less than a year before the Lyceum speech), Lincoln insisted that assaults on abolitionist meetings and presses endangered the liberty of all Americans.[64]

Four years passed after the Lyceum speech before Lincoln again addressed the issues of slavery and abolition. This came in his 1842 speech to the Springfield Washington Temperance Society, an organiza- tion of reformed drinkers dedicated to promoting temperance. As in other states, drink was a divisive issue in Illinois politics. Whigs, especially New England migrants in the northern part of the state, tended to support laws restricting the sale of alcohol or banning it altogether. Democrats, especially in southern Illinois, viewed drink as a personal matter, outside the purview of the government. Beyond temperance lay the broader issue of evangelical reform (including abolitionism) and its relationship to the state. Did one part of the public have the right to use the law to impose its moral standards on society at large?

In the frontier society of Lincoln's youth, liquor was ubiquitous. As he noted in the speech, "To have a rolling or raising, a hunkering or hoe- down, anywhere without it, was *positively insufferable.*" To middle-class professionals such as Lincoln had become, however, sobriety was a mark of self-control and excessive drinking an example of unrestrained passion. Lincoln, who personally abstained from imbibing liquor, made a num- ber of temperance speeches during the 1840s. But as the Washingtonian speech revealed, his approach differed significantly from that of other advocates of the cause.[65]

Rather than a warning against the evil of alcohol, most of the Washingtonian address consisted of Lincoln's critique of prior efforts to combat it. Speaking in a Presbyterian church, he proclaimed that the "old reformers"—the "preachers, lawyers, and hired agents" who had promoted temperance—had conveyed no "sympathy or feeling" for the very persons they hoped to persuade. They spoke the language of "anathema and denunciation," indicting drinkers as "the authors of all the vice and misery and crime in the land." They urged the "good and virtuous" to ostracize these sinners. So "repugnant to humanity, so uncharitable, so cold-blooded and feelingless" was their language that it alienated the very persons it sought to enlist. By contrast, Lincoln praised the Washingtonians, as former drinkers themselves, for understanding how to approach the objects of their campaign with sympathy and understanding.[66]

Lincoln's strong language about the self-righteousness of previous temperance advocates has been taken, with plausibility, as a more general critique of the strategy and language of evangelical reform, including abolitionism. "A drop of honey," he remarked in the speech, "catches more flies than a gallon of gall." Lincoln favored voluntary abstinence, not coercive laws, and had voted against prohibition measures in the Illinois legislature. When Stephen A. Douglas, during their 1858 debates, charged that Lincoln had "kept a grocery" as a young man (that is, a place where liquor was sold by the drink), Lincoln denied it. But, he added, "I don't know as it would be a great sin, if I had."[67]

As the temperance speech suggests, Lincoln disliked the intemperate language of evangelical reformers. This is one reason why he never identified himself with the abolitionists. In his own later speeches, he would denounce slavery but not slaveholders. He made it perfectly clear in the Lyceum speech that he preferred to appeal to the reason of his listeners rather than to their emotions. Nevertheless, Lincoln's critique came from a man who shared the goals of the temperance movement, and, implicitly, of abolitionism, if not their approach to achieving them. He embraced their understanding of genuine freedom as arising from self-discipline rather than self-indulgence—something violated by both drinkers and slaveholders, who allegedly lived according to their passions. Lincoln closed the temperance speech by looking forward to the "happy day" when reason would rule the world: "all appetites controlled, all passions subdued," and "when there shall be neither a drunkard nor a slave on the earth." Only then, he added, would the promise of the American Revolution, the triumph of mankind's "political and moral freedom," be fulfilled.[68]

But as with virtually every critic of slavery in the Upper South where Lincoln had been born and the Lower North where he lived, hope for an eventual end to slavery did not translate into a vision of a future American society where race no longer defined the rights of citizens. Lincoln may have differed from his legislative colleagues about slavery, but during his first term in the House, he voted in favor of a resolution, which passed 35 to 16, stating that all male citizens age twenty-one and over should enjoy the right to vote regardless of whether or not they owned real estate, but adding that "the elective franchise should be kept pure from contamination by the admission of colored voters."[69]

Lincoln said almost nothing about the rights of black Americans during the first part of his career, but he was not above appealing to prevailing racial prejudices for political purposes. During the 1836 and 1840 presidential campaigns, he and other Whigs seized on Democrat Martin Van Buren's support at the 1821 New York constitutional convention for a provision allowing blacks to vote if they owned $250 worth of property. This actually represented a severe restriction on the political rights of blacks in New York, previously the same as those of whites, since hardly any of the state's African-American population could meet the new qualification. Nonetheless, Whigs in Illinois and elsewhere accused Van Buren of favoring black suffrage. Lincoln repeated the charge in speeches and anonymous newspaper articles. In one 1840 debate, Stephen A. Douglas vehemently denied Lincoln's accusation. At their next encounter, Lincoln read from a campaign biography of Van Buren to substantiate the charge, whereupon Douglas declared the book a forgery, grabbed it from Lincoln's hands, and threw it into the crowd. The Old Soldier, a campaign newspaper edited by Lincoln and a group of other Whigs, also chastised Van Buren for allowing two blacks to testify in court against a white naval officer during his presidency. Clearly, whatever his beliefs about slavery, Lincoln shared his state's prevailing view that blacks did not belong to the "political nation."[70]

Eventually, Lincoln would come to see the abolitionists and himself as part of a common antislavery struggle. Many ideas first advanced by abolitionists found their way into his speeches. Without a direct personal connection to the abolitionist movement, however, Lincoln lacked exposure to the radical egalitarianism that pervaded the cause. This helps to explain why, if Lincoln early in his career made clear his dislike of slavery, it took him a long time to begin to glimpse the possibility of racial equality in America.

2

"Always a Whig":
Lincoln, the Law, and the
Second Party System

■

I

"ALWAYS A WHIG IN POLITICS." With these words, Lincoln in 1859 summarized the first part of his political career. Lincoln joined the Whig party at its birth in the 1830s and left only when it disintegrated in the mid-1850s. Throughout these years, Lincoln remained a party stalwart and perennial aspirant for public office. While many Whigs viewed party organization with discomfort, Lincoln became a skilled political manager. He pushed for the development of an effective Whig political machine down to local precinct captains throughout Illinois. He contributed literally hundreds of unsigned articles to the Whig newspaper in Springfield. Two decades before using the phrase in one of his most celebrated speeches, Lincoln, commenting on the need for better party discipline, declared, "A house divided against itself cannot stand." Lincoln took his own advice about grassroots party organizing. A Boston reporter who accompanied him on a stagecoach ride from Peoria to Springfield in 1847 noted that Lincoln (then a congressman-elect) "knew, or appeared to know, every body we met."[1]

Unfortunately, being a Whig in Illinois meant almost always ending up on the losing side. In the party's twenty-year history, never once was one of its candidates elected a governor or senator, nor did its presidential candidate ever carry the state. To be sure, central Illinois, where Lincoln lived, was the party's one reliable stronghold, consistently electing Whigs to the state legislature and Congress. But "the tendency in Illinois," Lin-

33

coln's law partner John Todd Stuart later remarked, "was for every man of ambition to turn Democrat." "I should as leave think of seeing one rise from the dead," Lincoln's friend David Davis wrote in 1845, as to expect to see Illinois "ever being Whig."[2]

Nonetheless, it is not surprising that a person with Lincoln's deeply rooted desire for self-improvement found the Whig outlook appealing. Both major parties in the Age of Jackson were broad coalitions, attracting support in every part of the country and across the social spectrum. But in general, social classes most attuned to the market revolution—merchants, industrialists, professionals, and commercial farmers, including, in the South, the largest planters—tended to vote Whig. Democratic support centered on urban laborers and small farmers isolated from national markets. Religious and ethnic identities also distinguished the parties. Whigs drew support from evangelical Protestants, including many attracted to the era's myriad social reform movements—temperance, school reform, and, in the North, antislavery. Democrats did well among more traditional Protestant sects as well as Roman Catholics, among them the growing number of immigrants from Germany and Ireland.[3]

The outlooks of the two parties reflected these social realities. Whigs, North and South, viewed government as an agent of economic development, moral improvement, and national unity. They rallied to Henry Clay's American System, a comprehensive program of government-sponsored economic modernization. The plan centered on a tariff on imported manufactured goods to aid industry and protect American workers from the competition of low-wage foreign labor; government aid to internal improvements like the roads, canals, and railroads that formed the infrastructure of the market economy; and a national bank to provide a stable currency. They also believed government should improve the moral character of the citizenry by building schools and discouraging drinking, violations of the Sabbath, and other vices.[4]

Whigs insisted that in an expanding economy all classes shared a harmony of interests. Government-promoted economic growth created the context in which "self-made men" (a phrase coined by Calvin Colton, Henry Clay's campaign biographer) could achieve economic success and assimilate into the republic of property holders. During the 1850s, this emphasis on individual opportunity would become the foundation of the Republican party's "free labor" ideology and be linked to a critique of slave society for stifling economic advancement. But during Lincoln's early career, northern Whigs celebrated social opportunity in contrast not so much to slavery as to the critique of growing class inequality advanced by the Democratic party and the early labor movement. The Whig economic outlook formed part of a broad vision of national unity undisturbed by class, regional, or sectional conflict.[5]

Democrats charged that Whig economic policies favored the rich and well connected. They warned that "non-producers" such as merchants and bankers sought to use government to advance their own interests at the expense of honest workingmen. Active government appeared to Democrats as a threat to personal liberty, and they preferred to allow individuals to pursue economic advancement without outside interference. Their hands-off economic policy complemented moral laissez-faire. Democrats adamantly defended the separation of church and state and insisted that government should not impose any single definition of morality on a heterogeneous nation.[6]

Of course, many exceptions existed to this general pattern of party support. Lincoln, who had grown up on a farm in the backwoods of Indiana and never embraced revivalist religion, seemed to fit the Democratic mold. Certainly, he did not share the evangelical outlook so prominent among northern Whigs. Lincoln had a deep familiarity with the Bible, which he quoted frequently in his speeches. He attended religious services but, quite unusually for a Whig, never became a member of a church. Lincoln's religious views evolved over time, but they had more in common with the deism of the Enlightenment, which posited a God who did not regularly intervene in human affairs, than the personal Jesus of revivalist Protestantism. According to local lore, as a young man in New Salem, Illinois, where he lived from 1831 to 1837, Lincoln read Tom Paine's great attack on revealed religion, *The Age of Reason*, and wrote a manuscript denying the divinity of the Bible, which he then destroyed at the urging of friends. Lincoln's one public statement about his religious beliefs before the Civil War came in 1846 during his campaign for Congress. His opponent Peter Cartwright, a Methodist preacher, accused him of infidelity. Lincoln responded by publishing a handbill denying ever speaking with "intentional disrespect of religion in general." What is remarkable about this document is that nowhere in it did Lincoln actually affirm any religious faith except for a fatalistic "doctrine of necessity" whereby "some power" worked out mankind's

destiny in ways human beings could not fathom. It was hardly the statement of a devout Christian.[7]

Lincoln may have differed from most northern Whigs in his religious
outlook, but he found appealing the party's vision of an integrated, modernizing economy that offered opportunities for hardworking individuals
to rise in society. He always considered himself one of the self-made men
celebrated by Whig ideology.

Lincoln's early life coincided with far-reaching changes in transportation, the early development of manufacturing, and the growing dominance
of a cash economy. Despite the rapid spread of market relations, however,
farm families like the Lincolns in the southern Northwest still concentrated on growing food for their own needs. During Lincoln's youth, little
money circulated and the barter of labor and goods was common. The
Indiana farm where Lincoln grew up lay sixteen miles north of the Ohio
River, quite a distance given the primitive state of transportation. Stocked
with hogs, cattle, horses, and sheep, and growing wheat and corn, it was
basically self-sufficient. The family tanned leather, sewed clothing, and
made its own cloth. The surrounding forest teemed with wild game that
they hunted for food. Physically strong, Lincoln was assigned to manual
labor from an early age. Indiana law, like the law of nearly every state in
the Union, gave parents the right to the "service" of their children until the
age of twenty-one, and Thomas Lincoln frequently sent his son to work
for neighbors to pay off debts. One of his acquaintances later recalled
Lincoln remarking, "I used to be a slave," a reference to his father's appropriation of his labor. In Lincoln's early experiences may lie the origins of
his intense later commitment to the idea that all persons have a natural
right to the fruits of their toil.[8]

Lincoln's two round-trip journeys to New Orleans (in which he traveled
by both flatboat and steamboat) illustrated how he grew to adulthood in a
period of transition between old and new technologies, and between the
household and market economies. Even when the Lincoln family moved
in 1830 to the rich farming land of Sangamon County in central Illinois,
river transport remained unreliable and commerce restricted. When frontier families produced a surplus, they were eager to market it to local
merchants, who, in turn, shipped it to New Orleans. In exchange, farm
families and residents of small towns acquired products that could not be
produced at home, including glass, tableware, and other consumer goods
transported from the East via Pittsburgh and the Ohio River, or from St.

Louis. Nonetheless, New Salem and Springfield, where Lincoln moved in 1837, were small communities isolated from larger markets. Merchants tended to fail, as Lincoln did when he ran a store in New Salem. Residents of Illinois stood poised between "rude unsophisticated life and a civilized comfort," in the words of a journalist who visited the state. Not until the 1840s, when the National Road reached Illinois from Maryland and railroad construction began, did the state become fully integrated into the national market economy.[9]

Lincoln never romanticized his backwoods youth. When his 1860 campaign biographer John L. Scripps asked about his upbringing, Lincoln replied with a line from the English poet Thomas Gray's *Elegy Written in a Country Churchyard*: "the short and simple annals of the poor." Early in life, Lincoln decided that he did not want to live like his father, who in his son's eyes exemplified the values of the pre-market world where people remained content with a subsistence lifestyle. From age twenty-one, Lincoln lived in towns and cities and evinced no interest in returning to the farm or to manual labor. He held jobs—storekeeper, lawyer, and surveyor—essential to the market economy. The storekeeper brought manufactured goods from afar to isolated communities. The bulk of legal work revolved around land titles, business arrangements, bankruptcy cases, and the credit and debt that oiled the market revolution. The surveyor transformed land into private property with clearly identified boundaries, ready to be bought and sold. Lincoln was so enmeshed in market society that during the 1840s and 1850s, even while pursuing his legal and political careers, he provided credit reports about his Springfield neighbors to the Mercantile Agency, a credit rating company founded in New York City by the abolitionist Lewis Tappan.[10]

Like many ambitious, successful sons, Lincoln did everything he could to distance himself from his father. He did not invite Thomas Lincoln to his wedding or, indeed, to visit his family in Springfield at any time. In 1851, when Lincoln's stepmother informed him that his father lay on his deathbed a hundred miles from Springfield, Lincoln declined to visit him, explaining that "if we could meet now, it is doubtful whether it would not be more painful than pleasant." In the autobiographical account he composed for Scripps, Lincoln wrote that his father "never did more in the way of writing than to bunglingly sign his own name," a description so uncharitable that Scripps chose not to include it in the biography he produced. Lincoln had a similar attitude toward his stepbrother, John D.

Johnston, another self-sufficient farmer. When Johnston asked for a loan in 1848, Lincoln chastised him for laziness and advised him to join the cash economy: "Go to work for the best money wages." He refused the loan but offered to match any income that Johnston earned.[11]

Lincoln, who enjoyed less than one year of formal schooling, was essentially self-educated. He read widely in nineteenth-century political economy, including the works of the British apostle of economic liberalism John Stuart Mill and the Americans Henry Carey and Francis Wayland. Although these writers differed on specific policies—Carey was among the most prominent advocates of a high tariff while Wayland favored free trade—all extolled the virtues of entrepreneurship and technological improvement in a modernizing market economy. (Wayland, the president of Brown University and a polymath who published works on ethics, religion, and philosophy, made no direct reference to slavery in his 400-page tome, *Elements of Political Economy*, but did insist that people did not work productively unless allowed to benefit from their own labor, an argument Lincoln would reiterate in the 1850s.) Throughout his life, Lincoln remained fascinated by technological innovations, even receiving a patent in 1849 for "a new and improved manner of combining adjustable buoyant chambers with steam boats." A decade later, he listed patent laws along with the art of writing and the "discovery" of America as the three greatest improvements in human history. When he delivered a lecture to the Wisconsin State Agricultural Society in 1859, Lincoln noted, "I have thought a good deal, in an abstract way, about a steam plow." He lauded the advantages of scientific, mechanized farming, urging agriculturalists to combine physical labor with "cultivated thought." These attitudes were characteristic of the Whig party.[12]

By the 1840s, having married a woman from a prosperous family and established a good career as a lawyer, Lincoln had achieved respectability. Yet along the way, he had experienced poverty and failure. In New Salem in the 1830s, he invested his meager funds in stores that "winked out" (went bankrupt), accumulating debts that took many years to repay. Lincoln took all sorts of odd jobs in New Salem, working at a grain and saw mill, harvesting crops, and splitting rails. He received assistance from his friends in fending off creditors and from the local, state, and national governments, relying on employment as a postmaster, surveyor, and member of the legislature to make ends meet. Like his idol Henry Clay, Lincoln saw government as an active force promoting opportunity and advancement. Its "legitimate object," he wrote in an undated memorandum, "is to do for a community of people, whatever they need to have done, but can not do . . . for themselves." He offered as examples building roads and public schools and providing relief to the poor. To Lincoln, Whig policies offered the surest means of creating economic opportunities for upwardly striving men like himself.[13]

Lincoln came of age as two great transformations unleashed by American independence—the market revolution and the democratic revolution—reached fruition, and he embraced them both. Many conservative Whigs retained a distaste for popular democracy inherited from the old Federalists. They preferred government by a "natural aristocracy" and disapproved of the elimination of property qualifications for voting, which occurred in nearly every state between 1800 and 1828. Lincoln was part of a younger generation of "New School Whigs" comfortable with the world of mass political democracy, and was convinced that the party could compete head-on with the Democrats for the votes of humble citizens. Another forward-looking young Whig, William H. Seward, later Lincoln's secretary of state, alarmed conservative members of his party by actively seeking the support of the state's poor immigrant voters when he served as governor of New York from 1839 to 1843.[14]

By the time of Andrew Jackson's presidency, the axiom that the people ruled had become a cliché of American politics. When he ran for reelection to the legislature in 1836, Lincoln took this principle further than most of his contemporaries by issuing a public letter stating that he favored "admitting all whites to the right of suffrage, who pay taxes or bear arms, (by no means excluding females)." Very few women, mainly property-owning widows, would qualify, since none served in the militia and married women did not pay taxes in their own name. Nonetheless, Lincoln's statement represented a remarkable departure from the prevailing gendered definition of "the people." Simultaneously, however, as his statement made clear, Lincoln accepted the legitimacy of the racial boundary that excluded blacks from participation in American democracy.[15]

As with so many contemporaries in Jacksonian America, including his great rival Stephen A. Douglas, Lincoln found in politics an unparalleled opportunity for social advancement. He ran for the Illinois House of Representatives for the first time in 1832 at the age of twenty-three—the only time, he later wrote, that he suffered defeat in a popular vote—and two years later was elected to the first of his four terms in the legislature.

His earliest campaign pronouncements identified him as a supporter of government-sponsored economic development and the creation of a public infrastructure. He dwelled at length on the value of internal improvements, specifically making the Sangamon River navigable by steamboat (a plan never implemented) so that New Salem could export farmers' surplus agricultural goods and import "necessary articles from abroad." Even "the poorest and most thinly populated counties," he added, could thrive through participation in the market economy. He also promoted public education—something he had barely enjoyed—as "the most important subject which we as a people can be engaged in."[16]

Lincoln rose rapidly in his party. As early as 1836, he had emerged as "the acknowledged leader of the Whigs in the House." He played a key role in the shift of the state capital from Vandalia to Springfield in 1837, and then moved his residence from New Salem to the new center of government. And he became a key advocate of a vast plan for state financing of canals, railroads, and river improvements, paid for by borrowing. Joshua Speed later recalled Lincoln saying he wanted to be the "DeWitt Clinton of Illinois," referring to the New York governor who built the Erie Canal, completed in 1825. The internal improvements scheme, expanded so that every corner of the state would receive some benefit from it, initially won support from both parties. But the economic depression that began in 1837 made it impossible for the state to pay interest on its bonds. Democrats called for scrapping the program while Lincoln, as he put it, tried to "save something to the State, from the general wreck." When the House, in 1840, voted 77 to 11 to abandon the system, Lincoln was among the minority. The following year, when interest due on the internal improvements bonds considerably exceeded the state's entire revenue, Illinois defaulted, essentially declaring bankruptcy. It took the state forty-five years to pay off the debt.[17]

During the 1840 presidential campaign, when Whigs passed over their leader Henry Clay to nominate the Indian-fighter William Henry Harrison for president, Lincoln made numerous speeches and participated in debates with prominent local Democrats, including Stephen A. Douglas, then the secretary of state of Illinois. With President Martin Van Buren weakened because of the economic downturn, Whigs repackaged themselves as supporters of popular democracy, portraying the wealthy Harrison as a man of the people and Van Buren, the son of a tavern keeper, as an aristocrat. "No one will seriously pretend that this was a campaign of ideas," the Indiana political leader George W. Julian later recalled.

Yet Lincoln's speeches in fact offered well-reasoned arguments for Whig economic policies. He defended the constitutionality of the Bank of the United States, blamed the economic crisis on its destruction, and analyzed the likely impact of the Independent Treasury, which Van Buren had installed to replace it.[18]

During his entire legislative career and for years thereafter, Lincoln's primary concern remained economic policy. Sharing Henry Clay's belief that the Whig economic program would benefit all Americans, as well as Clay's powerful devotion to national unity, Lincoln also knew that as an intersectional institution, his party's prospects at the national level (where questions concerning the Bank, tariff, and federal aid to internal improvements would be resolved) required cooperation between northerners and southerners, nonslaveholders and slaveholders. Even as the slavery issue made its way from the wings to the center stage of American politics during the 1840s, Lincoln would continue to view it essentially as a divisive influence, a danger to the success of his party and the stability and future of the Union.

II

WILLIAM HENRY HARRISON swept to victory in the 1840 election but, as usual, the Democrats carried Illinois. That year, Lincoln won election to his last term in the legislature. From 1842, when his career in the Illinois House ended, until he assumed the presidency in 1861, he held no public office with the exception of a single term in Congress. He remained, however, an active member of the Whig party, regularly campaigning for its candidates and continuing to emphasize its stance on economic issues. He made more speeches on the protective tariff than on any other subject, he later remarked. As late as 1846, when Lincoln ran for Congress and the issue of slavery was making its way into political debate in connection with the Mexican War, the tariff remained, as one newspaper reported, the "principal subject" of Lincoln's speeches.[19]

Nonetheless, the slavery issue could not be entirely avoided. Antislavery sentiment was "gaining ground in the public mind," the prominent Ohio Whig Thomas Corwin noted, a fact "that no one can overlook." Some observers blamed the Liberty party—founded in 1840 by abolitionists who, unlike the followers of William Lloyd Garrison, believed in running candidates for public office—for Henry Clay's defeat in 1844. The

15,000 votes cast in New York for James G. Birney, the Liberty party's presidential candidate, enabled Democrat James K. Polk to carry the state and win the presidential election. Liberty supporters were far less numerous in Illinois—in 1840, the party received all of 160 votes. By 1844, its total had risen to 3,433 in a turnout that exceeded 100,000. Yet in a few northern counties, the Liberty party polled a substantial vote and became a factor in local politics. Given the Whigs' minority status in Illinois, a shrewd observer of politics like Lincoln could not help thinking about how to attract Liberty voters to his party.[20]

In October 1845, Lincoln sent a long letter to the Liberty supporter Williamson Dudley in Putnam County, where Birney had received 23 percent of the vote the previous year. "I was glad to hear you say," Lincoln wrote, "that you intend to attempt to bring about, at the next election in Putnam, a union of the whigs proper, and such of the liberty men, as are whigs in principle on all questions save only that of slavery." Lincoln set out to delineate the differences between Whigs and "liberty men." Both viewed slavery as an evil and both opposed the annexation of Texas, which had joined the Union as a slave state the previous March. Yet, Lincoln continued, "I was never much interested in the Texas question." He failed to see how annexation would "augment the evil of slavery," since slaves in Texas—whether in the American Union or outside it—would remain slaves. As to promoting emancipation in the South, Lincoln continued, "I hold it to be a paramount duty of us in the free states, due to the Union of the states, and perhaps to liberty itself (paradox though it may seem) to let the slavery of the other states alone"—the paradox being that to agitate against slavery endangered the preservation of the Union and Constitution that themselves embodied freedom. At the same time, Lincoln continued, northerners should never act so as to prevent "slavery from dying a natural death," or finding "new places" in which to thrive.[21]

Like his 1837 "protest," Lincoln's letter anticipated a position he would articulate in far greater detail and with far greater force in the 1850s. The ideal of liberty was central to American nationhood. Thus, the compromises of the Constitution, including recognition of slavery in existing states, must be respected by northerners lest the continued existence of the Union, the embodiment of liberty, be placed in danger. Nonextension, not abolition, was the only constitutionally available position for critics of slavery. Yet Lincoln did look forward to an American future, perhaps quite distant, without slavery.

Despite its tiny vote totals, the Liberty party played an important part in the evolution of political antislavery. Although the party was composed of committed abolitionists, its adherents accepted the pre–Civil War consensus that the Constitution gave Congress no authority whatever to interfere with slavery in the states. So widespread was this view, in the North as well as the South, that only a small minority of abolitionists challenged it. Lysander Spooner, a Massachusetts-born radical whose causes included postal reform, anarchism, and the rights of labor as well as abolitionism, claimed that by affirming mankind's inalienable right to liberty, the Declaration of Independence had abolished slavery, which had not legally existed since. Alvan Stewart, a prolific writer and speaker against slavery from New York, developed the argument that the Constitution's Fifth Amendment, which barred depriving any person of "life, liberty, or property" without due process of law, made slavery unconstitutional. Slaves, said Stewart, should go to court and obtain writs of habeas corpus ordering their release from bondage.[22]

Very few Americans found this reading of the law persuasive. "Absurd" was how the Republican *Cincinnati Gazette* described it in 1860. Far more influential was a political-constitutional strategy for opposing slavery developed in the 1840s by the antislavery Whig politicians Joshua R. Giddings and William H. Seward and, most notably, by the Liberty party leader Salmon P. Chase. It went by the name "freedom national" and concentrated on ways to make the federal government "freedom's open, active, and perpetual ally" by attacking slavery in every jurisdiction outside the southern states—the District of Columbia, the territories, federal forts and arsenals, and the interstate trade in slaves. "The principle must be established," Chase wrote in 1842, "that the government is a nonslaveholding government, that the nation is a nonslaveholding nation, that slavery is a creature of state law . . . to be confined within the states which admit and sanction it." There, he believed, it would "perish."

In Chase's personality deep religious conviction intertwined with inordinate ambition and self-regard. Somehow the result was a lifelong commitment to promoting the rights of African-Americans, slave and free. As a lawyer in Cincinnati in the mid-1830s Chase had been drawn to abolitionism as an expression of outrage over a mob attack on the offices of James G. Birney, who was then editing an antislavery newspaper in the city. Chase's program, developed in conjunction with Birney, offered an indirect means of limiting the power of slavery and promoting eventual abolition without violating the Constitution. It laid the groundwork for the juridical outlook of the Republican party in the 1850s and during the Civil War.[23]

Chase based his argument on a reading of the legal and political principles of the Age of Revolution. He harkened back to the case of James Somerset, a West Indian slave who sued for his liberty after being brought to England by his owner. In a landmark 1772 decision, Lord Mansfield, the chief justice of England, freed Somerset. Since the decision predated the printing of official versions of court decisions, what Mansfield actually said remains a matter of dispute. His ruling appears to have been a relatively cautious one, stating that the laws of England did not allow a master to use force to capture and remove from the country a slave who had escaped. Mansfield tried to rule in Somerset's favor without freeing the thousands of other West Indian slaves present in England or asserting the general principle that slavery could not exist outside the jurisdiction that created it. But the Somerset decision took on a life of its own. The antislavery movement on both sides of the Atlantic seized on it as establishing the legal doctrine that slavery was "so odious" that whenever a person left a jurisdiction where local law recognized the institution, he automatically became free. The case came to be best remembered for a phrase used by Somerset's attorney: the air of England was "too pure for a slave to breathe." This idea, known as the Somerset principle or "freedom principle," quickly passed into English common law. It established a sharp distinction between the property right in slaves, which enjoyed only local legitimacy, and other forms of property, universally recognized as such.[24]

As an Ohio lawyer, Chase strove to persuade the courts to adopt his outlook, without much success. He took so many cases defending blacks who had escaped from bondage that he became known as a kind of "attorney general for fugitive slaves." In his 1837 defense of Matilda, who had accompanied her owner from Missouri and escaped in Cincinnati, and ten years later in *Jones v. Van Zandt*, a case involving an Ohio farmer fined for harboring nine fugitives, which Chase took all the way to the Supreme Court without a fee, he argued that despite the Constitution's fugitive slave clause, the moment an escapee entered a free state, he or she became free. Not surprisingly, Chase lost these cases. Matilda was returned to her owner and most likely sold at a slave market. Van Zandt paid his fine. Yet, as Charles Sumner, a young Massachusetts lawyer just embarking on a career in antislavery politics, commented about the Van Zandt ruling, Chase's argument "will seriously influence the public mind."[25]

In one legal context, the Somerset principle slowly came to be recognized in northern courts. This concerned the right of "transit"—that is, whether southern slaveholders had the right to bring their slaves into states that had abolished the institution. Until the 1830s, northern states generally recognized the right of transit, although some limited the amount of time an owner could keep a slave within their borders. Increasingly, however, northern courts began to deny that slave law reached into the free states. Chief Justice Lemuel Shaw of Massachusetts in 1836 declared free all slaves entering the state, except for those who were fugitives. Connecticut courts adopted the same principle the following year, as did New York's legislature in 1841. Other states soon followed.[26]

In Illinois, the courts whittled away at the legal defenses of slavery, but very slowly. As late as 1843, the state supreme court explicitly affirmed the extraterritorial reach of the laws of slave states, noting that "thousands [of owners] from Kentucky, Virginia, Maryland," and elsewhere had "sought and found free and safe passage with their slaves" across Illinois. At this point, Illinois accorded more recognition to the right of slave transit than any northern state except New Jersey. But the 1843 decision proved to be the last of its kind. Two years later, for the first time, the Illinois Supreme Court declared that no person born after the date of the Northwest Ordinance—that is, 1787—could be held as a slave in Illinois and that any slave brought into the state by his or her owner automatically became free.[27]

These victories arose from the determined efforts of a group of lawyers who risked public odium by defending fugitive slaves in court and challenging the long-standing system of black indentured servitude. John M. Palmer, Gustave Koerner, and Orville H. Browning, all future Republican politicians, argued that blacks held to long-term indentures were free, and fought their cases in court without charge. In the 1850s, Lincoln's law partner William Herndon represented fugitive slaves pro bono. The state's most prominent antislavery lawyer was Lyman Trumbull, a native of Connecticut who taught in Georgia in the 1830s before moving to Illinois, where he established a law practice and entered Democratic party politics. In the 1840s, Trumbull represented numerous blacks held to servitude under indentures. Like Lincoln, Trumbull lived in a part of the state settled by migrants from Kentucky and Tennessee. His battle against the remnants of slavery in Illinois required political courage, but his experience also demonstrated that it was possible to be identified as a friend of the slave and still win elections. Trumbull ran successfully for the state supreme court in 1848 and won reelection with virtually no opposition in 1852.[28]

After 1842, when he decided not to run for reelection and his legislative career ended, Lincoln's livelihood derived from his law practice. Any lawyer in states bordering the Ohio River could, if he wished, devote part of his practice to cases involving fugitive slaves. Lincoln was not among those who in the 1840s and 1850s sought out cases involving blacks, or who volunteered to aid the antislavery cause. During his legal career, he handled more than 5,000 cases, mostly minor disputes about debts, land titles, and marital difficulties. Only 34 of these cases involved black persons in any way. Most were routine matters—a divorce, debt collections, issues relating to contracts, and several property transactions involving William Florville, a Springfield barber Lincoln befriended and whose tax matters he sometimes handled.[29]

Two of Lincoln's cases reflected how "whiteness" possessed concrete legal significance in Illinois. Thus, white persons accused of having intimate relations with a black person, or of being black, took action to defend their reputations and legal status. In 1844, Lincoln represented Ambrose Edwards and his wife, who sued another couple for slander for saying that Mrs. Edwards had "raised a family of children by a negro." A jury concluded that this accusation did indeed constitute slander and ruled in the Edwardses' favor. When the other couple appealed, the Edwardses hired Lincoln to represent them. Lincoln urged the Illinois Supreme Court to consider the accusation of engaging in interracial sex in the context of the almost universal disapproval of miscegenation in the state. But the court rejected his argument and reversed the judgment, arguing that the words themselves did not necessarily accuse Mrs. Edwards of fornication across racial lines or adultery, both of which would have subjected her to criminal penalties.

In a similar 1855 case, Lincoln represented William Dungey, a dark-complexioned man who sued his brother-in-law for slander on the grounds that he had referred to Dungey as "Black Bill," a "negro." Lincoln challenged the veracity of depositions presented to the court claiming that Dungey was known to be of mixed racial ancestry. Dungey was actually Portuguese, Lincoln told the jury. "My client is not a Negro," he added,

"tho it is no crime to be a Negro—no crime to be born with black skin."
Lincoln won an award of $600 plus legal costs. Had he lost the case,
Dungey would have been stripped of the right to vote and been subject
to penalties under the Illinois Black Laws, since he had married a white
woman. Illinois law did make it a crime, under certain circumstances, to
be "born with black skin."[30]

Many of Lincoln's cases left only a fragmentary historical record. He
seems to have represented a few individuals indicted for harboring fugitive
slaves; in one such case, in 1845, a jury acquitted the accused and Lincoln
and Herndon received a fee of five dollars.[31] On two well-documented
occasions, Lincoln became involved in the contentious issue of whether
residence in Illinois automatically made a slave free.

The first such case, *Bailey v. Cromwell and McNaughton*, argued in
1841, revolved around whether a black person could still be sold in Illinois.
David Bailey had signed a promissory note for the purchase of a black
woman, Nance Legins-Cox, from Nathan Cromwell. The parties agreed
that Cromwell would provide proof of her status as an indentured servant
or slave. Thirteen years earlier, Legins-Cox had unsuccessfully sued for
her freedom. Clearly a determined individual, she now refused to work
for Bailey without being paid wages, and abandoned him altogether after
six months, "asserting and declaring all the time that she was free." Subsequently, Cromwell died and his estate sued Bailey for payment of the
promissory note. Bailey refused, and retained Lincoln and his partner,
John Todd Stuart, to represent him.

Lincoln argued that Cromwell had never provided the required proof
of the woman's slave status and therefore violated the contract; hence
Bailey did not have to pay. The local court, however, ruled that Bailey had
to satisfy the debt and he appealed. The circuit court reversed the decision. The judges noted that in their previous term they had decided that
in the absence of evidence to the contrary, "the presumption of law was,
in this state, that every person was free, without regard to color." Since
no countervailing proof had been offered, this presumption must apply to
Legins-Cox, and "the sale of a free person is illegal." Legins-Cox subsequently gave birth to eight children, all of them, she proudly affirmed late
in life, "born in freedom." The decision did not outlaw slavery or servitude
in Illinois, but placed the burden of proof squarely on those claiming
ownership of such persons.[32]

In October 1847, six years after obtaining Legins-Cox's freedom, Lincoln represented a slaveholder who sought to regain possession of run-away slaves. Robert Matson, a resident of Kentucky, in 1836 purchased a large tract of land in Coles County, Illinois. Each year he brought slaves to work his farm and then returned them to Kentucky, bringing another contingent the following year so as to avoid legal difficulties. One slave, Anthony Bryant, however, remained in Illinois for an extended period, obtained his freedom, and acted as Matson's foreman. In 1845, Anthony's slave wife Jane joined him with their five children. Evidently, some time in 1847 an altercation took place between Jane Bryant and Matson's white housekeeper, who threatened to have Bryant and her children sold "down South in the cotton fields." Matson then sent one child back to Kentucky. The alarmed Anthony Bryant sought the aid of two local abolitionists, Gideon Ashmore, an innkeeper in Oakland, Illinois, and Hiram Ruther-ford, a physician. They advised Bryant to bring his family to the inn, even though harboring fugitive slaves was a crime under the Black Laws of Illinois. Bryant did so, and to recover them, Matson engaged as his lawyer Usher F. Linder, the former attorney general who a decade earlier had led the mob that broke up the first meeting of the state antislavery society. Formerly a Democrat, Linder had recently joined the Whigs and become a friend of Lincoln's. (In the 1850s Linder would return to the Democratic fold.) Linder persuaded a local justice of the peace to lodge Jane Bryant and her children in the local prison, where they remained during the fall of 1847. In accordance with another provision of the Black Laws, Matson sued the abolitionists for $2,500 for enticing his slaves to escape.

The two cases, *In Re Bryant* and the suit against the abolitionists, came before the Coles County Circuit Court in October 1847. The abolition-ists asked Lincoln to represent them. He replied, according to Ruther-ford's later recollection, that he could not do so, as he had already been approached by Linder to represent Matson. Shortly afterward, Lincoln obtained his release from Matson, but Rutherford, from a sense of injured pride, refused Lincoln's offer to represent him. So Lincoln took Mat-son's case, serving as co-counsel with Linder regarding both the legal status of Jane Bryant and her children and Matson's lawsuit against the abolitionists. The abolitionists' lawyer, Orlando B. Ficklin, a Democratic member of the U.S. House of Representatives from Illinois, cited the English precedent that any person who sets foot on free soil automatically becomes free. Lincoln argued that the principle of "transit" applied: The Bryants were only in Illinois temporarily and Matson intended to take them back to Kentucky. Therefore, they should be returned to Matson. Lincoln also presented testimony showing Matson to be, as the court put it, "an extremely kind and indulgent master."

The Coles County judges insisted that the case involved the law, not "the abstract question of slavery." Slavery, they continued, echoing Ficklin's argument, was a local institution, and except for fugitives from other states, the moment a slave arrived in free territory "the rights of the master cease, and the slave becomes free." (Since Matson had brought the Bryants into Illinois, the Constitution's fugitive slave clause did not apply to them.) The Bryants' two years in Illinois far exceeded any conceivable right of transit, but even if they had remained "but a day," their status as slaves ended. The judges also dismissed Matson's suit against the abolitionists. Thus, thanks to Orlando B. Ficklin, not Lincoln, the Somerset principle came to Illinois. Ironically, Lincoln's position—that residence in a free state did not automatically make a slave free—was adopted, to widespread dismay in the North, by Chief Justice Roger B. Taney in the *Dred Scott* decision ten years later. Eventually, the Bryant family made its way to Liberia, an outcome that may have affected Lincoln's subsequent belief that emancipated slaves would be willing to be colonized outside the United States.[33]

Overall, in his few cases involving blacks, Lincoln stuck to the facts and the letter of the law rather than seeking to establish antislavery principles or make a political point. In the Dungey slander case, Lincoln argued on the basis of the evidence; he did not challenge the Black Laws, but in effect got his client exempted from them. In the Bailey case he concentrated on the lack of evidence that Legins-Cox was a slave. The Matson case remains perhaps the most controversial of Lincoln's career. Lincoln not only sought to return a woman and her four children to slavery, but also represented a client who claimed damages under the Black Laws from those who had assisted the family. Lincoln did not mind working with Linder, an extreme anti-abolitionist, as co-counsel. He took a position at odds with recent precedents throughout the northern states. As Frederick Douglass noted about this case (without mentioning Lincoln by name), "We should suppose that this whole subject had been rendered so clear by repeated decisions, all going to confirm the same principle, that not another case of the kind would ever again come up."[34]

Lincoln's willingness to represent Matson does not mean that he was a supporter of slavery. Dr. Rutherford later recalled that he sought out

Lincoln, "his views and mine on the wrong of slavery being in perfect accord." Yet unlike antislavery lawyers such as Lyman Trumbull and Salmon P. Chase, Lincoln made a sharp distinction between his personal outlook and his practice of the law. Of course, lawyers frequently represent clients whose beliefs and interests are at odds with their own sentiments. The adversary system depends on every person called to court enjoying legal representation. On the other hand, nothing required Lincoln to take this particular case. In an effort to exonerate him, Lincoln's late-nineteenth-century biographer Jesse W. Weik claimed that the future president, uncomfortable with his role, in effect threw the case, presenting a weak argument on Matson's behalf. If true, this would represent a serious violation of legal ethics. In fact, the court's opinion noted that on both sides, counsel had presented their arguments "with unusual ability." In any event, if Lincoln represented Matson because he needed to pursue his livelihood, he ended up disappointed. Matson left Illinois in disgust, without paying Lincoln's fee.[35]

Lincoln's decision to represent Matson in seeking to return to slavery a family entitled to their freedom under Illinois law seems inexcusable. By 1847, Lincoln was no longer a fledgling lawyer but a respected member of the Illinois bar who was about to leave for Washington to take a seat in Congress. In the 1850s, Lincoln would repeatedly condemn Stephen A. Douglas and his famous statement that he did not care if slavery were "voted up or down." But in the Matson case, in which Lincoln proved willing to represent either side, he came perilously close to precisely this moral and ideological neutrality regarding slavery.[36]

If the Matson case proves anything, it is, as Lincoln's biographer David Donald argues, that up to this point Lincoln had not given consistent thought to the issue of slavery.[37] He had, to be sure, established an antislavery reputation, in large measure because of his 1837 "protest." But his antislavery sentiments had not yet developed to the point where they affected either his commitment to the Whig party or his law practice. But he was now entering, for the first time, an arena where he would be forced to clarify his views and make political decisions regarding slavery.

Lincoln argued the Matson case on October 16, 1847. The following day he returned to Springfield, and a week later he and his family departed for Washington to assume his seat as a member of Congress. On the way, they spent three weeks with Mary Lincoln's family in Lexington, Kentucky. Lincoln was almost certainly in the audience when Henry

Clay spoke in Lexington on November 13. Clay condemned as an act of American "aggression" the Mexican War initiated by President James K. Polk the previous year and affirmed that had he been in Congress when the declaration of war had been considered, "I never, never could have voted for that bill." He went on to oppose the acquisition of territory for the expansion of slavery and to reiterate his "well-known" belief that slavery was "a great evil." "I should rejoice," he added, "if not a single slave breathed the air or was within the limits of our country." But, he continued, abolitionist agitation only damaged the prospects for gradual emancipation. The American Colonization Society offered the "benevolent" solution to the slavery question and obviated the greatest obstacle to emancipation, "the continuance of the emancipated slaves to abide among us." Clay reminded the audience that nearly fifty years earlier, he had proposed a plan of gradual emancipation for Kentucky.[38]

Twelve days later, the Lincoln family departed for Washington, where Lincoln would make his first appearance on the national stage and present his first concrete plan for addressing the issue of slavery.

III

IT WAS A PECULIARITY of nineteenth-century politics that more than a year elapsed between the election of a Congress and its initial meeting. The Thirtieth Congress, elected in 1846, assembled in December 1847 to confront the complex questions arising from the Mexican War. Although Democrats in the Senate outnumbered their opponents by almost two to one, the Whig party enjoyed a narrow margin in the House—the only time in his entire legislative career that Lincoln found himself in the majority. Both parties, however, were internally divided, especially on the question of the future expansion of slavery. In August 1846, just as the previous Congress drew to a close, Congressman David Wilmot of Pennsylvania had proposed an amendment to an appropriation bill requiring that slavery be prohibited in any territory acquired from Mexico. The Wilmot Proviso, which passed the House but failed in the Senate, split both parties along sectional lines and ushered in a new era in which the slavery issue moved to the center stage of American politics.

In one form or another, the Proviso came before the House numerous times during Lincoln's term in Congress. Every northern Whig supported it, while northern Democrats, evidently more wary of offending the southern wing of their party, split. For example, when a motion came before the House in February 1848 to kill the Proviso by tabling it, all seventy-one northern Whigs, including Lincoln, voted no while northern Democrats divided 26 to 21 in favor. For their part, representatives of slaveholding states from both parties united in defense of slavery. In this case, they cast seventy-eight votes for tabling the Proviso and one against (the lone dissenter being John Houston, a Whig from Delaware). Lincoln supported the Wilmot Proviso throughout his term in Congress. "I think I may venture to say," he remarked in 1854, with some exaggeration, "I voted for it at least forty times."[39]

Feverish debate on slavery dominated congressional proceedings. "It would really seem," complained one member, "there is no other subject claiming the deliberations of this House but negro slavery. . . . From morning to night, day after day, and week after week, nothing is talked of here, nothing can get a hearing that will not afford an opportunity to lug in something about negro slavery."[40] Members from every state delivered long speeches, printed in the *Congressional Globe* and usually distributed in pamphlet form to their constituents. But one searches the *Globe* in vain for a significant contribution to the debate by Lincoln.

The first session of Congress, which lasted from December 1847 to August 1848, took place in the shadow of the upcoming presidential election. Lincoln quickly became associated with the Young Indians, a group of Whig congressmen (most of them southerners, including the future vice president of the Confederacy, Alexander H. Stephens) who pushed for the nomination of the victorious Mexican War general Zachary Taylor, owner of a Louisiana sugar plantation and over 100 slaves. Lincoln may have remained silent on slavery for fear of endangering the unity and electoral prospects of the Whig party. When he made his maiden speech, he chose not slavery but an issue on which northern and southern Whigs agreed—the Mexican War.[41]

By the time Congress assembled, fighting had ceased, American forces occupied the Mexican capital, and negotiations for a peace treaty were under way. Nonetheless, most Whigs continued to believe that President Polk had initiated the conflict by deceiving the American public. During his campaign for Congress in 1846, Lincoln had said little about the war, although he spoke at a rally to promote enlistment in the army. The war was popular in Illinois, where the spirit of Manifest Destiny ran high. But in Washington, the war had become, in the words of one congressman, "a party question." If evidence were needed, it came on January 3, 1848, when the House voted on a resolution of thanks to General Taylor and his army. George Ashmun, a Massachusetts Whig, proposed to add to the preamble the words "in a war unnecessarily and unconstitutionally begun by the President of the United States." Ashmun's amendment passed the House 82 to 81. Every Democrat, northern and southern, voted against it, and every Whig (Lincoln included) except one voted in favor.[42]

Nine days later, Lincoln delivered his first speech, a full-fledged attack on the president. Earlier Lincoln had introduced resolutions demanding that Polk inform Congress of the precise "spot" of American soil where, the president claimed, Mexican aggression had initiated the war. The speech dissected Polk's claims about the boundary between Texas and Mexico and his failure to offer proof that "the soil was *ours* where war began." Polk's whole discussion of the issue, Lincoln charged, rested on "the sheerest deception." In uncharacteristically emotional language, Lincoln continued: "He is deeply conscious of being in the wrong . . . he feels the blood of this war, like the blood of Abel, is crying to Heaven against him."[43]

Lincoln worked very hard on his speech. He hoped, he wrote his law partner William Herndon, to "distinguish myself." His mode of delivery—described by a New York newspaper as marked by "rapidity of utterance [and] abundance of gesture"—reflected his excitement. But despite Lincoln's overheated rhetoric, the speech repeated ideas that dozens of his Whig colleagues, from all parts of the country, were also saying. In the same month that Lincoln spoke, one Whig member of Congress described Polk as the second-worst president in history (Jackson presumably being the worst); another called the president's claims about the war "monstrous"; a third charged that Polk had committed "acts of injustice, cruelty, and wrong." Many Whigs echoed Lincoln's claim that the place where war began "was *not* American soil." Indeed, Lincoln's "spot resolutions," calling for further information from the president, seemed mild compared with the demand of some Whig colleagues that the president order the immediate withdrawal of all American troops from Mexico.[44]

In Illinois, however, which sent more volunteers to Mexico than any state other than Missouri, Lincoln's speech created a furor. One Democratic meeting described it as "treasonable." Herndon informed him of the unhappiness of many Illinois Whigs, himself included. Earlier in the 1840s, Whigs in Lincoln's district had agreed that the congressional seat would be occupied for a single term by a series of party leaders. Lincoln, therefore, could not be renominated. But his position on the Mexican War seems to have contributed to the defeat of Stephen T. Logan, his party's nominee to succeed him, in 1848. For the rest of his career, Lincoln would be dogged by accusations about his course during the Mexican War. In their 1858 debates, Stephen A. Douglas charged him several times with siding with the enemy in wartime. As late as 1863, when Lincoln approved the arrest of Congressman Clement Vallandigham of Ohio for an antiwar speech on the grounds that his words would discourage enlistments, Democrats responded that on the same principle, Lincoln ought to have been arrested during the Mexican War.[45]

Lincoln's attack on Polk dealt with the origins of the war, not its consequences. Unlike many other northern Whigs, he did not charge Polk with acting in order to acquire territory from Mexico to promote the expansion of slavery. Indeed, he explicitly denied that the war had "originated for the purpose of extending slave territory." Lincoln did not want the divisive slavery question to play a part in the 1848 campaign. Many northern Whigs disagreed. Calling the convention that nominated Zachary Taylor the "slaughter-house of Whig principles," the so-called Conscience Whigs joined with Democrats opposed to the expansion of slavery to form the Free Soil party, with Martin Van Buren and Charles Francis Adams as its nominees. The party aroused great enthusiasm, and to blunt its appeal, Democrats and Whigs throughout the North promised that they would prevent the westward expansion of slavery. Nonetheless, Van Buren won around 15 percent of the northern vote, a remarkable showing for a new party. The fact that a former president and the son and grandson of another had agreed to bolt their respective parties and run on a platform embracing not only non-extension but also the Liberty party's call for the divorce of the federal government from slavery demonstrated, William H. Seward observed, that antislavery had at length become "a respectable element in politics."[46]

In August 1848, as soon as the congressional session ended, Lincoln embarked on a tour of Massachusetts to give campaign speeches for Taylor. To counteract the Free Soil appeal, Lincoln called the Whigs the real antislavery party. Taylor may not have spoken in favor of the Wilmot Proviso, he argued, but as a Whig who believed in legislative supremacy, he would not veto it if passed by Congress. Democrats, on the other hand, would allow slavery to spread into the West. Thus, to avoid the mistake of 1844, when a split antislavery vote enabled Polk to win the election, Free Soilers should support Taylor.[47]

During this campaign tour, Lincoln shared the platform with William H. Seward, who also supported Taylor but whose speeches went much further on the slavery question. Seward had a far more extensive antislavery record than Lincoln; as governor of New York he had refused to extradite accused fugitive slaves and had supported the elimination of the property qualification for black voters. Now, he identified the Whigs as the party of emancipation and looked forward to the day when slavery would be abolished "by moral force, peacefully, and in full accordance with public opinion." Seward seemed to envision the future of the Whig party as a coalition of antislavery northerners and forward-looking southerners united in a commitment to a gradual end to slavery. By contrast, Lincoln still viewed the slavery controversy as, in his own words, a "distracting question," a threat both to the unity of his party and to the survival of the Union and Constitution he revered.[48]

The second session of the Thirtieth Congress convened in December 1848, shortly after Taylor's election. The slavery issue immediately reasserted itself, this time in the form of demands for abolition in the nation's capital. The first place where Lincoln had lived with a significant black population, the District of Columbia had a population of 52,000, including 3,700 slaves and 10,000 free blacks. Since the 1830s, slavery there had been a focal point of the abolitionist struggle. Many northern congressmen deemed the presence of slavery and of slave-trading establishments, some of which plied their business within sight of the Capitol, unseemly in the seat of government of a land of liberty.

The antislavery campaign in Washington was directed by Joshua R. Giddings, an abolitionist who represented the Western Reserve of Ohio, an area settled by New Englanders and one of the North's most antislavery constituencies. In 1842, after being censured by the House for introducing resolutions affirming slaves' right to rebel, Giddings had resigned his seat and been triumphantly reelected. Six years later, he attended the Buffalo convention that launched the Free Soil party, where he saw, he wrote his wife, "thousands of good and virtuous citizens, throwing aside party prejudices, declare for freedom and humanity." Like Lincoln, Giddings campaigned in Massachusetts that fall, but for the Free Soilers, not the Whigs. But in an unusual coincidence, Lincoln had found lodgings in Washington in the same boardinghouse in which Giddings resided and where a group of his antislavery allies frequently gathered, among them Congressmen Amos Tuck of New Hampshire, John G. Palfrey of Massachusetts, Daniel Gott of New York, and David Wilmot of Proviso fame. Lincoln was far more moderate than they on the politics of slavery. But living in the house with Giddings led to an expansion of Lincoln's views. Acting in cooperation with Giddings, he decided to promote his own plan for abolition in the nation's capital.[49]

Less than a week after Congress convened, Palfrey requested permission to introduce a bill to abolish slavery and the slave trade in the District of Columbia, but the House refused to grant it. A few days later, on December 18, 1848, Giddings presented his own bill, which called for a plebiscite on slavery's future in Washington in which "all male inhabitants" would cast ballots marked either "Slavery" or "Liberty." When Patrick Tompkins of Mississippi asked if he meant to allow slaves and free blacks to vote, Giddings replied that he did. If Tompkins, he continued, wished to exclude slaveholders as well as slaves from the referendum, he would agree, but he "never would submit to give one man the control of another man's liberty." The House quickly tabled Giddings's bill. Even the *National Era*, Washington's antislavery newspaper, called it too extreme. Then, on December 21, Daniel Gott introduced a resolution directing the Judiciary Committee to report a bill abolishing not slavery but the slave trade in the District. The resolution's preamble denounced the trade as "contrary to natural justice," Christianity, and "republican liberty." A move to table the Gott resolution failed, and the House then approved it. But a few days later, the members agreed to vote in two weeks on whether to reconsider their approval.

Both partisan and sectional loyalties affected these debates. In the wake of the strong showing by the Free Soil party, many northern congressmen desired to demonstrate their antislavery credentials. Lincoln had always feared the disruptive effects of sectional antagonism on party politics. Moreover, with his congressional term soon coming to an end, he was actively seeking a patronage appointment from President-elect Taylor, whose allies were attempting to suppress discussion of slavery. How these considerations influenced his course it is impossible to say. But in these December votes, Lincoln diverged sharply from nearly all the other northern Whigs. Thus, forty-nine northern Whigs voted in favor of allowing Palfrey to introduce his bill abolishing slavery in the District; only six, including Lincoln, opposed. Lincoln was one of ten northern Whigs to vote to table Giddings's bill for abolition, while fifty-five opposed. Only four northern Whigs, Lincoln among them, voted in favor of tabling the Gott resolution, while fifty-five voted against. And when the House adopted the Gott resolution, the votes of northern Whigs stood 65 to 3, with Lincoln among the tiny minority. Only George W. Dunn and Richard W. Thompson of Indiana, among the most conservative of northern Whigs, matched Lincoln's voting record. Lincoln's "anti-slavery education," the Radical Republican George W. Julian later remarked in his memoirs, "had scarcely begun."[50]

Had the debate ended here, Lincoln would probably be remembered as one of those politicians Giddings chastised as so desperate for jobs with the new administration that they went along with the president-elect in seeking to suppress the slavery issue. But early in January 1849, even as Lincoln continued his quest for a government job, Giddings recorded in his diary that Lincoln had begun "preparing resolutions to abolish slavery in the D. C." Lincoln met at least twice with Giddings at their boardinghouse for advice on a draft bill, and the two visited Washington's Whig mayor, William W. Seaton, to talk about the plan. On January 10, 1849, when the motion to reconsider the vote approving the Gott resolution for the abolition of the slave trade in the District came before the House, Lincoln announced that if reconsideration passed (thus killing the resolution), he planned to introduce his own bill. He claimed it had been approved by fifteen "leading citizens" of the capital. He then read his bill to the House.[51]

Lincoln's plan provided that all slave children born in the District after January 1, 1850, would labor as "apprentices" for their owners until they reached adulthood (the exact age to be determined), when they would become free. All living slaves would remain in that condition unless freed by the owners, in which case the federal government would pay monetary compensation. Slaves could not be removed from the District or brought in from outside it, except by officers of the government and citizens of slaveholding states in transit. At the same time, Washington's authorities would provide "active and efficient" support for the capture of fugitive slaves. The entire proposal would be voted on by the "free white male citizens" of the capital the following April. Later that day, Lincoln voted with the majority to reconsider and thus kill the Gott resolution. He was one of seventeen northern Whigs to do so, while fifty opposed the motion.[52]

Lincoln never explained why he suddenly shifted from voting "squarely on the side of the South," as Julian later put it, to collaborating with Giddings. Nor did Lincoln reveal how he drew up his proposal. But its various elements clearly reflected both his own long-standing views and the experience of previous emancipations. In providing for approval by the white residents Lincoln adhered to the condition he had laid out in his 1837 "protest." Compensation, as noted in chapter 1, was a feature of most previous emancipations. One of Lincoln's 1860 campaign biographies explained that Lincoln had opposed the earlier Palfrey bill for abolition in the District because it did not provide compensation to slaveowners. The clause concerning fugitive slaves reflected Lincoln's conviction that the compromises of the Constitution, no matter how distasteful, had to be obeyed. In providing freedom only for the children of slaves born after a certain date, Lincoln followed the precedent of emancipation in the northern states as well as Henry Clay's well-known preference for such a method. The apprenticeship clause seemed reminiscent of British emancipation in the West Indies. All these provisions would remain elements of Lincoln's approach to the slavery question for years to come. In the Lincoln-Douglas debates he would reiterate his support for abolition in the District along the lines he had proposed in 1849. During the first two years of the Civil War, he would present for the approval of slaveholders a number of plans for gradual, compensated emancipation. Not until January 1, 1863, when he issued the Emancipation Proclamation, would Lincoln embark on a different road to black freedom, and even after that date, he would continue to speak on occasion of gradual abolition, compensation to slaveowners, and apprenticeship as a halfway house on the road to freedom.[53]

Giddings considered Lincoln's plan "as good a bill as we could get at this time." Abolitionists outside Congress, however, were appalled. Controversy surrounding it resurfaced when Lincoln ran for president in 1860. In that year, the abolitionist orator Wendell Phillips would dub him "the Slave-Hound of Illinois" because of the bill's clause relating to fugitives from bondage. Lincoln's plan, Phillips charged, "is no credit to any man, being one of the poorest and most confused specimens of pro-slavery compromise." Giddings immediately rose to Lincoln's defense, chastising Phillips for failing to take into account the political circumstances of 1849. Giddings considered it "heroic" that Lincoln had "cast aside the shackles of party, and took his stand . . . with those who were laboring in the cause of humanity." Giddings's strong affirmation of Lincoln's antislavery credentials, inspired by the events of January 1849, helped to persuade Radical Republicans in 1860 that Lincoln shared their hatred of slavery.[54]

Southerners had no more interest in Lincoln's plan than those of Palfrey, Giddings, or Gott. Years later, Lincoln recalled that as soon as his bill became public, his "former backers" in the District deserted him.[55] He never actually introduced the bill. After Lincoln left Congress, the Compromise of 1850, originally proposed by Henry Clay and piloted to passage by Stephen A. Douglas, now a senator from Illinois, abolished the slave trade in the nation's capital, while also providing for a strong Fugitive Slave Act and the organization of territories acquired from Mexico without reference to slavery. Slave dealers, however, simply moved their businesses across the Potomac River to Alexandria. Slavery in the District survived until 1862. When in that year Lincoln signed the measure that abolished it, he noted his pleasure that the law respected the principle of monetary compensation for slaveholders.

Even as the debate over slavery in the District ran its course early in 1849, a different version of the compensation issue came before Congress. This involved a slave, Lewis, who had been hired as a guide by the U.S. Army in Florida during the Second Seminole War (1835–42) and later either was captured by the Seminoles or escaped to them. The heirs of Lewis's owner, Antonio Pacheco, requested a monetary payment of $1,000 from Congress.

The Pacheco case anticipated a major public question of the early years of the Civil War: Is the federal government obligated to compensate slaveholders for slaves lost as a result of military operations? Or, as an Illinois Democrat defined the "main issue" of the debate, "Does the Constitution of the United States recognize the right of property in slaves?" In an impassioned speech against payment, Joshua R. Giddings insisted that the Declaration of Independence and the principle of natural rights barred the federal government from acknowledging such a property right. Many northern congressmen agreed, at least in this particular case, since Florida, then a territory, had been under congressional control at the time of the Seminole War and therefore no state law applied. Every member of the House, declared William Duer of New York, understood that slaves "were property within the slaveholding states." But the Constitution, he argued, "had not nationalized in any degree the institution." Thus, when the army hired Lewis, it was obligated to consider him a human being, not property, and no compensation was in order. In a sense, in the Pacheco case, the Liberty party principle of "freedom national" suddenly entered the mainstream of congressional debate.[56]

Southern members found this alarming. "Every civilized nation on earth," claimed Richard K. Meade of Virginia, agreed that governments had an obligation to indemnify owners for property lost through military operations. To refuse was to deny the legitimacy of property in slaves. In these discussions, Lincoln remained silent. But along with nearly all the northern Whigs and a majority of northern Democrats, he voted consistently against providing compensation. In one instance, where the closeness of the vote created confusion about the outcome, Lincoln spoke up to ensure that he had been recorded in the negative. Eventually, the House approved the claim of Pacheco's heirs. But Lincoln had made clear that for him, as for many other northerners by 1849, property in slaves differed significantly from other forms of property.[57]

The adjournment of the Thirtieth Congress in 1849 appeared to mark the end, at the age of forty, of Lincoln's political career. He failed to get the job he sought from the Taylor administration and failed again at the end of 1850, when his name was mentioned for an appointment by Millard Fillmore, who had become president after Taylor's death. Lincoln's political ambitions appeared hopelessly blocked, and he returned to Illinois to devote himself to his law career. For the next five years, Lincoln said little about slavery. But in July 1852 it became clear that he was clarifying his ideas on the subject. The occasion was his eulogy for Henry Clay, which Lincoln delivered in Springfield a week after the death of his political idol and which offered his most extended public discussion so far on slavery. His speech differed from most of the innumerable tributes to Clay that summer. Most eulogists hailed Clay as the Great Compromiser, the man who had almost single-handedly saved the Union in a series of sectional crises. Lincoln, by contrast, ignored both Clay's work as a sectional conciliator and his economic program, to which Lincoln had devoted so much attention in the past. Instead, he devoted a significant portion of his speech to a (somewhat exaggerated) account of Clay's devotion to the "cause of human liberty."

Reflecting on Clay's career, Lincoln identified "negro slavery" as the main source of "discord" in the republic. He took note of Clay's efforts in 1799 and again in 1849 to persuade Kentucky constitutional conventions to adopt plans for gradual emancipation. Lincoln hailed Clay for occupying a position between two "extremes"—the abolitionists, whose assaults on slavery threatened the Union, and proslavery zealots who had begun to repudiate the very idea of human equality embedded in the Declaration of Independence, which Lincoln called the "white man's charter of liberty." He quoted extensively from Clay's speech before the American Colonization Society in 1827 in which he charged that those who looked to no end to slavery must "blow out the moral lights around us"—an evocative phrase Lincoln would appropriate in his own speeches later in the 1850s. And for the first time in his career, he publicly embraced the idea of returning both free and emancipated blacks to their "long-lost fatherland" in Africa. Indeed, Lincoln implied that Americans, like the ancient Egyptians, might one day suffer divine punishment for "striving to retain a captive people" (a theme to which he would return in his second inaugural in 1865). Lincoln had not previously coupled emancipation with colonization—his abolition bill of 1849 made no mention of sending freed slaves out of the country. But he would henceforth support the idea until well into the Civil War. Like Clay, Lincoln at this point in his career seemed to view blacks as a people who had been violently and unnaturally removed from their homeland, not as part of American society.[58]

In retrospect, Lincoln's speech appears as a eulogy not only for Clay but also for the kind of antislavery politics Clay represented. Surely, Lincoln recognized that Clay's half century of advocacy of gradual emancipation had accomplished nothing. Between 1799, when Clay first proposed his plan to rid Kentucky of slavery, and 1849, when another constitutional convention met and Clay again urged it to take up his idea, the state's slave population had grown from 40,000 to 210,000. Lincoln had been in Lexington, Kentucky, on legal business during the convention's deliberations in 1849. Slavery had been much discussed in the press. The majority of the delegates, however, displayed more interest in strengthening the institution than eliminating it.

Lincoln drew a lesson from these events. Three years later he would write that he had despaired of the "peaceful extinction of slavery. . . . The signal failure of Henry Clay, and other good and great men [including his late father-in-law], in 1849, to effect any thing in favor of gradual emancipation in Kentucky, together with a thousand other signs, extinguishes that hope utterly." "Not a single state," Lincoln noted, had rid itself of slavery since the revolutionary era. "That spirit which desired the peaceful extinction of slavery, has itself become extinct. . . . The Autocrat of all the Russias will resign his crown, and proclaim his subjects free republicans sooner than will our American masters voluntarily give up their slaves."

Lincoln concluded on a note of desperation: "The problem is too mighty for me." "Peaceful, voluntary emancipation" appeared to be impossible.[59]

Yet what was the alternative? In effect, in outlining Clay's position on slavery Lincoln described his own. Until well into the Civil War, Lincoln would continue to adhere to the outlook he associated with Clay in this speech—blacks were entitled to the basic human rights outlined in the Declaration of Independence, slavery should be ended gradually and with the consent of slaveholders, and abolition should be accompanied by colonization.

As to the Whig party, to which Clay and Lincoln had devoted their political careers, it too needed a eulogy. Its presidential candidate, Winfield Scott, another Mexican War hero, suffered a disastrous defeat in the 1852 presidential election, carrying only four states. In that year, Lincoln's brother-in-law Ninian Edwards defected to the Democrats. Lincoln served as a Whig elector but took a smaller part in this campaign than any presidential election since 1836. His few speeches dealt mostly with traditional economic issues that no longer seemed to matter to most voters.[60] Yet in 1852, Whig congressional candidates did carry four districts in northern Illinois by running candidates who could attract abolitionist and Free Soil voters. The *Western Citizen*, the abolitionist newspaper published in Chicago, urged its readers to vote for Elihu B. Washburne, an antislavery Whig whose victory launched a career of eight consecutive terms in the House of Representatives.[61]

By 1852, Lincoln had developed antislavery ideas but not a coherent antislavery ideology; he had cast antislavery votes but had not yet devised a way to pursue antislavery goals within the political system. If Winfield Scott's defeat threw into question the future of the Whig party, Elihu B. Washburne's success offered a harbinger of a new alignment of northern parties that in the next few years would transform the politics of Illinois and the nation and sweep Lincoln back into public life as his state's foremost opponent of the expansion of slavery.

3

"The Monstrous Injustice":
Becoming a Republican

On the evening of October 16, 1854, Lincoln stood before an audience in Peoria, Illinois, and delivered a powerful indictment of the nation's new policy regarding the westward expansion of slavery. Nine months earlier, Stephen A. Douglas had introduced a bill in the U.S. Senate to organize the Nebraska Territory, a part of the old Louisiana Purchase from which slavery had been barred by the Missouri Compromise of 1821. By the time the bill became law in May, it had evolved into the Kansas-Nebraska Act, which explicitly repealed that compromise, substituting for the ban on slavery what Douglas called "popular sovereignty"—the right of settlers to decide for themselves whether to allow or prohibit the institution. Douglas had made a name for himself through bold, sometimes impetuous, actions. In 1850, after Henry Clay failed to get his plan for resolving sectional issues through Congress, Douglas had seized the political initiative and steered the Compromise measures to passage. This time, however, he seriously miscalculated. The Kansas-Nebraska Act aroused a storm of protest throughout the North. Suddenly, the prospect beckoned of slavery spreading not simply into the faraway lands recently acquired from Mexico, but into the heart of the trans-Mississippi West, an area long regarded as the domain of free labor.

Many northerners saw the Kansas-Nebraska Act as the first step in an "atrocious plot" to spread slavery throughout the western United States. These were the words of the *Appeal of the Independent Democrats*, issued in January 1854 by Salmon P. Chase, Joshua R. Giddings, and a handful of other antislavery members of Congress. It called on northerners to unite across party lines to oppose the bill.[1] Over the course of the next two years, the furor aroused by Douglas's measure redrew the nation's political map. The Whig party disappeared and in its place arose the Republican, dedicated to halting once and for all the expansion of slavery.

The year 1854 marked the turning point in Lincoln's pre–Civil War career. "At last," a friend wrote to Chase in February 1854, "the great opportunity of your life has crossed your path."[2] The same could be said of Lincoln. He brilliantly seized the opportunity to revive his dormant life in politics. Before 1854 he had remained essentially a local politician. His name had rarely appeared in newspapers in Chicago, let alone outside Illinois. By 1860 he had become one of the North's major political leaders, part of a generation that included Douglas and William H. Seward, men, like Lincoln, who built or rebuilt their careers on the basis not of the economic issues of the Jacksonian era but their positions regarding slavery.

During these years, Lincoln held no office; he rose to prominence on the basis of oratory, not a record of public service. Many factors contributed to his emergence, among them the good luck of inhabiting the same political space as Douglas, the most prominent politician of the 1850s. Virtually every major speech of Lincoln's between 1854 and 1860 originated as a response to some action or statement by Douglas. In Springfield, where Lincoln delivered his critique of the Kansas-Nebraska Act a few days before presenting it in Peoria, he did so as a reply to Douglas's long defense of the measure in the same city that very afternoon. Four years later, Lincoln acquired a national reputation by virtue of his debates with Douglas. As one newspaper put it in 1859, "Without Douglas, Lincoln would be nothing."[3] Yet Lincoln's rise also reflected his success at fashioning a position on slavery that articulated the shared principles of those who were joining the new Republican party.

In the aftermath of the Kansas-Nebraska Act, Lincoln's public statements underwent a profound transformation. He had long believed slavery to rest "on both injustice and bad policy" (as he put it in his 1837 "protest") but had never considered opposition to its expansion the basis on which a political party could or should be formed. Now, he concluded, "that question [slavery] is a paramount one." In language that achieved an eloquence and moral power not presaged in his previous speeches, Lincoln condemned slavery as a violation of the nation's founding prin-

ciples as enunciated in the Declaration of Independence: human equality
and mankind's natural right to life, liberty, and the pursuit of happiness.
He spoke openly of achieving slavery's "ultimate extinction," although he
acknowledged that he had little idea how this could be accomplished.
During the 1850s, Illinois, a state divided between a southern section
closely tied to the Border South and a rapidly growing northern region
populated from the Northeast, became, in the words of Lincoln's law
partner William Herndon, "the battleground for the Slave Power and for
the Republicans."[4] And no one played a more important part in the battle
for Illinois, and therefore the nation, than Abraham Lincoln.

I

LINCOLN did not immediately raise his voice in opposition to Douglas's
bill. While "anti-Nebraska" meetings sprang up throughout the North in
the first few months of 1854, he remained silent. But Lincoln was hardly
inactive. He contributed unsigned editorials condemning Douglas's measure to the *Illinois State Journal*, Springfield's Whig newspaper. According to a Democratic journalist writing in the early fall, Lincoln had been
"nosing around for weeks in the state library." There, he consulted the
founders' statements about slavery, previous congressional debates, Douglas's own speeches, and even census returns. He began speaking publicly
in mid-August. Fragmentary newspaper accounts report that he urged
opponents of slavery's expansion to unite to achieve repeal of the Kansas-
Nebraska Act, while insisting on respect for the constitutionally guaranteed rights of slaveowners. He probably delivered much the same speech
at a number of venues. But not until he presented it at Peoria did a full
copy, provided by Lincoln himself, appear in the press. At 17,000 words
it was the longest speech he ever delivered. To publish it in its entirety,
the *State Journal* devoted a considerable part of seven consecutive issues
to the speech.[5]

Lincoln had finally found a subject worthy of his intellectual talent
and political ambition. The Peoria speech entirely ignored the economic
issues that had dominated his career until 1854. It said nothing about
other questions roiling the political landscape, such as temperance,
immigration, and anti-Catholicism. Instead, Lincoln offered a prolonged
examination of the history of the slavery question and a series of reflec-
tions on how to think about slavery's place in American life. His basic

argument was straightforward: Douglas's bill represented a profound departure from the original intention of the founding fathers, who sought to restrict the spread of slavery and hoped to see it eventually die out. In the Declaration of Independence, they had established a set of maxims about equality and liberty that defined the essence of the American experiment and that slavery violated fundamentally. The Constitution contained unavoidable compromises that protected slavery, and thus the North must respect the rights of slaveholders where the institution already existed. But no such obligation applied to the territories. Lincoln emphasized his determination to maintain an iron-clad "distinction" between "the existing institution, and the extension of it." Yet at several points in the speech he moved seamlessly from the right and wrong of the expansion of slavery to the right and wrong of slavery itself. His language and the logic of his argument unavoidably called into question the future of slavery in the United States.

Douglas's willingness to see slavery spread, Lincoln declared, violated the core principles of American nationality and fatally compromised the country's world-historical mission:

> This *declared* indifference, but as I must think, covert real zeal for the spread of slavery, I can not but hate. I hate it because of the monstrous injustice of slavery itself. I hate it because it deprives our republican example of its just influence in the world—enables the enemies of free institutions, with plausibility, to taunt us as hypocrites—causes the real friends of freedom to doubt our sincerity, and especially because it forces so many really good men amongst ourselves into an open war with the very fundamental principles of civil liberty—criticising the Declaration of Independence, and insisting that there is no right principle of action but *self-interest*.

Earlier in his career, Lincoln had described slavery as unjust, but never before had he referred to it as a "monstrous injustice." This was the language of abolitionism, not party politics. Yet just as, in his Washingtonian speech, he had advocated temperance without denigrating drinkers, Lincoln differentiated himself from those whose condemnation of slavery extended to slaveholders: "I have no prejudice against the Southern people. They are just what we would be in their situation. . . . If [slavery] did now exist amongst us, we should not instantly give it up."

And what of the future of slavery? Here, Lincoln candidly admitted his own uncertainty:

> If all earthly power were given me, I should not know what to do, as to the existing institution. My first impulse would be to free all the slaves, and send them to Liberia,—to their own native land. But a moment's reflection would convince me, that whatever of high hope, (as I think there is) there may be in this, in the long run, its sudden execution is impossible. . . . What then? Free them all, and keep them among us as underlings? Is it quite certain that this betters their condition? . . . Free them, and make them politically and socially, our equals? My own feelings will not admit of this; and if mine would, we well know that those of the great mass of white people will not. Whether this feeling accords with justice and sound judgment, is not the sole question, if indeed, it is any part of it. A universal feeling, whether well or ill-founded, can not be safely disregarded. We can not, then, make them equals. It does seem to me that systems of gradual emancipation might be adopted; but for their tardiness in this, I will not undertake to judge our brethren of the south.

Lincoln then turned to a dissection of popular sovereignty. He condemned the idea of leaving the issue of slavery to the voters of a territory as specious and unworkable. History demonstrated that to keep it out, slavery must be prohibited from the first days of settlement, as the Northwest Ordinance had done for Illinois (and even then, slavery had lingered for many years). The Kansas-Nebraska Act, moreover, failed to explain when and by whom the decision on slavery would be made—by a few dozen initial settlers, a few hundred, the territorial legislature? But beyond practicality lay the question of morality. Douglas had repeatedly insisted that by allowing residents of the territories to decide on their own local institutions, popular sovereignty exemplified "the great fundamental principle of self-government." Clearly, Lincoln responded, most issues of concern to communities should be decided locally—this was the essence of democracy. But because of its moral gravity, slavery was different:

> The doctrine of self government is right—absolutely and eternally right—but it has no just application. . . . Or perhaps I should rather say that whether it has such just application depends upon whether a negro

is *not* or *is* a man. . . . If the negro *is* a man, is it not to that extent, a total destruction of self-government, to say that he too shall not govern *himself?* When the white man governs himself that is self-government; but when he governs himself, and also governs *another* man . . . that is despotism. If the negro is a *man*, why then my ancient faith teaches me that "all men are created equal"; and that there can be no moral right in one man's making a slave of another.

Yet, after what could only be taken as a critique of slavery wherever it existed and, indeed, of racial inequality, Lincoln immediately drew back: "Let it not be said I am contending for the establishment of political and social equality between the whites and the blacks. . . . I am combating what is set up as moral argument for allowing them to be taken where they have never yet been."

Douglas's policy, moreover, defined whether slavery expanded into Kansas and Nebraska as a matter of purely local concern. In fact, Lincoln insisted, it must be decided by a national majority (that is, by the North). "The whole nation," he declared, "is interested that the best use shall be made of these territories. We want them for the homes of free white people . . . for poor people to go to and better their condition." Were slavery permitted, this avenue of self-improvement would be closed off.

At various points in the Peoria speech, Lincoln insisted that despite the injustice of slavery, the issue must be approached within the existing constitutional framework. Even as he claimed that the framers of the Constitution had intentionally omitted the word "slave" because of their distaste for the institution, Lincoln also acknowledged that they had had no choice but to include protections for the institution where it had already been established. It followed that northerners must adhere, "not grudgingly, but fully, and fairly," to the constitutional rights of the slave states. He described the recapture of men and women who had escaped from slavery as "a dirty, disagreeable job" but affirmed that because of the Constitution's fugitive slave clause, he would support "any legislation, for the reclaiming of their fugitives, which should not, in its stringency, be . . . likely to carry a free man into slavery." (This was a veiled rebuke of the Fugitive Slave Act of 1850, which accorded no due process rights whatever to accused runaways.) Indeed, Lincoln went on, he would even consent to the extension of slavery if the alternative were "to see the Union dissolved, just as I would consent to any great evil, to avoid a greater one." Yet what really endangered the Union, Lincoln insisted, was Douglas's precipitous abrogation of a time-honored sectional compromise. The remedy was to reenact the Missouri Compromise and, by so doing, return to the nation's original policy regarding slavery, thereby restoring "the national faith, the national confidence, the national feeling of brotherhood."

The Peoria speech closed with a powerful peroration that summarized Lincoln's argument against both Douglas and slavery:

> Our republican robe is soiled, and trailed in the dust. Let us repurify it. . . . Let us turn slavery from its claims of "moral right," back upon its existing legal rights, and its arguments of "necessity." Let us return it to the position our fathers gave it; and there let it rest in peace. Let us re-adopt the Declaration of Independence, and with it, the prac-tices, and policy, which harmonize with it. Let north and south—let all Americans—let all lovers of liberty everywhere—join in the great and good work. If we do this, we shall not only have saved the Union; but we shall have so saved it, as to make, and to keep it, forever worthy of the saving.

Juxtaposed with Lincoln's sweeping condemnation of slavery, his actual policy aim—restoring the Missouri Compromise—seemed anticlimactic. But he recognized that to accomplish even this required a reordering of northern politics. Identifying himself as "an old Whig," Lincoln urged members of his party not to be afraid to unite with others, including abo-litionists. "Stand with anybody that stands right," he advised his listeners, "and part with him when he goes wrong."[6]

Lincoln's expression of kind regard for southerners and his willingness to adhere fully and without reservations to the Constitution's provisions regarding slavery distinguished him from more radical northerners. So did his repudiation of the idea of "political and social equality" for blacks and his embrace of colonization. Yet clearly, despite Lincoln's insistence on maintaining the "distinction" between them, the Peoria speech was as much an attack on slavery as on its expansion. Its language, a Democratic newspaper complained, could easily "have come from Giddings or Sum-ner, and that class of abolitionists."[7]

With the Peoria speech (delivered in essentially the same form in various parts of Illinois in the fall of 1854) Lincoln emerged as his state's most eloquent opponent of the expansion of slavery. His public presentations, Lincoln later recalled, attracted "more marked attention than they had ever done before." In part, this resulted from his exceptional clarity of expression and his reliance on the logic of his argument rather than rhetorical ornamentation to persuade his listeners. In his preference for direct speech and the language of ordinary life he resembled Thomas Paine, whose works he had read and admired as a younger man. As a writer, Lincoln was indeed a conscious craftsman who chose his words, as a friend later wrote, to "make himself understood by all classes." Horace White, then a young antislavery journalist and later editor-in-chief of the *Chicago Tribune*, heard Lincoln deliver his address in Springfield, twelve days before he did so in Peoria. He described it as the "greatest" speech ever delivered in Illinois, "for vigor of thought, strength of expression, comprehensiveness of scope . . . rarely equalled in the annals of American eloquence." Half a century later, White would write that "the speech of 1854 made so profound an impression on me that I feel under its spell to this day."[8]

Although Lincoln subsequently deepened and expanded his arguments, the Peoria speech laid the foundation for his approach to the slavery question for the next six years. Before 1854, Lincoln had mentioned the Declaration of Independence only twice in public remarks—a passing reference in his Lyceum speech of 1838 and a more extended one in the Clay eulogy of 1852. Henceforth, he would repeatedly invoke the Declaration as the basis of what he had once called America's "civil religion." He knew that the Declaration's theme of equality had a powerful effect on ordinary northerners. In 1858, he would describe the Declaration as the "electric cord . . . that links the hearts of patriotic and liberty-loving men together." In Philadelphia on the way to assuming the presidency in 1861, Lincoln would declare that all his political sentiments sprang from the Declaration of Independence.[9]

Lincoln was hardly alone among critics of slavery in claiming inspiration from Jefferson, who in 1784 had unsuccessfully proposed to bar the institution from all the western territories then part of the United States. (The Northwest Ordinance, enacted in 1787 when Jefferson was in Paris, included Jefferson's rejected language, but applied it only to territories north of the Ohio River).[10] Nor did Lincoln originate the idea that the founders had launched the nation on an antislavery course. Garrisonian abolitionists, who "ransacked the past for the needs of the present," repeatedly made this argument. So did Liberty party leaders such as Salmon P. Chase. In 1850, Chase filled three single-spaced pages of the *Congressional Globe* with quotations from letters by Jefferson and Madison, town meeting resolutions, congressional debates, and other documents to demonstrate the antislavery convictions of the revolutionary era. In the 1850s no Republican campaign speech or political platform could be considered complete without references to Jefferson and other founders to demonstrate that they hoped for an end to slavery. By 1860, one Republican member of Congress could assure his colleagues that he would not "weary" them with such quotations since the evidence would "readily occur to all intelligent men." Lincoln did not originate this part of the Republican outlook, but he played a key role in disseminating it to a broad popular audience.[11]

History, it has been said, is what the present chooses to remember about the past. Like any narration of history inspired by the search for a "usable past," Lincoln's and other Republicans' account of the attitudes of the revolutionary generation toward slavery was highly selective. It required them to transform a hesitant, ambiguous commitment into a coherent antislavery credo. In fact, the debates over slavery at the Constitutional Convention of 1787 were conspicuously devoid of a moral component. Many of the founders did profess antislavery ideas, but few did anything to implement them and some had no desire whatever to see slavery end. Douglas, who called popular sovereignty the "Jeffersonian plan" because it rested on the principle of local self-government, also claimed the founders' legacy. So, too, in 1861, did southern secessionists, who said they were acting out the right of revolution enshrined in the Declaration.

Just as Lincoln had exaggerated Henry Clay's antislavery record, so he made Jefferson's far more consistent than it actually had been. Jefferson, to be sure, had written the egalitarian preamble of the Declaration of Independence and the proposal in the 1780s to ban slavery in the western territories. But a full reckoning with his career would have to take into account his persistent reluctance to endorse action against slavery in Virginia, the protection for slave property written into the Louisiana Purchase treaty of 1803, and his support, at the time of the Missouri debates, for slavery's westward "diffusion" on the patently absurd grounds that this would improve the condition of the slaves and weaken the institution. (Jefferson, however, had opposed Edward Coles's plan, mentioned in chapter 1, to free his slaves and settle them in Illinois.) The same federal government that barred slavery north of the Ohio River sanctioned, indeed encouraged, its expansion into the Gulf states during the terms of the Virginia presidents Jefferson, Madison, and James Monroe in the early nineteenth century.[12]

Lincoln later stated that slavery had been "a minor question with me" before 1854 because he "always believed that everybody was against it, and that it was in course of ultimate extinction." This seemed an almost willful misreading of history when one reflected that between the ratification of the Constitution and 1854 nine new slave states had entered the Union and the slave population had grown from 700,000 to over 3 million. The black abolitionist H. Ford Douglas pointedly challenged Lincoln's account of history. "The Republicans," he remarked in 1860, "say they are bringing the government back to the policy of the fathers. I do not desire to do this; the policy of the fathers was not uncompromising opposition to oppression."[13]

Nonetheless, during the 1850s Jefferson joined and eventually supplanted Henry Clay as Lincoln's touchstone of political wisdom. And the argument that the founders had tried to place the institution on the road to extinction became the cornerstone of his case against Douglas and popular sovereignty. His selective reading of history allowed Lincoln to present his opposition to the expansion of slavery as "eminently conservative," a return to the policy inaugurated by the revolutionary generation, rather than what in fact it was—a form of antislavery advocacy that marked a radical departure from national policies that for decades had fostered the spread of slavery. Despite his insistence on respecting white southerners and their constitutional rights, Lincoln's account of history in effect erased proslavery Americans from the nation's founding. "We," he said in 1858, had created a nation based on principles enunciated in the Declaration, but "we" had to compromise with slavery to "get our constitution." Lincoln's "we"—his definition of the American nation—did not seem to include the proponents of slavery.[14]

II

SHORTLY BEFORE the 1860 election, Frederick Douglass offered a succinct summary of the dilemma confronting opponents of slavery, like Lincoln, committed to working within the existing political and constitutional system. Abstractly, Douglass wrote, most northerners would agree that slavery was wrong. The challenge was to find a way of "translating antislavery sentiment into antislavery action." At Peoria in 1854, Lincoln for the first time embraced the idea that moral revulsion against slavery had become "a great and durable element of popular action" and that northerners should unite in making opposition to the expansion of slavery their central political tenet. But this belief did not immediately produce a formula for political action. Eventually, the collapse of the Whig party freed Lincoln from the pressure of reconciling his views on slavery with the need for intersectional party harmony. But the dissolution of Whig-gery took place slowly. The Nebraska bill, declared the *New York Tribune* in 1854, "inaugurates the era of a geographical division of political parties." But not until late in 1855 did Lincoln commit his political future to a sectional antislavery party.[15]

The year 1854 witnessed an extremely complicated political revolution throughout the North. "Fusion" movements uniting Whigs, antislavery Democrats, Free Soilers, and advocates of prohibition and nativism swept to victory in nearly every free state. But the balance of power within these coalitions varied enormously. In some states, the new Know-Nothing party, dedicated to curtailing the influence of immigrants and Roman Catholics in American politics, emerged as the primary force. In others, antislavery advocates, some calling their new organization the Republican party, dominated.[16]

Whig leaders like Lincoln struggled to adjust to the rapidly changing political situation. Many Whigs hoped the furor over the Kansas-Nebraska Act offered their party an opportunity to resuscitate itself by advocating the restoration of the Missouri Compromise, thus appealing both to Americans who opposed the expansion of slavery and to those, including southerners, who dreaded the revival of sectional controversy. But it soon became clear that the political crisis had resulted in what a southern newspaper called the "denationalization of the Whig party." In February 1854, a caucus of southern Whig congressmen decided to support Douglas's measure. Northern Whigs were outraged. "We have no longer any bond to Southern Whigs," proclaimed William H. Seward. Even Seward, however, remained convinced that the Whigs could survive by refashioning themselves as the party of opposition to the expansion of slavery.[17]

Especially in central and southern Illinois, many Whigs looked aghast at the idea of their party "being abolitionized," as Lincoln's friend David Davis put it. When a group of abolitionists and Free Soilers from northern Illinois met in Springfield on October 5 to launch a Republican party in the state, Lincoln declined an invitation to address them, even though his powerful antislavery speech, which he had delivered in the same city the previous day, had included a call for political cooperation among all those opposed to the Kansas-Nebraska Act. He turned down an appointment to the executive committee of the new party. As Lincoln explained to the abolitionist Ichabod Codding, one of the gathering's organizers, "I suppose my opposition to the principle of slavery is as strong" as any member of the convention, but he felt unable to "carry that opposition, practically," in the way Codding desired. Lincoln could scarcely join a new party that seemed to have no support in his political base of central Illinois.[18]

"Probably not since the organization of the government," declared a Chicago newspaper, "were political parties in such a state of inextricable confusion." In the congressional races that fall, Illinois Whigs "fused" with Free Soilers in three northern congressional districts, offered their own candidates in five districts in the central and southern parts of the state, and in one race endorsed Lyman Trumbull, running as an anti-Douglas Democrat. Trumbull, the three fusionists, and one Whig were elected, but in the Springfield region Democrats defeated Richard Yates, for whom Lincoln had campaigned. To the *Free West*, Chicago's abolitionist newspaper, the lesson was clear: "the Whig party is dead."[19]

Further complicating Lincoln's situation was his emergence as a leading candidate for the U.S. Senate seat held by James Shields, an ally of Douglas's whose term was about to expire. It is not clear exactly when this possibility occurred to Lincoln. During the summer of 1854 he announced himself as a candidate for a seat in the legislature. Lincoln claimed he was running to help Yates's campaign for Congress. But in August and September Lincoln began making speeches to audiences far afield from his and Yates's district. Before the ratification of the Seventeenth Amendment in 1913, state legislatures, not the voters, chose U.S. Senators. In November 1854, when the voters of Illinois chose a legislature with an "anti-Nebraska" majority, Lincoln resigned the seat to which he had been elected so that he could seek election to the Senate, which Illinois law barred members of the legislature from doing.[20]

Lincoln calculated that the new legislature consisted of fifty-seven anti-Nebraska members and forty-three Democrats. But the new majority comprised what one member called "discordant elements"—men elected as Republicans, Whigs, fusionists, anti-Nebraska Democrats, temperance advocates, and nativists. Lincoln began writing to legislators and to local political leaders throughout Illinois seeking their support for his Senate candidacy. Sometimes he described himself as a Whig; sometimes he avoided identifying a party affiliation. Those who considered themselves Whigs expressed support for Lincoln. But anti-Nebraska Democrats preferred one of their own.[21]

Many abolitionists and Free Soilers from northern Illinois considered Lincoln insufficiently antislavery. In the *Free West*, Zebina Eastman advised antislavery members of the legislature not to vote for Lincoln "or any of the moderate men of his stamp." Lincoln, Eastman claimed, not only remained loyal to "that mummy of a Whig party," but also "dares not oppose the Fugitive Slave Law." Lincoln's Kentucky birth and family connections worried some antislavery advocates. "I must confess I am afraid of 'Abe,'" the Chicago editor Charles H. Ray wrote to Elihu B. Washburne, who had just won reelection to Congress. "He is southern by birth, southern in his associations, and southern, if I mistake not, in his sympathies. I have thought that he would not come squarely up to the mark in a hand to hand fight with southern influence and dictation. His wife, you, know, is a Todd, of a pro-slavery family, and so are all his kin."

At Lincoln's request, Washburne launched a campaign to swing northern Illinois radicals to Lincoln's candidacy. He approached Ohio congressman Joshua R. Giddings, who had admired Lincoln since they lived together and cooperated in seeking to end slavery in the nation's capital in 1849. Giddings, Washburne reported to Lincoln, "is your strongest possible friend and says he would walk clear to Illinois to elect you." Giddings promised to write on Lincoln's behalf to the abolitionist Owen Lovejoy, one of the newly elected members of the legislature. Washburne assured Eastman that Lincoln was "a man of splendid talents, of great probity of character, and . . . threw himself into the late fight on the *republican platform* and made the greatest speech in reply to Douglas ever heard in the state." "*I know he is with us in sentiment,*" Washburne added.[22]

Washburne and Giddings succeeded in convincing the "extreme Anti-Slavery men," as Lincoln called them, including Lovejoy. When voting began, they all supported Lincoln, who received forty-four votes on the first ballot. Senator Shields tallied forty-one; five anti-Nebraska Democrats, unwilling to back a Whig, supported Lyman Trumbull; and eight legislators scattered their votes among other candidates. As balloting continued, Lincoln found it impossible to gain the votes of Trumbull's supporters, and without them he could not reach the required majority.

Suddenly, Democrats abandoned Shields and appeared within reach of electing Governor Joel Matteson, a Democrat not associated with the Kansas-Nebraska Act. "Taken by surprise," as he put it, and unwilling to see the possibility of electing an antislavery senator disappear, Lincoln ordered his backers to cast their votes for Trumbull, ensuring his victory on the next ballot.[23]

If this episode demonstrated anything, it was that prior political affiliations constituted a major obstacle to antislavery cooperation. The outcome left Lincoln bitterly disappointed. But his willingness to sacrifice personal ambition for political principle reinforced his standing among those opposed to the expansion of slavery. Once a statewide Republican party emerged in 1856, he became its presumptive candidate for the Senate in 1858, when Douglas's term would expire. Meanwhile, Lyman Trumbull's election deepened the split in the Democratic party and earned him the bitter enmity of Douglas and his supporters, who viewed him as "the quintessence of political and moral turpitude." For their part, despite having backed Lincoln, the political abolitionists viewed the result as a triumph for their cause. At this point, because of his long record of defending the legal rights of the black community in Illinois, Trumbull had more of an antislavery reputation than Lincoln.[24]

Throughout 1855 and early 1856, the political situation in Illinois and throughout the North remained unsettled. "Bleeding Kansas"—violence between proslavery and antislavery settlers in the territory—kept the slavery issue on the front pages. But the successes of the Know-Nothings in state elections in 1855 suggested that they had as much chance of replacing the Whigs as the chief rival to the Democrats as a new antislavery coalition. Efforts to expand the fledgling Illinois Republican party made little headway. In August 1855, northern Illinois abolitionists, led by Owen Lovejoy, reached out to Lincoln, Trumbull, and other antislavery politicians, urging them to join the party they had created. Lovejoy promised that it would adopt a moderate platform, in recognition of the necessity of "not loading the middle and southern portions of the state with too heavy a load."

Neither Lincoln nor Trumbull responded favorably. "Not even you," Lincoln replied, "are more anxious to prevent the extension of slavery than I; and yet the political atmosphere is such, just now, that I fear to do any thing, lest I do wrong." The main problem, he continued, was that the Know-Nothing party had not yet "tumbled to pieces." Lincoln found the party's views reprehensible but did not wish to attack it openly. In central Illinois, where the party attracted many Old Line Whigs who saw it as a way of suppressing the dangerous slavery question, the Know-Nothings, Lincoln wrote, consisted mostly of his "old political and personal friends" whose participation would be essential to any successful antislavery coalition. A few days later, Trumbull also rejected Lovejoy's plea. He identified as the main obstacles to "fusion" the persistence of "old party associations, and side issues, such as Know-Nothingism and the Temperance question." Trumbull, along with other prominent Illinois Democrats who had broken with Douglas, remained reluctant to join a new organization in which, they feared, they would occupy a position "at the tail end of the old Whig party."[25]

Also in August 1855, Lincoln penned his often-quoted letter to Joshua Speed about the political situation:

> You enquire where I now stand. That is a disputed point. I think I am a whig; but others say there are no whigs, and that I am an abolitionist. . . . I now do no more than oppose the extension of slavery. I am not a Know-Nothing. That is certain. How could I be? How can any one who abhors the oppression of negroes, be in favor of degrading classes of white people? Our progress in degeneracy appears to me to be pretty rapid. As a nation, we began by declaring that *"all men are created equal."* We now practically read it, "all men are created equal, *except negroes.*" When the Know-Nothings get control, it will read "all men are created equal, except negroes, *and foreigners, and catholics.*" When it comes to this I should prefer emigrating to some country where they make no pretense of loving liberty—to Russia, for instance, where despotism can be taken pure, and without the base alloy of hypocracy.[26]

Clearly, Lincoln despised the nativists. As early as 1844, he had helped to organize a public meeting in Springfield that denied that the Whig party harbored "hostility . . . to foreigners and Catholics." Ten years later, during his campaign for a seat in the legislature, he turned down the endorsement of the Sangamon County Know-Nothings. (Characteristically, he told a story to the party delegation that came to see him. He had asked his immigrant Irish gardener Patrick, Lincoln recounted, why he had not been born in the United States. "Faith, Mr. Lincoln," Patrick replied, "I wanted to be, but my mother wouldn't let me.") Nonetheless,

Lincoln said, the Know-Nothings were welcome to vote for him if they wished. He only expressed his strong antinativist views in private, knowing that no antislavery coalition could succeed without Know-Nothing support.[27]

As late as November 1855, the *Illinois State Journal* insisted that "this Republican movement" could never "prove the basis of a permanent party" in the state. But soon afterward, Lincoln decided that the time had come to "fuse." In January 1856, leading antislavery Whigs and Democrats, almost certainly including Lincoln, agreed to form a new party devoted to preventing the westward expansion of slavery. Meanwhile, Paul Selby, who ran a newspaper in Jacksonville, Illinois, had called for the state's antislavery editors to gather in Decatur on February 22, 1856, to plan a strategy for the upcoming state and national elections.

Because of a snowstorm, only a dozen newspapermen made it to Decatur. Lincoln was the only nonjournalist present, and he helped to draft resolutions that deftly covered both moderate and radical antislavery ground. The resulting platform disclaimed any intention to interfere with slavery in the southern states, affirmed the constitutionality of the Fugitive Slave Act, and called for the restoration of the Missouri Compromise rather than barring slavery from all territories. These were moderate positions. But the resolutions also adopted the "freedom national" doctrine of more radical Republicans, holding that in any place under national jurisdiction, freedom was "the rule" and slavery "the exception." In a nod to the Know-Nothings, the resolutions denounced "attacks" on the public school system (supposedly emanating from Catholics), while to appeal to immigrant voters it opposed any changes in the naturalization laws and defended the principle of religious freedom—positions advocated by a German-American editor and supported by Lincoln. "We have no doubt," proclaimed the *Chicago Tribune*, "that the platform laid down will be satisfactory to the Anti Nebraska men of all sections of the state, no matter what their political antecedents or present political affiliations." The editors called a convention to meet at Bloomington in May to nominate candidates for state office.[28]

Lincoln threw himself into the fusion movement, even as most of his local political associates held back. Three years later, a resident of Springfield would recall in a newspaper letter how Lincoln "started out in this city, almost solitary and alone, as a defender of the Republican party and the Republican faith." As the Bloomington convention approached,

Lincoln worked behind the scenes to make sure that antislavery Know-Nothings, Democrats, and Whigs attended, and that none of them were put off by the presence of abolitionists like Ichabod Codding and Owen Lovejoy. Trumbull, too, urged his political allies to participate. Republicans, he assured reluctant anti-Nebraska Democrats, would take their stand on the principle of opposition to the expansion of slavery and "will I think be willing to abandon their ultraisms" for this "one issue."[29]

As a Whig, Lincoln had seen the slavery question as a threat to party unity and economic policy as a source of party strength. Now, he realized, the situation was reversed. He worked to ensure that the new party with its heterogeneous membership ignored divisive issues like the Whig economic agenda, which he had strenuously advocated for two decades but which would alienate former Democrats. The platform, written by Lincoln's old Whig legislative colleague Orville H. Browning with the assistance of Lincoln and Trumbull, called for preventing the extension of slavery "into territories heretofore free," a less radical demand than barring the institution from all territories, and a far cry from Republican platforms in more radical states that called for the repeal of the Fugitive Slave Act and the complete divorce of the federal government from slavery. In the name of party unity, Lincoln pressed for the nomination of William H. Bissell, an anti-Nebraska Democrat from southern Illinois, for governor. To appeal to German-American voters, the convention nominated one of their leaders, Francis Hoffmann, for lieutenant governor, but the rest of the ticket consisted of former Know-Nothings. Nonetheless, the platform opposed all discrimination "on account of religious opinions, or in consequence of place of birth."

Lincoln delivered the convention's major speech. He electrified the audience with, in the words of one reporter, "the power of his argument, the intense irony of his invective, and the deep earnestness and fervid brilliancy of his eloquence." So "spell bound" were his listeners that journalists ceased taking notes—hence Lincoln's remarks have been known ever since as his "lost speech." Whatever Lincoln said, Zebina Eastman later claimed that after the convention "there was no longer any opposition to Mr. Lincoln from the most radical of the abolitionists."[30] To be sure, the abolitionists and Free Soilers who had tried to create a Republican party in 1854 had little influence in the newly reconstituted organization. But Lovejoy did address the Bloomington convention, and Lincoln made clear that he and his supporters must be a part of the broad antislavery coalition. Meanwhile, Ichabod Codding shrewdly predicted that disappointing as the platform seemed, "the Republicans will be driven to take the whole Anti-Slavery issue before they are through with this controversy."[31]

The Bloomington convention appointed delegates to the upcoming Republican National Convention, which met in June 1856 in Philadelphia. There, the atmosphere proved distinctly more radical than in Illinois. The temporary president, Robert Emmet of New York, opened the proceedings by proclaiming, to "long continued cheering," that any "honest man . . . who respects the immortal Declaration of Independence" hoped to see the day when slavery "shall not exist in the world." The resolutions called on Congress to admit Kansas as a free state and to prohibit in the territories the "twin relics of barbarism—Polygamy, and Slavery" (an appeal to anti-Mormon sentiment). It insisted that neither Congress nor a territorial legislature had the power to "give legal existence to slavery" in any territory. In a mild slap at the Know-Nothings, the platform reaffirmed the right of all Americans to "liberty of conscience" and opposed legislation impairing the "security" of any group.

Frederick Douglass condemned the Republican platform for ignoring every critical question except Kansas: "Nothing said of the Fugitive Slave Bill—nothing said of slavery in the District of Columbia—nothing said of the slave trade between the states." Yet the radical element within the party announced itself pleased with the language, evidently drafted by Joshua R. Giddings, that described slavery as unconstitutional outside of state jurisdiction. Salmon P. Chase wondered whether the delegates fully understood "what broad principles they were avowing." They had endorsed, he noted, "the denationalization entire," an idea "first promulgated by the Liberty party" in the early 1840s. George W. Julian, the leading Indiana Radical (and Giddings's son-in-law), claimed that the logic of the Republican platform would lead inexorably to abolition in the District of Columbia and the repeal of the Fugitive Slave Act.[32]

When it came to choosing the party's first presidential candidate, the convention eschewed established political leaders of all kinds and settled on John C. Frémont, whose claim to fame lay in having explored the Far West and playing a role in the conquest of California during the Mexican War. (Lincoln preferred Supreme Court Justice John McLean of Ohio, whose reputation as a moderate Whig, he felt, would appeal to voters in Illinois and throughout the Lower North.) Since Frémont's brief career in politics, a stint in the Senate from California in 1850–51, had been as a Democrat, the convention needed to choose a former Whig for vice president. The Illinois delegation asked John Allison of Pennsylvania to nominate Lincoln. Few at the convention had heard of him. All Allison could say about Lincoln's qualifications was that "he knew him to be the prince of good fellows, and an Old-line Whig." William B. Archer of Illinois seconded the nomination. He described Lincoln as fifty-five years old (in fact, he was forty-seven), "as pure a patriot as ever lived," and a man whose presence on the ticket would enable the party to carry Illinois. John M. Palmer of Illinois added, "I know he is a good man and a hard worker in the field, although I never heard him." Despite these less-than-ringing endorsements, Lincoln received 110 votes on the first ballot, far behind the eventual nominee, William Dayton of New Jersey, but well ahead of political luminaries such as Nathaniel P. Banks, David Wilmot, and Charles Sumner. Lincoln's support from his own delegation reflected the standing he had achieved as a party leader in Illinois; his strong showing elsewhere underscored how crucial his state would be in the upcoming campaign.[33]

The three-way election of 1856 that pitted Frémont against Democrat James Buchanan and ex-president Millard Fillmore, running as the candidate of the American party, as the Know-Nothings were officially known, proved to be the most boisterous since the log-cabin campaign of 1840. Like the nation itself, Illinois emerged as a house divided, with Republicans certain to carry the northern counties and Democrats the southern. The "central counties . . . are to be the battle ground," Richard Yates reported to Lincoln in August. And there Fillmore offered a refuge for conservative Whigs alarmed by the sectional nature of the Republican party but unwilling to vote for a Democrat. "I regret to say," Yates wrote, "that the Fillmore division is large in this section of the State—splitting the Anti Nebraska vote *right* in the *middle*."[34]

Lincoln threw himself into the campaign, all but abandoning his law practice in the fall to deliver over 100 speeches for Frémont. ("I lost nearly all the working part of last year," he wrote in 1857, "giving my time to the canvass.") He concentrated on his political base of central Illinois, but also gave a major address in Chicago. He even ventured into the southern part of the state, to places where, one newspaper remarked, "such a thing as a Fremont speech . . . [had] never been heard." In general, Lincoln repeated the themes he had advanced in 1854, although the language now seemed more strident. Slavery, he claimed, was seeking not simply to expand into the West but to become the "ruling element" in the government. To counteract the Democrats' description of the Republicans as a "sectional party" that endangered the Union, which he called "the most difficult objection we have to meet," Lincoln drew attention to his own Kentucky birth and Whig background and to his party's disavowal of any intention to interfere with slavery where it already existed. He begged Fillmore supporters to "unite" with the Republicans, even proposing the formation of a joint electoral ticket that would pledge to throw its support to whichever of the two candidates received more popular votes in the state.[35]

In the end, Frémont carried eleven northern states—all of New England, New York, Ohio, and the upper Northwest. But this was not enough, as Buchanan won every slave state except Maryland (Fillmore's only victory), as well as California, Illinois, Indiana, Pennsylvania, and New Jersey—the moderate and conservative bastions of the Lower North. Within Illinois, the results reflected the national pattern. Frémont carried northern Illinois by an overwhelming margin—Elihu B. Washburne's congressional district gave Frémont the largest majority of any in the country. But enough former Whig voters in the southern and central parts of the state voted for Fillmore or Buchanan to produce a Democratic victory. Even John Todd Stuart, Lincoln's former political mentor and law partner and his wife's cousin, could not bring himself to vote for the Republicans, a party he associated with abolitionism. Overall, Frémont received 74 percent of the vote in northern Illinois, 37 percent in the central counties, and 23 percent in the southern part of the state.[36]

The disappointing outcome nonetheless offered grounds for Republican optimism. It represented a remarkable showing for a party that had not existed two years earlier. In key northern states, Buchanan enjoyed only a narrow margin of victory. His plurality over Frémont in Illinois slightly exceeded 9,000 votes (around 3 percent of the total turnout), but William Bissell, the Republican candidate for governor, was elected along with the rest of the state ticket. Clearly, the key to the state's future politics lay with the 37,000 voters, almost all of them in southern and central Illinois, who had chosen Fillmore. With the Know-Nothings disintegrating under the pressure of the same slavery issue that had destroyed the Whig party, it did not seem unrealistic to assume that a significant part of the Fillmore vote could be attracted to the Republicans the next time around.[37]

Moreover, rapid changes in the state's economy and its population augured well for future Republican success. By the mid-1850s, great East-West trunk lines connected Chicago with Baltimore, Philadelphia, and New York; the Illinois Central Railroad traversed the state from north to south; and feeder lines crisscrossed the prairies. The development of the rail network catalyzed a transformation of economic life in Illinois, bringing the final triumph of the market revolution. Milton Hay, the uncle of Lincoln's secretary John Hay, later recalled the coming of the railroad as the "dividing line in point of time between the old and the new. Not only our homemade manufactures, but our homemade life and habits to a great measure disappeared. . . . We farmed not only with different implements but in a different mode. Then we began to inquire what the markets were and what product of the farm we could raise and sell to the best advantage."

The railroad transformed Chicago's agricultural hinterland, a vast area including northern and central Illinois and parts of Iowa and Wisconsin, into one of the world's preeminent centers of commercial agriculture. By 1860, Illinois led the nation in corn and wheat production. Its economy reoriented itself from south to east. Railroads shipped farm goods previously sent to New Orleans to the burgeoning cities of the Atlantic seaboard, weakening the state's ties to the slave South. Fewer and fewer men would take goods down the river for sale, as Lincoln had done in his youth. Indeed, in one of his most celebrated legal cases of the 1850s, Lincoln successfully defended a company that had built a railroad bridge across the Mississippi River against a suit by owners of a steamboat that had crashed into the bridge and burned. He had "no prejudice against steamboats or steamboatmen," Lincoln told the jury, but "there is a travel from East to West, . . . growing larger and larger" and essential to the continuation of "the astonishing growth of Illinois."[38]

Lincoln's rise coincided with that of Illinois. The 1850 population of 851,000 doubled to 1.7 million ten years later, making Illinois the nation's fourth largest state. Much of this increase occurred in the rapidly growing counties of northern Illinois, the heartland of the new Republican party. Farmers and laborers poured into Illinois from New England, New York, Pennsylvania, and overseas. By 1860, only 10 percent of the state's population had, like Lincoln and most of the early settlers, been born in the South; a full 20 percent hailed from Ireland and Germany. Even southern Illinois attracted northern migrants, bringing "certain uncomfortable and antagonistical political maxims" to illuminate its "time-honored darkness," as one Republican newspaper rather condescendingly put it. Of course, not every northerner gravitated to the Republican party (Stephen A. Douglas himself had been born in Vermont). But anyone examining the statistics of economic and population growth—which a politician as shrewd as Lincoln could hardly ignore—would conclude that like its economy, the state's political geography had been fundamentally transformed. This was the context that made possible the rise of the Republican party and the emergence of Lincoln.[39]

III

DURING THE 1850s, Lincoln established an approach to the slavery issue that situated him squarely in the middle of the spectrum of northern antislavery opinion. At one end of this spectrum stood abolitionists who sought to arouse public opinion by working outside the political system and insisted that free African-Americans must be recognized as equal citizens. Closely connected to abolitionists were the Radical Republicans, politicians who generally represented districts in New England or the belt of New England migration that stretched across upstate New York and the upper Northwest. Here, the abolitionist movement sank deep roots, and Republicans favored more drastic action against slavery than merely preventing its westward expansion. Radicals like Charles Sumner, George W. Julian, and Salmon P. Chase repeatedly avowed that the federal government had no right to interfere with slavery in the southern states. But, as we have seen, they insisted that constitutionally permissible actions beyond non-extension—the divorce of federal government from slavery, abolition in the District of Columbia and elsewhere within federal jurisdiction, repeal of the Fugitive Slave Act—could promote their avowed goal, "the emancipation of the bondsmen in America."[40]

At the other end of the antislavery spectrum stood conservatives, most of them former Whigs, who joined the Republican party believing that so long as the federal government remained under the control of the "slave power," measures important to the country's economic growth such as a protective tariff and federal aid to internal improvements could never be enacted. They opposed the expansion of slavery but feared that any agitation beyond this would endanger the survival of the Union.[41] Lincoln's speeches of the mid-1850s, with their emphasis on the intentions of the founders, the principles of the Declaration of Independence, and the need to prevent slavery's expansion so that free white laborers could inhabit the western territories, articulated ideas common among Republican politicians and newspapers. In some ways, however, he carved out an approach that was very much his own.

Abolitionists and Radical Republicans spoke movingly of the harsh cruelty of slavery. Their understanding of natural rights included the right to be free from physical abuse. Their speeches, newspapers, pamphlets, and lithographs overflowed with accounts of slave suffering: whippings, denial of access to literacy, and, especially in works produced by female abolitionists, the sexual abuse of black women and the separation of families. Radicals delivered long speeches in Congress about the "barbarism" of the "diabolical system" and dwelled luridly on "the flesh galled by manacle . . . the human form mutilated by knife," and similar injustices. Lincoln privately, as in his 1855 letter to Joshua Speed, commented on how witnessing the sale of slaves and the hunting down of fugitives to be "carried back to their stripes" made him "miserable." But he almost never spoke in public of the violations of slaves' bodies and family ties. Occasionally, as in a March 1860 speech in Hartford, Lincoln warned against ignoring the reasons that inspired a slave to run away, including "the lashes he received." But generally, Lincoln discussed slavery as an abstraction, a violation of basic principles of self-determination and equality, not as a living institution that rested on day-to-day violence.[42]

As a politician, Lincoln worked to harness the moral energies of the North's evangelical churches for the Republican cause. But unlike most Radicals, religious doctrine played little role in his political outlook. The "little New Englands," including northern Illinois, where Radical Republicanism flourished, had been swept in the decades before the Civil War by religious revivals that instilled a commitment to ridding the world of sins of all kinds, including slavery. Joshua R. Giddings believed in "the absolute oneness of religion and politics" and identified "religious truth" as "the only basis of free government." Even moderate Republicans like Henry L. Dawes of Massachusetts called slavery a sin, echoing what abolitionists had been saying for decades. Lincoln spoke of slaveholders not as reprobates and sinners but as men and women enmeshed in a system from which they could not disentangle themselves. "They are just what we would be in their situation," he said at Peoria. In 1858 he reminded one audience that he had never "expressed any harsh sentiment towards our

Southern brethren." Lincoln knew the Bible well, but to condemn slavery he appealed not so much to Scripture or religious precepts as to American history and the Declaration of Independence.[43]

Lincoln's single-minded focus on the question of slavery's expansion also differentiated him from the Radicals. Unlike them, he rarely complained about the Constitution's three-fifths clause, nor did he embrace the "freedom national" doctrine that envisioned an assault on slavery wherever it existed under federal jurisdiction. Lincoln eschewed language, common among the Radicals and, indeed, more moderate Republicans, that portrayed slavery as an obstacle to human progress and southerners as economically and socially backward and lacking in morality. During the 1850s, Republicans mobilized census statistics—everything from economic output and railroad mileage to the number of educational institutions and the circulation of books and newspapers—to demonstrate that the South lagged far behind the North in every index of civilization. The typical Republican speech, quipped Robert Winthrop, a longtime Whig leader in Massachusetts, consisted of one-third repeal of the Missouri Compromise, one-third outrages in Kansas, "and one-third disjoined facts, and misapplied figures . . . to prove that the South is, upon the whole, the very poorest, meanest, least productive, and most miserable part of creation."

On this score, the contrast is striking between Lincoln and William H. Seward. During the Civil War, Seward, as secretary of state, would become Lincoln's closest confidant in the cabinet and would be regarded by congressional Radicals as a conservative influence on administration policy. During the 1850s, however, Seward was widely considered the most prominent Radical Republican, thanks to his long career of antislavery politics and his penchant for using provocative phrases such as "higher law" and "irrepressible conflict" and for forthrightly challenging the South to a contest for the future of the territories and the nation. Both Lincoln and Seward traveled in the South as young men. What impressed Seward was how slavery impaired the region's economic development. Virginia's soil had been exhausted by overreliance on tobacco, and as for New Orleans, which he visited a few years after Lincoln, Seward concluded that because of slavery "the city is secondary" compared to what it might have become. In his speeches of the 1850s, Seward termed slavery a "blight," a "pestilence," an "element of national debility and decline," and repeatedly contrasted western economic development with what he called the stagnation of the South. Lincoln did not describe the South in this manner.[44]

In his Lyceum speech of 1838, Lincoln had proclaimed his commitment to the rule of law. He rejected talk of a "higher law" than the Constitution. Seward had used this phrase during the debates over the Compromise of 1850 to condemn the proposed Fugitive Slave Act as illegitimate. In 1852, Lincoln distanced himself from Seward's doctrine: "In so far as it may attempt to foment a disobedience to the constitution, or to the constitutional laws of the country, it has my unqualified condemnation." Radicals like Owen Lovejoy avowed that in obedience to a higher law, they would never assist in returning a fugitive to bondage. Lincoln, as we have seen, found the hunting down of fugitives outrageous, but, he wrote, "I bite my lip and keep quiet."[45]

Thus, in overall outlook, specific policies, and personal temperament, Lincoln differed considerably from the more radical members of the Republican party. Yet in persistently emphasizing both the moral dimensions of the sectional controversy and how the institution undermined the heritage of democratic self-government, and in seeking to exclude from political debate any issue that might divert attention from the centrality of slavery, he found himself allied with them. Lincoln's language and his concentration on the slavery question made him appear more radical than his actual policy proposals. He may not have spoken of slavery as a sin, but during the 1850s he referred to it as a "monstrous injustice" (his words in the Peoria speech), "a vast moral evil," an "odious institution," a "cancer" capable of destroying the republic. He compared slavery to a "venomous snake" found in bed with a child—it could not be attacked directly but its activity must be constrained. By the mid-1850s, a gulf had opened between Lincoln and conservative Whigs such as Richard W. Thompson of Indiana. The two had voted almost identically on questions relating to slavery in the Thirtieth Congress. But Thompson now explicitly denied that "slavery, as it exists in this country, presents a *moral* question for our consideration." Lincoln insisted this was precisely what it did.[46]

Lincoln was undoubtedly familiar with radical antislavery ideas. His law partner William Herndon, ten years Lincoln's junior and somewhat in awe of his associate, later claimed to have been an abolitionist. This was perhaps an exaggeration, but he did correspond with Theodore Parker, Charles Sumner, Wendell Phillips, and other eastern foes of slavery. In one letter of 1857, Herndon described how, in response to the events of the 1850s, he had evolved from one who "hated . . . the very name of Anti-Slavery," to an advocate of "universal freedom." Herndon subscribed to abolitionist periodicals such as the *National Anti-Slavery Standard*, *National Era*, and Chicago's *Western Citizen* as well as more mainstream antislavery newspapers like the *New York Tribune*. He purchased copies of the speeches of Joshua R. Giddings, William H. Seward, Charles Sumner, and other Radicals, which accumulated in the law office he shared with Lincoln.[47]

After his emergence as a Republican leader early in 1856, Lincoln struggled to maintain unity in a party riven by internal discord. He found himself mediating disputes between former Democrats and former Whigs, nativists and immigrants, conservatives, moderates, and radicals. This was one reason why he stressed so single-mindedly the issue of slavery's expansion, the lowest common denominator of Republican opinion and the one position on which these various elements could agree. Thus, he found himself making common cause with party Radicals, who had long desired, as one put it, "to make slavery the *first* question in our political affairs."[48]

As he made the transition from a local to a statewide political leader, Lincoln recognized that the Republican party could not succeed without mobilizing the radical antislavery constituencies of northern Illinois. In July 1856, the Republican convention in the Third Congressional District, which included counties in both northern and central parts of the state, nominated the abolitionist Owen Lovejoy as its candidate for Congress, passing over Lincoln's friend Leonard Swett, who was preferred by moderate former Whigs. Some of Swett's supporters decided to nominate Judge T. Lyle Dickey, a Kentucky-born Old Line Whig who abhorred abolitionists, as an independent candidate, thereby splitting the Republican vote. Lincoln acted immediately to dissuade them.

"When I heard that Swett was beaten and Lovejoy nominated, it turned me blind," Lincoln wrote to David Davis, who "hated" abolitionists and initially favored a Dickey candidacy. But, Lincoln continued, "on reaching that region, and seeing the people there—their great enthusiasm for Lovejoy—considering the activity they will carry into the contest with him . . . I really think it best to let the matter stand." After receiving Lincoln's letter, Davis urged Dickey to withdraw. Events like "the outrages in Kansas," he wrote, had "made abolitionists of those who never dreamed they were drifting into it." Meanwhile, Lovejoy took matters into his own hands by appearing at a gathering called by the dissidents and disclaiming any right to interfere with slavery in the states. In the end, Dickey abandoned the contest. Lincoln appeared on the same platform with Lovejoy a number of times during the campaign, and the voters elected Lovejoy to Congress.[49]

A similar set of events transpired in 1858. Once again, conservative Republicans, led by Davis, plotted to run an independent candidate in alliance with local Democrats. Even though it placed him at odds with Davis, Ward Hill Lamon, and other "highly valued friends," Lincoln privately warned Lovejoy that spring not to be complacent about his renomination. It would be better for all concerned, Lincoln wrote to Charles H. Ray of the *Chicago Tribune*, to renominate Lovejoy "without a contest." When Lamon conveyed to Lincoln his fear that Lovejoy's election would "put this Congressional District irredeemably in the hands of the Abolitionists," Lincoln beseeched Lamon not to support an independent: "It will result in nothing but disaster all round." Lovejoy might be "known as an abolitionist," but, Lincoln pointed out, he "is now occupying none but common ground." Partly as a result of these events, Lovejoy and Lincoln developed a close political relationship. Lovejoy closed one letter to Lincoln with a salutation expressing how, in his view, they agreed on the fundamental question: "Yours for the *'ultimate extinction of slavery.'*" During the Civil War, when other Radicals voiced harsh criticism of Lincoln's policies, Lovejoy would always defend his antislavery credentials.[50]

More was involved here than Lincoln's recognition of the paramount importance of party unity in the elections of 1856 and 1858 (when he was a candidate for the Senate). In July 1856, the *Chicago Tribune* observed that the "charge of abolitionism" constituted one of the greatest obstacles to Republican success. Fear of being "caught in cooperation with some abolitionist" had led "timid souls" to remain "aloof from the Republican movement." Yet Lincoln was not afraid to work with abolitionists. He understood that without the public sentiment generated by abolitionist agitation outside the political system and by Radical Republicans within it, his new party could never succeed and that it needed to harness the intense commitment that Lovejoy's supporters would bring to the campaign.

Lincoln was a moderate Republican, not a Radical. But during the 1850s, he came to see himself as part of a long struggle against slavery that stretched back to the eighteenth century and might, he said, continue for another hundred years. Every schoolboy, he wrote in 1858, recognized the names of William Wilberforce and Granville Sharp, leaders of the earlier struggle in Great Britain to outlaw the Atlantic slave trade. "But who," he asked, "can now name a single man who labored to retard it?" (In the context of his Senate race with Stephen A. Douglas in 1858, this remark implied that Douglas, by far the more famous of the two at that point, would be forgotten and Lincoln remembered by posterity.) Lincoln, who had always craved recognition, had found his life's purpose. The "higher object of this contest," he wrote, "may not be completely attained within the term of my natural life. But . . . I am proud . . . to contribute an humble mite to that glorious consummation, which my own poor eyes may not last to see." There was no mistaking that the "consummation" Lincoln envisioned was the eventual eradication of slavery, not simply a halt to its expansion.[51]

In December 1856, a month after Frémont's defeat, Lincoln addressed a Republican banquet in Chicago. He described the recent campaign as a battle not so much over specific public policies, but over bedrock political and moral principles. Republicans, he insisted, adhered to the idea, which, as always, he traced back to the revolutionary generation, of "the equality of men." Democrats sought to "discard that central idea" and substitute "the opposite idea that slavery is right" and therefore ought to be perpetuated and extended. Which would triumph? "Our government," Lincoln declared, "rests on public opinion. Whoever can change public opinion can change the government." The task of Republicans was to counteract Democrats' "gradual and steady debauching of public opinion" until it no longer valued the central ideal of equality.[52]

Like the abolitionists, Lincoln saw public sentiment as the terrain on which the crusade against slavery was to be waged. This was his most fundamental objection to Douglas's doctrine of popular sovereignty—its moral "indifference," its assumption that it did not matter whether the people of a territory voted slavery "up or down." "Moral principle," Lincoln believed, was what "unites us in the North." By the same token, the agitation of abolitionists and Radical Republicans helped to embed moral principle in the public mind, enabling—or compelling—politicians to take antislavery ground.

In the mass political system created during the Age of Jackson, leading politicians like Lincoln both reflected and helped to create public opinion. Speaking of William H. Seward, Wendell Phillips observed, "It is worth while to understand his course. . . . His position decides that of millions." But by the same token, as Phillips knew well, the abolition-ists helped to "create a public sentiment which will embolden men like Seward to speak their thoughts." Never had the power of public opinion in a democracy been more evident than in the political earthquake of 1854–56, when leading politicians struggled to fathom and keep up with rapid shifts in popular sentiments.[53]

During the 1856 campaign, John Murray Forbes, a Boston railroad mag-nate and investor in southern plantations (and the man who handled the American investments of Alexis de Tocqueville), commented warily on the transformation he observed overtaking northern public opinion. Abo-litionists, he wrote to a business associate, had little "direct influence" on party politicians. But the idea of "the wrong of slavery," twenty years earlier confined to "a few fanatic men, and . . . enthusiastic women," had now penetrated the northern consciousness. Forbes hoped for a Frémont victory so that the issue of expanding slavery could be settled once and for all before the future of the institution itself came into question. For were "northern feeling" against slavery to grow in the next four years "as fast as it has grown for four years past," a "flood more dangerous and more sweeping than now" might well ensue, endangering slavery and the Union (and, of course, Forbes's southern holdings).[54]

Between 1854 and 1856, unforeseen developments—the Kansas-Nebraska Act, bleeding Kansas, the rise and fall of Know-Nothingism—had shattered the old party system and impelled Lincoln to articulate far more fully and forcefully than in the past his views about slavery and its place in American life and politics. Beginning in 1857 another cascade of events, among them the *Dred Scott* decision, the Buchanan administra-tion's attempt to force slavery into Kansas, and his Senate race against Stephen A. Douglas, would propel Lincoln to address directly questions he had until then touched on only tangentially—the rights and future status of black Americans, and the underlying differences between two societies resting on antagonistic systems of slave and free labor.

4

"A House Divided":
Slavery and Race in the Late 1850s

■

I

Two DAYS AFTER the inauguration of James Buchanan in March 1857, the Supreme Court handed down one of the most infamous decisions in its history. During the 1830s, Dred Scott, a slave of Dr. John Emerson of Missouri, resided with his owner in Illinois, where state law prohibited slavery, and the Wisconsin territory, from which it had been barred by the Missouri Compromise. He married another slave, Harriet Scott, and in 1846, after returning to Missouri, the Scott family, by now consisting of husband, wife, and two daughters, went to court claiming that residence on free soil had made them free. In time, the case made its way to the Supreme Court. Chief Justice Roger B. Taney, supported by six other members of the court, concluded that the Scotts must remain slaves. No black person, Taney declared, could be a citizen of the United States and thus the Scotts had no standing to sue in court. The case could have ended there. Taney, however, went on to argue that because the Constitution "distinctly and expressly affirmed" the right to property in slaves, slaveholders could bring them into the federal territories. The Missouri Compromise—repealed three years earlier by the Kansas-Nebraska Act—had therefore been unconstitutional. Only once before, in the landmark case of *Marbury v. Madison*, which established the principle of judicial review, had the Court invalidated an act of Congress on constitutional grounds. John McLean of Ohio and Benjamin R. Curtis of Massachusetts dissented; Curtis was so outraged by the decision that he resigned from the bench.

Much of Taney's opinion consisted of a historical discussion purporting to demonstrate that the founding fathers had not recognized black persons as part of the American people. The framers of the Constitution, he insisted, regarded blacks, free and slave, as "beings of an inferior order, and altogether unfit to associate with the white race . . . and so far inferior, that they had no rights which the white man was bound to respect." (This statement, Thaddeus Stevens later remarked, "damned [Taney] to everlasting fame; and, I fear, to everlasting fire.") States could make free blacks citizens if they wished, but this did not require the federal government or other states to recognize them as such. No state could unilaterally "introduce a new member into the political community created by the Constitution"—a community, according to Taney, limited to white persons.[1]

"The most important decision ever made by the Supreme Court," as the *New York Times* described it, *Dred Scott* was the work of a chief justice who belonged to a long-established planter family in Maryland. Taney had manumitted his own slaves in the 1820s but strongly believed in black inferiority. He seems to have thought that the Court could restore sectional harmony by resolving the slavery controversy. The decision had precisely the opposite effect. As a Georgia newspaper exulted, it "covers every question regarding slavery and settles it in favor of the South."[2] Taney had declared unconstitutional the platform of the nation's second largest political party. His ruling also seemed to undercut Stephen A. Douglas's popular sovereignty doctrine, for if Congress lacked the authority to deprive slaveholders of their constitutionally guaranteed right to bring slaves into a territory, how could a territorial legislature created by Congress do so?

Until after the Civil War, there existed no commonly agreed understanding of citizenship or of the rights it entailed. People derived different kinds of rights from different levels of citizenship: local, state, and national. The Constitution mentioned but did not enumerate the "privileges and immunities" of citizens. Although popular usage identified citizenship with voting, legal doctrine did not (in some states, immigrants could vote before becoming citizens, and everywhere, white women were citizens but could not vote). The Court's denial of black citizenship did not lack for legal precedents. Before the Civil War, virtually every state,

North as well as South, excluded free blacks from some fundamental rights. Only five states, all in New England, allowed blacks to vote on the same basis as whites. Outside New England, nearly every state court that had ruled on the question before 1857 concluded that free blacks should not be considered citizens either of the state or of the nation. Four attorneys general, including Taney himself during Andrew Jackson's presidency, had taken the same position.[3]

Abolitionists, who had pioneered an alternative reading of the Constitution based on a uniform national citizenship not limited by race, responded bitterly to the *Dred Scott* decision. James McCune Smith, a black physician, author, and antislavery activist, carefully dissected Taney's reasoning, citing legal precedents going back to "the annals of lofty Rome" to demonstrate that all free persons born in the United States, black as well as white, "must be citizens." Many Republicans agreed. Taney's ruling on this issue was "villainously false," declared the *Cleveland Leader*. The Republican legislatures of New Hampshire, Vermont, New York, and Ohio adopted resolutions recognizing black citizenship in their states, joining Massachusetts, where state courts had long affirmed this position. Maine's legislators adopted a resolution declaring the decision "not binding, in law or in conscience, upon the government or citizens of the United States." When the State Department in 1858 refused to issue a passport to the black physician John Rock of Boston on the grounds that he was not an American citizen, the *Springfield Republican* condemned the action as an insult to the entire state of Massachusetts.[4]

Republicans objected even more vociferously to Taney's reversal of the "freedom national" doctrine. They accused the Supreme Court of making slavery the norm and freedom the exception, transforming the South's "peculiar institution" into a national one that must exist everywhere it had not been prohibited by state law. The decision, they claimed, even threw into question whether states possessed the constitutional authority to prohibit slavery. The Supreme Court, declared John Murray Forbes, had "passed into the hands of the South, and . . . become simply a political body whose opinions deserve no more weight than those of any other sectional caucus of partisans."[5]

The *Dred Scott* decision propelled to the forefront of public debate questions that would dominate politics until the outbreak of the Civil War: the founders' intentions regarding slavery; whether slavery should be viewed as a local or national institution; and the constitutional authority of the federal government to prohibit slavery in the territories. Lincoln had already expressed his opinions on these issues and would continue to do so between 1857 and 1860. But the decision inspired him to elaborate his views on a subject about which he had previously said very little, the place of blacks in American society. Lincoln knew this question carried an explosive political charge. Soon after the Court issued its ruling, Stephen A. Douglas delivered impassioned speeches proclaiming that the Declaration of Independence and Constitution had been written for whites and charging that Republicans who opposed the *Dred Scott* decision favored "perfect and absolute equality of the races." Lincoln believed that rhetoric of this kind had played a role in Frémont's defeat in the presidential election of the previous November. Republicans, Lincoln wrote, had been "constantly charged with seeking an amalgamation of the white and black races; and thousands turned from us . . . *fearing* to face it themselves." If others would not "face it," he would.[6]

Lincoln later called *Dred Scott* a "burlesque upon judicial decisions."[7] On June 26, 1857, two weeks after Douglas spoke in Springfield in its support, Lincoln responded in the same city. The decision, he argued, was so erroneous that it could not be viewed as having established a "settled doctrine for the country." Nearly all Republican leaders agreed. But unlike most Republican politicians, who preferred to attack Taney for having taken on the territorial question when he need not have done so and who devoted most of their attention to the constitutional power of Congress to bar the institution in the territories, Lincoln addressed head-on the vexatious question of black citizenship. He denied that Taney had presented a plausible account of the founders' racial outlook. Free blacks, he pointed out, echoing Justice McLean's dissent, had voted in several states at the time the Constitution was ratified, indicating that they were then viewed as members of the body politic. Taney, moreover, was "grossly incorrect" to imply that "the public estimate of the negro" had improved since the revolutionary era; in fact, "the change between then and now is decidedly the other way." Lincoln conspicuously failed to mention the deteriorating situation in Illinois, whose voters and legislature within the past decade had approved measures barring free blacks from entering the state. Instead, he turned to the condition of the slaves. In the revolutionary era, he said, emancipation seemed a real possibility; now the prospect had almost been extinguished. Lincoln offered an elaborate metaphor to show how the slave's prospects had receded:

> All the powers of earth seem rapidly combining against him. Mammon is after him; ambition follows, and philosophy follows, and the Theology of the day is fast joining the cry. They have him in his prison house; they have searched his person, and left no prying instrument with him. One after another they have closed the heavy iron doors upon him, and now they have him, as it were, bolted in with a lock of a hundred keys, which can never be unlocked without the concurrence of every key; the keys in the hands of a hundred different men, and they scattered to a hundred different and distant places; and they stand musing as to what invention, in all the dominions of mind and matter, can be produced to make the impossibility of his escape more complete than it is.

In probing the founders' intentions, Lincoln said almost nothing of the Constitution's relationship to slavery, which he would later analyze in detail in his Cooper Institute address of February 1860. Instead, to refute Taney he turned to the Declaration of Independence. During the era of the Revolution, he insisted, the Declaration had been "held sacred by all." Now, in the hands of Taney, Stephen A. Douglas, and supporters of slavery, "it is assailed, and sneered at, and . . . torn, till, if its framers could rise from their graves, they could not at all recognize it." In the Peoria speech, Lincoln had asserted that the Declaration's promise of equality applied to blacks. Now, for the first time, he elaborated what he meant—equality should be understood as an open-ended process, not an idea fixed at a single moment in time:

> I think the authors of that notable instrument intended to include *all* men, but they did not intend to declare all men equal *in all respects*. They did not mean to say all were equal in color, size, intellect, moral development, or social capacity. They defined with tolerable distinctness, in what respects they did consider all men created equal—equal in "certain inalienable rights, among which are life, liberty, and the pursuit of happiness." . . . They meant to set up a standard maxim for free society, which should be familiar to all, and revered by all; constantly looked to, constantly labored for, and even though never perfectly

attained, constantly approximated, and thereby constantly spreading and deepening its influence.[8]

Lincoln meant his emphasis on the timeless truth of the Declaration to counter not only Douglas's racialized reading of the document but also proslavery "philosophy" and "theology." In 1848, John C. Calhoun had attacked the idea that "all men are born free and equal" as "the most false and dangerous of all political error." Such statements became increasingly common in the South in the 1850s. Lincoln regularly read the *Charleston Mercury* and *Richmond Enquirer* as well as the writings of the southern ideologue George Fitzhugh, who described the idea of equality as a disastrous mistake. Lincoln was also familiar with *Slavery Ordained by God*, a militant defense of slavery by the Alabama minister Frederick A. Ross. In an undated manuscript, Lincoln imagined Dr. Ross, seated "in the shade, with gloves on his hands," ruminating on whether slavery harmonized with the will of God, while his slave Sambo worked in "the burning sun." Lincoln doubted that under the circumstances Dr. Ross would be "actuated by that perfect impartiality, which has ever been considered most favorable to correct decisions." Douglas's view that the Declaration applied only to whites seemed to Lincoln essentially the same as the arguments of proslavery ideologues; he considered both a repudiation of "our national axioms."[9]

As Isaac N. Arnold, a Radical Republican from Chicago who would serve two terms in Congress during the Civil War, later wrote, "It required some nerve in Lincoln, in a state where the prejudice against the negro was so strong . . . to stand up and proclaim the right of the negro to all the rights in the Declaration." But what did those rights amount to? The right to life in Jefferson's triad needed no explanation; liberty stood as a rebuke to the institution of slavery. The equal right to the pursuit of happiness, Lincoln explained, meant enjoyment of the fruits of one's labor. To drive home his point, he chose to refer to a black woman, implying that this right was bounded by neither gender nor race: "In some respects she certainly is not my equal; but in her natural right to eat the bread she earns with her own hands without asking leave of any one else, she is my equal, and the equal of all others."

Lincoln also directly confronted Douglas on the charge that by speaking of blacks enjoying any rights at all, Republicans promoted "amalgamation"—that is, interracial sexual relations. In fact, Lincoln

responded, it was slavery that produced such mixing. He noted sardoni-
cally that by returning the Scotts' two teenage daughters to slavery, Taney's
decision exposed them to the danger of "the forced concubinage of their
masters," one of the few times in his career that he referred even obliquely
to the sexual abuse of slave women. The best way to prevent "amalgamation" was to "keep them apart." At the end of his speech, as he had done
at Peoria, Lincoln called for "the separation of the races" through colonization. Blacks might be entitled to the natural rights of mankind, but
ultimately they should enjoy them outside the United States.[10]

The Springfield speech was Lincoln's sole major address of 1857. He
devoted the rest of the year to his law practice. He reentered the political
arena in the Senate campaign of 1858. Then, he would elaborate what
"equality" did and did not imply. He would make explicit that blacks
were not entitled to the civil and political rights white Americans took for
granted. But he would not retreat from his insistence that the principles
enunciated in the Declaration of Independence applied to every human
being.

II

As LINCOLN PREPARED for his second run for the Senate, a political
earthquake dramatically altered the landscape of party politics. In the
wake of the *Dred Scott* decision, President Buchanan announced that
slavery now existed in all the territories, "by virtue of the Constitution."
In the spring of 1858, when Buchanan attempted to bring Kansas into the
Union as a slave state under the Lecompton Constitution, which patently
flouted the wishes of the majority of the territory's residents, Stephen
A. Douglas denounced the move as a violation of popular sovereignty.
Douglas and his supporters joined with Republicans in Congress to block
approval of the constitution.

Douglas's stance outraged the president and southern Democrats and
made it almost inevitable that his party would fracture along sectional
lines in 1860. But by reinventing himself with an antisouthern (if not antislavery) political persona, Douglas created a dilemma for the Republican
party in Illinois and for Lincoln's senatorial ambitions. Horace Greeley,
perhaps the most influential Republican journalist, whose *New York Tribune* circulated widely throughout the North, urged Illinois Republicans
to support Douglas's reelection to the Senate. Lincoln was dismayed.

"What does the New-York Tribune mean," he wrote anxiously to Lyman Trumbull, "by its constant eulogizing, and admiring, and magnifying [of] Douglas? Does it, in this, speak the sentiments of the republicans at Washington? Have they concluded that the republican cause, generally, can be best promoted by sacrificing us here in Illinois?" Trumbull responded that, in his view, no "honest Republican" could embrace Douglas: "The idea is preposterous."[11]

Most Illinois Republicans agreed. When the Republican state convention met in Springfield on June 16, 1858, party leaders decisively rebuffed eastern calls to embrace Douglas. The platform made no concessions to popular sovereignty: it called for barring slavery from all the territories and denounced the *Dred Scott* decision and the entire idea of the "extra-territorial operation" of slave law. In an unprecedented move, the delegates named Lincoln the party's candidate for the U.S. Senate. (Normally, such a decision awaited the convening of the next legislative session.) Half a century before a constitutional amendment provided for the popular election of senators, the Illinois legislative campaign of 1858 in effect became a referendum on whether Lincoln or Douglas should represent the state in Washington.[12]

The highlight of the convention was Lincoln's speech launching his campaign. In May he had written to a fellow Republican, "There remains all the difference there ever was between Judge Douglas and the Republicans." Now he set out to demolish the idea that Republicans could in good conscience support Douglas, by linking his opponent to the designs of the slave South and denying that any middle ground existed between the friends and foes of slavery. Underlining his words for vocal emphasis, Lincoln began by addressing the consequences of Douglas's Kansas-Nebraska Act of 1854:

We are now far into the *fifth* year, since a policy was initiated, with the *avowed* object, and *confident* promise, of putting an end to slavery agitation. Under the operation of that policy, that agitation has not only, *not ceased*, but has *constantly augmented*. In *my* opinion, it *will* not cease, until a *crisis* shall have been reached, and passed.

"A house divided against itself cannot stand." I believe this government cannot endure, permanently half *slave* and half *free*. I do not expect the Union to be *dissolved*—I do not expect the house to *fall*— but I *do* expect it will cease to be divided. It will become *all* one thing, or *all* the other. Either the *opponents* of slavery, will arrest the further spread of it, and place it where the public mind shall rest in the belief that it is in course of ultimate extinction; or its *advocates* will push it forward, till it shall become alike lawful in all the States, old as well as new—North as well as South.

Have we no tendency to the latter condition?[13]

That last seemingly anticlimactic sentence was crucial. In the remainder of the speech, Lincoln spelled out the "tendency" toward the nationalization of slavery. He accused Douglas of participating in a broad conspiracy involving Presidents Pierce and Buchanan and Chief Justice Taney, to make slavery legal throughout the United States. Already, the Supreme Court had deprived blacks of the protection of the Constitution's comity clause requiring states to accord citizens of other states the same rights as their own. It had ruled that slavery could not be barred from any territory and that Scott's temporary residence in the free state of Illinois had not made him free. The final step would be a ruling that a master could lawfully bring his slaves into any free state for any length of time he desired. Once the *Dred Scott* decision had been "apparently indorsed by the people" (presumably by Douglas's reelection), such a ruling would be inevitable. "We shall *lie down*," Lincoln warned, "pleasantly dreaming that the people of *Missouri* are on the verge of making their State *free*; and we shall *awake* to the *reality*, instead, that the *Supreme* Court has made *Illinois* a *slave* State."

Lincoln's point in the House Divided speech was not the imminence of civil war but that Illinois voters, and all Americans, must choose between supporting or opposing slavery. As he had since 1854, Lincoln identified not Congress or the courts but public sentiment as the key battleground where the fate of slavery would be decided. The entire conspiracy rested on Douglas's effort to "*mould* public opinion" to accept the moral equivalence of freedom and slavery. Once that had been accomplished, northerners would join Douglas in not caring "whether slavery is voted *down* or voted *up*." Here was the reason no Republican should consider supporting Douglas for reelection: "Our cause . . . must be intrusted to, and conducted by [those] . . . who do *care* for the result."

Frederick Douglass later identified the House Divided speech as the moment when "the friends of freedom" recognized in Lincoln a "statesman" who could unite "all the moral and political forces [opposed to] the slave power." Some of Lincoln's friends feared the speech would injure his chances in central Illinois, enabling Democrats to portray him as a dangerous radical. But Lincoln, as always, chose his words with care. He wanted to draw a sharp distinction between himself and Douglas. To do so, as he had in the past, Lincoln invoked ideas common in antislavery circles while formulating the argument in his own distinctive way. Henry Clay, as Lincoln well knew, had used the words "ultimate extinction" as had such Republicans as David Wilmot, Salmon P. Chase, and Senator Solomon Foot of Vermont.[14] The image of a "house divided" was hardly unfamiliar. It appears three times in the Bible, most prominently in Jesus's rebuke to the Pharisees in the Gospel of Matthew. (When Douglas objected to its use in 1858, Lincoln replied that if "a question of veracity" existed, it lay not between himself and Douglas but "between the Judge and an authority of a somewhat higher character.") Lincoln had, in a sense, anticipated the idea in his Lyceum speech of 1838, when he spoke of a future tyrant choosing between "emancipating slaves or enslaving free men." He had employed the phrase itself as early as 1843 (referring to the Whig party, not the nation), and it had been invoked before 1858 by the antislavery minister Theodore Parker and by the proslavery writer George Fitzhugh.[15]

The idea that Pierce, Buchanan, Douglas, and Taney had entered into a proslavery conspiracy strained credibility, not least because of the bitter conflict between Buchanan and Douglas over Kansas. But by 1858, the notion of a vast plot to spread slavery throughout the nation had become standard fare in Republican circles. Lincoln considered the accusation so powerful a rhetorical weapon that he urged Republican editors not to refer to it during the campaign until he could directly confront Douglas with the charge. The Republican press, in Illinois and throughout the North, was already warning of a new *Dred Scott* decision that would make it illegal for states to prohibit the introduction of slaves. Newspapers identified as the likeliest candidate the Lemmon case, in which a New York court had freed eight slaves brought by their Virginia owners to New York City for shipment to Texas. In October 1857, an appellate court upheld the original decision, whereupon the state of Virginia appealed, pledging to take the case all the way to Taney's Supreme Court. Many Republicans worried that the Court would use it to establish a nationwide right to slave "transit." Lincoln did not mention the Lemmon case in his House Divided speech, but he referred to it in a footnote in the printed version of his 1860 Cooper Institute address. (The case had not yet come before the Court when the Civil War broke out and Virginia seceded, rendering it moot.)[16]

By the time of the House Divided speech, the idea that slavery and freedom were locked in mortal combat and that one or the other would dominate the nation's future was already familiar. Along with Lincoln's, the most widely publicized statement of this idea also came in 1858, in a speech by William H. Seward in Rochester, New York. The very economic integration promoted by the market revolution, Seward maintained, was bringing the slave and free states—two "radically different" civilizations—into closer contact and placing a greater premium on national unity. "Shall I tell you," he asked his audience, "what this collision means? . . . It is an irrepressible conflict between opposed and enduring forces, and it means that the United States must and will, sooner or later, become either entirely a slaveholding nation, or entirely a free-labor nation."[17]

Unlike Lincoln, Seward was a self-conscious empire-builder who envisioned a future American nation, having rid itself of slavery, embracing the whole of the North American continent and the Caribbean, as well as "distant islands in either ocean." He saw the slave South as a relic of a bygone era; aristocratic and economically retrograde, it was out of step with the progressive currents sweeping the nineteenth-century world. Lincoln also saw slavery as an impediment to American destiny, but his sense of the nation's mission centered less on future imperial power than on demonstrating to the world the superiority of free political institutions. He had little interest in territorial expansion and indeed ridiculed the pretensions of Young America—a group of ebullient nationalists that included Douglas—and their vision of incessant territorial aggrandizement. Unlike Seward, Lincoln's belief in future national homogeneity rested on political and moral premises, not economic and civilizational ones. But the two concurred that a clash between freedom and slavery was inevitable. As Lincoln wrote in 1860, while he did not accept Seward's "higher law" doctrine, "I agree with Seward in his 'Irrepressible Conflict.' "[18]

In the House Divided speech, Lincoln did not address the rights of black Americans, except when he appeared to suggest that they ought to be covered by the Constitution's comity clause. But four weeks later, in a speech in Chicago, he tried, once again, to outline his views on this question. Like so many of Lincoln's other major addresses, this one came in response to a speech by Douglas, delivered in the city the previous day.

Douglas had condemned the House Divided speech as a call for civil war by a man who had revealed himself to be a radical abolitionist. Douglas did not mince words in appealing to racism: "This government of ours is founded on the white basis, . . . for the benefit of the white man, to be administered by white men." He accused Lincoln of opposing the *Dred Scott* decision because he favored racial equality. Lincoln's talk of national uniformity, moreover, revealed a misunderstanding of the essential principle of self-government—"the right of every community to judge and decide for itself, whether a thing is right or wrong." Douglas challenged Lincoln's effort to appropriate the founders to the antislavery cause. Popular sovereignty, he insisted, descended from Jefferson's vision of a decentralized empire of liberty. Why, he asked, could the nation not continue to exist half-slave and half-free, as it had for over half a century?[19]

The day after Douglas spoke, Lincoln addressed his rival's charges head-on, in one of his most eloquent speeches. First, he responded to Douglas's argument about national diversity. The future of slavery, a "vast moral evil," could not be equated with "the cranberry laws of Indiana, the oyster laws of Virginia, or the Liquor Laws of Maine." On such issues, each locality could and should determine policy for itself. But slavery was a national question—later in the campaign he would call it a "wrong" to "the whole nation"—that demanded a national solution.

Chicago was a center of Radical Republicanism. Lincoln knew his audience would not object when he declared, "I have always hated slavery I think as much as any Abolitionist." But when he turned to the rights of blacks he took a calculated risk. In opposition to Douglas's racialized definition of American nationhood, Lincoln counterposed a civic nationalism grounded in the ideals of the Declaration of Independence. Not race or ethnicity but principle bound Americans to one another. Douglas in 1857 had explained the Declaration's preamble as a claim that American colonists should enjoy equality with Englishmen. Lincoln seized on this formulation to argue that Douglas's repudiation of the universality of the Declaration's principles endangered the liberties of all Americans, including immigrants not descended from the population of 1776:

> Perhaps half our people . . . are men who have come from Europe—German, Irish, French and Scandinavian . . . finding themselves our equals in all things. If they look back through this history to trace their connection with those [revolutionary] days by blood, they find they have

none, . . . but when they look through that old Declaration of Independence . . . they feel that that moral sentiment taught in that day
evidences their relation to those men. . . . That is the electric cord in
that Declaration that links the hearts of patriotic and liberty-loving men
together, . . . as long as the love of freedom exists.

Douglas's repudiation of the Declaration's universality, Lincoln continued, threatened the foundations of democratic government:

It does not stop with the negro. . . . So I say in relation to the principle
that all men are created equal, let it be as nearly reached as we can. . . .
Let us discard all this quibbling about this man and the other man—
this race and that race and the other race being inferior, and therefore
they must be placed in an inferior position. . . . Let us discard all these
things, and unite as one people throughout this land, until we shall
once more stand up declaring that all men are created equal. . . . I leave
you, hoping that the lamp of liberty will burn in your bosoms until there
shall no longer be a doubt that all men are created free and equal.[20]

These words, with which Lincoln ended his speech, constituted the most
forthright affirmation of equality of Lincoln's entire career.

Lincoln's practice of following Douglas around Illinois to respond to
his speeches struck Republicans as demeaning. Soon after the Chicago
speech and a similar encounter in Springfield, Lincoln challenged Douglas to meet him in a series of debates. They quickly agreed on a series of
seven encounters to take place between late August and mid-October in
towns scattered across Illinois. The Great Debates attracted immense
national attention as they were taking place and became part of the lore of
American politics. Newspapers from throughout the country sent reporters to cover them, and transcripts quickly appeared in the press. Thousands of listeners attended each debate.

The two candidates could not have cut more different figures. The
short, stocky Douglas dressed in elegantly tailored suits, spoke with great
force, tried to be constantly on the attack, and appealed unabashedly
to the racial prejudices of his listeners. Accompanied by his fashionable
second wife, Adele, a grand-niece of first lady Dolley Madison and at
twenty-two less than half his age, Douglas arrived at each debate in a
private railcar and was greeted by the firing of cannons by his supporters.

Lincoln, tall and angular, and often dressed in rumpled clothing, traveled alone, seated with the regular passengers. Having long perfected ways of establishing rapport with his audience, Lincoln self-consciously adopted the persona of the judicious and rational underdog. His "appearance is not comely," one newspaper commented, but "he has no superior as a stump speaker."[21]

Unlike modern presidential debates where the candidates offer brief, pre-programmed answers to questions posed by a moderator or members of the audience, the Lincoln-Douglas debates consisted of a series of set speeches. One candidate opened with an hour-long address. The other responded for an hour and a half. The first then had thirty minutes to reply. The speeches were repetitious and sometimes tedious. Each candidate made unsubstantiated charges against the other. Douglas, according to Lincoln, had joined in a plan to nationalize slavery (although somewhat incongruously, Lincoln also condemned him for indifference as to whether slavery did or did not spread into the territories). Lincoln and Lyman Trumbull, Douglas declared, had conspired to destroy the Whig and Democratic parties in order to "abolitionize" Illinois and satisfy their hunger for political office. Each presented himself as a moderate while accusing the other of being too radical for their state. Lincoln, Douglas asserted, advocated "monstrous" doctrines that threatened to bring on "warfare between the North and the South." Lincoln accused Douglas of diverting the nation from the course regarding slavery on which the founding fathers had embarked. With former Whig voters in central Illinois holding the balance of power, each claimed the political mantle of Henry Clay (oddly in the case of Douglas, who had opposed most of what Clay stood for during his long political career).

Yet despite their imperfections, there was something remarkable about the Lincoln-Douglas debates. Carl Schurz, who had emigrated from Germany after the failed revolution of 1848 and emerged in the 1850s as a prominent western Republican, recorded in his memoirs having been "deeply impressed by the democratic character of the spectacle. . . . Here were two men, neither of whom had enjoyed any of the advantages of superior breeding or education . . . [who] contended for . . . mastery by appealing to the intelligence and patriotism of the people." The debates, as Republican political leader James G. Blaine later noted, exemplified how American politics had been transformed in the preceding two years. Despite the onset in 1857 of an economic downturn whose effects still lingered in Illinois, the candidates completely ignored economic matters. As Blaine recounted, they did not mention "protection, free trade, internal improvements, the subtreasury, all the issues, in short, which had divided parties for a long series of years." The debates focused on "one issue" and one alone, Blaine continued, thus reflecting "the public mind" of the late 1850s. Indeed, in Lincoln's correspondence with constituents and party leaders in 1858, slavery and the rights of blacks were virtually the only matters to receive attention. Overall, the debates offered a serious public discussion of the most fundamental problem dividing the nation and the first real gauge of the impact of the *Dred Scott* decision on American politics. As a Washington newspaper observed, thanks to the Lincoln-Douglas debates, Illinois "becomes, as it were, the Union."[22]

The first debate took place on August 21 at Ottawa, a town in northern Illinois whose population of around 9,000 more than doubled on the day of the encounter. A few days earlier, an old friend had advised Lincoln that thus far in the campaign he had "acted too much on the defensive." He urged him to "assail" Douglas "at every vulnerable point." But as the opening speaker, Douglas immediately seized the initiative with a scattershot series of charges: Lincoln had sided with the country's enemies during the Mexican War; was responsible for radical resolutions adopted by a local Republican convention in 1854 that included calls for the repeal of the Fugitive Slave Act and abolition in the District of Columbia; and intended to "make all the institutions uniform, and set the niggers and white people to marrying." Thrown on the defensive, Lincoln seemed to have difficulty responding.[23]

The night before the second debate, scheduled for August 27 in the small town of Freeport (population around 5,000) located in northern Illinois, a group of Republican leaders met to plot strategy. They urged Lincoln to counterattack vigorously. He should repudiate the more radical planks of the 1854 platform, ask Douglas "a few ugly questions," and portray him "as a traitor & conspirator, a proslavery, bamboozelling demagogue." So, after beginning by stating that he favored modification but not repeal of the Fugitive Slave Act and in other ways staking out his position as a moderate, Lincoln posed a series of questions to Douglas. In view of the *Dred Scott* decision, which Douglas had endorsed, could the people of a territory legally prohibit slavery? If not, what became of Douglas's vaunted principle of popular sovereignty? This was the famous "Freeport question," intended to drive a further wedge between Douglas and the Buchanan administration and to force Douglas to alienate either the South, by repudiating Taney's ruling, or northern supporters, by abandoning popular sovereignty.[24]

Lincoln surely anticipated Douglas's response since, as his rival remarked, he had already given his answer "a hundred times from every stump in Illinois." The people of a territory, Douglas declared, could lawfully prohibit slavery by refusing to enact the "local police regulations" without which owners would not risk bringing slaves into an area, or by enacting "unfriendly legislation." A few weeks earlier, Jefferson Davis had said much the same thing in a speech in Maine. Douglas was so pleased with his formula, which enabled him to claim fealty to both *Dred Scott* and popular sovereignty, that he repeated it in subsequent debates. On one occasion he directly quoted Davis's Maine speech to demonstrate the national appeal of his "Freeport doctrine."[25]

In a letter on the eve of the Freeport debate conveying the recommendations of Republican strategists, the Chicago editor Joseph Medill urged Lincoln to "make short work of . . . nigger equality charges by telling him . . . that it is humbug, slang and trash." But Lincoln was already receiving letters from supporters in central and southern Illinois about the political impact of these charges, and urging him to make clear in no uncertain terms that "the Republicans are not in favor of making the blacks socially and politically equal with the whites." As the debates proceeded, Douglas relied more and more on race baiting. He claimed, for example, that Frederick Douglass had been seen in Illinois campaigning for Lincoln, "reclin[ing]" in a carriage next to the white driver's wife.[26]

At the fourth debate in Charleston, a town of 14,000 in the heart of Old Whig territory in central Illinois, Lincoln tried to neutralize Douglas's assaults with an explicit statement on the question of racial equality:

I will say then that I am not, nor ever have been in favor of bringing about in any way the social and political equality of the white and black races,—that I am not nor ever have been in favor of making voters or jurors of negroes, nor of qualifying them to hold office, nor to intermarry with white people; and I will say in addition to this that there is a physical difference between the white and black races which I believe will for ever forbid the two races living together on terms of social and political equality. And inasmuch as they cannot so live, while they do remain together there must be the position of superior and inferior, and

I as much as any other man am in favor of having the superior position assigned to the white race.

Later in the debate, Lincoln stated that while he believed states had the constitutional right to make blacks citizens, he was "opposed to [its] exercise" in Illinois.[27]

Several times during the debates, Douglas accused Lincoln of altering his positions according to the political geography of Illinois. Certainly, a marked difference existed between the principled affirmation of equality in his Chicago speech early in the campaign and Lincoln's remarks at Charleston, where he even omitted his usual statement that blacks were entitled to the kind of equality outlined in the Declaration. At the next debate, at Galesburg in north-central Illinois, Lincoln did return to this theme, insisting that no one until the past few years had denied that the language of the Declaration about natural rights was meant to apply to blacks. But for the rest of the campaign he continued to deny that he favored black citizenship. Abolitionists found Lincoln's comments appalling. "He forsook principle and planted himself on low prejudice," lamented the *Congregational Herald*, published in Chicago. On the other hand, conservative Republicans were delighted. David Davis wrote Lincoln that he found the way he handled the issue "admirable."[28]

Seeking to fight on the most favorable political terrain, Douglas persistently maintained that the question of "what shall be done with the free negro" far exceeded the slavery controversy in importance. For his part, having answered to his own satisfaction the charge of "Negro equality," Lincoln in the last three debates pushed to the forefront the subject he felt most fully exemplified his differences with Douglas—the morality of slavery. At Galesburg he declared that the "real difference" between himself and Douglas was that "every sentiment he utters discards the idea that there is anything wrong in slavery." He said much the same thing six days later at the Quincy debate.[29] The seventh and final encounter took place at Alton, where Elijah P. Lovejoy had met his death two decades earlier. Neither man mentioned the martyred editor, although Douglas referred in passing to his brother Owen Lovejoy. Lincoln tried to appeal to the broadest spectrum of the antislavery electorate. To adopt Douglas's policies, he said, would make it impossible for "free white people," including immigrants—"Hans and Baptiste and Patrick"—to find new homes and "better their conditions in life" by moving to the West. Here was a racialized antislavery that seemed to view the peculiar institution primarily as a threat to the future prospects of white Americans. But at the same time, Lincoln repeated that the natural rights of the Declaration of Independence applied to blacks. He accused Democrats of attempting to "dehumanize the negro—to take away from him the right of ever striving to be a man . . . to make property, and nothing but property of the Negro *in all the states of this Union.*" In the rhetorical high point of the seven debates, he identified the long crusade against slavery with the global progress of democratic egalitarianism:

> That is the real issue. That is the issue that will continue in this country when these poor tongues of Judge Douglas and myself shall be silent. It is the eternal struggle between these two principles—right and wrong— throughout the world.`. . . The one is the common right of humanity and the other the divine right of kings. . . . It is the same spirit that says, "You work and toil and earn bread, and I'll eat it." No matter in what shape it comes, whether from the mouth of a king who seeks to bestride the people of his own nation and live by the fruit of their labor, or from one race of men as an apology for enslaving another race, it is the same tyrannical principle.[30]

While their debates attracted the most attention, Lincoln and Douglas campaigned incessantly throughout the state. Both traveled thousands of miles by rail, but both concentrated their efforts in central Illinois. The northern counties, Lincoln wrote, "we take to ourselves, without question." As for parts of southern Illinois, "no use trying." To woo the pivotal Old Line Whigs of central Illinois, Lincoln read "extract after extract" from Henry Clay's speeches and letters, insisting that he "stood on the very ground occupied by that statesman" while Douglas "was as opposite to it as Beelzebub to an Angel of Light." For their part, Democrats harped increasingly on the House Divided and Chicago speeches to portray Lincoln as a dangerous radical. Douglas asserted that Republicans planned to repeal Illinois's Negro exclusion law, opening the door "for all the negro population to flow in and cover our prairies; in mid-day they will look dark and black as night." "No man of his time," Frederick Douglass would remark when Douglas died in 1861, "has done more than he to intensify hatred of the negro."[31]

Lincoln's supporters feared Democratic racism was having a political impact. All Republican speakers, David Davis insisted, must "distinctly and emphatically disavow negro suffrage, negro holding office, serving on juries, and the like." As election day neared, William Brown, a former Whig member of the Illinois legislature now running as the Republican candidate for his old seat, asked Lincoln for material he could use to fend off these charges. Lincoln assembled a scrapbook of passages that, he wrote, "contain the substance of all I have ever said about 'negro equality,'" beginning with excerpts from his Peoria speech of 1854 and ending with selections from the recent debates.[32]

In a letter accompanying the book, Lincoln explained his position on racial equality. "I think the negro," he wrote, "is included in the word 'men' used in the Declaration of Independence," and that slavery was therefore wrong. But natural rights were one thing, political and social rights quite another. As Lincoln explained, "I have expressly disclaimed all intention to bring about social and political equality between the white and black races." Lincoln added that these views were essentially the same as those of Henry Clay. On the day before the election, the *Illinois State Journal* devoted four columns on its front page to demonstrating that Clay and Lincoln held the same positions on slavery, racial equality, and "the separation of the races."[33]

On election day, the Democrats carried seventeen of the formerly Whig legislative districts in central Illinois compared to only eight for Lincoln. "Thus was Lincoln slain in old Kentucky," wrote the *Chicago Democrat*. William Herndon blamed a letter endorsing Douglas written by Senator John J. Crittenden of Kentucky, Clay's self-styled political heir, for the outcome. "Thousands of Whigs," he lamented, "dropped us just on the eve of the election, through the influence of Crittenden." But there were additional reasons why Republicans failed in 1858 to gain control of the Illinois legislature, ensuring Douglas's reelection. Many eastern Republicans, including the influential Greeley, gave Lincoln only lukewarm support. Among the party's national leaders, only Salmon P. Chase, who had been elected governor of Ohio in 1855, came to Illinois to campaign for Lincoln. (Two years later, when Lincoln sought the presidential nomination, he directed an Ohio supporter to "do no ungenerous thing towards Governor Chase, because he gave us his sympathy in 1858, when scarcely any other distinguished man did.") Douglas's strong opposition to the admission of Kansas under the Lecompton Constitution blunted Lincoln's efforts to portray him as a supporter of slavery. Even the *Chicago Press and Tribune*, in its election postmortem, admitted that Douglas "stood right on the great vital issue of the day."[34]

Nonetheless, had the senator been chosen by popular vote, it seems likely that Lincoln would have emerged victorious. Taken together, the Republican legislative candidates significantly outpolled their opponents. But because the apportionment of seats failed to reflect the rapid increase in population in the northern counties since 1850, Democrats retained control of both houses. The Republican candidates for treasurer and superintendent of public instruction, the only statewide offices contested in 1858, defeated their Democratic rivals by around 125,000 votes to 121,000. Because of the state's "antique apportionment law," wrote the *Press and Tribune*, Douglas was reelected, but "Illinois is a Republican state."[35]

Outside Illinois, 1858 ushered in a historic electoral realignment. Republicans swept to power not only in their strongholds in the Upper North, but in the key swing states of New York, Pennsylvania, and Indiana. With the Lecompton battle having discredited the Buchanan administration in the North and Douglas in the South, prospects for a Republican victory in 1860 seemed bright. As for Lincoln, 1858 made him a national figure for the first time. "Your speeches are read with great avidity by all political men," the Chicago editor Charles H. Ray reported from upstate New York in the midst of the campaign. Despite his refusal to embrace equal rights for blacks, many Radicals and abolitionists praised Lincoln for the forthrightness of his moral critique of slavery, his refusal to compromise the party's principles by withdrawing in favor of Douglas, and his insistence that the institution must eventually come to an end. Even though Lincoln twice stated during the debates that abolition might not occur "in less than a hundred years," the juxtaposition of the phrases "house divided" and "ultimate extinction" gave his speeches a radical edge he may not have entirely intended. The House Divided speech, Frederick Douglass proclaimed in August—his first known direct mention of Lincoln—was "well and wisely said. . . . Liberty or slavery must become the law of the land."

Lincoln seems to have assumed that the defeat marked the end of his aspiration for higher office. The battle "must go on," he wrote, but he expected to "fight in the ranks." But other Republicans already had a different idea. Three days after the election, George W. Rives, a party activist in Paris, Illinois, wrote, "My God, it is too bad. Now I am for Lincoln for the nomination for president in 1860."[36]

III

By 1859, Lincoln had a five-year record of public opposition to the expansion of slavery. That summer and fall, when he resumed public speaking, most of what he said was familiar. But in these speeches Lincoln placed new emphasis on what had previously been a subordinate theme in his political arsenal—the rights of northern "free labor." He found that this resonated powerfully with his audiences.

Ever since the party's creation, Republicans had contrasted the economic growth of the North with what they saw as the South's stagnation, and explained the difference by the superiority of free to slave labor. "It is the energizing power of free labor," Lincoln's friend Richard Yates told Congress in 1854, "which has built our railroads, set the wheels of machinery in motion, added new wings to commerce, and laid the solid foundation for our permanent prosperity and renown."[37] As the decade progressed, discussions of free labor and the differences between free and slave society became more and more frequent. A key reason was the increasing stridency of southern defenders of slavery, who insisted that the freedom of the northern wage-earner amounted to little more than the opportunity either to be exploited or to starve.

Proslavery ideologues like George Fitzhugh insisted that the northern laborer was in fact "the slave of the *community*," a situation far more oppressive than to be owned by a single paternalistic master who shielded his workers from the exploitation of the competitive marketplace. The very titles of Fitzhugh's books constituted an assault on northern market capitalism: *Sociology for the South, or the Failure of Free Society* (1854) and *Cannibals All!, or, Slaves Without Masters* (1857). By the late 1850s, the critique of free labor as inherently exploitative had become increasingly common among the defenders of slavery. In one widely quoted speech before the Senate in March 1858, James Hammond of South Carolina accused the antislavery movement of hypocrisy for ignoring the plight of workers at home. He hurled an explosive accusation: "Your whole class of manual laborers and operatives, as you call them, are slaves."[38]

In the 1830s, the description of northern workers as victims of "wage slavery" had been employed by the northern labor movement, Democratic politicians, and others uneasy with the consequences of the market revolution. Their critique had inspired defenders of market society to celebrate the harmony of interests that allegedly united all classes in the North. The free-labor ideology that emerged as a central tenet of the Republican party in the 1850s drew on this tradition. But unlike in the 1830s, the glorification of free labor and its opportunities for advancement in a free society was directed not against critics in the North, but the slave South. Republican newspapers and political leaders tried to refute southern charges by insisting that northern workers enjoyed an opportunity for social mobility unknown to slaves. "Our paupers of today, thanks to free labor, are our yeomen and merchants of tomorrow," declared the *New York Times* in November 1857. Invoking an economic argument that harkened back to the writings of Adam Smith, Republicans insisted that the opportunity to rise in the social scale provided a more effective incentive to work than the lash; hence free labor was inherently more productive than slave. Few Republicans associated freedom with social opportunity or developed the glorification of free labor into a critique of southern slave society more effectively than Lincoln.[39]

As early as the mid-1840s, Lincoln had invoked God's words to Adam—"in the sweat of thy face thy shall earn bread"—to vindicate the right of the worker to "the whole product of his labor." Then, however, he was discussing the tariff; free trade, he claimed, allowed those who lived "without labor" (merchants, bankers, etc.) to siphon off "a large proportion of the fruits."[40] In the 1850s, Lincoln returned to this theme, but as a powerful argument against slavery. He now described the slave as a worker illegitimately denied the fruits of his or her labor. Slavery, in other words, was a form of theft. Adding the contrast between free and slave labor to his preexisting critique of the moral and political foundations of slavery enabled Lincoln to crystallize his particular version of northern nationalism. The protection of the rights of free labor emerged as a fundamental reason why slavery must be confined to its existing locale and placed on the road to ultimate extinction.

Lincoln was fascinated and disturbed by the works of proslavery ideologues. In a speech in Michigan during the 1856 presidential campaign, Lincoln cited the *Richmond Enquirer* to argue that southerners erroneously believed that "their slaves are far better off than Northern freemen."[41] He expanded greatly on this theme in 1859.

When Lincoln accepted an invitation to travel to Ohio to aid Republicans there in the fall 1859 campaign, one motivation, as so often seemed to be the case, was to counter Stephen A. Douglas. In September, Douglas contributed a long article to *Harper's New Monthly Magazine*. The choice of venue, an important literary periodical published in New York City rather than a political journal, suggested the significance Douglas attached to the piece. Douglas insisted that the doctrine of popular sovereignty arose directly from the policies of the founders and their commitment to "local self-government." In his speeches in Ohio and elsewhere in the Northwest, Lincoln took issue with the argument of what he sarcastically called Douglas's "copy-right essay." He hammered away at arguments by now familiar in his speeches: slavery was a wrong "to the nation," requiring a national policy "that deals with the institution as being wrong." He challenged Douglas's account of the founders' intentions. "Choose ye between Jefferson and Douglas," he implored his audience at Columbus.[42]

In 1858, Charles H. Ray had urged Lincoln to refer to his humble origins to enhance his reputation: "If you have been the architect of your own fortunes, you may claim the most merit." Now, in repudiating the southern critique of free labor, Lincoln invoked his own rise from hired laborer to economic independence to offer a portrait of a society of unbounded opportunity:

> The assumption that the slave is in a better condition than the hired laborer, includes the further assumption that he who is once a hired laborer always remains a hired laborer; that there is a certain class of men who remain through life in a dependent condition. . . . In point of fact that is a false assumption. There is no such thing as a man who is a hired laborer, of a necessity, always remaining in his early condition. The general rule is otherwise. I know it is so, and I will tell you why. When at an early age, I was myself a hired laborer, at twelve dollars per month. . . . A young man . . . works industriously, he behaves soberly, and the result of a year or two's labor is a surplus account. Now he buys land on his own hook. . . . There is no such thing as a man being bound down in a free country through his life as a laborer. . . . Improvement in condition . . . is the great principle for which this government was really formed.

Slaveowners, Lincoln continued, had taken labor, "the common *burthen* of our race," and placed it on "the shoulders of others." In so doing they had degraded their own society, for "*hope*" was a far more powerful incentive to "human exertion" than "the rod."[43]

In these speeches, Lincoln elaborated more fully than at any other time in his career a vision of northern society and "the true, genuine principle of free labor." In the free states, Lincoln told an audience at the Wisconsin State Fair in late September 1859,

> a large majority are neither *hirers* nor *hired*. Men, with their families— wives, sons and daughters—work for themselves, on their farms, in their houses and in their shops, taking the whole product to themselves, and asking no favors of capital on the one hand, nor of hirelings or slaves on the other. . . . This, say its advocates, is free labor—the just and generous, and prosperous system.[44]

Lincoln's ideal America, the world of small independent producers, should not be confused with the humble self-sufficiency of his youth. In his Wisconsin address and in a lecture on discoveries and inventions he delivered a number of times between 1858 and 1860, Lincoln spoke, rather, of an interconnected society of farms, shops, and mercantile establishments, of new inventions, improving agriculture, and a constantly rising standard of living. He advised farmers to abandon traditional ways in favor of new methods of plowing and crop rotation and new fertilizers, seeds, and agricultural machinery. Lincoln chided Young America for excessive materialism, but could not suppress his own enthusiasm for the globalized consumerism the market revolution had brought to the United States— "cotton fabrics from Manchester and Lowell, . . . silk from France; furs from the Arctic regions . . . tea from China, and spices from India." Inventions and the circulation of material goods, Lincoln declared, had made possible not only a continual improvement in the standard of living, but intellectual advancement as well—liberation from the "slavery of the mind." This was the engine of progress in free society.[45]

Lincoln's vision of northern life arose from the world he knew: agrarian and small-town Illinois, with its widely dispersed farm ownership, small-scale manufacturing, numerous family-owned businesses, and rising living standards during the decade of the 1850s. In Springfield, where Lincoln had become one of the wealthiest residents, the gap between the classes was growing, and what his wife called "palaces of homes" were rising during the 1850s. But many of the richest residents had in fact begun life in humble circumstances. In Illinois as a whole, the majority of male heads of household (although not the seven-eighths

Lincoln claimed in one speech) owned productive property. Lincoln's understanding of wage labor as a permanent feature of northern life, but a temporary status for individuals, still seemed plausible. The free-labor ideology seemed far less appropriate to the urban centers and factory towns of the Northeast, where a permanent wage-earning class had come into existence, inequalities of wealth were increasing, and wages had stagnated during the 1850s. This was not a world Lincoln knew or found easy to explain. In free society, he believed, every man controlled his own destiny. If one did not rise above the condition of wage-earner, it was "not the fault of the system," as advocates of slavery claimed, "but because of either a dependent nature which prefers it, or improvidence, folly, or singular misfortune."[46]

Lincoln had little sense of the emerging class relations of an industrializing society. He spoke of economic relations as a "race of life," a metaphor that dated back at least as far as Adam Smith and that encapsulated a meritocratic view of social justice in which individuals competed for advancement and success went to the most talented, so long as the competition was fair. In March 1860, Lincoln lectured in Connecticut at the height of a strike that paralyzed shoe manufacturing throughout New England (involving 20,000 workers, it was the largest strike in American history before the Civil War). Fitzhugh saw strikes as symptoms of the failure of free society. To Lincoln, they exemplified the superiority of free labor to slave: "I am glad to see that a system of labor prevails in New England under which laborers *can* strike." But as the speech made clear, Lincoln understood striking essentially as leaving one's job to find another. He never really confronted the implications for "free society" if wage labor was not simply a way station for a young "beginner" on the road to economic independence, but a large and permanent feature of economic life. Ironically, the Civil War would give a powerful impetus to the very economic forces that undermined the free-labor world of Lincoln's America.[47]

Despite its palpable limitations, Lincoln's invocation of the free-labor ideology added a powerful new dimension to his antislavery outlook. It took the slavery controversy out of the realm of moral judgments and made it, as the *New York Times* put it, a matter of "social and political economy," emphasizing the threat the institution posed to the economic self-interest of white northerners and the prosperity of the entire nation. Whether or not one cared about the plight of the slave, the prospect of

slavery expanding westward threatened the promise of social advancement, the key attribute of free society. As Lincoln explained,

> In the exercise of this right you must have room. . . . Where shall we
> go to? . . . To those new territories which belong to us, which are God-
> given for that purpose. . . . Can they make that natural advance in their
> condition if they find the institution of slavery planted there?[48]

And without the safety valve of westward expansion, would not northern
society eventually come to resemble the rigidly class-stratified economic
order of the Old World, thus fatally undermining the promise of American
exceptionalism?

Some Republicans invoked the idea of free labor in an explicitly racist
manner. Their language suggested that the presence of blacks in the territories, not the presence of slavery, degraded white labor. A month after
Lincoln spoke in Ohio, Salmon P. Chase expressed his concern over a
tendency in the party "to lower our principles . . . to talk of white labor
against negro labor rather than of free labor against slave labor." Lincoln
himself on occasion spoke of the importance of "free white men" having
access to the territories. But he continued to insist that the Declaration
of Independence, America's "Charter of Freedom" with its bedrock principle of a universal right to the pursuit of happiness—now defined as
enjoyment of the fruits of one's labor—"applies to the slave as well as to
ourselves." "I want every man," he said at New Haven in March 1860, "to
have the chance—and I believe a black man is entitled to it—in which he
can better his condition."[49]

IV

THE SENATE CAMPAIGN and his speeches of 1859 offered the first full
airing of Lincoln's views on the rights of black Americans and of how he
situated himself on the spectrum of contemporary racial thought. In a
society deeply imbued with racism, incessant Democratic charges that
"Negro equality" was "the necessary, logical, and inevitable sequence of
[Republican] policies," as one congressman put it, posed a serious problem for the party. Lincoln was hardly the only Republican leader to struggle to find a consistent response. "If we suffer the Dems to present the
issue which Douglas offers . . . to wit the equality of the black with the

white race," wrote an Indiana Republican, "we shall be beaten . . . from this time forward."

Compounding the Republican dilemma was the fact that in antebellum America ideas about race and nationality were confused and contested. Contradictions abounded even in advanced antislavery circles. Benjamin F. Wade, the Radical senator from Ohio, for example, supported civil equality for blacks but freely used the word "nigger" in his private correspondence. Throughout his political career, William H. Seward defended the right of free blacks to vote. Under the Constitution, he maintained, "a white man . . . was no better than a black man." But Seward also described the "African race" as an exotic element in American life, incapable of "assimilation and absorption."[50]

As Benjamin Stanton, a Republican member of Congress from Ohio, put it in 1859, a "great variety of sentiment" existed within the party "as to the political and civil rights" to which blacks were entitled. Some Republicans tried to ignore the entire question, dismissing Democratic racism as an appeal to "low, vulgar prejudice." Others insisted that their party's goal was not so much to benefit blacks as to preserve the western territories for free white labor. A few Radicals, most notably Senator Charles Sumner of Massachusetts, forthrightly condemned racism and insisted that free blacks ought to enjoy precisely the same rights as white Americans.[51]

Complicating the situation further, most Americans distinguished sharply between different kinds of rights. Nearly all Republicans, like Lincoln, agreed that blacks were entitled to the natural rights of mankind, as enumerated in the Declaration of Independence. Most, but by no means all, also felt that basic civil rights—protections of individual liberty and security of person and property—ought to be enjoyed by free blacks. Political rights were another question entirely. These were regulated by the individual states, and Republicans differed widely on whether they should be extended to free blacks. Social rights were even more contentious. "Social equality" was more a term of abuse than a legal or analytical category. It implied support for interracial sexual relations and marriage, which most white Americans viewed with disgust and which nearly every state, North and South, prohibited by law. Even the most radical Republicans believed that social rights stood outside the ken of legislation.[52]

Republicans' racial outlooks were strongly affected by geographical and ideological differences and differences in political antecedents. Former

Democrats seemed more prone to use overtly racist language than former Whigs. Radical Republicans were far more committed to civic and political equality for free blacks than other members of the party. Salmon P. Chase, Thaddeus Stevens, Joshua Giddings, George Julian, and Republican leaders in New England like Sumner had long fought to repeal laws discriminating against northern blacks and to guarantee their right to vote. Chase insisted on the repeal of Ohio's Black Laws as part of the 1849 political bargain that elevated him to the U.S. Senate in exchange for Free Soilers, who held the balance of power in the state legislature, throwing their support to the Democrats. The repeal allowed free blacks to enter Ohio without posting a bond, send their children to public schools, and testify in court against whites. Overnight, Ohio went from being one of the most restrictive northern states with regard to black rights to one of the most tolerant.[53]

Even in New England, where five states allowed black men to vote, a Republican newspaper described the organization as "the white man's party" and charged the Democrats with "fighting for more niggers and slavery." Nonetheless, racism seemed far more prevalent among western Republicans than eastern. Benjamin Stanton of Ohio told Congress in 1860 that in the entire Northwest not one Republican in a thousand favored "extending equal social and political privileges to the negroes." He went on to add, however, that blacks were entitled to "certain natural, inherent, and inalienable rights. . . . The right to live, the right to the enjoyment of a man's own earnings, the right of locomotion, to go from place to place" (the rights, that is, of free labor).[54]

Similar crosscurrents characterized the Illinois Republican party. When the legislature enacted its "Negro exclusion" law in 1853, which included a provision for auctioning black persons who entered the state and could not pay a fine, Norman Judd, soon to become the state Republican chairman, told the Senate that the title should be amended to read "An Act to establish perpetual slavery in Illinois." In 1857 and 1859, a majority of the Republican members of the legislature supported amending the Black Laws to allow blacks to testify in court and attend public schools, but unanimous Democratic opposition plus the votes of more conservative Republicans defeated the proposals. Richard Yates, like Lincoln a party leader in central Illinois, denounced the Black Laws as inhumane and called for their repeal; this did not prevent his election as governor in 1860. On the other hand, many Republicans, including

Lyman Trumbull, who had fought to eradicate the state's indenture system in the 1840s, freely employed antiblack rhetoric. Republicans, Trumbull declared in 1858, "want . . . nothing to do with" blacks. A year later he reiterated, "We are for the free white man, and for making white labor acceptable and honorable, which it can never be when negro slave labor is brought into competition with it." Trumbull's "noble stand" against "negro suffrage, personal negro rights, etc.," one constituent reported, had had a "telling effect" among voters previously reluctant to support the Republican party.[55]

Efforts to assess Lincoln's own racial outlook run the danger of exaggerating the importance of race in his thinking. Race is our obsession, not Lincoln's. Other than in 1857–58, this was not a subject to which he devoted much attention before the Civil War. Many aspects of the slavery controversy—the rights of free labor, domination of the federal government by the Slave Power, the way slavery violated basic American values—were only marginally related to race. Although he carefully read proslavery books and newspapers, Lincoln evinced no interest in his era's extensive literature of racial theorizing, with its predictions about racial destinies and debates over ethnography, separate genesis, and inborn racial difference. What was "political" or "strategic" in Lincoln's statements during the 1858 campaign was not his disavowal of racial equality, but that he felt the need to outline his views on race at all.[56]

Nonetheless, it is clear that while Lincoln had disengaged from many aspects of frontier culture and was hardly unwilling to take unpopular political positions—as his long career as a Whig stalwart demonstrated—he shared many of the prejudices of the society in which he lived. Lincoln used the word "nigger" privately and, occasionally, in public. He enjoyed going to blackface minstrel shows, and his seemingly endless repertoire of stories and jokes included overtly racist humor.[57] As we have seen, when pressed by Douglas in the campaign of 1858, Lincoln disavowed belief in black citizenship and civil and political equality. There is no reason to think that Lincoln, at this point in the development of his ideas, was not sincere in these statements. On the other hand, he consistently emphasized that blacks were entitled to enjoy the natural rights of mankind, especially the right to the fruits of their labor, a position that undoubtedly cost him votes in parts of Illinois. His definition of equality as an aspirational principle whose full accomplishment lay in the future could be taken to imply the possibility of improvement in the black condition.

In some respects, what Lincoln did not say is as important as what he did. He could turn racism into a political weapon, as he had done early in his career against Van Buren and again in 1852 in a speech quoting a sailor's sea chanty about a "bright Mullater" to criticize Franklin Pierce, the Democratic presidential candidate, for seeking antislavery votes by criticizing the Fugitive Slave Act. In the 1858 debates, Lincoln charged that Douglas's policies, by promoting the spread of slavery, would also encourage "amalgamation." But generally speaking, in the 1850s Lincoln's comments on race came in response to Democratic charges of "Negro equality." Unlike many contemporaries, he was not given to orations on the glories of the Anglo-Saxon "race" and its supposed love of liberty. He did not express contempt for free blacks, or refer to them as a vicious and degraded group, descriptions ubiquitous among Democrats and hardly unknown among Republicans. In his 1852 eulogy for Henry Clay he spoke of the "troublesome presence of the free negroes." But later in the same paragraph, when he identified a "dangerous presence" in the United States, Lincoln referred not to free blacks, but to slavery itself. Lincoln justified discrimination on the basis not of innate racial inferiority but the will of the (white) majority in a political democracy. When speaking of black capacity his remarks were usually cautious and tentative. In his Springfield speech of July 1858, he said, "Certainly, the negro is not our equal in color—perhaps not in many other respects." Even in the debate at Charleston, when he said the two races could never coexist in the same country on the basis of equality, the reason he advanced was "physical," not moral or intellectual, difference.[58]

Lincoln's personal dealings with blacks did not reveal prejudice. Springfield when Lincoln lived there was a small city (its population had not reached 10,000) with a tiny black population (171 persons in 1850). Nonetheless, Lincoln could not have been unaware of the black presence. In the 1850s, more than twenty black men, women, and children lived within three blocks of his house. He and his wife employed at least four free black women to work as domestic servants at one time or another. Lincoln befriended and gave free legal assistance to William Florville, the city's most prosperous black resident, known as "Billy the Barber." In 1857, Lincoln and Herndon paid a fine incurred by John Shelby, a free black resident of Springfield who had been jailed in New Orleans while working on a Mississippi River steamboat, securing his release. W. J. Davis, a former slave who lived in Bloomington, Illinois, and claimed during the

Civil War to have been "personally acquainted" with Lincoln since the mid-1850s, described him as "a kind-hearted, sociable kind of man."[59]

In 1860, the black community of Illinois numbered fewer than 8,000 in a population of over 1.7 million. How Lincoln in his heart of hearts viewed black people probably mattered less to this tiny group than his refusal to take a principled stand against racial inequality. He may not have fully embraced racism, but he did not condemn it. The most he would say, as at Peoria, was that in a democratic society, a "universal" prejudice could not be "safely disregarded," regardless of whether it accorded with "justice and sound judgment." This was an oddly agnostic position for a politician who repeatedly emphasized that the fundamental difference between Democrats and Republicans lay in the former's refusal to address the morality of slavery.

In at least some of his responses to the *Dred Scott* decision, Lincoln seemed to endorse the idea of free black citizenship. But, at a time when nearly all the rights of citizens derived from the states, Lincoln was not among the Illinois Republicans who spoke out against his state's oppressive Black Laws, nor did he assist the members of the legislature who tried to have them modified. The black abolitionist H. Ford Douglas, a Virginia-born slave who escaped from bondage and moved to Chicago, claimed that in 1858 he asked both Lincoln and Trumbull to sign a petition for repeal of the Black Laws, whose provisions, Douglas observed, "would disgrace any Barbary State." Both, Douglas related, refused. Lincoln had not thought through how free blacks could enjoy the opportunity to rise if denied physical mobility, access to education, testifying in court, and serving on juries—essential attributes of free society. Was there really a difference, asked Henry L. Dawes, a prominent Massachusetts Republican, between discriminatory laws like those of Illinois and the idea that "the negro has *no* rights which the white man is bound to respect"?[60]

Abolitionists saw the fights against slavery and racism as symbiotically related. Racism, as Frederick Douglass put it, constituted "the greatest of all obstacles in the way of the anti-slavery cause," and he accused Republicans of betraying their own moral beliefs when they stood "opposed to Negro equality, to Negro advancement, to Negro suffrage, to Negro citizenship." Lincoln, by contrast, saw the question of "Negro equality" as a false one, an attempt to "divert the public mind from the real issue—the extension or non-extension of slavery." "Negro equality! Fudge!" Lincoln wrote in notes for a speech in 1858. "How long . . . shall there continue knaves to vend, and fools to gulp, so low a piece of demagoguism as this?"[61]

In an undated fragment written in the 1850s, Lincoln mused on the logical absurdity of proslavery arguments:

> If A. can prove, however conclusively, that he may, of right, enslave B.—why not may B. snatch the same argument, and prove equally that he may enslave A? You say A. is white, And B. is black. . . . Take care. By this rule, you are to be the slave to the first man you meet, with a fairer skin than your own.[62]

The same problem, he continued, existed if the right to enslave another were grounded in superior intelligence, or simply in self-interest. But Lincoln failed to acknowledge that precisely the same argument could be made against laws, like those of Illinois, in which the white majority imposed all sorts of disabilities on the free black population. Lincoln challenged prevailing prejudices when it came to blacks' enjoyment of natural rights, but he would go no further. As was typical of Lincoln in the 1850s, his position occupied the middle ground of Republican opinion. In the context of the North as a whole, Lincoln's views on race fell far short of abolitionist egalitarianism, but differed substantially from the virulent and gratuitous racism of the Democrats, not to mention Chief Justice Taney's ruling in the case of *Dred Scott*. At this point in his career, Lincoln had not yet given serious thought to the role blacks might play in a post-slavery America. He distinguished between an entitlement to natural rights, which he always claimed for blacks, and membership in the American nation. "What I would most desire," he explained at Springfield in 1858, "would be the separation of the white and black races"—that is, the colonization of blacks outside the United States.[63]

V

BY THE LATE 1850s, the American Colonization Society seemed moribund. The *New York Herald* called its annual convention an "old fogy affair." In 1859, out of a black population, slave and free, of well over four million, the Society sent around 300 persons to Liberia. "Can anything be more ridiculous," the *Herald* asked, "than keeping up such a society as this?"[64] Yet at this very moment the idea of colonization experienced a revival within the Republican party. As in the days of Henry Clay, support for the idea centered in the border slave states and the lower Northwest.

The most avid Republican promoters of colonization were the Blair family: the venerable Francis P. Blair, once a close adviser to President Andrew Jackson and editor of the *Washington Globe*, the Democratic party's organ in the nation's capital, and his sons Francis Jr. (Frank) and Montgomery. As an editor and member of Jackson's unofficial "kitchen cabinet," the elder Blair had exerted enormous political influence in the 1830s and 1840s. Having joined the Republican party, he expected to do so again, as did his sons. The Blairs were self-important, indomitable, and, as critics of slavery living in slave states, courageous. In 1856, Frank Blair won election to Congress from St. Louis as an antislavery Democrat but soon switched parties, becoming the first Republican representative from a slave state. Two years later he began to manumit slaves he had inherited from his mother. Montgomery represented Dred Scott before the Supreme Court and his fellow Marylander Chief Justice Taney. The Blairs saw themselves as the vanguard of a movement that would rid the Upper South, and eventually the nation, of slavery and the black presence.

Colonization was central to the Blairs' plan to speed the rise of the Republican party and the progress of gradual, compensated emancipation in border states where slavery was weak or in decline. The Blairs looked to Central America, not Africa, as the future homeland of black Americans and hoped that the promise of land and financial aid would make a colony attractive enough for a large number of blacks to settle there. Frank Blair developed an elaborate scheme, not unlike a proposal of Henry Clay's in the 1830s, for Missouri to use the proceeds of public land sales to purchase the state's slaves and transport them to Central America. This would be followed by an influx of white immigrants into Missouri and a restructuring of its economy on the model of the free-labor North. The Blairs believed that the United States should be reserved for "the Anglo-Saxon race," while blacks, "worse than useless" in this country, would flourish in the tropics, to which they were naturally suited. They attacked slavery not on moral grounds but for degrading nonslaveholding whites and retarding southern economic development.[65]

The colonization movement had long been divided between those who saw it as a way of ridding the country of free blacks and others for whom it formed part of a long-term strategy for ending slavery. Despite their overt racism, the Blairs were firmly in the latter camp. Before the Civil War, no one, except perhaps John Brown, could conceive of a way to end slavery without the consent of slaveowners; there was simply no constitutional way that this could be accomplished. And it seemed impossible that whites would ever consent to emancipation unless coupled with the removal of the black population. Republican endorsement of colonization, the Blairs insisted, would be "an enabling act to the emancipationists of the South." Colonization would refute the charge that abolition meant racial equality. In the late 1850s, Republican conventions in the border states endorsed colonization while simultaneously repudiating "negro equality and . . . all who favor negro equality."[66]

The Blair plan would have the added bonus of expanding the American commercial presence in the Caribbean (the region would become "our India," said Frank Blair) and blocking southern efforts to create a slave empire embracing the West Indies, Mexico, and Central America, an idea that gained increasing currency during the 1850s. In mid-decade, the filibusterer William Walker conquered Nicaragua, established himself as president, and during his brief reign legalized slavery and reopened the slave trade. Similar expeditions landed in Mexico, Ecuador, Honduras, and Cuba. Colonization, Frank Blair told Congress in 1858, would enable black emigrants to secure American access to "the intertropical region" while preventing "the propagation of slavery" there.[67]

During the late 1850s, Frank Blair tirelessly promoted the idea of colonization in speeches throughout the North and in letters to prominent Republicans. In 1860, he delivered a major speech at New York's Cooper Institute one month before Lincoln's celebrated oration at the same venue. In it, Blair touted colonization as "the only solution to the Negro question" and presented a curious proposal for the acquisition of tropical areas that would be open to settlement only by owners who emigrated with their slaves and promised them eventual freedom and landownership.[68]

The idea of colonization remained highly controversial in Republican ranks. Many Radicals shared the abolitionists' conviction that such proposals, by denying that blacks were part of the American nation, added to the obstacles to racial equality within the United States. After Blair spoke in Chicago in 1858, the *Press and Tribune* felt compelled to chide him for "ignoring the moral and religious aspects of the slavery question, and basing all anti-slavery movements on the superior claims of the white race." Others deemed the idea unworkable. But Blair won the support of a number of Republican leaders, including Senator James R. Doolittle of Wisconsin, the governors of Iowa, Wisconsin, Illinois, and Ohio, and such prominent members of Congress as Lyman Trumbull and James Ashley. Trumbull told the Senate that the "idea of the deportation of the free negro population" would become "part of the creed of the Republican party." Most but by no means all of the Blairs' supporters were western-ers. But Hannibal Hamlin of Maine endorsed the plan, and even Charles Sumner, the party's most stalwart defender of black rights, concluded that it did not violate "any principle of justice," so long as emigration remained voluntary. Eastern Republican newspapers such as the *New York Times* and *New York Tribune* spoke favorably of the Blair plan.[69]

A variety of motives inspired these endorsements, including political expediency, racial prejudice, the belief that blacks were innately suited to a tropical climate, and a desire to assist slave-state Republicans. After Benjamin F. Wade told the Senate that he wanted his party to include colonization in its platform, a constituent commended him: "I like this new touch of colonizing the niggers. I believe practically it is a d——n humbug. But it will take with the people." Whatever one thought of the idea, Charles Francis Adams wrote in 1859 after hearing Frank Blair speak in Boston, "we must respect it as coming from an earnest and sincere emancipationist in a slave state."[70]

Many Republicans accepted the Blairs' argument that an embrace of colonization would enable the party to expand into the Border South. Like Lincoln, most Republicans envisioned a distant future without slavery. But, as the *New York Tribune* observed, even "our wisest statesmen" could not "tell us how slavery is to be abolished in the southern states." Were the Blairs harbingers of a new generation of southern Republicans who would set in motion the abolition of slavery? Many northern Republicans believed a significant number of border residents were anxious to make common cause with their party. They celebrated, and exaggerated, the importance of the Blairs and other border-state critics of slavery, such as Cassius M. Clay of Kentucky, another advocate of colonization. William H. Seward, who thought the idea of sending a large part of the nation's labor force out of the country absurd, nonetheless called Frank Blair "the man of the West, of the age." Within eight years of a Republican national victory, declared the *Chicago Press and Tribune*, Delaware, Maryland, and Missouri would "rid their states" of slavery, and Kentucky and Virginia would soon follow. Some southerners feared the same outcome. One congressman from Mississippi declared in 1859 that in parts of the border, slavery was already "almost a nominal thing."[71]

By 1858, Lincoln had emerged as a public spokesman for colonization. His first extended discussion, as we have seen, came in 1852, in his eulogy of Henry Clay. By the next year, Lincoln was closely enough identified with the idea that when Reverend James Mitchell, a prominent colonization organizer from Indiana, traveled to Springfield seeking allies to promote the cause, a local minister referred him to Lincoln. Lincoln addressed the annual meeting of the Illinois Colonization Society in 1853 and again in January 1855, even as his first bid for election to the Senate unfolded. No record has survived of the first speech and only a brief outline of the second. In 1858, when he ran for the Senate, Lincoln's was the first name listed among the eleven members of the society's Board of Managers. (The vice presidents included Chicago Republican editor John L. Scripps and William Brown, at whose behest Lincoln compiled his "book" on racial equality.) In his first debate with Douglas, Lincoln read aloud the passage from his Peoria speech of 1854 in which he said his "first impulse" in dealing with slavery would be to free the slaves and send them to Africa.[72]

There is no reason to doubt the sincerity of Lincoln's advocacy of colonization or to explain it solely as a way of deflecting Douglas's accusation that Republicans favored racial equality. When Lincoln made his first extended remarks on the subject in 1852, he was not a candidate for office and his political career appeared to have reached a dead end. Unlike many other advocates of colonization, Lincoln never countenanced compulsory deportation and expressed little interest in creating an American empire in Central America or in the Christianization of Africa. Nonetheless, he believed that blacks would welcome the opportunity to depart for a place where they could fully enjoy their natural rights. Lincoln seemed to envision the bulk of the black population eventually emigrating. In his Springfield speech of 1857, he cited biblical precedent: "The children of Israel," in numbers comparable to American slaves, "went out of Egyptian bondage in a body."[73] For many white Americans, including Lincoln, colonization was part of a plan for ending slavery that represented a middle ground between abolitionist radicalism and the prospect of the United States existing forever half-slave and half-free.

Lincoln's thought seemed suspended between a civic conception of American nationality, based on the universal principle of equality (and thus open to immigrants with no historic roots in this country and, in principle, to blacks), and a racial nationalism that saw blacks as in some ways not truly American. He found it impossible to imagine the United States as a biracial society. When he spoke of returning blacks to Africa, their "own native land," Lincoln revealed that he did not consider them an intrinsic part of American society. In fact, by the 1850s, the vast majority of black Americans—a far higher percentage, indeed, than of the white population—had been born in the United States.

The Blairs made a special effort to enlist Lincoln in their cause. In February 1857, Frank Blair, whose wife Appeline was a Kentuckian and relative of Mary Lincoln, traveled to Springfield, where he met with "the leading men of the party," Lincoln doubtless among them. Blair advised them, he wrote his father, "to drop the negro and go the whole hog for the white man . . . the ground we have always taken here in St. Louis." In April, Lincoln and William Herndon met in their law office with "one of the leading emancipationists of Missouri," probably Blair, and developed a plan to promote the Republican party in the Upper South. Two months after this meeting, in his speech at Springfield on the *Dred Scott* decision, Lincoln called for "the separation of the races," adding that while the Republican party had not officially endorsed the idea, "a very large proportion of its members" favored it. Blair and Lincoln met again in December 1857. They agreed that John Hay, then studying law in Lincoln's office, would become a correspondent for the *Missouri Democrat*, St. Louis's Republican newspaper. In 1858, Hay reported on the Lincoln-Douglas debates for the *Democrat*. Despite the urging of some Republicans, the Illinois party did not endorse colonization at the state convention of 1858, following Trumbull's advice not to "get mixed up with the free negro question" at all. But Blair returned to the state to campaign for Lincoln, perhaps to the neglect of his own political fortunes, as he was defeated for reelection to Congress.[74]

These encounters seem to have affected both men. Visiting Illinois reinforced Blair's conviction that Missouri must rid itself of slavery. "No resident of a slave state," he wrote, "could pass through the splendid farms of Sangamon and Morgan, without permitting an enormous sigh to escape him at the evident superiority of free labor." As for Lincoln, he clearly saw colonization as part of a broader antislavery strategy aimed, initially at least, at the Upper South. Perhaps the Blairs offered a way of placing slavery in the course of "ultimate extinction," of which Lincoln had spoken but without any real explanation of how it would take place. Based on the surviving outline, his 1855 address to the Illinois Colonization Society surveyed the history of slavery beginning in the fifteenth century and went on to describe the spread of antislavery sentiment, culminating in the formation of the American Colonization Society in 1816. In the fifth debate with Douglas, Lincoln quoted Henry Clay to the effect that colonization would help prepare the way for emancipation. When Lincoln advanced his own program during the Civil War for gradual, compensated abolition in the border states, coupled with colonization, it was the culmination of many years of thinking.[75]

For decades, colonization had faced the seemingly insuperable difficulty that most free blacks repudiated the idea. In the 1850s, however, the resurgence of interest in colonization among whites coincided with a rising tide of nationalism among northern blacks as well as deep despair about their future in the United States. With the Fugitive Slave Act threatening their freedom, the *Dred Scott* decision denying that they could be citizens, and the prospect of abolition as remote as ever, a number of northern blacks now embraced emigration. "We must have a nationality," one wrote. "I am for going anywhere, so we can be an independent people." Martin R. Delany, an abolitionist editor and lecturer whose pessimism about the prospects for blacks in the United States was strengthened when, as a student at Harvard Medical School, he was dismissed because white classmates protested his presence, advocated the creation of a new homeland for black Americans in the Caribbean, Central America, or Africa. Henry H. Garnet founded the African Civilization Society to promote emigration. James T. Holly advocated emigration to Haiti. Like the Blairs, Delany envisioned mass emigration from the United States. Most black emigrationists of the 1850s, however, looked to a select group of migrants, a talented tenth, to bring to Africa, Haiti, or Central America the benefits of Christian civilization and American economic enterprise. Success abroad, they believed, would redound to the benefit of the descendants of Africa in "our own country," as the constitution of the African Civilization Society put it.[76]

Like earlier colonizationists, the Blairs gathered endorsements from black leaders, among them Delany and Garnet. Their emigration efforts sparked a sharp debate within the black community. Black conventions engaged in heated discussions of the future of the race in the United States. Early in 1861, the *Weekly Anglo-African*, a black-run newspaper published in New York City, apologized to its readers for having devoted so much space to lengthy letters, pro and con, about emigration that "our usual editorial matter is crowded out." The editor urged correspondents to remember that "brevity is the soul of wit." The most prominent opponent of colonization, in lectures, editorials, and letters throughout the 1850s, was the black abolitionist Frederick Douglass. "No one idea has given rise to more oppression and persecution to the colored people of this country," he wrote, "than that which makes Africa, not America, their home." Douglass argued that the idea of colonization allowed whites to devise plans for ending slavery while avoiding thinking about its aftermath in the United States. This certainly seems to have been the case for Lincoln.[77]

Despite its harsh Black Laws and the growth of the emigration movement elsewhere in the North, Illinois offered scant evidence for Lincoln's belief that free blacks could be persuaded to leave the United States voluntarily. In 1848, the black Baptist Association of Illinois sent Reverend Samuel Ball of Springfield to visit Africa and report on prospects for emigration. On his return, Ball published a pamphlet praising Liberia as "the brightest spot on this earth to the colored man." But at the time of Ball's death in 1852, only thirty-four black persons had emigrated from Illinois to Liberia under the auspices of national or local colonization societies during the previous twenty years.[78]

Blacks in Illinois held their first statewide conventions in the 1850s, beginning with a gathering in Chicago in 1853. Primarily aimed at organizing to seek repeal of the Black Laws, the conventions also spoke out against colonization. The Chicago delegates denounced all such "schemes" as "directly calculated to increase pro-slavery prejudice." A second convention in Alton in 1856 and a public meeting of Springfield blacks in February 1858 expressed similar views. "We believe," the Springfield gathering declared, "that the operations of the Colonization Society are calculated to excite prejudices against us, and they impel ignorant or ill disposed persons to take measures for our expulsion from the land of our nativity. . . . We claim the right of citizenship in this, the country of our birth. . . . We are not African." Another black convention in Chicago in August 1858 decisively defeated a resolution proposed by H. Ford Douglas favoring emigration to some locale "on this continent." It is likely that Lincoln was aware of these gatherings, which were reported in the Republican press, but there is no record of a comment from him about them. They did not alter his public commitment to colonization.[79]

Shortly after Lincoln's election as president in 1860, a New Orleans newspaper castigated him as a "thorough radical abolitionist." As evidence, it cited a speech Lincoln had supposedly delivered in Cincinnati during the 1840s, when the local black community presented a silver pitcher to Salmon P. Chase to honor his legal work on behalf of fugitive slaves. The following month, William C. Smedes, a member of the Mississippi legislature, mentioned this report in a letter justifying secession to Henry J. Raymond, the editor of the *New York Times*. Raymond forwarded the letter to Lincoln, who replied by describing Smedes as a "mad-man." "I was never in a meeting of negroes in my life," Lincoln insisted. This was a revealing comment. Unlike Chase and other white abolitionists and Radical Republicans, Lincoln had no real contact with politically active free blacks before the Civil War.[80]

James McCune Smith, the black abolitionist, wrote in despair in 1860 of the pervasiveness of both prejudice and sheer ignorance among white Americans. "Our white countrymen do not know us," he observed; "they are strangers to our characters, ignorant of our capacity, oblivious to our history."[81] Here is where Lincoln's lack of involvement in the abolitionist movement affected his point of view. The experience of interracial cooperation was crucial both in persuading white opponents of slavery to abandon the idea of colonization and in enabling them to outgrow racism by being exposed to and working with talented black counterparts. Despite his deep hatred of slavery, Lincoln did not share this experience. Only during the Civil War would he come into contact with black Americans of political experience and wide-ranging accomplishment. Partly as a result, his outlook regarding the place of blacks in American society would finally begin to change.

5

"The Only Substantial Difference": Secession and Civil War

■

By 1859, as a result of his debates with Douglas, Lincoln had become a prominent figure in the national Republican party. Out-of-state Republicans eagerly sought his political advice as their thoughts turned to the upcoming presidential election. The "great problem," Schuyler Colfax wrote from Indiana, was how to consolidate into a "victorious phalanx" a party that encompassed "all shades and gradations of opinion from the Conservative, who almost fears to defend his principles for fear of imperiling peace, to the bold radical, who strikes stalwart blows, regardless of policy or popularity." Lincoln had a solution. The key to success lay in setting aside what he considered peripheral questions and concentrating on the lowest common denominator of Republican opinion—opposition to the "*spread* and *nationalization* of slavery."[1]

In his letters and speeches of 1859 and early 1860 Lincoln succeeded in positioning himself as a viable candidate for his party's nomination. So effectively did he do this that George White, a Massachusetts lawyer, described him as a "cunning, sly, crafty designing man," whose public record "seems to have been made up for the express purpose of being a successful presidential candidate."[2] White felt that Lincoln had "no deep convictions"—certainly an unfair judgment. But Lincoln did shrewdly manage to make himself acceptable to all wings of his party. Occupying the Republican middle ground ideologically and geographically, he was moderate enough to carry the entire North and therefore the Electoral College, yet enough of a radical that his election triggered the crisis of the Union. In that crisis, besieged by conflicting advice from throughout the country, Lincoln once again located himself on the middle ground of Republican opinion. He proved willing to compromise on what he considered subordinate questions but refused, even at the risk of war, to sacrifice his and his party's core commitment to halting slavery's expansion.

I

In an era of intense partisan loyalties, Lincoln had always been a party man. He had remained a Whig, he said, "from the origin to the end of that party." Now he committed himself to promoting Republican unity as the essential precondition to victory in 1860. "My main object," he explained to Schuyler Colfax, "[is] to hedge against divisions in the Republican ranks generally, and particularly for the contest of 1860. The point of danger is the temptation in different localities to '*platform*' for something which will be popular just there, but which, nevertheless, will be a firebrand elsewhere." Lincoln urged Republicans throughout the North to steer clear of subsidiary and divisive issues and not to adopt positions in one state that would injure the party in others.[3]

In the spring of 1859, Massachusetts held a referendum on an amendment to the state constitution establishing a two-year waiting period before naturalized citizens could vote. In a state with a powerful nativist movement, many Republican leaders supported the amendment. The measure was a considerably watered-down version of a twenty-one-year waiting period originally promoted by the Know-Nothings. Nonetheless, Lincoln joined numerous out-of-state Republicans in urging its rejection. Passage of the amendment, he feared, would identify his party throughout the North with anti-immigrant sentiment and alienate German-Americans, a pivotal voting bloc in the Northwest, especially Illinois. The amendment passed; shortly thereafter, Lincoln arranged the funding to establish a German-language newspaper in Springfield devoted to promoting the Republican cause.[4]

The bruising Senate battle of 1858 had also convinced Lincoln that Republicans must not allow themselves to become identified with "Negro equality." He told Elihu B. Washburne that he wished his brother Israel, a Republican congressman from Maine, had "omitted" a portion of a speech criticizing Oregon's new constitution for limiting the suffrage to whites. Lincoln himself said virtually nothing about race or colonization in 1859, although on one occasion he did reiterate his opposition to black suffrage. He continued to characterize Democrats' appeals to racism as "flimsy diatribes" intended to "divert the public mind from the real issue—the extension or the non-extension of slavery—its localization or its nationalization."[5]

Another divisive issue arose from the efforts of Radicals in a number of northern states to prevent enforcement of the federal Fugitive Slave Act of 1850. Ironically, as the *New York Times* pointed out, by nationalizing the right to property in slaves the *Dred Scott* decision made "the doctrine of state rights, so long [slavery's] friend, . . . its foe." A number of northern states had already enacted personal liberty laws that prohibited public officials from cooperating in the rendition of fugitive slaves; some tried to ensure accused fugitives a trial by jury, which the federal law denied them. Now, Radicals in some states invoked the Virginia and Kentucky Resolutions of 1798–99, in which Jefferson and Madison had claimed for the states the power to challenge or even override national legislation. The Maine Republican convention in 1858 passed a resolution terming the states "essentially independent sovereignties," a position previously associated with defenders of slavery. Some Republicans spoke of nullification. "The fact is," one Radical wrote in 1859, that to prevent enforcement of the Fugitive Slave Act, "we have got to come to Calhoun's ground."[6]

The issue came to a head in Wisconsin and Ohio. In the former, the state supreme court declared the Fugitive Slave Act unconstitutional, and when the U.S. Supreme Court reversed the ruling in 1859, the Republican legislature denounced its decision, quoting the Kentucky Resolution to reaffirm the state's sovereignty. In Ohio, the Republican state convention of 1859 demanded repeal of the federal law and denied renomination to a judge who had upheld its constitutionality.[7]

Moderate and conservative Republicans were aghast. "Almost the whole country," wrote Timothy O. Howe of Wisconsin, "has declared *nullification* to be an unconstitutional remedy," and it would be suicidal for Republicans to allow themselves to become associated with the doctrine. Lincoln, always a strong nationalist and believer in the rule of law, fully agreed. He had no liking for the 1850 act, which was heavily weighted against the accused fugitive, but he had long affirmed the South's right to "an efficient fugitive slave law." To repudiate one clause of the Constitution, he said during the Lincoln-Douglas debates, would undermine the entire document. In 1859, Lincoln complained to Ohio Republican leaders that their demand for repeal seriously imperiled the party's chances elsewhere by suggesting that it stood "in disregard of the constitution." "I assure you," he wrote, "the cause of Republicanism is hopeless in Illinois, if it can be in any way made responsible for that plank."[8]

But if Lincoln warned against Radicals' efforts to add to the Republican platform positions of dubious legality, he also opposed efforts by conservatives to "lower the Republican standard" by deemphasizing the slavery question altogether. The economic downturn that began in 1857 revived demands for tariff protection among manufacturers, especially Pennsylvania iron-makers. Conservative Republicans, most of them former Whigs, promoted the tariff as an issue that could broaden the party's base by attracting voters more interested in economic recovery than slavery. It might even win votes in border states like Maryland and Virginia, where industry was growing. "An attempt is making from the old Whig side," Charles Francis Adams warned, "to stuff in the protective tariff as a substitute for the slave question." Radicals like Adams strongly opposed such plans, as did the numerous former Democrats in the Republican party, long advocates of free trade. Despite his previous enthusiasm for the tariff, Lincoln sided with them. "I was an old Henry Clay tariff Whig," he wrote, and "in olden times I made more speeches on that subject, than on any other." But, he insisted, the revival of the tariff question "will not advance the cause." As Lincoln explained to Thomas Corwin, the venerable Ohio Whig who had been elected to Congress as a Republican in 1858, slavery was "the living issue of the day" and it would be as disastrous to abandon it for the tariff or other "old issues" as to create a *"rumpus"* within the party over fugitive slaves.[9]

Ever since the 1858 election, local newspapers in Illinois had promoted Lincoln as a potential president. In April 1859, Lincoln rebuffed one editor who wanted to endorse his candidacy, explaining, "I must, in candor, say I do not think myself fit for the Presidency." Lincoln still harbored political ambitions. But another term as a freshman member of Congress lacked appeal, and he could not challenge Trumbull's reelection in 1860 without wrecking the party, even though, he wrote, "I would rather have a full term in the Senate than in the Presidency." Certainly, Lincoln's speaking tour outside his home state in the fall of 1859 could hardly be explained by political requirements in Illinois. His purpose, he explained to a Pennsylvania correspondent, was to promote "the Republican cause." He would "labor faithfully in the ranks" to this end, "unless, as I think not probably, the judgment of the party shall assign me a different position." He did not say what other "position" he had in mind. Perhaps the vice presidency, for which he would be a plausible choice if an easterner became the Republican standard-bearer. But at some point in the fall of 1859, Lincoln began to think of himself as a contender for the presidential nomination.[10]

Early in 1860, the opportunity to lecture in New York City offered the chance to enhance his national standing. The invitation had been arranged by a group of New York Republicans hostile to William H. Seward, the frontrunner for the party's nomination. They first asked Lincoln to speak at the Plymouth Church in Brooklyn, where Reverend Henry Ward Beecher, perhaps the nation's most prominent clergyman, held forth every Sunday. But when Lincoln arrived in New York he discovered that the venue had been moved to Cooper Institute in Manhattan. The institute had been founded the previous year by Peter Cooper, whose life, like Lincoln's, seemed to exemplify the opportunities for social advancement offered to men of ambition by northern society. The son of a New York City crafts-man and a coach-maker's apprentice as a youth, Cooper had acquired great wealth as a railroad entrepreneur and industrialist. His institute provided education, free of charge, to aspiring workingmen and women. In 1876, at the age of eighty-five, convinced that the free-labor ideal was receding in post–Civil War America, Cooper would run for president as the candidate of the Greenback party.

On February 27, 1860, Horace Greeley of the *Tribune*, long Seward's critic, helped escort Lincoln to the platform, and William Cullen Bryant, editor of the *New York Evening Post* and another member of the anti-Seward faction, introduced him. When Lincoln rose to speak, the insti-tute's 1,800-seat Great Hall was filled almost to capacity, "crowded with distinguished Republicans" as well as "a considerable number of ladies." Lincoln used the occasion to strike blows against two rivals for the presi-dency, Seward and Stephen A. Douglas, as well as Chief Justice Taney, and to demonstrate to a demanding eastern audience his command of the slavery question, commitment to Republican principles, and availability as a candidate should Seward falter.[11]

Lincoln framed the Cooper Institute speech as a response to Douglas's article in *Harper's Magazine* the previous fall, and especially its claim that popular sovereignty represented a continuation of the founders' policy with regard to slavery. Lincoln spent much of the time preceding his trip in the Illinois State Library in Springfield, where he exhaustively researched the public statements, votes in Congress, and writings of men

who had framed the Constitution. The result was a surprisingly schol-
arly presentation, complete, when published, with numerous footnotes.
Lincoln concluded that the vast majority of the founders who expressed
an opinion on the subject viewed slavery as an evil whose existence had
to be tolerated but whose expansion could and should be prevented by
Congress. Moreover, contrary to Taney's ruling in *Dred Scott* that the
Constitution recognized property in slaves, Lincoln pointed out that the
document referred to slaves not as property but as "other persons," and
intentionally avoided using the words "slave" and "slavery." If a conflict
existed between "the rights of property" and "the rights of men," Lincoln
had written in 1859, precedence must go to the latter. Now he insisted
that the founders held the same view.

"What is conservatism?" Lincoln asked. "Is it not adherence to the
old and tried, against the new and untried?" On this basis, he insisted,
Republicans were the conservative party. This familiar reassurance he
considered doubly necessary in the wake of John Brown's raid on Harper's
Ferry, Virginia, the previous November, when this deeply religious abolitionist and a band of nineteen followers seized the federal arsenal, hoping
to spark a slave insurrection. Democrats, North and South, had blamed
Brown's private war against slavery on the dissemination of Republican
doctrines. Douglas had even introduced a bill in the Senate to outlaw
agitation against slavery. But, Lincoln replied, Democrats had "failed
to implicate a single Republican" in the failed enterprise. In any event,
Brown's effort to incite a slave insurrection was "so absurd that the slaves,
with all their ignorance, saw plainly enough it could not succeed."

But there was more to the Cooper Institute speech than an erudite,
legalistic exposition of history. In remarkably forceful language, Lincoln
accused the South of planning to "destroy the Government" unless it
prevailed on "all points in dispute between you and us." The implication
was clear: the North would not let it do so. As he had done so often,
Lincoln denied that Republicans planned to interfere with slavery where
it existed. But, he continued, southerners remained unpersuaded. What
would convince them? "This, and this only: cease to call slavery *wrong*,
and join them in calling it *right*. . . . [A] sedition law must be enacted and
enforced, suppressing all declarations that slavery is wrong." This Republicans would not do. The address concluded with a clarion call for the
party not to abandon its bedrock beliefs in the face of threats of secession
and charges of radicalism. Lincoln had been experimenting with dramatic

perorations at least since March 1859, when he ended a speech in Chicago with the words "Stand by your principles; stand by your guns; and victory complete and permanent is sure at the last." Now, he closed with far more resonant language: "Let us have faith that right makes might, and in that faith, let us, to the end, dare to do our duty as we understand it."[12]

The Cooper Institute speech was an immediate success. It quickly appeared in pamphlet form and four major New York newspapers, with a combined circulation of 150,000 readers, reprinted it in its entirety. They included the pro-Douglas *Herald*, which charged Lincoln with offering a selective reading of history. If the founders were as antislavery as Lincoln claimed, it observed, "they took a very curious way of showing it, by holding slaves themselves, and by drawing up a pro-slavery constitution." On the other hand, although he continued to favor Edward Bates of Missouri for the Republican nomination, Horace Greeley called the speech "one of the happiest and most convincing political arguments ever made in this city." Immediately after its delivery, Lincoln traveled to New England, where he reiterated the same ideas, often in the same language he had employed at Cooper Institute, adding, as well, the free-labor arguments he had not mentioned in New York.[13]

"Mr. Lincoln," *Harpers Weekly* would observe a few months later, "was comparatively unknown to the people of this section of the Union" until the Cooper Institute address and his New England tour. He returned to Illinois widely viewed as a presidential candidate—still a dark horse, but a possibility nonetheless. Shortly before his departure for New York, the Chicago Republican editor John Wentworth offered sage advice: "Look out for prominence. When it is ascertained that no one of the prominent candidates can be nominated, then ought to be your time." And by May 1860, when the Republican convention assembled in Chicago, it had become clear that all the leading candidates suffered from serious liabilities. Seward was undoubtedly the country's most prominent Republican, the man whose election, one supporter wrote, would "effectually symbolize the triumph of our cause." But because of his long career of opposition to slavery and his "higher law" and "irrepressible conflict" speeches that seemed to suggest a lack of regard for the constitutional protections of slavery, Seward had acquired a reputation for radicalism. Republicans in Pennsylvania, Indiana, and Illinois feared he could not carry their states and would drag down local candidates with him. Moreover, Seward's outspoken efforts years earlier to bring immigrants into the Whig party had made him anathema to nativists, while his support for the right to vote for

New York's black population inspired "strong objection" among western Republicans.[14]

Many Republicans also considered Salmon P. Chase of Ohio too radical. Chase had launched his political career in the Liberty party, worked to secure blacks' rights in Ohio, and supported efforts to combat the Fugitive Slave Act. On the other hand, Edward Bates of Missouri, the favorite of conservatives and Republicans like Greeley who feared the northern electorate would never accept a true antislavery candidate, had been closely associated with the Know-Nothings, thus alienating immigrant voters. Bates did not appear to be a Republican at all; he had voted for Millard Fillmore in 1856 and his nomination was certain to antagonize the Radicals.

In discussing the politics of Illinois, a microcosm of the North, Lincoln outlined the situation of the front-runners: "I think Mr. Seward is the very best candidate we could have for the North of Illinois, and the very worst for the South of it. The estimate of Gov. Chase here is neither better nor worse than that of Seward. . . . Mr. Bates, I think, would be the best man for the South of our State, and the worst for the North of it." Less prominent candidates also had weaknesses. Simon Cameron of Pennsylvania was widely considered corrupt, and Benjamin F. Wade, another Radical, could not rely on the united support of his home state of Ohio with Chase in the running. Justice John McLean, also of Ohio, at age sixty-five was too old, and John C. Frémont had failed four years earlier.[15]

Lincoln, as Illinois congressman John Farnsworth reported, seemed to be "the second choice of everybody." His private life was "unimpeachable," and his humble origins appealed to working-class voters (who before Republicans began to identify him as the "Rail Splitter" knew Lincoln as "the Flatboatman"). Lincoln had defended the rights of immigrants and was popular among German-Americans, but had not been "too severe" in public on the nativists. He opposed black suffrage, reassuring western voters, yet his principled condemnations of slavery and opposition to efforts to water down the party platform appealed to the Radicals. Indeed, because of the House Divided speech many conservatives, according to Lyman Trumbull, declared, "If you are going to nominate a man of that stamp, why not take Seward?" Overall, as Mark Delahay, a supporter from Kansas, explained to Lincoln, "You represent the middle" of the party and "could hold the head and tail on and beat the Democracy," especially since "Penna, Ills, and Indiana will be the field of battle," none of which Seward could carry.[16]

For many, Lincoln's appeal boiled down to the fact that he seemed electable. "I don't care a fig for any of the candidates," wrote George Ashmun of Massachusetts a month before he departed for Chicago as a delegate, "except as they may give assurance of success." Lincoln had already proved he could fight Douglas, still the presumptive Democratic candidate, to a draw. (By the time the Republicans met, the Democratic National Convention had broken up along sectional lines without making a nomination and was set to reconvene in June.) As Republicans gathered in mid-May 1860, the *Chicago Press and Tribune* printed a long editorial recapitulating the arguments for Lincoln's nomination and gave it the title "The Winning Man." The delegates chose him on the third ballot. With no input from Lincoln, they selected as his running mate Hannibal Hamlin of Maine, who as an easterner and former Democrat balanced the ticket. Hamlin professed himself "astonished"—he had not campaigned for the post and "neither expected nor desired it."[17]

The platform adopted by the convention that nominated Lincoln avoided most divisive issues while seeking to broaden the party's electoral appeal. In deference to Pennsylvania, it included a carefully worded resolution that avoided mention of "protection" but called for an adjustment of import duties to "encourage the industrial interests of the whole country." It also endorsed a homestead act offering free land to settlers in the West, and the construction of a railroad to the Pacific, proposals with broad support among all parties in the North but widely rejected in the South.

The most controversial plank opposed any change in national or state laws abridging the rights of immigrants, a repudiation of Massachusetts's two-year amendment. Carl Schurz served on the platform committee and later claimed he had been given carte blanche to compose this resolution "so that the Republican party be washed clean of the taint of Know-Nothingism." Lincoln received numerous reports of nativist displeasure. "I wish our German friends could have been satisfied without such a resolution," Trumbull wrote to Lincoln after the convention adjourned. A Boston Republican newspaper sympathetic to the Know-Nothings commented that it would have been just as legitimate for easterners to demand a plank opposing the impairment of rights by any state on account of race. In fact, the platform entirely avoided mention of free blacks, although at the insistence of Joshua R. Giddings it included an affirmation of the Declaration's language about human equality. Despite the hopes of the Blairs and their supporters, it did not endorse colonization. "It was too large a scheme and involved too many details to be introduced," the elder Francis P. Blair explained. But the border states where colonization was so central a part of the Republican appeal played a major role in the convention. Ninety delegates—one-fifth of the total—hailed from below the Mason-Dixon Line. Republicans could be excused for believing that, as one Connecticut delegate put it, many southerners agreed with their party "if they dare express it."[18]

When it came to the core issue—slavery—the platform avoided the inflammatory language of four years earlier about "relics of barbarism" and condemned John Brown's raid. The platform, claimed the *New York Times*, was "eminently conservative in tone." But the key plank embraced the "freedom national" position long associated with the Radicals. It went beyond non-extension by declaring freedom the "normal condition of all the territories" and denying the power of either Congress or a territorial legislature to give slavery "legal existence" there. "We have assumed the doctrine," exulted the Radical Henry Wilson, a senator from Massachusetts, "that a slave cannot tread the soil of the Territories of the United States . . . a position in advance of the Wilmot Proviso."[19]

George W. Julian, the Indiana Radical leader, later commented on "the amazing diversity of opinion" among those who campaigned for Lincoln. Most former Know-Nothings, despite feeling "humiliated" by the platform, "reluctantly swallowed the pill." Rejoicing in the rejection of Seward and his "extreme opinions," Old Line Whigs such as Richard W. Thompson and Thomas Ewing worked for a Republican victory, describing Lincoln as "a sound conservative man" who had no connection with the "abolitionists, higher-law and irrepressible-conflict men." But Radical Republicans campaigned with equal enthusiasm. "I am inclined to think," wrote the Boston correspondent of the *New York Tribune*, "that Mr. Lincoln is ahead of the anti-slavery sentiment of the Republican party, rather than behind it." As noted in chapter 2, when Wendell Phillips called Lincoln the "Slave-Hound of Illinois" because his 1849 bill for gradual emancipation in the District of Columbia envisioned strict enforcement of the Constitution's fugitive slave clause, Giddings rebuked him and affirmed the strength of Lincoln's antislavery beliefs.[20]

Some abolitionists condemned Lincoln for his 1858 statements opposing suffrage and other rights for free blacks. No candidate, the black abolitionist H. Ford Douglas declared, "is entitled to the sympathy of anti-slavery men, unless that party is willing to extend to the black man all the rights of a citizen." Yet even Douglas hoped for Lincoln's success, because his election would strengthen the genuine "anti-slavery element" in the Republican party. Against Lincoln's stated opposition to black civil and political rights, his abolitionist admirers counterposed his commitment to racial equality in enjoying the fruits of one's labor. Lydia Maria Child wrote that she trusted Lincoln because during his debates with Douglas, he had said that "a negro is my equal; as good as I am" (an imperfect paraphrase, to be sure). Considering that Illinois "is *very* pro-slavery," she added, "I think he was a brave man to entertain such a sentiment and announce it." Frederick Douglass could not bring himself to vote for Lincoln, but praised him in his monthly magazine as "a man of will and nerve." Even though Lincoln fell far short of the principle of equal rights for all, he added, "it will be a great work accomplished when this government is divorced from the active support" of slavery.[21]

Four candidates contested the election of 1860. After the split in their party proved unresolvable, northern Democrats nominated Stephen A. Douglas while southerners put forward John C. Breckinridge of Kentucky, who pledged congressional enforcement of owners' right to bring their slaves into all the territories. The hastily organized Constitutional Union party chose John C. Bell of Tennessee on a platform pledging to preserve national unity by loyalty to the Constitution and the enforcement of the laws. The new party appealed to many voters in the Upper South desperate to avoid disunion. The conservative Philadelphia diarist Sidney George Fisher, however, noted its flaw: it did not represent "any definite principles or opinions." The "overwhelming and exciting subject before the country is slavery," Fisher wrote, and no party "that passes this question by" could "hope for success." Far from the Democratic split ensuring Lincoln's election, it actually made victory more difficult. Even though he expected Lincoln to win, Trumbull warned in June that "by cutting loose from the administration and the Fire Eaters, [Douglas] will be less assailable than if he were the candidate of the united Democracy." Facing a Democratic candidate who had acceded to southern demands in order to obtain the nomination would have made Lincoln's task much easier.[22]

The election campaign was intense. "Town meetings, stump oratory, torchlight processions, and all other means of excitement are rife throughout the state," wrote Fisher about Pennsylvania. Along with the themes their party had perfected during the 1850s—the rights and opportunities of free labor, the necessity of halting slavery's expansion—Republicans also emphasized their refusal to countenance southern secession in the event of Lincoln's election, while simultaneously downplaying the danger of disunion. And while insisting they would not interfere directly with slavery in the states, numerous Republican newspapers and speakers predicted that Lincoln's election would launch a slow process of abolition in the states of the Upper South. The southern press reported such statements with alarm.[23]

In effect, two presidential elections took place in 1860. Breckinridge captured most of the slave states, but Bell carried about 40 percent of the southern vote and three states of the Upper South. Lincoln solidly defeated Douglas in the free states by holding on to the gains Republicans had achieved in the elections of 1858. He won 54 percent of the northern

The Presidential Election of 1860

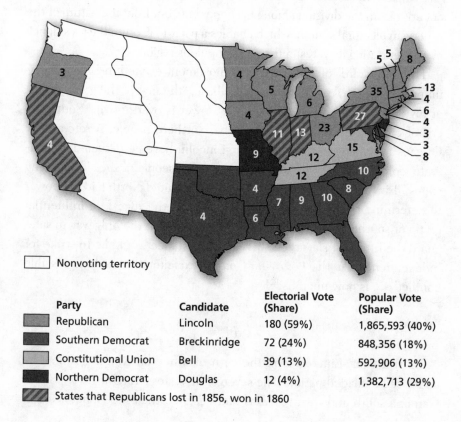

		Electorial Vote (Share)	Popular Vote (Share)
Party	Candidate		
Republican	Lincoln	180 (59%)	1,865,593 (40%)
Southern Democrat	Breckinridge	72 (24%)	848,356 (18%)
Constitutional Union	Bell	39 (13%)	592,906 (13%)
Northern Democrat	Douglas	12 (4%)	1,382,713 (29%)
States that Republicans lost in 1856, won in 1860			

Nonvoting territory

popular vote, carrying every county in New England (the only time a candidate achieved this feat between 1832 and 1896) and an absolute majority in every state of the Old Northwest. But Lincoln was not even on the ballot in a majority of the slave states and won only 2 percent of the southern vote. Republicans who believed their party was poised to make inroads in the Border South could find encouragement from the results in Delaware, which gave Lincoln 23 percent of the vote, and Missouri (the only state carried by Douglas), where Lincoln polled 10 percent, mostly in St. Louis and its vicinity. But the results in Maryland, Kentucky, and Virginia, where Lincoln received less than 3 percent of the total, did not suggest the existence of significant Republican sentiment. Overall, Lincoln received 1,866,000 votes, more than any other man who had run for president and half a million more than Frémont polled four years earlier. This represented only 40 percent of the national total. But under the Electoral College system, Lincoln's sweep of the North was more than enough to secure victory. Indeed, if the electoral votes for Bell, Breckinridge, and Douglas had been united on a single candidate, Lincoln would still have been elected. His victory did not arise from the division among his opponents but from the nature of the American electoral system, which enables a party to capture the presidency by concentrating its votes in the most populous region.

The "old guard" of the antislavery movement exulted in Lincoln's triumph. "At length," wrote Salmon P. Chase, "the first of the great wishes of my life is accomplished. The Slave Power is overthrown." Southerners, of course, reacted differently. "The Northern people," wrote a New Orleans newspaper, "in electing Mr. Lincoln, have perpetuated a deliberate, cold-blooded insult and outrage on the people of the slaveholding states." Lincoln's victory demonstrated that a united North had the power to determine the nation's future. Throughout the 1850s, an influential group of southern political leaders had insisted that the only way to safeguard the future of slavery in such a circumstance would be to strike for independence. As the *Louisville Courier* exclaimed, "The 'irrepressible conflict' . . . is now upon us."[24]

II

BY THE TIME Lincoln took the oath of office on March 4, 1861, he addressed a divided nation. The seven slave states stretching from South Carolina south and west to Texas had declared their independence and formed a new nation, the Confederate States of America. As the states seceded, they seized federal property: post offices, forts, arsenals, and the U.S. Mint in New Orleans, whose holdings of gold and silver financed the Confederacy in its initial months. In this unprecedented crisis, Lincoln struggled to develop a consistent policy to prevent the contagion of secession from spreading and to keep his party from splintering. Although his stance evolved as the crisis developed, he proved willing to be conciliatory on what he deemed nonessential questions, but steadfastly refused to compromise on the non-extension of slavery. And he unwaveringly insisted on the permanence of the Union and his right to assume the presidency.

North and South, the secession crisis energized the public sphere. By the tens of thousands, ordinary Americans took part in mass meetings and petition drives, penned letters to political leaders, and anxiously followed deliberations in Congress and state legislatures. As soon as the election results were announced, advice flooded into the mailboxes of Lincoln and other Republicans. Overall, grassroots Republicans seemed adamant against compromise. From Galesburg, Illinois, Alfred Babcock, a former Whig member of Congress, informed Lincoln that "all the Republicans with whom I have conversed" believed that any concession would simply "give more strength to the institution of slavery and correspondingly weaken the principles established by our fathers in the erection of this government." No compromise, Senator James W. Grimes of Iowa, a Republican moderate, wrote in December, would satisfy the secessionists because the North's real offense was its hostility to slavery. The only way to keep the Lower South in the Union would be to "agree to the proposition that slavery is a benign, constitutional system, and that it shall be extended in the end all over this continent."[25]

Republicans of Democratic ancestry seemed to view the secession winter as a replay of the nullification crisis of the 1830s. They insisted that the South needed to be taught a lesson. "In these trying times," wrote one former Democrat, "there is need of Jacksonism." Many Republicans of Whig backgrounds also invoked Old Hickory's legacy. As a result of the crisis, as the *New York Times* put it, Andrew Jackson had become "the favorite hero" of Republicans opposed to compromise. Throughout the winter, some Republicans spoke of war as the inevitable consequence of secession. "If nothing but blood will prevent [disunion]," declared an Indianapolis newspaper in December, "let it flow." In the House Divided speech, Lincoln had predicted that the slavery controversy would not cease "until a crisis shall have been reached and passed." The crisis had arrived. "Settle it now," wrote the *Chicago Tribune*.[26]

A few Republicans, notably the mercurial Horace Greeley, believed that only by letting the seceding states depart in peace could a demeaning compromise be avoided. In December, on the eve of South Carolina's decision to leave the Union, Greeley's *New York Tribune* commented that if the principle of government by the consent of the government were to be taken seriously, "we do not see that it would not justify . . . secession." If the states of the Lower South declared their intention to leave, "we shall feel constrained by our devotion to human liberty to say, Let them go!" (Greeley, however, insisted that secession must come only after popular referendums in each state, which he thought advocates of southern independence would lose.)[27]

Many abolitionists, who had never shared the mystical devotion to the Union so common among their countrymen, also welcomed peaceable secession as preferable to compromise. "If the Union can only be maintained by new concessions to the slaveholders," said Frederick Douglass early in December, "let the Union perish." William Lloyd Garrison, who had long advocated disunion in order to free the North from its connection to slavery, insisted that the time had come for "a separation from the South. . . . Is it not evident that we are, and must be . . . two nations?" In a series of widely noted speeches, Wendell Phillips argued that disunion would bring nearer the day of emancipation. The Union, he said, protected and enriched the slave states; "disunion is abolition!"[28]

On the other hand, northern business leaders, especially those with commercial ties to the South, bombarded Lincoln with calls for compromise. The election was followed by falling stock and commodity prices as investors panicked at the possibility of civil war. In December and January, eastern businessmen made frantic efforts to save the Union. As in the 1830s, gentlemen of property and standing led mobs that disrupted gatherings of abolitionists, whom they blamed for the crisis. They held mass meetings where speakers (most of them Democrats, but with a fair representation of Republicans) called for compromise to avert secession. They circulated petitions that gathered tens of thousands of signatures in Boston, New York, and Philadelphia, and dispatched delegations to Washington to lobby Republican congressmen. In January, a special train brought thirty leading New York merchants to the nation's capital bearing a petition for compromise signed by 40,000 New York businessmen. "The perpetuity of the Union," it declared, was more important than "this or that subject of controversy." Hamilton Fish, a prominent conservative Republican in New York City, expressed "surprise" at "the extent of concessions" merchants were willing to make. Many called for the repeal of the North's personal liberty laws, which sought to impede the operation of the Fugitive Slave Act, and the extension of the old Missouri Compromise line to the Pacific—"a plan . . . manufactured in Wall Street," according to William Cullen Bryant, who opposed the idea. Others spoke of accepting the validity of the *Dred Scott* decision and allowing slavery to expand throughout the West.[29]

Despite calls for compromise to avoid both secession and civil war, very few northerners of either party acknowledged a state's right to secede or denied the government's authority to employ force as a last resort to maintain the Union. During the secession winter, northern Democratic newspapers and party leaders blamed Republicans' "agitation . . . of the slavery question" for the crisis and tried to assure the South that it enjoyed broad sympathy in the North. But at the same time, no less than Republicans, they warned southerners that the election of a president did not justify secession and that they would not allow the Union to be destroyed. "If your feelings and opinions are the common feelings and opinions of the North," Senator James A. Bayard of Delaware responded to a letter from one prominent northern Democrat, "then civil war is upon us."[30]

To the surprise of secessionists and many northerners, even President James Buchanan refused to recognize the legality of secession. His annual message to Congress in early December insisted that Lincoln's election did not constitute a "just cause" for dissolving the Union. Buchanan approved an attempt to resupply federal troops stationed at Fort Sumter, in Charleston harbor. The *Star of the West* sailed from New York on January 5, 1861, but was driven away by fire from the shore three days later. Ironically, as southerners resigned from government posts, Buchanan ended his presidency presiding over a northern, Unionist administration.[31]

When Congress assembled early in December 1860, members brought forth compromise proposals of every description. One barred future legislation related in any way to slavery; another called for replacing the office of president with an executive council elected from different regions of the country; a third would establish a national police to enforce the Fugitive Slave Act. One member of Congress presented no fewer than

seventeen constitutional amendments, protecting slavery from every conceivable interference. The House and Senate appointed committees to
sift through the proposals.

The most widely supported plan emanated from John J. Crittenden of
Kentucky. It consisted of six unamendable constitutional amendments
designed to deal with all the points at which federal authority touched
slavery. Crittenden's plan would deny Congress the power to abolish
slavery in the states or on government property such as military forts;
bar abolition in the District of Columbia unless Virginia and Maryland
emancipated their own slaves; prevent federal interference with the interstate slave trade; and extend the Missouri Compromise line to the Pacific
Ocean so as to divide between freedom and slavery all current territories
and any "hereafter acquired." At the end of December, Stephen A. Douglas endorsed Crittenden's proposals and added his own elements. Douglas's plan required a vote by two-thirds of Congress for the acquisition of
new territory; prohibited states from conferring the right to vote on free
blacks (South Carolina had listed the grant of suffrage to blacks in some
northern states as one of its grievances in its Ordinance of Secession);
and provided federal aid to any state that wished to "remove" its free black
population to Africa or South America. Douglas also revived the "sedition"
bill he had introduced in the previous session, criminalizing speeches and
writings hostile to slavery.[32]

With Lincoln in Springfield, William H. Seward assumed the self-
appointed role of party leader in Washington. On January 12, 1861, Seward
gave a widely anticipated Senate speech before packed galleries and the
"whole diplomatic corps," pleading for calm and offering his own list of
concessions to the South, including the repeal of northern personal liberty
laws; an amendment barring any future change in the Constitution to
give Congress power over slavery in the states; and a promise that within
two years a national convention would be called to resolve other disputed
matters. Later that month, Seward and Charles Francis Adams, who represented Massachusetts in the House, proposed the immediate admission
of New Mexico as a slave state as a further step toward reconciliation.[33]

Given his radical reputation, Seward's stance came as a surprise to
many observers. "What do you think of Seward?" Carl Schurz wrote to
his wife. "The mighty is fallen. He bows before the slave power." Seward
insisted that his proposals would strengthen Unionists in the eight Upper
South slave states that had not seceded, isolate the secessionists, and
ensure Lincoln's peaceful inauguration. He had always believed that

inexorable historical forces made slavery's doom inevitable. Lincoln's election, he believed, marked a historic turning point that could not be reversed. It had forever broken the Slave Power's hold on the federal government and no concessions would alter this fact. When "freedom was in danger," he explained to one critic, he had spoken so single-mindedly in its defense that "men inferred that I was disloyal to the Union." Now, freedom had triumphed and the nation was in danger, so "I speak single for the Union." At the very least, if compromise failed, Seward wanted "to cast the responsibility on the party of slavery." Most Republicans, he feared, did not appreciate the seriousness of the crisis.[34]

Unionists in the Upper South rallied to the Crittenden plan and hailed Seward's speech as a harbinger of reconciliation. Most Republican members of Congress, however—and, the evidence suggests, most Republican voters—rejected all these proposals. Grassroots Republicans, Russell Errett, an editor of the *Pittsburgh Gazette*, reported at the end of January, were "bitter against all efforts at concession. . . . Those who are familiar with the public sentiment at Harrisburg, Philadelphia, N. Y. and Washington can have no idea of the fierceness of the sentiment here." From deep in southern Illinois, one constituent reported to Lyman Trumbull that Republicans in his neighborhood unanimously opposed any compromise recognizing slavery as right in principle, or as a national institution. Any such concession, another writer from Illinois informed Trumbull, "*dissolves* the Republican party." Crittenden's reference to territory "hereafter acquired," many Republicans believed, offered a thinly veiled invitation for renewed filibustering expeditions to add slave states to the Union.[35]

As to Douglas's proposed "sedition" act, Republicans took this as an indication that the South's "real grievance," as the *Chicago Tribune* put it, was not so much the election of Lincoln, but northern public sentiment—"it is . . . the eradication of ideas that is demanded." Indeed, during the crisis, members of Congress from the South frequently referred to the growth of antislavery public opinion as the reason their states could not safely remain in the Union, a position reiterated in the official declarations justifying secession. "Why not make the concession which they really want?" the Republican entrepreneur John Murray Forbes wondered sarcastically after Seward's January 12 speech: a constitutional amendment allowing federal judges to determine "what it is proper to write or say" about slavery. Already, a number of Republican congressmen were warning that slavery could not survive a civil war. "The standard of revolt," declared Sidney Edgerton of Ohio, "will be the signal of emancipation."[36]

Buffeted by these crosscurrents of opinion, Lincoln struggled to keep abreast of the rapidly evolving crisis and to devise a consistent policy for dealing with it. At the same time, he began the process of selecting a cabinet, a task not completed until the very eve of his inauguration. In keeping with tradition, he offered the post of secretary of state to his chief rival for the presidential nomination, William H. Seward. He used the other appointments to satisfy the various political and regional factions in his party. Salmon P. Chase, perhaps the party's leading Radical, became secretary of the Treasury; the more conservative Attorney General Edward Bates of Missouri and Postmaster General Montgomery Blair of Maryland represented crucial border slave states. Lincoln appointed Gideon Welles, a former Democrat from Connecticut, as secretary of the navy, and Caleb B. Smith, a former Whig from Indiana, to head the Interior Department. The most controversial choice was Simon Cameron of Pennsylvania as secretary of war. Cameron had a well-earned reputation for corruption, and a number of leading Republicans in his own state opposed his inclusion. The Chicago editor Horace White later called the choice of Cameron a "colossal blunder"; within a year he would be replaced by Edwin M. Stanton, also of Pennsylvania. Some of Lincoln's selections, including his rivals for the 1860 nomination, Seward, Chase, and Bates, had far more experience in national affairs than he, and Lincoln hoped their presence would reassure those who doubted his own administrative abilities. From the outset, Lincoln's cabinet was marked by political rivalries and personal jealousies. It never really functioned as a unit. As president, Lincoln gave each member wide latitude in running his own department. But when it came to slavery, while from time to time he asked the cabinet's advice, he would decide on policy himself.[37]

Until his departure for Washington on February 11, 1861, Lincoln remained in Springfield. To gauge public sentiment and political developments he relied on letters, newspapers, and conversations with a steady stream of visitors. It is not clear if Lincoln fully understood the severity of the crisis before his inauguration. Along with many other Republicans, he overestimated the strength of Unionism in both the seceded and non-seceded slave states and underestimated the willingness of the Deep South to go to war. Republicans had long believed that the mass of white southerners did not share the interests of the Slave Power. They had denigrated threats of secession as a ploy to intimidate the North into granting southern demands. John Bell's victories in Virginia, Kentucky, and Tennessee and near-victories in Maryland and North Carolina, and Douglas's capture of Missouri, strengthened Republicans' conviction that the Upper South, at least, was strongly pro-Union. More than once, Lincoln referred to the crisis as "artificial," suggesting that if "let alone" it would dissipate by itself.

A few days after the election, the *Illinois State Journal*, whose editorials were widely regarded as reflecting Lincoln's views, assured its readers that the "conservative majority" of southerners would "put down any batch of traitors" bent on breaking up the Union. Even after states began to secede, Lincoln seems to have believed that if he did nothing to provoke the secessionists, the majority of slave states would remain in the Union and the Lower South would eventually return. Unlike his idol Henry Clay, he did not devote himself to pursuing a compromise that would resolve a national crisis.[38]

Lincoln received numerous pleas to issue public statements reassuring southerners that he had no intention of interfering with slavery or in other ways abridging their rights under the Constitution. He seemed to bristle at such demands. As he explained to one correspondent, his views were readily available in published speeches but had been persistently misrepresented in the South. He did compose a few lines for a speech Lyman Trumbull delivered at Springfield on November 20, 1860, with Lincoln sitting on the platform. Lincoln's contribution pledged that his administration would not abridge the constitutional rights of the South, and indicated that talk of secession was the work of a minority. It even welcomed the "military preparation" being undertaken in southern states on the grounds that this would "enable the people" to suppress secessionist "uprisings." Trumbull, who paraphrased Lincoln's sentences rather than reading them verbatim, omitted this curious observation. Trumbull added an assurance that Republicans did not favor "negro-equality or amalgamation, with which political demagogues have so often charged them."[39]

The speech did not have the desired effect. Not a single newspaper, Lincoln complained, used it to "quiet public anxiety." "It is a mockery for Lincoln or his friends," wrote a New Orleans journal, "to say [the South's] rights will be respected, when we know that *their* interpretation of our rights is exactly the reverse of *our own*." Lincoln resolved to make no further public statements. Rather than doing good, he believed, they "would do positive harm. The secessionists, per se believing they had alarmed me, would clamor all the louder." Lincoln assumed that a dispassionate reading of his speeches would mollify southerners. In fact, it alarmed them, because he had consistently coupled assurances that he would not interfere with slavery in the states with a moral condemnation of the institution and hope for its ultimate extinction. Many southerners believed Lincoln posed as much a threat to the long-term existence of slavery as the abolitionists.[40]

Throughout the crisis, the *Illinois State Journal* published bellicose editorials widely thought to reflect Lincoln's views and some possibly written by him. On December 20, the day South Carolina seceded, it warned that "treason must and will be put down at all hazards." Another editorial predicted that civil war would result in "the total overthrow of slavery," as slaves would escape to the North and might even rise against their masters. The paper denied that a Lincoln administration planned to interfere with slavery in the states or favored "the equality of the black and white race." But it insisted that Lincoln "stands immovably upon the Chicago platform" and had no interest in any "compromise whatever." The president-elect, the paper declared, using words that would find their way into Lincoln's inaugural address, would have "an oath registered in Heaven" to uphold and enforce the laws. When William Kellogg, an Illinois Republican congressman, proposed a compromise including extension of the Missouri Compromise line, the paper denounced him: "He has sold himself to the slave power."[41]

Two weeks before Lincoln's inauguration, the *New York Times* complained that the Republican party lacked a "settled plan" for dealing with secession. In fact, throughout the crisis Lincoln displayed remarkable consistency. He proved willing to compromise on issues he had always considered inessential, but refused to countenance any concession that ran the risk of sundering the Republican party and surrendering the results of the election before his administration began. In December 1860 and January 1861, he intervened forcefully in congressional deliberations, something no previous president-elect had done, to delineate what kinds of conciliatory measures he would and would not support. On December 10, only one week after Congress assembled and talk of compromise began to circulate, Lincoln made his position clear to Lyman Trumbull in Washington: "Let there be no compromise on the question of extending slavery. If there be, all our labor is lost, and, ere long, must be done again. . . . Stand firm. The tug has to come, and better now, than any time hereafter." Three days later he sent the same instructions to Elihu

B. Washburne, who had written to alert Lincoln to the "imminent peril" that several states would soon secede, but also warning that on the question of compromise, Seward was "misrepresenting your position." Lincoln reiterated his opposition to "compromise of any sort" on the expansion of slavery. "On that point," he instructed Washburne, "hold firm, as with a chain of steel."[42]

Lincoln did draw up resolutions to be introduced by Seward in the Senate committee considering the crisis, which he handed to Seward's political alter ego Thurlow Weed, who visited Springfield in late December to plead for compromise. Apart from an affirmation that the Union "must be preserved," they dealt entirely with the issue of fugitives from bondage. Lincoln called for effective measures for their return with "safeguards" against "free men . . . being surrendered as slaves," as well as the repeal of northern personal liberty laws. Lincoln wrote to Trumbull that he thought the resolutions would "do much good." "They do not touch the territorial question," he pointed out. For this very reason, as Lincoln could have anticipated, they had no impact on congressional discussions.[43]

Another indication of Lincoln's position on conciliation came in his responses to letters from John A. Gilmer of North Carolina and Alexander H. Stephens of Georgia, both avid opponents of secession (although after Georgia left the Union, Stephens would become the Confederacy's vice president). Gilmer asked for reassurances regarding Lincoln's intentions on a range of issues—abolition in the District of Columbia, the future of the interstate slave trade, federal interference with slavery in the states, the use of federal patronage, and "the disturbing question of Slavery in the Territories." In his response, which soon became public, Lincoln remarked that Gilmer could hardly expect him to "shift the ground upon which I have been elected." But he went on to promise to "accommodate" southern views on all the issues mentioned except one. "On the territorial issue," he noted, "I am inflexible." Repeating in somewhat different language a point he had made at Cooper Institute, Lincoln identified the "only substantial difference" between North and South: "You think slavery is right and ought to be extended; we think it is wrong and ought to be restricted." Lincoln repeated these very words a few days later in his letter to Stephens, whom he had befriended years earlier when they both served in Congress and who now asked him to make a public statement to help "save our common country."[44]

Unionists in the Upper South begged Lincoln to support the Crittenden plan when it came before Congress in January. Opinion in "the whole southern states," wrote Neill S. Brown, a former governor of Tennessee, was so inflamed that only in this way could the Union be saved. But Lincoln did not budge. As he explained to James T. Hale, a Republican member of Congress from Pennsylvania who urged him to support the proposal, he considered demands for compromise under threat of secession a kind of extortion:

> We have just carried an election on principles fairly stated to the people. Now we are told in advance, the government shall be broken up, unless we surrender to those we have beaten, before we take the offices. . . . If we surrender, it is the end of us, and of the government. They will repeat the experiment upon us ad libitum [as they desire]. A year will not pass, till we shall have to take Cuba as a condition upon which they will stay in the Union.[45]

On February 1, 1861, Lincoln replied to a long letter from Seward, who pleaded with him to respond to "the appeals from the Union men in the Border states for something of concession or compromise." Lincoln began by reaffirming his inflexibility on the territorial issue—compromise on that point would "put us again on the high-road to a slave empire." As to fugitive slaves, the nation's capital, and so on, "I care but little," so long as the measures adopted were not "altogether outrageous." But in a significant shift in policy, Lincoln added that he could accept the plan to admit New Mexico as a slave state "if further extension were hedged against." Seward took Lincoln's letter as a green light to continue his compromise efforts. But realizing that Lincoln's concession would not satisfy southerners who preferred the Crittenden plan, he did not make it public. Nothing came of the New Mexico idea, but Congress did in February organize three new territories—Colorado, Nebraska, and Nevada—with no mention of slavery. This reflected not a sudden embrace of Douglas's popular sovereignty doctrine, but Republicans' conviction, stated in the 1860 platform, that slavery could not legally exist under federal jurisdiction.[46]

After delivering a moving farewell speech to his Springfield neighbors, in which he said he was about to "assume a task more difficult than that which devolved upon General Washington," Lincoln on February 11 departed on a journey by train to the nation's capital. The circuitous 2,000-mile trip took Lincoln to state capitals such as Indianapolis, Columbus,

Albany, Trenton, and Harrisburg, and numerous other cities, large and small. It lasted twelve days, during which time Lincoln made more than 100 impromptu speeches. Generally delivered before large, enthusiastic crowds, his remarks gave hundreds of thousands of northerners their first real glimpse of Lincoln himself and of his thinking on the crisis. Lincoln repeatedly tried to persuade southerners that his administration would pose no threat to them or to slavery, while seeking to satisfy Republican demands for firmness. But overall, his speeches did not augur well for reconciliation. Nothing, he said, "can ever bring me willingly to consent to the destruction of this Union." He did not threaten war but neither did he reject that possibility, and he denied that retaking federal property seized by the Confederacy or enforcing federal laws would constitute "coercion." Already, Lincoln was positioning the Union as the victim, not the aggressor, if war broke out. There would be no bloodshed, he announced, unless "forced upon the government."[47]

Lincoln's speeches dismayed Seward and other advocates of compromise, who considered their tone far too belligerent. Lincoln's audiences, however, responded enthusiastically to his expressions of resolve. When Lincoln told the Democrat-dominated New Jersey General Assembly that while he cherished peace, "it may be necessary to put the foot down," the legislators broke out in wild, prolonged cheering. It is worth noting, however, that Lincoln's speeches were less bellicose than those delivered at the same time by Jefferson Davis as he made his way to Montgomery, Alabama, for his swearing-in as president of the Confederacy. Northerners, Davis warned, would soon "smell southern gunpowder and feel southern steel."[48]

During his journey, Lincoln said nothing directly about slavery. But in a speech on George Washington's birthday at Independence Hall in Philadelphia, where the Declaration of Independence had been signed, Lincoln reaffirmed his oft-stated conviction that the Declaration's affirmation of human equality had kept the United States "so long together." He identified that idea with the free-labor ethos, the "promise that in due time the weights should be lifted from the shoulders of all men, and that *all* should have an equal chance." Even if it were the only way to settle the secession crisis without bloodshed, he said, he would not surrender that principle.[49]

As March 4, the date of Lincoln's inauguration, neared, supporters of compromise desperately sought to hammer out a settlement. Throughout February, delegates to a national peace conference in Washington, called by Virginia, debated the situation, with little result. Because of the advanced age of many delegates—the chair, ex-president John Tyler, was seventy-one—Horace Greeley dubbed it the "Old Gentlemen's Convention." The debates did not suggest that a meeting of minds was likely. James A. Seddon of Virginia, later the Confederacy's secretary of war, condemned northerners for seeking the "final extinction of slavery," which he described as a beneficent institution that brought "Christian civilization" to "colored barbarians." Most Republican delegates were playing for time, hoping the discussion would prevent further acts of secession before Lincoln's inauguration. As the convention drew to a close at the end of February, it approved a revised version of the Crittenden plan, a single, multipart constitutional amendment reworded to apply only to territory currently owned by the United States, not "hereafter acquired." But the Senate rejected the proposal and it never came before the House.[50]

In the end, the only substantive result of all these deliberations was a single constitutional amendment, originally drafted by Seward but known as the Corwin amendment after Thomas Corwin of Ohio, the head of the House committee deliberating on the crisis. This explicitly denied Congress the power to abolish slavery in the states, although in keeping with the language of the original document it avoided the words "slave" and "slavery" in favor of circumlocutions: "domestic institutions" and "persons held to labor." Radicals like Owen Lovejoy, who predicted that in time Virginia, Maryland, and other states of the Border South would request federal aid in emancipating their slaves, opposed the amendment. But the proposed Thirteenth Amendment received the necessary two-thirds majority in the House on February 28 and the Senate three days later. The sole compromise measure adopted by Congress, it hardly sufficed to settle the secession crisis.[51]

"Your refusal to adopt the Crittenden compromise measures produced war," charged Senator Willard Saulsbury, a Delaware Democrat, addressing his Republican colleagues in 1862. In any of its permutations, the Crittenden plan never attracted much support from Republican members of Congress. Given the state of Republican opinion, Hiland Hall, a Republican delegate from Vermont to the Peace Convention, wrote in February, Congress would approve it only "*if Mr. Lincoln wishes it and makes his wishes known*, but not otherwise." Although rumors circulated that Lincoln had endorsed the Peace Convention's version of the plan, he never did so publicly. Indeed, Lincoln later told Carl Schurz that he did not call

Congress back into special session after it adjourned on March 4 "for fear of reopening the compromise agitation."[52] Whether approval of the Crittenden plan would have resolved the crisis, however, may be doubted. It certainly would have strengthened the hand of Unionists in the Upper South but would not have brought back the seven seceded states. As long as they insisted on their independence, some sort of armed confrontation was almost certainly unavoidable. And as events would reveal, four of the eight slave states that remained in the Union on the day of Lincoln's inauguration were prepared to secede rather than see force used against the Confederacy, even if the latter struck the first blow. No compromise could alter these facts.

III

ON MARCH 1, with Lincoln set to assume the presidency in three days, the *New York Times* announced, "We have turned the most difficult corner. We have obtained delay." Lincoln, it continued, must now announce a conciliatory policy. The *Times* often reflected Seward's views, and in the days leading up to the inauguration Seward proposed numerous changes to a draft of Lincoln's inaugural address, all of them intended, as he wrote, to "soothe the public mind" by toning down what he considered needlessly provocative language. The draft had ended with a startling statement: "With you, and not with me, is the solemn question of 'Shall it be peace or a sword?'" At Seward's insistence, Lincoln modified this, although the eventual wording—"in your hands, my dissatisfied fellow countrymen, and not in mine, is the momentous issue of civil war"—still struck many observers as unnecessarily threatening. At the urging of Orville H. Browning, Lincoln also omitted a pledge to "reclaim" public property that had been appropriated by the seceded states, promising simply to "hold" places still in Union hands.[53]

On the sunny, chilly afternoon of March 4, 1861, a crowd estimated at 50,000 persons, the majority residents of slaveholding jurisdictions—Maryland, Virginia, and the District of Columbia—gathered at the Capitol for Lincoln's inaugural address. In a voice described by a reporter as "clear and emphatic," Lincoln went to great lengths to allay southern fears that his administration would endanger the South's property in slaves, and attempted to rally northerners and southern Unionists, especially in the eight unseceded slave states, to support national authority.[54]

Lincoln reiterated at the outset that he had neither power nor inclination to interfere with slavery where it existed. He stated that the mails would be delivered unless repelled and that federal laws would be enforced unless the attempt to do so would cause conflict. Near the end, he took note of the proposed constitutional amendment permanently barring federal interference with slavery, stating that since it simply made explicit what was already "implied" constitutional law, he had no objection to its passage. Lincoln and other Republicans had always assumed that slavery would end by state action, which the amendment did nothing to inhibit. Nonetheless, this was not a minor concession. Republicans had long claimed that the Constitution did not explicitly recognize property in slaves. Despite its careful avoidance of the word "slavery," the amendment violated this principle, and for this reason a large number of Republicans had opposed its passage. It would "engraft upon the Constitution an express recognition of property in man," said one congressman. On March 7, Lincoln sent the proposed amendment to the states. Only three states ratified it—Ohio in May 1861, and Maryland and Illinois in 1862. When a Thirteenth Amendment was finally added to the Constitution in 1865, rather than making slavery permanent it irrevocably abolished it.[55]

Despite this concession, it is easy to understand why many southerners did not view Lincoln's inaugural address as conciliatory. When it came to what he considered the central issue of the controversy, Lincoln again refused to compromise. Repeating almost verbatim the language of his letters to Gilmer and Stephens the previous December, Lincoln declared, "One section of our country believes slavery is right, and ought to be extended, while the other believes it is wrong, and ought not to be extended. This is the only substantial dispute." He repeated his commitment to the South's right to retrieve fugitive slaves, but suggested not only that the law be modified so as to prevent free blacks from being enslaved, but also that legislation should enforce the Constitution's requirement that each state respect the rights of citizens of other states. Free blacks, Lincoln appeared to be saying, must be viewed as entitled to recognition as citizens under the comity clause. No president, the *Liberator* pointed out, had ever made such an assertion, which repudiated the *Dred Scott* decision. Indeed, Lincoln went on to insist that when it came to vital issues "affecting the whole people," Americans could not "resign their government into the hands" of judges. All this was said in the presence of Chief Justice Taney, who had administered the oath of office moments earlier, looking, according to one reporter, like a "galvanized corpse."[56]

The heart of Lincoln's first inaugural consisted of a lengthy repudiation of the right of secession and an affirmation of national sovereignty and majority rule. In preparing the address he had consulted Henry Clay's speech to the Senate on the Compromise of 1850 and President Buchanan's December 1860 message to Congress, some of whose phraseology made its way into his speech. But the two key influences were classic documents of American nationalism dating from the early 1830s: Andrew Jackson's Proclamation on Nullification and Daniel Webster's reply to South Carolina Senator Robert Hayne. Drawing on the arguments of Jackson and Webster, which generations of northern children had learned in school and Republicans had reiterated throughout the 1850s, Lincoln insisted that the nation had been created by the American people rather than the states, and had been meant from the outset to be perpetual. No state, therefore, could unilaterally dissolve it. The audience, one newspaper reported, greeted Lincoln's passages on the necessity of maintaining the Union with "vociferous applause."[57]

Lincoln couched his argument as a defense of a basic principle of democracy—that the minority must acquiesce in the rule of the majority, so long as that rule accords with constitutional principles. The deep national division over the morality of slavery could be decided only by a democratic process, such as the one that had placed him in office. Secession, by contrast, not only was illegal but would lead to an endless splintering of authority as disgruntled minorities seceded from polities they deemed oppressive. No government could function in such circumstances. Over two decades earlier, as a young legislator, Lincoln had condemned "the increasing disregard for law" as the greatest threat to American institutions and the American experiment in democratic self-government. Then, the culprit was mob violence; now it was the claim that a state could decide to leave the Union. "Plainly," he declared, "the central idea of secession, is the essence of anarchy."

But Lincoln also appealed to the spirit of American nationalism that he believed remained as powerful in the South as elsewhere in the country. More than a constitution, more than a set of ideals, the nation was also a physical reality that could not be sundered. Here, he abandoned abstruse legal arguments for the language of everyday life:

Physically speaking, we cannot separate. We cannot remove our respective sections from each other, nor build an impassable wall between them. A husband and wife may be divorced, and go out of the presence, and beyond the reach of each other; but the different parts of our country cannot do this.

Lincoln closed with an eloquent call for reconciliation, based on a paragraph suggested by Seward but reworked into a poetic conclusion to an otherwise impersonal speech:

> I am loth to close. We are not enemies, but friends. We must not be enemies. Though passion may have strained, it must not break our bonds of affection. The mystic chords of memory, stretching from every battle-field, and patriot grave, to every living heart and hearthstone, all over this broad land, will yet swell the chorus of the Union, when again touched, as surely they will be, by the better angels of our nature.[58]

The diarist Sidney George Fisher found this "fine sentiment and beautiful image" so moving that he commented, "He who wrote it is no common man."[59]

Some abolitionists criticized Lincoln for failing to address the real cause of the crisis. Borrowing Lincoln's own words, the *Weekly Anglo-African* noted that the "only substantial dispute" was not the "mere question of extension," but the very existence of slavery. But the address rallied Republicans and seems to have reassured Unionists in the Upper South and Democrats and conservative former Whigs in the North. Under the circumstances, commented a Jersey City newspaper that had supported John C. Bell for president in 1860, "it was hardly possible for Mr. Lincoln to speak with more mildness." In New York City, according to one letter to the White House, reactions to the speech were universally enthusiastic, except for one "stock broker" who thought "there is too much fight in it."[60]

But if Lincoln thought his speech would persuade secessionists to abandon their ways, he was sorely disappointed. To Confederates and their supporters, Lincoln's refusal to recognize the legitimacy of secession and his insistence on retaining control of federal property in the seceded states amounted to a decision for confrontation. Two days after Lincoln delivered the speech, the Confederate Congress authorized the raising of 100,000 troops. Americans, wrote one North Carolina newspaper, "might as well open their eyes to the solemn fact that war is inevitable." Frederick

Douglass chided Lincoln for failing to include any statement of his personal feelings "against slavery." But, he added, while Lincoln complained that his intentions had been misunderstood in the South, the real problem was that "the slaveholders understand the position of the Republican party" all too well. Secessionists were not "such fools" as to believe that Lincoln would suddenly issue a proclamation abolishing slavery, but they knew "that the power of slavery" in the federal government had been broken. Lincoln had insisted that in a democratic government, the "majority" must rule. Of course, Lincoln's was an extremely unusual majority, comprising only 40 percent of the popular vote. But his election indicated that the free states, when united, now constituted a self-conscious national majority and here, Douglass suggested, lay the real cause of secession.[61]

When Lincoln assumed the presidency, four forts in Confederate states remained in Union hands within Confederate territory—Taylor and Jefferson in the Florida Keys and in no danger of attack; Pickens on an island off Pensacola, Florida; and Sumter, in Charleston harbor, very much within range of Confederate shore batteries. Moreover, the *Star of the West* episode in January left little doubt as to how Confederates would respond to an attempt to resupply Sumter. In his letter of February proposing changes in a draft of the inaugural address, Orville H. Browning had observed that no matter what policy Lincoln announced, war would still be possible. Thus, it was "very important that the traitors shall be the aggressors. . . . The first attempt that is made to furnish supplies or reinforcements to [Fort] Sumter will induce aggression by South Carolina, and then the government will stand justified, before the entire country, in repelling that aggression."

As early as March 15, the *Chicago Tribune* suggested that Lincoln send a ship "with provisions, but not with reinforcements" to Sumter and make "no secret of its undertaking." This, it noted, would "place upon Mr. Jefferson Davis the responsibility of firing on a provision-ship going to the relief of American citizens, or suffering it to quickly accomplish the object of its mission." After a month of indecision, with his cabinet deeply divided as to the best course of action, Lincoln adopted this very course. He announced a humanitarian venture to send food and medicine, but not arms, to the beleaguered troops. Unwilling to acquiesce in this show of federal authority, the Confederate president on April 12 ordered the bombardment of Sumter. Civil War had begun.

With the fort's surrender, Lincoln declared that an "insurrection" existed in the seceded states. To suppress it, on April 15 he called for the states to supply 75,000 militia volunteers, ordered an expansion of the regular army and navy, proclaimed a blockade of the southern coast, authorized the expenditure of millions of dollars for military purposes, and suspended the writ of habeas corpus along the railroad line from Philadelphia to Washington. He also ordered federal troops stationed in the West to move to the East, thereby alienating Indian tribes whom the soldiers were there to protect from white incursions on their land, and, ironically, abandoning a number of Union forts. Congress had adjourned (Lincoln called it into special session beginning on July 4), and these were among the boldest unilateral exercises of executive authority in American history, doubly remarkable for a man who had entered politics as a member of a party opposed to what it considered abuses of presidential power. By the end of May, four more slave states—Virginia, North Carolina, Tennessee, and Arkansas—seceded rather than take part in the coercion of their southern brethren.[62]

Whether Lincoln craftily maneuvered the South into firing the first shot or simply took a calculated risk of war, creating a situation that placed the onus of striking the first blow on Jefferson Davis rather than himself, the result galvanized public sentiment in the North. The attack on Fort Sumter crystallized in northern minds the direct opposition between free and slave societies that abolitionists and many Republicans had long insisted on. In time, serious divisions would emerge in the North over the conduct of the war. But in the early weeks, contemporaries were struck by the virtual unanimity of opinion. Stephen A. Douglas rushed to the White House to offer his support and then traveled to Illinois, where, only a few weeks before his untimely death, he addressed the legislature, calling for undivided loyalty to the Union. In Quincy, Illinois, a mass meeting of Democrats and Republicans unanimously adopted resolutions drawn up by Browning pledging "ardent support" to the administration in its efforts for "the suppression of rebellion, preservation of the Union, chastisement of treason, etc." In Philadelphia, Sidney George Fisher recorded in his diary, "the streets are all of a flutter with flags, streaming from windows, hotels, stores. . . . It is at the risk of any man's life that he utters publicly a sentiment in favor of secession." "Ten days ago great differences of opinion existed among our people," Elias B. Holmes, who had served in the 1840s as a Whig member of Congress, reported from upstate New York. "Today they are a unit. . . . The latent sparks of patriotism all over the land are being ignited."[63]

In none of his proclamations did Lincoln mention the word "slavery" or indicate that military efforts had any purpose other than to suppress "insurrectionary combinations" that prevented the execution of the laws. In his call for 75,000 militiamen issued two days after Sumter surrendered, he explicitly stated that the "utmost care" would be taken to avoid any "interference" with property in the seceded states. Two weeks after the war began, Lincoln assured Garrett Davis, a Unionist senator from Kentucky, that he intended to "make no attack, direct or indirect" on the domestic institutions of "any state." Lincoln believed that making slavery a target of the war effort would drive all the states of the Upper South to secede and shatter northern unanimity. In the immediate aftermath of Sumter, northern Democrats made it abundantly clear that, as one newspaper put it, "we are not fighting for negro freedom or negro abolition." Even in staunchly antislavery Wayland, Massachusetts, when the abolitionist David Child told a town meeting that slaves should be allowed "to fight on our side," his audience responded that the war was about national unity, "and they wouldn't hear a word about the niggers." As so often, Lincoln sought the lowest common denominator of public sentiment—in this case, a war to preserve the Union.[64]

War, however, has a way of producing unanticipated consequences. Even in these early weeks, antislavery rhetoric made its appearance in patriotic pronouncements, and not simply among Radicals. "The time is not yet," his friend Orville H. Browning, one of the more conservative Republicans, advised Lincoln, "but it will come when it will be necessary for you to march an army into the South and proclaim freedom to the slaves." One Ohio journal that had supported Breckinridge in 1860 and denounced Lincoln's inaugural address as a "virtual declaration of war upon the institution of slavery," now called on him to punish the "vile traitors" who "would convert the land of the free into a chattel mart." "If the people become satisfied," Senator James R. Doolittle informed Lincoln from Wisconsin, "that either slavery or the union and constitution must perish," they would readily sacrifice slavery. The Confederacy had adopted a constitution that explicitly protected slave property; its vice president, Alexander H. Stephens, had called slavery and belief in black inferiority the new nation's "cornerstone." What was the point, wondered the Washington correspondent of the *New York Times*, in seeking an "end to the present war . . . which leaves the cause of it in existence?"[65]

Four decades earlier, at the time of the Missouri debates, John Quincy

Adams, with remarkable prescience, had confided in his diary that differences over slavery might lead to civil war, a "calamitous" eventuality that, however, would inevitably result in "the extirpation of slavery from this continent." He repeated the thought in 1836 and 1842 in the House of Representatives. Were the slaveholding states to become "the theatre of a war, civil, servile, or foreign," Adams announced, the "war power" would supercede all the barriers "so anxiously erected" in the Constitution for the protection of slavery. In 1836, he assigned the power of emancipation to Congress, but six years later he identified the commander in chief of the army as possessing the authority to "emancipate all the slaves in the invaded territory." During the secession crisis, John A. Bingham of Ohio read excerpts from Adams's speeches on the floor of the House.

With the outbreak of war, Radical Republicans and abolitionists hastened to remind Lincoln of Adams's words. As soon as he heard of the attack on Fort Sumter, Senator Charles Sumner rushed to the White House and told the president "that under the war power the right had come to him to emancipate the slaves." A few days later, Wendell Phillips spoke in Boston. Like William Lloyd Garrison, Phillips had long advocated disunion in order to free the North from its connection with slavery. To support the war, he told a fellow abolitionist, would be to "renounce my past . . . start anew with a new set of political principles, and admit that my life has been a mistake." But that is what he did. "Today," Phillips proclaimed, "abolitionist is merged in citizen, in American." The war would sweep away slavery and for the first time create a unified nation with a common nationality based on free-labor ideals. Phillips, too, referred to John Quincy Adams's prophecy: "When the South cannonaded Fort Sumter, the bones of Adams stirred in his coffin. . . . That hour has come to us." He even declared that he had "always believed in the sincerity of Abraham Lincoln," which must have surprised listeners familiar with his previous orations.[66]

Frederick Douglass, too, experienced a remarkable change of heart. The course of events in the late 1850s, he had written in August 1860, filled him with "doubt and gloom." Lincoln's election failed to dissipate his sense of "hopelessness." During the secession crisis, Douglass modified his long-standing opposition to black emigration. In January 1861, he accepted an invitation to visit Haiti from James Redpath, the white abolitionist who headed the Haitian Emigration Bureau. But at the last minute, after the firing on Sumter, Douglass postponed the trip. For the first time, his monthly magazine appeared bedecked with an engraving of the American flag and a cap of liberty and alongside them the slogan "Freedom for All, or Chains for All." The Civil War, Douglass wrote, portended "a tremendous revolution in . . . the possible future of the colored race of the United States." "This is no time," he added, "for us to leave the country." Instead, he would remain and fight for emancipation: "Fire must be met with water, darkness with light, and war for the destruction of liberty must be met with war for the destruction of slavery."[67]

In its issue after the war began, the black-owned *Weekly Anglo-African* also carried an image of the American flag on its editorial page, with the words "Emancipation or Extermination" superimposed on it. "Out of this strife," it predicted, "will come freedom, although the methods are not yet clearly apparent." Moreover, it added prophetically, "the millions 'bowed and bound' in slavery" should not be viewed as "impassive observers" of the strife. The administration might deem it "a white man's war," but the slaves "have a clear and decided idea of what they want—Liberty." They, too, the paper predicted, would play a role in the outcome of the Civil War.[68]

As for Lincoln, he believed that because secession was illegal, the states remained in the Union with all their constitutional rights intact. "Some of our northerners," he remarked after receiving the letters from Browning and Doolittle, "seem bewildered and dazzled by the excitement of the hour. Doolittle seems inclined to think that the war is to result in the entire abolition of slavery." Such an idea did seem far-fetched in the spring of 1861. Yet, Lincoln's refusal to compromise his core antislavery commitment had helped to produce the war in the first place. Not long after the conflict began, the *National Anti-Slavery Standard* predicted that as Union armies advanced into the South, the question of slavery "will rapidly turn from abstract into the concrete."[69] Far sooner than he anticipated, Lincoln would have to make policy decisions about the South's peculiar institution, and how to place it on the road to ultimate extinction.

6

"I Must Have Kentucky":
The Border Strategy

■

I

On March 11, 1861, a week after Lincoln's inauguration and a month before the Civil War began, a canoe arrived at Fort Sumter carrying a "negro boy" who had heard that the new president intended to free the slaves. The commanding officer ordered him immediately turned over to the authorities in Charleston. The following day, four slaves appeared at Fort Pickens in Florida, "entertaining the idea," according to Lieutenant Adam Slemmer, "that we were placed here to protect them and grant them their freedom." Determined to "teach them the contrary," Slemmer ordered the men delivered to the marshal at Pensacola (like Charleston, part of the Confederate States of America).[1]

The outbreak of the Civil War in April did nothing to change the army's policy. "The Fugitive Slave Act," *Harper's Weekly* pointed out, "is not to be found in the Army Regulations." Nonetheless, by the end of the month some thirty Florida slaves who had escaped to Fort Pickens suffered the same fate as the initial four. In April and May, as Union forces made their way through Maryland to protect Washington, hundreds of slaves flocked to their lines or took the occasion to escape to Pennsylvania. Seeking to ensure the loyalty of local whites, Union commanders in the border states, and in enclaves of Confederate territory where the army ventured, issued strict orders to their troops to respect private property and return runaway slaves, and assured residents that they harbored no "animosity" toward them or their institutions. Enforcement of the Fugitive Slave Act continued. A week after the war began, the U.S. marshal appointed by Lincoln arrested several fugitives in Chicago. Three months into the conflict, a Maryland newspaper pointed out that more escaped slaves had been returned to their owners under Lincoln "than during the whole of Mr. Buchanan's presidential term."[2]

The flight of slaves should not have come as a surprise. Thousands had sought refuge with British forces during the struggle for independence and the War of 1812. Whatever the announced policies of the Lincoln administration, slaves, as a Kansas newspaper put it, viewed the Civil War as their "hour of opportunity," the dawn of freedom. Acting on this belief, they took actions that placed the issue of slavery on the national agenda and helped to propel America down the road to emancipation.[3]

The war, the *New York Times* would observe a year and a half into the conflict, shattered many myths. Despite southern propaganda, slaves turned out to be "earnestly desirous of liberty," possessed a keen understanding of "the questions at issue in this war," and had "far more rapid and secret" ways of disseminating news among themselves "than ever was dreamed of at the North." As the war progressed and Union armies occupied larger and larger portions of the South, the trickle of runaways became a flood. "Slave labor is disappearing so rapidly," a member of Maryland's legislature complained early in 1862, "that our lands must go untilled." As the navy patrolled the southern coast to enforce the blockade, slaves came to the shore hoping to escape to their ships. Some succeeded in doing so. When a small Union flotilla sailed up the Stono River in South Carolina in May 1862, the crew observed cavalry pursuing a "stampede of slaves" fleeing to avoid relocation inland. After opening fire on the Confederate forces and dispersing them, the naval commander took more than seventy slaves on board. He settled them in a safe location near the coast. That same month, in one of the war's most celebrated acts of individual daring, Robert Smalls, the slave pilot of the Confederate naval vessel *Planter*, brought on board his wife, child, and a dozen other slaves, guided the ship out of Charleston harbor, and surrendered it to the Union navy.[4]

By 1864, nearly 400,000 slaves had made their way to Union lines. Long before then, the escape of slaves powerfully affected both sides in the Civil War. Most slaves did not have the opportunity to flee, but the escape of those who did made those who remained "restless and discontented." Fear of escape caused owners to remove slaves to the southern interior, far from the battle lines, and prompted the Confederate government to reinforce plantation discipline by exempting one adult male from military service for every twenty slaves. These measures disrupted the institution of slavery and caused serious dissension in southern white society. The situation also undermined discipline within the Union army, as some soldiers defied orders by encouraging fugitives and refusing to assist in "returning a poor wretch to slavery," in the words of Colonel Harvey Brown, the commander at Fort Pickens.[5]

As the *New York Herald* explained at the end of 1861, the slavery question had been "forced upon the administration by these . . . negroes in our army camps." The strategic importance of the four border slave states that remained in the Union, where most runaways originated in 1861, heightened the urgency of dealing with the issue. When Lincoln began to make policy about slavery, he drew on ideas he had long embraced, advancing a plan for gradual, compensated emancipation in these states, coupled with the colonization of the freed slaves outside the country. For Lincoln, as for most Republicans, the road to emancipation still ran through the border states.[6]

In retrospect, Congressman Isaac N. Arnold of Illinois commented in 1866, it seemed difficult to understand the administration's initial reluctance to endanger slavery. But, he noted, for the nation's entire history "the claim of the master to his slave had been protected by extraordinary guarantees," embedded in the Constitution and recognized as lawful by almost every American. Most northerners, including Lincoln, desired to conduct the war, at least at the beginning, in a constitutional manner. Lincoln's initial definition of the conflict, moreover, seemed to rule out action against slavery. Convinced that secession was a rebellion of individuals, not states, he insisted that the Union remained intact, with the states retaining all their constitutional rights. To be sure, the proclamation of a blockade and the decision to treat captured southerners as prisoners of war rather than criminals seemed to recognize the Confederacy as a belligerent power. And under the laws of war, many northerners argued from the outset, slavery in the Confederacy no longer enjoyed constitutional protection.[7]

Whatever the legal status of the seceded states, Lincoln appreciated the crucial importance to the Union war effort of securing the loyalty of Delaware, Maryland, Kentucky, and Missouri, where the Constitution undoubtedly still applied. These states had a white population of 2.6 million—a little less than half that of the Confederacy—and about 420,000 slaves. Maryland and Kentucky, with their diverse economies and key strategic positions, were especially crucial to Union prospects. "I hope to have God on my side," Lincoln is said to have quipped, "but I must have Kentucky." Lincoln took many steps early in the war to bolster Union control of the border states. He appointed opponents of secession to patronage posts without regard to their party affiliation. With the army occupying much of Maryland, he moved swiftly and forcefully to suppress disunion sentiment, allowing soldiers to arrest Confederate sympathizers and administer loyalty oaths to voters, steps that helped to produce a Unionist victory in the state's June 1861 elections. He adopted a quite different approach in Kentucky, tacitly accepting its declaration of "armed neutrality" and keeping Union soldiers out of the state. His forbearance paid dividends when Confederate forces invaded Kentucky at the beginning of September 1861 and the legislature threw its support to the Union. Making emancipation a war aim, Lincoln believed, would drive the border to secession.[8]

Nonetheless, the status of escaping slaves could not be ignored, especially as the Confederacy set slaves to work for its armies. On May 23, 1861, three black men made their way to Fortress Monroe, where General Benjamin F. Butler had assumed command the previous day. Situated in Virginia at the mouth of the James River, Monroe was one of the largest forts in the United States. It stood near the spot where twenty slaves had been landed from a Dutch ship in 1619, marking the beginning of slavery in England's North American colonies. Until the outbreak of war, nearby Norfolk was a fashionable resort and "gay promenaders" had crowded the fort's parapets every evening.

The three fugitives told Butler that they were about to be sent "to Carolina" to labor for the Confederate army. Other slaves, Butler ascertained, were building Confederate fortifications in Virginia. Having "great need" for manpower himself, Butler decided not to return the men; instead, he put them to work. Shortly thereafter, an agent of Colonel Charles K. Mallory, their owner and the Confederate commander in the area, arrived under a flag of truce asking for the return of his human property. Butler replied that the Fugitive Slave Act "did not affect a foreign country, which Virginia claimed to be." But if Mallory took an oath of allegiance to the United States, Butler would return the men. This offer Mallory declined.[9]

Butler called the escaped slaves "contrabands of war." He claimed to be drawing on international law, even though the term "contraband" means goods used for military purposes that a neutral country ships to one side in a conflict, and which the other combatant may lawfully seize. Butler's legal reasoning broke down further as escaping slaves who had not labored for the Confederate military, including women and children, joined male fugitives. Nonetheless, Butler had introduced a new word into the political lexicon. Soon, there would be contraband camps, contraband schools, and extended debate about the status and future of "the contrabands." His policy won wide support in the North, including, wrote the Boston Radical Edward L. Pierce, among those who "would be repelled by formulas of broader and nobler import." Butler's actions did not imply a broad attack on slavery. He recognized the fugitives as property but used that very status to release them from service to their owners. Since it deprived the Confederacy of manpower, the strongly anti-abolitionist *New York Herald* approved of Butler's order. But, the *Chicago Tribune* predicted, "if the war continues one year or more, 'what shall we do with the slaves?' will . . . become the question of the day."[10]

Butler was an unlikely initiator of a new policy regarding slavery. A well-to-do Massachusetts lawyer and staunch Democrat, he had run unsuccessfully for governor in 1859 and the following year voted for John C. Breckinridge, the most pro-southern of the four candidates for president. When he marched into Maryland in April, Butler assured the state's governor that his troops would help to suppress any slave insurrection. Nonetheless, word of his action at Fortress Monroe spread quickly among local slaves. On May 27, forty-seven more, including a three-month-old infant, arrived at what blacks now called the "freedom fort." Butler set as many to work as servants or laborers as he could and requested instructions from Washington. "As a political question and a question of humanity," he asked, could he continue to receive runaway slaves? "Of the humanitarian aspect I have no doubt. Of the political one, I have no right to judge." Thus, less than two months into the war, the actions of runaway slaves had created a "political question" for the Lincoln administration.[11]

Postmaster General Montgomery Blair reported to Butler that Winfield Scott, the Union's southern-born general in chief, wanted to overturn his contraband policy. Blair himself felt it should apply only to able-bodied fugitives, leaving nonworking slaves as a financial burden on

*Abraham Lincoln in a photograph taken on
May 7, 1858. Earlier that day, wearing the
same white suit, he argued a case in court.
(Picture History)*

Right. Orville H. Browning, who served in the Illinois legislature with Lincoln and became a leading conservative Republican. (Courtesy of the Library of Congress)

Below. Lyman Trumbull, elected in 1855 to a Senate seat sought by Lincoln and chairman of the Senate Judiciary Committee during the Civil War. (Chicago History Museum, ICHi-24885)

Left. Lincoln's great antagonist, Stephen A. Douglas. (Picture History)

Right. Owen Lovejoy, brother of the murdered abolitionist editor Elijah P. Lovejoy, leader of the Illinois Radical Republicans, and Lincoln's political ally during the 1850s and Civil War. (Courtesy National Archives, photo no. 111-BA-1128)

ABRAHAM LINCOLN,

REPUBLICAN CANDIDATE FOR PRESIDENT OF THE UNITED STATES.

Above. An 1860 campaign placard. The images and text emphasize Lincoln's commitment to justice, the Union, the Constitution, and liberty. (Courtesy of the Library of Congress)

Opposite. The Railsplitter, *an 1860 painting by an unknown artist, portrays Lincoln as a symbol of northern free labor, emphasizing his humble origins even though by this time he had achieved middle-class status as an attorney. The flatboat on the river recalls Lincoln's early journeys to New Orleans. The painting was displayed during the campaign; the White House is barely visible in the background, just above the boat. (Chicago History Museum, ICHi-52428)*

The Dis-United States, *a cartoon published the day
after the attack on Fort Sumter, shows a black man,
depicted in the racist imagery common at the time,
tearing a map of the United States, suggesting that
slavery is the cause of the nation's disintegration.*
(*Provided courtesy HarpWeek, LLC.*)

Stampede of Slaves from Hampton to Fortress Monroe,
a depiction of slaves seeking refuge at the Virginia fort where
General Benjamin F. Butler initiated wartime emancipation by
declaring fugitives "contraband of war" and refusing to return
them to their owners. (Provided courtesy HarpWeek, LLC.)

*Left. Charles Sumner, leader of the Radical Republicans
in Congress who pressed for emancipation from the outset
of the Civil War. (Chicago History Museum,
ICHi-52582)*

*Right. Wendell Phillips, the celebrated abolitionist orator
and Lincoln's frequent critic, who met with Lincoln in
March 1862 to argue the case for emancipation.
(Chicago History Museum, ICHi-52581)*

First Reading of the Emancipation Proclamation of President Lincoln.
*An 1864 painting by Francis B. Carpenter that commemorates the moment
on July 22, 1862, when Lincoln presented an emancipation order to his
cabinet. At the advice of Secretary of State William H. Seward and others,
he postponed issuing it until September. From left to right, those pictured
are Secretary of War Edwin M. Stanton, Secretary of the Treasury Salmon P.
Chase, Lincoln, Secretary of the Navy Gideon Welles, Secretary of the
Interior Caleb B. Smith, Seward, Postmaster General Montgomery Blair,
and Attorney General Edward Bates. The artist also includes a portrait of
Andrew Jackson (on the far left wall); a copy of the Constitution (on the
table); a military map of Virginia (before Bates); and a map showing
the distribution of the slave population (lower right corner). The Cabinet
is arranged by political outlook, with Radicals on the left and more
conservative members on the right. Chase later complained that the
painting gave too much emphasis to Seward. (U.S. Senate Collection)*

Abe Lincoln's Last Card, *a cartoon in the English*
magazine Punch, *depicts the Preliminary Emancipation*
Proclamation as the last card of a desperate gambler.
(Chicago Historical Museum, ICHi-22094)

Despite the Preliminary Emancipation Proclamation, which
promised to free slaves in the Confederacy on January 1, 1863,
Lincoln's annual message to Congress of December 1862
proposed a plan of gradual emancipation that would not be
completed until 1900. The caption of this cartoon reads:
"Sensation among 'Our Colored Brethren' on ascertaining
that the Grand Performance to which they had been invited
on New Year's Day, was unavoidably postponed to the
year 1900!" (Harper's Weekly, December 20, 1862, provided
courtesy HarpWeek, LLC.)

Left. Frederick Douglass in an 1856 photograph. The great black abolitionist and editor met three times with Lincoln during the war. (National Portrait Gallery, Smithsonian Institution/Art Resource, NY.)

Right. Alexander Crummell, a prominent pan-Africanist, discussed black emigration to Africa with Lincoln in April 1862. (Print Collection, Miriam and Ira D. Wallach Division of Art, Prints and Photographs, The New York Public Library, Astor, Lenox and Tilden Foundations)

Right. Martin R. Delany, an abolitionist whom Lincoln called "this most extraordinary and intelligent black man." Delany visited the White House early in 1865 and became the army's first black commissioned officer. (Ohio Historical Society)

Left. William H. Johnson accompanied Lincoln from Springfield to Washington as his valet. When Johnson, an African-American, died in 1864, Lincoln arranged for him to be buried at Arlington Cemetery and chose the one-word inscription, a direct refutation of the Dred Scott decision. (Courtesy Anne Cady)

THE MISCEGENATION BALL

at the Headquarters of the Lincoln Central Campaign Club, Corner of Broadway and Twenty Third Street New York Sept. 22 ¼ 1864 being a perfect fac simile of the room &c. &c. [From New York World Sept. 23 ¼ 1864) No sooner were the formal proceedings and speeches hurried through with, than the room was cleared for a 'negro ball,' which then and there took place.' Some member the 'Central Lincoln Club 'left the room before the mystical and circling rites of languishing glance and many dance commenced. But that MANY remained is also true. This fact WE CERTIF that on the floor during the progress of the ball were many of the accredited leaders of the Black Republican party, thus testifying their faith by their works in the hall and headquarters of their politi gathering. There were Republican OFFICE-HOLDERS, and prominent men of various degrees, and at least one PRESIDENTIAL ELECTOR ON THE REPUBLICAN TICKE

The Miscegenation Ball, *a Democratic campaign lithograph from 1864 that depicts white men dancing with black women at the "Lincoln Central Campaign Club,"* supposedly at a ball celebrating the second anniversary of the Preliminary Emancipation Proclamation. Two reporters for the New York World *invented the word "miscegenation" as part of a plan to associate Republicans with "social equality" between the races. (Courtesy of the Library of Congress)*

Above. Negro Volunteers Enrolling in Gen. Grant's Army Corps, *an engraving from the French periodical* Le Monde Illustré *in 1863. The service of black soldiers strongly affected Lincoln's evolving ideas about the role of blacks in postwar American life. (Chicago History Museum, ICHi-22053)*

Right. Uncle Abe's Valentine Sent by Columbia *shows Lincoln opening a Valentine's Day envelope, out of which spills the Thirteenth Amendment and broken chains. The House of Representatives had approved the amendment, which abolished slavery throughout the United States, on January 31, 1865. (Provided courtesy HarpWeek, LLC.)*

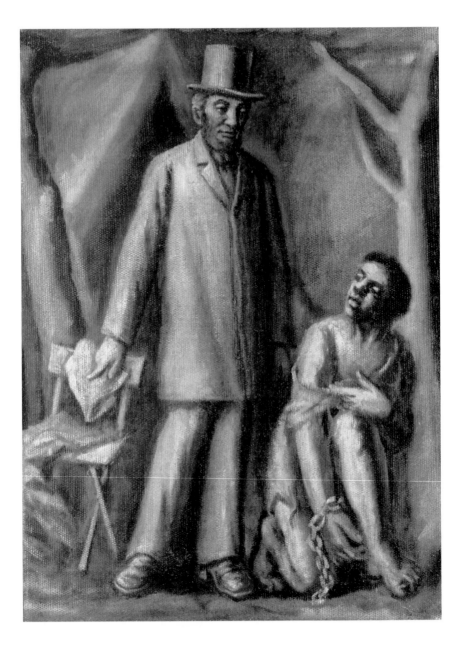

Lincoln and the Female Slave, *an 1863 painting by David B.*
Bowser, a black artist living in Philadelphia, depicts Lincoln
conferring freedom on a kneeling slave. It offers an early example
of the apotheosis of Lincoln, among both black and white
Americans, as the Great Emancipator. (Wadsworth Atheneum
Museum of Art/Art Resource, NY)

Confederate owners. But Lincoln approved of what Butler had done. He laughingly called the order "Butler's fugitive slave law," adding, however, that the question required further consideration because of the large numbers the Union army would soon "have on hand in virtue of this new doctrine." On May 30, 1861, in a convoluted letter that reflected the complexities of the situation, Secretary of War Simon Cameron informed Butler that his policy "is approved" (he did not say precisely by whom). Butler could employ slaves as workers, but he should keep a record of the value of their labor and the expense of their maintenance. Their "final disposition," Cameron wrote, would be left for future determination. The letter said nothing about Butler's offering refuge to women and children. And no public announcement followed, in order, Blair explained, to "escape responsibility from acting at all at this time." (Predictably, reports of the cabinet discussion appeared immediately in the press anyway.) Lincoln, according to the *New York Herald*'s Washington correspondent, preferred to leave the issue to local commanders. As a result, some officers continued to return fugitives, while others refused to do so.

By the end of July, over 850 blacks had escaped to Fortress Monroe. "Are these men, women, and children slaves?" Butler wondered. "Are they free?" For the moment, no answer was forthcoming. "*Where* we are drifting, I cannot see," the abolitionist Lydia Maria Child would write a few months later, "but we are drifting *somewhere*; and our fate, whatever it may be, is bound up with these . . . 'contrabands.' "[12]

I

FOR NEARLY THREE MONTHS after the firing on Fort Sumter, Lincoln and the executive branch, in effect, were the national government. But once Congress assembled for the special session Lincoln called to begin on July 4, 1861, he had to share power with other politicians, many of whom had far more experience in national affairs than he and thought of themselves as equally attuned to northern public sentiment and the interests of the nation, and equally qualified to judge military and political strategy. Thanks to the departure of the seceded states, Republicans now held substantial majorities in both houses. Throughout his presidency, Lincoln strove to forge as close a working relationship with congressional Republicans as possible. Generally, he ceded economic matters to the lawmakers, while attempting to retain control over the issues he believed fell within the rubric of presidential power—especially the conduct of the war. Eventually, he became convinced that he, not Congress, possessed authority over the slavery question. Yet Congress persistently tried to shape national policy regarding slavery. The special session of the Thirty-seventh Congress was no exception.

Lincoln greeted the legislators with a long message detailing his actions since the outbreak of war and offering a philosophical and legal justification for the Union cause. Acknowledging that some of his actions might not have been "strictly legal," he insisted that all had been demanded by "public necessity." To critics, he posed a pointed challenge: "Are all the laws, but one, to go unexecuted, and the government itself go to pieces, lest that one be violated?" He asked for retroactive approval of his conduct. This was soon forthcoming for all of Lincoln's military measures, although Congress notably failed to endorse his suspension of the writ of habeas corpus. This did not stop Lincoln from continuing to suspend the writ when he thought proper.[13]

Lincoln's message reiterated arguments from his inaugural address about the permanence of the Union, the nation's supremacy over the states, and the illegality of secession. He rejected the idea that any seceded state except previously independent Texas had ever been a sovereign entity, which he defined as "a political community without a political superior"—a description so "terse and complete," the lawyer and political essayist Sidney George Fisher wrote in his diary, "that it deserves a place in the science of politics." Northern newspapers, as well as many ordinary soldiers, had already insisted that the effort to maintain the Union embodied "the cause of self-government throughout the world." Lincoln offered a powerful affirmation of this understanding of the war's meaning:

> This issue embraces more than the fate of these United States. It presents to the whole family of man, the question, whether a constitutional republic, or a democracy—a government of the people, by the same people—can, or cannot, maintain its territorial integrity, against its own domestic foes.

Lincoln went on to link the idea of democracy directly with the familiar free-labor ethos, which he had not mentioned in his inaugural. Democracy was not simply a structure of government but a promise of economic opportunity and social justice:

> This is essentially a People's contest. On the side of the Union, it is a struggle for maintaining in the world, that form, and substance of government, whose leading object is, to elevate the condition of men—to lift artificial weights from all shoulders—to clear the paths of laudable pursuit for all—to afford all, an unfettered start, and a fair chance, in the race of life.[14]

Lincoln's celebration of free labor implicitly conveyed a critique of its opposite, slave labor. But apart from a reference to "slave states," the message to Congress contained no reference to slavery as a cause of the war or to abolition as a potential result. Indeed, Lincoln promised that after the conflict ended, the states would enjoy all their traditional constitutional rights. "Any one reading that document, with no previous knowledge of the United States," Frederick Douglass complained, "would never dream . . . that we have a slaveholding war waged upon the Government. . . . Thus do we refuse to see even what it is impossible to hide." To be sure, many northern newspapers praised the message for precisely this reason. But *Harper's Weekly* greeted the assembling lawmakers with an editorial entitled "The Slavery Question." "This," it declared, "without doubt, will be the most difficult problem with which Congress will have to grapple." The disposition of runaway slaves, the editors continued, could not be left to individual military commanders—the government must adopt a "uniform policy."[15]

A uniform policy, however, proved difficult to arrive at. Indeed, during the five-week session, Congress adopted measures that seemed patently contradictory. Five days into the session, Owen Lovejoy presented to the House a resolution declaring it "no part of the duty of the soldiers of the United States to capture and return fugitive slaves," and calling for repeal of the Fugitive Slave Act. The resolution was tabled, but the following day, after the second part had been omitted, the House approved it 93 to 55, with nearly every Republican voting in favor and Democrats and border Unionists opposed. The resolution never came before the Senate and did not have the force of law, but it indicated widespread Republican dissatisfaction with military commanders who returned runaway slaves.[16]

On the other hand, shortly after the battle of Bull Run on July 21, the war's first significant encounter and a shocking defeat for the Union army, both houses approved by overwhelming margins a resolution affirming that the war was being waged solely to maintain the supremacy of the Constitution and not "for the purpose of overthrowing or interfering with the rights or established institutions of these states." Introduced in the House by John J. Crittenden of Kentucky and in the Senate by Andrew Johnson of Tennessee, the lone senator from a seceded state to remain in his seat, and supported by Lincoln, it passed the House, 117 to 2, on July 22, and the Senate, 30 to 5, three days later. According to James G. Blaine, the resolution accurately reflected "the popular sentiment throughout the North" in mid-1861. Presumably for this reason, James Ashley, George W. Julian, Owen Lovejoy, Thaddeus Stevens, and Charles Sumner, the leading Radicals in Congress, abstained rather than opposing it (a decision Ashley later called "the most cowardly act of my life").[17]

The special session mainly concerned itself with fiscal and military matters. The question of "the future relations of the government with slavery," *Harper's Weekly* observed when Congress adjourned in August, had "by general consent" been postponed to December, when the members would reconvene. Yet the debates in July and August indicated that if Republicans did not see emancipation as the war's "purpose," many believed it might well become a consequence. Senator James H. Lane of Kansas warned that when "the army of freedom" penetrated the South, "it will be the tocsin . . . for an insurrection of the slaves." To the alarm of border-state Unionists, even moderate Republicans like Senator James Dixon of Connecticut declared that if slavery interfered with the success of the war effort, "let slavery perish." No one sought abolition, said the moderate Henry S. Lane of Indiana, but emancipation might well be "one of the results of the war." This, he added, was "precisely the position of the administration." Even Garrett Davis, the Unionist senator from Kentucky, who described himself as having "always been a pro slavery man," informed Lincoln that if it came to a choice between preserving slavery or saving the Union, he would sacrifice slavery even if it meant that "another fibre of cotton should never grow in our country."[18]

Especially after the fiasco at Bull Run, constituents inundated members of Congress with letters calling for invigoration of the war effort, a demand echoed in northern newspapers. Even moderate journals like the *New York Times* hinted that emancipation might become necessary to win the war. Reports also circulated of slaves "by the thousands" employed by Confederate armies. As the session neared adjournment, Congress on August 6 responded to this pressure by passing the Confiscation Act. Enacted over the objections of Democrats and border Unionists, it confiscated property (including slaves) utilized for Confederate military purposes and declared that the owner would "forfeit his claim" to any slave so employed.[19]

"This bill," John J. Crittenden complained, "will be considered as giving an anti-slavery character and application to the war." To be sure, as a measure of abolition it was extremely limited. The act confiscated individual slaves but did not affect the law of slavery. It said nothing about the status of the large majority of slaves within Union lines, who had not been employed by Confederate armies. An early version described confiscated slaves as "discharged from service"—that is, emancipated—but this clause did not make it into the bill as passed. Undoubtedly, slaves to whom the law applied thought of themselves as freed. But their legal status remained unclear. They no longer owed labor to their owners, but the act did not explicitly emancipate them.

For all its limitations, however, the Confiscation Act represented an early turning point in the relations of the federal government to slavery. It treated slaves as persons "held to labor," rather than chattel property. The confiscation of other property required a court proceeding, but the termination of the master-slave relationship did not—that was meant to be self-executing. The law, moreover, applied not only in the seceded states but also in the loyal border if owners allowed the Confederacy to utilize their slaves. Fearing it would alienate the border states (and possibly violate the Constitution's prohibitions against the seizure of property without due process of law and confiscation beyond the lifetime of the owner), Lincoln signed it "with great reluctance," according to the *New York Times*. But given that virtually every Republican member of Congress had voted for the bill, he felt he had no alternative.[20]

When Congress adjourned in early August, the administration still lacked a consistent policy regarding slavery, as Lincoln no doubt preferred. Immediately after the passage of the Confiscation Act, Secretary of War Cameron, claiming to speak for the president, advised Butler that while the army could not receive fugitives from states that remained in the Union, the rights of slaveholders in the Confederacy must be "subordinated to the military exigencies created by the insurrection." Butler himself had already decided to treat arriving slaves as "free, . . . never to be reclaimed." All this went well beyond the letter of the Confiscation Act. But early in August, Lincoln suddenly appointed General John E. Wool commander at Fortress Monroe, dispatching Butler to New England to raise troops. Butler assumed that this insulting demotion arose from "my views on the negro question." In fact, it resulted from a debacle in which he had sent untrained troops to try to capture a Confederate outpost.

Wool continued Butler's contraband policy, paying wages to both male and female fugitives employed by his forces. Military commanders elsewhere, however, still barred runaways from entering their lines and returned them to their owners. In the nation's capital, Ward Hill Lamon, an old friend from Illinois whom Lincoln had appointed U.S. marshal, enforced the Fugitive Slave Act, jailing blacks who sought refuge from nearby Virginia and Maryland. "Thus far," complained Francis E. Spinner, the treasurer of the United States, "our army has been but an armed police, whose duty has seemed to be to arrest and return runaway slaves to their rebel masters." Spinner consoled himself with the reflection that "this will work itself out. There can be but one result to this contest, and it is only a question of time, and the manner of its being done."[21]

II

ALLOWING INDIVIDUAL military commanders to make policy about dealing with slaves had the advantage of enabling the administration in Washington to avoid the issue. But since every such decision unavoidably made a political statement, it could lead to unanticipated problems. The disadvantages became strikingly evident at the end of August 1861, when John C. Frémont, commanding Union forces in Missouri, issued an order declaring martial law in the state, providing for the summary execution of rebels, and confiscating the property and emancipating the slaves owned by Confederates. Frémont had been dispatched in May to bring Missouri firmly under Union control. He found the state, he reported to Lincoln, "in disorder, nearly every county in an insurrectionary condition." Frémont believed the administration had given local commanders a free hand. But his order went well beyond both Butler's contraband policy, which applied only to fugitives, and the recently enacted Confiscation Act, which dealt with slaves employed for military purposes. Although it freed only slaves of rebels, not those of Unionists, Frémont's was the war's first proclamation of emancipation.[22]

Military emancipation—liberating slaves as a means of weakening a foe in wartime—was hardly a new idea. As early as the seventeenth century,

Spain had used it as a weapon against other slaveholding powers in the New World. The British had done so during the War of Independence. In the Second Seminole War, the U.S. Army itself had offered freedom to black Seminoles, most of them fugitive slaves from Florida, who surrendered to its forces. Nonetheless, Frémont's proclamation, issued at the very moment that the Kentucky legislature was considering throwing in its lot with the Union, raised a furor throughout the border. Lincoln's old friend Joshua Speed, now a prosperous Kentucky slaveholder, had opposed Lincoln's election but in 1861 helped to rally his state's Unionists. Speed warned the president that Frémont's order would inspire border slaves to "assert their freedom" and would "crush out every vestige of a union party" in Kentucky. Freeing the slaves of Confederates would destroy Unionists' hold on their own slaves: "You cannot declare my neighbor's negroes free—without affecting mine." After all, Speed pointed out, slaves differed from every other kind of property: "It is the only property in the world that has locomotion with mind to control it." Other Kentucky Unionists also pleaded with the president, including Robert Anderson, the former commander of Fort Sumter, who warned that unless the order were immediately reversed, "Kentucky will be lost to the Union."[23]

Lincoln, who was born in Kentucky, who married a Kentuckian, and who had lived among migrants from Kentucky in Illinois, paid a great deal of attention to opinion in that state. (Critics accused him of being "president of Kentucky.") Even before receiving Speed's letter, Lincoln, "in a spirit of caution and not of censure," asked Frémont to modify his order. Lincoln wanted him to seek presidential approval before executing Confederates (otherwise the enemy would "very certainly shoot our best man in their hands in retaliation") and to modify the provisions relating to property, including slaves, to conform to the Confiscation Act. If he did not, "our rather fair prospect for Kentucky" would be ruined. Frémont, a man of considerable stubbornness, refused. If the president wanted the order modified, he replied, he should do it himself. Frémont dispatched his wife, Jessie, the daughter of former senator Thomas Hart Benton of Missouri, to plead his case. Lincoln received her coolly. When she made the point that emancipation would win the support of Great Britain, which otherwise might recognize the Confederacy, he called her, according to her later account, "quite a female politician." The next day, Lincoln directed Frémont to modify his proclamation in the ways he had earlier requested. Six weeks later, Lincoln removed Frémont from his command.[24]

Lincoln must have been surprised by the enthusiasm Frémont's proclamation aroused. To Radicals, it represented a telling blow against slavery; to others, a justified punishment of rebels and a legitimate means of weakening the Confederate war effort. Senator William P. Fessenden of Maine, a moderate Republican, noted its "electric effect" on public opinion in "all parts of the country." "It is wonderful to see the general approval of the act," James Bowen, the police commissioner of New York City, wrote. "I have not yet seen the man democrat or republican who doubts its wisdom." In the Northwest, Senator James W. Grimes of Iowa reported, "everybody of every sect, party, sex, and color approves it." Orestes Brownson, the philosopher and educator who had strongly opposed abolitionism before the war, now wrote that Frémont had forced the government to confront the question of slavery, which "everybody knows . . . is at the heart of the whole controversy." Perhaps, he added, in a sentiment that Lincoln himself would later echo, "all-wise Providence" had brought about the war because of the country's long indifference to "the cry of the enslaved."[25]

Frémont's order and its modification inspired more letters to Lincoln than any other event of his presidency. Many Democrats, including those who had initially welcomed the proclamation, applauded Lincoln's action. So did the *New York Times*, although it had to admit that Frémont's action was "in harmony with public sentiment throughout the North." Lincoln's correspondence bore this out. Charles Reed, who had served as a Whig legislator alongside Lincoln in the 1830s, informed the president that his instructions to Frémont had "produced the deepest sadness and consternation among all parties and classes" and "put a decided check upon men's volunteering for the war." Many writers presented cogent arguments against Lincoln's action. "No wonder Europe looks on the struggle with indifference," read a letter from Delaware, "while we fight the slave interest . . . and sustain slavery."[26]

No one knows which letters Lincoln actually read—his secretaries screened his voluminous correspondence and passed along only a small sampling. But one that he probably saw since it came from John L. Scripps, his 1860 campaign biographer who had recently been appointed postmaster of Chicago, must have arrested his attention:

"This nation cannot endure part slave and part free." . . . To you sir has been accorded a higher privilege than was ever before vouchsafed to man. The success of free institutions rests with you. The destiny not alone of four millions of enslaved men and women, but of the great American people . . . is committed to your keeping. *You must either make yourself the great central figure of our American history* for all time to come, or your name will go down to posterity as one who . . . proved himself unequal to the grand trust.[27]

Years earlier, in his Lyceum speech, Lincoln had warned of the emergence of a tyrant who would seek to outdo the achievements of the founders by emancipating the slaves. Yet Lincoln had always wanted to make his mark on history. How better to do so than by completing the founders' work by placing slavery on the road to extinction?

Whatever thoughts he may have harbored along such lines, in September 1861 Lincoln had more immediate concerns: the war effort, Kentucky, and civilian control of the military. Among the letters praising Frémont, one arrived from Lincoln's conservative friend Orville H. Browning. Twenty-five years earlier, Browning had written the Illinois legislative resolutions affirming owners' "sacred" right to their slave property, from which Lincoln had dissented. Now he wrote from his home in Quincy, Illinois, that Frémont's proclamation had "the unqualified approval of every true friend of the Government. . . . I do not know of an exception." The administration, he charged, had shown "too much tenderness toward traitors and rebels." Lincoln took the time to draft a long response justifying his decision. Browning's letter, he wrote, "astonished me." Congress, Lincoln pointed out, had determined the limits of action against slavery in the Confiscation Act. A general could seize property, including slaves, used for military purposes, but it was up to Congress to "fix their permanent future condition" (something the Confiscation Act had failed to do). To allow a general—or a president—to go beyond the law and "make permanent rules of property by proclamation" would turn the government into a "dictatorship." Moreover, in a more practical vein, he had reason to believe that Frémont's order would irrevocably alienate Kentucky. "I think to lose Kentucky is nearly the same as to lose the whole game," Lincoln wrote. "Kentucky gone, we cannot hold Missouri, nor, as I think, Maryland. These all against us, and the job on our hands is too large for us." But, he insisted, he had not acted "*because* of Kentucky." The "liberation of slaves" was a "political" question, and he would not allow generals to make political decisions.[28]

Lincoln's letter to Browning offered the most elaborate explanation of his thinking on the war's relationship to slavery in the late summer of 1861. Later, his outlook would change. He would end up doing what the letter indicated he could not do—abolish property in slaves "by proclamation" in the absence of legislative authority. All this proves is that five months into the Civil War, Lincoln, like the vast majority of his countrymen, had not yet arrived at a coherent policy regarding how to deal with slavery.

The controversy over Frémont's order opened the floodgates of public discussion of slavery. As William O. Stoddard, one of Lincoln's three secretaries, wrote in a New York newspaper, it reconfigured northern politics, dividing it "as by a saber cut, *permanently*, into the new shape of 'conservatives' and 'radicals.' " For the moment, Stoddard added, the conservatives, led by Lincoln, had things "their own way." Yet, he noted, the distinction was less rigid than heated rhetoric sometimes suggested. "For the most part," the two groups sought "the same ends but by different means."[29]

Nonetheless, this difference was significant. Radicals and abolitionists, many of whom had refrained during the summer from direct criticism of the administration, condemned Lincoln's modification of Frémont's order. "Where is the war power now?" wondered the *Weekly Anglo-African*. Some comments included disdainful remarks of a kind that would resurface again and again during Lincoln's presidency. Benjamin F. Wade wrote of Lincoln's "imbecility and perverseness," claiming he had done "more injury to the cause of the Union . . . than [General Irvin] McDowell did by retreating at Bull Run." Lincoln's action, Wade added, "could only come of one born of 'poor white trash' and educated in a slave state."[30]

For months, abolitionists had insisted that the war could not be won without emancipation. Now they embarked on a campaign to persuade the administration and the northern public. A group in Boston formed the Emancipation League to present the case for abolition in terms that would attract the widest support. "I have been advocating of late," wrote the abolitionist editor Charles G. Leland, "emancipation for the sake of the Union—and of free white labor," not the slaves. On October 1, Charles Sumner, who to the surprise of many constituents had said nothing about slavery during the special session of Congress, called for emancipation in a speech at the Republican state convention in Massachusetts.

Even in Massachusetts, however, most Republicans had no desire to break with the president. The moderate Republican press denounced

Sumner's speech, and the delegates rejected a resolution that advocated freeing all slaves within Union lines, with compensation for loyal owners. Yet Sumner also received many letters of support, not all of them from Radicals. Even Montgomery Blair praised his remarks: "Your speech is noble, beautiful, classical, sensible. I would have timed it differently, but I will take it now." In any event, the debate had become public, and it would not go away. In October, his former congressional colleague Richard W. Thompson reported to Lincoln from Indiana that "public sentiment" had reached a "peculiar" condition, marked by "a very free examination and discussion of the policy of the administration." No president, he added, had "ever been subjected to a severer or more searching scrutiny." People of all parties strongly supported the war effort, but they demanded "vigorous policy—decided and prompt action" against the South. Ironically, Thompson observed, Lincoln's strongest support came from his former opponents, while "Republicans, thus far, complain the most."[31]

III

LINCOLN WAS unquestionably thinking seriously about slavery in the fall of 1861. In November, George Bancroft, the noted historian and former member of James K. Polk's cabinet, conveyed to Lincoln his conviction that "Divine Providence" had brought on the war as a way to "root out social slavery." Lincoln replied that the matter "does not escape my attention." He promised to deal with it "in all due caution, and with the best judgment I can bring to it."[32]

In fact, Lincoln had already settled on tiny Delaware as the place where emancipation could be launched with the greatest prospect of success. The state's population in 1860 included 90,500 white persons (only 587 of them slaveowners), 19,800 free blacks, and just under 1,800 slaves. Even this last figure was something of an exaggeration, as Delaware had created a legal category of half-freedom whereby slaves whose owners agreed to manumit them served a term as indentured servants before being liberated. Alone among the slave states, Delaware had barred the sale of slaves outside its borders, resulting in a decline in the value of its human property since excess labor could not be shipped farther south. Abolition, Senator James A. Bayard had told the Senate several months earlier, would have no effect on his state's prosperity. Delaware, moreover, had a significant Quaker population and, in the northern part of the state, a long antislavery tradition. In 1847, a bill for gradual emancipation had failed in the legislature by one vote. On the other hand, the state had also enacted harsh black codes. Free blacks could not vote, testify in court, or send their children to public schools, and the law presumed all black persons to be slaves unless they could demonstrate their free status. The main obstacle to abolition in the state, according to Bayard, was fear it would lead to "the equality of races."[33]

Early in November 1861, Lincoln met at the White House with George P. Fisher, Delaware's lone member of the House of Representatives, and Benjamin Burton, whose twenty-eight slaves made him the state's largest slaveholder. Both were strong Unionists. Lincoln pressed them to initiate a process of gradual, compensated emancipation, which the federal government would finance. Once Delaware acted, other border states would follow, shattering the Confederacy's hope of weaning them from the Union and leading to the end of the war in the "cheapest and most humane" manner. Their state, the two men told Lincoln, would be delighted to rid itself of slavery in this manner, whereupon Lincoln drafted two bills that could be introduced in the Delaware legislature. One abolished slavery in five yearly stages, culminating in 1867, with slave children to serve apprenticeships until adulthood. The second bill immediately freed slaves above the age of thirty-five but extended the process of emancipation for the remainder all the way to 1893. Both bills required the federal government to compensate owners with about $400 per slave, and both barred the sale of soon-to-be-emancipated slaves out of state. In keeping with his long-established preference for gradual emancipation, Lincoln noted, "on reflection, I like No. 2 the better."[34]

The idea of compensated emancipation had a long lineage. Even though abolitionists had attacked such plans for surrendering the "great fundamental principle that man cannot hold property in man," the Constitution's Fifth Amendment distinctly required "just compensation" if the federal government appropriated private property. In one form or another compensated emancipation had been implemented in the British West Indies and most of Latin America. Even as Americans debated the question, the Netherlands early in 1862 adopted a plan for compensated emancipation in its Caribbean colonies. Lincoln had included compensation in his 1849 proposal for abolition in the District of Columbia. All these plans shared an essential characteristic—recognition of the local laws that defined slaves as property.[35]

During the 1850s, the "learned blacksmith" and veteran reformer Elihu Burritt had organized a Compensated Emancipation Convention in Cleveland. Unlike most such proposals, Burritt's plan would provide money not only to owners, but, in smaller amounts, to emancipated slaves as well. Burritt lectured widely on the scheme in the northern and border states, including twice in Springfield, where he conferred with William Herndon, Lincoln's law partner. (There is no record of Lincoln having met Burritt or attending his lectures.)[36]

In August 1861, with the war now under way, Daniel R. Goodloe, an abolitionist from North Carolina who was working in Washington, D.C., as a reporter for the *New York Times*, published a pamphlet urging the federal government to propose compensated emancipation to the loyal border states. The editor of the *Times*, Henry J. Raymond, published and distributed it without charge. To counter white concerns about the creation of a large free black population, Goodloe predicted that the emancipated slaves would voluntarily migrate to the Deep South, which would become their "Eldorado." It is not known if Lincoln saw this pamphlet, but he later appointed Goodloe to chair the commission that allocated compensation to slaveowners after Congress abolished slavery in the District of Columbia.[37]

Compared with later developments, Lincoln's proposal to Delaware, which envisioned slavery surviving for thirty additional years, seems cautious indeed. Yet in November 1861, when no significant military action had yet taken place, it was a bold initiative. Never before had a president committed the federal government to promoting abolition. Moreover, in aiming not simply to free individual slaves but to abolish the institution, it advanced well beyond Butler's contraband policy and the Confiscation Act. And, in Lincoln's view, it was constitutionally unassailable since it relied on the action of state authorities and did not seize property without compensation. In effect, the plan made slaveholders partners in, rather than opponents of, emancipation, and offered a way of ending the institution without violence or social revolution.

Lincoln's proposal for Delaware, which he soon extended to the entire border, should not be viewed simply as an attempt to outflank the Confederacy. It represented a continuation of prewar Republican plans to promote the demise of slavery in the border region. And when it came to the future status of the freed slaves, Lincoln also thought along prewar lines. When he presented his proposal to Fisher in November 1861, Lincoln did not mention colonization. But he told Orville H. Browning, who had been elected to the Senate from Illinois, that colonization "should be connected with it." Lincoln was well aware that, as Joshua Speed had warned him from Kentucky, white public opinion in the border would never countenance "allowing negroes to be emancipated and remain among us." "You might as well," Speed commented, "attack the freedom of worship in the North or the right of a parent to teach his child to read, as to wage war in a slave state on such a principle."[38]

Once Fisher prepared a bill, under whose terms slavery in Delaware would end in 1872 with apprenticeship until adulthood for slave children, debate began in the state's newspapers. Opponents warned that emancipated slaves would demand citizenship rights and that the end of slavery would lead to "equality with the white man." Fisher went to great lengths to fend off this charge, insisting that not equality but colonization, of blacks already free as well as emancipated slaves, would follow abolition. But by February 1862 it had become apparent that the bill could not pass, and it was never actually introduced in the legislature. Slavery survived in Delaware until December 1865, when the Thirteenth Amendment became part of the U.S. Constitution (and the owners received no monetary compensation).[39] The outcome in Delaware offered an early indication that Lincoln's hope of border owners voluntarily surrendering their slaves was doomed to failure. It also demonstrated that proponents of emancipation needed to have a persuasive answer to the inevitable question of what would happen to slaves once freed. This brought to the fore, once again, the prospect of colonization.

For years, colonization had been one element of a strategy for promoting gradual abolition in the border states pressed by the Blair family and their followers and embraced, although without their fervor, by Lincoln. His cabinet included three strong advocates of the idea: Edward Bates, Montgomery Blair, and Caleb B. Smith. From the very beginning of his administration, Lincoln considered ways of laying the groundwork for colonization. In March 1861, a month before the outbreak of the war, Elisha Crosby, the new minister to Guatemala, departed for his post carrying secret instructions "conceived by old Francis P. Blair" and endorsed by Lincoln, to secure land for a colony of blacks "more or less under the protection of the U.S. Government." Crosby found the presidents of Guatemala and Honduras unreceptive. One asked why the Lincoln administration did not settle blacks in its own western territory, "a question,"

Crosby related, "which I must confess I found very difficult to answer." On April 10, even as the crisis at Fort Sumter reached its climax, Lincoln found time to meet at the White House with Ambrose W. Thompson, who claimed to have acquired several hundred thousand acres of land in Chiriqui on the Isthmus of Panama, then part of New Granada (today's Colombia). Thompson touted the region's suitability for a naval station because of its fine harbor and rich coal deposits, which colonized blacks could mine.[40]

After fighting began, the Blairs pressed the colonization initiative. The increasing numbers of "contrabands" who could neither be returned to their owners nor be brought to the North given prevailing prejudices there, increased their urgency. They hoped to use as guinea pigs the refugees at Fortress Monroe. "I am in favor of sending them straight to Hayti," Montgomery Blair wrote to General Butler on June 8, 1861. "Suppose you sound some of the most intelligent, and see how they would like to go with their families to so congenial a clime." Lincoln apparently agreed. On July 8, Browning, a longtime advocate of colonization, recorded in his diary that he and the president had discussed "the negro question" at the White House. Both agreed, Browning wrote, that the government should not send fugitives back to slavery and that at the end of the war they should be colonized. Around the same time, Blair approached Matías Romero, the Mexican chargé d'affaires in Washington, about establishing a black colony in the Yucatán. But given that Mexico had recently surrendered one-third of its territory to the United States, the prospect of further intrusions on its soil aroused insurmountable opposition.[41]

Chiriqui seemed to offer a more promising prospect. Lincoln, according to Secretary of the Navy Gideon Welles, was "much taken" with Ambrose W. Thompson's proposal and pressed Welles to look into the matter. The secretary responded that the navy had no interest in a coaling station in Chiriqui, that there was "fraud and cheat in the affair," and that he doubted blacks desired to become coal miners. Undeterred, Lincoln turned the matter over to Secretary of the Interior Caleb B. Smith. In October 1861, he authorized Smith to agree to a contract for "coal and privileges" in Chiriqui, which, Smith hoped, would not only benefit the federal government but also help "to secure the removal of the negroes from this country." Lincoln also asked Mary Lincoln's brother-in-law Ninian Edwards and Francis P. Blair Sr. to look into the Chiriqui matter. Both reported positively. Edwards seemed mainly interested in saving the government money on coal. Blair waxed enthusiastic about Chiriqui as the "pivot" for an American empire in the Caribbean and a site for the "deportation" of the "African race," thus "removing the element that convulses the whole system." Soon after meeting with Congressman Fisher, Lincoln informed Secretary of the Treasury Salmon P. Chase that he was anxious to have the "Chiriqui coal contract . . . closed." But in view of Welles's opposition, the project was shelved. It would be revived in 1862.[42]

Any doubt that at this point colonization remained part of Lincoln's plan for dealing with slavery and its aftermath was dispelled when Congress reassembled. In his annual message, sent to the lawmakers on December 3, 1861, Lincoln urged them to provide funds for the colonization of slaves freed under the Confiscation Act or whom the border states decided to emancipate, as well as blacks already free who might desire to emigrate. He asked them to consider acquiring new territory for the purpose. A Washington newspaper suggested that the proposed black colony be called Lincolnia. Lincoln also called for extending diplomatic recognition to Haiti and Liberia, partly, it is plausible to assume, to improve prospects for black emigration to these countries. (The *New York Herald* objected that such recognition would result in a "strapping negro" arriving in Washington as an ambassador.)[43]

Overall, commented the Washington correspondent of the *New York Times*, the message took "the ancient ground of Henry Clay in regard to slavery . . . combined with the plan of Frank P. Blair, Jr." "No plan of emancipation," the reporter added, "unless accompanied by a practical scheme for colonization, will ever meet the President's assent." Editorially, however, the *Times* viewed colonization as thoroughly impractical. The country, it insisted, could not afford to lose so much labor, and "perfectly harmonious relations" between the races could be established once slavery ended. But other voices of Republican moderation praised this part of the message. And colonization societies were overjoyed by the president's embrace of their program.[44]

In the annual message, Lincoln approached the future of slavery cautiously. John J. Crittenden had urged him to say nothing at all about it: "It is a topic which has been the bane of our country, and it must be wise, therefore, to shut off" discussion. Lincoln reiterated that the war's "primary object" was to preserve the Union. He reminded the lawmakers that he had avoided "radical and extreme measures." Nonetheless, the message contained a subtle expansion of his position regarding slavery and the war. It built on the Delaware plan to offer financial aid to any state that agreed to gradual emancipation. Payment would take place in a curious manner, as an offset against "direct taxes" owed to the federal government as if, the *Chicago Tribune* remarked, slaves could "be used as currency by the State." The message also included the startling statement that slaves covered by the Confiscation Act had been "liberated"—a description that went beyond the letter of that ambiguous law. Lincoln mentioned the possibility of Congress passing a "new law" regarding slavery, perhaps inviting it to do so. And he included a passage celebrating the strength of border-state Unionism that inadvertently, perhaps, suggested that future policy need not be tailored to border sensibilities.[45]

Reactions to Lincoln's annual message underscored divisions among Republicans over the relationship of slavery to the war as well as their bases of unity. Moderate and conservative Republicans praised the president's sagacity. A policy of general emancipation would destroy the "unanimity of public sentiment" essential for prosecution of the war, the *New York Times* declared, and lead to border secession and the disbandment of half the army. Not surprisingly, abolitionists and Radicals found the message "sorely disappointing." Lincoln "has evidently not a drop of anti-slavery blood in his veins," William Lloyd Garrison commented. "I shudder at the possibility of the war terminating without the utter extinction of slavery." Lyman Trumbull received numerous letters from constituents complaining about the absence of a "battle cry" in the message. "It would seem that Mr. Lincoln had his face *Southward* when he wrote this *thing*," one observed. "If this struggle ends with slavery still in existence, the Battle of Liberty has been only half fought."[46]

Radicals were further dismayed by what Charles H. Ray of the *Chicago Tribune* called a "horrible *fiasco*" regarding the annual report of Secretary of War Simon Cameron. This related to the extremely delicate issue of enlisting blacks in the Union army. Black men had served in the navy before the war, but had been barred from the militia by a federal statute dating back to 1792, and from the regular army by tradition even though no law required it. Throughout 1861, northern free blacks offered their services, only to be turned away. So did runaway slaves. Early in the war, Henry Jarvis, who escaped to Fortress Monroe, offered to enlist. General Butler, Jarvis later recalled, "said *it wasn't a black man's war*. I told him it *would* be a black man's war before they got through." Disgusted, Jarvis

emigrated to Africa. He returned two years later and, federal policy having changed, enlisted in the Union army. In fact, the Confederacy raised
black soldiers before the Union did. New Orleans had a long tradition
of free black militia service, dating back to the period of French rule.
Early in 1862, officials there began to enroll black soldiers into the First
Native Guards to help defend the city. (When federal forces captured
New Orleans, these soldiers proclaimed their allegiance to the Union,
saying they had been coerced into serving the Confederacy.)[47]

Lincoln said nothing when Secretary Welles in September 1861 authorized the navy to begin enrolling blacks at its lowest rank, "boy." But in
October, when Cameron allowed General T. W. Sherman to utilize the
"services" of blacks in any capacity he saw fit in the expedition to the
South Carolina Sea Islands, Lincoln added a sentence that this did not
include "a general arming of them for military service." Lincoln left intact
the rest of Cameron's language, which seemed to imply that if necessary, some blacks could be armed. But Lincoln feared reaction in the
border states and the army itself to a policy of welcoming black recruits.
Undeterred, Cameron included in his annual message a recommendation
for freeing the slaves and enlisting blacks in the army. Lincoln ordered
Cameron to remove the offending passage, and government censors tried
to block publication of the original draft. Both versions of the report from
the Secretary of War appeared in the press, to Lincoln's considerable
annoyance. In January 1862, Lincoln replaced Cameron with Edwin M.
Stanton, a far more capable secretary of war.[48]

Clearly, no consensus about dealing with slavery as yet existed within
the Republican party. Justin S. Morrill, a moderate Republican member
of the House from Vermont, illustrated how constitutional scruples and
doubts about blacks' readiness for freedom counterbalanced the widespread desire for action against slavery. "I hope and pray," he wrote, "that
the institution of slavery may receive its deathblow in this great struggle,
and I believe it will." But Congress should "make haste slowly." Morrill
approved acting against the slaves of rebels, but the idea of freeing those
of "loyal men," even with monetary compensation, struck him as "a wild
and utterly impracticable scheme," far beyond the lawmakers' constitutional authority. Moreover, loose talk about emancipation might arouse
"the passions of these poor degraded Africans," with consequences no one
could foresee. Nevertheless, as the correspondent of the *New York Times*
in the capital noted, even moderates who praised the president favored "a

very radical treatment of the disease" (slavery). This, he added, "cannot fail to influence the policy of the administration."[49]

IV

APART FROM the capture in February of Forts Henry and Donelson in Tennessee by Union forces under Ulysses S. Grant, the winter of 1861–62 witnessed little significant military action. But public discussion of slavery intensified. In part, this resulted from frustration at the lack of military progress, in part from renewed agitation by the abolitionists. Lincoln's secretary John Hay ridiculed the "little handful of earnest impracticables" clamoring for a policy of emancipation. But their efforts began to have an impact in the North. By early 1862, petitions with thousands of signatures calling for action against slavery began piling up in Washington. "Rousing anti-slavery meetings" took place at the Smithsonian Institution. Lincoln himself sat on the podium during Horace Greeley's talk there on January 3, to the dismay of one Democratic congressman, who demanded an immediate halt to these "abolition lectures." While abolitionists remained a small minority, they were increasingly treated with respect, their meetings now covered extensively by mainstream Republican newspapers. Orestes Brownson, who called for emancipation as the only way to establish a "permanent Union of freedom," spoke for many when he reconsidered his prewar sentiments. Abolitionists, he wrote, had been justly criticized for giving too little consideration to "political expediency," but "we who have opposed them are, perhaps, even more chargeable with having made too little account in our political calculations of justice."[50]

That winter, Wendell Phillips received almost 200 invitations to lecture on the war and emancipation. He may have been heard by as many as 50,000 people, and via publication in newspapers and pamphlets, his words reached many more. When he spoke at Cooper Institute, people lined up for hours and many had to be turned away. Even John Hay, who held the abolitionists as responsible as the "slavery propagandists" for bringing on the war, noted that listeners who had hissed Phillips a year earlier now applauded him, an example, Hay wrote, of "the progress of ideas in a revolution." Again and again, Phillips hammered home his message: the war must not only destroy slavery but create a new nation that "knows neither black nor white, . . . [and] holds an equal sceptre over all." Phillips criticized Lincoln's reluctance to act against slavery and called on Congress to take the lead. In March 1862, for the first time in his life, Phillips lectured in Washington. Charles Sumner introduced him on the floor of the Senate, he spoke at the Capitol in the presence of Vice President Hamlin and many members of Congress, and had an interview with Lincoln. Frederick Douglass, William Lloyd Garrison, and other abolitionists also lectured to large audiences.[51]

As part of their campaign to influence public opinion, proponents of abolition defended the results of prior emancipations. They made a particular effort to refute the "prevailing notion," as *Harper's Weekly* put it, that emancipation in the British West Indies had been a "failure" because it had been followed by a sharp decline in sugar exports. They publicized William G. Sewell's *Ordeal of Free Labor in the British West Indies*, a series of letters that originally appeared in the *New York Times* and was published in book form in 1861. Sewell blamed poor management by planters for post-emancipation economic problems and insisted that "freedom, when allowed fair play," benefitted black and white alike. Freedpeople in the British Caribbean, John P. Hale of New Hampshire assured the Senate, had become "an industrious, contented and prosperous peasantry." Advocates of emancipation also pointed to the South Carolina Sea Islands, where the 10,000 or so slaves who remained behind when their masters fled the approach of the Union navy appeared eager for education and understood that they must "work for a living." After a visit to the islands to investigate prospects for resuming cotton production, John Murray Forbes proclaimed himself convinced that "the negro has the same selfish element in him which induces other men to labor."[52]

"The rebellion," Gideon Welles later recalled, "rapidly increased the anti-slavery sentiment everywhere, and politicians shaped their course accordingly." Pressure for more dramatic action against slavery came not only from abolitionists and Radicals but also the Republican mainstream. Members of all wings of the party viewed Lincoln as too cautious and irresolute. The president, wrote James C. Conkling, the former chair of the Illinois Republican party, "does not seem disposed to assume any responsibility." Even the attorney general, Edward Bates, feared the president "lacked *will* and *purpose*."[53]

When Congress assembled in December 1861, journalists predicted a "stormy session" in which "the slave question" would occupy "the most prominent part in . . . discussion." It was clear from the outset that sentiment about slavery had shifted. Three days into the session, the House killed a motion to reaffirm the Crittenden-Johnson resolution of the previous July, which had disavowed the idea that interference with slavery was a "purpose" of the war. Radicals launched a campaign for vigorous action. Anyone who doubted that slavery was "the very *sole* cause of the war," wrote Horace White, the Washington correspondent of the *Chicago Tribune*, was a "lunatic." Martin F. Conway of Kansas offered a penetrating critique of the legal "fiction" under which the administration continued to operate. Lincoln's insistence that the seceded states remained in the Union, he declared, "binds us to slavery." Unless this understanding of the conflict changed, Union victory would restore the "slave power" to its former domination.[54]

In the early days of the session, Radicals introduced numerous measures dealing directly or indirectly with slavery. Thomas Eliot of Massachusetts presented a resolution urging Lincoln, under the war power, to emancipate the slaves in areas under rebellion. John P. Hale called for abolishing the current Supreme Court and replacing it with another one. Owen Lovejoy advocated enlisting black men in the Union army. Proposals circulated for abolition in the nation's capital, repeal of the Fugitive Slave Act, and the confiscation and emancipation of the slaves of Confederates. Lyman Trumbull, who introduced a confiscation bill early in December, received numerous letters of support. "I honestly believe," declared a writer from Cairo at the southern tip of Illinois, "that the people are far ahead of the leaders today in their readiness to take the proper steps to put down this rebellion." Throughout December debate continued. The *New York Herald* urged members to devote themselves to war measures "instead of wasting their precious time, by day and night, upon fruitless discussions upon the negro."[55]

One contentious issue concerned the status of fugitive slaves who sought refuge in the nation's capital. Following complaints about conditions in the city jail, where marshal Ward Hill Lamon had incarcerated some sixty escaped slaves to await return to their masters, Secretary of State Seward, stating that he acted on instructions from Lincoln, reminded civil and military authorities in the District that runaways should not be arrested merely "upon presumption arising from color." Those who had been employed by Confederate forces, he pointed out, were entitled to protection under the Confiscation Act. An embarrassing power struggle followed. After the Senate launched an investigation, Lamon ordered that no senator should be allowed access to the jail without his permission. The lawmakers responded with a unanimous vote declaring the marshal "in contempt of its rightful authority." When senators asked Lamon to justify his policy toward runaways, Lincoln, who may have feared the situation was needlessly complicating the administration's relationship with Maryland, where many fugitives originated, drafted for the marshal an evasive response stating that he acted "upon an old and uniform custom here." (The District's laws required free blacks to carry certificates of freedom or face arrest, and slaves to have the permission of their owners when away from home.) The situation led to considerable resentment in Congress. Senator James W. Grimes, who had been refused permission by the jailor to enter the premises, called Lamon a "foreign satrap, who has been brought here from the State of Illinois and fastened upon the seventy thousand people of this District."[56]

The consideration of antislavery measures continued throughout the winter and spring of 1862. These prolonged and widely reported debates, eagerly listened to by black and white visitors in the galleries, helped to educate the northern public about the relationship of slavery to the rebellion. Democrats, including staunch supporters of the war effort, were appalled by the tenor of Republican sentiment. "The conservative men of the country must make themselves felt in Congress and without a moment's delay," wrote General John A. Dix, one of the numerous Democrats Lincoln had appointed to key military positions. Border-state Unionists, too, expressed increasing alarm at the Republicans' overtly antislavery tone. Congress, they insisted, had no more power to interfere with slavery "than with the common school system, or any other local institution." Talk of abolition, declared Augustus W. Bradford, the Unionist governor of Maryland, amounted to "treason."[57]

The debates also exposed fissures within the Republican majority. Moderate Republicans—the majority of the party—deplored what they considered Radical "fanaticism." William P. Fessenden of Maine spoke with annoyance of the "gentlemen on this floor" who seemed to think "that they are the representatives of all righteousness." What was clear, however, as Senator Timothy O. Howe of Wisconsin advised his nephew, a colonel in the Union army, was that change had become the order of the day: "Don't hitch yourself to any measure. Don't anchor yourself to any policy. Don't tie up to any platform. The very foundations of the government are cracking. . . . No mere policy or platform can outlast this storm."[58]

Recognizing that the war had created a fluid and unpredictable situation, Lincoln tried to keep track of public opinion. He read newspapers and some of the letters that poured into the White House, and inquired about popular sentiment from the innumerable individuals and delegations who waited on him. He resented Radical attacks on his policies, at one point referring to "the Jacobinism in Congress." But he also did what he could to avoid a split in the party. He used patronage to try to solidify the new and still-fragile Republican coalition, adhering to the motto "justice for all." Recognizing the importance of winning antislavery opinion abroad to the Union cause, Lincoln appointed veteran Radicals and abolitionists to diplomatic positions. Zebina Eastman, the most prominent Illinois abolitionist, Lincoln told Secretary of State Seward, was "just the man to reach the sympathies of the English people." Seward named Eastman the U.S. consul at Bristol. Radical Republican appointments included Joshua R. Giddings as consul general in Canada, William Slade as consul at Nice, and ambassadors Charles Francis Adams in Britain, Carl Schurz in Spain, Cassius M. Clay in Russia, George G. Fogg in Switzerland, and Anson Burlingame in China.[59]

Lincoln appears to have used his conversations with the stream of visitors who came to the White House to hear various points of view without committing himself. Regardless of their position on the political spectrum, most came away persuaded that Lincoln was on their side. George Bancroft reported that Lincoln told him during a conversation in early December 1861 that slavery had already "received a mortal wound." In January, the abolitionist Moncure D. Conway called on Lincoln along with W. H. Channing, the chaplain of the Senate, to promote compensated emancipation. Four years later, he recalled Lincoln saying that "when the hour comes for dealing with slavery, I trust I shall be willing to act." But by the same token, the banker and railroad entrepreneur Henry D. Bacon, a far more conservative man than Conway, reported after a conversation with the president, "Lincoln thinks just as I do about the disposition of the slaves of the rebels." Sometimes, as a member of one delegation that pressed him for action against slavery related, Lincoln simply "told us a lot of stories." One of his favorites concerned a group of travelers in Illinois who debated for hours how to cross a distant river until one declared, "I never cross a river until I come to it."[60]

Despite heated criticisms of the administration (Frederick Douglass's lead editorial for January 1862 bore the title "The Slave Power Still Omnipotent at Washington"), important parts of the abolitionist press recognized Lincoln as "drifting" toward further action against slavery. One sign was the administration's reinvigoration of efforts to suppress the illegal slave trade from Africa. On assuming office, Lincoln instructed Secretary of the Interior Smith to enforce federal laws to this effect, which, despite increased enforcement by the Buchanan administration, had essentially remained dead letters under his predecessors. In February 1862, ignoring numerous pleas for clemency, including one from the Republican governor of New York, Lincoln refused to intervene to prevent the execution of Captain Nathaniel Gordon, an illicit slave trader whose ship carrying nearly 900 slaves had been captured off the coast of West Africa by a U.S. naval vessel. A week after Lincoln's election, a New York jury had convicted Gordon of international slave trading, a crime legally equivalent to piracy and punishable by death. Gordon became the first and only American to be hanged as a slave trader. (President Buchanan had pardoned the only man previously sentenced to death in 1857.) Meanwhile, Secretary of State Seward negotiated a new treaty with Britain to strengthen enforcement of the ban. It provided for American participation in the international courts that tried slave traders, in which the United States had previously refused to take part. And for the first time, it allowed the British navy to stop and search ships flying the American flag, a practice traditionally resented by Americans—half a century earlier it had helped to bring on the War of 1812. These actions sent a strong antislavery message. The hanging of Gordon, wrote the *Weekly Anglo-African*, offered "the most solid indication of character" Lincoln had yet displayed.[61]

Lincoln and Congress also reached agreement about the status of slaves who escaped to Union lines. The Washington correspondents of both the New York and Chicago *Tribunes* reported in January 1862 Lincoln's view that the government had no obligation to return fugitive slaves and that in any event public opinion would not allow it to do so. Nonetheless, the problem cried out for a consistent official policy. It could not be solved, *Harper's Weekly* noted, "by the whim of this General, and the prejudice of that. There can not be thousands, and presently millions of people who have no recognized status, hanging around and within the lines of the army." Some commanders refused to return fugitive slaves; others still sent them back to their owners. Major General Henry Halleck, who had replaced Frémont in Missouri, explained that the Fugitive Slave Act remained on the books and it was up to Congress, not the army, to change the law.[62]

In February 1862, Francis P. Blair Jr. reported from the House Committee on Military Affairs a new article of war that forbade army and navy officers from returning fugitive slaves under threat of court-martial. It received congressional approval, with virtually unanimous support from Republicans, and Lincoln signed it on March 13, 1862. The session's first significant antislavery measure, the new article of war established for the first time a uniform policy regarding runaways and fundamentally altered the army's relationship to slavery. In effect, it superceded the Fugitive Slave Act, even though that law would not be repealed until 1864. It made no distinction between fugitives from loyal and disloyal owners, or between those who escaped in Union and Confederate states. It did not explicitly free any slaves. But enacted just as the army was expanding its presence in the Mississippi Valley, it made Union lines a safe haven for fugitives. Since it did not offer compensation to the owners of fugitives sheltered by the army, it underscored how respect for the property right in slaves was declining. Henceforth, said Trumbull, an army officer must treat a fugitive slave not as property but "as a person," exactly like "other persons whom he may meet in the country."[63]

V

PREOCCUPIED WITH military matters and the long illness of his young son Willie, who died on February 20, 1862, Lincoln nonetheless pressed ahead with the idea of compensated emancipation in the border states. At the end of November 1861, Lincoln had told Charles Sumner that "in a month or six weeks we should all be together" on the question of slavery. A month later, Sumner reported Lincoln alerting him to expect an "early message" proposing that the federal government purchase the slaves of the loyal border states. On March 6, Lincoln sent the promised message to Congress.

Lincoln asked Congress to adopt a joint resolution pledging to provide financial compensation to any state that enacted a plan for the "gradual abolishment of slavery." Such a measure, he argued, would help to preserve the Union, since Confederates continued to expect the border states to join them. "To deprive them of this hope," which the adoption of a plan of emancipation would accomplish, "substantially ends the rebellion." Lincoln made clear his preference for "gradual, and not sudden emancipation." He reiterated that the federal government had no right to "interfere with slavery within state limits," and that the border states had complete "free choice" whether to accept or reject his idea. Yet he also included a not-too-veiled warning: so long as the war continued, no one could foresee the consequences.[64]

Determined to keep leading Radicals on his side, Lincoln called Sumner to the White House and read the message aloud before sending it to Congress. To everyone else, the announcement came as a complete surprise, as "unexpected," Wendell Phillips said, "as a thunderbolt in a clear sky." If Lincoln had "not entered Canaan," Phillips told one audience, "he has turned his face Zionward." Other abolitionists were even more enthusiastic. On the day Lincoln dispatched his message to Congress, a New York meeting sponsored by the Emancipation League greeted word of his action with "transports of joy." "We could hardly believe the news," declared the *Weekly Anglo-African*. "Who could have prophesized this three months ago?"[65]

Lincoln seemed to have gauged the state of public opinion precisely. All the major New York newspapers, including the radical *Tribune*, Democratic *World*, anti-abolitionist *Herald*, and ever-cautious *Journal of Commerce*, applauded his plan. The *Tribune*'s correspondent in the capital called the message "perhaps the most important document ever addressed to Congress." Conservatives saw the message as a counter to "the drift of abolition schemes" in Congress. They praised Lincoln for envisioning gradual, not immediate, emancipation, and for acknowledging the states' exclusive power to determine slavery's future. Many northern Democrats, to be sure, criticized his plan as unwarranted by the Constitution. But for the moment, Lincoln had "given the Republican party a *policy*," presenting "ground where all might stand, the conservative and the radical," declared Owen Lovejoy. Lovejoy and other Radicals remained determined to press for further action against slavery. But Lincoln's proposed resolution quickly won congressional approval, with virtually every Republican voting in favor (but not Thaddeus Stevens, who abstained, thinking the plan far too weak). Overshadowed by later events, Lincoln's March 6 message marked an important milestone on the road to abolition. While Lincoln had privately been promoting border emancipation since the previous November and had asked Congress to provide funds for this purpose in his annual message of December, he now publicly made the eventual end of slavery a national goal, and claimed a new national authority to promote it. *Frank Leslie's Illustrated Weekly* explained why it considered Lincoln's message important enough to publish in full, rather than providing only a summary, its usual practice with public documents: gradual emancipation had become "the policy of the nation."[66]

Lincoln moved to drum up support for his proposal when he met with Wendell Phillips at the White House late in March. The meeting lasted an hour, with Lincoln doing most of the talking. He seemed to feel that Phillips did not appreciate "quite enough" the March 6 message. According to Phillips, Lincoln affirmed his hatred of slavery and that he *"meant it should die."* Lincoln assured the abolitionist that runaways would not be returned: "The Negro who has once touched the hem of the government's garment shall never again be a slave." The words sound more like Phillips than Lincoln, but the sentiment was the president's.[67]

More important to the success of the initiative was the response in the border states. Four days after sending his message to Congress, Lincoln met with a delegation of border congressmen. Shortly afterward, John W. Crisfield of Maryland wrote a summary of Lincoln's remarks. Lincoln, Crisfield recorded, stated that he was "constantly annoyed by conflicting and antagonistic complaints" about how to deal with the slaves who kept coming into Union lines. Were the border states to embrace his proposal, this "irritation" would be removed and the war shortened. Crisfield, himself a large slaveholder, replied that white Marylanders would be willing to give up slavery if provision were made so that "they could be rid of the race." Asked what would happen if the border rejected his proposal, Lincoln replied that he had no further "designs" on slavery. The delegation asked Lincoln to state this publicly, to which he responded that he could not do so without getting into a "quarrel" with the Radicals. He "did not pretend to disguise his antislavery feeling," Lincoln added, but he "recognized the rights of property which had grown out of it, and would respect those rights."[68]

Shortly after the beginning of the Civil War, Frederick Douglass had written, "Our rulers do not yet know slaveholders." Lincoln would quickly learn that he had considerably overestimated the willingness of the border states to embrace emancipation. Some border Unionists did support Lincoln's plan, including George P. Fisher, his ally in promoting abolition in Delaware. The majority, however, rejected it. Kentucky seemed especially adamant. The legislature voted to disenfranchise any resident who "may advocate the doctrine of the abolition or emancipation of slavery" in the state. In Maryland, even officeholders appointed by Lincoln denounced anyone who supported the plan as an "abolitionist and not worthy of the confidence of any gentleman." When Congress passed the resolution Lincoln had requested, border members voted against it with "almost perfect unanimity." The border, wrote the *New York Times*, had proved "unequal to the occasion."[69]

On one thing border Unionists agreed: emancipation, gradual or not, must be accompanied by the removal of the black population. On the day before Lincoln sent his message to Congress, Montgomery Blair urged him to include a provision for "colonizing the blacks." Even though he had mentioned the idea in his annual message of the previous December, Lincoln did not do so. But his border supporters immediately linked the two ideas. Blair himself published a letter in a Baltimore newspaper claiming that Lincoln's plan included "the separation of the races." A meeting in Missouri to endorse the president offered its "hearty support" to "the gradual emancipation and colonization of the slaves." Senator Willard Saulsbury of Delaware voted against the resolution, but noted that he would be happy to see slavery ended in his state if the government would "take the free negroes off our hands."[70]

The *Liberator* charged Lincoln with bringing forth his gradual emancipation proposal to forestall more radical action by Congress.[71] This hardly seems likely. Numerous antislavery measures were about to reach the floor, and there was no reason to believe that Congress would abandon them because of Lincoln's initiative. In fact, less than a week after Congress approved the resolution offering financial aid to states that agreed to abolish slavery came passage of another historic measure, the abolition of slavery in Washington, D.C.

When Lincoln arrived as president in 1861, the District of Columbia, with Georgetown, had a population of 75,000, including 11,100 free blacks and a little under 3,200 slaves. The United States, Lot Morrill of Maine told the Senate, was the only "civilized nation" to tolerate slavery in its capital. Lincoln himself, it will be recalled, had advanced a plan for abolition in the District during his term in Congress. At the opening of the December 1861 session, Henry Wilson of Massachusetts introduced an emancipation bill, which came before Congress the following March. It received final approval on April 11, but not before spirited debate over its method and consequences. Taking the two houses together, every northern Republican voted for the bill, and all but five northern Democrats against. Most representatives of the border states strenuously opposed it, charging that it would drive Unionist southerners to embrace the Confederacy, lower the wages of white workers, and produce "a war of extermination between the two races." Blacks, they insisted, had only one understanding of freedom, "freedom from labor," and would become "lazy, indolent, thievish vagabonds," in the words of Garrett Davis of Kentucky.[72]

To avert this supposed fate, Davis proposed an amendment for the compulsory colonization outside the United States of all persons freed under the act. This touched off a debate on colonization that revealed sharp disagreement between Radical and moderate Republicans. Orville H. Browning, probably the most conservative Republican senator, said that compulsory deportation might become necessary. Many moderates believed, as Senator John Sherman of Ohio declared, that given the strength of prevailing prejudice, emancipation would grant blacks a freedom "stripped of everything but the name." Colonization, Sherman believed, should be voluntary, but every antislavery bill should include a provision making it possible for blacks who so desired to "seek freedom elsewhere." Most Radicals agreed with James Harlan, who told the Senate, "I am disposed to leave them where they are." Davis's compulsory colonization amendment failed, as, initially, did a substitute offered by James R. Doolittle to provide $100,000 to promote voluntary black emigration. Later, some Radicals changed their votes for fear Lincoln would veto the measure without it, and Doolittle's proposal became part of the bill. "My amendment *saved* and *carried through*" the abolition of slavery in the nation's capital, Doolittle claimed.[73]

Lincoln exerted little direct influence on the deliberations. "I do not talk to members of congress on the subject," he wrote, "except when they ask me." He feared, however, that immediate abolition in the District would arouse opposition to his border policy. Privately, he expressed the hope that one or more border states might move toward gradual emancipation before Congress acted. If this did not happen in a "reasonable time," he preferred that the bill have "three main features—gradual—compensation—and vote of the people" (like his 1849 draft legislation and, in part, his 1837 legislative "protest"). But Congress disregarded Lincoln's preferences. The measure did provide for compensation to loyal owners, up to a maximum of $300 per slave (well below their market value, critics charged). But emancipation was immediate, not gradual, and the law made no provision for a popular vote on the subject.

For a few days, Lincoln hesitated. "I really sympathize with him," Con-

gressman John W. Crisfield of Maryland wrote to his wife. "He is sur-
rounded [by] immense difficulties." Crisfield claimed after a meeting at
the White House that while Lincoln "greatly" objected to some of the
bill's features, he felt a veto would do more harm than good. He hoped
Maryland would understand. Lincoln feared that immediate abolition
might result in chaos. He told Browning that he had qualms about dis-
rupting the lives of white families and about whether blacks could truly
make their way in freedom. According to Browning's account, Lincoln
remarked, "Now families would at once be deprived of cooks, stable boys,
etc., and [slaves] of their protectors without any provision for them." On
April 16, Lincoln finally signed the D.C. emancipation measure into law,
informing Congress of his gratification that "the two principles of compensation, and colonization, are both recognized, and practically applied."
"Only the damnedest of 'damned abolitionists' dreamed of such a thing a
year ago," wrote the New York diarist George Templeton Strong on hearing the news.[74]

Lincoln soon appointed a three-man commission, headed by Daniel R.
Goodloe, to allocate federal compensation payments. Their proceedings
were rife with irony. Unsure how to assess the market value of slaves, the
commission hired a slave trader from Baltimore to advise them. To ascertain slaveholders' loyalty or lack thereof, the commission turned to the
emancipated slaves (barred by District of Columbia law from testifying
in court against whites), who reported conversations they had overheard
in their owners' homes. The commissioners worked quickly by Washington standards, and awarded compensation for slightly over 3,000 slaves,
who ranged in age from infants to a ninety-three-year-old. At the end
of January 1863, hundreds of former slaveholders lined up at the Treasury Department to receive their checks, amounting in total to around
$900,000. When Goodloe informed the president that the commission
had completed its labors, Lincoln replied that he was "glad to know that
somebody had finished something."[75]

But if the allocation of compensation was resolved expeditiously, the
future status of the emancipated slaves was not. Some Republicans
believed colonization would solve (or avoid) the problem. But the $100,000
appropriation, with a maximum of $100 for any individual, would have
paid for the emigration of only 1,000 of the 14,000 black residents in the
Districts. In any event, this part of the law proved to be an abject failure.
Immediately after passage, the American Colonization Society offered to

assist potential emigrants. "The number known to entertain that desire," it discovered, "was *one*. The colored people . . . are waiting, in the hope of changes which will make their condition here as good as that of white men." And soon after passing the emancipation act, Congress repealed the District's black code, which had barred free blacks from certain occupations, required them to post bonds for good behavior, and limited their freedom of assembly. It soon directed local authorities to establish schools for black children, financed from black property tax payments. Early in May, Lincoln's secretary William O. Stoddard commented perceptively that the District's black residents "begin, the best of them, to feel and cherish the notion of their *nationality. . . .* The blacks refuse to regard themselves as *Africans*."[76]

The first federal statute to grant immediate freedom to any group of slaves, the law ending slavery in Washington, D.C., fulfilled a long-standing abolitionist dream and marked a significant change in federal policy. It abolished slavery as an institution, rather than releasing individual slaves from their obligations to their owners as the Confiscation Act had done, and freed the slaves of loyal as well as disloyal owners. It ended the anomalous situation that had existed since the beginning of the century in which the civil and criminal laws, including slave codes, of Virginia and Maryland continued in force in the parts of the District these states had ceded to the government to create the national capital. It offered one example of how the war was inexorably expanding federal power.

Abolition in Washington further undermined slavery in nearby Virginia and Maryland, inspiring a new wave of runaways. One Maryland congressman complained to Lincoln that his constituents were "hourly suffering great losses from their slaves being entered into this District." He demanded to know if Lincoln planned to enforce the Fugitive Slave Act. The situation remained unclear and volatile. James S. Wadsworth, the military governor of the District and a strong opponent of slavery, sent troops to arrest the city jailor and release blacks from prison, whereupon Marshal Ward Hill Lamon organized a posse to apprehend the military detachment. Lincoln tried to persuade civil and military authorities to come to some sort of accommodation, but to no avail. In July 1862, Washington's mayor ordered a Maryland fugitive "remanded to his legitimate claimant," whereupon soldiers rescued the man and brought him before a provost marshal, who freed him, stating that henceforth no escaped slave would be arrested in the District. "This policy," one owner complained, "will be tantamount to issuing an Emancipation Proclamation" in the counties surrounding Washington.[77]

With abolition in the District of Columbia, however, the antislavery initiative in Congress temporarily ground to a halt. When the Indiana Radical George W. Julian introduced a resolution in June calling for the repeal of the Fugitive Slave Act, the House tabled it by a vote of 66 to 41. Charles Sumner pressed for repeal of an 1825 law limiting employment as mail carriers to white persons. The Senate approved the measure, but the House rejected it, with Republicans divided among themselves.[78]

Congress also failed to reach agreement on the enlistment of black troops in the Union army. The employment of slave soldiers was hardly unfamiliar. Britain had established a Caribbean slave army numbering more than 10,000 men during the wars of the Age of Revolution, and Parliament in 1807 emancipated them, paying compensation to the owners. Spain had also used slave soldiers in Caribbean wars. Black soldiers had served under George Washington in the War of Independence and Andrew Jackson at the battle of New Orleans. "Why [is it] offensive to employ colored men to fight for the Union," Senator James Harlan asked in January 1862, "any more than for independence?" Harlan's Iowa colleague James W. Grimes believed black enlistment would mean "the end of slavery." Other Republicans supported the idea on purely military grounds. "When a negro rushes in to save the life of my brother or my son from the bayonet of a traitor," said Lyman Trumbull, "I will say 'God speed.'" Democrats were appalled. Blacks, they insisted, were unfit to be soldiers. Armed slaves would commit barbarous acts against their owners yet flee the first sign of combat, said Robert Mallory of Kentucky. How was it, Thaddeus Stevens responded, "that they are so dangerous to their masters, when a single cannon shot will put ten thousand to flight?"[79]

Even more contentious was the debate that raged throughout the session over further confiscation of Confederate property. This raised thorny political, legal, and constitutional questions. Early in December 1861, Lyman Trumbull introduced a bill for the "absolute and complete forfeiture forever" of "every species of property" of "rebels," including their slaves, who would be "made free." Trumbull's proposal envisioned a far more radical attack on slavery than the first Confiscation Act, which applied only to slaves used for military purposes. Most members of the Republican caucus, the *New York Herald* reported, favored passage of a confiscation measure, but "the general shape of such a law was not agreed on." This was, to say the least, an understatement. During the course of the next seven months, Congress spent more time debating confiscation than any other question. Radicals pressed for sweeping confiscation as a means of liberating the vast majority of the slaves in the Confederacy. Rebels, declared one congressman, "are entitled to no rights whatever, and least of all to the right of domination over others." But many moderates held back, fearing that Trumbull's bill violated the Constitution's bar on bills of attainder—legislative acts declaring a person guilty of a crime and punishing him without benefit of a trial—as well as its provision limiting forfeiture of property for treason to the lifetime of the offender. Property rights, moderates insisted, were inviolable, even for rebels, unless the property was used directly to support the southern war effort.[80]

The leading Republican opponent was Lincoln's old friend Orville H. Browning, who delivered interminable speeches outlining the legal objections to confiscation. Slavery, Browning told the Senate, was "the sole, original cause" of the war and were it "blotted from the American continent," the conflict could not last another thirty days. But under the Constitution, he insisted, only the president, as military commander in chief, possessed the authority to act against the institution. "From hour to hour," Benjamin F. Wade complained, Browning held the floor arguing "that the President has all power in war, and we none." At one point John Sherman exclaimed, "I am sick and tired of this debate." Grassroots Republicans seemed to agree. "Do let us have *some* kind of confiscation measure, and that speedily," wrote a constituent of Trumbull's. "By the way, does it never occur to Congress that . . . they are frittering away month after month in bickerings and twaddle unworthy of a country-school debating society?"[81]

In fact, in the two months after the abolition of slavery in Washington, D.C., only one further piece of antislavery legislation won approval. In May 1862, Isaac N. Arnold of Illinois introduced a bill to abolish slavery in all places of exclusive federal jurisdiction—the territories, forts, dockyards, federal buildings, and American vessels on the high seas. The purpose, said Arnold, was "to render freedom national, and slavery sectional." But moderates considered the bill too broad. Owen Lovejoy quickly proposed a substitute narrowing its scope to slavery in the territories, the issue that had always united the Republican party. This passed the House on May 12 and the Senate on June 9. The breakdown of votes had by now become familiar. Every Republican was in favor, while every Democrat and nearly all the border Unionists voted against.[82]

Abolition in the territories, which directly repudiated the *Dred Scott* decision, affected only a handful of slaves. The Census of 1860 counted fifteen in Nebraska and twenty-nine in Utah. (New Mexico had already repealed its slave code in December 1861, freeing the few slaves within its borders.) Nonetheless, the measure had great symbolic importance. It finally settled the question that, as Congressman William D. Kelley put it, "has kept the nation boiling with agitation for the last thirty years." The bill provided for immediate abolition and made no mention of compensation to owners or the colonization of those freed. Nonetheless, on June 19 Lincoln signed it into law. Together with other measures of this session— the Morrill Act, which provided states with public land grants to fund the establishment of agricultural colleges; the Homestead Act, which offered free public land to settlers; and the Pacific Railroad Act—abolition in the territories sought to implement the free-labor vision of the American West, as a region free from the presence of slavery and populated by small farmers engaged in forward-looking market agriculture.[83]

All in all, the first sixteen months of Lincoln's presidency—the period from March 1861 through June 1862—witnessed noteworthy changes in the government's relationship to slavery. Lincoln had become the first American president to send to Congress a plan for abolition and had signed measures ending slavery in the nation's capital and territories and superseding the Fugitive Slave Act. At this point, however, the course of future policy remained uncertain. The war and its consequence, the flight of slaves to Union lines, had weakened but by no means dissolved slavery's traditional legal protections. The Confiscation Act of 1861 and the additional Article of War dealt with slaves in terms of their relationship to the military situation. Other measures, such as the resolution offering assistance to states that adopted emancipation plans and abolition in the District of Columbia and the territories, operated within the well-established constitutional framework. They attacked slavery either through action by slave states themselves or in places where Republicans believed the federal government enjoyed undisputed authority. Thus far, federal actions had no bearing on slaves in the Confederacy other than those set to work for the military or who managed to escape to Union lines. Nonetheless, the presidential initiatives and congressional enactments of the spring of 1862 portended large changes in American life. "Hereafter," declared a writer for a northern periodical, "the thinking on the subject of American Slavery will be only in one line—how shall it be done away?"[84]

That outcome, however, depended on Union victory. And in the spring of 1862, this by no means appeared inevitable. In April, General George B. McClellan began the laborious process of moving the immense Army of the Potomac from the vicinity of Washington down to the Virginia Peninsula, from which he planned to march on Richmond, the Confederate capital. A two-month campaign began early in May, culminating in the Battles of the Seven Days at the end of June. A staunch Democrat, McClellan never developed an understanding of the relationship between politics and the war effort. He strongly opposed talk of abolition and insisted that the war could and should be won without touching slavery.[85] Had McClellan defeated the Confederate army and captured Richmond, the war might have ended then and there, with slavery weakened but intact. McClellan's failure inspired Lincoln and Congress to rethink the Union's military and political strategy, opening the door to general emancipation.

7

"Forever Free":
The Coming of Emancipation

EVEN AS THE ARMY of General George B. McClellan embarked on the Peninsular campaign, a military commander with a very different political outlook compelled Lincoln to clarify yet again his policy toward slavery. In March 1862, Major General David Hunter, a West Point graduate from Illinois and one of the few abolitionists in the officer corps, was appointed commander of the Department of the South. On paper the department encompassed all of South Carolina, Georgia, and Florida; in reality, the army's control did not extend much beyond the South Carolina Sea Islands, captured the previous November. Before departing for his new post, Hunter asked Secretary of War Stanton for permission to "have my own way on the subject of slavery," including the authority to "arm such loyal men as I can find in the country." Since the entire white population of the islands had fled, Hunter clearly intended to enlist black soldiers. When Stanton failed to reply, Hunter took his silence as permission to proceed. On May 9, 1862, he declared all the slaves in his department (over 900,000 men, women, and children) "forever free," and instructed his officers to accept black volunteers.[1]

Hunter may have been a talented general, but when it came to politics he displayed a certain naiveté. When he asked Stanton's permission to attack slavery he added, "The administration will not be responsible." Of course, his proclamation, if not revoked, became administration policy. When Secretary of the Treasury Chase urged Lincoln not to overturn the order, the president sent a sharp reply: "No commanding general shall do such a thing upon *my* responsibility without consulting me." At a time when he was energetically promoting his plan of border emancipation based on the principles of gradualism, compensation, and colonization— every one of which Hunter's order violated—it was inconceivable that Lincoln would allow the edict to stand. With Stanton's assistance, Lincoln drew up a statement revoking Hunter's order, which he made public on May 19. Like his order rescinding John C. Frémont's emancipation decree in August 1861, it denied that army officers had the authority "to make proclamations declaring the slaves of any State free." This time, however, Lincoln appealed directly to the people of the border states to take up his offer of compensated emancipation: "The change it contemplates would come gently as the dews of heaven, not rending or wrecking anything. Will you not embrace it?" The death of slavery, he strongly implied, had become inevitable: "You cannot if you would, be blind to the signs of the times."[2]

Carl Schurz, back in the United States after a stint as ambassador to Spain, had urged Lincoln, if he overturned Hunter's order, not to preclude future action. "You can hardly tell at the present moment," Schurz wrote, "how far you will have to go six weeks hence. . . . The arming of negroes and the liberation of those slaves who offer us aid and assistance are things which must and will inevitably be done." And in his proclamation, Lincoln for the first time claimed the right as commander in chief to abolish slavery if "it shall become a necessity indispensable to the maintenance of the government." This marked a significant change in his view of presidential authority. Interestingly, Lincoln never officially communicated the revocation to Hunter. "I wanted him to *do* it, not say it," Schurz reported Lincoln remarking when the two met in June. Some Radicals took note of Lincoln's language holding out the possibility that he might in the future exercise the power he denied to Hunter. Lincoln's statement, declared the *Chicago Tribune*, "sounds like a prophet's word," warning slaveowners that freedom "will soon dawn."[3]

The Hunter imbroglio had an unusual afterlife. On June 9, 1862, the House of Representatives called on Stanton for information about whether Hunter had in fact formed a black regiment. Stanton replied that he had no information to that effect, but forwarded Hunter's justification of his policy: the white masters had fled the Sea Islands, thus abandoning their self-proclaimed responsibility to feed and clothe their slaves. In the absence of a "fugitive master law," Hunter had no alternative but to arm "hardy and devoted" slaves in the hope of retrieving their owners. Radicals in Congress laughed and applauded when the letter was read; border representatives denounced their reaction as "disgraceful to the American Congress."[4]

I

WHAT WERE the "signs of the times" portending the doom of slavery to which Lincoln referred? In the spring and early summer of 1862, pressures for a change in government policy intensified. As the army pushed into new parts of the Confederacy—coastal North Carolina, portions of Tennessee, Arkansas, and Louisiana—slaves viewed its arrival as a sign of "their approaching millennium," and thousands fled to Union lines. The war's destructive impact on slavery was dramatically evident in the sugar plantation region near New Orleans, where the arrival of Union forces inspired mass escapes, strikes, and demands to be paid wages. Even officers who strongly opposed action against slavery found themselves employing more and more black refugees as laborers. Moreover, fugitive slaves provided intelligence about the disposition of Confederate forces, the location of hidden supplies, and routes through unmapped terrain, making commanders reluctant to turn them away. General Ormsby Mitchel, who in March 1862 expelled fugitives from his camp in Tennessee, soon realized the "absolute necessity of protecting slaves who furnish us valuable information."[5]

Encounters with runaway slaves strongly affected opinion regarding slavery in the army. "When the Union soldier meets the negro in the enemy's country," wrote George E. Stephens, one of the few black war correspondents, "he knows him as a friend." Stephens did not fail to convey to his readers the deep-seated racism of many soldiers. But witnessing firsthand slaves' loyalty to the Union and encountering evidence of the cruelty of slavery increased emancipation sentiment. Samuel F. DuPont, who had led the naval expedition that captured Port Royal in the Sea Islands, remarked that he "accounted himself a conservative until he had seen the institution in all its horrors." He now called himself an abolitionist. James A. Garfield, commanding an Ohio unit in Tennessee, reported that he found "the rank and file of the army steadily and surely becoming imbued with sympathy for the slaves and hatred for slavery." In this war of "thinking bayonets," in which soldiers eagerly debated political issues and wrote numerous letters home, sentiment in the army could not but affect northern politics.[6]

As in 1861, dissension over dealing with slavery flared within the army. The most dramatic incident took place in southern Louisiana. Hoping to conciliate local whites, General Benjamin F. Butler abandoned his earlier contraband policy and ordered most fugitives barred from Union lines. But at Camp Parapet just outside New Orleans, Brigadier General John W. Phelps, a strong opponent of slavery, refused to carry out Butler's policy and welcomed escaped slaves. After considerable back and forth between the two officers, Butler in June 1862 referred the whole matter to Washington. On July 3, Stanton replied. Saying he spoke for Lincoln, Stanton reminded Butler that army officers were no longer allowed to return escaped slaves. "In common humanity," they must be provided with food and shelter and those capable of labor put to work and "paid reasonable wages." "In directing this to be done," Stanton added, "the President does not mean, at present, to settle any general rule in respect to slaves or slavery."[7]

But a general rule was becoming more and more necessary. Radicals and abolitionists kept up demands for general emancipation. Some denounced Lincoln as "irresolute" and a "coward," in the heated words of Chicago journalist Horace White. Radicals close to Lincoln defended him against these assaults. In June, in a speech in New York City, Owen Lovejoy assured the Emancipation League of Lincoln's intentions. The president, he said, was riding in a carriage being pulled by "the Radical steed. . . . If he does not drive as fast as I would, he is on the same road."[8]

More surprising than the continuing campaign by longtime advocates of emancipation was that moderate Republicans now expressed increasing impatience with the administration. Even those who professed "unbounded confidence" in Lincoln's integrity wished he would "strike rebellion with a little more force." Thomas J. Sizer, a moderate from Buffalo, New York, published a pamphlet noting that northerners themselves were being "emancipated"—from their "mental thralldom to slavery." "The great phenomenon of the year," the anti-abolitionist *Boston Daily Advertiser* remarked in August, "is the terrible intensity which this [emancipation] resolution has acquired. A year ago men might have faltered at the thought of proceeding to this extremity." Now they were "in great measure prepared for it." The reason, the paper added, was the "process of education which is going on with every day of the war." But growing support for the idea of attacking slavery, expressed in newspapers, pamphlets, and letters to Republican congressmen and the president, did not translate into a clear policy. "The government seems to us," wrote the abolitionist but generally pro-Lincoln *Independent*, "to be in the position of men who don't know what to do."[9]

Despite the gathering pressure for action against slavery, Lincoln hesitated. He feared that the northern public was not prepared for more radical steps. Lincoln valued the support of War Democrats like the New York investment banker August Belmont, who used his extensive connections in Europe to help forestall recognition of the Confederacy but urged Lincoln not to yield to "extremists" demanding emancipation. Lincoln also feared the repercussions of an emancipation edict on the army, knowing the opposition of the officer corps and perhaps mistaking their views for those of ordinary soldiers. Steeped in antebellum legal culture, he harbored doubts whether even under the war power, an emancipation edict would be constitutional. Lincoln told Carl Schurz that he feared he was too radical for Democrats and not radical enough for Republicans and would end up without political support.[10]

Lincoln worried that since most of the Confederacy lay outside the control of the Union army, a proclamation of emancipation would be seen as a sign of desperation. When a delegation of Quakers visited the White House on June 20, 1862, to express their "earnest desire that he might . . . free the slaves and thus save the nation from destruction," Lincoln responded that he shared their belief "that slavery was wrong" and recalled that he had publicly anticipated its ultimate extinction. But "if a decree of emancipation" could abolish slavery, he added, "John Brown would have done the work effectively." In the *Liberator*, Wendell Phillips Garrison, the editor's son, wondered how "any sensible man" could equate an edict issued by John Brown at Harper's Ferry with one emanating from "the Commander-in-Chief of the whole army, and invested by the Constitution with the absolute, undisputed control of the War Power?" Lincoln's point, however, was that an unenforceable proclamation would be taken as an exercise in futility.[11]

Lincoln remained wedded to his border emancipation plan and his fear that a direct assault on slavery would drive the border to secede, even as the Union's hold on the region tightened and the prospect of border secession receded. When Charles Sumner urged him to celebrate July 4, 1862, by issuing a proclamation of general emancipation, Lincoln replied that he would do so if he did not worry that "half the army would lay down their arms and three other states would join the rebellion." Lincoln also feared that precipitous action against slavery would undermine efforts to woo wavering Confederates to the Union cause. He praised an article in the *Continental Monthly* which acknowledged that slavery could hardly be "let alone" during the conflict but made a sharp distinction between "the results of the war in relation to slavery" and the official "purpose of the North," preserving the Union. It also argued that respect for the constitutional right of states to determine their domestic institutions would help to swell the ranks of "loyal citizens" in the South.[12]

Lincoln hoped to encourage Unionists in parts of the South to establish civilian governments after the federal army gained control. Early in the war, he extended recognition to the Restored Government of Virginia, a convention of Unionists who met in Wheeling after the secession of their state and chose Francis H. Pierpont, a prominent antislavery attorney, as Virginia's new governor. (Pierpont's authority, in fact, extended only to western Virginia, the immediate vicinity of Washington, and the area around Norfolk.) In 1862, Lincoln appointed military governors for Tennessee, Louisiana, Arkansas, and North Carolina. He hoped they would rally loyal sentiment and restore their states to full participation in the Union. At the beginning of July 1862, he urged Andrew Johnson, Tennessee's military governor, to hold elections as preparation for the state's restoration. "If we could, somehow, get a vote of the people of Tennessee and have it result properly," Lincoln explained, "it would be worth more to us than a battle gained." Lincoln's expectation that military governors could win over local whites militated against further steps toward abolition. "In all attempts to soothe southern wrath," one northern reporter shrewdly noted, "the negro is thrown in as the offering." Andrew Johnson, for example, did not hesitate to take strong action against rebels—he jailed disloyal local officials and ministers who preached support for secession. But he assured the people of Tennessee that he aimed to restore them to the Union in "the same condition as before the existing rebellion," with their slaves "still in subordination."[13]

Some of the steps taken by these governors displayed an alarming sensitivity to local white opinion. In April 1862, Lincoln appointed Edward Stanly, a former Whig congressman, as North Carolina's military governor (his rule extended only to a small area along the Atlantic seaboard). Stanly ordered the closing of schools for blacks that the army had established after capturing New Bern. Under the laws of North Carolina, he explained, it was illegal to teach blacks to read and write. In any event, the schools' presence "would do harm to the Union cause." Stanly also allowed owners to retrieve fugitives from army camps. He told Stanton that he had been "sent to restore the old order of things" in North Carolina and that this could not be done if local whites believed emancipation was in the offing. Large numbers of whites visited Stanly to congratulate him "upon the auspicious beginning of his administration." But his actions created a furor in the North. "All the world," noted the *New York Evening Post*, regarded the ban on education as among "the most abhorrent features of . . . slavery."[14]

Early in June, Vincent Colyer, who had set up the schools as the army's superintendent of the poor, traveled to Washington and, accompanied by Charles Sumner, called at the White House to complain about Stanly's actions. Lincoln, Colyer later related, at first seemed annoyed to be asked to deal with the matter. "Do you take me for a School-Committeeman?" the president asked. Lincoln's tone changed when told about the return of fugitive slaves. Stanly, he said, had misunderstood his instructions. "I have hated slavery from childhood," Colyer recalled Lincoln remarking, and no "fugitive from a rebel, shall ever be returned to his master." But Lincoln rejected calls to remove Stanly and viewed the controversy as a distraction from weightier matters. Horace Maynard, a member of Congress from East Tennessee, reported to Andrew Johnson that Lincoln "expresses himself gratified in the highest degree that you do not raise any 'nigger' issues to bother him."[15]

Nonetheless, with emancipation sentiment rising, Lincoln redoubled his efforts to promote his plan for gradual, compensated abolition. On July 12, he invited to the White House over two dozen congressmen from the border states, Virginia, and Tennessee, and read to them from a carefully prepared manuscript. Had their states embraced his proposal when he announced it in March, he told them, somewhat hyperbolically, "the war would now be substantially ended." Lincoln noted that regardless of the constitutional protections slavery enjoyed, the institution was eroding because of the war and would eventually be destroyed "by mere friction and abrasion." How much better it would be to make "a *decision* at once to emancipate *gradually*," thereby allowing for monetary compensation. Moreover, land for colonization could easily be obtained, and "the freed people will not be so reluctant to go." Clearly, Lincoln was trying to make his plan as appealing as possible to the border states. Yet he also noted that by reversing General Hunter's order in May, he had given "dissatisfaction, if not offence, to many whose support the country cannot afford to lose." Moreover, "the pressure, in this direction, is still upon me, and is increasing." He begged them to act, and quickly.[16]

That evening, when the delegation gathered to draft a response, a "stormy debate" ensued. Lincoln must have been sorely disappointed by the outcome. Eight members of Congress endorsed Lincoln's plan and said they would advise their constituents to "consider" it. But the majority, Lincoln's supporter George P. Fisher of Delaware remarked with "great disgust," opposed "the liberation of a single slave." Their report, written by John W. Crisfield of Maryland and signed by twenty-one congressmen, contained a scathing rejection of what they called the "radical change of our social system" Lincoln envisioned. The president's proposal, Crisfield wrote, intruded on a matter that "exclusively belonged to our respective States." The report lectured Lincoln on how to conduct himself: "Confine yourself to your constitutional authority; confine your subordinates within the same limits; conduct this war solely for the purpose of restoring the constitution to its legitimate authority."[17]

Lincoln still believed that the border states held the key to abolition nationwide. Four years later Isaac N. Arnold recalled Lincoln remarking to him and Owen Lovejoy on the day after the July 12 meeting that if the border would only accept his proposal, then "the labor of your life, Lovejoy, would be crowned with success—you would live to see the end of slavery." On July 14, Lincoln sent to Congress the draft of a bill pledging to provide compensation in the form of federal bonds to any state that adopted a plan of abolition. One new feature was that Lincoln now considered the possibility that a state might later decide to "reintroduce" slavery, in which case the bonds would become "null and void." Republican leaders were not impressed. Some, wrote a reporter for the *New York Tribune*, thought the proposal "ridiculous," and Congress took no action on it before adjourning.[18]

If the border states rejected Lincoln's offer, one participant in the July 12 meeting told a northern journalist, the president would "irresistibly be swept into the vortex of the revolution." The military situation heightened the pressure for a new departure. By early July, it had become apparent that McClellan's Virginia campaign launched the previous spring had failed. The impact was traumatic. "A profound gloom . . . settled upon the public mind," declared the *New York Times*, "in regard to the conduct and prospects of the . . . war." Lincoln's friend Richard Yates, now the governor of Illinois, issued a public letter calling for a more vigorous effort to save the Union: "The crisis of the war and our national existence is upon us. The time has come for the adoption of more decisive measures." John Sherman, the moderate from Ohio, told the Senate that while he respected "the rights of the southern people," it had become imperative to confiscate the slaves and other property of "the disloyal" and mobilize the full power of the nation to "enter into the war in earnest." It was in the context of a broad shift in thinking about how the war should be conducted that Congress broke the long logjam on the use of black troops and the confiscation of Confederate property, and Lincoln made the decision for emancipation.[19]

With manpower needs now extending into the indefinite future, Congress in July moved forward on the contentious issue of raising black soldiers, which Radicals had advocated, to no effect, since the session began. As adjournment neared, it began debate on a bill amending the Militia Act of 1795 to authorize the president to receive blacks for "constructing intrenchments, or performing camp service or any other labor, or any military or naval service for which they may be found competent." If owned by supporters of the Confederacy, black men who enlisted along with their immediate families (identified as the mother, wife, and children) would become free. This was a remarkable acknowledgment that slaves *had* families, even though no state accorded them legal recognition. While opening the door to black recruits serving in combat, the bill envisioned them mainly as military laborers, freeing white troops for combat. Hence it set their pay at ten dollars per month minus a three-dollar clothing ration, six dollars less than that of white soldiers. Representatives of the border states, where the measure offered an immediate path to freedom for many male slaves and their families, objected vociferously. Willard Saulsbury of Delaware called the bill "the most magnificent scheme of emancipation yet proposed." White soldiers, he warned, would never "fight side by side with negroes."[20]

But moderate Republicans lined up behind the proposal. The war, declared Senator William P. Fessenden, must be fought on "different principles." Fessenden's long speech in favor of admitting blacks into military service marked a crucial turning point. It "amazed the Radical Republicans," reported one northern journalist, noting that Fessenden, "a crabbed conservative," was among the Senate's most influential members: "When *he* moves, it signifies that the whole glacier has started." Lincoln signed the Militia Act on July 17. But for it to go into effect, a presidential order was needed.[21]

On July 11 and 12, 1862, after months of ideological deadlock, Congress also approved and sent to the president the Second Confiscation Act. The importance of this law, Congressman Isaac N. Arnold of Illinois would later write, "has not been fully appreciated." This resulted, in part, from the fact that it consisted of contradictory elements, drawn from divergent proposals of the previous few months. Early sections of the measure provided for fines, imprisonment, and possible death sentences, as well as the loss of slaves, for anyone convicted of assisting the rebellion, and for the immediate seizure and sale of the property of high-ranking Confederate officials. The bill also authorized the president to warn all supporters of the Confederacy to abandon the rebellion or face the confiscation and sale by federal courts of their property. The ninth section declared "forever free of their servitude" all rebel-owned slaves who escaped to Union lines or lived in Confederate territory subsequently occupied by Union troops. The bill also forbade the army from returning fugitives to disloyal owners, and allowed Lincoln to employ blacks in any way he deemed "necessary and proper for the suppression of this rebellion." Finally, it asked the president to provide for the colonization "in some tropical country" of liberated slaves willing to emigrate.[22]

In some ways the most striking feature of the Second Confiscation Act was its sharp distinction between the confiscation of other property and the emancipation of slaves. For most property it established a cumbersome judicial process that helps to explain why little land was actually seized and sold under its provisions. Yet the section freeing rebel-owned slaves who came within Union lines did not require court proceedings: it was self-enforcing. Slaves would become free, wrote the *Springfield Republican*, "as fast as the armies penetrate the Southern section." Henceforth, the newspaper added, "every victory is a victory of emancipation." To be sure, the number of slaves freed by the act would depend on how much Confederate territory the Union army succeeded in occupying. But to their critics, it seemed that Republicans were bent on the emancipation of "almost the entire slave population" of the United States.[23]

For all its ambiguities, the Second Confiscation Act embodied a major shift in national policy. Orville H. Browning, the Senate's leading Republican critic of the bill, badgered Lincoln to veto it. The moment had arrived, he said, to decide whether the president "was to control the abolitionists and radicals, or whether they were to control him." Lincoln responded that he wished Congress had not legislated on confiscation at all. But given that nearly all Republicans, unlike Browning, had voted for the bill, Lincoln was reluctant to disapprove it. Instead, he adopted an unusual course of action. Lincoln drafted a veto message outlining his objections. It criticized not only the permanent confiscation of the property of rebels but also the lack of any provision for determining whether runaway slaves belonged to Confederate or Unionist owners. Then, after asking Congress, which was about to adjourn, to remain in session an extra day, he met with a few members, including the influential Fessenden, and asked them to secure a resolution stating that the forfeiture of real estate would not extend beyond the life of the owner, as the Constitution required. Congress passed the resolution and then adjourned. On July 17, the same day that he approved the Militia Act, Lincoln signed the Second Confiscation Act, but also dispatched his draft veto message.[24]

Many members of Congress found Lincoln's demand for a resolution and his decision to send a veto message without actually vetoing the bill "inexpressibly provoking." The House refused to print extra copies of Lincoln's message, the usual courtesy, and the Senate refused to print it at all. Nonetheless, once Lincoln signed the bill, all slaves of rebels who came within Union lines automatically became free. By the time Congress adjourned, Charles Sumner declared, the president and Congress agreed on two things: "The blacks are to be employed [in the military], and the slaves are to be freed." Lincoln, wrote *Harper's Weekly*, "has represented the average feeling of the people. Now as that feeling changes, we may expect a change of conduct on the part of the Administration." And, in fact, a few days before he signed the Second Confiscation Act, Lincoln had embarked on a new approach to slavery and emancipation.[25]

When Lincoln decided to issue a proclamation of emancipation remains unknown. According to Hamlin family lore, he read a draft of such a document to his vice president as early as mid-June 1862 (an unlikely story, given that when Lincoln finally made his decision public that fall, Hamlin seemed surprised). Owen Lovejoy also claimed to have been told about it in advance. On July 1, 1862, on the other hand, Orville H. Browning recorded in his diary that Lincoln had read to him a draft paper about how to conduct the war "in its relations to slavery." Rather than containing any new departures, this document reiterated existing policy. No fugitives who escaped during the war were to be returned to slavery; no blacks would be armed; and Congress had "no power over slavery in the states." According to Browning, Lincoln even stated that whatever remained of slavery once the war ended would "be left to the exclusive control of the states where it may exist." Three days later, as noted earlier, Lincoln rebuffed Charles Sumner's plea for the "reconsecration" of Independence Day "by a decree of emancipation."[26]

On July 7, Lincoln traveled to Harrison's Landing on the James River to confer with General McClellan, commander of the Union's main eastern army. McClellan presented him with a letter insisting that the war must be conducted "upon the highest principles known to Christian Civilization." Violation of civilian property rights and the "forcible abolition of slavery," he insisted, were beneath the dignity of civilized armies. But the visit seems to have led Lincoln to the opposite conclusion from what McClellan intended. He departed convinced that the war could not possibly be won in this manner, and that what would come to be called "hard war"—war not simply of army against army but of society against society—had become necessary. This meant abandoning previous efforts to shield southern civilians from the consequences of secession.[27]

Lincoln returned to Washington on July 10, as Congress completed work on the Second Confiscation Act, with its emancipation provisions. Two days later, Lincoln met with the border-state delegation to press his plan for gradual abolition. The following day, July 13, while sharing a carriage with Secretaries Welles and Seward en route to the funeral of Stanton's infant son, Lincoln for the first time broached the subject of emancipation by presidential proclamation. Welles later recollected that Lincoln "dwelt earnestly on the gravity" of the subject, saying that "it was a military necessity absolutely essential for the salvation of the Union." Two factors, Welles believed, were uppermost in Lincoln's mind: lack of military success, which had convinced him that the nation could no longer pursue a "forbearing policy" toward Confederates, and the failure of his border initiative. Lincoln had "concluded that emancipation in rebel areas must precede that in the border, not the other way around." In a letter to his wife that day, Welles wondered why he had been chosen to hear the momentous announcement. "I scarcely know what to make of it," he wrote.[28]

On July 21, 1862, four days after he signed the Second Confiscation Act and the Militia Act, Lincoln informed the cabinet that he had resolved on decisive new measures. He presented the drafts of four new orders. The first gave field commanders the authority to live off the land in hostile territory (that is, to appropriate civilian property). The others authorized the use of blacks as military laborers; required the army to keep records of confiscated property, including slaves, so loyal owners could receive compensation; and envisioned "the colonization of negroes in some tropical territory." The first three, which essentially executed provisions of the confiscation and militia acts, received the cabinet's unanimous approval. The colonization proposal garnered little support and was, for the moment, dropped. The cabinet also discussed another request from General Hunter to enlist black soldiers. Cabinet members were favorably disposed, but Lincoln "expressed himself as averse to arming negroes."[29]

The next day, July 22, the discussion continued. Lincoln had prepared a new draft order, which he read to the cabinet. It consisted of three sentences. The first, citing the Second Confiscation Act, warned Confederates to cease the rebellion within sixty days or face the confiscation of their property, including slaves. The second reaffirmed Lincoln's support for compensated, gradual emancipation. The third, invoking his authority as commander in chief, declared that on January 1, 1863, "all persons held as slaves within any state or states" still under Confederate control "shall then, thenceforward, and forever, be free."[30]

Presented without fanfare and appearing almost an afterthought, this final sentence constituted the initial version of the Emancipation Proclamation. It went well beyond anything Congress or Lincoln had previously envisioned. Apart from the act freeing a few slaves in the territories, previous steps toward emancipation had carefully distinguished between loyal and Confederate owners. They kept up, one northern newspaper complained, "the confounded distinction between the slaves of one class of people and those of another," making emancipation a punishment for rebellion and permitting slaveowning "as a *reward* for devotion to the government."[31] Moreover, the Second Confiscation Act, despite its potential for future emancipation, did not apply to the vast majority of slaves until they came within Union control. Now, Lincoln audaciously proposed to extend wartime emancipation to all the slaves in most of the places where the institution existed. Abolition would be immediate and without compensation. Whether the owner was loyal to the Union or a rebel would make no difference.

Lincoln's cabinet seems to have been stunned by this announcement. Chase, the most radical member, remained silent. He admitted shortly after the meeting that the plan went "beyond anything I have recommended." But he worried that state courts would not recognize the freedom of those liberated by such a proclamation, and feared the proposal would lead to "depredation and massacre." He preferred incremental emancipation by local commanders as the army occupied southern territory. Stanton, who had favored emancipation for months, supported the immediate promulgation of the document. Montgomery Blair expressed opposition, fearing that emancipation would cost Republicans votes in the fall elections. Welles said nothing. Lincoln's plan, he later wrote, was "fraught with consequences, immediate and remote, such as human foresight could not penetrate." It would bring about "a revolution of the social, civil, and industrial habits and condition of society in all the slave states."[32]

Perhaps most surprising was Secretary of State Seward's reaction. On the day before Lincoln presented his draft proclamation to the cabinet, Seward had written to James Watson Webb, the ambassador to Brazil, stating bluntly, "Slavery is the cause of this civil war." For months, American diplomats had been recommending that emancipation be made an explicit war aim in order to forestall foreign recognition of the Confederacy or some kind of international mediation proposal. Britain, the leading world power, which had abolished slavery in its own empire in the 1830s, would be far less likely to assist the Confederacy if the issue were changed from the South's right to self-determination to the future of slavery. Given the international situation and his long career of anti-slavery politics, Seward would have been expected to offer enthusiastic support to Lincoln's proposal. But Seward had long believed that the war had doomed slavery, making government action unnecessary. Now, he argued that the announcement of an emancipation policy would actually make foreign interference more likely, since Britain would fear a permanent disruption of its cotton supply. Moreover, issuing the proclamation immediately, as Lincoln intended, would seem an act of desperation. It would be far better to wait for a military victory. That evening, Lincoln met with Seward's political alter ego, the Albany editor and "wizard of the lobby" Thurlow Weed, who warned that the proposed proclamation would produce serious "disaffection" in the border states and could not be enforced in the Confederacy.[33]

With the cabinet divided, and perhaps still uncertain himself, Lincoln decided to put his emancipation order aside. Nonetheless, news of the proceedings, if not the actual result, quickly found its way into the press. A correspondent for the *New York Evening Post* reported that the cabinet had agreed on "total abolition" in the Confederate states "or I am grossly misinformed." Over the next few weeks, other newspapers related that Lincoln had decided on emancipation but had delayed his announcement because of the "determined opposition" of Seward and Blair.[34]

Despite shelving his emancipation edict, Lincoln did issue the proposed orders allowing military commanders to seize or destroy private property (although not "in wantonness or malice") as well as the warning to the South of the coming implementation of the Second Confiscation Act. Meanwhile, Major General John Pope, newly appointed to command the Army of Virginia, issued his own orders directing his soldiers as far as possible to live off the land, punish civilians for guerrilla activity in their communities, and deport disloyal men from occupied areas to the Confederacy. When McClellan complained to General in Chief Henry Halleck about these departures from "civilized" warfare, Halleck responded that he could not revoke the orders as he understood they had been seen and approved by the president. Pope, however, had little time to implement his policy. After his defeat at Second Bull Run at the end of August, he was transferred to the West. Not until 1864, under the far more capable Ulysses S. Grant and William T. Sherman, would the "hard war" really come into its own.[35]

Nonetheless, the character of the war had clearly changed, and emancipation was part of the transformation. Despite having postponed his edict, Lincoln expressed increasing exasperation with southerners who professed loyalty to the Union but demanded that he not interfere with slavery. When a prominent citizen of New Orleans complained about the actions of General John W. Phelps, who, it will be recalled, was encouraging slaves to flee to Union lines, Lincoln fired back: "What would you do in my position? . . . Would you give up the contest, leaving any available means unapplied?" On July 31, he sent a similar letter to August Belmont. "Broken eggs cannot be mended," Lincoln wrote, and if Louisiana wanted to prevent slavery from being destroyed, it must quickly resume its place in the Union. The government, he added, "cannot much longer play a game in which it stakes all, and its enemies stake nothing."[36]

II

LINCOLN'S SHIFT to a policy of general emancipation in the Confederate South did not automatically imply the abandonment of his previous plan for the border states, where his proposed proclamation would not apply. This, according to his secretary John Hay, remained "the object nearest the President's heart." Indeed, both his commitment to the border plan and his impending new policy for the Confederate South heightened Lincoln's long-standing interest in the colonization of the freed slaves. The border states remained adamantly opposed to any increase in their free black population. According to the *New York Tribune*'s Washington correspondent, Lincoln frequently quoted the comment by Senator Garrett Davis of Kentucky that his state's Unionists "would not resist his gradual emancipation scheme if he would only conjoin it with his colonization plan." Moreover, fear in the North that liberated slaves would flock into the region and become "roaming, vicious vagabonds" constituted, according to the *Chicago Tribune*, the greatest obstacle to support for general emancipation. Thus, with his border proposal still pending and emancipation in the offing, if not yet announced, Lincoln redoubled his efforts to promote colonization. This does not mean that he acted insincerely or purely for political reasons. His public support for colonization was by now a decade old. And he had yet to give serious thought to the future place of emancipated slaves in American society. Nor had most other Republicans.[37]

During the spring and early summer of 1862, as Congress pressed ahead with antislavery legislation, colonization played an important part in its debates. There was far more discussion of where freed slaves would reside than what rights they would enjoy. The desire to demonstrate the practicality of colonization led its advocates to strange mathematical calculations. Robert Patterson, the treasurer of the U.S. Mint in Philadelphia, purported to demonstrate that "deporting *females* alone" when they "arrive at the child bearing age" would make the black population "disappear" entirely sometime in the early twentieth century. (Patterson acknowledged the "inhumanity" of his idea and the disadvantages of leaving the South with "an enormous disproportion of male slaves," but still hoped Congress would consider it.) In the Senate, James R. Doolittle presented elaborate tables showing that if 150,000 were colonized each year, the "last remnants of the slave population" would be gone by 1907.[38]

Both the law providing for abolition in the District of Columbia and the Second Confiscation Act included provisions for the colonization of those willing to emigrate. During 1862, Congress appropriated a total of $600,000 to aid in the transportation overseas of African-Americans. With unanimous Republican support, it also approved Lincoln's request to establish diplomatic relations with Haiti and Liberia. On July 12, the day he met with the delegation of border congressmen, Lincoln appointed a consul general for Haiti. Radicals hailed the step for recognizing the black republic as an equal member of the "family of nations." But many members of Congress were motivated in part by the hope of facilitating colonization.[39]

In Congress, colonization was most strongly promoted by border Unionists and moderate Republicans from the Northwest. Lyman Trumbull, who included a colonization provision in the original version of the Second Confiscation Act, explained candidly, "There is a very great aversion in the West . . . against having free negroes come among us. Our people want nothing to do with the negro." Numerous constituents, including the prominent Illinois Republican James C. Conkling, wrote to Trumbull praising his stance as a way of counteracting Democrats' "constant hue and cry of negro worshipers etc." Radical Republicans, most of whom had long defended the rights of northern free blacks, tended to oppose colonization. "The idea of removing the whole colored population from this country is one of the most absurd ideas that ever entered into the head of man or woman," declared John P. Hale, the Radical senator from New Hampshire. But many Radicals went along to placate the president, the border states, and western Republicans.[40]

Some Republicans in Congress spoke of blacks as "natural-born citizens," who, while not entitled to political or social equality, "shall be equal to the white race in their right to themselves and the enjoyment of the proceeds of their own labor" (Lincoln's own position in the 1850s). Even those who opposed colonization, however, generally maintained that because of a preference for a warm climate, family ties, or some other reason, blacks who became free would remain in the South. Although Lincoln appears to have had little direct influence on congressional deliberations, proponents of colonization invoked the president's name. The *New York Times* declared that Lincoln and Frank Blair were in perfect accord "on the entire subject."[41]

Numerous colonization schemes surfaced in 1862. From Brazil, ambassador James Watson Webb, who as the pro-colonization editor of the *New*

York Courier and Enquirer had helped to whip up the city's anti-abolition riot of 1834, proposed the creation of a joint stock company to settle black Americans along the Amazon River. The Danish chargé d'affaires in Washington asked the administration to encourage black emigration to St. Croix, whose sugar plantations had suffered from a "want of manual labor" since Denmark abolished slavery there in 1848.[42]

The Chiriqui project, which Lincoln had discussed in 1861 with Ambrose W. Thompson, who claimed to own land suitable for colonization in this province of Colombia, now came back to life. Thompson's son, a captain in the Union army, sent Lincoln a long letter detailing the region's attractions, including its soil, climate, coal mines, even the abundant "turtles and fish" in its harbors. In a more practical vein he predicted that an American colony there would exert "a preponderating influence in Central and South America." In April 1862, Secretary of the Interior Caleb B. Smith recommended that the government advance $300,000 to Thompson to enable him to open the coal mines in Chiriqui. This, he wrote to the president, would begin "a great national scheme which may ultimately relieve the United States of the surplus colored population." Lincoln seemed more enthusiastic about Smith's report than any member of the cabinet. In June 1862, Lincoln appointed Reverend James Mitchell, the Indiana colonizationist he had met nine years earlier, commissioner of emigration in the Department of the Interior.[43]

As talk of colonization increased, so did black opposition. "No considerable number of colored people have manifested any wish to be colonized," one Massachusetts newspaper observed. To Mitchell's dismay, he found blacks who had obtained their freedom in 1861 and 1862 "to a great extent satisfied with their new liberties and franchises." To counteract this reluctance to emigrate, Lincoln, for the first and only time, took the idea of colonization directly to black Americans. Early in July, he asked his emigration commissioner to gather a black delegation at the White House. Mitchell conveyed the invitation to an audience assembled at one of Washington's black churches. The group adopted a resolution calling discussion of colonization "inexpedient, inauspicious, and impolitic." But as it would be discourteous to refuse to meet with the president, a committee of five was appointed. On August 14, 1862, in Mitchell's words, "in the goodness of his heart, for the first time in the history of the country," an American president "received and addressed a number of colored men."[44]

This was not, in fact, the first time Lincoln had met with prominent

African-Americans. In April 1862 he had a forty-five-minute conversation with the black theologian Daniel A. Payne about the District of Columbia emancipation bill. That same month, he discussed colonization with two representatives of the government of Liberia, one of them the prominent pan-Africanist Alexander Crummell. A newspaper report that the two had urged Lincoln to support "compulsory transportation" inspired "severe comments" from black Americans, and Lincoln dashed off a letter to the two to repair the damage. "Neither you nor any one else," he affirmed, "have ever advocated, in my presence, the compulsory deportation of freed slaves to Liberia or elsewhere."[45]

What Lincoln said on August 14 to the black delegation made the meeting one of the most controversial moments of his entire career. "You and we are different races," Lincoln told them. Because of white prejudice, "even when you cease to be slaves, you are yet far removed from being placed on an equality with the white race. . . . It is better for us both, therefore, to be separated." Lincoln offered a powerful indictment of slavery: "Your race are suffering in my judgment, the greatest wrong inflicted on any people." But he refused to issue a similar condemnation of racism, although he also declined to associate himself with it. Blacks, he said, could never "be placed on an equality with the white race" in the United States; whether this "is right or wrong I need not discuss" (a remarkable comment from one who had so vehemently condemned Stephen A. Douglas for moral agnosticism regarding slavery). Lincoln seemed to blame the black presence for the Civil War: "But for your race among us there could not be war." He offered their removal as the remedy. Although not mentioning Chiriqui by name, he touted Central America as an area of fine harbors and "rich coal mines" where even a small band of colonists might succeed. Invoking the memory of George Washington and the "hardships" he had endured in the War of Independence, Lincoln urged blacks to "sacrifice something of your present comfort" by agreeing to emigrate. To refuse would be "extremely selfish." Despite his powerful endorsement of colonization, Lincoln, unlike Bates, the Blairs, and many other border emancipationists, continued to insist that any such plan must be voluntary, in effect leaving the decision to blacks themselves. Nonetheless, as the Washington correspondent of the *New York Times* observed, Lincoln's statement "committed him more strongly than ever to the colonization policy as the surest solution of negro complications."[46]

A stenographer was present and Lincoln's remarks quickly appeared in the nation's newspapers, as he undoubtedly intended. Edward M. Thomas, the delegation's spokesman, wrote to Lincoln that he found his remarks persuasive: "We were entirely hostile to the movement until all the advantages were so ably brought to our views by you." But overall, the meeting had the same result as Lincoln's conference a month earlier with the border congressmen: failure. The bulk of the antislavery public, along with many others, greeted the publication of Lincoln's little speech with dismay. "The scheme is simply absurd," wrote James Bowen, the police commissioner of New York City, "and is either a piece of charlatanism or the statesmanship of a backwoods lawyer, but disgraceful to the administration." Secretary of the Treasury Chase found the encounter shocking. "How much better," he remarked in his diary, "would be a manly protest against prejudice against color." A. P. Smith, a black resident of New Jersey, wrote to the president: "Pray tell us, is our right to a home in this country less than your own, Mr. Lincoln? . . . Are you an American? So are we. Are you a patriot? So are we." Blacks considered it a "perfect outrage" to hear that their presence was "the cause of all this bloodshed" and their desire to remain in "the land of their birth" a result of fear of "making sacrifices."[47]

Most indignant of all was Frederick Douglass. His vision of a society that had transcended the determinism of race stood as the polar opposite of the "pride of race and blood" that Lincoln, he wrote, had revealed. "Mr. Lincoln," Douglass complained, "assumes the language and arguments of an itinerant colonization lecturer, shows all his inconsistencies, . . . his contempt for Negroes and his canting hypocrisy." Douglass pointed out that blacks had not caused the war; slavery had. The real task of a statesman was not to patronize blacks by deciding what was "best" for them, but to allow them to be free. Fourteen years later, when Douglass delivered his famous speech at the unveiling of a statue of Lincoln in Washington, the 1862 meeting still rankled. He could not forbear to mention the day when the president "strangely told us that we were the cause of the war . . . [and] were to leave the land in which we were born."[48]

Commenting on the meeting with the black delegation, a London newspaper observed, "If ever a public man was aware of the weight of his own words . . . President Lincoln must have been so." But Lincoln failed to consider that his remarks might reinforce racism and encourage racists to act on their beliefs. Northern blacks reported that since the publication of the president's comments they had been "repeatedly insulted, and told that we must leave the country." The summer of 1862 witnessed a series of violent outbreaks targeting blacks. Lincoln's meeting with the black delegation, wrote the *Chicago Tribune*, "constitutes the wide and gloomy background of which the foreground is made up of the riots and disturbances which have disgraced within a short time past our Northern cities." The "kindly" Lincoln, it went on, "does not mean all this, but the deduction is inevitable."[49]

Heedless of this reaction, Lincoln pressed forward. A few days after the meeting, he discussed colonization at length with Senator Samuel C. Pomeroy of Kansas and accepted Pomeroy's offer to organize black emigration parties to Central America. Previously, Pomeroy had opposed colonization—if anybody should be sent out of the country, he quipped, it was slaveholders, "a class whose absence shall be least felt." Now, on August 26, 1862, Pomeroy issued a public address, "sanctioned by the President," inviting 100 black families to accompany him to Chiriqui. Within a few days he had received more than enough applications. Indeed, Frederick Douglass wrote to Pomeroy that his two sons desired to be included, even though Douglass himself opposed the idea. On September 11, even as a pivotal military campaign in Maryland unfolded, Lincoln authorized Secretary Smith to sign an agreement with the Chiriqui company for the U.S. government to purchase land for the colonists and advance funds for the development of coal mines. The document envisioned the eventual dispatch of 10,000 emigrants. By October, Pomeroy claimed to have the names of more than 13,000 potential participants. Even if he exaggerated, it seems evident that some black Americans found the idea appealing. Most of the volunteers appear to have been northerners, not contrabands or newly emancipated slaves in the nation's capital.[50]

Lincoln's meeting with the black delegation and stepped-up promotion of colonization formed parts of an unusual sequence of events between his decision in July to shelve the emancipation edict and the issuance of the Preliminary Emancipation Proclamation two months later. During this period, the military situation showed little improvement and pressure for emancipation continued to mount. Even as Lincoln privately intimated that he was "pretty well cured of objections," he made a series of widely reported statements that cast doubt on his willingness to issue such a proclamation. In retrospect, he appears to have been preparing the northern public for the coming announcement.

Throughout these two months, northern newspapers, Republican as well as Democratic, criticized the administration's "want of decision and purpose." Republican congressmen who returned home after adjournment found public opinion demanding "a vigorous prosecution of the war." From Ohio, John Sherman wrote to his brother, General William T. Sherman, "You can form no conception of the change of opinion here as to the Negro Question. . . . I am prepared for one to meet the broad issue of universal emancipation." Letters poured into the White House demanding action against slavery. "The rebellion cannot be crushed without a general emancipation of the slaves," wrote Benjamin Bannan, an influential editor from Pennsylvania.[51]

The will of God now became a consideration in the debate, an odd situation for a man like Lincoln whose religious views were, to say the least, unorthodox. Northern ministers, including many who could hardly have been described as abolitionists before 1861, delivered sermons and dispatched petitions and delegations to the White House explaining the war as a divine chastisement for the sin of slavery and assuring Lincoln that God intended him to free the slaves. At one meeting with two representatives of "Chicago Christians of all denominations," Lincoln gently ridiculed the idea that God's purposes were self-evident. He pointed out that prelates on different sides of the question had been pressuring him, "equally certain that they represent the Divine will." Confederates also believed that God was on their side. He wondered why God had revealed his wishes to the delegation but not to him, since he must make the decision, although he quickly added that he did not expect "a direct revelation."

Lincoln then discussed the pros and cons of emancipation; he almost seemed to be arguing with himself. On the one hand, slavery was undoubtedly "the root of the rebellion." Emancipation would "help us in Europe," "help somewhat in the North," and weaken the Confederacy. On the other hand, he still feared that the border states would "go over to the rebels." Moreover, issuing a proclamation that could not be enforced would be seen by the "whole world" as a sign of weakness, "like the Pope's bull against the comet." Lincoln seemed put off by the ministers' statement that emancipation would give the North a principle around which to rally. "We already have an important principle," he declared, "the fact that constitutional government is at stake."[52]

On August 20, six days after Lincoln's meeting with the black delegation at the White House, Horace Greeley published in the *New York*

Tribune a long open letter addressed to the president, entitled "The Prayer of Twenty Millions" (more or less the population of the North). It touched on many issues, including Lincoln's supposed deference to the "fossil politicians" of the border states. But essentially, it urged him to enforce the Second Confiscation Act, including its "emancipating provisions." This was an odd request, since in late July Lincoln had in fact issued a proclamation giving Confederates sixty days to abandon the rebellion or face the confiscation of their property under that law, a time limit that still had a month to run. Lincoln could have simply replied that he was in the process of doing what Greeley demanded. He could have pointed out, as the *Chicago Tribune* did, that under the Second Confiscation Act slaves of rebels entering Union lines were legally "already free" and that "their title to freedom" did not depend on any action by the president. Instead, Lincoln chose to interpret Greeley's letter as a call for immediate and total abolition. He replied with his most often-quoted public letter, which, in what Greeley must have considered an affront, Lincoln released to a rival newspaper, the Washington *National Intelligencer*:

> I would save the Union. I would save it in the shortest way under the Constitution. . . . My paramount object in this struggle *is* to save the Union, and is *not* either to save or to destroy slavery. If I could save the Union without freeing *any* slave I would do it, and if I could save it by freeing *all* the slaves I would do that. What I do about slavery, and the colored race, I do because I believe it helps to save the Union. . . . I have here stated my purpose according to my view of official duty; and I intend no modification of my oft-expressed personal wish that all men everywhere could be free.[53]

Moderate Republicans hailed Lincoln's response to Greeley's "impertinent" letter as the "best enunciation" yet of slavery's relationship to the war effort. Because of what he considered its indifference to the fate of slavery, Wendell Phillips called it, in a letter to the managing editor of the *New York Tribune*, abolitionist Sydney Howard Gay, "the most disgraceful document that ever came from the head of a free people." But Gay himself congratulated Lincoln. The "general impression" in the North, Gay wrote, was that Lincoln would soon announce the "destruction of slavery" as necessary to save the Union.

Gay's response was insightful. There is no question that winning the war and preserving the Union were uppermost in Lincoln's mind, and that as far back as his law career he had always maintained a distinction between professional responsibilities and personal beliefs. Yet the response to Greeley should be understood not as a statement of principle from which Lincoln was determined never to depart so much as a way of preparing northern public opinion for a change in policy on which he had already decided. Certainly, it suggested that freeing all the slaves was now a real option, something that had not been the case a year or even six months earlier. But perhaps the most telling comment came from the *Springfield Republican*. The editors praised Lincoln's position but pointed out that the very notion of "saving" the Union required rethinking: the prewar Union was gone forever.[54]

One indication of vast changes on the horizon was the administration's movement in the summer of 1862 toward the use of black soldiers. The War Department's call for 300,000 volunteers in July produced disappointing results; on August 4 it asked for another 300,000 and threatened to draft members of state militias if necessary. Leading members of Congress had been advocating black enlistment for months, and the militia and confiscation acts had opened the door, should Lincoln desire to cross the threshold. But for the time being, he authorized the employment of blacks only as "laborers." Lincoln had long resisted calls to enroll black soldiers. He knew the border states, most of the officer corps, and many white soldiers bitterly opposed such a move. He remained unsure of blacks' military capacity. "If we were to arm them," he told the Chicago clergymen, "I fear that in a few weeks the arms would be in the hands of the rebels."[55]

The beginnings of a change in policy came in August 1862. Lincoln preferred to let local commanders lead the way, so long as they did so quietly. The irrepressible General John W. Phelps requested arms from Benjamin F. Butler for black units he had been drilling in Louisiana without permission. Butler refused and Phelps resigned. But Secretary of the Treasury Chase warned Butler that the enlistment of blacks was inevitable. "Phelps's policy prevails instead of yours," Butler's politically astute wife, Sarah, wrote him on August 8. Sensing a shift in the political winds, Butler informed Stanton that he was enlisting into Union service the First Native Guards, the free black militia units of Louisiana that had previously served the Confederacy. But not all the enrollees were free, since, as a Treasury official in New Orleans noted, "nobody inquires whether the recruit is (or has been) a slave."

Ironically, the first blacks to take part in Civil War battles did so in Indian Territory, present-day Oklahoma. In November and December 1861, Unionists from the Creek and Seminole nations who repudiated treaties of alliance their tribal leaders had signed with the Confederacy fought pitched battles against pro-southern forces, after which they retreated into Kansas. In these encounters, some three hundred black men—former slaves and free men who lived with the Indians—fought on the Union side. Senator James H. Lane of Kansas immediately advocated the enlistment of Indians into the Union army, but fearing an adverse reaction among white residents of the West, the War Department held back. But in May 1862, the First Indian Home Guard was mustered into the Union army. Despite its name this was a triracial unit. Whites from Kansas, Indians, and blacks fought side by side when the unit invaded Indian Territory in July 1862 in an unsuccessful effort to wrest it from Confederate control.[56]

Meanwhile, Lane, without explicit permission, was also recruiting soldiers in Kansas for a black unit. According to the *New York Tribune's* Washington correspondent, both Secretary of War Stanton and Lincoln told Lane they would not interfere, although for months Lane felt obliged to "keep [the soldiers] from public view." On August 25, Stanton authorized General Rufus Saxton in South Carolina to recruit up to 5,000 black soldiers. Stanton attached a note to his order: "This must never see daylight, because it is so much in advance of public opinion." These steps were meant to ease manpower shortages in specific areas, not to initiate a general policy of black enlistment. But the military's ever-increasing need for men suggested that the widespread recruitment of black troops could not be postponed forever.[57]

III

"From the tenor of his remarks," one reporter commented on Lincoln's letter to Horace Greeley, "if the next battle in Virginia results in a decided victory for our army," an emancipation proclamation "will be forthwith issued." A few days later, Union forces suffered a humiliating defeat at Second Bull Run. Not until September 17 at Antietam, where George B. McClellan turned back the Confederate invasion of Maryland in the bloodiest day of fighting of the entire war, did the Union achieve the success for which Lincoln had been waiting. On September 22, 1862, he informed his cabinet that the decision to issue an emancipation edict postponed in July could no longer be delayed. "My mind has been much occupied with this subject," he told them. "I think the time has come now." Lincoln said he had promised God that if Robert E. Lee's army were driven out of Maryland, he would issue the proclamation. Lincoln did not mention it, but the sixty-day notice given to rebels after the passage of the Second Confiscation Act expired the next day, so some further action seemed to be called for. In any event, the decision had been made, but he invited the cabinet to offer stylistic suggestions.[58]

Like the postponed order of July, the Preliminary Emancipation Proclamation Lincoln presented to the cabinet gave the Confederate states until January 1 to cease the rebellion or see their slaves freed. It again offered the alternative of gradual emancipation and endorsed the colonization of freed slaves, although at Seward's insistence, Lincoln revised the language to make clear that this would proceed only with the consent of the colonists and of Central American governments. Unlike its predecessor, however, the new edict quoted the Article of War of March and the Second Confiscation Act of July and directed military personnel to enforce their provisions regarding fugitive slaves and emancipation (as Greeley had demanded). The draft Lincoln presented to the cabinet stated that the freedom of the slaves would be sustained during the term of "the present incumbent," an odd formulation for someone normally so precise in the use of language. What would be the status of these persons after Lincoln left office? Seward and Chase objected to this phrase, and Lincoln dropped it. The final version promised that those to whom it applied would be "forever free."[59]

With the exception of Montgomery Blair, the cabinet endorsed Lincoln's decision. "It is a despotic act in the cause of the Union," Welles wrote, "and I may add of freedom." The proclamation, a correspondent of New York Democratic leader Samuel L. M. Barlow reported from Washington, portended a "Northern Revolution." "No one here," he added, "talks conservatism any longer, or speaks of the old Constitution." Overall, however, the announcement on September 22, 1862, of the preliminary proclamation launched a two-pronged approach to ending slavery. It envisioned general emancipation in the rebel states, but adhered to the program of gradual, compensated emancipation for the border. To be sure, abolition in the Confederacy would fatally undermine slavery everywhere. Once slavery died in the Deep South, *Harper's Weekly* pointed out, it was "utterly impossible that Maryland, Kentucky, and Missouri can continue to maintain the institution." Thus, wrote the *Springfield Republican*, the proclamation offered a glimpse of a "stirring" future, whose exact contours remained to be determined: "[A] great social, political, and financial revolution is to be effected in every rebellious state."[60]

The Preliminary Emancipation Proclamation, one newspaper noted, had been "somewhat anticipated, from recent rumors and unofficial reports." Nonetheless, public reaction was intense. The announcement, the *New York Tribune* predicted, would "separate the sheep from the goats." Certainly this seemed to be the case in the border states and occupied South, where it drove a wedge into the Unionist coalition. Thomas A. R. Nelson, a former Whig congressman and one of Tennessee's most prominent Unionists, accused Lincoln of setting out to "destroy the last vestige of freedom among us," and switched his allegiance to the Confederacy. Although the proclamation did not apply to the border states, the reaction there was mostly hostile. "The measure is wholly unwarrantable and wholly pernicious," wrote the *Louisville Journal*. "Kentucky cannot and will not acquiesce in this measure. Never!" On the other hand, Missouri Radicals, who had been calling for emancipation as part of a battle with the Blairs for control of state politics, hailed the announcement. It was "the noblest act of the age on this continent," one of their leaders, B. Gratz Brown, wrote from St. Louis.[61]

Most northern Republicans welcomed the proclamation. Twelve governors were meeting at Altoona, Pennsylvania, to discuss war policy when it was released. They voted to adjourn and sent a delegation to Washington to offer congratulations. "Men vastly more conservative than I have ever been," reported Senator Ira Harris of New York, embraced Lincoln's policy. So did many War Democrats. "If they lose their negroes it is their own fault not ours," one wrote from Illinois. Some abolitionists and Radicals lamented the absence of any moral statement against slavery in the document. It was "merely a war-measure," complained Lydia Maria Child, with "no recognition of principles of justice or humanity." But most were overjoyed, including some of Lincoln's harshest critics. "Hurrah for Old Abe and the *proclamation*," exulted Benjamin F. Wade. "From the date of this proclamation," declared the *Chicago Tribune*, "begins the history of this Republic as . . . the home of freedom." A month after excoriating the president for his embrace of colonization, Frederick Douglass called the Preliminary Emancipation Proclamation the most important document ever issued by an American president, the "first chapter" in a new national history. Lincoln, Douglass assured his readers, "will take no backward step." Commendations poured into the White House ("all that a vain man could hope for," Lincoln wrote).[62]

"The liberated men are to have rights before the law," declared the *Springfield Republican*. But the preliminary proclamation left unresolved their future status. Lincoln still assumed that large numbers would agree to be colonized outside the country. On September 24—two days after they considered the proclamation—and again on the twenty-sixth, the cabinet discussed colonization. Lincoln, according to Secretary of the Navy Welles, thought it essential "to provide an asylum for a race which we had emancipated but which could never be recognized or admitted to be our equals." He thought a treaty could be worked out with a government in West Africa or Central America "to which the Negroes could be sent." It was "distinctly understood," Welles recorded in his diary, that emancipation and colonization were linked. Attorney General Bates again proposed compulsory deportation ("the more the better," he thought), but Lincoln demurred: "Their emigration must be voluntary and without expense to themselves."[63]

By the time of the cabinet discussion, numerous questions had arisen about the validity of Ambrose W. Thompson's land grant in Colombia, his grandiose accounts of the region's natural resources, and the attitude of the local government. Welles considered the entire plan "a rotten remnant of an intrigue of the last administration." The House Ways and Means Committee had determined that the area was "uninhabitable" and that in any event, Thompson "had not a particle of a title to an inch of it." The Smithsonian Institution reported that samples of Chiriqui coal examined by a leading scientist were worthless. If loaded onto naval vessels, the coal "would spontaneously take fire." Since 1860, Colombia had been engaged in its own civil war, albeit one less bloody than that of the United States, making it uncertain who possessed the authority to sign an agreement to settle emancipated slaves in Chiriqui. Moreover, other Central American governments had been complaining to Secretary of State Seward about public discussion of colonies on their soil. The cabinet agreed that colonization could not go forward without the agreement of the relevant governments. On September 24, the administration suspended Pomeroy's colonization expedition, which had been set to embark the following week.[64]

Despite sharing the Blair family's enthusiasm about establishing an American empire in the Western Hemisphere, Seward had long harbored "grave doubts" about colonization, which is probably why Lincoln had previously circumvented him in pursuing the idea. Seward did not believe that any significant number of blacks would emigrate voluntarily, and felt the United States needed all the workers it could find. "I am always for bringing men and States *into* this Union," he once remarked, "never for taking any *out*." Indeed, in 1861 Seward had begun to issue passports to black northerners stating that they were citizens of the United States, a repudiation of the *Dred Scott* decision and a different vision of the black future than colonization. Lincoln and Seward had become very close; as Seward's secretary George E. Baker recalled soon after Lincoln's death, they "never disagreed in but one subject—that was the colonization of the negroes."[65]

Nonetheless, given Lincoln's desire to work out a colonization treaty, Seward on September 30 addressed a circular to the governments of Britain, France, the Netherlands, and Denmark—owners of colonial possessions in the Caribbean basin—offering to enter into agreements to colonize American blacks on their territory. The numerous requirements he listed for any treaty almost ensured rejection: homes must be ready on arrival; adequate compensation must be paid; schools and medical care must be available; the emigrants must enjoy all the rights of citizens. Few of the governments were interested. By the end of October 1862, Secretary of the Interior Smith was forced to admit that the administration now had "no settled policy" regarding colonization. But a month later, Lincoln was writing to Chase of his hope that a Chiriqui contract still could be arranged.[66]

If Lincoln anticipated that his embrace of colonization would reconcile his critics to emancipation, the elections of 1862 proved him wrong. As in any electoral campaign, numerous issues affected voters' decisions, including infringements on civil liberties such as the suspension of habeas corpus, the economic impact in the Northwest of the suspension of commerce on the Mississippi River, and lack of military success. But Democrats spent much of their time denouncing Republicans as "Nigger Worshippers." Lincoln, they charged, had unilaterally and unconstitutionally altered the war's purpose. Emancipation would produce "scenes of lust and rapine" in the South and unleash "a swarthy inundation of negro laborers and paupers" on the North. Raising lurid racial fears paid electoral dividends. Democrats captured the governorships of New York and New Jersey, won control of the Illinois and Indiana legislatures, and gained thirty-four seats in the House of Representatives. Among those ousted from Congress was Lincoln's ally George P. Fisher, in what was taken as a repudiation of the president's compensated emancipation plan by Delaware voters.[67]

The results, however, had no effect on what a Washington newspaper called "the majestic march of events" that was "overwhelming" the carefully wrought policies of politicians and generals. Indeed, reflecting the contradictions inevitable at a moment of radical change, even as Lincoln pressed his colonization plan the administration moved toward recognizing blacks as free laborers and American citizens. Within military lines, officers were now treating all blacks as free under the Second Confiscation Act and paying them wages. In the Mississippi Valley, General Grant appointed John Eaton, a Dartmouth graduate and former superintendent of schools in Toledo, Ohio, to "take charge" of the escaped slaves who were congregating around army posts. Eaton enrolled thousands of them in schools in "contraband camps." In Louisiana, Benjamin F. Butler established an "experiment of free labor," with blacks working for wages for loyal planters. When Lincoln requested information about the system, Butler replied that he was convinced that black labor could be "as profitable in a state of freedom as in slavery." The entire army, he added, now believed "that slavery is doomed." Meanwhile, moves toward the use of black soldiers inevitably raised the question of their postwar status. As one newspaper noted, "It would hardly be treating the African like a man to use him as a soldier and then banish him."[68]

Nowhere were the shifting crosscurrents of policy more evident than in the course of Attorney General Edward Bates. More than once, Bates had advocated compulsory deportation of emancipated slaves. Yet in November 1862, he issued an opinion affirming the citizenship of free black persons born in the United States. Bates had asked the advice of the distinguished jurist and political philosopher Francis Lieber, who responded that there was "not even a shadow of a doubt" that American citizenship included blacks. Bates agreed. The *Dred Scott* decision, he boldly declared, had "no authority" outside the specific circumstances of that case. Bates added that citizenship did not imply either equality before the law or political rights (women and children, after all, were citizens). Nonetheless, Salmon P. Chase, who had requested Bates's ruling, immediately dispatched it to Louisiana, where free black activists had been demanding civil and political rights. The opinion, a striking change in public policy, was published early in December. "It properly precedes and ushers in," wrote Greeley's *Tribune*, "that other great act which is to come from the president on the 1st of January."[69]

The electoral setback did not affect Lincoln's outlook. His old friend David Davis visited the White House at the end of November 1862. He found Lincoln's "whole soul . . . absorbed in his plan for remunerative emancipation." Lincoln, Davis reported, remained certain that if Congress authorized the issuance of compensation bonds, the border states would take steps to abolish slavery and "the problem is solved." Lincoln's annual message to Congress, which reconvened on December 1, reflected this conviction. This was, to say the least, a curious document. It said almost nothing about the progress of the war, but included an elegiac reverie on the land itself, how it endured while "passing generations of men" and their ephemeral disputes came and went. Half its pages, a Democratic member of Congress complained, were "devoted to the negro."[70] But Lincoln did not discuss the impending proclamation. Instead, he devoted most of this section to reiterating his commitment to compensated emancipation and colonization. He asked for constitutional amendments authorizing Congress to appropriate funds for colonization, authorize payment to states that provided for emancipation by the year 1900 (with provision for repayment if they reintroduced slavery), and compensate loyal owners of slaves who gained freedom as a result of the war. This plan, he said, offered a "compromise" between advocates of abolition with the freed-people remaining "with us," and those who favored gradual abolition and their "removal." It would enable freed slaves to avoid the "vagrant destitution" that would likely follow "immediate emancipation."

"I cannot make it better known than it already is," Lincoln declared, "that I strongly favor colonization." Three times, he used the ominous word "deportation," although he also spoke of his administration's continuing efforts to sign treaties for the "voluntary emigration" of blacks. He gently chided them for not being willing to leave the country, adding that he hoped a "considerable migration" would eventually take place. Colonization, he maintained, would benefit whites: "Labor is like any other commodity on the market. . . . Reduce the supply of black labor by colonizing the black laborer . . . and . . . you increase the demand for and the wages of white labor." But at the same time, Lincoln directly addressed the racial fears stirred up in the fall political campaign, offering an extended argument as to why, if freed slaves remained in the United States, they would pose no threat to the white majority. He referred obliquely to exclusion laws such as that of Illinois: "In any event, cannot the north decide for itself whether to receive them?"

The December message contained a last offer to the border and Confederate states of a different path to abolition than immediate emancipation. Lincoln's scheme would have had the government issue interest-bearing bonds to be presented to slaveowners, with the principal due when slavery ended in their state. He offered elaborate calculations of costs, benefits, and population trends to prove that despite the economic value of slave property—over three billion dollars, an enormous sum—the growth of the white population through natural increase and immigration would make the burden of taxation to pay off the bonds less and less onerous as time went on. Lincoln was betting that the white population would grow faster than the black, an outcome that colonization would ensure. The adoption of his proposals, he said, would "end the struggle now, and save the Union forever."

Lincoln closed the message with a stirring peroration:

The dogmas of the quiet past, are inadequate to the stormy present. The occasion is piled high with difficulty, and we must rise with the occasion. As our case is new, so we must think anew, and act anew. We must disenthrall our selves, and then we shall save our country.

Fellow-citizens, we cannot escape history. We of this Congress and this administration, will be remembered in spite of ourselves. . . . The fiery trial through which we pass, will light us down, in honor or dishonor, to the latest generation. . . . We—even *we here*—hold the power, and bear the responsibility. In *giving* freedom to the *slave*, we *assure* freedom to the *free*—honorable alike in what we give, and what we preserve. We shall nobly save, or meanly lose, the last best, hope of earth. Other means may succeed; this could not fail. The way is plain, peaceful, generous, just.

These words, proclaimed the *Continental Monthly*, should be "committed to memory and constantly recalled by every man." A century and a half later, they remain among the most eloquent ever composed by an American president. Lincoln implored Americans to embrace the end of slavery—not, however, through the impending Emancipation Proclamation, which he failed to mention, but via his thirty-seven-year plan of compensated abolition. The message to Congress revealed Lincoln's thinking at a crucial moment of transition. He clung to a proposal he had been promoting for a year with no success, yet pleaded with Americans to abandon the "dogmas" of the past. He again endorsed colonization, yet referred to prospective emigrants as "free Americans of African descent" rather than alien members of some other nationality, and argued that the nation had nothing to fear if former slaves remained in the United States.[71]

Many observers found the message puzzling and disappointing. "What becomes of the president's [Preliminary Emancipation] proclamation of the 22nd of last September?" wondered Orestes Brownson. Some Republicans "gently laughed" at Lincoln's "astounding scheme." "I could hardly credit my ears," wrote Colonel James A. Garfield, who heard the reading of the message while visiting Washington. Chase had urged Lincoln, to no avail, not to suggest constitutional amendments that could never be adopted. As Chase anticipated, the proposals went nowhere.[72]

For Lincoln, December 1862 was among the most trying months of the entire war. Between December 11 and 15, Union forces suffered a disastrous defeat at Fredericksburg, Virginia. This precipitated a full-fledged political crisis, with cabinet members scheming against one another and a congressional delegation demanding the ouster of Secretary of State Seward, whom many Republicans blamed for the administration's failures.

Lincoln weathered the crisis. He assured members of Congress that he would not retreat from his pledge to issue the proclamation on January 1. But the weeks leading up to the new year witnessed an unseemly scramble for exemptions. In the Preliminary Emancipation Proclamation, Lincoln had alluded to the possibility that parts of a state could escape its impact. He offered a precise guideline as to how to do so: a congressional election would have to be held in which a majority of "qualified voters" took part. Lincoln saw this as a way of encouraging white southern Unionism. He urged military commanders in the occupied South to schedule elections before January 1 and to remind local residents that by participating they could "avoid the unsatisfactory prospect before them"—that is, the freeing of their slaves.[73]

At Lincoln's urging, Louisiana's military governor, George F. Shepley, organized an election in December in and around New Orleans in order, as he impolitically put it, to enable residents to avail themselves of "the benefits" of exemption from emancipation. The turnout of 7,700 amounted to 60 percent of the vote cast in 1860. Military Governor Andrew Johnson called elections for late December in parts of Tennessee, but Confederate raids made holding them impossible. Nonetheless, Johnson and other Tennessee Unionists "urgently" requested Lincoln to exempt the entire state from the proclamation. Joseph Segar, whom Congress had earlier seated to represent eastern Virginia, pressed Lincoln to exempt that region. Lincoln seemed anxious to comply. On December 31, he wired General John A. Dix that time was "nearly up" but he had received no word of an election. Dix replied that one had just been held in Norfolk.[74]

Western Virginia took a different route to exemption. Early in the war, as previously related, Unionists there had created the Restored Government of Virginia, which Congress and Lincoln recognized as the state's legitimate regime. Early in 1862, the legislature called for the creation of a separate state of West Virginia, whose population of 378,000 included about 18,500 slaves and 2,800 free blacks. In June, the U.S. Senate approved the idea, so long as West Virginia provided for the emancipation of the children of slaves born after July 4, 1863. In December 1862, the resolution passed the House. Lincoln then had to decide whether to sign it.[75]

The Constitution allows for the division of a state if authorized by its legislature. But the idea that the Restored Government truly represented Virginia, as Thaddeus Stevens remarked, was a "mockery." Asked by Lincoln for its opinion about the creation of this new state, the cabinet divided. Seward thought it essential to "plant a free state south of the Ohio." Bates declared the entire proceeding unconstitutional. Welles agreed, and pointed out that were West Virginia not admitted, all its slaves "would probably be free by Tuesday when the Proclamation emancipating slaves would be published." To Lincoln, the key issue was not constitutionality, but whether admission would assist the war effort. Deciding that it would, on December 31 he signed the resolution admitting West Virginia to the Union. In February 1863, the state amended its constitution to incorporate the required plan for gradual emancipation.[76]

Also on the final day of 1862, Lincoln took his most concrete step to implement the idea of colonization. With James R. Doolittle, one of the idea's most avid proponents, present, Lincoln signed a contract with Bernard Kock, a businessman originally from Charleston, to transport blacks to Île à Vache (Cow Island), located just off the coast of Haiti. Kock had persuaded the Haitian government to grant him the right to cut timber there. In the fall he had issued a public letter to Lincoln waxing poetic about the resources of his "beautiful, healthy, and fertile island." Lincoln's commissioner of emigration, James Mitchell, lobbied on Kock's behalf. Less enthusiastic was Attorney General Bates, who told the president, "This *Governor* Kock is an errant humbug . . . a charlatan adventurer." But Lincoln arranged for Kock to be paid $250,000 for transporting 5,000 blacks to Cow Island. Doolittle and the Blairs were overjoyed. They believed, wrote Elizabeth Blair Lee, the sister of Frank and Montgomery Blair, "it is the beginning of the 2nd great Exodus."[77]

IV

THE NEXT DAY, January 1, 1863, Lincoln presided at the annual White House New Year's reception. Beginning in late morning, he greeted "an immense line" of visitors that included the diplomatic corps, justices of the Supreme Court (led by Chief Justice Taney), military officers, and members of the general public who managed to enter before the doors were closed at two o'clock. Later that afternoon, Lincoln retired to his study to sign the Emancipation Proclamation. The first time he attempted to affix his signature, he stopped and laid down his pen. His hand was shaking, not from nervousness, but because of exhaustion. "I do not want it to appear as if I hesitated," he said. After a moment of repose, he signed the proclamation. Ever concerned with his place in history, Lincoln knew he would be remembered for this act. In 1863 and 1864 he would make himself available to artists, photographers, and sculptors who portrayed him as the Emancipator. He allowed the artist Francis B. Carpenter to live in the White House for four months while painting *The First Reading of the Emancipation Proclamation.*[78]

The proclamation declared that all the slaves in the areas to which it applied—over three million men, women, and children—"are and henceforth shall be free." (Why Lincoln chose not to use the more direct phrase "forever free" from the preliminary proclamation remains unknown.) It ordered the army and navy to "recognize and maintain" that freedom. It enjoined emancipated slaves to refrain from violence, except in "necessary self-defence," and urged them to "labor faithfully for reasonable wages." For the first time, it authorized the enrollment of black soldiers into the "armed service" of the United States.

So many layers of myth have enveloped the Emancipation Proclamation that its actual content is often misunderstood. Couched in dull, legalistic language, much of it consists of a long quotation from the preliminary proclamation of September 22. Unlike the Declaration of Independence, it contains no preamble enunciating the rights of man. Only at the suggestion of Secretary of the Treasury Chase did Lincoln at the last minute add a conclusion invoking the "considerate judgment of mankind and the gracious favor of Almighty God" on this "act of justice."[79]

Lincoln did not, as is sometimes thought, free all the slaves with a stroke of his pen. The proclamation had no bearing on the nearly half-million slaves in the four border states and West Virginia. It applied only

THE EMANCIPATION PROCLAMATION

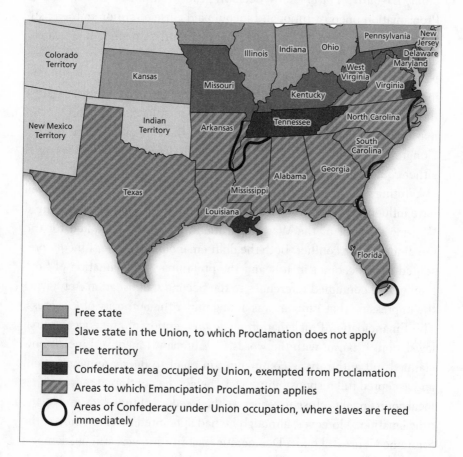

Free state

Slave state in the Union, to which Proclamation does not apply

Free territory

Confederate area occupied by Union, exempted from Proclamation

Areas to which Emancipation Proclamation applies

Areas of Confederacy under Union occupation, where slaves are freed immediately to the Confederacy and almost exclusively to areas outside Union control. Despite objections from a majority of the cabinet, it exempted a number of areas occupied by the Union army: seven counties in Tidewater Virginia (where Benjamin Butler had inaugurated the contraband policy and with it wartime emancipation), thirteen parishes in southern Louisiana, and the entire state of Tennessee. These places contained another 300,000 slaves, bringing to nearly 800,000 the number to whom the proclamation did not apply, of a total of 3.9 million.[80]

The Proclamation rested not on the rights of mankind but "upon military necessity." The previous May, in his order rescinding General David Hunter's emancipation edict, Lincoln had claimed the right, as commander in chief, to take such action himself if it became necessary to save the government. But in the fall of 1862, former Supreme Court justice Benjamin R. Curtis, a dissenter in *Dred Scott*, had issued a pamphlet, *Executive Power*, flatly declaring the Preliminary Emancipation Proclamation unconstitutional. Lincoln paid close attention to the ensuing legal debate. Around the same time that Curtis's pamphlet appeared, the Boston attorney William Whiting published a detailed examination of presidential war powers. Slavery, Whiting insisted, was a legitimate military target since it enabled the Confederacy to carry on "war against the Union" and forced "three millions of loyal subjects" owned by rebel masters to act as if they were traitors. Under the Constitution, he argued, Congress and the president possessed independent war powers, and either could legitimately abolish slavery "as an act of war."[81]

Whiting's treatise, which went through numerous printings, may well have influenced Lincoln's outlook. In November 1862, Lincoln appointed Whiting solicitor of the War Department, a post he occupied for the remainder of the conflict. Both the draft emancipation order Lincoln presented to the cabinet in July and the preliminary proclamation of September had contained references to the Second Confiscation Act, giving the impression that Lincoln was acting under the authority of Congress. The Emancipation Proclamation made no mention of any congressional legislation. It began with the words, "I, Abraham Lincoln." Lincoln now claimed full authority as commander in chief to decree emancipation, and accepted full responsibility. Nonetheless, he continued to worry that local courts might refuse to recognize the freedom of those covered by the proclamation. Moreover, although he had appointed three members, the Supreme Court still had a Democratic majority and was still headed by a chief justice who had declared in no uncertain terms that the Constitution protects slavery. Lincoln was convinced, as one Washington reporter wrote the day before the document was issued, that the proclamation could only survive judicial scrutiny "as a war measure," not "one issuing from the bosom of philanthropy." To ground emancipation, he later remarked to Chase, on anything other than military necessity, including the notion that it was "politically expedient and morally right," would "give up all footing upon constitution or law."[82]

In fact, however, the Emancipation Proclamation was as much a political as a military document. Attorney General Bates had cautioned Lincoln that its provisions about which areas were or were not in rebellion "must be truly declared." Yet Lincoln's decision to exempt parts of the Confederacy reflected not only the actual military situation but also his judgment about the prospects for winning over white support. Even the Unionists who pleaded with Lincoln to exempt all of Tennessee acknowledged that large portions of the state remained "in possession of the rebel army." But in order to bolster Andrew Johnson's regime and attract cooperation from slaveholders, Lincoln acceded to their wish. In the process, he sacrificed, for the time being, the interests of Tennessee's slaves.[83]

Critics at home and abroad charged that the proclamation actually freed no slaves at all, since it applied only to areas under Confederate control. In fact, Lincoln did not exempt occupied areas where the number of white Unionists was small or nonexistent and political reconstruction had made little or no progress—parts of Arkansas, Florida, Mississippi, North Carolina, and the Sea Islands of South Carolina. Here, emancipation was immediate. The failure to exempt eastern North Carolina surprised many observers. Military Governor Stanly resigned as a result. Overall, tens of thousands of slaves—50,000 according to one estimate—gained their freedom with the stroke of Lincoln's pen. To be sure, on the day it was issued, there was no way to enforce the proclamation in most of the South; its implementation would await Union victories. But as the Boston entrepreneur and Republican activist John Murray Forbes wrote, "In such a Proclamation words become *things* and powerful things too."[84]

The Emancipation Proclamation differed dramatically from Lincoln's previous policies regarding slavery and emancipation, some of which dated back to his days in the Illinois legislature and Congress. It abandoned the idea of seeking the cooperation of slaveholders in emancipation, and of distinguishing between loyal and disloyal owners. It was immediate, not gradual; contained no mention of monetary compensation for slaveowners; did not depend on action by the states; and made no reference to colonization (in part, perhaps, because gradualism, compensation, and colonization had no bearing on the "military necessity" that justified the document). Lincoln had long resisted the enlistment of black soldiers; now he welcomed them into the Union army. The proclamation addressed slaves directly, not as the property of the country's enemies but as persons with wills of their own whose actions might help win the Civil War.

Lincoln had not entirely abandoned his previous thinking, elements of which would reappear in the next two years. From time to time he would speak again of gradualism and compensation, but these no longer formed parts of a comprehensive plan of emancipation. Embarking on a different path to ending slavery rendered that plan irrelevant. As his contract with Bernard Kock demonstrated, Lincoln still retained an interest in colonization. But he would never again publicly advocate this policy. The language of the proclamation repudiated fears that freed slaves would become a threat to public order or succumb to "idle vagabondage," as the *New York Times* warned they might.[85] Putting some black men into the military and asking others to labor for wages implied a very different vision of their future place in American society than plans for settling them overseas. Lincoln made no effort to define the future status of the emancipated slaves, but the proclamation unavoidably placed that question on the national agenda.

Even apart from the 800,000 persons to whom it did not apply, the Emancipation Proclamation by itself hardly guaranteed the irrevocable end of slavery; for that, Union military victory would have to follow. Slavery is a remarkably resilient institution. It had survived the dislocations of the War of Independence (including the flight of tens of thousands of slaves to British lines) only to enter a period of unprecedented growth. France decreed abolition in its West Indian colonies in 1794, Napoleon restored it in 1802, and except for independent Haiti, the institution survived until 1848.[86] Were the Confederacy to gain its independence, slavery would undoubtedly continue to exist.

The proclamation's "great characteristic," declared Wendell Phillips, was that it did not make emancipation a punishment for individual rebels but treated slavery as "a system" that must be abolished. Legally speaking, this was not quite accurate, since, as William Whiting pointed out in his treatise on the war power, freeing slaves, even millions of them, did not abrogate the local laws that established and protected slavery. Further action beyond presidential emancipation, he noted, would be necessary to "render slavery unlawful."[87]

Nonetheless, the Emancipation Proclamation, as the *New York Herald* commented, marked a watershed in American life, "a new epoch, which will decisively shape the future destinies of this and of every nation on the face of the globe." Never before had so large a number of slaves been declared free. The proclamation altered the nature of the Civil War, the relationship of the federal government to slavery, and the course of American history. It liquidated without compensation the largest concentration of property in the United States. It made a negotiated settlement impossible unless the Union were willing to retract the promise of freedom. It crystallized a new identification between the ideal of liberty and a nation-state whose powers increased enormously as the war progressed. Indeed, emancipation presupposed the existence of a nation capable of enforcing such a measure, something that had not existed before 1860. Henceforth, freedom would follow the American flag. As Frederick Douglass proclaimed, "The cause of the slaves and the cause of the country" had become one. Whatever the proclamation's limitations, by making the army an agent of emancipation and wedding the goals of Union and abolition, it ensured that northern victory would produce a social transformation in the South and a redefinition of the place of blacks in American life. In his message to Congress of December 1861, Lincoln had said that he did not wish to conduct the war as a "violent and remorseless revolutionary struggle." The proclamation announced that this was precisely what it must become.[88]

"I claim not to have controlled events," Lincoln would later write, "but confess plainly that events have controlled me." Among the most important of the events that propelled him and the country down the road to emancipation were the actions of slaves wherever the Union army ventured; the pressure of abolitionists and Radicals; the desire to eliminate the possibility of European intervention; the failure of efforts to fight the war without targeting the economic foundation of southern society; the need for additional manpower; the rejection of his gradual emancipation plan by the border states; and the antislavery measures of what one newspaper called "the Congress of the Revolution." But Lincoln was hardly a passive observer of the actions of others. In October 1862, a black writer had shrewdly observed that although Lincoln's actions seemed "rather equivocal," in fact "by close observation, there could be seen a constant under-current in favor of freedom."[89]

Lincoln's course in the first two years of the war was not without miscalculations. He succumbed to wishful thinking about the extent of southern Unionism, the willingness of border slaveholders to accept any plan of emancipation, and the receptivity of black Americans to the fantastic scheme of colonization. But early in the war, he had made public a plan for emancipation that, while unsuccessful, committed the federal government to seeking an end to slavery. He made clear numerous times his wish that "all men everywhere could be free," and signed every piece of antislavery legislation enacted by Congress, including highly controversial measures like the Militia and Second Confiscation Acts. Lincoln lagged behind the abolitionists and Radicals in recognizing the necessity of general emancipation. While celebrating the proclamation, the *Christian Recorder* urged its black readers to give thanks to Sumner, Stevens, Lovejoy, Chase, and other "apostles of liberty" for their role in changing public opinion and government policy. But popular sentiment does not exist independently of political leadership. "Your personal influence upon public opinion," Carl Schurz had written to Lincoln in May 1862, "is immense; you are perhaps not aware of the whole extent of your moral power." In his own way, Lincoln helped to create the public sentiment that made emancipation possible.[90]

Despite its palpable limitations, the proclamation set off scenes of jubilation among free blacks in the North and contrabands and slaves in the South. At Beaufort on the Sea Islands, over 5,000 African-Americans celebrated their freedom by singing what a white observer called "the Marseillaise of the slaves": "In that New Jerusalem, I am not afraid to die; We must fight for liberty, in that New Jerusalem." In the North, blacks gathered in their churches. "I have never witnessed," the abolitionist Benjamin R. Plumly wrote to Lincoln from Philadelphia, "such intense, intelligent and devout 'Thanksgiving.'" The mention of Lincoln's name "evoked a spontaneous benediction from the whole Congregation" and the singing of "The Year of Jubilee." "The Black people all trust you," Plumly reported. "They believe you desire to do them justice." When one person suggested that Lincoln might pursue "some form of colonization," a woman shouted, " 'God won't let him,' . . . and the response of the congregation was emphatic." The process of deifying Lincoln as the Great Emancipator had begun.[91]

During the Civil War, Europeans carefully observed events in the United States. The announcement of the Emancipation Proclamation produced expressions of gratitude from across the continent. In ornateness of rhetoric, none surpassed the message from the Italian patriot Giuseppe Garibaldi and his two sons:

> Heir of the thought of Christ and [John] Brown, you will pass down to posterity under the name of the Emancipator! More enviable than any crown and any human treasure! An entire race of mankind yoked by selfishness to the collar of Slavery is, by you, at the price of the noblest blood of America, restored to the dignity of Manhood, to Civilization, and to Love.

No American in the debates of 1861 and 1862 had linked emancipation with the restoration of Love—it took an Italian to do so. More down to earth was the comment of Karl Marx in one of his occasional dispatches from London for the *New York Tribune*: "Up to now, we have witnessed only the first act of the Civil War—the constitutional waging of war. The second act, the revolutionary waging of war, is at hand."[92]

8

"A New Birth of Freedom": Securing Emancipation

▪

ON JANUARY 9, 1863, a little over a week after Lincoln signed the Emancipation Proclamation, General Richard J. Oglesby, a former member of the Illinois legislature and a future governor of the state, spoke at a war rally in Springfield. The proclamation, he said, "is a great thing, perhaps the greatest thing that has occurred in this century. It is too big for us to realize."[1] Despite his awkward language, Oglesby understood that if emancipation opened a new chapter in American history, its long-term consequences were impossible to predict or even, in some ways, to comprehend.

When Oglesby spoke, emancipation was neither complete nor secure. The Confederate government vowed not to recognize the liberty of the slaves Lincoln had declared free. Indeed, as the fortunes of war ebbed and flowed, blacks who had tasted freedom behind Union lines sometimes found themselves reenslaved by advancing Confederate forces. In the North, Democrats denounced the edict as a violation of the Constitution and an unwarranted redefinition of the war's purposes. When it assembled on January 8, 1863, the Democratic-controlled legislature of Indiana demanded that the proclamation be revoked. Even some Republicans refused to accept emancipation as a fait accompli. In the days after it was issued, representatives of the party's conservative wing, including Orville H. Browning, David Davis, James R. Doolittle, and Thomas Ewing, implored Lincoln to withdraw the proclamation, arguing that it had strengthened Confederate resolve and divided the North. Lincoln refused; it was a "fixed thing," he told them. "The proclamation," he assured one group of visitors to the White House, "has knocked the bottom out of slavery."[2]

"All the logic of the struggle," wrote the *New York Times* in 1863, "leads us more and more toward universal freedom." Lincoln embraced that logic. In his message to Congress of the previous December, Lincoln had called on Americans to rethink their basic assumptions. And between January 1863 and his death, Lincoln would abandon or modify many of his previous beliefs. Even as the military situation remained uppermost in his mind, Lincoln began to address questions the proclamation had left unresolved. These included the fate of slavery in the border states and the exempted parts of the Confederacy, the conditions for "rebel" states to return to the Union, and the system of labor that would replace slavery. As the disintegration of slavery continued and Union victory grew more likely, these questions became increasingly urgent. To secure complete emancipation, Lincoln again encouraged the border states to take action against slavery and made abolition a requirement for the readmission of Confederate states. In public letters and his messages to Congress he sought to persuade the American people of the wisdom of emancipation (he even encouraged Bayard Taylor, a noted poet, dramatist, and former diplomat in Russia, to give public lectures on the liberation of the serfs).[3] Lincoln's racial views began to change, and for the first time in his life, he began to think seriously about the role of blacks in a post-slavery America.

I

AMONG THE MOST RADICAL PROVISIONS of the Emancipation Proclamation was Lincoln's invitation to African-American men to enlist in the Union army. The recruitment of blacks, remarked Congressman William P. Cutler of Ohio, "is a recognition of the Negro's *manhood* such as has never before been made by this nation." For this very reason, the arming of black soldiers inspired as much controversy as emancipation itself. On January 12, 1863, Thaddeus Stevens introduced a bill in the House authorizing Lincoln to raise 150,000 black soldiers. Slaves who enlisted would become free, as would their families, with the government paying monetary compensation to loyal owners.

Only "partisan demagogues," Stevens declared, failed to realize that "if we are to continue this war, we must call in the aid of Africans." But during the next few weeks, Congress engaged in rancorous debate over black military service. "No such strife has been produced by any other measure during this Congress," remarked one member. Democrats and border Unionists denounced black enlistment as the "despairing cry" of a discredited administration, part of a Radical plan to "exterminate" the white people of the South or, at the very least, elevate blacks to full equality. They predicted that white soldiers would find themselves taking orders from "Colonel Sambo," an intolerable insult. They used innumerable quorum calls and motions for adjournment to delay a vote. Amended to bar the enlistment of the slaves of loyal owners in the border states and Tennessee, Stevens's bill finally passed the House. But in the Senate, it ran into further difficulty. Finally, Henry Wilson, chair of the Committee on Military Affairs, withdrew the measure, declaring it redundant since the Militia Act of July 1862 had already empowered the president to employ black men in any military capacity he saw fit.[4]

Having previously opposed black recruitment and doubted blacks' military capacity, Lincoln in 1863 became an avid proponent. In January, he authorized Governor John Andrew of Massachusetts to organize a black regiment. With Robert Gould Shaw, the son of a prominent Boston abolitionist, as its commanding officer, the Fifty-fourth Massachusetts infantry enlisted black volunteers from throughout the North. Abolitionists urged blacks to enlist. "A century may elapse," wrote the *Weekly Anglo-African*, "before another opportunity shall be afforded of reclaiming and holding our withheld rights. . . . Freedom is ours. And its fruit, equality, hangs temptingly on the tree beckoning our own brave arms to rise and clutch it."[5]

Shortly after Lincoln issued the Emancipation Proclamation, the Washington correspondent of the *New York Tribune* reported that the president still planned to use black troops primarily in noncombat roles, not "to put arms in their hands." But Lincoln soon changed his mind. Early in March 1863, he received a long letter from Thomas Richmond, a former member of the Illinois legislature, urging him to press forward immediately with enrolling "the muscle and sinew of the slave population." Unless the government speedily armed the slaves, Richmond warned, "the Confederates will." On the envelope in which the letter arrived, Lincoln wrote, "Good advice." That month, the War Department authorized a massive recruiting effort in the occupied South. This decision may have been influenced by the success on the battlefield of the First and Second South Carolina Volunteers, nearly all of them former slaves, who occupied Jacksonville, Florida, early that month. Lincoln sent a congratulatory message to General David Hunter, noting the importance of black units: "The enemy will make extra efforts to destroy them; and we should do the same to preserve and increase them." Shortly after the battle, Lincoln dispatched a letter to Andrew Johnson, the military governor of Tennessee, urging him to begin enrolling black troops. "The colored population," Lincoln wrote, "is the great *available* and yet *unavailed* of, force for restoring the Union. The mere sight of fifty thousand armed and drilled black soldiers on the banks of the Mississippi, would end the rebellion at once."[6]

Lincoln also instructed Secretary of War Stanton to have Adjutant General Lorenzo Thomas move forward with recruiting in the Mississippi Valley. In April 1863, Thomas delivered a speech to Ulysses S. Grant's army, then in northern Louisiana. Stating that he spoke "with full authority from the president," Thomas declared that the Union army must enforce emancipation and recruit black troops. Any soldier, whatever his rank, who mistreated the freedmen would be dismissed. The performance of black soldiers that spring and summer at Port Hudson and Milliken's Bend in Louisiana and Fort Wagner in South Carolina dispelled lingering doubts about their abilities. Only the operation at Milliken's Bend (where black soldiers rescued beleaguered white troops) was a military success. The Fifty-fourth Massachusetts lost half its men in the failed assault on Fort Wagner. But in all these places, black soldiers performed heroically, proving themselves, Stanton wrote, "among the bravest of the brave in fighting for the Union." Fort Wagner, in particular, was a turning point in recognition of blacks' capacity to serve in the army. The battle, commented the *New York Tribune*, would become for them what Bunker Hill had been for whites during the War of Independence (forgetting that blacks had also fought at Bunker Hill).[7]

By August 1863, Lincoln was writing to General Grant that he hoped "at least a hundred thousand" could quickly be enrolled. Grant responded that emancipation was "the heaviest blow yet given to the Confederacy" and that "by arming the negro we have added a powerful ally." His letter reflected a broad evolution of opinion within the army. To be sure, "aversion to the negro," as *Harper's Weekly* reported, remained widespread in the ranks. Two of Grant's officers resigned rather than cooperate in raising black troops. But Grant himself recognized that the new policy required not only enlisting black soldiers but also "removing prejudice against them."[8]

Increasingly, the army actively encouraged the disintegration of slavery, even in places exempted from the proclamation. "While in the field I am an abolitionist," one officer wrote to his wife from Tennessee in 1863. More and more Union soldiers embraced the change in the character of the war. Few whites had joined the army to abolish slavery. But increasing numbers saw the institution as a barrier to the country's mission of exemplifying "the great principles of liberty and self-government." They now fought for a new nation without slavery rather than the restoration of the prewar Union and accepted the necessity of using black soldiers to that end. Encountering the harsh reality of bondage in the plantation South reinforced support for emancipation. "Since I am here," a Democratic colonel wrote from Louisiana," I have learned and seen . . . what the horrors of slavery was. . . . Never hereafter will I either speak or vote in favor of slavery." All in all, as James A. Garfield declared in January 1864, "the rapid current of events has made the army of the republic an Abolition army."[9]

Black soldiers played a part in this transformation. By the war's end, more than 180,000, the large majority recently emancipated slaves, had served in the Union army—over one-fifth of the nation's adult male black population under age forty-five and about 10 percent of all the soldiers who fought for the Union. Many originated in the border states and Tennessee, where the Emancipation Proclamation did not apply and military service, for most of the war, offered the only legal route to freedom. Here, black enlistment pushed the administration's commitment to abolition beyond the terms of the proclamation. At first, Lincoln authorized only the enrollment of free blacks and the slaves of disloyal owners. In October 1863, however, he extended recruitment to all slaves in Delaware, Maryland, Missouri, and Tennessee, with compensation to loyal owners of $300 (the same amount a free person could pay to secure exemption from the draft). All slaves who enlisted "shall forever thereafter be free." Because of vehement opposition from Kentucky, the War Department did not set up a recruiting post for black soldiers in the state until January 1864, and not until June did it begin enlisting slaves there without the consent of their owners. Governor Thomas E. Bramlette informed Lincoln that anyone encouraging a slave to leave his master, including military officers, would be prosecuted under state law. But by the end of the war, nearly 24,000 black soldiers had served from Kentucky, a majority of the state's eligible black men and a total second only to that of Louisiana. Early in 1865, Congress freed the families of all black soldiers. Well before its legal demise, black enlistment undermined slavery in Kentucky.[10]

"The government," wrote Orestes Brownson early in 1864, "by arming the negroes, has made them our countrymen." To be sure, black soldiers, organized into segregated regiments, often found themselves subjected to abuse from white officers. Even after proving themselves in battle, blacks could not advance into the ranks of commissioned officers until the final months of the war. Their pay, as established by the Militia Act of 1862, which anticipated blacks serving largely as military laborers, was considerably less than that of white soldiers. Black regiments also faced unique dangers. The Confederate government refused to recognize them as prisoners of war (to do so, one southern newspaper declared, would violate the premises of "the social system for which we contend") and threatened them with enslavement, or execution as slave rebels. Some Confederate officers refused to take black prisoners; the murder of black soldiers after surrender occurred in every theater of the war.[11]

Nonetheless, black soldiers played a crucial role not only in winning the Civil War but also in defining its consequences. Just as runaway slaves had forced the administration to begin to make policy about slavery in 1861, black military service put the question of postwar rights squarely on the national agenda. Its "logical result," the Missouri Radical Charles D. Drake observed in 1864, was that "the black man is henceforth to assume a new status among us." This transformation happened first in the army. For the first time in American history, large numbers of blacks were treated as equals before the law, if only military law. In army courts, they could testify against whites, something unknown in the South and much of the North. Demanding to be treated identically with other Union soldiers, the Fifty-fourth and Fifty-fifth Massachusetts regiments refused to accept their monthly stipends and continued to do so after the state legislature voted to make up the difference in pay. Soldiers flooded black newspapers with complaints about the pay issue, dispatched petitions to Congress and the president, and enlisted Governor John Andrew to lobby Lincoln and the War Department on their behalf. The issue, declared a petition signed by seventy-four enlisted men, was not money, but "liberty, justice and equality." The soldiers' campaign persuaded Congress in June 1864 to enact a measure for equality in pay, enlistment bounties, and other compensation retroactive to the time of enlistment for free-born blacks and to the beginning of 1864 for former slaves. In March 1865, Congress provided for full retroactive pay equality. These were among the first federal statutes based on the principle of equal rights regardless of race.[12]

The issue of equal treatment came before Lincoln in 1863 and 1864, pressed by the black soldiers, their families, and white allies. From the outset, Lincoln worried about how Confederates would deal with captured black soldiers. He received numerous pleas to order retaliation if the Confederacy mistreated black prisoners of war, including a letter from Francis G. Shaw, whose son Robert had died with dozens of his soldiers in the assault on Fort Wagner. Another arrived from Hannah Johnson, the daughter of a fugitive slave and mother of a soldier in the Fifty-fourth Massachusetts:

> I have but poor edication but I never went to schol, but I know just as well as any what is right between man and man. Now I know it is right that a colored man should go and fight for his country, and so ought to a white man. I know that a colored man ought to run no greater risques. . . . So why should not our enemies be compelled to treat him the same, Made to do it. . . . I thought of this thing before I let my boy go but then they said Mr. Lincoln will never let them sell our colored soldiers for slaves.

Unbeknownst to Mrs. Johnson, on July 30, 1863, the day before she wrote, Lincoln had signed a military order condemning the enslavement of black soldiers as "a relapse into barbarism and a crime against the civilization of the age." This was unusually emotional language for Lincoln. He went on to threaten to execute a Confederate prisoner for each captured Union soldier put to death, and to assign a southern prisoner of war to hard labor for each black soldier sold into slavery.[13]

The treatment of black troops provided the occasion for Lincoln's first meeting with Frederick Douglass, the black abolitionist and editor of a monthly periodical widely read in antislavery circles. On August 10, 1863, Douglass went to the White House to argue for equal pay and promotion opportunities and the protection of captured black soldiers. In the most recent issue of his magazine, Douglass had excoriated Lincoln for indifference to "the slaughter of blacks taken as captives." At their meeting, Lincoln explained "his policy respecting the whole slavery question." Regarding the pay issue, Lincoln remarked that blacks continued to be widely "despised" and that their enlistment remained highly controversial; unequal pay, he said, helped to "smooth the way," and in time they would receive the same wages as white soldiers. He had been charged with being slow and vacillating, Lincoln added, but "I think it cannot be shown that when I have once taken a position, I have ever retreated from it." As for retaliation for the mistreatment of black soldiers, despite his order of July 30, he viewed this as a "terrible remedy," which would invite an ever-worsening spiral of retribution: "Once begun, I do not know where such a measure would stop."[14]

In the event, neither Lincoln nor the army enforced the retaliation order. Even when Confederate troops under General Nathan B. Forrest massacred dozens of black soldiers who surrendered at Fort Pillow, Tennessee, in April 1864, Lincoln warned publicly of retribution, but it did not come. In May 1863, however, Lincoln suspended prisoner-of-war exchanges, which had been carried on since the previous July according to a formal arrangement between the Union and Confederate governments, unless the Confederacy agreed to include captured black soldiers. Despite Democratic criticism of this policy and petitions from white soldiers in southern prison camps asking him to resume exchanges, Lincoln did not relent for the remainder of the conflict. Early in 1865, the Confederacy finally agreed to exchange black prisoners of war.[15]

In a public letter of 1864, Lincoln identified the need for black soldiers as a crucial catalyst for emancipation. Faced with the alternative of "either surrendering the Union, . . . or of laying strong hand upon the colored element," he chose the latter course. A year after widespread recruiting began, he wrote, "We have the men; and we could not have had them" without emancipation. He came to value immensely black soldiers' contributions to Union victory. Lincoln was drawn to logical, quantitative reasoning. When most Americans visited Niagara Falls, they were overwhelmed by the awesome grandeur of nature. When Lincoln traveled to the falls in 1848, his response was to try to calculate the power unleashed by the waters and how much solar energy was needed to cause evaporation. In 1864, he defended the employment of black troops as a matter of "physical force," which could be "measured and estimated" exactly like "steam-power." But beyond mere numbers, Lincoln's sense of blacks' relationship to the nation began to change. In May 1864, Lincoln recommended that Congress provide that the widows and children of black soldiers who fell in the war be "placed in law, the same as if their marriages were legal," so that they could receive the same pensions as white soldiers. A law to this effect was soon enacted. One of Lincoln's secretaries, William O. Stoddard, wrote that "arming the negroes" was creating a "new race of freemen, who will take care of the South and of themselves too" when the war ended. As we will see, Lincoln's first, cautious embrace of black suffrage involved extending the right to vote to soldiers.[16]

In 1864, the reformer Robert Dale Owen wrote of how the war had produced events "which no human foresight could anticipate," including rapid changes in whites' "opinion of the negro." Nothing, he added, "has tended so much to these results as the display of manhood in negro soldiers." Racism, of course, still ran deep, as evidenced most dramatically by the New York City draft riots of July 1863, when black residents were "literally hunted down like wild beasts" and forced to take refuge in Central Park or New Jersey. But two months later, a Washington newspaper wrote of "the dissolving prejudices against the colored man," attributing this development to the service of black soldiers. The widely publicized exploits of black troops helped to shatter long-standing images of docile or barbaric slaves. Even in New York, the presentation of colors to a black regiment a year after the riots drew a large, appreciative crowd to Union Square.[17]

Partly because of the value he placed on the contribution of black soldiers, Lincoln's own racial views seemed to change. There were other reasons as well. Frederick Douglass left his meeting with Lincoln impressed, he later wrote, with the president's "entire freedom from popular prejudice against the colored race," his willingness to engage in discussion without ever "remind[ing] me of the . . . difference in color." Lincoln may have recognized in Douglass a self-made man like himself; according to John Eaton, who supervised freedmen's affairs for General Grant, the president remarked that considering his origins, Douglass was "one of the most meritorious men in America."[18]

Douglass was only one of many accomplished African-Americans who met with Lincoln during the war, the first such encounters of Lincoln's life. Before the war he had had almost no contact with prominent blacks. In November and December 1860, the hundreds of well-wishers, politicians, and office-seekers who visited him in Springfield after his election did not include a single black person. But Lincoln opened the White House to black guests as no president had before. In 1862, as we have seen, he discussed emancipation in the District of Columbia with Bishop Daniel E. Payne of the African Methodist Episcopal Church, and colonization with Alexander Crummell (not to mention the black delegation he urged to leave the country). Subsequently, in addition to Douglass, Lincoln received the black abolitionists Sojourner Truth and Martin R. Delany (whom he called "this most extraordinary and intelligent black man"); black diplomats from Haiti and Liberia; a delegation of five African-Americans from North Carolina presenting a petition for the right to vote; a number of groups of black clergymen; five leaders of the African Civilization Society; and two emissaries from the free black community of New Orleans. In 1864 he allowed blacks onto the White House grounds to take part in marking a national day of "humiliation and prayer." He had daily contact with Elizabeth Keckley, his wife's seamstress and confidante and an educated former slave who headed the Contraband Relief Association that assisted needy blacks in Washington.[19]

Lincoln's encounters with talented, politically active black men and women seemed to soften the prejudices with which he had grown up. To be sure, he never became a full-fledged racial egalitarian. In private, he continued to use words like "nigger" and "darky" and tell racially inflected stories. But not infrequently his humor used irony to undercut racism. One of his stories related how a Democratic orator in prewar Illinois had warned his audience that Republicans would extend political rights to blacks. Lincoln mimicked the speaker who related what would transpire: "Here comes forward a white man. . . . I will vote for [Stephen A.] Douglas. Next comes up a sleek pampered negro. Well Sambo, who do you vote for? I vote for Massa Lincoln. . . . What do you think of that?" Whereupon, Lincoln continued, a farmer shouted from the audience, "I think the darky showed a damd sight of more sense than the white man." Another instance of employing humor to express impatience with overt expressions of racism came in Lincoln's response to a telegram from Pennsylvania that bluntly stated, "Equal Rights & Justice to all white men in the United States forever—White men is in Class number one & black men is in Class number two & must be governed by white men forever." Lincoln drafted a reply to be sent by one of his secretaries:

The President has received yours of yesterday, and is kindly paying attention to it. As it is my business to assist him whenever I can, I will thank you to inform me, for his use, whether you are either a white man or black one, because in either case, you can not be regarded as an entirely impartial judge. It may be that you belong to a third or fourth class of *yellow* or *red* men, in which case the impartiality of your judgment would be more apparent.

When Lincoln moved to Washington to take up the presidency, William H. Johnson, a black resident of Springfield who had been working as his valet, accompanied him. Lincoln arranged for him to be placed on the Treasury Department payroll, describing him as a "colored boy" even though Johnson was a grown man. When Johnson died in 1864, Lincoln arranged for him to be buried at Arlington Cemetery, paid for a tombstone with Johnson's name on it, and chose a one-word inscription: "Citizen."[21]

Lincoln also abandoned the idea of colonization. When the Emancipation Proclamation was issued, the black abolitionist H. Ford Douglas predicted that the progress of the war would "educate Mr. Lincoln out of his idea of the deportation of the Negro." The change Douglas predicted did come, but gradually. After January 1, 1863, Lincoln made no further public statements about colonization, perhaps realizing that such statements had failed both to persuade blacks to emigrate or to reconcile his critics in the northern and border states to emancipation. But later that month, after meeting with an official of the Pennsylvania Colonization Society, Lincoln directed the Interior Department to advance money to a black minister who wanted to establish a settlement in Liberia. In February, Lincoln told Congressman William P. Cutler of Ohio that he was still "troubled to know what we should do with these people—Negroes—after peace came." Cutler replied that he thought the plantations would continue to need their labor.[22]

Throughout the spring of 1863, John P. Usher, a proponent of colonization who had succeeded Caleb B. Smith as secretary of the Interior, continued to promote various schemes. In April, he met with John Hodge, a representative of the British Honduras Company, "comprising . . . some of the leading banker capitalists, and merchants of London" and owner of "valuable lands" in desperate need of labor. Hodge hoped the administration would help him transport 50,000 black indentured laborers to that colony or even "a much larger number." Lincoln gave Hodge permission to visit contraband camps in Virginia "to ascertain their willingness to emigrate." But Secretary of War Edwin M. Stanton refused to allow

Hodge's visit, since the army was now recruiting able-bodied men for military service. "The mission failed," reported the *New York Times*, "and the gentleman went home."[23]

"The recent action of the War Department," Usher commented, "prevents the further emigration from the U.S. of persons of African descent for the present." If James Mitchell, the emigration commissioner, is to be believed (a rather large if), as late as August 1863 Lincoln remained committed to colonization. The president, Mitchell later claimed, alluded to the draft riots one month earlier: "It would be far better to separate the races than to have such scenes as those in New York the other day, where negroes were hanged to lamp posts." Nonetheless, placing black men in the army suggested a very different future for them than colonization.[24]

The fiasco at Île à Vache also contributed to the demise of colonization. Early in 1863, Secretary of State Seward convinced Lincoln to delay the implementation of the colonization contract he had signed with Bernard Kock on the eve of issuing the Emancipation Proclamation. In March, Kock transferred the agreement to two Wall Street brokers, Paul S. Forbes and Charles K. Tuckerman, whom he had convinced that Île à Vache, off Haiti, was the perfect place to grow Sea Island cotton. Later that month, Tuckerman met with Lincoln and persuaded him to approve a new contract with himself and Forbes for the transportation of 500 blacks to the island, even without approval from the Haitian government. Tuckerman then appointed Kock to oversee the project.[25]

On April 17, 1863, Kock and more than 450 men, women, and children embarked from Fortress Monroe in Virginia. Reports soon began to filter back of destitution and unrest among the colonists. It turned out that Kock had declared himself "governor," taken the emigrants' money, and issued scrip printed by himself. When they disembarked, the settlers found three dilapidated sheds; funds that were supposed to have been used to build housing had instead been spent on "handcuffs and leg-chains and the construction of stocks for their punishment." The irate colonists soon drove Kock from the island. Dozens of emigrants perished, and others left for the mainland of Haiti. In July 1863, at a meeting with John Eaton, Lincoln spoke at length of the "failure" of colonization and his distress over the suffering on Île à Vache. In February 1864, Lincoln ordered the War Department to send a ship to bring the survivors home.[26]

Thus ended the only colonization project actually undertaken by the Lincoln administration. The *Chicago Tribune* entitled an editorial on the debacle "The End of Colonization." The disaster convinced Secretary Usher to abandon the entire policy. As he explained to Lincoln, despite "the great importance which has hitherto been attached to the separation of the races," colonization was dead. He viewed its demise philosophically: "Time and experience, which have already taught us much wisdom, and produced so many consequent changes, will, in the end, solve this problem for us also." The Senate launched an investigation, and Congress froze its previous appropriation for colonization. On July 1, 1864, John Hay noted in his diary, "I am glad that the President has sloughed off the idea of colonization. I have always thought it a hideous and barbarous humbug." (The last sentence was not accurate, as Hay, whose opinions generally reflected Lincoln's, had strongly favored the idea in 1862.)[27]

By 1864, although Lincoln still saw voluntary emigration as a kind of safety valve for individual blacks dissatisfied with their condition in the United States, he no longer envisioned large-scale colonization. In a message to the ambassador to the Netherlands that coyly absolved Lincoln of responsibility for his previous advocacy of the idea, Secretary of State Seward explained why: "The American people have advanced to a new position in regard to slavery and the African race since the President, in obedience to their prevailing wishes, accepted the policy of colonization. Now, not only their free labor but their military service also is appreciated and accepted." When Congress that spring debated the constitutional amendment abolishing slavery, almost everyone supporting the proposal assumed that the emancipated slaves would remain in the United States. A few, such as Congressman John Broomall of Pennsylvania, still predicted that blacks would eventually depart voluntarily for a "promised land" in the tropics. This, however, would be "the work of ages."[28]

As Seward's letter indicated, Republicans were increasingly convinced of the need for black labor in the postwar South. Fears of a national labor shortage led Congress to pass the Act to Encourage Immigration, which Lincoln signed on July 4, 1864, allowing employers to bring workers from abroad under short-term contracts. (The act, the *New York Times* assured wary readers, contemplated Europeans, not "Chinese, Hindoos or Turks.") Black labor was essential to what a writer in the *Continental Monthly* called "the vital and momentous question of cotton production." If the cultivation of cotton, by far the nation's leading prewar export, did not resume, economic disaster would follow. Of course, another reason for the shift in policy was that blacks showed no interest in emigration.

The president of the American Colonization Society lamented early in 1864 that many Americans, black and white alike, believed that as a result of the war, "the condition of the negro will be so much modified . . . that the separation of the two races . . . will be no longer necessary; and that whites and negroes will come to be regarded as equals."[29]

To be sure, equality remained a distant dream. The idea of a white America did not die with the Civil War, nor did blacks' own emigration efforts. But colonization as an official policy was dead. Frederick Douglass offered the most fitting obituary. In a reply to a public letter by Postmaster General Montgomery Blair promoting the idea, Douglass dismantled one by one the arguments for colonization. Neither racism nor race conflict were immutable, and there was no such thing as a people being naturally fitted for a particular climate. More profoundly, the idea of colonization allowed whites to avoid thinking about the aftermath of slavery. It was an "opiate" for a "troubled conscience," Douglass wrote, which deflected attention from the necessity of confronting the consequences of emancipation.[30]

The continuing evolution of Lincoln's attitudes regarding blacks stands in stark contrast to the lack of change when it came to Native Americans. Lincoln's paternal grandfather, Abraham, after whom he was named, had been killed by an Indian while working on his Kentucky farm, an event witnessed by the seven-year-old Thomas Lincoln. Not surprisingly, this traumatic incident became part of family lore, "impressed upon my mind and memory," Lincoln later wrote. He mentioned it in the autobiographical sketches he produced for the 1860 campaign. But unlike many frontiersmen and military officers, Lincoln was never an Indian hater. He did not share the outlook, for example, of General John Pope, who wrote in August 1862 when he was dispatched to put down a Santee Sioux uprising in Minnesota, "It is my purpose utterly to exterminate the Sioux if I have the power to do so," or of the state's governor, Alexander Ramsey, who urged Lincoln to approve the execution of all 300 Indians condemned to death by courts-martial in the aftermath of that conflict. Lincoln carefully reviewed the trial records and commuted the sentences of all but thirty-eight. (Nevertheless, this still constituted the largest official execution in American history.) Lincoln subsequently signed a bill for the removal of the Sioux and Winnebago (who had nothing to do with the uprising) from their lands in Minnesota. Overall, not surprisingly, Lincoln devoted little attention to Indian policy during his presidency. He allowed army commanders free rein when it came to campaigns against Indians in the West, with the predictable result that the Civil War witnessed events like the 1864 Sand Creek Massacre in Colorado, where soldiers under the command of Colonel John Chivington attacked a village of Cheyenne and Arapaho Indians, killing perhaps 400 men, women, and children.[31]

Lincoln may not have had any special animus toward Indians but he shared the widespread conviction that they lacked civilization and constituted an obstacle to the economic development of the West. The influences that operated to change his views regarding blacks had no counterpart when it came to Native Americans. Blacks came to be identified with the fate of the Union, but key Indian tribes like the Cherokee, Choctaw, and Creek sided with the Confederacy, making them enemies of the nation's survival. Indeed, Indian claims to independent sovereignty, while guaranteed by treaty, increasingly seemed at odds with the unified nation-state that emerged from the war. Although some 5,000 Indian soldiers fought for the Union on the western frontier, their numbers were too small to raise the issue of postwar citizenship. Lincoln had virtually no contact with Native Americans either before or during his presidency. He spoke in 1862 with the Cherokee leader John Ross, but nothing came of the encounter. In March 1863, he did hold a meeting at the White House with a group of fourteen western chiefs. His remarks were patronizing and illogical. He informed them that the world is round, as if they were unaware of this fact; urged them to take up farming; and ignoring the carnage going on around him, advised them to become less warlike and adopt the peaceful ways of white people. The Cheyenne chief, Lean Bear, pointed out that whites were responsible for most of the violence in the West. While many Americans recognized the need for reform of the notoriously corrupt Office of Indian Affairs (Lincoln mentioned this in his annual messages of 1862 and 1863), the future status of Native Americans was not the focus of a large social movement that pressured the White House for a change in national policy. Perhaps most important, the free-labor vision of the West, implemented in wartime measures such as the Pacific Railroad and Homestead Acts, meant continuing encroachment on Indian land. In his messages to Congress, Lincoln spoke of the need to extinguish the "possessory rights of the Indians to large and valuable tracts of land" and to encourage the exploitation of the West's land and mineral resources by whites, while providing for "the welfare of the Indian." He did not acknowledge that these aims were mutually contradictory.[32]

But if Lincoln's Indian policies are depressingly similar to those of virtually every nineteenth-century president, when it came to African-Americans, he began during the last two years of the war to imagine an interracial future for the United States.

I I

THE SUMMER OF 1863 witnessed significant Union military victories. In the greatest battle ever fought on the North American continent, the Army of the Potomac turned back Robert E. Lee's incursion into northern territory at Gettysburg, Pennsylvania. On July 4, the same day that Lee's final assault was repelled, Vicksburg, the last major Confederate outpost on the Mississippi River, fell to the forces of Ulysses S. Grant. Severing the eastern and western parts of the Confederacy and opening the entire Mississippi to Union naval and commercial vessels, the battle at Vicksburg was "the most important northern strategic victory of the war." These successes contributed to growing support for the administration in the North and a widespread embrace of emancipation and the arming of black troops. At the same time, however, Democrats, emboldened by their electoral gains the previous year, continued their harsh criticism of the administration. During his presidency, Lincoln no longer gave long public speeches to disseminate his views. But he did issue widely reprinted public letters to explain his policies. These played a major role in wartime politics and in solidifying support for emancipation.[33]

In May 1863 a group of New York Democrats headed by the banker and railroad magnate Erastus Corning dispatched a letter to the president protesting the arrest and trial by military tribunal of former congressman Clement Vallandigham of Ohio. Convicted of violating an order of General Ambrose Burnside, who commanded the Department of the Ohio, which included Ohio, Indiana, and Illinois, prohibiting the expression of "sympathy for the enemy," Vallandigham was exiled to the Confederacy. His ordeal made him a rallying point for Lincoln's critics. Vallandigham made his way to Canada, ensconced himself in a hotel just across from Detroit, and received a steady stream of visitors from the United States. In June, Ohio Democrats nominated him as their candidate for governor. Democrats, joined by some Republicans, also expressed unhappiness with other restrictions on civil liberties, such as the suspension of the writ of habeas corpus, the holding of military trials where civilian courts were in operation, and the suppression of Democratic newspapers like the *Chicago Times*, temporarily closed by the overzealous Burnside around the time of Vallandigham's nomination. Such policies, wrote Secretary of the Navy Welles in his diary, "disregard those great principles on which our government and institutions rest."[34]

Welles was certain that Lincoln regretted what had been done, and indeed, the president ordered Secretary of War Stanton to allow the *Chicago Times* to resume publication. But on June 11, 1863, Lincoln sent to the *New York Tribune* a reply to the Corning protest, strongly defending his limitation of civil liberties. He accused Vallandigham of giving speeches that actively discouraged enlistment and promoted desertion, which was why, Lincoln claimed, he came under military jurisdiction. In an oft-quoted sentence, he asked, "Must I shoot a simple-minded soldier boy who deserts, while I must not touch a hair of a wiley agitator who induces him to desert?" But Lincoln went well beyond this one case. He condemned persons guilty of disloyalty, among whom he identified individuals who actively aided the Confederacy as well as those who dared to raise the issue of freedom of speech or who did not avow support for the war effort. Not only the outright critic, but the man who "talks ambiguously" in support of the Union or "stands by and says nothing" assisted the enemy. Two weeks later, Lincoln addressed a similar letter to another group who condemned violations of "free thought, free speech, and a free press." "Your attitude," Lincoln responded, "encourages desertion, resistance to the draft, and the like."[35]

Lincoln was no dictator. Elections took place as scheduled throughout the war, and the Democratic press continued to criticize the administration in the harshest terms. But neither did he possess a modern sensitivity to the importance of civil liberties. He believed that actions that in normal times would violate the Constitution became legal in wartime, emancipation itself being a salient example. His stance reflected how the war, which created a newly empowered nation-state with an unprecedented impact on Americans' everyday lives, also inspired an upsurge of patriotism and a new identification of democracy and liberty with national authority. "One nation—one government—one universal freedom" would be the war's result, declared a writer in the *Continental Monthly*. This frame of mind flowed easily into the equation of dissent with treason and of patriotism with unquestioning support for government policies. Republicans harped on these themes in political campaigns. One 1863 pamphlet, entitled *Unconditional Loyalty*, declared that in times of crisis, the "first and most sacred duty of loyal citizens" was "to rally round the president—without question or dispute." Given his own intense nationalism, it is not surprising that Lincoln seemed to share this outlook. Of course, by 1863, support for the nation and the president also meant support for emancipation. "If we are not now abolitionists, in the old sense," the political essayist Sidney George Fisher wrote in his diary in October 1863, "we are emancipationists and wish to see slavery destroyed since it has attempted to destroy the nation."[36]

Lincoln designed his public letters to influence public opinion, not just respond to a few individuals. He had already done this in his reply to Horace Greeley in 1862 and would do so again in August 1863, when he sent a letter to James C. Conkling declining an invitation to speak at the Illinois Republican Convention. Lincoln crafted the language with care and instructed Conkling to "read it slowly." He was mortified when a copy appeared in a number of newspapers "botched up." The Conkling letter offered a sharp rebuke to those "dissatisfied with me about the negro" and a long defense of the Emancipation Proclamation and black military service. Borrowing language from a letter he had recently received from General Grant, Lincoln called these policies "the heaviest blow yet dealt to the rebellion." He directly challenged criticism of the proclamation's legality: slaves were property, he wrote, and "the law of war" enabled a commander in chief to seize property "when needed." He celebrated the patriotism of black soldiers, contrasting it with the disloyalty of his white critics:

> Negroes, like other people, act upon motives. Why should they do any thing for us, if we will do nothing for them? If they stake their lives for us, they must be prompted by the strongest motive—even the promise of freedom. And the promise being made, must be kept. . . .
>
> Peace does not appear so distant as it did. . . . And then, there will be some black men who can remember that, with silent tongue, and clenched teeth, and steady eye, and well-poised bayonet, they have helped mankind on to this great consummation; while, I fear, there will be some white ones, unable to forget that, with malignant heart, and deceitful speech, they have strove to hinder it.[37]

Lincoln's public letters proved enormously popular. "No document issued since your inauguration," wrote a Republican from Philadelphia of the Corning letter, "has done more to satisfy the public mind." "All the loyal papers" printed the letter and the Loyal Publication Society circulated over half a million copies. A Republican newspaper praised the "penetrating common sense" of the Conkling letter, predicting that its "plain and honest language" would resonate more deeply among northerners than the "rhetorical artifices" of other politicians. The wide circulation of Lincoln's letters contributed to the stunning reversal of the results of 1862 in the state elections of 1863. These, in effect, amounted to a referendum on the vast changes the country had experienced in the past year. Republicans carried every major statewide race and increased their majority in Congress. In the closely watched governor's election in Ohio, Vallandigham received only 40 percent of the vote, well below the Democrats' usual total.[38]

Two weeks after the Republican triumph, Lincoln traveled by train to Gettysburg to dedicate a military cemetery at the site of the battle in which 8,000 men had lost their lives. This was one of the very few times during his presidency that Lincoln left Washington to deliver a speech. On the day of his address, November 19, 1863, Lincoln had to wait while the featured speaker, the orator Edward Everett, delivered a florid two-hour speech presenting a detailed history of the battle interspersed with references to classical antiquity and political philosophy. Then followed a period in which the crowd of 15,000 stretched their limbs, moved about, and relaxed, followed by an ode performed by the Maryland Musical Association. Finally, his friend Ward Hill Lamon, marshal of the District of Columbia, introduced the president. Lincoln's remarks took a little over two minutes. His theme was the war's transcendent significance:

Four score and seven years ago our fathers brought forth on this continent, a new nation, conceived in Liberty, and dedicated to the proposition that all men are created equal.

Now we are engaged in a great civil war, testing whether that nation, or any nation so conceived and so dedicated, can long endure. We are met on a great battle-field of that war. We have come to dedicate a portion of that field, as a final resting place for those who here gave their lives that that nation might live. It is altogether fitting and proper that we should do this.

But, in a larger sense, we can not dedicate—we can not consecrate—we can not hallow—this ground. The brave men, living and dead, who struggled here, have consecrated it, far above our poor power to add or detract. The world will little note, nor long remember what we say here, but it can never forget what they did here. It is for us the living, rather, to be dedicated here to the unfinished work which they who fought here have thus far so nobly advanced. It is rather for us to be here dedicated to the great task remaining before us—that from these honored dead we take increased devotion to that cause for which they gave the last full measure of devotion—that we here highly resolve that these dead shall not have died in vain—that this nation, under God, shall have a new birth of freedom—and that government of the people, by the people, for the people, shall not perish from the earth.[39]

Some observers immediately recognized the genius of the Gettysburg Address. It was "a perfect gem," declared the *Springfield Republican*, "deep in feeling, compact in thought and expression," a model of "verbal perfection and beauty" that would "well repay" multiple readings. The day after the dedication, Edward Everett wrote to Lincoln, "I should be glad, if I could flatter myself that I came as near to the central idea of the occasion, in two hours, as you did in two minutes." Many Democrats, however, denounced Lincoln for unilaterally redefining the war's purpose, which, they insisted, had nothing to do with equality. The founders, wrote the *Chicago Times*, rejected the idea "that negroes were their equals. . . . How dare, he, then, standing on the [soldiers'] graves, misstate the cause for which they died, and libel the statesmen who founded the government?"[40]

As early as his Lyceum speech of 1838, Lincoln had identified the United States as "a political edifice of liberty and equal rights" and the idea of democratic self-government as the core principle of the American polity. In other ways, however, his language and argument at Gettysburg were new. The cadences and language—hallow, consecrate, a new birth—were more overtly biblical than in past speeches. He had never before used the opening language, which recalled a passage from one of the Psalms but perhaps was suggested by Speaker Galusha Grow's remarks at the convening of the special session of Congress in July 1861. (Grow, like Lincoln, identified July 4, 1776, as the date of the nation's creation, but his math was faulty—his "fourscore years ago" counted back to 1781.) The Gettysburg Address also contained a subtle but significant shift in wording. Since the mid-1840s, in referring to the United States

Lincoln had generally used the word "Union," a polity composed of individual states, rather than "nation," a unitary entity. In his message to Congress of July 1861, Lincoln had referred to the Union over forty times and the nation only three. Now, he spoke of the nation five times and did not mention the Union at all. In this, the speech reflected the explosive growth of national self-consciousness that arose from the Civil War.[41]

Lincoln did not explicitly mention either slavery or emancipation at Gettysburg. But no one could mistake the meaning of the "new birth of freedom" to which he alluded. The Gettysburg Address offered a powerful definition of the reborn nation that was to emerge from the Civil War as a land of both liberty and equality. Left unanswered was the question of how fully blacks would share in that promise in a nation where they had never known it, and whether they would finally be recognized as part of "the people" on whom, Lincoln's concluding words declared, the government rested. But so long as emancipation remained incomplete, securing abolition, not defining equality, remained Lincoln's immediate concern. Three weeks after he spoke at Gettysburg, Lincoln returned to this question when he outlined for the first time a plan for what was already being called Reconstruction: how to govern southern areas that came under federal control and under what conditions to restore them to the Union.

Lincoln had insisted from the war's outset that legally the Confederate states remained in the Union, which, among other things, meant that they retained authority over slavery within their borders. In the first part of 1862, Radicals in Congress had advanced an alternative approach. Charles Sumner presented resolutions to the Senate stating that the seceding states had committed suicide as political entities and reverted to territorial status. This meant that Congress could govern them directly, and implied the termination of those "local institutions" that depended for their existence on state law, chief among them slavery. In the House, James Ashley, the Radical from Ohio, introduced a bill to establish territorial governments in the occupied South. Democrats, border-state members of Congress, and moderate Republicans vehemently opposed these measures, considering them "virtually an ordinance of secession," since they seemed to accept the idea that Confederate states were no longer fully parts of the Union. With no agreement in sight, the House in March 1862 tabled Ashley's proposal.[42]

The Emancipation Proclamation transformed the problem of Reconstruction, for it implied that the Confederate states could not resume their prewar status without acknowledging the destruction of slavery. During 1863, Lincoln repeatedly urged military governors in the South to organize loyal governments that abolished slavery, even in states all or part of which he had exempted from the proclamation. "Get emancipation into your new state government—Constitution," he urged Andrew Johnson, Tennessee's military governor, in September. Two months later, he insisted that any new government established in Louisiana must be committed to the end of slavery. People had to take sides, he wrote, "be *for* and not *against* . . . permanent freedom."[43]

At the same time, however, Lincoln repeatedly suggested in 1863 that he would prefer a gradual end to slavery and a probationary period of black apprenticeship, as he had proposed in his 1849 bill for abolition in the District of Columbia. He had long feared that immediate emancipation would produce chaos. A week after issuing the Emancipation Proclamation, he wrote to Major General John A. McClernand, who commanded part of Grant's army engaged in the attack on Vicksburg, that southern states were welcome to "adopt systems of apprenticeship for the colored people, conforming substantially to the most approved plans of gradual emancipation." In July 1863, he suggested to General Stephen A. Hurlbut that "some plan, substantially being gradual emancipation, would be better for both white and black," and urged him to press Arkansas Unionists to move in this direction. In November, on the day he departed for Gettysburg, Lincoln told a Texas Unionist that the sudden destruction of slavery would "be attended with great ruin." He would be "glad to see" the state adopt a plan of "gradual emancipation."[44]

How gradual abolition would work remained quite unclear. Would those who had been declared free on January 1, 1863, revert for a time to slavery or apprenticeship? Gradual emancipation had been carried out by northern states in the early republic. But its recent history, especially in the British Caribbean, was hardly encouraging. In Illinois, as Lincoln must have known, apprenticeship had served as a means of continuing slavery, not a pathway to freedom. Rather than carefully thought-out proposals, Lincoln's references to gradualism and apprenticeship were efforts to make emancipation and reunion palatable to white southerners even as he insisted that Confederate states could not return to the Union without taking steps to ensure the future end of slavery. Secretary of the Treasury Chase thought the effort misguided. "The Southern people whom we must conciliate," he wrote in April 1863, "are the black Americans" and those whites willing to adjust immediately to a free-labor system. "All others," he believed, "are naturally in sympathy with the rebellion." Orestes Brownson pointed out that to allow slaveholders to retain control of black labor for a time appeared inconsistent with the logic of the Emancipation Proclamation. If the justification for ending slavery was military necessity, he observed, then abolition "must be immediate."[45]

Despite Lincoln's talk of gradualism and other actions to encourage southern Unionism, his efforts to create loyal governments in the South in 1863 failed to produce results. Andrew Johnson did not create a functioning civilian government in Tennessee, and nothing was accomplished by military governors in North Carolina, Arkansas, or Louisiana. A new approach seemed imperative. Moreover, in the wake of Union victories in the summer of 1863, the question of Reconstruction suddenly moved to the forefront of political debate, exacerbating factionalism within the Republican party. "The whole political community," noted the *New York Times*, "seems to be plunging headlong into this discussion." The *Times* urged Lincoln not to make the abolition of slavery a requirement for reunion. In October, Postmaster General Montgomery Blair delivered an intemperate speech at Rockville, Maryland, denouncing an article in the *Atlantic Monthly* by Charles Sumner that outlined the doctrine of state suicide and called for equal rights for the emancipated slaves. Blair condemned Radicals who, he claimed, wished to "amalgamate" blacks and whites and enfranchise the freedmen, subjecting whites to their rule. He insisted that the seceded states had lost none of their traditional rights, including the authority to regulate the suffrage, and equated Confederates and abolitionists as "equally despotic" extremists bent on overthrowing the Constitution.[46]

One of a series of addresses in 1863 in which Blair, claiming (without authority) to speak for the president, sought to counter "revolutionary attempts . . . to abolish the state governments for the interest of Negrodom," the Rockville speech led to an angry counterattack from Radical Republicans. In November, Senator Zachariah Chandler of Michigan urged Lincoln to "*stand firm*" against conservative pressure, pointing out that Republicans had succeeded in the recent elections by taking "bold *radical*" positions in favor of emancipation and against "slaveholders." As always, Lincoln sought to maintain party unity. On reading the Rockville speech, he remarked that the controversy between Blair and Sumner "is one of mere form and little else." To Chandler, Lincoln responded, "I hope to 'stand firm' enough not to go backward, and yet not go forward fast enough to wreck the country's cause."[47]

On December 2, 1863, to the roar of 100 cannons, Thomas Crawford's colossal *Statue of Freedom* was hoisted to the top of the Capitol dome. Eight years earlier, Jefferson Davis, then the secretary of war, had ordered the statue's original design changed, for the female figure wore a cap of liberty, a symbol in ancient Rome of emancipated slaves. Crawford replaced the cap with a feathered helmet. He could hardly have imagined that by the time the statue was completed, the liberty of hundreds of thousands of slaves would be real, not simply allegoric. Six days after the statue was put in place, Lincoln sent his annual message to the opening session of the Thirty-eighth Congress, along with the Proclamation of Amnesty and Reconstruction intended to secure the reuniting of the nation. Senator William E. Chandler of New Hampshire had written in November that Republicans desired "a policy radical enough *to destroy slavery*, conservative enough *to save the nation*." This is what Lincoln sought to provide.[48]

Lincoln's annual message included a long defense of emancipation and the enlisting of black soldiers. When announced the previous January, he reflected, these initiatives "gave to the future a new aspect, about which hope, and fear, and doubt contended." Now, eleven months later, fear and doubt had dissipated. There had been no "servile insurrection," and black soldiers had proven themselves in battle. The northern public had endorsed the new policy in the recent elections. Thus, what remained was hope. And for the nation to turn its back on the promise of freedom would not only relinquish an important "lever of power," but constitute "a cruel and an astounding breach of faith."

Lincoln then announced a new approach to Reconstruction. He offered full pardon and the restoration of all rights "except as to slaves" to Confederates who took an oath of future loyalty and pledged to accept the abolition of slavery "so long and so far as not modified or declared void by decision of the Supreme Court"—an odd statement that reflected his continuing fear of the possible abrogation of the Emancipation Proclamation. Lincoln excluded from pardon high-ranking civil and military officers and those who had abused Union soldiers, including black troops, whom he specifically singled out. When in any state the number of loyal southerners, defined as those who took the oath, amounted to 10 percent of the votes cast in 1860, this minority could establish a new state government. Voting qualifications from before the war would apply, excluding blacks from the franchise. The new state constitution must abolish slavery and provide for the education of the freedpeople, but it could also adopt temporary measures regarding the freedpeople "consistent . . . with their present condition as a laboring, landless, and homeless class." This, Lincoln observed, would limit the "confusion and destitution" resulting from a "total revolution of labor." The new governments would be entitled to representation in Washington, although Lincoln took care to note that each house of Congress possessed the right to judge the qualifications of its own members. As for the border states to which Reconstruction did not apply since they remained in the Union, Lincoln declared that he remained committed to the plan he had "so earnestly urged upon this subject"—gradual, compensated emancipation.[49]

Clearly, Lincoln did not envision Reconstruction as embodying a social and political revolution beyond the abolition of slavery. His approach recognized the traditional power of the states to determine the civil and political rights of their inhabitants. He had always believed in the existence of a considerable body of Unionist whites and reluctant secessionists in the Confederacy and assumed that they would step forward to accept his terms. This militated in favor of leniency and against any pressure for black rights in the reconstructed South. Black suffrage would alienate such men, while the invitation to regulate the transition from slave to free labor, Lincoln explained, would make them "more ready" to accept his terms.

Lincoln's Ten Percent Plan would soon arouse considerable opposition from the Radicals. But when it was announced, as the *Chicago Tribune* observed, "all shades of opinion among loyal men" endorsed it. The conservative Republican press called the plan "the best that has yet been proposed." It praised Lincoln for avoiding "abstract dogmas" like state suicide or the reversion of states to territories. While Lincoln eschewed their reckless race-mongering, the Blairs expressed approval since Lincoln had endorsed "*our speciality*": state control over "local law"—law, that is, regulating blacks. Radicals, however, also praised the plan, since it recognized that the states were not in their traditional constitutional position. "If the old state is still a state in the Union," Orestes Brownson asked, how could the president authorize one-tenth of the voters to establish a new government? Noting the praise Lincoln received from both wings of his party, the *New York Herald* quipped, "The art of riding two horses is not confined to the circus."[50]

With the fate of emancipation still in some ways in the balance, the "pivotal point of the whole message," the journalist Whitelaw Reid wrote, was its treatment of slavery. Charles Sumner was thrilled. "He makes emancipation the corner-stone of reconstruction," he wrote, "and I am ready to accept any system which promises this result." Because in this respect it rejected the position of conservative Republicans, one Boston newspaper declared that the message announced Lincoln's "conversion to the radical programme." Before Lincoln sent his message to Congress, Secretary of the Treasury Chase urged him, unsuccessfully, to drop the allusions to apprenticeship (which he considered "virtual reenslavement") and a possible court ruling revoking the proclamation, and to modify it to allow "loyal citizens" to vote. But black suffrage had not yet become a major public issue. More important to most Radicals was that the idea of restoring the prewar Union—a Union with slavery—was dead.[51]

It would be a mistake to see Lincoln's message as announcing a blueprint for Reconstruction from which he was determined never to deviate. The reporter Noah Brooks, who spoke regularly with the president, described the program as an outline, not a "finality." Indeed, he wrote, "it is obvious that we are at sea in this whole matter of Reconstruction." Rather than a design for the postwar South, the Ten Percent Plan, in the words of the *Philadelphia Inquirer*, was "a war measure," a strategy to encourage southern Unionism and make emancipation secure. Denying participation to both blacks and the disloyal majority of whites, the governments established under Lincoln's proclamation would clearly lack full legitimacy. The *New York World* called these governments inverted pyramids in which a few thousand voters would determine the destiny of entire states. Fourteen hundred men, it pointed out, could establish a government in Florida and send two senators to Washington. Lincoln offered no explanation of how he had arrived at the 10 percent figure, although it clearly suggested a desire to organize new governments quickly. But in strictly military terms, for 10 percent of the voters of 1860 to pledge loyalty to the Union and detach their state from the Confederacy would constitute a significant victory. The adoption of state constitutions that abolished slavery, moreover, would counteract doubts about the legal foundations of emancipation and its fate if Democrats captured the presidency in 1864. As a military order, the Emancipation Proclamation could be rescinded by a future president. It was impossible, Lincoln reminded

Andrew Johnson, to know "who is next to occupy the position I now hold, nor what he will do."[52]

The decision to establish loyal governments that abolished slavery had unanticipated consequences, producing serious divisions among southern Unionists and allowing long-excluded groups to demand a share of political power. In both the border states and the Confederate South, Lincoln had to navigate complex political factionalism while promoting the goal of state-enacted emancipation. In doing so, he would allow Reconstruction in some states to diverge in significant ways from the Ten Percent Plan. Despite his stated preference for gradualism, he ended up supporting those who favored immediate emancipation. By the end of the war, with Lincoln's strong backing, slavery had been abolished by state action in the border states of Maryland, Missouri, and West Virginia, and in occupied Arkansas, Louisiana, Tennessee, and Virginia. The willingness to abolish slavery, however, did not necessarily imply a willingness on the part of southern Unionists to grant former slaves equality before the law or recognize them as members of the postwar body politic.

III

THE BORDER STATES that remained unaffected by the Emancipation Proclamation and Ten Percent Plan were the first to reveal the consequences of tying Reconstruction to abolition. As the editor of the *New York Times*, Henry J. Raymond, observed in a speech in Delaware in November 1863, the presence of the Union army had already made "abolition a practical question of local politics" there. But the results varied dramatically from state to state. Delaware and Kentucky remained under the control of conservative Unionists who clung to the dying body of slavery. "Kentucky loyalty," observed Jesse W. Fell, Lincoln's longtime friend from Illinois, "means *loyalty to slavery*." Even though the recruitment of black soldiers undermined slavery in these two states, it survived as a legal institution until the ratification of the Thirteenth Amendment in December 1865.[53]

Elsewhere in the border, by contrast, new groups came to power eager to overthrow slavery and revolutionize state politics. West Virginia, which had entered the Union in 1863 committed to gradual abolition, decreed immediate emancipation by statute early in 1865. But instead of enfranchising African-Americans (a tiny percentage of the state's population),

Republicans sought to retain their hold on power by requiring voters to take an oath of past loyalty to the Union, thus disqualifying thousands of Confederate sympathizers. The same pattern held true in the other border and Upper South states that abolished slavery.[54]

In 1864, emancipation came to Maryland, a state divided between plantation counties that dominated the government thanks to a gerrymandered legislature, and a large region of small farms plus the industrial city of Baltimore, where much of the population resented slaveholder control. Federal troops occupied Maryland from the outset of the war. The "great army in blue," one antislavery leader wrote, brought in its wake "a great army of ideas." By 1863, with large numbers of slaves enlisting in the army or escaping to Washington, slavery in the state was disintegrating. Maryland Unionists accepted the inevitability of emancipation. But conservatives, headed by Montgomery Blair, hoped to institute a plan of gradual, compensated abolition, while Radicals, led by Congressman Henry Winter Davis, demanded immediate emancipation with no payment to slaveowners. Abolition, Davis insisted, would transform Maryland into a prosperous free-labor society and destroy the domination of "aristocratic" planters over yeomen and urban workers. To owners' demands for compensation, Davis replied, "Their compensation is the cleared lands of all Southern Maryland, where everything that smiles and blossoms is the work of the negro that they tore from Africa."[55]

Blair's screeds against the Radicals were motivated in equal part by national and Maryland politics. His aim, he explained, was to "get rid of the slavery question in order that we may get at the negro question which lies immediately behind it." He warned Augustus W. Bradford, Maryland's governor and a Unionist reluctant to move against slavery, that the only way to "foil [the Radicals'] schemes entirely" was "by taking ground for emancipation." By seizing the initiative, Blair believed, Maryland could prevent Congress from interfering in post-emancipation race relations. Lincoln tried to remain aloof from the contest between the followers of Blair and Davis, dividing patronage between the two factions and satisfying neither.[56]

Buoyed by strict loyalty oaths required of voters by the army, Unionists committed to abolition swept the Maryland elections of 1863 and proceeded to call a convention to rewrite the state constitution. In March 1864, shortly before it assembled, Lincoln made his own position clear: "I am very anxious for emancipation to be effected in Maryland," he wrote to Congressman John A. J. Creswell, noting that this "would aid much to end the rebellion." Lincoln added that his "preference for *gradual* over *immediate* emancipation" had been "misunderstood." He still thought that gradual abolition would "produce less confusion, and destitution," but if the convention should "prefer the *immediate*, most certainly I have no objection." The main point was for the friends of emancipation not to allow "jealousies, rivalries, and consequent ill-blood" to derail the abolition of slavery.

In April 1864, shortly before the convention assembled, Lincoln traveled to Baltimore to deliver remarks at the opening of the Sanitary Fair (an exposition to raise money for medical supplies and to assist needy and disabled Union soldiers) and to promote the cause of emancipation. He reflected on how the war had revealed the contested nature of the core American value, freedom:

> We all declare for liberty; but in using the same word we do not all mean the same thing. With some the word liberty may mean for each man to do as he pleases with himself, and the product of his labor; while with others the same word may mean for some men to do as they please with other men, and the product of other men's labor. . . .
>
> The shepherd drives the wolf from the sheep's throat, for which the sheep thanks the shepherd as a liberator, while the wolf denounces him for the same act as the destroyer of liberty, especially as the sheep was a black one. . . . Hence we behold the processes by which thousands are daily passing from under the yoke of bondage, hailed by some as the advance of liberty, and bewailed by others as the destruction of all liberty. Recently, as it seems, the people of Maryland have been doing something to define liberty; and thanks to them that, in what they have done, the wolf's dictionary, has been repudiated.[57]

In this parable, Lincoln himself was the shepherd; the sheep were slaves advancing toward freedom; the wolf, the slaveholding South; and the voters of Maryland, agents of the triumph of the free-labor understanding of liberty. The description of slaveholders as wolves was not the kind of language Lincoln had used before the Civil War, when he generally went out of his way to deny any personal animus toward white southerners. It could be taken to imply that reconciliation would prove difficult after the war.

Over the objections of delegates who proclaimed it "robbery," the convention abolished slavery immediately and prohibited the legislature from compensating the former owners. Reflecting the shift in political power that had taken place, it reapportioned the legislature to reduce the power of the plantation counties, established the state's first free, tax-supported school system, and limited voting to those who took a loyalty oath far more stringent than the one Lincoln had included in his Ten Percent Plan. But only a handful of emancipationists demonstrated any concern for the fate of the state's 80,000 slaves. The school system excluded their children, and suffrage was limited to whites.[58]

In the fall of 1864 Lincoln urged Maryland voters to approve the new constitution. They did so on October 13 by the narrowest of margins, 400 votes in a turnout of 60,000. On the day before the election, Chief Justice Roger B. Taney, a Marylander, died. Many Republicans shared the reaction of George Templeton Strong, the opinionated New York diarist: "Two ancient abuses and evils were perishing together." On November 1, the day the constitution went into effect, Lincoln addressed a group of blacks who paraded to the White House. "It is difficult to realize," he remarked, "that in the state, where human slavery has existed for ages . . . the soil is made forever free." He urged former slaves to "improve yourselves, both morally and intellectually." The air of celebration, however, was soon dispelled as Maryland's courts assigned thousands of black children, against the vociferous objections of their parents, to labor under long-term indentures for their former masters in a blatant attempt to continue planters' access to unfree labor.[59]

The other border state to experience wartime reconstruction was Missouri, whose Unionists remained even more hopelessly divided than Maryland's by what Lincoln called a "pestilent factional quarrel." Conservatives pressed for gradual, compensated emancipation and lenient treatment of Confederates; Radicals for immediate abolition and the disenfranchisement of rebels. Each group bombarded Lincoln with complaints about the other. Lincoln sought without success to reconcile them and expressed exasperation with their ongoing feud. He had been "tormented . . . beyond endurance" by Missouri factionalism, he complained at one point. "Neither side pays the least respect to my appeals to . . . reason."[60]

In June 1863 the Missouri state convention, which in 1861 had become a rallying point for Unionists against the pro-secessionist legislature, reassembled and adopted a plan of gradual emancipation that would not begin until 1870. As a form of nonmonetary compensation, elderly slaves would remain in bondage for life and young ones would work as indentured servants until the age of twenty-three. As the delegates deliberated, General John M. Schofield, the military commander in Missouri, asked for instructions. Lincoln replied by reiterating his belief that "*gradual* can be made better than *immediate* for both black and white, except when military necessity changes the case," but that the delay before abolition took hold should be "comparatively short." Missouri slaves, however, did not desire to wait seven more years for freedom. "The slaves are leaving by hundreds every day," James S. Rollins, one of the state's congressmen, reported. The "self-emancipated 'chattels,'" quipped a Kansas City newspaper, "seem to prefer emancipation without compensation."[61]

Missouri Radicals now launched a campaign for immediate emancipation. In September 1863 the Radicals sent a seventy-man delegation, headed by the St. Louis lawyer Charles D. Drake, to lobby Lincoln for the removal of General Schofield, whom they accused, with justification, of siding with their foes. Two days before their meeting with Lincoln, Frank Blair, in a speech in St. Louis, lashed out at the Radicals, opposing immediate emancipation. Despite his long association with the Blairs, Lincoln tried to avoid taking sides. He would not, he declared, get involved in "the political differences between radicals and conservatives." He refused to oust Schofield but expressed regret that the onset of emancipation in Missouri had been put off to 1870. According to John Hay, Lincoln in October remarked that the Radicals would probably win control of Missouri, "and I do not object to it. They are nearer to me than the other side, in thought and in sentiment, though bitterly hostile personally. They are utterly lawless—the unhandiest devils in the world to deal with—but after all their faces are set Zionwards." In December 1863 Lincoln did remove Schofield, replacing him with General William Rosecrans, who he hoped would play a more even-handed role in Missouri politics.[62]

The following fall, after many more months of charges and countercharges between the two factions, Radical Unionists elected Thomas C. Fletcher as governor. In January 1865, a constitutional convention decreed immediate abolition in Missouri as well as other reforms, including the establishment of a public school system and the end of imprisonment for debt. Thanks to Drake, who insisted that while blacks could not be "lifted into equality," many "disqualifications, prohibitions, and degradations are to be removed," to ensure that "freedom . . . is no empty name," the new constitution granted blacks equal access to the courts and empowered the legislature to establish schools for black children. Drake himself favored black suffrage. But instead of expanding the right to vote, the convention established stringent loyalty requirements. Those entitled to vote approved the new constitution in June 1865.[63]

Unlike in the border states (other than Missouri, where martial law persisted for the entire war), wartime Reconstruction took place in the occupied Confederacy under the auspices of military rule. Here, too, Lincoln pressed for abolition by state action. The first Confederate state to embrace emancipation was the Restored Government of Virginia. Early in 1864, a diminutive constitutional convention of sixteen delegates abolished slavery, restricted suffrage to loyal whites, and provided for a system of public education for white children. Although it had no authority in most of Virginia and could not muster anywhere near the support of 10 percent of the voters of 1860, Lincoln continued to recognize this regime as Virginia's legitimate government.[64]

Lincoln had long seen Arkansas, with considerable Unionist sentiment in its mountainous northwestern counties, as a promising place to create a loyal state government. As soon as he announced his Reconstruction plan, Lincoln dispatched a military officer to the state with forms to record the names of those who took the oath of loyalty. Lincoln advised the military commander, General Frederick Steele, to be sure to have a "free State constitutional provision in some unquestionable form" when a new government was established. A few days later, mindful of developments elsewhere, Lincoln added, "Of all things, avoid, if possible, a dividing into cliques." Bypassing the holding of an election under the Ten Percent Plan, Arkansas Unionists organized a self-appointed constitutional convention, which assembled in Little Rock in January 1864. Lincoln directed Steele to cooperate with it. The delegates quickly approved a new constitution that abolished slavery, restricted suffrage to whites, and authorized the legislature to establish an indenture system for blacks modeled on the one in the Illinois constitution of 1818. They also passed an ordinance prohibiting the further entrance of blacks into the state, except under federal authority. The constitution was ratified in March 1864, with more than 20 percent of the 1860 voters participating. Although it had not been created in accordance with his Ten Percent Plan, Lincoln directed General Steele to recognize the authority of the new state government.[65]

Lincoln devoted the greatest attention to Reconstruction in Tennessee and Louisiana. By the fall of 1863, Military Governor Andrew Johnson, who had persuaded Lincoln to exempt Tennessee from the Emancipation Proclamation, had, at the president's urging, declared for emancipation. But when Lincoln announced the Ten Percent Plan, Johnson and his supporters were dismayed. Horace Maynard, a member of Congress from East Tennessee, where pro-Union families had suffered severely under Confederate rule, complained that the plan displayed "excessive liberality" to rebels. On his own initiative, Johnson added to Lincoln's oath of future loyalty "a hard oath—a tight oath" whereby prospective voters had to pledge that they "ardently" desired Confederate defeat and the abolition of slavery. Despite numerous complaints from Tennessee, Lincoln allowed Johnson's requirement to stand. He saw "no conflict," he observed, between Johnson's policy and his own.[66]

Johnson's conversion to emancipation did not imply a sudden interest in the welfare of Tennessee's blacks. He had risen to prominence in Tennessee politics as a self-proclaimed tribune of nonslaveholding yeomen and condemned the "slaveocracy" for monopolizing political power and oppressing poor whites. He would rather, he said in 1863, see all the slaves sent to "their fatherland . . . and Africa distinct from this earth, as a planet, out of the world's orbit, rather than any injury should happen to the government." But as white Tennesseans resisted his efforts to form a state government while blacks enlisted in the Union army, his outlook seemed to change. Johnson rejected demands by black leaders in Nashville, Memphis, and Knoxville for the right to vote (which free blacks had enjoyed in Tennessee until 1835). But he sketched out a vision of Tennessee's future in which the end of slavery would bring an "era of freedom" for both ordinary whites and emancipated slaves. The freedman would work for wages, enjoy "the fruits of one's labor," and "if he can rise by his own energies, in the name of God let him rise." In October 1864, addressing a black gathering, Johnson, by then Lincoln's vice presidential running mate, unilaterally decreed the end of slavery in Tennessee. "I will indeed be your Moses," he promised, "and lead you through the Red Sea of war and bondage to a promised future of liberty and peace." Early in 1865, having failed to get civilian government functioning, Johnson bypassed elections altogether and endorsed the assembling of a self-appointed convention of Unionists, which adopted a constitutional amendment abolishing slavery without compensation. This was approved in February by those Tennesseans allowed to vote under Johnson's requirements.[67]

Of all the states where wartime Reconstruction was attempted, only Louisiana lay in the heart of the Confederacy. Here Lincoln invested his greatest hopes. Union forces, it will be recalled, in 1862 had occupied New Orleans and the nearby sugar parishes, a region with a considerable population of reluctant Confederates—former Whig planters, European immigrants, and northerners. The city was also home to a community of 11,000 free persons of color, many of them prosperous and well educated. Descended from unions between early French settlers and slave women or from free black immigrants from Haiti, they were strongly influenced by the currents of radical thought that swept the Atlantic world in the Age of Revolution and again in 1848. If the Unionists could cooperate, the prospects for creating a loyal government seemed bright. In the fall of 1862 New Orleans voters sent Michael Hahn, an immigrant from Bavaria, and Benjamin Flanders, a New Hampshire–born teacher and newspaper editor, to Congress. They represented a Free State movement that saw emancipation as the key to remaking Louisiana in the image of the free-labor North.[68]

In order to encourage white Unionism, Lincoln exempted southern Louisiana from the Emancipation Proclamation. But in August 1863, as he was promoting abolition in the border and Upper South, Lincoln instructed General Nathaniel P. Banks to organize a constitutional convention that would abolish slavery in Louisiana. Lincoln reiterated his preference for "gradual, and not sudden emancipation," and his promise that the state could adopt "some practical system by which the two races could gradually live themselves out of their old relation to each other." Nothing, however, transpired. On November 5, Lincoln again wrote to Banks, expressing frustration at the lack of progress and urging him to "waste no more time" in establishing a loyal government. Lincoln made it clear that abolition was the sine qua non of Reconstruction—he would not cooperate with "professedly loyal men" who did not accept the end of slavery.[69]

Lincoln's Ten Percent Plan was motivated, in considerable measure, by a desire to speed up Reconstruction in Louisiana by attracting as many whites as possible to the process. He implored Louisiana Unionists, to no avail, to "stoutly eschew cliquism" and cooperate toward the common goals of reunion and emancipation. Unfortunately, as in other states, Lincoln soon had to deal with an acrimonious division within Unionist ranks. The split began in a dispute over whether a constitutional convention should precede or follow the creation of a civilian government. It was exacerbated by Secretary of the Treasury Chase's use of patronage appointments to build support for his unannounced bid for the presidency in 1864. But increasingly, it came to focus on what rights blacks would enjoy in a free Louisiana.[70]

The contentious issue of black suffrage first came to national attention via Louisiana. The free black community demanded the right to vote in elections to create a new state government. Lincoln, who up to this point had never supported black suffrage, did not object. In August 1863, Secretary of War Stanton, with Lincoln's approval, sent instructions to Louisiana authorizing the registration of "all the loyal citizens" as voters, with no mention of race. Even though the Ten Percent Plan, announced in December, ruled out black suffrage, Stanton sent another such authorization in January 1864. General Banks, however, feared that allowing free blacks to vote would alienate the vast majority of white residents, including most Unionists. "Legislation in regard to the negro, beyond emancipation," he informed Lincoln, would be "unacceptable to moderate men," whose support he considered indispensable. In February 1864, Banks organized an election for a new state government under the prewar constitution, which recognized slavery and severely restricted the rights of blacks. Hahn and Flanders presented themselves as candidates for governor. Hahn's campaign freely used racist language, calling his opponent's supporters "Negro-heads" and "Negro-Equality men," thus exacerbating the split among Unionists and alarming Radicals in the North. In fact, at this point, only a handful of white Radicals in Louisiana supported black voting rights. ("I am only sorry that the epithets were not better deserved," Chase remarked.) Hahn was elected governor, and Banks pressed ahead with plans for a constitutional convention.[71]

Meanwhile, two representatives of the free black community of New Orleans, Arnold Bertonneau, a wealthy wine dealer, and Jean Baptiste Roudanez, a plantation engineer, traveled to Washington to present a petition with more than 1,000 signatures advocating suffrage for free-born blacks like themselves. Once in the capital, the two came into contact with Charles Sumner, at whose behest they added a request that "those born slaves," especially black soldiers, should also be enfranchised. On March 12, 1864, Lincoln met with the two men at the White House. According to newspaper reports, he told them that he had no objection to intelligent black men voting but that to impose this requirement on Louisiana would jeopardize his primary task, suppressing the rebellion.

The next day, however, Lincoln wrote to Governor Hahn, suggesting "for your private consideration, whether some of the colored people not be let in." He singled out "the very intelligent"—men like Bertonneau and Roudanez—but added, "and especially those who have fought gallantly in our ranks." This was the only occasion on which Lincoln intervened in a state's Reconstruction process to promote blacks' civil or political rights rather than the abolition of slavery. Hardly a ringing endorsement of black suffrage, it nonetheless represented a major departure for him. It underscored his growing conviction that in fighting for the Union, black soldiers had staked a claim to citizenship in the postwar nation. And it envisioned a significant departure from the terms of the Ten Percent Plan.[72]

The Louisiana constitutional convention assembled in April 1864. It not only abolished slavery immediately but also tried to reconstruct the politics and society of the state. The constitution made New Orleans the capital and sharply increased its representation in the legislature at the expense of plantation counties. It included forward-looking provisions such as a minimum wage on public works, a system of free public education, and a progressive income tax. "We have changed all the elements of society," Banks wrote. "Rhode Island or Massachusetts is as likely to become a slave state, as Louisiana is to reestablish the institution." But when it came to extending rights to blacks, resistance to change dominated. "Prejudice against the colored people is exhibited continually," reported a correspondent of Chase, "prejudice bitter and vulgar." Some delegates who favored abolition also called for the expulsion of the entire black population from the state, even though black soldiers were guarding the convention hall. The convention petitioned Congress to compensate loyal owners for their loss and ignored Lincoln's "suggestion" regarding partial black suffrage. Only after intense lobbying by Governor Hahn, who showed Lincoln's letter to key delegates, did the delegates authorize the legislature to extend the right to vote in the future and to give black children access to a separate system of public schools.[73]

To Lincoln, the key provision was abolition. He urged the swift ratification of the new constitution and insisted that all federal appointees in Louisiana support it. Early in September, voters in and around New Orleans approved it and elected a legislature and members of Congress. Lincoln hailed the outcome and urged General Stephen A. Hurlbut, who had replaced Banks, to cooperate with the new government. The constitution, Lincoln observed, was "better for the poor black man than we have in Illinois." But Radical Unionists and free blacks denounced the new regime and called on Congress to repudiate it, setting the stage for a battle in Washington over Reconstruction.[74]

IV

A GROWING CONTROVERSY over the army's policies toward black laborers further complicated discussions of Reconstruction. Shortly after Lincoln decreed emancipation, the *New York Times* observed that "if the Proclamation makes the slaves actually free, there will come the further duty of making them work." "This," it added, "opens a vast and most difficult subject."[75]

All Republicans agreed that free labor must replace slave, a conviction reinforced by the war. But many doubted that the freedpeople, having been reduced to a state of "infantile weakness and inexperience" by slavery, could be expected to compete immediately as free laborers. Such observers envisioned a prolonged period in which blacks, under federal oversight, would learn the rules and discipline of the market economy. Others believed that federal assistance created dependence; blacks, they insisted, had the same capacities and motives as white persons and would work efficiently if treated fairly and allowed to rise in the social scale. "What the freedman wants," declared the *Philadelphia Inquirer*, "is education, instruction, and an opportunity to earn a fair day's wages for a fair day's work." "The whole subject," noted the *Inquirer*, "is yet in its infancy."[76]

In March 1863, the War Department, at the behest of Charles Sumner, created the American Freedmen's Inquiry Commission (AFIC) to suggest policies for dealing with the emancipated slaves. Its members— Samuel Gridley Howe, James McKaye, and Robert Dale Owen—were prominent reformers. Howe was an abolitionist and advocate of education for the blind; McKaye, part of Charles Sumner's antislavery circle in Boston; and Owen, an advocate of women's rights and the rights of labor. The commission took testimony from both races in the North and occupied South, sent questionnaires to the commanders of black troops, and pored over histories of abolition in the West Indies. It issued a preliminary report in June 1863 and a final one eleven months later. The commission's recommendations, transmitted to Congress by Secretary of

War Stanton and widely publicized in the North, illustrated the tension between the laissez-faire and interventionist approaches to the aftermath of slavery. The reports called for the creation of a Bureau of Emancipation to exercise benevolent guardianship over the freedpeople, but warned that it must not be a "permanent institution," lest blacks fail to become self-reliant. They emphatically rejected the idea of apprenticeship, pointing to the disastrous results of that experiment in the West Indies, and concluded that the best way of protecting blacks' rights was to grant them civil and political equality and the opportunity to purchase farms. McKaye went further, advocating the confiscation of the planters' land and its redistribution to poor whites and former slaves, bringing about a thorough "social reconstruction of the Southern states."[77]

Lincoln made no public comment on the AFIC reports. He had long insisted that blacks deserved the right to the fruits of their labor. In the Emancipation Proclamation he had urged the former slaves to go to work for reasonable wages. But, as Sumner pointed out, he did not "undertake to say how this opportunity shall be obtained" or how the freedpeople's rights as free laborers would be protected.[78] As the Union army occupied significant plantation regions and conflicts over control of black labor arose involving former slaves, former slaveholders, military commanders, and northern entrepreneurs, Lincoln was forced to begin confronting these crucial problems.

The Civil War witnessed a variety of experiments in free labor in the occupied South. The most highly publicized of these "rehearsals for Reconstruction" took place on the South Carolina Sea Islands, where reformers from the North established schools for blacks and tried to aid them in acquiring land, while northern investors put blacks to work as free laborers on abandoned plantations. Far more former slaves, however, were affected by labor policies implemented in the Mississippi Valley. Benjamin F. Butler had inaugurated this program in 1862, requiring blacks to labor on the estates of loyal planters, where they would receive wages according to a fixed schedule as well as food and medical care. In 1863, General Banks extended this system throughout occupied Louisiana. Banks saw it as "the first step in the transition from slave to free labor." He banned corporal punishment and required that education be provided for black children, while also promising that the army would enforce "perfect subordination" on the part of the laborers. Many freedmen resented the year-long contracts they were required to sign, the low wages, and the rules forbidding laborers to leave plantations without the permission of their employers. They viewed the system as a disguised form of slavery.[79]

In 1863 Banks's experiment was extended to the entire Mississippi Valley. Hoping to relieve the army of the expense and burden of supervising contraband camps and to secure Union control of the Mississippi Valley by settling a loyal population there, General Lorenzo Thomas decided to lease plantations to northerners and local planters who took Lincoln's amnesty oath. Thomas's system of compulsory free labor offered black men the choice of joining the army, working as military laborers, or signing plantation contracts. They could choose their employers, but once having done so they could not leave until the end of the year, or they would forfeit their wages.[80]

After numerous complaints of mistreatment of the freedpeople by unscrupulous lessees, the War and Treasury departments sent emissaries to investigate conditions in the Mississippi Valley. General James Wadsworth, dispatched by Stanton in October 1863, advocated settling blacks on plantations and arming them to help develop a "manly self-dependence." He approved of the leasing system but insisted that wages should be high enough to enable blacks eventually to purchase their own farms. The "great danger," he concluded, was "the tendency to establish a system of serfdom" in the name of supervised free labor. The reformer James Yeatman, sent by Secretary Chase, reported that blacks on leased plantations remained in "a state of involuntary servitude." He urged the Treasury Department, which supervised abandoned lands, to establish a more humane program that would include some land distribution.[81]

In December 1863 Chase briefly took control of the labor system. New rules raised wages significantly and contemplated leasing the plantations directly to groups of blacks. But after an appeal from the army, Lincoln at the end of February restored military authority, giving General Thomas command of "the contraband and leasing business." The Treasury plan, Lincoln wrote, "doubtless is well intended," but he viewed it as unworkable. Because of constant disputes between employers and employees and Confederate raids that disrupted production, Thomas's system did not work very well either. Indeed, the most successful freedmen in the Mississippi Valley were the small number of "independent Negro cultivators," especially those at Davis Bend, the site of plantations owned by Jefferson Davis and his brother Joseph, where the land was leased to freedmen to work as they saw fit.[82]

The administration, in Stanton's words, lacked a "well defined system" for dealing with the transition to free labor. But Lincoln, despite remaining far more concerned with the military situation and securing emancipation, expressed increasing interest in how the experiments fared. In February 1862, when he met with Edward L. Pierce, who had traveled to the Sea Islands and written articles about conditions there for the northern press, Lincoln listened for a few moments and then said he "did not think he ought to be bothered with such details." A year and a half later, however, when he met with John Eaton, whom Grant had sent to Washington to describe his policies for dealing with the former slaves, Lincoln's attitude had changed. He questioned Eaton closely "in regard to those who were coming into our lines: What was their object; how far did they understand the changes that were coming to them, and what were they able to do for themselves?"[83]

Occasionally, Lincoln took steps toward assisting former slaves in acquiring land. Preparations were under way at Port Royal, South Carolina, to auction land seized by the army for nonpayment of a direct tax Congress had imposed in 1862. In September 1863, and again in December, Lincoln directed that plots of land be set aside for preemption by black families at a price of $1.25 per acre, to give them "an interest in the soil." The plantation system would be destroyed, declared the *Washington Morning Chronicle*, and the "heir of the lash" would become a landowner, thus "assimilat[ing] our institutions to the noble doctrine of Freedom." The commissioners in charge of the sales, however, refused to carry out Lincoln's orders. One described the idea of allocating land to blacks as "a wild scheme, that out-radicals all the radicalism I ever heard of." "Sharp sighted speculators" from the North also objected. They persuaded Secretary of the Treasury Chase, who oversaw the land sales, to amend the instructions. When the auction took place in February 1864, some black families acquired farms, but most of the land ended up in the hands of army officers and northern investors.[84]

The Sea Islands, where no native white population remained to conciliate, was a special case. Elsewhere, Lincoln feared that talk of land redistribution would undermine efforts to win southern white support. His Reconstruction and amnesty plan had offered restoration of "all rights of property," other than slaves, to Confederates who took the oath of loyalty. In February 1864 he directed the acting attorney general to exempt from the operation of the two confiscation acts southerners who did so.[85]

By 1864, with support for gradual emancipation and apprenticeship fading, Lincoln was moving toward the idea (anticipated in the Emancipation Proclamation) that former slaves should immediately go to work as free laborers under equitable conditions. That January he responded to an inquiry from Arkansas by writing that he would view "with great favor" a situation in which plantation owners accepted emancipation and hired their former slaves to "re-commence . . . cultivation . . . by fair contracts." He would treat the freedpeople, he added, "precisely as I would treat the same number of free white people in the same relation and condition." Such a step toward instituting "the free-labor system," Lincoln continued, would help to secure the twin aims of the war: to "advance freedom, and restore peace and prosperity."[86]

Soon afterward, mindful, perhaps, of the growing criticism of the labor systems of Generals Banks and Thomas, Lincoln advised the latter that when plantations were leased to loyal men in the Mississippi Valley, care should be taken to ensure "fairness to the laborers." In February 1864 Lincoln sent General Daniel E. Sickles to the Mississippi Valley to report on how many Confederates were taking up his offer of amnesty, how Andrew Johnson's regime in Tennessee was faring, and "the colored people—how they get along as soldiers, as laborers in our service, on leased plantations, and as hired laborers with their old masters." The redoubtable Sickles, who had lost a leg at the battle of Gettysburg, embarked on a tour that took him to parts of Tennessee, Arkansas, and Louisiana. He enjoyed a lavish reception at a plantation near New Orleans, complete with "some grotesque dancing by the youthful darkies." Whether this enabled Sickles to assess the labor situation in the occupied South may be doubted. When he returned to Washington, he gave Lincoln his impressions of the journey verbally. Save for one letter about illicit trading with the enemy by army officers in Memphis, Sickles did not produce a written report. In August 1864 Lincoln met again with John Eaton and questioned him closely about the emancipated slaves. He asked about "the more remarkable colored men and women" who had escaped, what they might do when they returned home, and "what freedom meant to those who had attained it."[87]

By 1864 Lincoln's thoughts about ending slavery had changed in significant ways. In this, he reflected broader trends in northern public sentiment. Deeply rooted "theories and prejudices," the *New York Times* observed in February 1864, were rapidly being "discarded." "It is extraordinary," the editors noted, "how completely the idea of *gradual* emancipation has been dissipated from the public mind everywhere by the progress of events."[88] The same, it could have added, was true of colonization. No new consensus, however, on the role of the former slaves in the postwar world had emerged. Lincoln himself viewed this question less on its own merits than in terms of its effect on securing white loyalty in the South and emancipation by state action. But in 1864, with Congress back in session, a presidential election looming, and concerns rising in the North over the course of wartime Reconstruction, the question of what should follow the end of slavery emerged as a battleground in national politics.

9

"A Fitting, and Necessary Conclusion": Abolition, Reelection, and the Challenge of Reconstruction

I

"WHAT SHALL WE DO WITH THE NEGRO?" The *New York Times* posed this question on the eve of Lincoln's issuance of the Emancipation Proclamation, and as the end of the Civil War drew nearer, more and more Americans came to see it as the most difficult dilemma confronting the nation. But as Leonard Marsh, a northern pamphleteer, shrewdly observed at the war's outset, this question had as much to do with whites as with blacks. It really meant, Marsh wrote, "how will their freedom affect us?" Or, to put it another way, what kind of society was post-slavery America to be?[1]

The Civil War unleashed a dynamic debate over the meaning of American freedom and the definition and entitlements of American citizenship, a debate that continues to this day. When the Thirty-eighth Congress assembled in December 1863, a writer in the *Continental Monthly* declared, "Reconstruction sounds the key-note of American politics today." According to his secretary John Hay, Lincoln believed that Republicans agreed on most aspects of Reconstruction. "The only question," Lincoln remarked, "is who constitute the State?" But that was the crucial point. Abolitionists, black and white, maintained that emancipation would remain incomplete until black men had been guaranteed the right to vote. Without the ballot, wrote the *Weekly Anglo-African*, freedom would be "unworthy of the name." In a speech at Cooper Institute that December, Wendell Phillips objected to the lack of provision for black suffrage or equality before the law, indeed for any role whatever for blacks, in Lincoln's Ten Percent Plan. Lincoln's approach, Phillips complained, "frees the slave and ignores the negro." Presciently, he warned that the president's invitation to southern whites to control the transition from slavery to freedom opened the door to "poor laws, vagrant laws, laws for debt" that would reduce the freedpeople to a new condition of servitude. Phillips praised Lincoln as "a growing man" whose views had changed enormously since the war began and might well change again. Abolitionists, he concluded, must persuade Lincoln to adopt "a method of reconstruction much safer and better than the one he has suggested."[2]

The debate over Reconstruction was intimately connected to another political initiative in the first months of 1864. As Lincoln pressed for state-enacted emancipation in the border states and occupied South, abolitionists and many Republicans turned to a different route to full freedom: a constitutional amendment irrevocably abolishing slavery throughout the United States. Abolitionists had already launched a "fresh moral agitation" toward this goal, coordinated by the Women's National Loyal League, headed by the abolitionist-feminists Susan B. Anthony and Elizabeth Cady Stanton. In February 1864, two black men carried a "monster" petition with 100,000 signatures to the Senate floor and deposited it onto Charles Sumner's desk. More petitions followed; by mid-1864 the number of signers had reached 400,000. Support for an amendment reached far beyond abolitionist ranks. In March, a correspondent reported to Lincoln that Boston's merchants, who previously believed "that you must not interfere with the slave system," now agreed "that slavery must be utterly destroyed before there can be any solid peace."[3]

Just before Lincoln sent his annual message to Congress in December 1863, Congressman Isaac N. Arnold of Illinois urged him to include a recommendation for a change in the Constitution to rid the nation of slavery. Lincoln chose not to do so. As we have seen, he had decided to pursue abolition on a state-by-state basis as part of his plan for Reconstruction. Nonetheless, such amendments were quickly introduced in both houses. The final language, modeled on the Northwest Ordinance of 1787, was hammered out in the Senate Judiciary Committee, headed by Lyman Trumbull: "Neither slavery nor involuntary servitude, except as a punishment for crime whereof the party shall have been duly convicted, shall exist within the United States, or any place subject to their jurisdiction." (Thus, in the act of abolition, the amendment, for the first time, introduced the word "slavery" into the Constitution.) The Judiciary Committee rejected wording proposed by Charles Sumner based on the French Declaration of the Rights of Man and of the Citizen of 1791: "all persons are equal before the law, so that no person can hold another as a slave." Jacob Howard of Michigan urged Sumner to "dismiss all reference to French constitutions or French codes, and go back to . . . good old Anglo-Saxon language." But Trumbull did incorporate a second clause proposed by Sumner: "Congress shall have power to enforce this article by appropriate legislation."[4]

On February 10, 1864, Trumbull presented the amendment to the Senate. Various acts of Congress and the Emancipation Proclamation, he noted, had freed many slaves but had not destroyed the legal foundations of slavery. The only way of ridding the country of the institution and preventing its rebirth was to amend the Constitution. At first, not all Republicans agreed. Some, like Lincoln, preferred abolition to take place through state action. Others believed an amendment unnecessary; the war, they argued, gave Congress the power to abolish slavery by statute and it should do so immediately rather than going through the cumbersome amendment process. But as time went on, congressional Republicans rallied around the Thirteenth Amendment. Lincoln remained noncommittal. When John D. Defrees of Indiana asked him to endorse the proposal, Lincoln replied, "Our own friends have this under consideration now, and will do as much without a message as with it."[5]

At first, it seemed possible that the amendment would attract significant Democratic support. James Brooks, a Democratic congressman from New York, surprised the House in February by declaring the abolition of slavery "a fixed fact, a fact accomplished." Senator Reverdy Johnson of Maryland became the most prominent Democrat to endorse the amendment. Slavery, he declared, was "an evil of the highest character," and "a prosperous and permanent peace" could never be achieved "if the institution is permitted to survive." Johnson added that by escaping to Union lines at the first opportunity, slaves had demonstrated their "inextinguishable right to freedom."[6]

As the spring went on, however, and election-year politics moved to the fore, Democratic willingness to support the amendment faded. The party's congressmen increasingly reiterated the familiar arguments against abolition, among them that the end of slavery would lead inexorably to "amalgamation" and black political equality. These charges forced Republicans to try to delineate the basic rights that belonged to all Americans, which slavery had denied and emancipation would restore. All agreed that contractual relations must be substituted for the discipline of the lash and the master's authority over the personal and family lives of the former slaves abolished. All denied Democratic charges that freedom automatically conferred the right to vote; this, they insisted, was a matter for individual states to regulate.[7]

Here, agreement ended. In keeping with long-standing traditions of federalism, some supporters of the amendment, like John Henderson of Missouri, insisted, "We give him no right except his freedom, and leave the rest to the States." On the other end of the political spectrum, Radical Republicans embraced Sumner's egalitarian vision. "A new nation" would emerge from the war, declared Isaac N. Arnold, one "wholly free," in which "liberty, *equality before the law* is to be the great cornerstone." James Harlan of Iowa listed among the evils of slavery the denial of the rights to marry, own property, testify in court, and enjoy access to education; presumably emancipation would carry with it these essential human entitlements. No phrase was repeated more often in these discussions than one Lincoln had emphasized in the late 1850s: the right to the fruits of one's labor. Ebon Ingersoll of Illinois spoke of the "right to till the soil, to earn his bread by the sweat of his brow, and to enjoy the rewards of his labor." Republicans assumed that the amendment's second clause empowered Congress to prevent states from denying freed slaves these opportunities. The debates over the Thirteenth Amendment offered a foretaste of the more far-reaching discussion of the meaning of American freedom that would follow the Civil War.[8]

Much of the discussion covered familiar ground. One element, however, was new, reflecting the ideological changes unleashed by the war. Republicans condemned slavery not simply as a violation of basic human rights but as an affront to the nation itself. The institution violated the principle that each individual owed undivided loyalty to the nation-state. "The defiant pretensions of the master, claiming control of his slave," declared Sumner, "are in direct conflict with the paramount rights of the national government." The amendment's second clause embodied this new sense of national empowerment. Traditionally, the federal government had been seen as the greatest threat to individual liberty; thus, the Bill of Rights protected civil liberties by restricting the actions of Congress, not the states. But, as the *Chicago Tribune* observed, "events have proved that the danger to . . . freedom is from the states, not the Federal government." The second clause gave Congress seemingly unlimited authority to prevent actions by states, localities, and private individuals that sought to establish or restore slavery, a startling change in the federal system. The seemingly redundant words "or involuntary servitude" opened the door to congressional legislation against indentures or apprenticeship arrangements such as Lincoln had proposed.[9]

On April 8, 1864, the Senate approved the Thirteenth Amendment by a vote of 33 to 6. The four senators from Kentucky and Delaware and two northern Democrats voted no. The majority included all the Republicans, three Democrats from the North, and five border senators. Because the amendment envisioned immediate, uncompensated abolition by national action, the *New York Herald* called the result a rebuke to Lincoln, a declaration by Congress that "his petty tinkering devices of emancipation will not answer." But in June, in a vote almost entirely along party lines, the amendment mustered 93 votes in the House, 13 short of the necessary two-thirds' majority. Only four Democrats voted in favor.[10]

The Thirteenth Amendment was one of a number of measures relating to blacks' postwar status debated in the first months of 1864. When Congress assembled, George W. Julian, chairman of the House Committee on Public Lands, launched a campaign to repeal the joint resolution of 1862 that limited the confiscation of land to the owner's lifetime. Long an enemy of "land monopoly," Julian insisted that without economic autonomy the former slaves would be reduced to a situation "more galling than slavery itself." Many members still resented what they considered Lincoln's high-handedness when he insisted that Congress adopt the joint resolution before he agreed to sign the Second Confiscation Act. In 1864, each house approved a different measure repealing the 1862 resolution, although no joint measure was enacted. In any event, Lincoln saw the restoration of confiscated land as a means of promoting white southern Unionism. His promise to restore property other than slaves to southerners who took an oath of loyalty meant that the amount of land available for redistribution remained negligible.[11]

Also the subject of prolonged debate was the recommendation by the American Freedman's Inquiry Commission that Congress establish a Bureau of Emancipation to oversee the transition from slavery to freedom. Supporters insisted that emancipation had made blacks "wards of the republic" and that the federal government, as B. Gratz Brown, the Radical senator from Missouri, put it, had an obligation to prevent them "from being made serfs or apprentices" after the war ended. Democrats characterized the proposed bureau as a "sweeping and revolutionary" expansion of federal power. Even among Republicans, the idea encountered resistance from those who believed that long-term guardianship would undermine blacks' self-reliance. "Are they free men, or are they not?" asked Senator James W. Grimes. "If they are free men, why not let them stand as free men?" Lincoln did not express his own views, and Congress took no action before the session ended.[12]

Congress did manage to enact other measures weakening slavery and expanding the rights of black Americans. In June 1864 it repealed the Fugitive Slave Act, which had incongruously remained on the books despite emancipation. The session also enacted the law, mentioned in the previous chapter, providing equal pay for black soldiers. Charles Sumner pushed a number of other measures to purge racial discrimination from the statute book. At one point, Reverdy Johnson complained that half the Senate's time was taken up with Sumner's equal rights proposals. Congress rescinded the prohibition on the employment of blacks to carry the mails (a step Sumner had unsuccessfully proposed in 1862) and allowed testimony by blacks in federal courts and judicial proceedings in the District of Columbia. The Senate also agreed to Sumner's proposal to bar streetcar companies in the District from excluding black passengers, but the bill died in the House. Lincoln was a passive observer of Sumner's crusade; the president, Sumner complained, was "not moved to help" on any of these matters when "a word from him . . . would have saved me much trouble." But Lincoln signed into law those bills that managed to pass.[13]

Another harbinger of postwar debates in the spring of 1864 came when Congress considered a bill to create a territorial government for Montana. No blacks were known to reside there, but Radicals insisted that the suffrage not be restricted by race. The nation, complained Senator John P. Hale, was "calling on this colored race to fight for us" yet remained unwilling to confront the "absurd and barbarous prejudice" that denied them one of the basic "privileges of freemen." But Democrats and conservative Republicans warned of starting down the road to "negro social as well as political equality." Senator James R. Doolittle pointed out that regulating the suffrage was universally regarded as a "right which belongs to a state," not to Congress. Moreover, he reminded Republicans, "a presidential canvass" was on the horizon and the party must not saddle itself with advocacy of black suffrage. Doolittle's argument resonated with many Republicans. The *New York Times* reprinted his speech and the editor, Henry J. Raymond, wrote, "I agree with every word of it." Raymond found it "amazing" that Radicals were bent on "forcing the country into new contests of negro suffrage and negro rights of all kinds." In the event, the House adopted the Montana bill with suffrage limited to whites; the Senate removed the racial qualification; the House refused to recede; and its version became law.[14]

Clearly, Republicans had not arrived at a consensus about the status of blacks in the postwar world. Their differences affected how they viewed the upcoming election. No sitting president had run for reelection since Martin Van Buren in 1840; none had won a second term since Andrew Jackson. Many Republicans seemed uneasy about the prospect of a second Lincoln administration. "You would be surprised in talking with public men," Lyman Trumbull wrote in February 1864, "to find how few when you come to get at their real sentiments are for Mr. Lincoln's reelection. There is a distrust and fear that he is too undecided and inefficient ever to put down the rebellion." Some Republicans suspected that Lincoln was not fully committed to ending slavery. "His emancipation," charged Martin F. Conway, the Radical congressman from Kansas, "is that of Henry Clay, . . . gradual and 'compensatory,' " unsuited to the "new world" the war had brought into being. The moderate John Sherman told the Senate that Lincoln had acted only after the country "became wearied" by his reluctance to move against slavery.[15]

To be sure, Lincoln enjoyed deep support among the Republican rank and file. "The people desire the reelection of Mr. Lincoln," wrote James A. Garfield, now serving as a member of Congress from Ohio. The *New York Times* castigated the president's critics as "monomaniacs" who thought patriotism meant "devotion to the negro." Some Radicals strongly defended Lincoln's antislavery credentials. In a long address in January 1864, Isaac N. Arnold cited the House Divided speech to demonstrate that one of the "great objects" of Lincoln's life had always been to "eradicate slavery." "He is a radical," Arnold insisted, claiming that Lincoln had "exerted a greater influence . . . in forming public opinion" than any other person: "His speeches and writings, plain, homely, and unpolished as they sometimes are, have become the household words of the people, and crystallized into the overwhelming public sentiment which demands the extinction of slavery." Owen Lovejoy also spoke up on Lincoln's behalf. When Lovejoy died in March 1864, Lincoln remarked, "I have lost the best friend I had in the House."[16]

Lincoln's critics found it difficult to settle on an alternative candidate. For at least a year, Salmon P. Chase had been using Treasury Department patronage appointments to build support for an effort to replace Lincoln as the Republican nominee. Chase was notorious for ambition and self-regard, but these qualities had not led him to compromise his commitment to black suffrage, and some Radicals saw him as more likely to implement a racially egalitarian Reconstruction policy than Lincoln. Chase's candidacy, however, collapsed in February when Senator Samuel C. Pomeroy of Kansas circulated an intemperate manifesto calling for Lincoln to be replaced at the head of the ticket. Lincoln's renomination, Pomeroy wrote, would undermine "the cause of human liberty, and the dignity and honor of the nation." Republican reaction was so negative that Chase announced that he would not seek the presidency.[17]

As always, Lincoln sought to keep the party united behind him. In an effort to explain the evolution of his policy toward slavery and burnish his antislavery credentials while retaining support from conservatives, Lincoln in April 1864 issued another of his influential public letters. This one was addressed to Albert G. Hodges, a Kentucky newspaper editor and delegate to the upcoming Republican National Convention. Lincoln, in essence, reiterated the position he had taken in his 1862 letter to Horace Greeley about the primacy of preserving the Union and the distinction between his public responsibilities and his personal hatred of slavery:

> I am naturally anti-slavery. If slavery is not wrong, nothing is wrong. I can not remember when I did not so think, and feel. And yet I have never understood that the Presidency conferred upon me an unrestricted right to act officially upon this judgment and feeling. . . . And I aver that, to this day, I have done no official act in mere deference to my abstract judgment and feeling on slavery. . . . I did understand however, that my oath to preserve the constitution to the best of my ability, imposed upon me the duty of preserving, by every indispensable means, that government—that nation—of which that constitution was the organic law. . . . When, in March, and May, and July 1862 I made earnest, and successive appeals to the border states to favor compensated emancipation, I believed the indispensable necessity for military

emancipation, and arming the blacks would come, unless averted by that measure. They declined the proposition; and I was, in my best judgment, driven to the alternative of either surrendering the Union, and with it, the Constitution, or of laying strong hand upon the colored element. I chose the latter.[18]

The Hodges letter helped to solidify Lincoln's support. Some Radicals, however, continued to hope for a new nominee. At the end of May 1864, an aggregation of Radicals, War Democrats, and others estranged from the administration gathered at Cleveland and nominated John C. Frémont for president. Their platform called for a constitutional amendment not only abolishing slavery but also establishing "absolute equality before the law," although it avoided mention of black suffrage. It also advocated the confiscation of Confederates' land and its redistribution to soldiers and former slaves. This last plank was the only one to cause dissension in the platform committee, and Frémont quickly repudiated it.[19]

Among those who participated in the Frémont movement were Wendell Phillips and Frederick Douglass, both of whom dispatched letters to Cleveland. Phillips condemned Lincoln's Reconstruction policy, which "puts all power into the hands of the unchanged white race [and] makes the freedom of the negro a sham." His course was quite a departure for a man who had previously insisted that abolitionists should remain aloof from electoral campaigns and concentrate on changing public opinion. As one commentator reminded Phillips, his influence rested on his "absolute independence of politics. . . . I think you sacrifice your position, the moment you pronounce decisively for any man as president."[20]

Assembling a week before the national convention of the Union party (as the Republicans had rechristened themselves to attract Democrats) was to meet in Baltimore, the Cleveland gathering had little chance of derailing Lincoln's nomination. Most Radical Republicans remained aloof from the Frémont movement. The *Chicago Tribune*, Lincoln's frequent critic, called the convention "the protracted and noisy travail of a few hundred malcontents." Sumner, the Senate's leading advocate of black rights, did not endorse Frémont, partly because of his close personal relationship with Lincoln and his wife. Nor did Thaddeus Stevens, the most outspoken Radical in the House.[21]

Nonetheless, the prospect of a split in the party posed a serious problem for Lincoln's reelection campaign. No doubt as a response to Frémont's nomination, Lincoln directed Senator Edwin Morgan, chair of the National Union Executive Committee, to make a constitutional amendment abolishing slavery the "key note" of his speech opening the national convention. Morgan did so, and the platform included a plank demanding the "utter and complete extirpation" of slavery via such an amendment. "Tremendous applause" greeted the reading of this provision. The platform went on to demand the "unconditional surrender" of the Confederacy and singled out for praise the Emancipation Proclamation and enlistment of black soldiers. It said nothing about the divisive issue of Reconstruction and avoided the question of equality before the law for blacks other than soldiers, who, it proclaimed, were entitled to the protection of the laws of war "without regard to distinction of color." In his letter accepting the nomination, Lincoln for the first time called for the passage of the Thirteenth Amendment, describing it as "a fitting, and necessary conclusion" to the war effort that would make permanent the joining of the causes of "Liberty and Union."[22]

Lincoln's nomination was a foregone conclusion, but two other questions aroused controversy at the convention: the seating of contested delegations and the choice of vice president. Predictably, rival delegations presented themselves from Missouri. The convention voted overwhelmingly to seat the Radicals, demonstrating how thoroughly the Blairs' racist screeds had alienated mainstream Republicans. The twenty-two Missouri delegates then proceeded to cast their votes for General Grant, the only departure from unanimity in Lincoln's renomination. Delegations also presented themselves from six Confederate states. Some Republicans welcomed them as harbingers of their party's future extension into the South. But critics of Lincoln's wartime Reconstruction policy claimed that no legitimate loyal governments existed in these states. By a two-to-one margin, the convention admitted the delegations from Louisiana, Arkansas, and Tennessee as full members, and those from Virginia and Florida as nonvoting participants. It refused recognition to a biracial group from Beaufort, South Carolina (a state, like Florida, where no loyal government had been established), that included the black naval hero Robert Smalls.[23]

To the surprise of many observers, the delegates jettisoned Vice President Hannibal Hamlin and in his place nominated Andrew Johnson, the military governor of Tennessee. Lincoln made no public comment on the vice presidency before the convention and instructed John Hay, who attended the meeting, "not to interfere about V. P." Had Lincoln worked behind the scenes for Johnson's nomination? It is certain that if he had expressed a desire to retain Hamlin on the ticket the convention would have obliged. Hamlin, however, did not expect to be renominated. His office, he later remarked, was a "nullity," and he had played no role whatever in decision making. More to the point, many Republicans believed that a War Democrat would add strength to the ticket, and Johnson had the added advantage that he was the country's most prominent southern Unionist. When the balloting began, the Massachusetts delegation executed an unexpected gambit. It pushed for the War Democrat Daniel Dickinson of New York, hoping that Hamlin (who lived in Maine) would return to the Senate, replacing the conservative William P. Fessenden, and that the election of Dickinson would force Secretary of State Seward to resign, since two top offices could not be held by persons from the same state. Whereupon Thurlow Weed, to protect Seward, swung the New York delegation to Johnson and other states followed.[24]

This maneuvering should not obscure Johnson's widespread popularity in Republican ranks. All wings of the party admired his "splendid stand against secession." As early as February 1864, the *Chicago Tribune* had reported that "a large and influential party in the Union ranks" favored Johnson as Lincoln's running mate. In any event, most Republicans considered the vice presidential nomination "of comparatively little moment." Time would reveal this to be a tragic error. "I did think it was good policy to place some one living in a southern state—who had been true—on the ticket and favored Johnson," wrote John D. Defrees of Indiana in 1866, after Johnson had unexpectedly become president. "For which the Lord forgive me."[25]

William Lloyd Garrison, who attended the Union convention, was delighted by the enthusiasm with which the delegates greeted speeches denouncing slavery. After the gathering adjourned he headed to Washington, where he had an hour-long meeting at the White House. He left convinced of Lincoln's "desire to do all that he can . . . to uproot slavery." Departing from his previous conduct as fully as Phillips, Garrison endorsed Lincoln's reelection as essential to securing abolition. But if the delegates thought that the Baltimore convention would restore party harmony, events soon proved them wrong. The debate over admitting delegates from the southern states was a precursor to further Republican divisions over Reconstruction. Indeed, shortly after the convention seated the Arkansas delegation, Congress refused to admit senators and representatives who had been elected from that state, declaring the government Lincoln recognized there illegitimate. Lincoln instructed the local military commander to support it anyway.[26]

As noted in the previous chapter, Lincoln's Ten Percent Plan, announced in December 1863, had initially won support from all parts of the Republican party. But the racism openly expressed by members of the Louisiana constitutional convention in the spring of 1864, and disturbing reports about the treatment of black laborers in the state, raised concerns in Washington, as did the visit of the black emissaries from New Orleans requesting the right to vote. The Reconstruction question languished for a time as Congress concentrated on the Thirteenth Amendment and other matters. But on the eve of adjournment in July 1864, Congress passed the Wade-Davis Bill, a repudiation of Lincoln's course regarding Reconstruction. The bill proposed to delay the start of Reconstruction until a majority, not 10 percent, of a state's white males had taken an oath to support the Constitution. Only then could elections take place for a constitutional convention, with suffrage limited to white southerners who could take the Ironclad Oath of past, as well as future, loyalty. (Benjamin F. Wade, who sponsored the measure along with Henry Winter Davis, favored black suffrage but said that to include it would "sacrifice the bill.") Coming two weeks after the House rejected the Thirteenth Amendment, the Wade-Davis Bill also granted freedom to all slaves in the Confederacy, and contained guarantees for equality before the law for the freedmen under reconstructed southern governments.[27]

Viewing abolition by congressional enactment as unconstitutional and fearing that the bill would force him to repudiate the new regimes in Arkansas and Louisiana, Lincoln pocket vetoed it (allowed it to die by not signing it before Congress adjourned). Lincoln obviously felt strongly about the measure. He almost always went along with congressional enactments; this was one of only a handful of vetoes during his entire presidency and the only one of a bill of any significance. In his veto message, Lincoln called again for ratification of the Thirteenth Amendment and added that he had no objection if any southern state voluntarily adopted the Wade-Davis plan, hardly a likely occurrence. If this was an effort at conciliation, it did not succeed. The bill's authors issued a public statement accusing Lincoln of exercising "dictatorial usurpation" and of surreptitiously seeking to keep slavery alive despite the Emancipation Proclamation. Like the

Pomeroy circular of the previous February, the Wade-Davis manifesto backfired; even Radical newspapers denounced it as "ill-tempered." But this should not obscure the fact that the bill had won overwhelming support among congressional Republicans. Even moderates were convinced that Congress had a role to play in Reconstruction and desired "something more Radical" than Lincoln's Ten Percent Plan.[28]

These debates revealed significant differences in Republicans' approach to Reconstruction. Lincoln saw Reconstruction primarily as an adjunct of the war effort—a way of undermining the Confederacy, rallying southern white Unionists, and securing emancipation. Radicals believed Reconstruction should be postponed until after the war (as the Wade-Davis Bill clearly envisioned in the requirement that a majority of whites take an oath of loyalty) and that the federal government should attempt to ensure basic justice to the emancipated slaves. At this point, equality before the law, not black suffrage, was the key issue for most congressional Republicans. But some already wondered whether truly loyal governments could be established without black votes, given that, as the Massachusetts Radical George Boutwell pointed out, in many parts of the South the freedmen "are almost the only people who are trustworthy supporters of the Union." "The whole subject of Reconstruction is beset with difficulty," Secretary of the Navy Welles noted in his diary. But the immediate task for Republicans was the coming presidential campaign.[29]

II

THE MILITARY SITUATION cast a dark shadow over Lincoln's prospects for reelection. In May 1864, Ulysses S. Grant, who had been brought east to take command of the Army of the Potomac, launched an assault against Robert E. Lee's forces in Virginia. Rather than limiting the campaign to a few days of combat as his predecessors in the eastern theater did, Grant was determined to keep pressure on the Confederate army. Every day saw bloody engagements. After a month of fighting, Grant's casualties numbered more than 40,000, almost the size of Lee's army. Eventually, Grant broke off contact and headed for Petersburg, the rail junction south of Richmond. Lee got there first, and Grant began a siege. Meanwhile, Nathaniel P. Banks failed in an effort to bring the Red River valley in Louisiana under Union control, and William T. Sherman seemed to be making little progress as his army moved out of Tennessee toward

Atlanta. Early in July, a Confederate division under Jubal Early reached the outskirts of Washington, further reinforcing the sense that the war was not being won. A week later, Lincoln issued a call for 500,000 additional troops.[30]

"No man," declared *Harper's Weekly*, "will complain that we are not now making war in earnest." But much of the northern public saw no need for bloodshed of such magnitude, especially with victory nowhere in sight. The result was a crisis of morale and a growing clamor for peace. Even Martin F. Conway, the congressional Radical who had excoriated Lincoln for failing to pursue the war more vigorously, now begged him, "For god's sake try and arrange [peace] with the South, on any basis short of their resumption of federal power on the cornerstone of slavery. . . . The war-spirit is gone."[31]

Almost from the beginning of the war, what the *New York Herald* called "amateur peace negotiators" had sought to bring an end to the conflict. In May 1863, James F. Jaquess, an army chaplain from Illinois, persuaded Lincoln to authorize him to travel to Richmond in the hope of arranging terms of reunion. Two months later, Lincoln approved a letter written by James R. Gilmore, publisher of the *Continental Review*, to Zebulon Vance, the governor of North Carolina, proposing "a reunion of all the States on the basis of the abolition of slavery . . . and the full reinstatement of every Confederate citizen in all the rights of citizenship."[32]

Nothing came of these initiatives. But early in July 1864, with a sense of desperation over the course of the war taking hold in the North, the mercurial Horace Greeley informed Lincoln that two Confederate emissaries "empowered to negotiate for peace" had arrived at the Canadian side of Niagara Falls. (In fact, there were three, and they had been instructed to "harass the Northern government in every possible way" and do what they could to encourage peace sentiment in view of the coming northern election.) Greeley proposed his own "plan of adjustment": the restoration of the Union, the abolition of slavery, amnesty to all Confederates, $400 million in compensation to slaveowners, representation in Congress based on total population (which would increase southern political power, since the entire former slave population would now be counted rather than three-fifths), and a national convention to propose changes in the Constitution. Surely realizing that nothing would come of the initiative but not wanting to seem averse to peace, Lincoln designated Greeley to travel to Canada to meet the emissaries. On July 18, Lincoln sent Greeley a letter, addressed "To Whom It May Concern," offering to receive "any proposition which embraces the restoration of peace, the integrity of the whole Union, and the abandonment of slavery." When Greeley presented the letter, the commissioners issued a public statement expressing "profound regret" that Lincoln had proposed terms the Confederacy could never accept.[33]

While these events were transpiring, Jaquess and Gilmore traveled to Richmond, where they met with Jefferson Davis to present peace terms approved by Lincoln. These closely followed Greeley's proposals with one alteration: the number of congressmen would be based not on the total population of a state but on the number of voters, presenting the South with the choice of seeing its congressional representation reduced or allowing black men to vote. (In somewhat different form, the Fourteenth Amendment passed by Congress in 1866 would also offer the southern states this choice.) Gilmore later claimed that Lincoln approved of the mission in order to demonstrate the impossibility of a negotiated peace. If this was Lincoln's aim, Davis obliged. He indignantly told the emissaries that the war would continue until the Union acknowledged "our right to self-government."[34]

Lincoln felt vindicated. But Democrats seized on the To Whom It May Concern letter to argue that the only thing preventing peace was Lincoln's unwillingness to withdraw the Emancipation Proclamation. Lincoln, charged the *New York World*, preferred to "continue a war for the abolition of slavery rather than entertain a proposition for the return of the seceded states with their old rights." Of course, neither the Confederate agents nor Davis had made any such proposal. But many Republicans feared that Lincoln's prospects for reelection had been seriously damaged. The president, wrote the *New York Times*, should have insisted only on the restoration of the Union, leaving every other question, including the fate of slavery, "open to discussion" once the war ended. Meanwhile, Greeley continued to badger Lincoln to take steps to "stop this useless carnage."[35]

As July gave way to August, northern morale sank to its lowest level of the war. Calls for Lincoln to step down in favor of another candidate proliferated. "Lincoln's election is beyond any possible hope," his old Illinois friend Leonard Swett wrote to his wife. Pressure on Lincoln to modify his position on peace negotiations mounted. On August 16, 1864, two Republican leaders from Wisconsin, former governor Alexander Randall and Judge Joseph T. Mills, visited the White House and delivered a letter from the prowar Democrat Charles D. Robinson complaining that Lincoln's declaration that there could be no peace without abolition "puts the whole war question on a new basis, and takes us War Democrats clear off our feet, leaving us no ground to stand on."[36]

These developments forced Lincoln to clarify his own thinking on the relationship of emancipation to the war effort. He drafted a sharp reply to Robinson, outlining the moral and practical reasons why he could not go back on the proclamation. He linked abolition directly to the recruitment of black soldiers:

> I am sure you will not, on due reflection, say that the promise being made, must be *broken* at the first opportunity. . . . As a matter of morals, could such treachery . . . escape the curses of Heaven, or of any good man? As a matter of policy, to *announce* such a purpose, would ruin the Union cause itself. All recruiting of colored men would instantly cease, and all colored men now in our service, would instantly desert us. And rightfully too. Why should they give their lives for us, with full notice of our purpose to betray them? . . . [Without them] we can not longer maintain the contest.

Yet at the end of this letter, Lincoln added, "If Jefferson Davis wishes . . . to know what I would do if he were to offer peace and re-union, saying nothing about slavery, let him try me."[37] This seems to have been an attempt to shift the burden of prolonging the war to Davis, rather than truly opening the door to a retreat from emancipation. When Lincoln showed the draft to Randall and Mills on August 19, he made clear his exasperation with those urging him to change course. The war was for the Union, Lincoln said, but "no human power can subdue this rebellion without using the Emancipation lever as I have done." Were he to return black soldiers to slavery, "I should be damned in time and eternity."[38]

That same day, Lincoln also read the draft letter to Frederick Douglass, whom he had invited to the White House. Douglass urged Lincoln not to send it. He objected strongly to the final sentence, warning that it "would be given a broader meaning than you intend to convey" and be taken as "a complete surrender of your antislavery policy." Lincoln's main purpose in initiating this meeting, however, was to seek Douglass's advice on how to increase the number of blacks who, in the event that he lost the election, could not be returned to bondage. Slaves, Lincoln said, were not coming into Union lines as quickly as he hoped. He asked Douglass to devise a plan to send black "scouts" behind Confederate lines to spread news of the Emancipation Proclamation and encourage slaves to escape—a kind of official institutionalization of the prewar Underground Railroad. A few days after their meeting, Douglass forwarded to Lincoln a proposal for putting into effect the president's remarkable idea, although nothing came of it as the military and political situation shortly turned more favorable. Soon after their meeting, Douglass wrote that on this occasion, Lincoln "showed a deeper moral conviction against slavery than I had ever seen before in anything spoken or written by him." Yet Douglass found alarming Lincoln's apparent belief that to be free when the war ended, slaves must have come within Union lines.[39]

Lincoln decided not to send the letter to Robinson. But demands for a change of policy continued to mount. On August 22 the Republican National Committee, meeting in New York, concluded that Lincoln could not be reelected. They dispatched Henry J. Raymond to Washington to urge the president to send a peace commissioner to Richmond to propose an end to the war on the "sole condition" of reunion. Raymond assured Lincoln that this would involve "no sacrifice of consistency" and would be a shrewd political move. Jefferson Davis would reject any such overture, thus dispelling "all the delusions about peace that prevail in the North."[40]

Lincoln was convinced he faced defeat. He asked his cabinet to affix their signatures to an envelope containing a document whose contents remained hidden. Only after his reelection did he reveal what they had signed:

> This morning, as for some days past, it seems exceedingly probable that this Administration will not be re-elected. Then it will be my duty to so co-operate with the President elect, as to save the Union between the election and the inauguration; as he will have secured his election on such ground that he can not possibly save it afterwards.[41]

The "blind memorandum" did not mention slavery; it could be interpreted as envisioning a situation in which emancipation might be sacrificed to save the Union. On August 24, 1864, the day after the cabinet signed it, Lincoln composed a letter authorizing Raymond to proceed to Richmond to propose "that upon the restoration of the Union and the national authority, the war shall cease at once, all remaining questions to be left for adjustment by peaceful modes." Were this rejected, Raymond should ascertain "what terms of peace" the Confederacy would accept. The following day, Lincoln discussed the draft letter with Raymond, Senator William P. Fessenden, and Secretaries Seward and Stanton. Overnight, it appears, Lincoln had changed his mind. He and the others agreed that the Raymond mission should not go forward; it would amount to an "ignominious" surrender, "worse than losing the Presidential contest." Thus, after a moment of hesitation, Lincoln reaffirmed the transformation that had taken place in the character and purpose of the Civil War. Begun as a means of preserving the Union, the war, as Seward put it, had evolved into "a popular revolution against African slavery." Emancipation had become an end in itself, which Lincoln would not abandon even if it meant risking his own reelection.[42]

The painful events of August 1864 forced Lincoln to define with greater precision his understanding of the scope and permanence of the Emancipation Proclamation. He had always worried about its constitutionality and what would happen to it when the war ended. The quest to make emancipation more secure helps to explain why he pressed in 1863 and 1864 for the writing of new state constitutions that abolished slavery and why he eventually came to support abolition by constitutional amendment. As the *New York Times* noted, while the Emancipation Proclamation had "set free" all the slaves in areas in rebellion, many had not yet been "*made* free." Lincoln made a similar distinction. He had always insisted that black soldiers could not be reenslaved. He had announced that he would not "return to slavery any person who is free by the terms of that proclamation, or by any of the acts of Congress," by which he seemed to mean those who had actually enjoyed freedom within Union lines. He assumed that such persons would remain free even if the Democrats won the coming election, which is why he asked Douglass to devise a means of increasing their number.

The stark fact remained, however, that in August 1864, a majority of the 3.1 million slaves covered by the proclamation still resided in parts of the South where the Union army had not yet penetrated. What would happen to them if the Confederacy suddenly gave up the struggle or a Democrat were elected in 1864? In an undated memorandum, Lincoln mused on this problem. He would "dread," he wrote, to see slavery survive the war. So long as he remained in office, the government would not return to slavery any person "who is free according to the proclamation, or to any of the acts of congress," unless the Supreme Court ordered it to do so. In that case, "I will promptly act as may then appear to be my personal duty." The implication was that he would resign.[43]

On August 29, four days after Lincoln decided not to dispatch the peace mission to Richmond, the Democratic National Convention gathered in Chicago. The nomination of General George B. McClellan was already assured but the "ultra peace men," led by Clement Vallandigham, who had returned to the United States from exile in Canada, controlled the platform committee. They drafted a document that called the war a failure and demanded a "cessation of hostilities" and a convention of all the states to restore peace and "the Federal Union of the States." Republicans immediately characterized this as a recipe for surrender. McClellan's letter of acceptance repudiated the "peace plank." While implying that he was willing to abandon emancipation (the war, he said, should be conducted for the "sole object" of national unity), McClellan affirmed that there could be no armistice until the South agreed to the restoration of the Union.[44]

On August 31, a New York Republican reported Lincoln as declaring, "I am a beaten man, unless we can have some great victory." Two days later, William T. Sherman's army finally occupied Atlanta, a key railroad hub and the communications and transportation center for the entire Southeast. Sherman's triumph made him a Union hero and dispelled the northern public's sense of futility about the war. The combination of the Democratic convention and Sherman's victory reinvigorated Republican optimism and "had a magical effect towards uniting our friends," as one politician reported. "We are going to win the Presidential election," exulted Theodore Tilton, the editor of the *Independent*, who had been among those hoping to have Lincoln replaced at the head of the ticket. "I have never seen such a sudden lighting up of the public mind as since the late victory at Atlanta. This great event, following the Chicago platform—the most villainous political manifesto known to American history!—has secured a sudden unanimity for Mr. Lincoln." Now it was the Democrats' turn to worry. One party leader reported from Albany, "The Republicans gather heart, resume the aggressive, and are confident enough to bet on the result."[45]

Leaving nothing to chance, Lincoln moved to shore up his support from Radicals. On September 23, he asked Montgomery Blair, whose racist tirades had made him "odious" to Radical voters, to resign from the cabinet. This was part of an agreement, brokered by Senator Zachariah Chandler, by which John C. Frémont abandoned the race (but not before denouncing the administration as a "failure"). The Republican party was now united behind Lincoln's candidacy.[46]

In the fall campaign, McClellan's supporters continued to harp on the To Whom It May Concern letter to demonstrate that Lincoln's "abolition policy" was needlessly prolonging the war. In the event of McClellan's election, declared party leader August Belmont at a rally at Cooper Institute, "you will see State after State leave the Confederacy." But along with promising to restore peace, Democrats in 1864 conducted what one historian has called "the most explicitly and virulent racist campaign by a major party in American history." At the convention that nominated McClellan, speaker after speaker referred to blacks in the most derogatory terms. One spoke of the "flat-nosed, long-heeled, cursed of God and damned of men descendants of Africa." Democratic speakers and newspapers warned of the danger of "miscegenation," a term two journalists for the *New York World* had coined to describe the sexual mixing of the races, which, they claimed, abolitionists and Republicans desired. One campaign lithograph, "The Miscegenation Ball," depicted white men dancing with black women at the Lincoln Central Campaign Club in an atmosphere of debauchery. As in the past, Democratic speakers warned that emancipation would flood the north with an influx of unwanted blacks.[47]

Union, military victory, and Democratic "treason" formed the keynotes of the Republican campaign. "The platform of the Chicago Convention," announced *Harper's Weekly*, "will satisfy every foreign and domestic enemy of American Union and Liberty." Stung by Democratic charges that emancipation was the sole reason the war continued, Republicans initially tried to play down the subject of slavery, although as the campaign neared its conclusion more and more speakers defended abolition on moral and pragmatic grounds. But even Radicals like William D. Kelley, who insisted that the war was "a conflict between two orders of civilization" in which slavery must perish, added that once emancipation had been secured, not only would southern blacks lose any desire to move to the North, but "there are not a thousand negroes in Pennsylvania who would not leave [for] the tropics." Republicans, Frederick Douglass wrote in disgust in October, seemed "ashamed of the Negro." But, along with nearly all the abolitionists, Douglass ended up supporting Lincoln's reelection. He would have preferred a candidate "of more decided anti-slavery convictions," Douglass wrote, but since the choice had come down to Lincoln and McClellan, "all hesitation ought to cease."[48]

Partly to get discussion of the postwar rights and status of blacks onto the political agenda, a national black convention, the first since 1855, assembled in October in Syracuse, New York, with delegates from throughout the North and parts of the South. Some, including Abraham H. Galloway of North Carolina (who had led a black delegation to the White House in May to present a petition for the right to vote), James H. Ingraham of Louisiana, and Francis L. Cardozo of South Carolina, would go on to play major roles in Radical Reconstruction. Written by Douglass, the address of the convention demanded complete abolition, equality before the law, and black suffrage. It condemned the racism of the Democratic party but complained that Republicans, too, remained "largely under the influence of the prevailing contempt for the character and rights of the colored man." It noted that neither Lincoln's Reconstruction plan nor the Wade-Davis Bill recognized blacks as having "any political existence or rights whatever." The convention established the National Equal Rights League to press the cause of equality.[49]

In keeping with tradition, Lincoln did not campaign, although he delivered impromptu remarks to a number of army units in Washington and penned public letters. He spoke of the need to preserve a form of government based on "liberty and equality," which guaranteed to all "an open field and a fair chance . . . in the race of life." "Mr. Lincoln," observed the *North American Review*, "represents and contends for the democracy of free labor." When he received resolutions of support from a group of Methodists opposed to slavery, Lincoln responded, "I trust it is not too early for us to rejoice together over the speedy removal of that blot upon our civilization." Lincoln also sent a letter to be read to a mass meeting in Maryland supporting ratification of the state's new antislavery constitution. "I wish all men to be free," he wrote. "I wish the material prosperity of the already free which I feel sure the extinction of slavery would bring. I wish to see, in process of disappearing, that only thing which ever could bring this nation to civil war."[50]

As late as mid-October, Lincoln expected to lose half a dozen or more states and to be reelected by only three electoral votes. But early in November, he swept to a resounding victory, carrying every state except New Jersey, Delaware, and Kentucky. Lincoln won 55 percent of the popular vote, the largest majority since Andrew Jackson in 1828. Nineteen states counted the votes of the soldiers cast in army camps, and Lincoln won over 70 percent of these ballots. The soldiers, one officer wrote, believed in Lincoln because he recognized that "this war is *not* a failure, that slav-

THE PRESIDENTIAL ELECTION OF 1864

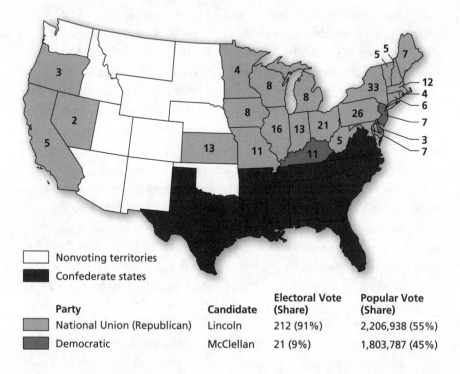

	Nonvoting territories
	Confederate states

Party	Candidate	Electoral Vote (Share)	Popular Vote (Share)
National Union (Republican)	Lincoln	212 (91%)	2,206,938 (55%)
Democratic	McClellan	21 (9%)	1,803,787 (45%)

ery must die." Republicans also strengthened their control of Congress, ensuring that if the second session of the Thirty-eighth Congress did not ratify the Thirteenth Amendment, the Thirty-ninth would certainly do so. To a crowd that gathered at the White House to celebrate his victory, Lincoln called the fact that elections had been held in the midst of the war a vindication of popular self-government. The aristocratic New York diarist George Templeton Strong agreed. The result of "the most momentous election ever held since ballots were invented," he wrote, had somewhat mitigated "my contempt for democracy and extended suffrage."[51]

III

DESPITE REPUBLICANS' rather cautious embrace of emancipation during the campaign, they chose to interpret the election as an endorsement of irrevocable abolition. Richard J. Oglesby, who had just been elected governor of Illinois, assured Lincoln that he was now "at liberty to say to the rebels about what you said to 'whom it may concern.'" Lincoln himself understood the result in this way. In his annual message to Congress in early December 1864, he claimed that "the voice of the people" had been heard in favor of ratification of the Thirteenth Amendment. Since "the next Congress will pass the measure if this does not," he added, "may we not agree that the sooner the better?" Lincoln then discussed prospects for peace, reiterating his offer of amnesty to rank-and-file Confederates who took an oath of loyalty but also warning that the day would "probably" come when he would adopt "more rigorous measures" to secure reunion. He repeated his previous declarations that he would not return to slavery any person freed by the Emancipation Proclamation or Congress. The message made no mention of colonization. "We shall hear no more of that suicidal folly," wrote a correspondent of the black-owned *New Orleans Tribune*.[52]

Lincoln took further steps to cement party unity and ensure the completion of emancipation. In December he appointed James Speed of Kentucky, the brother of his friend Joshua Speed, as attorney general. Unlike his brother, James Speed was one of the most radical Kentucky Unionists; early in the war, he had described himself to Lincoln as "almost an abolitionist." And Lincoln named Salmon P. Chase chief justice of the Supreme Court. He did so in part to placate the Radicals, who had bombarded him with letters urging Chase's appointment, but also, Lincoln told a group of visitors, to guarantee that the Court did not challenge the constitutionality of the Emancipation Proclamation. "You at the head of the Nation—and Chase at the head of the Supreme Court," Lincoln's old friend Norman D. Judd exulted. Judd was not the only person who could scarcely believe how the national government had been transformed since 1860. "Mr. Speaker," a Democratic member of Congress proclaimed, "the anti-slavery party is in power. We know it; we feel it."[53]

The first order of business of the Republican majority when Congress reconvened in December 1864 was to reconsider the House vote of the previous June that had failed to approve the Thirteenth Amendment. Lincoln threw his support to the endeavor, intervening more directly in the legislative process than at any other point in his presidency. He pressured border Unionists, most of whom had opposed the amendment in June, to change their position. Congressman John Alley of Massachusetts later claimed that Lincoln told him to procure votes in any way he chose, remembering that the president is "clothed with immense power."

One border congressman who voted for the amendment was subsequently appointed ambassador to Denmark. Lincoln also authorized Speaker of the House Schuyler Colfax to announce that if the amendment failed again, Lincoln would call a special session of the next Congress in March, as soon as the current one adjourned.[54]

Current and former cabinet members joined in the lobbying campaign. Seward promised patronage appointments to Democrats who had been defeated for reelection and agreed to vote for the amendment. Montgomery Blair urged the influential Samuel L. M. Barlow to swing Democratic votes in its favor, arguing that passage would enable the party to recoup its fortunes "on the *negro* question as contradistinguished from the *slave* question." In December 1864, "around a table at Delmonico's," leading New York Democrats including Barlow, Samuel J. Tilden, and *New York World* editor Manton Marble debated whether the amendment's passage would benefit their party. Barlow remained unconvinced, but the *World* wrote almost nothing about the amendment as the vote neared, to the relief of the measure's supporters.[55]

When the decisive moment came on January 31, 1865, spectators ranging from members of the cabinet and Supreme Court to ordinary black residents of Washington packed the House chambers. By a vote of 119 to 56, slightly more than the required two-thirds majority, the House approved the Thirteenth Amendment. Every Republican voted in favor, along with sixteen Democrats, all but two of them lame ducks who had been defeated or had chosen not to run in 1864. Lincoln's former law partner John T. Stuart, now a Democratic congressman from Illinois, rejected a personal appeal from the president and voted no. Lincoln's lobbying did, however, pay dividends among border congressmen. The five border states (including West Virginia) produced 19 votes for the amendment and only 8 against. During the debates, border congressmen who had previously opposed passage explained their change of heart. "War," said John A. J. Creswell of Maryland, "is as subversive of theories as it is of mere physical obstacles," and the Civil War had dispelled the idea that "the negro race" was unfit for freedom. James S. Rollins of Missouri, once "a large owner of slaves," declared, "We can never have an entire peace in this country as long as the institution of slavery remains. . . . We may as well unsheathe the sword and cut the Gordian knot!" Green C. Smith of Kentucky identified slavery as the reason Ohio had "outstripped" his own state in prosperity. Thus, the old nightmare of the Lower South came to pass: the northern tier of slave states joined the North in bringing about the abolition of slavery.[56]

"Regardless of parliamentary rules," the staid reporter for the *Congressional Globe* noted, the House erupted in "an outburst of enthusiasm" when the final tally was announced. Congressmen "wept like children" while in the galleries men threw their hats in the air and "the ladies . . . rose in their seats and waved their handkerchiefs." The names of those who voted for the amendment, the *Washington Morning Chronicle* proclaimed, would go down in history beside the signers of the Declaration of Independence. Lincoln offered impromptu remarks to a group that came to the White House to celebrate. The Thirteenth Amendment, he declared, went well beyond the Emancipation Proclamation as a way to "eradicate slavery" and would erase any doubts as to the proclamation's "legal validity." He said that the proclamation was "inoperative" on slaves who did not come within Union lines and might have no effect on their children. "But this amendment," he added, "is a King's cure for all the evils."[57]

The debate over the amendment reached its climax as one of the more unusual episodes in Lincoln's presidency unfolded. In his message to Congress of the previous December, Lincoln had flatly rejected negotiations with the Confederacy, since the "insurgent leader" had made it clear that he would accept nothing short of "the severance of the Union." A few days later, however, Lincoln gave Francis P. Blair Sr. permission to travel to Richmond to meet with Jefferson Davis. Blair had devised a bizarre scheme whereby the Union and Confederacy would declare an armistice and send a joint army to overthrow the regime the French had established in Mexico. Davis told Blair he was willing to "enter into conference with a view to secure peace to the two countries."[58]

Lincoln adamantly denied that "two countries" existed. Nonetheless, he agreed to meet with a three-man peace delegation headed by Confederate vice president Alexander H. Stephens, his old congressional colleague. News of the impending conference leaked out and threatened to derail House passage of the Thirteenth Amendment, which Democrats charged would create an obstacle to peace. James Ashley, the Ohio Radical who had been rounding up votes for the amendment, implored Lincoln to deny that peace was at hand. On January 31, the day of the vote, Lincoln sent a note for Ashley to read to the House: "So far as I know, there are no peace commissioners in the city, or likely to be in it." This was literally true since the commissioners were not coming to Washington, but certainly misleading. In any event, on February 3, Lincoln and Secretary of State Seward met with the three envoys on a naval vessel anchored off Hampton Roads, Virginia. The southerners arrived, wrote a Union army officer, accompanied by "the *bone of contention* . . . in the shape of a black man carrying a valise."[59]

The Hampton Roads conference lasted for several hours and the participants agreed not to take notes. They all eventually recorded accounts of what had transpired, which generally coincide although they differ on some significant points. Seward and Stephens rambled on about the Monroe Doctrine and Blair's Mexican scheme until Lincoln became impatient and made clear he had no interest in the idea. Lincoln insisted that no consideration of "terms and conditions" could take place until the Confederacy recognized national authority, but promised to be lenient in issuing pardons and restoring confiscated property. When one negotiator cited Charles I as an example of a ruler who entered into an agreement with rebels before a war ended, Lincoln replied, "All I distinctly recollect about the case of Charles I, is, that he lost his head in the end."[60]

Alexander H. Stephens later claimed that Lincoln urged him to persuade Georgia to withdraw from the Confederacy and ratify the Thirteenth Amendment with the proviso that it go into effect in five years. This seems highly unlikely; Lincoln was too good a lawyer not to know that such a codicil would have no legal effect. In Seward's account, Lincoln simply told the Confederates that there was every reason to expect the Thirteenth Amendment soon to become part of the Constitution. Lincoln also mentioned his long-standing idea of compensated emancipation. Indeed, immediately after his return to Washington, Lincoln presented to the cabinet a proposal to distribute $400 million (the sum Greeley had proposed in his peace initiative of the previous July) to the slave states, including the border, if the war ended by April 1. The document also promised to restore all confiscated property, other than slaves, that had not been sold to third parties. The cabinet unanimously rejected Lincoln's idea. Secretary of the Navy Welles observed that while the desire for peace was admirable, "there may be such a thing as overdoing." "You are all against me," Lincoln remarked, and abandoned the proposal. He failed to mention it in his report to Congress on the peace conference.[61]

The Radical senator Zachariah Chandler considered the Hampton Roads proceedings "disgraceful." But most Republicans praised Lincoln's conduct, which they understood as an uncompromising insistence on reunion and emancipation. The outcome reinforced Republicans' determination to press ahead with ratification of the Thirteenth Amendment to settle once and for all the fate of slavery. For it to become part of the Constitution required the approval of three-fourths of the states. The admission of Nevada on the eve of the 1864 election (when some Republicans thought its three electoral votes might provide the margin of victory) had increased the number of states to thirty-six, including the eleven of the Confederacy. Thus, were the seceded states to be counted, as Lincoln insisted they must be (to do otherwise, he thought, would recognize the legitimacy of secession), ratification required twenty-seven approvals. It seemed unlikely that the three states carried by McClellan would ratify; thus five Confederate states would have to do so. The four with new governments recognized by Lincoln could be counted on—Arkansas, Louisiana, Tennessee, and Virginia. Where the fifth state would come from depended on the progress of Reconstruction.[62]

Appropriately, Illinois was the first state to ratify. Delaware, the border state where Lincoln had begun his emancipation initiative in 1861, became the first to reject the amendment; not until 1901, long after it had become part of the Constitution, would it gain Delaware's approval. Kentucky, with a government, one correspondent informed Lincoln, under the control of "the old secession party, and the relapsed portion of the Union party," also refused to ratify. The place of Lincoln's birth would have the distinction of being the only state to reject the Thirteenth, Fourteenth, and Fifteenth Amendments to the Constitution. Nonetheless, slavery in both these border states was clearly dying. Because of black enlistment in the army, Delaware was "practically free." As for Kentucky, "no family knows whether they have a servant to prepare breakfast for them or not," complained the *Louisville Journal*. Soon after the House approved the Thirteenth Amendment, moreover, Congress passed the bill, mentioned in chapter 8, to free the families of black soldiers. After soliciting the advice of Secretary of War Stanton, who affirmed that it would strengthen the army by relieving black soldiers of "great anxiety" about "those whom they love," Lincoln signed it. By the end of the war, despite slavery's continued legal existence, nearly three-quarters of the slaves in Kentucky and Delaware had become free. The remainder, however, would not enjoy liberty until the ratification of the Thirteenth Amendment in December 1865.[63]

"The one question of the age is *settled*," declared Congressman Cornelius Cole of California. But if the Thirteenth Amendment solved one problem, it raised a host of others. During the debates Democrats had asked repeatedly, "What is to be done with the negroes who may be freed?" Republicans showed little desire to discuss the precise rights that would come with freedom. But a number insisted that abolition would incorporate blacks into the "national citizenship" that would emerge from the war. For the moment, however, there was no agreement as to precisely what the rights of citizens were. Most Republicans agreed with Congressman John Farnsworth that "all questions of the consequences of emancipation" should be postponed.[64]

Nevertheless, the issue of blacks' postwar rights had a way of reappearing. The month of February 1865 witnessed remarkable breaches in the northern color line. On February 1, the day after passage of the Thirteenth Amendment, Chief Justice Chase admitted John S. Rock of Boston as the first black lawyer to practice before the Supreme Court, an "extraordinary reversal" of the *Dred Scott* decision, *Harper's Weekly* noted, and an "indication of the revolution which is going on in the sentiment of a great people." A few days later, on Lincoln's fifty-sixth birthday, Henry H. Garnet became the first black minister to preach a sermon in the hall of the House of Representatives. He used the occasion to claim for his people "every right of American citizenship." Not only blacks but the nation as a whole, he proclaimed, had embarked on an exodus after a long bondage to slavery. Also in February, Lincoln approved the appointment of Martin R. Delany as the army's first black commissioned officer, dispatching him to Beaufort, South Carolina, to raise additional black soldiers. And Illinois finally repealed its discriminatory Black Laws, the result of a campaign spearheaded by the black abolitionist John Jones of Chicago, who stationed himself at the door of the legislature "morn, noon, and evening" to lobby members. By the end of 1865, every northern state but Indiana would remove such laws from their statute books.[65]

Lincoln made no comment on the repeal or on the agitation by northern blacks for greater rights. But what John Cochrane, New York's attorney general, called "the great problem of *the free races*" unavoidably presented itself as Congress once again debated Reconstruction. The issue was made more urgent by the actions of the government of Louisiana, the showcase for Lincoln's Reconstruction initiative. The new legislature rejected the Quadroon Bill, which would have extended the right to vote to free men of color possessing three-quarters' white ancestry, and made no appropriation for black education. The free blacks of New Orleans found that "vagrancy" and curfew regulations issued as part of Nathaniel P. Banks's labor system did not distinguish between themselves and the freedpeople, placing severe restrictions on their traditional freedom of movement.[66]

Soon after the Louisiana constitutional convention of 1864, a group of free blacks established the *New Orleans Tribune* as a rallying point for Louisiana Radicalism. As editor they hired Jean-Charles Houzeau, a Belgian astronomer and journalist who had emigrated to the United States in 1858 and whose political outlook, like theirs, had been shaped by the heritage of the Enlightenment and the French Revolution. The *Tribune* launched an assault on the army's labor system as a reincarnation of slavery and demanded the right to vote not only for the free blacks but also for their "dormant partners," the emancipated slaves. Houzeau made the *Tribune* a journal widely respected among northern Republicans and known even in Europe (it received a letter in 1865 from the great French novelist Victor Hugo). In January 1865 a convention of the National Equal Rights League assembled in New Orleans, bringing together urban free blacks and freedpeople from the countryside to press for complete civil and political equality. "We no longer have classes or castes among us," declared the *Tribune*. "We are made one people and one nation. . . . Liberty must be the same for all."[67]

Although the government of Louisiana made no response to these developments, Lincoln remained committed to its success. Failure in Louisiana, he wrote in November 1864, would "gladden the heart" of every enemy of the Union and "every advocate of slavery." In his annual message to Congress the following month, Lincoln praised the "loyal State governments with free constitutions" that he had helped to establish. But complaints against the Louisiana regime received an increasingly sympathetic hearing in Congress, exacerbating divisions within the Republican party over Reconstruction. "The question of extending the right of universal suffrage to the colored race," observed the *Washington Morning Chronicle*, "is . . . more difficult of practical solution than any which has ever been presented to the people of this country." But events in Louisiana placed it on the political agenda.[68]

In December 1864 Charles Sumner and other Republican leaders held repeated discussions with Lincoln about "the duty of harmony between Congress and the Executive." Sumner thought they had reached agreement on a plan to recognize the legitimacy of the Louisiana government and at the same time require other Confederate states to accord "all citizens" equality before the law and the right to vote before readmission to the Union. "If this arrangement is carried out," Sumner remarked, "it will be an immense political act." Too immense, it turned out, to succeed.[69]

James Ashley soon introduced in the House of Representatives a Reconstruction bill embodying the arrangement described by Sumner. However, while Lincoln privately assured key legislators that he would use his influence to get Louisiana to enfranchise at least some blacks, he objected to putting black suffrage in the bill. Lincoln still believed that voting rights were a matter for the states, not the federal government, to determine. In an effort to make the bill acceptable to the president, whose standing with Congress had improved significantly because of his triumphal reelection, Ashley revised it to limit the right to vote to loyal whites and blacks who had served in the military. Weeks of debate followed, and the bill went through numerous incarnations. But with some Republicans insisting on black suffrage and others, along with all the Democrats, resisting it, it became "very clear," Ashley remarked, "that no bill providing for the reorganization of the governments of loyal State governments in the rebel States can pass this Congress."[70]

"The president's Reconstruction policy stands," declared the *Springfield Republican*. But Congress refused to count Louisiana's 1864 electoral vote, and on the eve of adjournment a filibuster by Sumner prevented the seating of the senators elected by what he called "the pretended State Government" there. Lincoln, the *Republican*'s Washington correspondent reported, was "indignant" over Sumner's action. But this did not seem to damage their cordial personal relationship. "Still he respects Mr. Sumner," the journalist continued, "confers with him, and perhaps fears him." A few days after the filibuster, Lincoln sent his private carriage to bring Sumner to the inaugural ball.[71]

When Congress adjourned at the beginning of March 1865, the issue of Reconstruction remained unresolved. With eight months set to elapse before the next Congress convened, Lincoln had a free hand in making and implementing policy. But Radicals preferred the issue to go over to the fall; in the meantime, said Ashley, "I hope the nation may be educated up to our demand for universal suffrage." As for Lincoln, Sumner believed that while he was "slow in accepting truths . . . his mind is undergoing change."[72]

Even the abolitionist movement could not agree on the next steps after emancipation. At the annual meeting of the Massachusetts Anti-Slavery Society in January 1865, Wendell Phillips and Frederick Douglass spoke "with unusual warmth of manner" of the necessity of keeping Louisiana out of the Union. Otherwise, the rest of the southern states would return with similar laws, and "we should have slavery back again, in spirit if not in form." In a nation that proclaimed itself an exemplar of democracy, Douglass declared, to deny blacks the right to vote "is to brand us with the stigma of inferiority." To which William Lloyd Garrison responded that the suffrage was "a conventional right . . . not to be confused with the natural right" to freedom. Political equality would come, he believed, only with "industrial and educational development." The *Liberator* embraced the "renovated" Louisiana regime. "O Garrison," wrote the *Boston Commonwealth*, "this is not abolitionism." The debate offered a preview of the split in the American Anti-Slavery Society that would take place the following May, when the members rejected Garrison's proposal to declare victory and dissolve, Phillips replaced him as president, and the *National Anti-Slavery Standard* appeared with a new motto on its masthead: "No Reconstruction without Negro Suffrage."[73]

In early 1865 an equally portentous question also appeared on the political horizon: should the federal government distribute land to the emancipated slaves? While the issue had been pressed by a few members of Congress in 1864, it acquired new urgency thanks to General William T. Sherman. Shortly after Lincoln's reelection, Sherman and his 60,000-man army set out from Atlanta on the celebrated March to the Sea. They arrived in Savannah at the end of December, accompanied by some 20,000 slaves who had abandoned the plantations to follow the army. On January 12, 1865, at the urging of Secretary of War Stanton, who had traveled to Savannah, Sherman met with twenty leaders of the local black community, most of them Baptist and Methodist ministers. The conversation revealed that the black leaders possessed clear conceptions of slavery and freedom. Asked what he understood by slavery, Garrison Frazier, the group's spokesman, replied that it meant "receiving by irresistible power the work of another man, and not by his consent." Freedom he defined as "placing us where we could reap the fruit of our own labor," a definition not unlike Lincoln's. The best way to accomplish this was "to have land and till it by our own labor."[74]

Four days later, Sherman issued Special Field Order No. 15, setting aside the Sea Islands and a large swath of land along the coasts of South Carolina and Georgia for the exclusive settlement of black families on forty-acre plots. He also offered them broken-down mules the army could no longer use. Here lay the origins of the phrase "Forty Acres and a Mule" that would reverberate throughout the South during Reconstruction. Sherman was no Radical; his aim was not to inaugurate a social revolution but to relieve his army of the burden of caring for black refugees and, in the process, punish Confederate planters. But black families hastened to take advantage of his order. By June some 40,000 freedpeople had been settled on "Sherman land."[75]

Warning that the black settlers would become "landed paupers" whose presence would prevent "the energy and industry of the North" from utilizing this valuable land, General John C. Robinson urged Lincoln to overturn it. Although Sherman's policy went well beyond anything Lincoln had previously envisioned or supported, he took no action one way or the other, whether from deference to the decisions of military commanders in the field or a desire to see how the experiment worked out is impossible to say. Lincoln did, however, continue to monitor free-labor experiments in the South. In February 1865 he met once again with John Eaton and directed him to continue his supervision of the freedpeople in the Mississippi Valley "on the same principle as in the past, making such improvements as experience may suggest." On March 1, after receiving a report from Thomas Conway, who had tried to make the labor system established by General Banks more equitable, Lincoln praised Conway's success "in the work of their moral and physical elevation," noting that wartime experiments were leading to "an earlier and happier consummation than the most sanguine friends of the freedmen could reasonably expect."[76]

Sherman's order left unclear whether his land grants were permanent or temporary. But the idea that the federal government would provide the former slaves with access to land was reinforced when, at the beginning of March, Congress finally approved and Lincoln signed the bill to establish a Bureau of Emancipation, now called the Freedmen's Bureau. The measure charged the bureau with distributing clothing, food, and fuel to destitute former slaves and overseeing "all subjects" relating to their condition in the South. To avoid the impression of giving preferential treatment to blacks, Congress at the last moment expanded its responsibilities to include white southern refugees as well.

Continuing fears about the former slaves becoming dependent on federal assistance led the lawmakers to limit the bureau's existence to one year (later extended to 1870). Nonetheless, the bureau represented an enormous expansion of federal authority. During its life it would set up its own courts, establish schools, regulate labor contracts, try to protect former slaves from violence, and in myriad other ways oversee matters traditionally considered local and state concerns. And as suggested by its full title—Bureau of Refugees, Freedmen, and Abandoned Lands—it was also authorized to divide abandoned and confiscated land into plots for rental to freedmen and loyal white refugees and eventual sale with "such title as the United States can convey," language that reflected the legal ambiguity surrounding southern land that had come into the government's possession. Hardly a commitment to widespread land distribution, the Freedmen's Bureau Act did envision the federal government settling some former slaves on farms of their own. A number of bureau officials soon proceeded to do so. But in the summer of 1865, in one of his early acts as president, Andrew Johnson would order all land in government hands that had not actually been sold, including that distributed by Sherman, returned to its former owners. Ironically, the only freedpeople to whom the federal government in the end guaranteed land were the former slaves of tribes like the Cherokee that had sided with the Confederacy during the war.[77]

"It seems our fate never to get rid of the Negro question," Sidney George Fisher, the Philadelphia lawyer and political commentator, observed in his diary. "What shall we do with the Negro?—seems as far from being settled as ever."[78] As the war neared its conclusion, it was apparent that the fate of the emancipated slaves would be the central issue of Lincoln's second term as president.

Epilogue

"Every Drop of Blood": The Meaning of the War

On March 4, 1865, Lincoln took the oath of office for the second time. The setting itself reflected how much had changed in the past four years. When Lincoln delivered his first inaugural address, the new Capitol dome, which replaced the original wooden one, was only half complete. Now the *Statue of Freedom* crowned the finished edifice, symbolizing the reconstitution of the nation on the basis of universal liberty. For the first time in American history, companies of black soldiers marched in the inaugural parade. According to one estimate, half the audience that heard Lincoln's address was black, as were many of the visitors who paid their respects at the White House reception that day.[1]

When Lincoln spoke, the end of the war and of slavery was finally in sight. Early in February, William T. Sherman's army had marched from Savannah into South Carolina, bringing, as one planter recorded in his journal, the "breath of Emancipation" to the heartland of secessionism. Only days later, Union forces, among them the celebrated Fifty-fourth Massachusetts singing "John Brown's Body," occupied Charleston. Meanwhile, Grant tightened his grip on Lee's army, still besieged at Petersburg, the gateway to Richmond.[2]

It must have been very tempting for Lincoln to use his inaugural address to review the progress of the war and congratulate himself and the nation on impending victory. Instead, he delivered a speech of almost unbelievable brevity and humility.[3] Lincoln began by stating that there was no need for an "extended address" or an elaborate discussion of "the progress of our

323

arms." He refused to make any prediction as to when the war would end. One week after the inauguration, Senator Thomas F. Bayard of Delaware wrote that he had "slowly and reluctantly" come to understand the war's "remote causes."[4] He did not delineate them, but in the second inaugural Lincoln did. Slavery, he stated forthrightly, was the reason for the war:

> One eighth of the whole population were colored slaves. Not distributed generally over the Union, but localized in the Southern part of it. These slaves constituted a peculiar and powerful interest. All knew that this interest was, somehow, the cause of the war. To strengthen, perpetuate, and extend this interest was the object for which the insurgents would rend the Union, even by war, while the government claimed no right to do more than to restrict the territorial enlargement of it.

Lincoln, as always, chose his words carefully. Referring to the slaves as one-eighth of the "population" suggested that they were part of the nation, not an exotic, unassimilable element, as he had once viewed them. "Peculiar," of course, was how southerners themselves had so often described slavery. "Powerful" seemed to evoke Republicans' prewar rhetoric about the Slave Power. To say that slavery was the cause placed responsibility for the bloodshed on the South. Yet Lincoln added simply, "And the war came," seemingly avoiding the assignment of blame. But the war, Lincoln continued, had had unanticipated consequences:

> Neither party expected for the war, the magnitude, or the duration, which it has already attained. Neither anticipated that the cause of the conflict might cease with, or even before, the conflict itself should cease. Each looked for an easier triumph, and a result less fundamental and astounding.

The "astounding" outcome, of course, was the destruction of slavery. Countless northern ministers had pointed to this as evidence of divine sanction for the Union war effort. Lincoln took a different approach. Rejecting self-congratulation, he offered a remarkably philosophical reflection on the war's larger meaning:

> Both [sides] read the same Bible, and pray to the same God; and each invokes His aid against the other. It may seem strange that any men

should dare to ask a just God's assistance in wringing their bread from the sweat of other men's faces; but let us judge not that we be not judged. The prayers of both could not be answered; that of neither has been answered fully. The Almighty has His own purposes. "Woe unto the world because of offences! for it must needs be that offences come; but woe to that man by whom the offence cometh!" If we shall suppose that American Slavery is one of those offences which, in the providence of God, must needs come, but which, having continued through His appointed time, He now wills to remove, and that He gives to both North and South, this terrible war, as the woe due to those by whom the offence came, shall we discern therein any departure from those divine attributes which the believers in a Living God always ascribe to Him? Fondly do we hope—fervently do we pray—that this mighty scourge of war may speedily pass away. Yet, if God wills that it continue, until all the wealth piled by the bond-man's two hundred and fifty years of unrequited toil shall be sunk, and until every drop of blood drawn with the lash, shall be paid by another drawn with the sword, as was said three thousand years ago, so still it must be said "the judgments of the Lord, are true and righteous altogether."

Despite having promised not to judge the South, Lincoln did so. For one last time he reiterated his condemnation of slavery as a theft of labor, combining this with the most direct allusion in all his writings to the institution's physical brutality. Lincoln was reminding the country that the "terrible" violence of the Civil War had been preceded by two and a half centuries of the terrible violence of slavery. Yet Lincoln called it "American slavery," not southern slavery, his point being that the nation as a whole was guilty of this sin. This may help to explain why he clung so long to the idea of compensated emancipation; in his letter to Albert G. Hodges of 1864 he had alluded to the possibility that the North would have to "pay fairly for our complicity in that wrong."[5] But the second inaugural implicitly shifted the moral equation from what was due to slaveholders to the nation's obligation to the slaves.

This long paragraph, one of the most remarkable in American letters, echoed the abolitionists' view of slavery as a national evil deeply embedded in all the institutions of society and of the war itself as a "judgment of the Lord" for this sin. Lincoln's words, an Illinois newspaper observed, "might claim paternity of Wendell Phillips." Or, it might have added,

Frederick Douglass, who in his great 1852 speech, "The Meaning of the Fourth of July to the Negro," had also spoken of "American slavery." Indeed, the Radical editors of the *Chicago Tribune* pointed out that they had said much the same thing as Lincoln two and a half years earlier in a piece entitled "Justice of the Almighty," although, they acknowledged, their exposition was not "so admirably condensed" as Lincoln's. The *Tribune* had referred to the likely destruction of "the sum total of profit that has been derived from slaveholding," and how "our own sufferings" were "balance[d]" by the "bloodshed and tears" of two centuries of slavery.[6]

Not for the first time, Lincoln had taken ideas that circulated in anti-slavery circles and distilled them into something uniquely his own. He was asking the entire nation to confront unblinkingly the legacy of the long history of bondage. What were the requirements of justice in the face of those 250 years of unpaid labor? What was necessary to enable the former slaves, their children, and their descendants to enjoy the pursuit of happiness he had always insisted was their natural right but that had been so long denied to them? Lincoln did not live to provide an answer. But even implicitly raising these questions suggested the magnitude of the task that lay ahead.

After this passage in which Lincoln, like Puritan preachers of old, struggled to understand the causes of God's anger with his chosen people, the second inaugural closed with the eloquent words for which it is most often remembered:

> With malice toward none; with charity for all; with firmness in the right, as God gives us to see the right, let us strive on to finish the work we are in; to bind up the nation's wounds; to care for him who shall have borne the battle, and for his widow, and his orphan—to do all which may achieve and cherish a just, and a lasting peace, among ourselves, and with all nations.

Lincoln had been thinking a great deal about the process of reconciliation. In the first weeks of 1865, he had urged military commanders and Governor Thomas C. Fletcher to encourage the people of Missouri to abandon their internecine violence and let bygones be bygones rather than seeking vengeance. Neighborhood meetings, Lincoln suggested, should be held where all would agree to forget "whatever they may heretofore have thought, said or done. . . . Each leaving all others alone, solves the problem." Fletcher rejected Lincoln's plea. The promises of rebels, he responded, could never be trusted. Left unresolved in Lincoln's Missouri initiative and in the second inaugural itself was the tension between mercy to the former slaveowners and justice to the former slaves. Would the pursuit of one inevitably vitiate the other? "Equality before the law," Charles Sumner insisted, must precede forgiveness. "Then at last will come *reconciliation*, and not before."[7]

Frederick Douglass, who was in the audience, called the second inaugural "more like a sermon than a state paper." In a speech of only 700 words, Lincoln had referred to God or the Almighty eight times and liberally quoted and paraphrased the Bible. "Woe unto the world," and "let us judge not" are the words of Jesus; "wring their bread" is a rewording of a passage from Genesis; the archaic usage "bond-man" (which Lincoln had never before employed) appears a number of times in Scripture. Lincoln, of course, had long since acquired a deep knowledge of the Bible. And during the war, while he never joined a church, he seems to have undergone a spiritual awakening. Especially after the death of his young son Willie in 1862, Lincoln moved away from his earlier religious skepticism. He began to compose private thoughts on the will of God and its relation to the war. Lincoln had long believed that a remote higher power controlled human destiny. He now concluded that God intervened directly in the world, although in ways men could not always fathom.[8]

An intensely private man, Lincoln did not readily reveal his religious convictions. "I have often wished that I was a more devout man than I am," he remarked in 1863 to a group of clerics, hastily adding that nonetheless, "I place my whole reliance in God." Of course, Lincoln also understood that revealed religion had a powerful claim on the northern public. During the war, he announced days of thanksgiving and fasting and called on Providence for assistance to himself and the country. Yet he managed to see the war as a divine punishment for slavery while avoiding the desire for blame and vengeance. If Lincoln's second inaugural was a sermon, it was quite different from those that northerners had grown accustomed to hearing during the Civil War.[9]

After the address, Douglass repaired with some 5,000 other persons to the White House. When he stepped forward to offer congratulations, Lincoln clasped his hand and said, "My dear Sir, I am glad to see you." Douglass called the speech a "sacred effort."[10] Not every listener was as kind. Particularly harsh was the *New York World*, which printed the speech "with a blush of shame." It was an "odious libel," the editors complained, to equate the blood that "trickled from the lacerated backs of the negroes" with the carnage of "the bloodiest war in history." "The president's theology," it added, "smacks as strongly of the dark ages as does Pope Pius's politics." But many Republicans also found the speech puzzling. Why, they asked, had Lincoln not promised an end to the war and laid out "some definite line of policy" regarding Reconstruction? A few contemporaries recognized the greatness of the address. Charles Francis Adams Jr., the colonel of a black regiment, wrote to his father, the ambassador in London, "That rail-splitting lawyer is one of the wonders of the day. . . . This inaugural strikes me in its grand simplicity and directness as being for all time the historical keynote of this war." Overall, however, as Lincoln himself recognized, the address was "not immediately popular," although he remained confident that it would "wear as well—perhaps better than—anything I have produced." Lincoln thought he knew why people did not like his speech: "Men are not flattered by being shown that there has been a difference of purpose between the Almighty and them." On one thing everyone agreed: as George Templeton Strong noted in his diary, the second inaugural was "unlike any American state paper of this century."[11]

Nine days after the inaugural, after prolonged debate, the Confederate Congress authorized the enlistment of black soldiers in the southern armies. A few days later, Lincoln took note of this act of desperation in remarks to an Indiana regiment in Washington. "I have always thought that all men should be free," he remarked, but if any deserved to be slaves it was those willing to fight to keep themselves or others in bondage.[12]

On April 3, 1865, Robert E. Lee's army finally abandoned Petersburg. The road to Richmond, twenty miles to the north, now lay open. As government officials fled the defenseless city and a fire raged out of control, destroying much of the business district, Union forces led by the all-black Fifth Massachusetts cavalry entered the capital of the Confederacy. Scenes never before witnessed on this continent followed. Blacks thronged the streets, dancing, praying, and singing, "Slavery chain done broke at last." Garland H. White, the chaplain of a black regiment, was called on to make a speech to a "vast multitude." He "proclaimed for the first time in that city freedom to all mankind. After which the doors of all the slave pens were thrown open, and thousands came out shouting and praising God, and Father, or Master Abe."

The next day Lincoln walked the streets of Richmond, accompanied only by a small detachment of sailors. "The colored population," wrote T. Morris Chester, a black war correspondent for the *Philadelphia Press*, "was wild with excitement." At every step, Lincoln was besieged by emancipated slaves, who, to his embarrassment, fell on their knees and hailed him as their messiah or pressed forward to kiss his hand. "I know that I am free," one black woman exclaimed, "for I have seen Father Abraham and felt him." The city's white residents remained indoors. Having always considered their slaves loyal and contented, they were stunned by the reception the black population gave to Lincoln and the conquering (or liberating) Union army. Charles Sumner hoped that Lincoln's reception in Richmond would affect his ideas about Reconstruction. "He saw with his own eyes," Sumner wrote to Salmon P. Chase, "that the only people *who showed themselves were negroes. . . .* Never was I more convinced of the utter impossibility of any organization which is not founded on the votes of the negroes."[13]

Hoping to bring the war to an immediate end, Lincoln met in Richmond on April 4 and 5 with John A. Campbell, a former justice of the Supreme Court and one of the emissaries who had taken part in the Hampton Roads conference. Campbell proposed that Lincoln allow Virginia's Confederate legislature to convene in order to repeal the ordinance of secession and withdraw the state's troops from southern armies, whereupon Lee would surrender. On April 6, Lincoln directed General Godfrey Weitzel to allow the lawmakers to assemble in Richmond for this purpose, also informing Grant about the action but adding, "I do not think it very probable that anything will come of this." Lincoln also met with Francis H. Pierpont to assure him that he would continue to recognize the Restored Government of Virginia Pierpont headed. According to Pierpont's later recollections, Lincoln asked questions rather than offering answers. How many Unionists really existed in the South? Would they join the Republican party? What would be the fate of the freedmen? If Pierpont is to be believed, Lincoln remarked that he "had no plan for reorganization."[14]

On April 9, Grant accepted Lee's surrender at Appomattox. Although the last Confederate force, Kirby Smith's army in Texas, would not capitulate until May, the Civil War had ended. Shortly after Lee's surrender, Lincoln revoked permission for the Confederate legislature of Virginia to convene, which the cabinet and Republican members of Congress who remained in Washington had unanimously opposed. To Lincoln's annoy-ance, Campbell had interpreted his gesture as an invitation to negotiate an armistice and peace terms, including Virginia's right to representation in Congress and "the condition of the slave population." In any event, Lee's surrender rendered the matter moot.[15]

Reconstruction now emerged as the foremost problem confronting the nation. On April 11, having returned to Washington, Lincoln delivered a speech on this subject to a large crowd that had gathered at the White House. According to one newspaper, he prepared it with "unusual care and deliberation." In part, it was a defense of the new government of Louisiana, to whose support Lincoln had devoted so much effort. In the past month, events in that state had taken an ominous turn. On the day of Lincoln's second inauguration, Governor Michael Hahn resigned after being elected to the Senate and was replaced by J. Madison Wells, a Unionist planter who had owned more than 100 slaves before the Civil War. Quickly taking stock of the political situation as the war neared its end, Wells realized that Confederates who took an oath of loyalty, thus restoring their right to vote, would soon vastly outnumber white support-ers of his regime. He promptly began replacing Hahn's appointees in local and statewide offices with conservative Unionists and former rebels.[16]

In his speech, Lincoln acknowledged that the problem of Reconstruc-tion was "fraught with great difficulty." Nonetheless, he again sought to bolster northern support for the Louisiana regime, while also trying to find common ground with his Republican critics. In fact, Lincoln had asked Charles Sumner to stand on the White House balcony while he delivered the address. Lincoln noted that when he issued his Ten Percent Plan, every member of the cabinet had approved it and he had received "many commendations . . . and not a single objection to it, from any professed emancipationist." (The next day, Chase wrote to Lincoln saying he had in fact objected to the exclusion of blacks from voting but admitted he had not done so strongly, not wanting to appear "pertinacious.") Lincoln praised Louisiana's accomplishments—the abolition of slavery, public education for both races, and the fact that abolition had been immedi-ate, without an apprenticeship program of the kind he himself had once favored. However, he continued, it was "unsatisfactory to some that the elective franchise is not given to the colored men." For the first time, Lin-coln acknowledged that "the colored man . . . desires" the right to vote. He now repeated the sentiment of his private letter to Governor Hahn in

1864: "I would myself prefer that [the vote] were now conferred on the very intelligent, and on those who serve our cause as soldiers." This was a remarkable statement. No American president had publicly endorsed even limited black suffrage. At this time only six northern states allowed black men to vote.[17]

What became known as his "last speech" (a description that, while factually accurate, suggests a finality scarcely anticipated when it was delivered) was in many ways typical of Lincoln. He urged Republicans to think of Reconstruction as a practical problem rather than a philosophical one. The question of whether the South was "in or out of the Union," he said, was not only "practically immaterial" but downright "mischievous," since all agreed that the seceded states were "out of their proper practical relation" to it. He insisted that the Louisiana regime should be supported, but denied being wedded to any "inflexible plan" for the other states. Even regarding Louisiana, he noted that "bad promises are better broken than kept," suggesting that the process he had set in motion there might have to be modified or even abandoned. Lincoln closed by telling his audience to expect a "new announcement" regarding Reconstruction.

It was significant that Lincoln spoke of "reconstruction" and not "restoration," as he had frequently done in the past. These terms carried very different implications. "Reconstruction," one Democratic party leader observed around this time, "is synonymous with radicalism, restoration conservatism." But if Lincoln expected the speech to quiet criticism of his course, he was disappointed. Lincoln, Sumner wrote to Chase, "had said some things better than any body else could have said them. But I fear his policy now." Other Radicals were even more critical. It would be "wicked and blasphemous," one wrote, "for us as a nation to allow any distinction of color whatever in the reconstructed states." Even the moderate *New York Times* wondered what would prevent the southern states, if restored with their traditional rights intact, from abusing blacks? "The government cannot, without the worst dishonor, permit the bondage of the black man to be continued in any form," it insisted.[18]

Many observers concluded from the speech that Lincoln remained undecided about Reconstruction. "Mr. Lincoln gropes . . . like a traveler in an unknown country without a map," were the unkind words of the *New York World*. In fact, as a Washington reporter noted, most Republicans at this point had not yet "made up their minds" about Reconstruction. Even the *Chicago Tribune*, which favored black suffrage, acknowledged that

under the Constitution, states had the right to set their own voting qualifications. One member of the audience, however, thought he understood
exactly what Lincoln intended. "That means nigger citizenship," the actor
John Wilkes Booth is said to have remarked. Booth and a group of pro-
Confederate conspirators had been plotting to kidnap the president and
demand the release of southern prisoners of war. "Now, by God," Booth
supposedly muttered, "I'll put him through."[19]

When the cabinet assembled on April 14, Lincoln noted that he had
"perhaps been too fast in his desires for early reconstruction." Before
the meeting, he showed Attorney General James Speed a letter he had
received from Chase urging the enfranchisement of all "loyal citizens"
regardless of race when new state governments were formed. Speed
thought Lincoln was moving toward the Radical position. "He [never]
seemed so near our views," Speed told Chase the next day. Lincoln now
appeared to believe that the immediate problem was the prospect of anarchy in the South. He had directed Secretary of War Stanton to draw up
a plan for interim military rule. Stanton presented to the cabinet a proposal to appoint a temporary military government for Virginia and North
Carolina. Since his plan put off the establishment of civilian rule, he "left
open" the question of whether blacks should vote. But Stanton's proposal
clearly implied that reliance on white Unionists might not be enough to
establish loyal, stable governments. Little discussion ensued, and Lincoln
urged his colleagues to devote their attention to "the great question now
before us," on which "we must soon begin to act." Stanton was directed
to redraft his proposal for consideration at the next cabinet meeting.[20]

That night, April 14, 1865, John Wilkes Booth mortally wounded Lincoln while he sat at Ford's Theatre. He was carried to a house across the
street, where his life slowly ebbed away. Before dawn, Secretary of the
Navy Welles left Lincoln's bedside and went outside. Already, mourn-
ers thronged the streets of Washington. "The colored people," Welles
wrote, "and there were at this time more of them perhaps than of whites,
were painfully affected." A little after seven in the morning, Lincoln died.
His passing inspired an unprecedented outpouring of grief, and the first
national funeral in the country's history. Millions of men, women, and
children viewed Lincoln's casket as his remains made their way on a circuitous 1,700-mile journey from Washington to Springfield, with stops in
more than 100 cities. It essentially retraced the route Lincoln had taken
in February 1861 on the way to his inauguration. Reading the accounts of

his funeral journey, one senses that Americans recognized that Lincoln's experience during the war mirrored their own. For, as his bitter critic the *New York World* noted after his death, "some have changed more rapidly, some more slowly than he; but there are few of his countrymen, who have not changed at all." Yet change was hardly total. When Lincoln's body reached New York, the city council sought to prevent blacks from marching in the procession, only to be overruled by the War Department.[21]

Coupled with the achievements of piloting the United States through its greatest crisis and presiding over the emancipation of the slaves, the manner of his death ensured Lincoln's place in the pantheon of the most revered American leaders. That the assassination occurred on Good Friday heightened the conviction that Lincoln had sacrificed himself to redeem a sinful nation. At the time of his death and for years thereafter, Lincoln was remembered primarily as the Great Emancipator. Not until the turn of the century, when the process of (white) reconciliation was far advanced, would Americans forget or suppress the centrality of slavery and emancipation to the war experience. Lincoln would then be transformed into a symbol of national unity, and the Gettysburg Address, which did not explicitly mention slavery, would, in popular memory, supplant the Emancipation Proclamation as the greatest embodiment of his ideas. More recently, we have returned to the insight Lincoln offered in the second inaugural: slavery was the war's cause and emancipation its most profound outcome. To which may be added that these questions were central to Lincoln's own rise to greatness.[22]

■　■　■

"WITH THE END OF THE WAR," wrote a northern editor in April 1865, "the real trial of our statesmanship, our patriotism, and our patience will begin."[23] No one knows what Lincoln would have done had he lived to complete his second term. As his last speech and final cabinet meeting demonstrated, Reconstruction policy was in flux when Lincoln died. Despite his determined support for the Louisiana regime, Lincoln had never been wedded to a single plan for Reconstruction. Different approaches had operated simultaneously in different parts of the South, all of them conceived as ways to weaken the Confederacy and secure the abolition of slavery rather than as fixed blueprints for the postwar South. None had been very successful. Lincoln had failed to bring a single reconstructed state back into the Union. The new governments he had initiated had not revealed a willingness to deal justly with the former slaves.

What we do know is that Lincoln was succeeded in office by a man who lacked all the qualities of greatness that he possessed. Lincoln was intellectually curious, willing to listen to criticism, attuned to the currents of northern public opinion, and desirous of getting along with Congress. Over the course of the war he had developed a deep sense of compassion for the slaves he had helped to liberate, and a concern for their fate—what the *New York Times* called, in commenting on the second inaugural, a "feeling for the bondmen and the sense of the great wrong done to them."[24] Andrew Johnson was self-absorbed, insensitive to the opinions of others, unwilling to compromise, and unalterably racist. If anyone was responsible for the downfall of his presidency it was Johnson himself. With Congress out of session until December 1865, Johnson took it upon himself to bring about Reconstruction, establishing new governments in the South in which blacks had no voice whatever. When these governments sought to reduce the freedpeople to a situation reminiscent of slavery, he refused to heed the rising tide of northern concern or to budge from his policy. As a result, Congress, after attempting to work with the president, felt it had no choice but to sweep aside Johnson's Reconstruction plan and to enact some of the most momentous measures in American history: the Civil Rights Act of 1866, which accorded blacks equality before the law; the Fourteenth Amendment, which put the principle of equality unbounded by race into the Constitution; the Reconstruction Act of 1867, which mandated the establishment of new governments in the South with black men, for the first time in our history, enjoying a share of political power. Johnson did everything in his power to obstruct their implementation. In 1868, fed up with his intransigence and incompetence, the House of Representatives impeached Johnson and he came within one vote of conviction by the Senate.[25]

It is impossible to imagine Lincoln, had he lived, becoming so isolated from Congress, the Republican party, and the northern public as to be impeached and nearly removed from office. Nor does it seem likely that Lincoln would have implemented a policy and then clung to it in the face of its self-evident failure. Lincoln had changed enormously during the Civil War. Had he "considered it too humiliating to learn in advanced years," one emancipated slave later wrote, "our race would yet have remained" in bondage. During Reconstruction, Lincoln's ideas would undoubtedly have continued to evolve. This is why Frederick Douglass, his frequent critic, in 1865 called his death "an unspeakable calamity" for black America.[26]

"Liberty has been won," Charles Sumner proclaimed in a eulogy after Lincoln's death. "The battle for Equality is still pending."[27] Unlike Sumner and other Radicals, Lincoln did not see Reconstruction as an opportunity for a sweeping political and social revolution beyond emancipation. He had long made clear his opposition to the confiscation and redistribution of land. He believed, as most Republicans did in April 1865, that voting requirements should be determined by the states. He assumed that political control in the South would pass to white Unionists, reluctant secessionists, and forward-looking former Confederates. But time and again during the war, Lincoln, after initial opposition, had come to embrace positions first advanced by abolitionists and Radical Republicans. Had he died early in 1862, it would be quite easy to argue today that Lincoln would never have issued a proclamation of emancipation, enrolled black solders in the Union army, or advocated allowing some black men to vote. Whatever the makeup of the new southern governments established during a second Lincoln term, had they passed laws, as those established by Johnson did, severely limiting the ability of the former slaves to choose their employment, acquire property, and enjoy the other basic rights Republicans believed essential to freedom, Lincoln undoubtedly would have listened carefully to the outcry for further protection for the former slaves.

Despite their differences, Lincoln had always tried to find common ground with the Republican majority in Congress. It is entirely plausible to imagine Lincoln and Congress agreeing on a Reconstruction policy that encompassed federal protection for basic civil rights plus limited black suffrage, along the lines Lincoln proposed just before his death. Radicals would have demanded more, but this would have been a far cry from what Lincoln's successor was willing to tolerate. Perhaps, confronted by a united Republican party and a president willing to enforce the law, white southerners would have learned to acknowledge the rights of the former slaves. Had they done so, blacks and the nation might have been spared the long nightmare of disenfranchisement, segregation, and racial violence that followed the end of Reconstruction. Or, perhaps, even this Reconstruction plan would have aroused violent opposition in the South. Lincoln would then have faced the alternative that in fact came to confront Congress: whether to move forward to full black suffrage and a vigorous federal commitment to protect blacks' rights as citizens, or relegate the freedpeople to quasi-freedom under the domination of their former masters. No one can say what would have happened then, for by now we have advanced far into the realm of the purely speculative.

Lincoln did not enter the White House expecting to preside over the destruction of slavery. A powerful combination of events, as we have seen, propelled him down the road to emancipation and then to a reconsideration of the place blacks would occupy in a post-slavery America. Of course, the unprecedented crisis in which, as one member of Congress put it, "the events of an entire century transpire in a year," made change the order of the day. Yet as the presidency of his successor demonstrated, not all men placed in a similar situation possessed the capacity for growth, the essence of Lincoln's greatness. "I think we have reason to thank God for Abraham Lincoln," the abolitionist Lydia Maria Child wrote one week before his death. "With all his deficiencies, it must be admitted that he has grown continuously; and considering how slavery had weakened and perverted the moral sense of the whole country, it was great good luck to have the people elect a man who was *willing* to grow."[28]

Two months after Lincoln issued the Emancipation Proclamation, one abolitionist wrote that "to make the proclamation a success, we must make freedom a blessing to the freed."[29] The question of how to do so would long outlive Lincoln and the Civil War.

Acknowledgments

■

BEGINNING WITH MY FIRST WORK OF HISTORY, a study of the ideology of the Republican party before the Civil War published four decades ago, Abraham Lincoln has played an important part in my historical scholarship. But until now, he has not occupied center stage. Nonetheless, like so many other students of the American past, I have always been fascinated by Lincoln and what his life tells us about our society and its history.

In writing this book, I owe my greatest debt to the legions of historians who have studied, from every possible angle, Lincoln and his era. I want to single out for special thanks a number of scholars who have published books during the past decade or so that make available previously inaccessible documentary sources related to Lincoln: Michael Burlingame, for editing a series of volumes of writings by persons close to Lincoln; Don E. Fehrenbacher and Virginia Fehrenbacher, for compiling and evaluating later recollections of Lincoln's words; Douglas L. Wilson and Rodney O. Davis, for gathering and publishing the interviews conducted by Lincoln's law partner William Herndon; and the staff of the Lincoln Legal Papers project, who have produced in digital form the records of Lincoln's law career.

Indeed, thanks to the digital revolution of the past decade, a vast array of primary sources relevant to the study of Lincoln are now readily available online, making the task of the researcher immeasurably less onerous. I thank John Tofanelli of the Columbia University Libraries for assisting me with research on digital sources. Incongruous as it may seem, much of the research for this book in online resources such as the *Official Records* of the Civil War, the *Congressional Globe*, and the Abraham Lincoln Papers at the Library of Congress, as well as Lincoln's *Collected Works* at the website of the Abraham Lincoln Association, was conducted in the spring of 2008 when I was fortunate enough to serve as a Leverhulme Visiting Scholar at Queen Mary University, University of London. I thank the Leverhulme Trust and my colleagues at Queen Mary for making this possible. Thanks, too, to the American Civilization Department at Harvard University, which invited me to deliver the 2009 William E. Massey, Sr., Lectures in the History of American Civilization, where I presented some of the ideas in this book, and to Columbia University, whose Tenured Faculty Research Program helped to defray research expenses.

I am deeply indebted to friends and colleagues who generously read the entire manuscript of this book and offered valuable corrections and suggestions: Alan Brinkley, Andrew Delbanco, Peter Field, Melinda Lawson, Olivia Mahoney, Bruce Miroff, Mark E. Neely Jr., and James Oakes. I have benefited from many conversations about the writing of history with Judith Stein on the way to and from our weekly tennis matches. I also wish to thank scholars who responded to my requests for information and shared the results of their own research: A. J. Aiseirithe, Gregory Baggett, Elizabeth Blackmar, Michael Burlingame, Eduardo Posada Carbo, Harold Holzer, Frank Safford, Lea VanderVelde, and John Witt. Thanayi Jackson and Benjamin Soskis tracked down elusive material for me at the Library of Congress and National Archives. Peter and Philip Kunhardt, Olivia Mahoney, and Susan Severtson helped me to assemble the images in this book.

I owe a special debt of gratitude to my literary agent, Sandra Dijkstra (my classmate at Long Beach High School a number of years ago), for her encouragement, and to Steve Forman, my editor at W. W. Norton, who offered sage advice at every stage of this project. Thanks also to his able assistant, Rebecca Charney, and to Mary Babcock, the excellent copy editor for this book.

As always, my greatest debt is to my wife, Lynn Garafola, and daughter, Daria Rose Foner, not simply for being willing to live with Lincoln, as it were, for several years, but for serving as sounding boards for my ideas and, not least, reading the manuscript and making numerous valuable suggestions.

The book is dedicated to my uncle, Henry Foner, the last survivor of four remarkable brothers, including my late father, Jack D. Foner, who devoted their lives to advancing social justice in this country.

Chronology of Lincoln, Slavery, and Emancipation

1787	U.S. Constitution does not mention the word "slavery" but includes protections for the institution including the fugitive slave and three-fifths clauses.
1808	January: Congress prohibits the importation of slaves into the United States.
1809	February 12: Lincoln is born in Hardin County, Kentucky.
1816	December: Lincoln family moves to southwestern Indiana.
	American Colonization Society is founded.
1820	Missouri Compromise prohibits slavery in Louisiana Purchase territory north of latitude 36°30'.
1828, 1831	Lincoln takes part in two flatboat trips to New Orleans.
1830	March: Lincoln family moves to Macon County, Illinois.
1831	July: Lincoln settles in New Salem, Illinois.
1833–38	Great Britain abolishes slavery throughout its empire.
1833	December: American Anti-Slavery Society is founded.
1834	Lincoln is elected to first of four terms in Illinois House of Representatives.
1837	January: Votes against proslavery legislature resolutions.
	March: With Dan Stone, issues "protest" explaining their votes.
	April: Moves to Springfield, Illinois.

October: Illinois Anti-Slavery Society is formed.

November 7: Abolitionist editor Elijah P. Lovejoy is killed by a mob in Alton, Illinois.

1838   January 27: Lincoln gives his speech "The Perpetuation of Our Political Institutions" at the Young Men's Lyceum, Springfield.

1841   July: Successfully argues case of *Bailey v. Cromwell and McNaughton* before Illinois Supreme Court, winning freedom for Nance Legins-Cox.

September: Encounters twelve chained slaves during a boat trip on the Ohio River.

1842   February 22: Gives a speech before a temperance society in Springfield.

November 4: Marries Mary Todd.

1846   August 3: Wins election to the U.S. House of Representatives.

1847   October: Unsuccessfully represents Robert Matson, who seeks to retain ownership of slaves he has brought from Kentucky to Illinois.

December: Introduces a resolution in the House of Representatives asking President James K. Polk to identify the "spot" of American soil where Mexico allegedly launched war against the United States.

1848   Campaigns in New England for Whig presidential candidate Zachary Taylor.

1849   January 10: Reads to the House of Representatives a bill for gradual abolition of slavery in Washington, D.C., but does not introduce it.

1852   July 6: Gives a eulogy on Henry Clay.

1853   Illinois enacts a law barring African-Americans from entering the state.

1854   January: Stephen A. Douglas introduces the Nebraska bill which, when passed in May as the Kansas-Nebraska Act, repeals the Missouri Compromises and applies the principle of "popular sovereignty" to these territories.

October 16: Lincoln gives a speech against the Kansas-Nebraska Act in Peoria.

1855   February: Fails in his bid for election to the U.S. Senate.

1856   May 29: Takes part in the Bloomington, Illinois, convention of the Republican party; delivers his "lost speech."

September–October: Campaigns for John C. Frémont, Republican candidate for president.

1857 March 6: Supreme Court issues its *Dred Scott* decision, stating that blacks cannot be citizens of the United States and that Congress lacks authority to bar slavery from any territory.

June 26: Lincoln gives a speech in Springfield criticizing the *Dred Scott* decision.

1858 Serves on the Board of Managers of the Illinois Colonization Society.

June 16: Gives his House Divided speech at the Republican state convention in Springfield.

August–October: Lincoln and Stephen A. Douglas debate.

November: Democrats retain control of the Illinois legislature, ensuring defeat of Lincoln's candidacy for the U.S. Senate.

1860 February 27: Lincoln gives a speech at Cooper Institute, New York City.

May 18: Is nominated for president by the Republican National Convention in Chicago.

November 6: Is elected the sixteenth president of the United States.

December 20: South Carolina secedes from the Union; six other southern states soon follow.

1861 February 4: Seceded states meet in Montgomery, form the Confederate States of America, and elect Jefferson Davis president.

March 2: U.S. Congress adopts the proposed Thirteenth Amendment forbidding future national action against slavery.

March 4: Lincoln gives his first inaugural address.

April 12: The attack on Fort Sumter begins the Civil War.

April 15: Lincoln calls for troops to put down the rebellion; four more states secede by May.

May 24: General Benjamin F. Butler declares that fugitive slaves at Fortress Monroe, Virginia, are "contraband of war" and will not be returned to their owners.

August 6: Lincoln signs the first Confiscation Act, which nullifies owners' claims to slaves employed by the Confederate army.

September 11: Lincoln orders General John C. Frémont to modify the order in which he had declared slaves of Confederates in Missouri free.

November: Proposes his plan to Delaware for gradual, compensated emancipation.

December 3: Gives his annual message to Congress, recommending a program of compensated emancipation and colonization of freed slaves outside the United States.

1862   March 6: Sends a message to Congress calling for aid to states that adopt plans of gradual, compensated emancipation.

March 13: Signs an additional article of war passed by Congress, forbidding the army from returning fugitive slaves.

April 16: Signs a bill for immediate abolition of slavery in the District of Columbia, with compensation to loyal owners and funds for colonization.

May 19: Nullifies the order of Major General David Hunter freeing slaves in South Carolina, Georgia, and Florida.

May 20: Signs the Homestead Act.

May–June: Peninsular campaign of General George B. McClellan fails.

June 19: Lincoln signs the bill for immediate, uncompensated abolition in the territories.

July 12: Meets with members of Congress from the border states to promote a plan for gradual, compensated emancipation with colonization.

July 13: Mentions his plan for general emancipation to cabinet members Gideon Welles and William H. Seward.

July 17: Signs the Second Confiscation Act freeing slaves owned by disloyal persons who come within Union lines and providing funds for colonization.

Signs the Militia Act authorizing enrollment of blacks in the war effort.

July 22: Presents to the cabinet an order for general emancipation in the Confederacy; issuance is postponed at the urging of Secretary of State Seward and others.

August 14: Meets at the White House with a black delegation and urges them to support the idea of colonization.

August 22: Releases his letter responding to Horace Greeley's "Prayer of Twenty Millions."

August 25: The War Department authorizes recruitment of black soldiers in the Sea Islands.

September 22: Five days after the battle of Antietam, Lincoln issues the Preliminary Emancipation Proclamation, warning that slaves in areas still in rebellion on January 1 will be freed, promising aid to states that adopt plans for gradual, compensated emancipation, and again referring to colonization.

November 29: Attorney General Edward Bates rules that free black persons born in the United States are American citizens.

December 1: Lincoln's annual message to Congress reiterates his support for gradual, compensated emancipation with colonization.

December 31: Lincoln signs the bill admitting West Virginia to the Union.

Signs a contract with Bernard Kock for the transportation of freed slaves to Île à Vache, Haiti.

1863   January 1: Issues the Emancipation Proclamation, freeing all slaves in the Confederacy except certain exempted areas, and authorizing enlistment of blacks into armed forces.

February: West Virginia provides for gradual emancipation; immediate abolition is enacted early in 1865.

March 16: American Freedmen's Inquiry Commission is appointed to recommend policies regarding emancipated slaves.

May–July: Black soldiers take part in battles at Port Hudson and Milliken's Bend, Louisiana, and Fort Wagner, South Carolina.

July 1–4: Union army wins battles at Gettysburg and Vicksburg.

July 30: Lincoln issues an order for retaliation for the mistreatment of black soldiers.

August 10: Meets with Frederick Douglass to discuss recruitment and treatment of black troops.

August 26: Lincoln's public letter to James C. Conkling defends his emancipation policy.

November 19: Lincoln gives the Gettysburg Address.

December 8: Outlines his Ten Percent Plan of Reconstruction and issues the Proclamation of Amnesty and Reconstruction.

1864   March 13: Sends letter to Michael Hahn, governor of Louisiana, favoring limited black suffrage.

March 16: Voters in Arkansas ratify the state constitution abolishing slavery.

April 8: The Senate approves the Thirteenth Amendment abolishing slavery.

May–June: General Ulysses S. Grant's campaign in Virginia leads to enormous casualties.

June 15: The House fails to approve the Thirteenth Amendment.

June 15: Lincoln signs the bill providing partial retroactive equal pay for black soldiers; full retroactive equal pay is enacted in March 1865.

July 4: Pocket vetoes Wade-Davis Bill.

August 16: Meets with Frederick Douglass about ways to spread news of the Emancipation Proclamation among slaves.

September 2: General William T. Sherman occupies Atlanta.

September 5: Voters of Louisiana ratify the state constitution abolishing slavery.

October 13: Voters of Maryland ratify the state constitution abolishing slavery.

November 8: Lincoln is reelected president.

1865   January 11: Missouri constitutional convention provides for abolition; constitution is ratified in June.

January 13: U.S. House of Representatives approves the Thirteenth Amendment.

January 16: General William T. Sherman issues Special Field Order No. 15 assigning plots of land to black families.

February: Illinois Black Laws are repealed.

February 3: Hampton Roads conference takes place.

February 22: Tennessee approves a constitutional amendment abolishing slavery.

March 3: Lincoln signs bill freeing wives and children of black soldiers.

Signs the bill establishing the Freedmen's Bureau.

March 4: Gives his second inaugural address.

April 9: General Robert E. Lee surrenders at Appomattox Court House, Virginia.

April 11: In the last speech before his death, Lincoln favors limited black suffrage in the South.

April 14/15: Lincoln is assassinated.

December 18: Thirteenth Amendment is ratified; slavery is abolished.

Abbreviations Used in Notes

ALP   Abraham Lincoln Papers, Library of Congress
ALPLM   Abraham Lincoln Presidential Library and Museum, Springfield, Ill.
BD   Theodore C. Pease, ed., *The Diary of Orville Hickman Browning* (2 vols.;
          Springfield, Ill., 1927)
CG   *Congressional Globe*
CP   John Niven, ed., *The Salmon P. Chase Papers* (5 vols.; Kent, Ohio, 1993–98)
CW   Roy P. Basler, ed., *The Collected Works of Abraham Lincoln* (8 vols.; New
          Brunswick, N.J., 1953–55)
CWH   *Civil War History*
GP   Sidney Howard Gay Papers, Rare Book and Manuscripts Library, Colum-
          bia University
HL   Huntington Library, San Marino, Calif.
JAH   *Journal of American History*
JALA   *Journal of the Abraham Lincoln Association*
JIH   *Journal of Illinois History*
JISHS   *Journal of the Illinois State Historical Society*
JSH   *Journal of Southern History*
LC   Library of Congress
LTP   Lyman Trumbull Papers, Library of Congress
NA   National Archives
OR   U.S. War Department, *The War of the Rebellion: A Compilation of the Offi-
          cial Records of the Union and Confederate Armies* (70 vols.; Washington,
          D.C., 1880–1901)
RG   Record Group
WD   Howard K. Beale, ed., *Diary of Gideon Welles* (3 vols.; New York, 1960)

Notes

Preface

1. Andrew Boyd, *A Memorial Lincoln Bibliography* (Albany, 1870).
2. Richard N. Current, *The Lincoln Nobody Knows* (New York, 1958), 12; T. J. Barnett to Samuel L. M. Barlow, June 6, 1863, Samuel L. M. Barlow Papers, HL.
3. For the perils of using "recollected words" attributed to Lincoln, see Don E. Fehrenbacher and Virginia Fehrenbacher, eds., *Recollected Words of Abraham Lincoln* (Stanford, 1996); and Don E. Fehrenbacher, "The Words of Lincoln," in John L. Thomas, ed., *Abraham Lincoln and the American Political Tradition* (Amherst, Mass., 1986), 31–49.
4. See Douglas L. Wilson, *Lincoln's Sword: The Presidency and the Power of Words* (New York, 2006).
5. *The Works of Charles Sumner* (15 vols.; Boston, 1870–83), 4: 10–11.
6. See, for example, William Lee Miller, *Lincoln's Virtues: An Ethical Biography* (New York, 2002), 151, 181, 192, 228; Joseph R. Fornieri, "Lincoln and the Emancipation Proclamation: A Model of Prudent Leadership," in Ethan Fishman, ed., *Tempered Strength: Studies in the Nature and Scope of Prudential Leadership* (Lanham, Md., 2002), 127–32; Jean Bethke Elshtain, "Forward," in Kenneth L. Deutsch and Joseph R. Fornieri, eds., *Lincoln's American Dream* (Washington, D.C., 2005), ix; Allen C. Guelzo, "Lincoln and the Abolitionists," *Wilson Quarterly*, 24 (Autumn 2000), 66–69. A significant recent counter to this point of view is James Oakes, *The Radical and the Politician: Frederick Douglass, Abraham Lincoln, and the Triumph of Antislavery Politics* (New York, 2007).
7. *CW*, 5: 318, 389.
8. Miller, *Lincoln's Virtues*, 105; *Chicago Tribune*, April 12, 1865; Peter Lassman and Ronald Speirs, eds., *Max Weber: Political Writings* (New York, 1994), 352–59, 369.

9. Matthew Pinsker, "Lincoln Theme 2.0," *JAH*, 96 (September 2009), 432–33.

10. *Chicago Daily Tribune*, May 15, 1858.

11. "Introduction," in Joseph R. Fornieri and Sara V. Gabbard, eds., *Lincoln's America, 1809–1865* (Carbondale, Ill., 2008), 3.

1 *"I Am Naturally Anti-Slavery"*

1. *CW*, 7: 281. We know little of Lincoln's early life. In David Donald's biography, Lincoln reaches the age of twenty-one in fewer than 20 pages. Donald, *Lincoln* (New York, 1995). In Michael Burlingame's 2,000-page *Abraham Lincoln: A Life* (2 vols.; Baltimore, 2008), his youth occupies fewer than 50 pages.

2. Marion B. Lucas, *A History of Blacks in Kentucky*, vol. 1: *From Slavery to Segregation, 1760–1891* (Frankfort, Ky., 1992), xv–xx, 2–3; Elizabeth Fox-Genovese and Eugene D. Genovese, *Slavery in White and Black: Class and Race in the Southern Slaveholders' New World Order* (New York, 2008), 7; Michael Burlingame, *The Inner World of Abraham Lincoln* (Urbana, Ill., 1994), 21; Richard L. Miller, *Lincoln and His World: The Early Years, Birth to Illinois Legislature* (Mechanicsburg, Pa., 2006), 17–29. For the division between Lower South, Upper South, and Border South, see William W. Freehling, *The Road to Disunion: Secessionists Triumphant, 1854–1861* (New York, 2007), 2–3.

3. Lowell H. Harrison, *The Antislavery Movement in Kentucky* (Lexington, Ky., 1978), 20–25; James F. Hopkins, ed., *Papers of Henry Clay* (10 vols.; Lexington, Ky., 1959–91), 1: 5–7; J. Blaine Hudson, "In Pursuit of Freedom: Slave Law and Emancipation in Louisville and Jefferson County, Kentucky," *Filson History Quarterly*, 76 (Summer 2002), 290–92; Kenneth J. Winkle, " 'Paradox Though it may Seem': Lincoln on Antislavery, Race, and Union, 1837–1860," in Brian Dirck, ed., *Lincoln Emancipated: The President and the Politics of Race* (DeKalb, Ill., 2007), 10.

4. Stephen Aron, *How the West Was Lost: The Transformation of Kentucky from Daniel Boone to Henry Clay* (Baltimore, 1996), 99–100; Monica Najar, " 'Meddling with Emancipation': Baptists, Authority, and the Rift over Emancipation in the Upper South," *Journal of the Early Republic*, 25 (Summer 2005), 157–87; Louis Warren, *Lincoln's Youth: Indiana Years* (New York, 1959), 13; Miller, *Lincoln and His World: Early Years*, 27; Ronald C. White Jr., *A. Lincoln: A Biography* (New York, 2009), 18.

5. *CW*, 4: 62; Thomas Cooper, *Some Information Respecting America* (London, 1794), 25; Kenneth J. Winkle, *The Young Eagle: The Rise of Abraham Lincoln* (Dallas, 2001), 11; Andrew R. L. Cayton, *Frontier Indiana* (Bloomington, Ind., 1996), 261–67.

6. Jeremy Adelman and Stephen Aron, "From Borderlands to Borders: Empires, Nation-States, and the Peoples in Between in North American History," *American Historical Review*, 104 (June 1999), 814–23; Nicole Etcheson, *The Emerging Midwest: Upland Southerners and the Political Culture of the Old Northwest, 1787–1861* (Bloomington, Ind., 1996), 4–5; William N. Parker, "From Northwest to Midwest: Social Bases of a Regional History," in David C. Klingaman and

Richard K. Vedder, eds., *Essays in Nineteenth Century Economic History: The Old Northwest* (Athens, Ohio, 1975), 23; J. L. Balen to Justin S. Morrill, March 11, 1859, Justin S. Morrill Papers, LC.

7. James E. Davis, *Frontier Illinois* (Bloomington, Ind., 1998), 157; *National Era*, August 19, 1847; *CW*, 3: 135.

8. Richard Yates and Catherine Yates Pickering, *Richard Yates: Civil War Governor* (Danville, Ill., 1966), 107; John Mack Faragher, *Sugar Creek: Life on the Illinois Prairie* (New Haven, 1986), 46–48; Etcheson, *Emerging Midwest*, 67.

9. Cayton, *Frontier Indiana*, 189–90; John C. Hammond, *Slavery, Freedom, and Expansion in the Early American West* (Charlottesville, 2007), 97–103, 116–21.

10. Paul Simon, *Lincoln's Preparation for Greatness* (Norman, Okla., 1965), 121; Paul Finkelman, "Evading the Ordinance: The Persistence of Bondage in Indiana and Illinois," *Journal of the Early Republic*, 9 (Spring 1989), 35–48; Arvah E. Strickland, "The Illinois Background of Lincoln's Attitude toward Slavery and the Negro," *JISHS*, 56 (Autumn 1963), 476.

11. Davis, *Frontier Illinois*, 167–68; Suzanne C. Guasco, " 'The Deadly Influence of Negro Capitalists': Southern Yeomen and Resistance to the Expansion of Slavery in Illinois," *CWH*, 47 (March 2001), 7–11; *CW*, 3: 455–57.

12. Paul M. Angle, ed., *Prairie State: Impressions of Illinois, 1673–1967, by Travelers and Other Observers* (Chicago, 1968), 81; N. Dwight Harris, *The History of Negro Servitude in Illinois* (Chicago, 1904), 48–52, 226–27; Simon, *Lincoln's Preparation*, 124–25.

13. Merton L. Dillon, "The Antislavery Movement in Illinois, 1809–1844" (unpub. diss., University of Michigan, 1951), 124; Harris, *History of Negro Servitude*, 229, 235; Elmer Gertz, "The Black Codes of Illinois," *JISHS*, 56 (Autumn 1963), 454–73; "Notes on Illinois: Laws," *Illinois Monthly Magazine* (March 1832), 244; *Liberator*, April 3, 1840.

14. Winkle, *Young Eagle*, 50.

15. For the market revolution and its impact, see Charles Sellers, *The Market Revolution: Jacksonian America, 1815–1846* (New York, 1991); and Melvin Stokes and Stephen Conway, eds., *The Market Revolution in America: Social, Political, and Religious Expressions, 1800–1880* (Charlottesville, 1996).

16. Burlingame, *Abraham Lincoln: A Life*, 1: 43–44, 56–57.

17. Thomas C. Buchanan, *Black Life on the Mississippi: Slaves, Free Blacks, and the Western Steamboat World* (Chapel Hill, 2004); *CW*, 4: 62.

18. Albert A. Fossier, *New Orleans: The Glamour Period, 1800–1840* (New Orleans, 1957); Joseph G. Tregle Jr., "Early New Orleans Society: A Reappraisal," *JSH*, 18 (February 1952), 20–36; J. P. Mayer, ed., *Journey to America*, trans. George Lawrence (New Haven, 1959), 164–65; Richard C. Wade, *Slavery in the Cities: The South, 1820–1860* (New York, 1964), 150.

19. Miller, *Lincoln and His World: Early Years*, 81–82; Wade, *Slavery in the Cities*, 5–6, 199–201; Walter Johnson, *Soul by Soul: Life inside the Antebellum Slave Market* (Cambridge, Mass., 1999).

20. Douglas L. Wilson and Rodney O. Davis, eds., *Herndon's Informants* (Urbana, Ill.,

1998), 457; Miller, *Lincoln and His World: Early Years,* 104–5; *CW,* 4: 64. Hanks also later claimed that Lincoln exclaimed after watching a New Orleans slave auction, "If I ever get a chance to hit that thing, I'll hit it hard." Don E. Fehrenbacher and Virginia Fehrenbacher, who have evaluated numerous such recollected statements by Lincoln, consider this one among the least credible. Don E. Fehrenbacher and Virginia Fehrenbacher, eds., *Recollected Words of Abraham Lincoln* (Stanford, 1996), 198. Allen Gentry's grandson claimed that his grandmother, Gentry's wife, related that Lincoln called a slave auction he witnessed in New Orleans a "disgrace." But the interview in which the grandson related this occurred in 1936, over a century after the alleged statement. Burlingame, *Abraham Lincoln: A Life,* 1: 44.

21. *BD,* 1: 138–39.

22. David Herbert Donald, *"We Are Lincoln Men": Abraham Lincoln and His Friends* (New York, 2003), 29, 44–47, 55; *CW,* 2: 320.

23. Joseph A. Harder, "The Lincoln-Douglass 'Debate': Abraham Lincoln, Frederick Douglass and the Rediscovery of America" (unpub. diss., University of Virginia, 2004), 27–28; *CW,* 1: 260–61.

24. Miller, *Lincoln and His World: Early Years,* 198, 231; Lucas, *History of Blacks in Kentucky,* 1: 89; Catherine Clinton, *Mrs. Lincoln: A Life* (New York, 2009), 15–17.

25. Richard E. Hart, "Springfield's African-Americans as a Part of the Lincoln Community," *JALA,* 20 (Winter 1999), 40–42; Stephen Berry, *House of Abraham: Lincoln and the Todds, a Family Divided by War* (Boston, 2007), xii–xiii, 40; William H. Townsend, *Lincoln and His Wife's Home Town* (Indianapolis, 1929), 192.

26. Berry, *House of Abraham,* x–xii, 41–42.

27. Townsend, *Lincoln and His Wife's Home Town,* 95, 140–55, 214, 226, 243.

28. In addition to the laws of Kentucky and Illinois mentioned earlier, see Paul Finkelman, "Prelude to the Fourteenth Amendment: Black Legal Rights in the Antebellum North," *Rutgers Law Journal,* 17 (Spring and Summer 1986), 425.

29. William Lee Miller, *Lincoln's Virtues: An Ethical Biography* (New York, 2002), 26–44.

30. Alexis de Tocqueville, *Democracy in America,* ed. J. P. Mayer, trans. George Lawrence (New York, 1966), 627.

31. Arthur Zilversmit, *The First Emancipation: The Abolition of Slavery in the North* (Chicago, 1967), 114–28; Stanley L. Engerman, "Emancipations in Comparative Perspective: A Long and Wide View," in Gert Oostine, ed., *Fifty Years Later: Antislavery, Capitalism and Modernity in the Dutch Orbit* (Pittsburgh, 1996), 227–29; Stanley L. Engerman, *Slavery, Emancipation and Freedom: Comparative Perspectives* (Baton Rouge, 2007), 4–5, 36–50; David Brion Davis, "The Emancipation Moment," in Gabor S. Boritt, ed., *Lincoln the War President* (New York, 1992), 75–79; *CW,* 6: 48–49. An article in the *New York Commercial Advertiser,* reprinted in *Douglass' Monthly* (April 1862), 636–37, summarizes the various measures that abolished slavery in the northern states.

32. Eric Foner, *The Story of American Freedom* (New York, 1998), 40–41; Winthrop D. Jordan, *White over Black: American Attitudes toward the Negro, 1550–1812* (Chapel

Hill, 1968), 354; Leonard P. Curry, *The Free Black in Urban America, 1800–1850* (Chicago, 1981), 260; Leon F. Litwack, *North of Slavery: The Negro in the Free States, 1790–1860* (Chicago, 1961), 31–54, 74–93; David W. Blight, *Frederick Douglass' Civil War: Keeping Faith in Jubilee* (Baton Rouge, 1989), 13.

33. Philip S. Foner, *Business and Slavery: The New York Merchants and the Irrepressible Conflict* (Chapel Hill, 1941); Steven Deyle, *Carry Me Back: The Domestic Slave Trade in American Life* (New York, 2005); James L. Huston, "Property Rights in Slavery and the Coming of the Civil War," *JSH*, 65 (May 1999), 254.

34. Betty L. Fladeland, "Compensated Emancipation: A Rejected Alternative," *JSH*, 42 (May 1976), 171–76; Robert P. Forbes, *The Missouri Compromise and Its Aftermath: Slavery and the Meaning of America* (Chapel Hill, 2007), 170.

35. *Harper's Weekly*, April 5, 1862; Forbes, *Missouri Compromise*, 28, 219, 251; David Brion Davis, "Reconsidering the Colonization Movement: Leonard Bacon and the Problem of Evil," *Intellectual History Newsletter*, 14 (1992), 3–4.

36. Philip S. Foner, ed., *The Life and Writings of Frederick Douglass* (5 vols.; New York, 1950–75), 1: 390; Merrill D. Peterson, ed., *Thomas Jefferson: Writings* (New York, 1984), 1484–87.

37. Isaac V. Brown, *Biography of the Rev. Robert Finley* (2nd ed.; Philadelphia, 1857), 103–15; Douglas R. Edgerton, "Averting a Crisis: The Proslavery Critique of the American Colonization Society," *CWH*, 43 (June 1997), 143–47; Daniel W. Howe, *The Political Culture of the American Whigs* (Chicago, 1979), 136.

38. Robert V. Remini, *Henry Clay: Statesman for the Union* (New York, 1991), 491–92, 508, 617–18, 772–73; Hopkins, *Papers of Henry Clay*, 8: 483; 9: 256–57, 779–80; 10: 356, 844–46; Harold D. Tallant, *Evil Necessity: Slavery and Political Culture in Antebellum Kentucky* (Lexington, Ky., 2003), 49; Edgerton, "Averting a Crisis," 147.

39. Schuyler Colfax to William H. Seward, April 27, 1850, William H. Seward Papers, Rush Rhees Library, University of Rochester; *CW*, 2: 79; 3: 29; Remini, *Henry Clay*, 8n.; Hopkins, *Papers of Henry Clay*, 10: 844–46.

40. Dixon D. Bruce Jr., "National Identity and African-American Colonization, 1773–1817," *Historian*, 58 (Autumn 1995), 15–28; Floyd J. Miller, *The Search for a Black Nationality: Black Emigration and Colonization, 1787–1863* (Urbana, Ill., 1975), 25–29, 49–50; Leonard I. Sweet, *Black Images of America, 1784–1870* (New York, 1976), 39–43.

41. William Lloyd Garrison, *Thoughts on African Colonization* (Boston, 1832), 5; *Proceedings of the American Anti-Slavery Society at Its Third Decade* (New York, 1864), 19–20; Manisha Sinha, "Black Abolitionism: The Assault on Southern Slavery and the Struggle for Equal Rights," in Ira Berlin and Leslie Harris, eds., *Slavery in New York* (New York, 2005), 243; Hopkins, *Papers of Henry Clay*, 8: 773, 793.

42. Robert Cover, *Justice Accused: Antislavery and the Judicial Process* (New Haven, 1975), 44–45; Wendell Phillips, *Speeches, Lectures, and Letters* (Boston, 1863), 110; Patrick Rael, *Black Identity and Black Protest in the Antebellum North* (Chapel Hill, 2002), 47.

43. Paul Starr, *The Creation of the Media* (New York, 2004), 86–88; Richard S. Newman, *The Transformation of American Abolitionism: Fighting Slavery in the Early Republic* (Chapel Hill, 2002), 131–32, 158–59.

44. Newman, *Transformation*, 6; Merrill D. Peterson, *The Jeffersonian Image in the American Mind* (New York, 1960), 172–73; *Liberator*, January 1, 1831; Zebina Eastman, "History of the Anti-Slavery Agitation, and the Growth of the Liberty and Republican Parties in the State of Illinois," in Rufus Blanchard, *Discovery and Conquests of the North-west, with the History of Chicago* (Wheaton, Ill., 1879), 663–65; C. Peter Ripley et al., eds., *The Black Abolitionist Papers* (5 vols.; Chapel Hill, 1985–93), 3: 191.

45. Larry Cephair, ed., *The Public Years of Sarah and Angelina Grimké: Selected Writings, 1835–1839* (New York, 1989), 194–95; William E. Nelson, *The Roots of American Bureaucracy, 1830–1900* (Cambridge, Mass., 1982), 51; Jacobus tenBroek, *The Antislavery Origins of the Fourteenth Amendment* (Berkeley, 1951), 71–90; Lydia Maria Child, *An Appeal in Favor of That Class of Americans Called Africans* (Boston, 1833).

46. Newman, *Transformation*, 120; Foner, *Life and Writings of Frederick Douglass*, 4: 167–68; Paul Goodman, *Of One Blood: Abolitionism and the Origins of Racial Equality* (Berkeley, 1998), 1, 57–62; *Colored American* (New York), May 9, 1840.

47. Sean Wilentz, *The Rise of American Democracy: Jefferson to Lincoln* (New York, 2005), 423–32; Leonard P. Richards, *"Gentlemen of Property and Standing": Anti-Abolition Mobs in Jacksonian America* (New York, 1970), 12–14.

48. Randolph A. Roth, *The Democratic Dilemma: Religion, Reform, and the Social Order in the Connecticut River Valley of Vermont, 1791–1850* (New York, 1987), 180; Richards, *"Gentlemen,"* 27–36; Hopkins, *Papers of Henry Clay*, 9: 81, 278–82.

49. Dillon, "Antislavery Movement," 132–44; Winkle, "Paradox," 14–15; Willard L. King, *Lincoln's Manager: David Davis* (Cambridge, Mass., 1960), 51; Charles N. Zucker, "The Free Negro Question: Race Relations in Antebellum Illinois, 1801–1860" (unpub. diss., Northwestern University, 1972), 191, 319.

50. *Liberator*, August 4, 1837; Dillon, "Antislavery Movement," 176–89; Wilentz, *Rise*, 486; Edward Magdol, *Owen Lovejoy: Abolitionist in Congress* (New Brunswick, N.J., 1967), 11.

51. Richard L. Miller, *Lincoln and His World: Prairie Politician, 1834–1842* (Mechanicsburg, Pa., 2008), 204–5; *Proceedings of the Ill. Anti-Slavery Convention: Held at Upper Alton on the Twenty-sixth, Twenty-seventh, and Twenty-eighth October, 1837* (Alton, 1838), 1–11.

52. *Proceedings of the Ill. Anti-Slavery Convention*, 14–22; Dillon, "Antislavery Movement," 294–95; Dana E. Weiner, "Racial Radicals: Antislavery Activism in the Old Northwest" (unpub. diss., Northwestern University, 2007), 319–20, 338–39.

53. James B. Stewart, "The Emergence of Racial Modernity and the Rise of the White North, 1790–1840," *Journal of the Early Republic*, 18 (Summer 1998), 197–201; Harris, *History of Negro Servitude*, 62–67, 97; *Chicago Tribune*, June 12, 1874; Winkle, *Young Eagle*, 257; Michael K. Curtis, "The 1837 Killing of Elijah Lovejoy by an Anti-Abolition Mob: Free Speech, Mobs, Republican Government, and the

Privileges of American Citizens," *UCLA Law Review*, 44 (April 1997), 1009–11, 1046–50.

54. Zucker, "Free Negro Question," 270–77; Weiner, "Racial Radicals," 129–31; Dana E. Weiner, "Anti-Abolition Violence and Freedom of Speech in Peoria, Illinois, 1843–1848," *JIH*, 11 (Autumn 2008), 179–81; *Liberator*, May 26, 1843.

55. Orville H. Browning to Isaac N. Arnold, November 25, 1872, Isaac N. Arnold Papers, Chicago History Museum.

56. *African Repository and Colonial Journal*, 13 (April 1837), 109; *Journal of the Senate of the Tenth General Assembly of the State of Illinois* (Vandalia, [1837]), 195–98; *Journal of the House of Representatives of the Tenth General Assembly of the State of Illinois* (Vandalia, [1837]), 238–44.

57. *CW*, 1: 74–75.

58. *CW*, 4: 65; *CG*, 36th Congress, 2nd Session, appendix, 248.

59. *Chicago Press and Tribune*, June 5, 1860; *Journal of the House of Representatives*, 238; Burlingame, *Abraham Lincoln: A Life*, 1: 122–27; Wilson and Davis, eds., *Herndon's Lincoln*, 119. David Donald calls the protest "a cautious limited dissent," which seems unfair. Donald, *Lincoln*, 63.

60. Davis, *Frontier Illinois*, 243; *CW*, 1: 108–15; Dorothy Ross, "Lincoln and the Ethics of Emancipation: Universalism, Nationalism, Exceptionalism," *JAH*, 96 (September 2009), 387; Michael Feldberg, *The Turbulent Era: Riot and Disorder in Jacksonian America* (New York, 1980), 3–4; Miller, *Lincoln and His World: Prairie Politician*, 210–11.

61. For example, George B. Forgie, *Patricide in the House Divided: A Psychological Interpretation of Lincoln and His Age* (New York, 1979); Donald, *Lincoln*, 81–82; Richard Striner, *Father Abraham: Lincoln's Relentless Struggle to End Slavery* (New York, 2006), 30; and William E. Gienapp, *Abraham Lincoln and Civil War America* (New York, 2002), 31–32. Burlingame suggests that Lincoln aimed his warning of a future tyrant against Douglas. Burlingame, *Abraham Lincoln: A Life*, 1: 140.

62. John Ashworth, *"Agrarians" and "Aristocrats": Party Political Ideology in the United States, 1837–1846* (London, 1983), 59–61.

63. *CW*, 1: 109–13; Neil Schmitz, "Murdered McIntosh, Murdered Lovejoy: Abraham Lincoln and the Problem of Jacksonian Address," *Arizona Quarterly*, 44 (Autumn 1988), 26.

64. Michael K. Curtis, *Free Speech, "The People's Darling Privilege": Struggles for Freedom of Expression in American History* (Durham, 2000), 10–13, 185–87, 260–61; Major L. Wilson, "Lincoln and Van Buren in the Steps of the Fathers: Another Look at the Lyceum Address," *CWH*, 29 (September 1983), 197.

65. Faragher, *Sugar Creek*, 152; Winkle, *Young Eagle*, 274–85; *CW*, 6: 487.

66. *CW*, 1: 271–79.

67. Gabor S. Boritt, *Lincoln and the Economics of the American Dream* (Memphis, 1978), 97–98; *CW*, 3: 5–6, 16.

68. *CW*, 1: 279.

69. *Journal of the House of Representatives of the Ninth General Assembly of the State of Illinois* (Vandalia, 1836), 236.

70. Burlingame, *Abraham Lincoln: A Life*, 1: 109–10, 154–55; Miller, *Lincoln and His World: Prairie Politician*, 53–54, 77; King, *Lincoln's Manager*, 38; Zucker, "Free Negro Question," 181–83; *The Votes and Speeches of Martin Van Buren, on the Subjects of the Right of Suffrage . . .* (New York, 1840).

2 *"Always a Whig"*

1. *CW*, 1: 180, 201–5, 315; 3: 511–12; Joel Silbey, " 'Always a Whig in Politics': The Partisan Life of Abraham Lincoln," *Papers of the Abraham Lincoln Association*, 8 (1986), 21–24; Michael Burlingame, "Lincoln Spins the Press," in Charles M. Hubbard, ed., *Lincoln Reshapes the Presidency* (Macon, Ga., 2003), 65; Harry E. Pratt, ed., *Illinois as Lincoln Knew It* (Springfield, Ill., 1938), 33.

2. Donald W. Riddle, *Lincoln Runs for Congress* (New Brunswick, N.J., 1948), 36–38; Douglas L. Wilson and Rodney O. Davis, eds., *Herndon's Informants* (Urbana, Ill., 1998), 480; Michael F. Holt, *The Rise and Fall of the American Whig Party* (New York, 1999), 214–15.

3. Daniel W. Howe, "Why Abraham Lincoln Was a Whig," *JALA*, 16 (Winter 1995), 27–38; Kenneth J. Winkle, *The Young Eagle: The Rise of Abraham Lincoln* (Dallas, 2001), 186–88, 247.

4. Daniel W. Howe, *The Political Culture of the American Whigs* (Chicago, 1979); John Ashworth, *Slavery, Capitalism, and Politics in the Antebellum Republic* (2 vols.; New York, 1995–2007), 1: 315–23.

5. Calvin Colton, *Labor and Capital* (New York, 1844), 36; John Ashworth, *"Agrarians" and "Aristocrats": Party Political Ideology in the United States, 1837–1846* (London, 1983), 62–71; Thomas Brown, *Politics and Statesmanship: Essays on the American Whig Party* (New York, 1985), 48, 120, 179; Eric Foner, *Free Soil, Free Labor, Free Men: The Ideology of the Republican Party before the Civil War* (New York, 1995 ed.), xx–xxi; Howe, *Political Culture*, 131.

6. Eric Foner, *The Story of American Freedom* (New York, 1998), 54–55; Robert W. Johannsen, ed., *The Letters of Stephen A. Douglas* (Urbana, Ill., 1961), 42–44.

7. Mark Noll, "Lincoln's God," *Journal of Presbyterian History*, 82 (Summer 2004), 79–80; Richard Carwardine, *Lincoln* (London, 2003), 30–36; Allen C. Guelzo, "A. Lincoln, Philosopher: Lincoln's Place in Nineteenth-Century Intellectual History," in Joseph R. Fornieri and Sara V. Gabbard, eds., *Lincoln's America, 1809–1865* (Carbondale, Ill., 2008), 75–86; Wilson and Davis, *Herndon's Informants*, 13, 61, 472; *CW*, 1: 382. Philip Ostergard lists every biblical reference in Lincoln's letters and speeches. Clearly, Lincoln was very familiar with Scripture. Philip L. Ostergard, *The Inspired Wisdom of Abraham Lincoln* (Carol Stream, Ill., 2008).

8. Darrel E. Bigham, *Towns and Villages of the Lower Ohio* (Lexington, Ky., 1998), 27–40; William E. Bartelt, *"There I Grew Up": Remembering Abraham Lincoln's Indiana Youth* (Indianapolis, 2008), 34; Winkle, *Young Eagle*, 12–18; Wilson and Davis, *Herndon's Informants*, 27, 39, 93; *CG*, 37th Congress, 2nd Session, 3338; Don E. Fehrenbacher and Virginia Fehrenbacher, eds., *Recollected Words of*

Abraham Lincoln (Stanford, 1996), 383. The Fehrenbachers are skeptical regarding the recollection of Lincoln referring to himself as a slave, while Michael Burlingame credits it as reflecting the origin of Lincoln's antislavery beliefs. Michael Burlingame, *Abraham Lincoln: A Life* (2 vols.; Baltimore, 2008), 1: 42.

9. Robert Mazrim, *The Sangamo Frontier: History and Archaeology in the Shadow of Lincoln* (Chicago, 2007), 116–19, 305; Winkle, *Young Eagle*, 43–54, 77, 99, 156–59; Benjamin P. Thomas, *Lincoln's New Salem* (Springfield, Ill., 1954), 6–37; Paul M. Angle, *"Here I Have Lived": A History of Lincoln's Springfield, 1821–1865* (New Brunswick, N.J., 1935), 23–35, 154–58; Pratt, *Illinois as Lincoln Knew It*, 79; James E. Davis, *Frontier Illinois* (Bloomington, Ind., 1998), 198–207.

10. Fehrenbacher and Fehrenbacher, *Recollected Words*, 395–96; Jean H. Baker, "Coming of Age in New Salem and Springfield: Lincoln Goes to Town," in Timothy P. Townsend, ed., *Papers from the Thirteenth and Fourteenth Annual Lincoln Colloquia* (Springfield, Ill., n.d.), 142–51; William Cronon et al., "Becoming West: Toward a New Meaning for Western History," in William Cronon et al., eds., *Under an Open Sky: Rethinking America's Western Past* (New York, 1992), 12–23; Scott A. Sandage, *Born Losers: A History of Failure in America* (Cambridge, Mass., 2005), 156–58.

11. William Lee Miller, *Lincoln's Virtues: An Ethical Biography* (New York, 2002), 60–61; *CW*, 2: 15–16, 96–97; 4: 61; John L. Scripps, *Life of Abraham Lincoln*, eds. Roy P. Basler and Lloyd A. Dunlap (New York, 1968), 26.

12. Emanuel Hertz, *The Hidden Lincoln* (New York, 1938), 117; Paul K. Conkin, *Prophets of Prosperity: America's First Political Economists* (Bloomington, Ind., 1980), 116–23; Francis Wayland, *The Elements of Political Economy* (2nd ed.; New York, 1838), 7, 105–6, 110–22, 417; *CW*, 2: 32; 3: 361, 472–80.

13. Kenneth J. Winkle, "The Middle-Class Marriage of Abraham and Mary Lincoln," in Fornieri and Gabbard, *Lincoln's America*, 94–114; *CW*, 4: 65; 2: 220–21; David Herbert Donald, *"We Are Lincoln Men": Abraham Lincoln and His Friends* (New York, 2003), 24–26; Thomas, *Lincoln's New Salem*, 88–110; Burlingame, *Abraham Lincoln: A Life*, 1: 78; Matthew W. Backes, "The Father and the Middle Class: Paternal Authority, Filial Independence, and the Transformation of American Culture, 1800–1850" (unpub. diss., Columbia University, 2005), 1–14.

14. Silbey, "Always a Whig," 28–29; Ashworth, *"Agrarians,"* 52–57, 117, 163–64; Sean Wilentz, *The Rise of American Democracy: Jefferson to Lincoln* (New York, 2005), 503–6.

15. *CW*, 1: 48. David Donald, unlike most biographers, thinks Lincoln included women as a joke and that his reference to paying taxes as a requirement for voting was meant to exclude propertyless Irish-born canal workers, who tended to vote Democratic. David Herbert Donald, *Lincoln* (New York, 1995), 59. Burlingame sees Lincoln as a "proto-feminist," no doubt a considerable exaggeration. Burlingame, *Abraham Lincoln: A Life*, 1: 104. The Illinois Constitution of 1818 contained neither a taxpaying nor a property qualification for voting, although it limited the suffrage to white males. Alexander Keyssar, *The Right to Vote: The Contested History of Democracy in the United States* (New York, 2000), appendix A.

16. *CW*, 1: 1–8; 3: 511.

17. Michael Burlingame, ed., *An Oral History of Abraham Lincoln: John G. Nicolay's Interviews and Essays* (Carbondale, Ill., 1996), 30–31; Wilson and Davis, *Herndon's Informants*, 476; Johannsen, *Letters of Stephen A. Douglas*, 68; Paul Simon, *Lincoln's Preparation for Greatness* (Norman, Okla., 1965), 48–53, 147–56, 184–86; Gabor S. Boritt, *Lincoln and the Economics of the American Dream* (Memphis, 1978), 26–25; *CW*, 1: 200–1.

18. Robert G. Gunderson, *The Log-Cabin Campaign* (Lexington, Ky., 1957), 109; George W. Julian, *Political Recollections, 1840 to 1872* (Chicago, 1884), 11–13; Boritt, *Lincoln and Economics*, 63–72; Richard L. Miller, *Lincoln and His World: Prairie Politician, 1834–1842* (Mechanicsburg, Pa., 2008), 342.

19. *CW*, 1: 307–11, 329, 334, 381–82; 3: 487.

20. Thomas Corwin to John McLean, September 8, 1845, John McLean Papers, LC; Theodore C. Pease, ed., *Illinois Election Returns, 1818–1848* (Springfield, Ill., 1923), 117, 149; Vernon L. Volpe, *Forlorn Hope of Freedom: The Liberty Party in the Old Northwest, 1838–1848* (Kent, Ohio, 1990), 64–69; Reinhard O. Johnson, *The Liberty Party, 1840–1848: Antislavery Third-Party Politics in the United States* (Baton Rouge, 2009), 197–201.

21. Pease, *Illinois Election Returns*, 149; *CW*, 1: 347–48.

22. Mark E. Brandon, *Free in the World: American Slavery and Constitutional Failure* (Princeton, 1998), 52–57; Lysander Spooner, *The Unconstitutionality of Slavery* (Boston, 1845), 36.

23. *Cincinnati Gazette*, March 26, 1860; George W. Julian, *The Life of Joshua R. Giddings* (Chicago, 1892), 118–19, 134, 417–23; *The Works of Charles Sumner* (15 vols.; Boston, 1870–83), 2: 288; *CP*, 2: 79–80, 87–88; Foner, *Free Soil*, 73–87.

24. T. K. Hunter, "Transatlantic Negotiations: Lord Mansfield, Liberty and Somerset," *Texas Wesleyan Law Review*, 13 (Symposium 2007), 711–27; Mark S. Weiner, *Black Trials: Citizenship from the Beginnings of Slavery to the End of Caste* (New York, 2004), 84–86; Douglas R. Egerton, *Death or Liberty: African Americans and Revolutionary America* (New York, 2009), 52–55.

25. John Niven, *Salmon P. Chase: A Biography* (New York, 1995), 51–54; *CP*, 1: xxi–xxiii; *Law Reporter* (Boston), 9 (April 1847), 553.

26. Leonard W. Levy, *The Law of the Commonwealth and Chief Justice Shaw* (Cambridge, Mass., 1957), 58–71; Paul Finkelman, *An Imperfect Union: Slavery, Federalism, and Comity* (Chapel Hill, 1981), 43–127.

27. Newton N. Newbern, "Judicial Decision Making and the End of Slavery in Illinois," *JISHS*, 98 (Spring–Summer 2005), 7–11; Finkelman, *Imperfect Union*, 97–99; Horace White, *The Life of Lyman Trumbull* (Boston, 1913), 28–29.

28. N. Dwight Harris, *The History of Negro Servitude in Illinois* (Chicago, 1904), 122–23; *BD*, 1: xvi; *Chicago Daily Tribune*, August 5, 1857; Martha L. Brenner and Cullom Davis, eds., *The Law Practice of Abraham Lincoln* (3 CDs; Urbana, Ill., 2000): *McElroy v. Clements* (1857), *Dickinson v. Canton* (1860); Mark M. Krug, *Lyman Trumbull, Conservative Radical* (New York, 1965), 57–68.

29. *CW*, 3: 518; Brian Dirck, *Lincoln the Lawyer* (Urbana, Ill., 2007), 56–61, 106;

Brenner and Davis, *Law Practice*. Lincoln's cases involving blacks included *Shelby v. Shelby* (1841), *Unknown v. Smith* (1845), *Flourville v. Stockdale et al.* (1849), *Flourville v. Allen et al.* (1853), and *People v. Hill* (1854).

30. Brenner and Davis, *Law Practice: Edwards et ux. v. Edwards et ux.* (1844), *Dungey v. Spencer* (1855); Stacey P. McDermott, " 'Black Bill' and the Privileges of Whiteness in Antebellum Illinois," *JIH*, 12 (Spring 2009), 2–26.

31. Brenner and Davis, *Law Practice: People v. Pond* (1845), *People v. Kern* (1847), *People v. Scott* (1847).

32. Carl Adams, "Lincoln's First Freed Slave: A Review of *Bailey v. Cromwell*, 1841," *JISHS*, 102 (Spring 2009), 235–59; Brenner and Davis, *Law Practice: Bailey v. Cromwell and McNaughton* (1841). By the time Lincoln argued the case, his partnership with John Todd Stuart had been dissolved and Lincoln was junior partner to Stephen T. Logan. Most accounts of the case refer to the woman simply as "Nance," but Adams identifies her full name.

33. Brenner and Davis, *Law Practice: In Re Bryant, et al.* (1847), *Matson for Use of Coles County Illinois v. Rutherford* (1847). Accounts of the case include Jesse W. Weik, "Lincoln and the Matson Negroes," *Arena*, 17 (April 1897), 752–58; Anton-Hermann Chroust, "Abraham Lincoln Argues a Pro-Slavery Case," *American Journal of Legal History*, 5 (October 1961), 299–308; and Mark E. Steiner, *An Honest Calling: The Law Practice of Abraham Lincoln* (DeKalb, Ill., 2006), 103–25.

34. *North Star*, February 4, 1848.

35. Weik, "Lincoln and the Matson Negroes," 755–58; Brenner and Davis, *Law Practice: In Re Bryant, et al.* (1847). For a relevant discussion of morality and the law, see Steve Sheppard, *I Do Solemnly Swear: The Moral Obligations of Legal Officials* (New York, 2009).

36. Michael Burlingame writes of lawyers' "ideological neutrality" to exonerate Lincoln in the Matson case. Burlingame, *Abraham Lincoln: A Life*, 1: 253. Dirck also excuses Lincoln's representation of Matson. Dirck, *Lincoln the Lawyer*, 147–49.

37. Donald, *Lincoln*, 133–35.

38. Robert V. Remini, *Henry Clay: Statesman for the Union* (New York, 1991), 692–93; James F. Hopkins, ed., *Papers of Henry Clay* (10 vols.; Lexington, Ky., 1959–91), 10: 361–73.

39. John S. Wright, *Lincoln and the Politics of Slavery* (Reno, 1970), 18–19; *CG*, 30th Congress, 1st Session, 391; *CW*, 2: 252.

40. *CG*, 30th Congress, 2nd Session, appendix, 79–80.

41. Holt, *Rise and Fall*, 285–308.

42. Wright, *Lincoln and the Politics of Slavery*, 23; *CW*, 1: 381–82; *CG*, 30th Congress, 1st Session, 523. The vote on the Ashmun resolution was reported as 85 to 81, but the actual list of ayes and nays shows only 82 in favor. *CG*, 30th Congress, 1st Session, 95.

43. *CW*, 1: 433–41.

44. *CW*, 1: 420–21; *Hudson River Chronicle* (Sing-Sing, N.Y.), August 15, 1848; *CG*, 30th Congress, 1st Session, 61–62, 175, 229; appendix, 156, 170.

45. William C. Harris, *Lincoln's Rise to the Presidency* (Lawrence, Kans., 2007), 41;

Herbert Mitgang, ed., *Abraham Lincoln: A Press Portrait* (Chicago, 1971), 57; Winkle, *Young Eagle*, 241–42; *CW*, 3: 6; 6: 300–305.

46. *CW*, 1: 475; Julian, *Political Recollections*, 53–63; Foner, *Free Soil*, 124–25; Frederick W. Seward, *Seward at Washington* (2 vols.; New York, 1891), 1: 71.

47. *CW*, 1: 505; 2: 3–9.

48. Seward, *Seward at Washington*, 1: 79–80; George E. Baker, ed., *The Works of William H. Seward* (5 vols.; New York, 1853–84), 3: 287–88, 301; *CW*, 1: 454.

49. Julian, *Life of Joshua R. Giddings*, 246; James B. Stewart, *Joshua R. Giddings and the Tactics of Radical Politics* (Cleveland, 1970), 88; Burlingame, *Abraham Lincoln: A Life*, 1: 284.

50. Stewart, *Joshua R. Giddings*, 168–70; *CG*, 30th Congress, 2nd Session, 31, 38, 55, 83–84; appendix, 127; Julian, *Life of Joshua R. Giddings*, 259–61. Lincoln did vote, along with all the other northern Whigs, against tabling antislavery petitions. *CG*, 30th Congress, 1st Session, 60, 73, 82, 180.

51. Joshua R. Giddings Diary, January 8 and 9, 1849, Joshua R. Giddings Papers, Ohio Historical Society; Paul H. Verdun, "Partners for Emancipation: New Light on Lincoln, Joshua Giddings, and the Push to End Slavery in the District of Columbia, 1848–49," in Townsend, *Papers*, 66–81.

52. *CW*, 2: 20; *CG*, 30th Congress, 2nd Session, 210.

53. Julian, *Life of Joshua R. Giddings*, 259–61; D. W. Bartlett, *Life and Public Services of Hon. Abraham Lincoln* (New York, 1860), 42; *CW*, 3: 39–40.

54. Giddings Diary, January 11, 1849, Giddings Papers; *Liberator*, June 22, July 13, and August 24, 1860.

55. *CW*, 2: 22.

56. *CG*, 30th Congress, 2nd Session, 239, 302.

57. *CG* 30th Congress, 2nd Session, 123–24, 129, 177, 247, 303.

58. William E. Gienapp, *Abraham Lincoln and Civil War America* (New York, 2002), 40–45; Carwardine, *Lincoln*, 22; *New York Tribune*, January 1, 1851; *CW*, 2: 126–32; 3: 424–25.

59. William H. Townsend, *Lincoln and His Wife's Home Town* (Indianapolis, 1929), 222; Hopkins, *Papers of Henry Clay*, 10: 574–80; Carwardine, *Lincoln*, 21; *CW*, 2: 318.

60. Winkle, *Young Eagle*, 290; Wright, *Lincoln and Politics of Slavery*, 47–48; *CW*, 2: 158; Wilentz, *Rise*, 684; Stephen L. Hansen, *The Making of the Third Party System: Voters and Parties in Illinois, 1850–1876* (Ann Arbor, 1980), 7–11.

61. Holt, *Rise and Fall*, 754; Elihu B. Washburne to Zebina Eastman, February 3, 1874, Zebina Eastman Papers, Chicago History Museum.

3 *"The Monstrous Injustice"*

1. Eric Foner, *Free Soil, Free Labor, Free Men: The Ideology of the Republican Party before the Civil War* (New York, 1970), 94.

2. J. W. Taylor to Salmon P. Chase, February 7, 1854, Salmon P. Chase Papers, LC.

3. Lewis E. Lehrman, *Lincoln at Peoria: The Turning Point* (Mechanicsburg, Pa., 2008), 37–38; Herbert Mitgang, ed., *Abraham Lincoln: A Press Portrait* (Chicago, 1971), 141–42.

4. *CW*, 2: 514; Joseph F. Newton, *Lincoln and Herndon* (Cedar Rapids, 1910), 82–83.

5. Michael Burlingame, *Abraham Lincoln: A Life* (2 vols.; Baltimore, 2008), 1: 370; Lehrman, *Lincoln at Peoria*, 33–44; *CW*, 2: 226–33; Douglas L. Wilson, *Lincoln's Sword: The Presidency and the Power of Words* (New York, 2006), 37.

6. *CW*, 2: 247–81; Robert W. Johannsen, ed., *The Letters of Stephen A. Douglas* (Urbana, Ill., 1961), 284.

7. Mitgang, *Abraham Lincoln: Press Portrait*, 71.

8. *CW*, 4: 67; Jacques Barzun, *On Writing, Editing, and Publishing: Essays Explorative and Hortatory* (Chicago, 1971), 57–73; Douglas L. Wilson and Rodney O. Davis, eds., *Herndon's Informants* (Urbana, Ill., 1998), 508; Joseph Logsdon, *Horace White, Nineteenth Century Liberal* (Westport, Conn., 1971), 21–22.

9. Ronald C. White, *A. Lincoln: A Biography* (New York, 2009), 198; *CW*, 2: 500; 4: 240–41.

10. Richard Beeman, *Plain, Honest Men: The Making of the U. S. Constitution* (New York, 2009), 217–25.

11. Robert Fanuzzi, *Abolition's Public Sphere* (Minneapolis, 2003), xvi, 7–12; Foner, *Free Soil*, 83–84; *CG*, 31st Congress, 1st Session, appendix, 469–71; Merrill D. Peterson, *The Jeffersonian Image in the American Mind* (New York, 1960), 199–203; *Speech of O. H. Browning, Delivered at the Republican Mass Meeting, Springfield, Ill., August 8, 1860* (Quincy, 1860), 5–8; Patrick W. Riddleberger, *George Washington Julian: Radical Republican* (Indianapolis, 1966), 127; *CG*, 36th Congress, 1st Session, 731.

12. John C. Hammond, *Slavery, Freedom, and Expansion in the Early American West* (Charlottesville, 2007), 1–7, 24–30; Peterson, *Jeffersonian Image*, 195, 216; Beeman, *Plain, Honest Men*, 213–15; John C. Miller, *The Wolf by the Ears: Thomas Jefferson and Slavery* (New York, 1977), 123, 143–45, 221–40; Lacy Ford, "Reconfiguring the Old South: 'Solving' the Problem of Slavery, 1787–1838," *JAH*, 95 (June 2008), 106; Merrill D. Peterson, ed., *Thomas Jefferson: Writings* (New York, 1984), 1343–46.

13. *CW*, 2: 492, 514; James Oakes, *The Radical and the Republican: Frederick Douglass, Abraham Lincoln, and the Triumph of Antislavery Politics* (New York, 2007), 70–72; C. Peter Ripley et al., eds., *The Black Abolitionist Papers* (5 vols.; Chapel Hill, 1985–93), 5: 91.

14. *CW*, 2: 499–501; 3: 404; Graham A. Peck, "Abraham Lincoln and the Triumph of an Antislavery Nationalism," *JALA*, 28 (Summer 2007), 2–6.

15. *Douglass' Monthly*, 3 (June 1860), 274; *CW*, 2: 282; *New York Tribune*, March 17, 1854.

16. Foner, *Free Soil*, 126–28, 237–39.

17. Foner, *Free Soil*, 193–95; *Richmond Enquirer* in *Ohio State Journal*, April 19, 1854; Frederick W. Seward, *Seward at Washington* (2 vols.; New York, 1891), 1: 120; *New York Times*, May 29, 1854; *New York Tribune*, November 9, 1854.

18. David Davis to Julius Rockwell, July 15, 1854, David Davis Papers, ALPLM; Paul Selby, "Republican State Convention, Springfield, Ill., October 4–5, 1854," *Transactions of the McLean County Historical Society*, 3 (1900), 43–47; William E. Gienapp, *The Origins of the Republican Party, 1852–1856* (New York, 1987), 84, 123–24; *CW*, 2: 288.

19. Chicago *Democratic Press*, August 30, 1854; Gienapp, *Origins*, 125; Edward Magdol, *Owen Lovejoy: Abolitionist in Congress* (New Brunswick, N.J., 1967), 116–17.

20. Don E. Fehrenbacher, *Prelude to Greatness: Lincoln in the 1850s* (Stanford, 1962), 37; Horace White to Abraham Lincoln, October 25, 1854, ALP.

21. *CW*, 2: 288–92, 304; Thomas J. Henderson to Lincoln, December 11, 1854; Augustus Adams to Lincoln, December 17, 1854, both in ALP.

22. Magdol, *Owen Lovejoy*, 118–20; Charles H. Ray to Elihu B. Washburne, December 24, 1854, Elihu B. Washburne Papers, LC; *CW*, 2: 293; Washburne to Lincoln, December 26, 1854, ALP; Washburne to Zebina Eastman, December 19, 1854, Zebina Eastman Papers, Chicago History Museum; William F. Moore and Jane Ann Moore, eds., *His Brother's Blood: Speeches and Writings, 1838–1864, Owen Lovejoy* (Urbana, Ill., 2004), xiii.

23. Roy F. Basler and Christian O. Basler, eds., *The Collected Works of Abraham Lincoln: Second Supplement, 1848–1865* (New Brunswick, N.J., 1990), 9–11; *CW*, 2: 304–6; Fehrenbacher, *Prelude*, 38.

24. George T. Allen to Lyman Trumbull, January 19, 1856, LTP; *Frederick Douglass' Paper*, March 2, 1855. At this point, Lincoln's name had almost never appeared in eastern abolitionist newspapers (at least, those now searchable online).

25. Gienapp, *Origins*, 189–237, 286; *CW*, 2: 316–17; Lyman Trumbull to Owen Lovejoy, August 20, 1855, Dr. William Jayne Papers, ALPLM; Silas Ramsey to Trumbull, March 7, 1856, LTP.

26. *CW*, 2: 322–23.

27. *CW*, 1: 337–38; N. Levering, "Recollections of Abraham Lincoln," *Iowa Historical Record*, 12 (July 1896), 495–96.

28. Gienapp, *Origins*, 239–40; Burlingame, *Abraham Lincoln: A Life*, 1: 411–12; Paul Selby, "The Editorial Convention of 1856," *JISHS*, 5 (July 1912), 343–46; George Schneider, "Lincoln and the Anti-Know-Nothing Resolutions," *Transactions of the McLean County Historical Society*, 3 (1900), 88–90; *Chicago Daily Tribune*, February 25, 1856.

29. *Chicago Press and Tribune*, April 8, 1859; Stephen L. Hansen, *The Making of the Third Party System: Voters and Parties in Illinois, 1850–1876* (Ann Arbor, 1980), 78.

30. Burlingame, *Abraham Lincoln: A Life*, 1: 417; Maurice Baxter, *Orville H. Browning: Lincoln's Friend and Critic* (Bloomington, Ind., 1957), 86; "Official Record of Convention," *Transactions of the McLean County Historical Society*, 3 (1900), 148–64; *Chicago Democratic Press*, May 31, 1856. Burlingame suggests that the failure to report Lincoln's speech may have been deliberate, as he spoke from notes and his remarks were not fully worked out. Burlingame, *Abraham Lincoln: A Life*, 1: 420.

31. Joseph Medill to Lincoln, August 9, 1860, ALP; Magdol, *Owen Lovejoy*, 147; John S. Wright, *Lincoln and the Politics of Slavery* (Reno, 1970), 100.

32. *Proceedings of the First Three Republican National Conventions* (Minneapolis, 1893), 7–20; Salmon P. Chase to George W. Julian, July 17, 1856, Giddings-Julian Papers, LC; Philip S. Foner, ed., *The Life and Writings of Frederick Douglass* (5 vols.; New York, 1950–75), 2: 392; George W. Julian, *The Life of Joshua R. Giddings* (Chicago, 1892), 335; George W. Julian, *Speeches on Political Questions* (New York, 1872), 146.

33. *CW*, 2: 342; Nathaniel G. Wilcox to Lincoln, June 6, 1864, ALP; *Proceedings of the First Three Republican National Conventions*, 61–64.

34. Richard Yates to Lyman Trumbull, August 3, 1856, LTP.

35. *CW*, 2: 347–50, 358, 365, 367, 379, 413.

36. Hansen, *Making of the Third Party System*, 83–85; CG, 35th Congress, 1st Session, 1346; William C. Harris, *Lincoln's Rise to the Presidency* (Lawrence, Kans., 2007), 80; Thomas J. McCormack, ed., *Memoirs of Gustave Koerner 1809–1896* (2 vols.; Cedar Rapids, 1909), 2: 22.

37. Sean Wilentz, *The Rise of American Democracy: Jefferson to Lincoln* (New York, 2005), 720; Gienapp, *Origins*, 416.

38. John Mack Faragher, *Sugar Creek: Life on the Illinois Prairie* (New Haven, 1986), 177–80, 221; Arthur C. Cole, *The Era of the Civil War, 1848–1870* (Springfield, Ill., 1919), 27, 75; Andrew R. L. Cayton and Peter S. Onuf, *The Midwest and the Nation* (Bloomington, Ind., 1990), 37–38; David C. Klingaman and Richard K. Vedder, eds., *Essays in Nineteenth Century Economic History: The Old Northwest* (Athens, Ohio, 1975), 25–28; *CW*, 2: 415. The jury proved unable to agree on a verdict and the case was not retried, so Lincoln's client did not have to pay damages.

39. Fehrenbacher, *Prelude*, 5–8; Olivier Fraysse, *Lincoln, Land, and Labor, 1809–60*, trans. Sylvia Neely (Urbana, Ill., 1994), 137; *New York Evening Post*, September 22, 1858.

40. Foner, *Free Soil*, 103–48; CG, 30th Congress, 1st Session, appendix, 518–19; 34th Congress, 3rd Session, 11.

41. Foner, *Free Soil*, 186–225.

42. Elizabeth B. Clark, " 'The Sacred Rights of the Weak': Pain, Sympathy, and the Culture of Individual Rights in Antebellum America," *JAH*, 82 (September 1995), 463–93; Philip S. Paludan, "Lincoln and Negro Slavery: I Haven't Got Time for the Pain," *JALA*, 27 (Summer 2006), 1–23; Julian, *Speeches*, 8; Magdol, *Owen Lovejoy*, 223; CG, 36th Congress, 1st Session, 202–6; *The Works of Charles Sumner* (15 vols.; Boston, 1870–83), 4: 11–13; *CW*, 2: 320; 4: 8.

43. Richard Carwardine, *Lincoln* (London, 2003), 91, 269–72; Foner, *Free Soil*, 108–9; Joshua R. Giddings to Sidney Howard Gay, March 3, 1858, GP; CG, 36th Congress, 1st Session, appendix, 224; *CW*, 2: 255; 3: 334.

44. Robert C. Winthrop Jr., *A Memoir of Robert C. Winthrop* (Boston, 1877), 188; Henry G. Pearson, *The Life of John A. Andrew* (2 vols.; Boston, 1904), 101–3; Foner, *Free Soil*, 41–44.

45. *CW*, 2: 156, 320; Magdol, *Owen Lovejoy*, 125.

46. *CW*, 2: 362, 494; 3: 313; 4: 10–11; *Speech of R. W. Thompson, Upon the Political Aspects of the Slavery Question* (Terre Haute, 1855), 6.

47. David Herbert Donald, *"We Are Lincoln Men": Abraham Lincoln and His Friends* (New York, 2003), 79; Paul M. Angle, ed., *Herndon's Life of Lincoln* (New York, 1949), 294–95; Carl F. Wieck, *Lincoln's Search for Equality* (DeKalb, Ill., 2002), 18–22; Newton, *Lincoln and Herndon*, 51; Robert Bray, "What Abraham Lincoln Read—An Evaluative and Annotated List," *JALA*, 28 (Summer 2007), 50.

48. Willard L. King, *Lincoln's Manager: David Davis* (Cambridge, Mass., 1960), 126–29; *CW*, 3: 355–56; Charles Francis Adams to Francis Bird, October 16, 1854, Letterbooks, Adams Family Papers, Massachusetts Historical Society.

49. Burlingame, *Abraham Lincoln: A Life*, 1: 424, 456; Roy F. Basler, ed., *The Collected Works of Abraham Lincoln: First Supplement, 1832–1865* (New Brunswick, N.J., 1974), 27; King, *Lincoln's Manager*, 103, 155–56; Lew Wallace, *Lew Wallace: An Autobiography* (2 vols.; New York, 1906), 1: 73–76; Moore and Moore, *His Brother's Blood*, 129.

50. *CW*, 2: 435–36, 458; Lincoln to Charles H. Ray, June 6, 1858, Papers of Abraham Lincoln (available online in New Document Discoveries section, website of Papers of Abraham Lincoln); Abraham Smith to Lincoln, May 31 and June 4, 1858; Ward Hill Lamon to Lincoln, June 9, 1858; Owen Lovejoy to Lincoln, August 4, 1858, all in ALP; Hans L. Trefousse, "Owen Lovejoy and Abraham Lincoln during the Civil War," *JALA*, 22 (Winter 2001), 15–32.

51. *Chicago Daily Tribune*, July 15, 1858; *CW*, 2: 482.

52. *CW*, 2: 385; 3: 423.

53. Wendell Phillips, *Speeches, Lectures, and Letters* (Boston, 1863), 353; *Liberator*, June 8, 1860.

54. Sarah F. Hughes, ed., *Letters (Supplementary) of John Murray Forbes* (3 vols.; Boston, 1905), 1: 167–78; Sarah F. Hughes, ed., *Letters and Recollections of John Murray Forbes* (2 vols.; Boston, 1899), 1: 153–55, 185.

4 *"A House Divided"*

1. Don E. Fehrenbacher, *The Dred Scott Case: Its Significance in American Law and Politics* (New York, 1978), 2–4, 324–49; Lea VanderVelde, *Mrs. Dred Scott: A Life on Slavery's Frontier* (New York, 2009), xiv; *CG*, 39th Congress, 1st Session, 75; J. R. Pole, *The Pursuit of Equality in American History* (2nd ed.; Berkeley, 1993), 182–84; Mark A. Graber, *Dred Scott and the Problem of Constitutional Evil* (New York, 2006), 57–59.

2. *New York Times*, March 7, 1857; Eric Foner and Olivia Mahoney, *A House Divided: America in the Age of Lincoln* (New York, 1990), 60.

3. Michael Vorenberg, "Abraham Lincoln's 'Fellow Citizens'–Before and After Emancipation," in William A. Blair and Karen F. Younger, eds., *Lincoln's Proclamation: Emancipation Reconsidered* (Chapel Hill, 2009), 151–52; Fehrenbacher, *Dred Scott*, 64–70; James H. Kettner, *The Development of American Citizenship,*

1608–1870 (Chapel Hill, 1978), 256–59; Noah Webster, *An American Dictionary of the English Language* (4th ed.; New York, 1830), 148; Graber, *Dred Scott*, 29–56.

4. *Anglo-African Magazine*, I (May 1859), 149–50; *Cleveland Leader*, March 27, 1857; *Chicago Daily Tribune*, April 10, 1857; Eric Foner, *Free Soil, Free Labor, Free Men: The Ideology of the Republican Party before the Civil War* (New York, 1970), 293; Charles W. Smith, *Roger B. Taney: Jacksonian Jurist* (Chapel Hill, 1936), 173; *Springfield Republican*, April 13, 1858.

5. *Springfield Republican*, March 11, 1857; Kenneth M. Stampp, *America in 1857: A Nation on the Brink* (New York, 1992), 105–8; Sarah F. Hughes, ed., *Letters (Supplementary) of John Murray Forbes* (3 vols.; Boston, 1905), I: 190.

6. James F. Simon, *Lincoln and Chief Justice Taney: Slavery, Secession and the President's War Power* (New York, 2006), 133–38; CW, 2: 391, 398–99.

7. CW, 2: 448.

8. CW, 2: 398–410; Fehrenbacher, *Dred Scott*, 406–8.

9. Richard K. Crallé, ed., *Works of John C. Calhoun* (6 vols.; Charleston, S.C., 1851–55), I: 507–8; Elizabeth Fox-Genovese and Eugene Genovese, *Slavery in White and Black: Class and Race in the Southern Slaveholders' New World Order* (New York, 2008), 8–21, 80–81; Merrill D. Peterson, *The Jeffersonian Image in the American Mind* (New York, 1960), 164–65; Paul M. Angle, ed., *Herndon's Life of Lincoln* (New York, 1949), 294–95; CW, 3: 204–5.

10. Isaac N. Arnold, *The History of Abraham Lincoln and the Overthrow of Slavery* (Chicago, 1866), 122–26; CW, 2: 405–9.

11. Foner, *Free Soil*, 131; Glyndon G. Van Deusen, *Horace Greeley: Nineteenth-Century Crusader* (Philadelphia, 1953), 225–28; CW, 2: 430; Lyman Trumbull to Lincoln, January 3, 1858, ALP.

12. Horace White, *The Life of Lyman Trumbull* (Boston, 1913), 87; Elihu B. Washburne to Lincoln, May 2, 1858, ALP; Don E. Fehrenbacher, *Prelude to Greatness: Lincoln in the 1850s* (Stanford, 1962), 54–63; *Proceedings of the Republican State Convention, Held at Springfield, Illinois, June 16, 1858* (Springfield, Ill., 1858), 8.

13. CW, 2: 446, 461–69.

14. Frederick Douglass, *Life and Times of Frederick Douglass* (Hartford, 1882), 300; William C. Harris, *Lincoln's Rise to the Presidency* (Lawrence, Kans., 2007), 94; John L. Scripps to Lincoln, June 22, 1858, ALP; Robert V. Remini, *Henry Clay: Statesman for the Union* (New York, 1991), 146; CG, 31st Congress, 1st Session, appendix, 943; *Speech of Hon. Salmon P. Chase, Delivered at the Republican Mass Meeting in Cincinnati, August 21, 1855* (Columbus, Ohio, 1855), 8; Solomon Foot, *Reasons for Joining the Republican Party* (New York, 1855), 6. The phrase "ultimate extinction" does not appear in Lincoln's *Collected Works* before the House Divided speech, except in a "fragment" that appears to be an early draft of that address. CW, 2: 453.

15. David Zarefsky, *Lincoln, Douglas and Slavery* (Chicago, 1990), 44; CW, 3: 17; Theodore Parker, *A Sermon of the Dangers Which Threaten the Rights of Man in America* (Boston, 1854), 27; Harvey Wish, *George Fitzhugh, Propagandist of the Old South* (Baton Rouge, 1943), 151.

16. Foner, *Free Soil*, 94–102; *Ohio State Journal*, March 11, 1857; George E. Baker, ed., *The Works of William H. Seward* (5 vols.; New York, 1853–84), 4: 294; John L. Scripps to Lincoln, July 3, 1858, ALP; Thomas J. Davis, "*Napoleon v. Lemmon*: Antebellum New Yorkers, Antislavery, and Law," *Afro-Americans in New York Life and History*, 33 (January 2009), 27–46; *Chicago Tribune*, October 13, 1857; *New York Times*, April 21, 1860; *New York Tribune*, April 21, 1860; *CW*, 3: 548n.

17. Foner, *Free Soil*, 70–72; Baker, *Works of William H. Seward*, 4: 289–92.

18. Baker, *Works of William H. Seward*, 4: 122, 226–27, 311–12, 333; Glyndon G. Van Deusen, *William Henry Seward* (New York, 1967), 204–9; *CW*, 3: 356–57; 4: 50.

19. Paul M. Angle, ed., *Created Equal? The Complete Lincoln-Douglas Debates of 1858* (Chicago, 1958), 14–21.

20. *CW*, 2: 487–501; 3: 254–55.

21. Zarefsky, *Lincoln, Douglas and Slavery*, 46–48; Allen C. Guelzo, *Lincoln and Douglas: The Debates That Defined America* (New York, 2008), 102; Waldo W. Braden, *Abraham Lincoln: Public Speaker* (Baton Rouge, 1988), 23–35; *Chicago Press and Tribune*, August 23, 1858; Willard L. King, *Lincoln's Manager: David Davis* (Cambridge, Mass., 1960), 122.

22. Fehrenbacher, *Prelude*, 104–9; *CW*, 3: 3, 111, 268; Zarefsky, *Lincoln, Douglas and Slavery*, 52–53, 156–60; Carl Schurz, *The Reminiscences of Carl Schurz* (3 vols.; New York, 1907–8), 2: 98–99; James G. Blaine, *Twenty Years of Congress* (2 vols.; Norwich, Conn., 1884), 1: 147–49; Allen C. Guelzo, "Houses Divided: Lincoln, Douglas, and the Political Landscape of 1858," *JAH*, 94 (September 2007), 391. The only other issue mentioned with any frequency in Republican correspondence in 1858 was Lincoln's conduct as a congressman during the Mexican War.

23. Leander Munsell to Lincoln, August 16, 1858, ALP; *CW*, 3: 1–29; Zarefsky, *Lincoln, Douglas and Slavery*, 56.

24. Joseph Medill to Lincoln, August 27, 1858, ALP; *CW*, 3: 39–40.

25. *CW*, 3: 43, 51–52, 295; Angle, *Created Equal?*, 58–59; Robert W. Johannsen, *Stephen A. Douglas* (New York, 1973), 670–71.

26. Joseph Medill to Lincoln, August 27, 1858; Jediah F. Alexander to Lincoln, August 5, 1858, both in ALP.

27. *CW*, 3: 145–46, 179.

28. *CW*, 3: 5, 140, 177, 213–14, 220, 299–300; Walter B. Stevens, *A Reporter's Lincoln*, ed. Michael Burlingame (Lincoln, Neb., 1998), 86; David Davis to Lincoln, September 25, 1858, ALP.

29. *CW*, 3: 11, 225–26, 254–55.

30. Guelzo, *Lincoln and Douglas*, 367; *CW*, 3: 284, 304–15.

31. Zarefsky, *Lincoln, Douglas and Slavery*, 49–52; *CW*, 2: 479–81, 545; Angle, *Created Equal?*, 33; Frederick Douglass to Susan B. Anthony, June 5, 1861, Harper Collection, HL.

32. David Davis to Lincoln, August 3, 1858, ALP; J. McCan Davis, *Abraham Lincoln: His Book* (New York, 1903).

33. *CW*, 3: 327–28; Christopher N. Breiseth, "Lincoln, Douglas, and Springfield in the 1858 Campaign," in Cullom Davis et al., eds., *The Public and the Private Lincoln: Contemporary Perspectives* (Carbondale, Ill., 1979), 16–17.

34. Guelzo, *Lincoln and Douglas*, 282–88; Michael Burlingame, *Abraham Lincoln: A Life* (2 vols.; Baltimore, 2008), 1: 548–49; Joseph F. Newton, *Lincoln and Herndon* (Cedar Rapids, 1910), 234; *New York Tribune*, June 24, 1858; *CW*, 4: 34; *Chicago Press and Tribune*, November 5, 1858.

35. Burlingame, *Abraham Lincoln: A Life*, 1: 546; *Chicago Press and Tribune*, November 5, 1858.

36. Roy F. Nichols, *The Disruption of American Democracy* (New York, 1948), 205–25; Charles H. Ray to Lincoln, July 27, 1858, ALP; *National Era*, November 18, 1858; *Independent*, October 21, 1858; Benjamin W. Arnett, ed., *Duplicate Copy of the Souvenir from the Afro-American League of Tennessee to Hon. James M. Ashley of Ohio* (Philadelphia, 1894), 17–18; Philip S. Foner, *The Life and Writings of Frederick Douglass* (5 vols.; New York, 1950–73), 5: 409–10; *CW*, 3: 18, 181, 337, 340; Guelzo, "Houses Divided," 417.

37. *CG*, 33rd Congress, 1st Session, appendix, 447. For a full discussion of the free-labor ideology of the Republican party, see Foner, *Free Soil*.

38. Marcus Cunliffe, *Chattel Slavery and Wage Slavery: The Anglo-American Context, 1830–1860* (Athens, Ga., 1979), 7; Manisha Sinha, *The Counterrevolution of Slavery: Ideology and Politics in Antebellum South Carolina* (Chapel Hill, 2000), 88–93, 140–42, 222–29; *CG*, 35th Congress, 1st Session, 962.

39. *New York Times*, November 18, 1857; *CG*, 35th Congress, 1st Session, 1093; Istvan Hont and Michael Ignatieff, "Needs and Justice in the *Wealth of Nations*: An Introductory Essay," in Istvan Hont and Michael Ignatieff, eds., *Wealth and Virtue: The Shaping of Political Economy in the Scottish Enlightenment* (Cambridge, U.K., 1983), 13–15; John Ashworth, "Free Labor, Wage Labor, and the Slave Power: Republicanism and the Republican Party in the 1850s," in Melvyn Stokes and Stephen Conway, eds., *The Market Revolution in America: Social, Political, and Religious Expressions, 1800–1880* (Charlottesville, 1996), 139–40.

40. *CW*, 1: 411–12.

41. *CW*, 2: 364.

42. Stephen A. Douglas, "The Dividing Line between Federal and Local Authority: Popular Sovereignty in the Territories," *Harper's New Monthly Magazine*, 19 (September 1859), 519–37; *CW*, 3: 405–6, 410, 435.

43. Charles H. Ray to Lincoln, n.d. [July 1858], ALP; *CW*, 3: 459–63.

44. *CW*, 3: 478.

45. *CW*, 3: 356–57, 363, 476–78.

46. James A. Stevenson, "Lincoln vs. Douglas over the Republican Ideal," *American Studies*, 35 (Spring 1994), 66–67; John Mack Faragher, *Sugar Creek: Life on the Illinois Prairie* (New Haven, 1986), 177–203; Kenneth J. Winkle, "The Voters of Lincoln's Springfield: Migration and Political Participation in an Antebellum City," *Journal of Social History*, 25 (Spring 1992), 604–6; Paul M. Angle, *"Here I Have Lived": A History of Lincoln's Springfield, 1821–1865* (New Brunswick, N.J., 1935), 175; Philip S. Paludan, *The Presidency of Abraham Lincoln* (Lawrence, Kans., 1994), 9–11; David A. Zonderman, *Aspirations and Anxieties: New England Workers and the Mechanized Factory System, 1815–1850* (New York, 1992), 293; *CW*, 3: 459, 479.

47. David Herbert Donald, *Lincoln* (New York, 1995), 234; *CW*, 2: 121; 3: 478–79; 4: 24; Mildred A. Beik, *Labor Relations* (Westport, Conn., 2005), 41–42.

48. *New York Times*, April 7, 1854; Roy F. Basler, ed., *The Collected Works of Abraham Lincoln: First Supplement, 1832–1865* (New Brunswick, N.J., 1974), 43.

49. *CP*, 3: 20–21; *CW*, 3: 437; 4: 16, 24.

50. *CG*, 36th Congress, 1st Session, appendix, 282; A. L. Robinson to Salmon P. Chase, November 30, 1857, Salmon P. Chase Papers, LC; Hans L. Trefousse, *Benjamin Franklin Wade: Radical Republican from Ohio* (New York, 1963), 119, 311–12; *Minutes of the State Convention of the Colored Citizens of Ohio* (Columbus, Ohio, 1851), 23; *Speech of Hon. William H. Seward at Jackson, October 4, 1856* (n.p., 1856), 12–13; Baker, *Works of William H. Seward*, 1: 56; Dorothy Ross, " 'Are We a Nation?' The Conjuncture of Nationhood and Race in the United States, 1850–1876," *Modern Intellectual History*, 2 (November 2005), 327–60.

51. *CG*, 35th Congress, 2nd Session, 1006; Foner, *Free Soil*, 264–67.

52. Foner, *Free Soil*, 290–92; *New York Tribune*, January 17, 1851; *Ohio State Journal*, May 22, 1857.

53. Foner, *Free Soil*, 281–84; *CP*, 1: 201–2, 239; Paul Finkelman, "Prelude to the Fourteenth Amendment: Black Legal Rights in the Antebellum North," *Rutgers Law Journal*, 17 (Spring and Summer 1986), 427.

54. *Hartford Courant*, March 13, 1860; *CG*, 36th Congress, 1st Session, 1910.

55. *African Repository*, 29 (April 1853), 106–7; Foner, *Free Soil*, 286; Linda Hartman, "The Issue of Freedom in Illinois under Gov. Richard Yates, 1861–1865," *JISHS*, 57 (Autumn 1964), 293; *Great Speech of Hon. Lyman Trumbull, On the Issues of the Day* (Chicago, 1858), 13; Eugene H. Berwanger, *The Frontier against Slavery: Western Anti-Negro Prejudice and the Slavery Extension Controversy* (Urbana, Ill., 1967), 124–32; A. N. Ballinger to Lyman Trumbull, February 16, 1860, LTP.

56. For an introduction to the voluminous literature on Lincoln and race, see Benjamin Quarles, *Lincoln and the Negro* (New York, 1962); Arthur Zilversmit, "Lincoln and the Problem of Race: A Decade of Interpretations," *Papers of the Abraham Lincoln Association*, 2 (1980), 21–45; Lerone Bennett, *Forced into Glory: Abraham Lincoln's White Dream* (Chicago, 2000) (which claims, on p. 66, that "racism was the center and circumference of his being"); George M. Fredrickson, *'Big Enough to be Inconsistent': Slavery and Race in the Thought and Politics of Abraham Lincoln* (Cambridge, Mass., 2008); Henry Louis Gates Jr. and Donald Yacovone, eds., *Lincoln on Race and Slavery* (Princeton, 2009); and James Oakes, "Natural Rights, Citizenship Rights, States' Rights, and Black Rights: Another Look at Lincoln and Race," in Eric Foner, ed., *Our Lincoln: New Perspectives on Lincoln and His World* (New York, 2008), 109–34. George M. Fredrickson discusses the burgeoning literature on race during the 1850s in *The Black Image in the White Mind: The Debate on Afro-American Character and Destiny, 1817–1914* (New York, 1971), 71–129,

57. *CW*, 3: 20, 28–29, 317; Bennett, *Forced into Glory*, 14, 90–100; David Mearns, *The Lincoln Papers* (2 vols.; Garden City, N.Y., 1948), 1: 169.

58. *CW*, 2: 132, 157, 520.

59. Richard E. Hart, "Springfield's African-Americans as a Part of the Lincoln Community," *JALA*, 20 (Winter 1999), 35–36, 45; Kenneth J. Winkle, *The Young Eagle: The Rise of Abraham Lincoln* (Dallas, 2001), 262–66; Kenneth J. Winkle, " 'Paradox Though it may Seem': Lincoln on Antislavery, Race, and Union, 1837–1860," in Brian Dirck, ed., *Lincoln Emancipated: The President and the Politics of Race* (DeKalb, Ill., 2007), 19–20; Elmer Gertz, "The Black Codes of Illinois," *JISHS*, 56 (Autumn 1963), 493; *Christian Recorder*, March 21, 1863.

60. *Liberator*, July 13, 1860; Christopher R. Reed, *Black Chicago's First Century* (Columbia, Mo., 2005–), 1: 105; *New York Journal of Commerce*, October 11, 1859.

61. *North Star*, June 13, 1850; Foner, *Life and Writings of Frederick Douglass*, 2: 490; *CW*, 3: 399; 4: 504.

62. *CW*, 2: 222–23.

63. *CW*, 2: 521; Dorothy Ross, "Lincoln and the Ethics of Emancipation: Universalism, Nationalism, Exceptionalism," *JAH*, 96 (September 2009), 391.

64. *New York Herald*, January 12, 1860.

65. Foner, *Free Soil*, 268–72; Francis P. Blair Jr., *The Destiny of the Races of This Continent* (Washington, D.C., 1859), 5–8, 23–27; William E. Parrish, *Frank Blair: Lincoln's Conservative* (Columbia, Mo., 1998), 66–68, 80; Francis P. Blair to Henry Ward Beecher, January 15, 1857 (draft), Blair-Lee Papers, Princeton University; *CG*, 35th Congress, 1st Session, 293–98.

66. Foner, *Free Soil*, 270; *New York Tribune*, July 3, 1858; *Chicago Press and Tribune*, March 4 and May 3, 1860; *Address of Montgomery Blair to the Maryland State Republican Convention* (Washington, D.C., 1860), 7.

67. Blair, *Destiny of the Races*, 24; Sharon H. Strom, "Labor, Race, and Colonization: Imagining a Post-Slavery World in the Americas," in Steven Mintz and John Stauffer, eds., *The Problem of Evil: Slavery, Freedom, and the Ambiguities of American Reform* (Amherst, Mass., 2007), 264; Robert May, *Manifest Destiny's Underworld: Filibustering in Antebellum America* (Chapel Hill, 2002); Matthew P. Guterl, *American Mediterranean: Southern Slaveholders in the Age of Emancipation* (Cambridge, Mass., 2008), 53; *CG*, 35th Congress, 1st Session, 293; Nicholas B. Wainwright, ed., *A Philadelphia Perspective: The Diary of Sidney George Fisher Covering the Years 1834–1871* (Philadelphia, 1967), 369.

68. Parrish, *Frank Blair*, 80; William W. Freehling, *The Road to Disunion: Secessionists Triumphant, 1854–1861* (New York, 2007), 327.

69. *Chicago Press and Tribune*, October 7, 1858; Richard H. Sewell, *Ballots for Freedom: Antislavery Politics in the United States, 1837–1860* (New York, 1976), 185; Foner, *Free Soil*, 276–78; James D. Bilotta, *Race and the Rise of the Republican Party, 1848–1865* (New York, 1992), 114–16; *CG*, 36th Congress, 1st Session, 60–61; Charles Sumner to James Russell Lowell, December 14, 1857, James Russell Lowell Papers, Houghton Library, Harvard University.

70. *CG*, 36th Congress, 1st Session, appendix, 154–55; D. R. Tilden to Benjamin F. Wade, March 27, 1860, Benjamin F. Wade Papers, LC; Charles Francis Adams Diary, January 26, 1859, Adams Family Papers, Massachusetts Historical Society.

71. *New York Tribune*, March 10, 1856; Foner, *Free Soil*, 120–23; *National Era*, August 14, 1856; William H. Seward to James Watson Webb, October 1, 1858, William H. Seward Papers, Rush Rhees Library, University of Rochester; *Chicago Press and Tribune*, May 31, 1860; *CG*, 36th Congress, 1st Session, appendix, 51.

72. *St. Louis Globe-Democrat*, August 26, 1894; *CW*, 2: 131–32, 255–56, 298–99; 3: 15; *African Repository*, 34 (April 1858), 122.

73. *CW*, 2: 409.

74. Catherine Clinton, *Mrs. Lincoln: A Life* (New York, 2009), 128; Francis P. Blair Jr. to Francis P. Blair, February 18, 1857, Blair Family Papers, LC; Newton, *Lincoln and Herndon*, 113–14; *CW*, 2: 409–10; William E. Smith, *The Francis Preston Blair Family in Politics* (2 vols.; New York, 1933), 1: 414–17; Wickliffe Kitchell to Lincoln, June 14, 1858; Lyman Trumbull to Lincoln, June 12, 1858, both in ALP; Parrish, *Frank Blair*, 73–74.

75. Walter B. Stevens, "Lincoln and Missouri," *Missouri Historical Review*, 10 (January 1916), 68; *CW*, 2: 298–99; 3: 233–34.

76. Vincent Harding, *There Is a River: The Black Struggle for Freedom in America* (New York, 1981), 173–87; *State Convention of the Colored Citizens of Ohio* (Oberlin, 1849), 8; Floyd J. Miller, *The Search for a Black Nationality: Black Emigration and Colonization, 1787–1863* (Urbana, Ill., 1975), 190–93, 268; "Thoughts on Hayti," by James T. Holly, which ran monthly in the *Anglo-African Magazine* from June to November 1859; African Civilization Society to Lincoln, November 5, 1863, ALP.

77. Philip S. Foner and George E. Walker, eds., *Proceedings of Black State Conventions, 1840–1865* (2 vols.; Philadelphia, 1979), 1: 335; *Weekly Anglo-African*, May 19 and 26, 1860, and February 23, 1861; *Douglass' Monthly*, 1 (February 1859), 19, and 5 (October 1862), 724–25.

78. *African Repository and Colonial Journal*, 24 (May 1848), 158; *African Repository*, 26 (April 1850), 113–15; Charles N. Zucker, "The Free Negro Question: Race Relations in Antebellum Illinois, 1801–1860" (unpub. diss., Northwestern University, 1972), 206.

79. Foner and Walker, *Proceedings of Black State Conventions*, 2: 60–64; Reed, *Black Chicago's First Century*, 1: 106; Hart, "Springfield's African-Americans," 53; *Chicago Press and Tribune*, August 16, 1858.

80. Dwight L. Dumond, ed., *Southern Editorials on Secession* (New York, 1931), 230–31; *The Address and Reply on the Presentation of a Testimonial to S. P. Chase, by the Colored People of Cincinnati* (Cincinnati, 1845), 4–5; William C. Smedes to Henry J. Raymond, December 8, 1860, in Raymond to Lincoln, December 14, 1860, ALP; *CW*, 4: 156.

81. James M. McPherson, ed., *The Negro's Civil War* (New York, 1965), 272–73.

5 *"The Only Substantial Difference"*

1. Schuyler Colfax to Abraham Lincoln, July 14, 1859, ALP; *CW*, 3: 391.

2. Diary of George White, October 7, 1860, Special Collections, Harvard Law

Library. I am grateful to my colleague Elizabeth Blackmar for bringing this diary to my attention. White himself did not seem to have fixed principles. A Free Soiler in 1848, he voted for James Buchanan in 1856 and voted "unwillingly" for Lincoln in 1860.

3. *CW*, 3: 390–91.

4. *CW*, 3: 380, 383; E. L. Pierce to Charles Sumner, May 31, 1859, Charles Sumner Papers, Houghton Library, Harvard University; Eric Foner, *Free Soil, Free Labor, Free Men: The Ideology of the Republican Party before the Civil War* (New York, 1970), 251–52.

5. *CW*, 3: 351, 403, 504.

6. *New York Times*, March 9, 1857; *Boston Atlas and Daily Bee*, June 26, 1858; David Donald, *Charles Sumner and the Coming of the Civil War* (New York, 1961), 232; George Hoadley to Salmon P. Chase, April 9, 1859, Salmon P. Chase Papers, LC. Edward McPherson lists the northern personal liberty laws as of December 1860 in his book *The Political History of the United States during the Great Rebellion* (2nd ed.; Washington, D.C., 1865), 45–47.

7. Foner, *Free Soil*, 135; Salmon P. Chase to Lincoln, June 13, 1859, ALP; Vroman Mason, "The Fugitive Slave Law in Wisconsin, with Reference to Nullification Sentiment," *Proceedings of the Wisconsin State Historical Society*, 43 (1895), 122–44.

8. Timothy O. Howe to George Rublee, April 3, 1859, Timothy O. Howe Papers, State Historical Society of Wisconsin; *Cincinnati Gazette*, November 17, 1859; *CW*, 3: 317, 384, 394–95, 460.

9. *CW*, 3: 379, 486–87; *Philadelphia North American and United States Gazette*, October 22, 1857, and August 14, 1858; Joseph H. Barrett to Salmon P. Chase, November 30, 1858, Salmon P. Chase Papers, LC; Charles Francis Adams to Charles Sumner, August 1, 1858, Letterbooks, Adams Family Papers, Massachusetts Historical Society; Lincoln to Thomas Corwin, October 9, 1859 (available online in New Document Discoveries section, website of Papers of Abraham Lincoln); Harold Holzer, "Lincoln Heard and Seen," *American Heritage*, 56 (February–March 2005), 16.

10. William C. Harris, *Lincoln's Rise to the Presidency* (Lawrence, Kans., 2007), 158; *CW*, 3: 377, 491, 505. Gary Ecelbarger claims that Lincoln pursued the nomination throughout 1859 but "hid his cards." Gary Ecelbarger, *The Great Comeback: How Abraham Lincoln Beat the Odds to Win the 1860 Republican Nomination* (New York, 2008).

11. *New York Tribune*, February 28, 1860; Michael T. Gilmore, "A Plot against America: Free Speech and the American Renaissance," *Raritan*, 26 (Fall 2006), 91–96. Harold Holzer gives the fullest account of the speech and the circumstances of its delivery in his book *Lincoln at Cooper Union* (New York, 2004).

12. *CW*, 3: 370, 374–76, 522–50.

13. Ecelbarger, *Great Comeback*, 147–53; *New York Herald*, February 29, 1860; *New York Tribune*, February 28, 1860; *CW*, 4: 17–19, 28–29.

14. *Harper's Weekly*, May 26, 1860; John Wentworth to Lincoln, February 7, 1860, ALP; John Bigelow to William Cullen Bryant, March 20, 1860, John Bigelow

Papers, New York Public Library; Foner, *Free Soil*, 211, 234–36; *Cincinnati Gazette*, May 5, 1860; *New York Times*, August 28, 1860.

15. Foner, *Free Soil*, 211–13; *Chicago Press and Tribune*, February 27 and May 11, 1860; *CW*, 4: 36.

16. John Farnsworth to Elihu B. Washburne, May 18, 1860, Elihu B. Washburne Papers, LC; *Chicago Press and Tribune*, February 16, 1860; *New York Tribune*, July 12, 1858; *Harper's Weekly*, May 12, 1860; Lyman Trumbull to Lincoln, April 24, 1860; Mark W. Delahay to Lincoln, March 26, 1860, both in ALP.

17. George Ashmun to Henry Wilson, April 22, 1860, Henry Wilson Papers, LC; *Chicago Press and Tribune*, May 15, 1860; Harold Holzer, *Lincoln President-Elect: Abraham Lincoln and the Great Secession Winter, 1860–1861* (New York, 2008), 25; Hannibal Hamlin to Ellen Hamlin, May 20, 1860, Hannibal Hamlin Papers, University of Maine.

18. *Proceedings of the First Three Republican National Conventions* (Minneapolis, 1893), 111–19, 131–35; Carl Schurz, *The Reminiscences of Carl Schurz* (3 vols.; New York, 1907–8), 2: 180; Lyman Trumbull to Lincoln, May 22, 1860; Schuyler Colfax to Lincoln, May 18 and 26, 1860; Francis P. Blair to Lincoln, May 26, 1860, all in ALP; Howard K. Beale, ed., *The Diary of Edward Bates, 1859–1866* (Washington, D.C., 1933), 128–29; *Boston Atlas and Daily Bee*, May 23, 1860; *Wisconsin State Journal*, May 8, 1860; George Dennison to Benjamin F. Wade, March 12, 1860, Benjamin F. Wade Papers, LC.

19. *New York Times*, May 13, 1860; Don E. Fehrenbacher, *Prelude to Greatness: Lincoln in the 1850s* (Stanford, 1962), 156n.; Richard Carwardine, *Lincoln* (London, 2003), 115; *Liberator*, July 13, 1860.

20. George W. Julian, *The Life of Joshua R. Giddings* (Chicago, 1892), 379–83; *Speech of the Hon. Thomas Ewing at Chillicothe, Ohio* (Cincinnati, 1860), 10–11; *New York Times*, August 31, 1860; Richard W. Thompson to Lincoln, June 12, 1860, ALP; James F. Babcock to Mark Howard, August 4, 1860, Mark Howard Papers, Connecticut Historical Society; *New York Tribune*, July 9, 1860; *Independent*, May 24, 1860; George W. Julian to Joshua Giddings, May 21, 1860, Giddings-Julian Papers, LC.

21. *Liberator*, July 13, 1860; C. Peter Ripley et al., eds., *The Black Abolitionist Papers* (5 vols.; Chapel Hill, 1985–93), 5: 91; Milton Meltzer and Patricia G. Holland, eds., *Lydia Maria Child: Selected Letters, 1817–1880* (Amherst, Mass., 1982), 352; Michael Burlingame, *Abraham Lincoln: A Life* (2 vols.; Baltimore, 2008), 1: 636–38; *Douglass' Monthly*, 3 (June 1860), 276, and (September 1860), 329.

22. Nicholas B. Wainwright, ed., *A Philadelphia Perspective: The Diary of Sidney George Fisher Covering the Years 1834–1871* (Philadelphia, 1967), 353; Lyman Trumbull to Lincoln, June 28, 1860, ALP.

23. Wainwright, *Philadelphia Perspective*, 361; *CG*, 36th Congress, 1st Session, 1913; *Springfield Republican*, October 20, 1860; *Wisconsin State Journal*, August 20, 1860; *Richmond Enquirer*, July 10, 1860.

24. Walter Dean Burnham, *Presidential Ballots, 1836–1892* (Baltimore, 1955), 79–80; *Springfield Republican*, November 3, 1860; Salmon P. Chase to E. L. Pierce,

November 7, 1860, Charles Sumner Papers, Houghton Library, Harvard University; Robert S. Harper, *Lincoln and the Press* (New York, 1951), 67–68; Dwight L. Dumond, ed., *Southern Editorials on Secession* (New York, 1931), 112.

25. Russell McClintock, *Lincoln and the Decision for War: The Northern Response to Secession* (Chapel Hill, 2008), 132; Alfred Babcock to Lincoln, December 7, 1860, Lincoln Collection, ALPLM; William Salter, *The Life of James W. Grimes* (New York, 1876), 132. The papers of Republican leaders are filled with letters from constituents opposing compromise with the South.

26. Foner, *Free Soil*, 180; George G. Fogg to William Butler, December 28, 1860, William Butler Papers, Chicago History Museum; *New York Times*, February 26, 1861; Howard C. Perkins, ed., *Northern Editorials on Secession* (2 vols.; New York, 1942), 1: 97; *CW*, 2: 461; *Chicago Tribune*, December 22, 1860.

27. *New York Tribune*, December 17, 1860; Glyndon G. Van Deusen, *Horace Greeley: Nineteenth-Century Crusader* (Philadelphia, 1953), 262–64.

28. *Douglass' Monthly*, 3 (January 1861), 388; Walter M. Merrill, ed., *The Letters of William Lloyd Garrison* (6 vols.; Cambridge, Mass., 1971–81), 5: 10–11; James B. Stewart, *Wendell Phillips: Liberty's Hero* (Baton Rouge, 1986), 212–13; Wendell Phillips, *Speeches, Lectures, and Letters* (Boston, 1863), 362.

29. Kenneth M. Stampp, *And the War Came: The North and the Secession Crisis, 1860–61* (Baton Rouge, 1950), 15, 126–28; James M. McPherson, *The Struggle for Equality: Abolitionists and the Negro in the Civil War and Reconstruction* (Princeton, 1964), 40–44; David Potter, *Lincoln and His Party in the Secession Crisis* (New Haven, 1942), 124–27; New York Republicans to Lincoln, January 29, 1861; William Cullen Bryant to Lincoln, December 25, 1860, both in ALP; Philip S. Foner, *Business and Slavery: The New York Merchants and the Irrepressible Conflict* (Chapel Hill, 1941), 251; William Dusinberre, *Civil War Issues in Philadelphia, 1856–1865* (Philadelphia, 1965), 102–10; Robert G. Gunderson, *Old Gentlemen's Convention: The Washington Peace Conference of 1861* (Madison, Wisc., 1961), 26–28.

30. Horatio Nelson Taft Diary, January 17, 1861, LC; Stampp, *And the War Came*, 33; Perkins, *Northern Editorials*, 1: 148; 2: 571–72; August Belmont, *A Few Letters and Speeches of the Late Civil War* (New York, 1870), 8–20; James A. Bayard to Samuel L. M. Barlow, December 26, 1860, Samuel L. M. Barlow Papers, HL.

31. *CG*, 36th Congress, 2nd Session, appendix, 1; Stampp, *And the War Came*, 54–55.

32. McPherson, *Political History*, 52–56; David E. Kyvig, *Explicit and Authentic Acts: Amending the U.S. Constitution, 1776–1995* (Lawrence, Kans., 1996), 146–49; *CG*, 36th Congress, 2nd Session, 114; appendix, 41, 44, 202; Frank H. Moore, ed., *The Rebellion Record* (11 vols.; New York, 1861–68), 1: 3–5.

33. *CG*, 36th Congress, 2nd Session, 344; *Chicago Tribune*, January 17, 1861; Martin Duberman, *Charles Francis Adams, 1807–1886* (Stanford, 1960), 224–43.

34. Joseph Schafer, ed., *Intimate Letters of Carl Schurz, 1841–1869* (Madison, Wisc., 1928), 242; Stampp, *And the War Came*, 172–75; *New York Tribune*, March 7, 1861; Frederick W. Seward, *Seward at Washington* (2 vols.; New York, 1891),

1: 496–97, 507; Thurlow Weed to Francis Granger, January 26, 1861, Francis Granger Papers, LC.

35. Russell Errett to Simon P. Cameron, January 23, 1861, Simon P. Cameron Papers, LC; A. B. Barrett to Lyman Trumbull, January 5, 1861; H. G. McPike to Trumbull, January 24, 1861, both in LTP; Salter, *Life of James W. Grimes*, 123–24, 133–35; *CG*, 36th Congress, 2nd Session, appendix, 127.

36. *Chicago Tribune*, February 15, 1861; *CG*, 36th Congress, 2nd Session, 3, 50, 187; Sarah F. Hughes, ed., *Letters (Supplementary) of John Murray Forbes* (3 vols.; Boston, 1905), 1: 230–31; *CG*, 36th Congress, 1st Session, 932.

37. Burlingame, *Abraham Lincoln: A Life*, 2: 52–58; David Herbert Donald, *Lincoln* (New York, 1995), 261–67.

38. Burlingame, *Abraham Lincoln: A Life*, 1: 692–93, 716; Potter, *Lincoln and His Party*, 141, 149–51; *CW*, 4: 211, 215, 238; William E. Barringer, *A House Dividing: Lincoln as President Elect* (Springfield, Ill., 1945), 55–56.

39. William H. Price to Lincoln, November 9, 1860; Joseph L. Bennett to Lincoln, November 10, 1860; Henry J. Raymond to Lincoln, November 14, 1860, all in ALP; *CW*, 4: 138–42; Holzer, *Lincoln President-Elect*, 94–95.

40. *CW*, 4: 139, 146; Dumond, *Southern Editorials*, 273; McClintock, *Lincoln and the Decision*, 50.

41. Perkins, *Northern Editorials*, 1: 121, 228; Burlingame, *Abraham Lincoln: A Life*, 1: 704–7; Michael Burlingame, ed., *Lincoln's Journalist: John Hay's Anonymous Writings for the Press, 1860–1864* (Carbondale, Ill., 1998), 351–52n.; *Illinois State Journal* in *Chicago Tribune*, January 31, 1861; McClintock, *Lincoln and the Decision*, 162–63.

42. *New York Times*, February 20, 1861; Holzer, *Lincoln President-Elect*, 158; McClintock, *Lincoln and the Decision*, 79–82, 94–95; *CW*, 4: 149–51; Elihu B. Washburne to Lincoln, December 9, 1860, ALP.

43. *CW*, 4: 156–58; McClintock, *Lincoln and the Decision*, 92–93.

44. John A. Gilmer to Lincoln, December 10, 1860, ALP; *CW*, 4: 151–52, 160–61.

45. Neill S. Brown to Lincoln, January 13, 1861, ALP; O. Ewing to Lincoln, January 24, 1861, both in Lincoln Collection, ALPLM; *CW*, 4: 172.

46. William H. Seward to Lincoln, January 27, 1861, ALP; *CW*, 4: 183; Burlingame, *Abraham Lincoln: A Life*, 1: 749–51; McClintock, *Lincoln and the Decision*, 166.

47. Holzer, *Lincoln President-Elect*, 389; David Davis to Sarah Davis, February 17, 1861, David Davis Papers, ALPLM; *CW*, 4: 191, 195, 233, 240–41.

48. McClintock, *Lincoln and the Decision*, 181; *CW*, 4: 237; Holzer, *Lincoln President-Elect*, 344.

49. *CW*, 4: 240–41.

50. Gunderson, *Old Gentlemen's Convention*, 13, 86; Lucius E. Chittenden, *A Report of the Debates and Proceedings in the Secret Sessions of the Conference Convention* (New York, 1864), 43–46, 94–97; Kenneth M. Stampp, ed., "Letters from the Washington Peace Conference of 1861," *JSH*, 9 (August 1943), 394–403.

51. *CG*, 36th Congress, 2nd Session, 1284–85, 1403; Appendix, 87.

52. *CG*, 37th Congress, 2nd Session, 2898; Hiland Hall to William H. Seward, Feb-

ruary 23, 1861; Carl Schurz to Lincoln, April 5, 1861, both in ALP; George S. Boutwell, *Reminiscences of Sixty Years in Public Affairs* (2 vols.; New York, 1902), 1: 274.

53. *New York Times*, March 1, 1861. *CW*, 4: 249–61, reprints Lincoln's first draft and indicates revisions. See also Orville H. Browning to Lincoln, February 17, 1861; William H. Seward to Lincoln, February 24, 1861; First Inaugural Address, Second Printed Draft with Seward's Suggested Changes in Red Ink, n.d., all in ALP.

54. *New York Tribune*, March 5, 1861; *CW*, 4: 262–70.

55. *CG*, 36th Congress, 2nd Session, 552, 1382; Kyvig, *Explicit and Authentic Acts*, 149–50. Ratification by Illinois was not valid, as it was done by a state constitutional convention, not the legislature as Congress had specified.

56. *Liberator*, March 8, 1861; Burlingame, *Abraham Lincoln: A Life*, 2: 61.

57. Holzer, *Lincoln President-Elect*, 256; William Lee Miller, *President Lincoln: The Duty of a Statesman* (New York, 2008), 10; *CG*, 33rd Congress, 1st Session, appendix, 321; 36th Congress, 1st Session, 1035; 2nd Session, 416; Kenneth M. Stampp, "Lincoln's History," in James M. McPherson, ed., *"We Cannot Escape History": Lincoln and the Last Best Hope of Earth* (Urbana, Ill., 1995), 26–27; *Independent*, March 7, 1861.

58. *CW*, 4: 247–71.

59. Wainwright, *Philadelphia Perspective*, 381.

60. *Weekly Anglo-African*, March 16, 1861; *CG*, 36th Congress, 2nd Session, 1442; Perkins, *Northern Editorials*, 2: 625–26; H. D. Faulkner to Lincoln, March 5, 1861, ALP.

61. Chandra Manning, *What This Cruel War Was Over: Soldiers, Slavery, and the Civil War* (New York, 2007), 27; Herbert Mitgang, ed., *Abraham Lincoln: A Press Portrait* (Chicago, 1971), 240–42; Doris Kearns Goodwin, *Team of Rivals: The Political Genius of Abraham Lincoln* (New York, 2005), 330; *Douglass' Monthly*, 3 (April 1861), 433.

62. Orville H. Browning to Lincoln, February 17, 1861, ALP; *Chicago Tribune*, March 15, 1861; Philip S. Paludan, *The Presidency of Abraham Lincoln* (Lawrence, Kans., 1994), 61–71; Don E. Fehrenbacher, "Lincoln's Wartime Leadership: The First Hundred Days," *JALA*, 9 (1987), 11–15; David A. Nichols, *Lincoln and the Indians: Civil War Policy and Politics* (Columbia, Mo., 1978), 27–29. Still valuable on the events leading to the outbreak of war is Richard N. Current, *Lincoln and the First Shot* (Philadelphia, 1963).

63. Earl J. Hess, *Liberty, Virtue, and Progress: Northerners and Their War for the Union* (New York, 1988), 26; Christopher Dell, *Lincoln and the War Democrats* (Rutherford, N.J., 1975), 52–59; Orville H. Browning to Lincoln, April 18, 1861; Elias B. Holmes to Lincoln, April 20, 1861, both in ALP; Wainwright, *Philadelphia Perspective*, 385.

64. *CW*, 4: 332, 353; Burlingame, *Abraham Lincoln: A Life*, 2: 154; Richard H. Sewell, *John P. Hale and the Politics of Antislavery* (Cambridge, Mass., 1965), 207; Meltzer and Holland, *Lydia Maria Child*, 381.

65. Orville H. Browning to Lincoln, April 30, 1861; James R. Doolittle to Lincoln,

April 18, 1861, both in ALP; Perkins, *Northern Editorials*, 2: 633–34, 727–30; Paul D. Escott, *"What Shall We Do with the Negro?": Lincoln, White Racism, and Civil War America* (Charlottesville, 2009), 9; *New York Times*, May 31, 1861.

66. Allan Nevins, ed., *The Diary of John Quincy Adams* (New York, 1928), 246–47; Burrus M. Carnahan, *Act of Justice: Lincoln's Emancipation Proclamation and the Law of War* (Lexington, Ky., 2007), 8–9, 14–15; *CG*, 36th Congress, 2nd Session, appendix, 83; Donald, *Charles Sumner*, 388; Stewart, *Wendell Phillips*, 219–22; Phillips, *Speeches*, 396–411; *Liberator*, April 26, 1861.

67. David W. Blight, *Frederick Douglass' Civil War: Keeping Faith in Jubilee* (Baton Rouge, 1989), 24; *Douglass' Monthly*, 3 (January 1861), 386–87, and (May 1861), 449–51; John R. McKivigan, "James Redpath and Black Reaction to the Haitian Emigration Bureau," *Mid-America*, 69 (October 1987), 139–53.

68. *Weekly Anglo-African*, April 27, 1861.

69. Michael Burlingame and John R. Ettlinger, eds., *Inside Lincoln's White House: The Complete Civil War Diary of John Hay* (Carbondale, Ill., 1997), 19; *National Anti-Slavery Standard*, July 13, 1861.

6 *"I Must Have Kentucky"*

1. *OR*, ser. 1, 1: 195; ser. 2, 1: 750.

2. *Harper's Weekly*, May 4, 1861; Milton Meltzer and Patricia G. Holland, eds., *Lydia Maria Child: Selected Letters, 1817–1880* (Amherst, Mass., 1982), 380; Michael Burlingame and John R. Ettlinger, eds., *Inside Lincoln's White House: The Complete Civil War Diary of John Hay* (Carbondale, Ill., 1997), 12; Nicholas B. Wainwright, ed., *A Philadelphia Perspective: The Diary of Sidney George Fisher Covering the Years 1834–1871* (Philadelphia, 1967), 387; Stephen V. Ash, *When the Yankees Came: Conflict and Chaos in the Occupied South, 1861–1865* (Chapel Hill, 1995), 26–32; *New York Tribune*, May 14, 1861; *Springfield Weekly Republican*, April 20, 1861; *Easton Gazette* (Maryland), July 13, 1861.

3. Howard C. Perkins, ed., *Northern Editorials on Secession* (2 vols.; New York, 1942), 2: 834; Armstead L. Robinson, *Bitter Fruits of Bondage: The Demise of Slavery and the Collapse of the Confederacy, 1861–1865* (Charlottesville, 2005), 41–43.

4. *New York Times*, September 28, 1862; John H. Bayne to Lincoln, March 17, 1862, ALP; Craig Symonds ed., *Charleston Blockade: The Journals of John B. Marchand, U.S. Navy, 1861–1862* (Newport, R.I., 1976), 175–81, 192; Craig Symonds, *Lincoln and His Admirals* (New York, 2008), 157–59.

5. Steven Hahn, *The Political Worlds of Slavery and Freedom* (Cambridge, Mass., 2009), 61–64; Ira Berlin et al., eds., *Freedom: A Documentary History of Emancipation, 1861–1867* (New York, 1982–), ser. 1, 3: 77–80; ser. 1, 1: 11–14; Robinson, *Bitter Fruits*, 184–87; *OR*, ser. 1, 51, pt. 2: 278–81; ser. 2, 1: 755–57.

6. *New York Herald*, December 4, 1861.

7. Isaac N. Arnold, *The History of Abraham Lincoln and the Overthrow of Slavery* (Chicago, 1866), 207–8; David Herbert Donald, *Lincoln* (New York, 1995), 302; Burrus M. Carnahan, *Act of Justice: Lincoln's Emancipation Proclamation and the Law of War* (Lexington, Ky., 2007), 43–49, 61.

8. William E. Gienapp, "Abraham Lincoln and the Border States," *JALA*, 13 (1992), 13–25; Richard H. Abbott, *The Republican Party and the South, 1855–1877: The First Southern Strategy* (Chapel Hill, 1986), 21–22; Charles L. Wagandt, *The Mighty Revolution: Negro Emancipation in Maryland, 1862–1864* (Baltimore, 1964), 9–18; William D. Foulke, *Life of Oliver P. Morton* (2 vols.; Indianapolis, 1899), 1: 134–35.

9. *OR*, ser. 2, 1: 752; Louis S. Gerteis, *From Contraband to Freedman: Federal Policy toward Southern Blacks, 1861–1865* (Westport, Conn., 1973), 11–13; *Harper's Weekly*, February 9, 1861; Edward L. Pierce, *Emancipation and Citizenship* (Boston, 1898), 20–23.

10. Pierce, *Emancipation and Citizenship*, 20–23; *Harper's Weekly*, June 8, 1861; Kate Masur, " 'A Rare Phenomenon of Philological Vegetation': The Word 'Contraband' and the Meanings of Emancipation in the United States," *JAH*, 93 (March 2007), 1054–59; Silvana R. Siddali, *From Property to Person: Slavery and the Confiscation Acts, 1861–1862* (Baton Rouge, 2005), 51–53; Christopher Dell, *Lincoln and the War Democrats* (Rutherford, N.J., 1975), 65; *New York Herald*, May 30, 1861; *Chicago Tribune*, June 5, 1861.

11. Pierce, *Emancipation and Citizenship*, 24–25; *OR*, ser. 2, 1: 750, 755; *Private and Official Correspondence of Gen. Benjamin F. Butler during the Period of the Civil War* (5 vols.; Norwood, Mass., 1917), 1: 112–13.

12. *Private and Official Correspondence*, 1: 116–17, 183–88; Montgomery Blair to Benjamin F. Butler, May 30, 1861, Benjamin F. Butler Papers, LC; *Cleveland Gazette*, May 30, 1861; *New York Herald*, May 31, 1861; *OR*, ser. 2, 1: 754–55; Meltzer and Holland, *Lydia Maria Child*, 401–2.

13. William E. Gienapp, "Abraham Lincoln and Presidential Leadership," in James M. McPherson, ed., *"We Cannot Escape History": Lincoln and the Last Best Hope of Earth* (Urbana, Ill., 1995), 71–73; *CW*, 4: 421–41; Philip S. Paludan, *The Presidency of Abraham Lincoln* (Lawrence, Kans., 1994), 81–82.

14. Wainwright, *Philadelphia Perspective*, 396; *Springfield Weekly Republican*, June 22, 1861; Henry F. Brownson, ed., *The Works of Orestes A. Brownson* (20 vols.; Detroit, 1882–87), 17: 143; Chandra Manning, *What This Cruel War Was Over: Soldiers, Slavery, and the Civil War* (New York, 2007), 40–41; *CW*, 4: 421–41. This, it is worth noting, was one of the very few times in his career that Lincoln used the word "democracy" other than to refer to the rival political party, the Democracy. Almost always, Lincoln spoke not of democracy but self-government.

15. *Douglass' Monthly*, 4 (August 1861), 497; *New York Herald*, July 7 and 9, 1861; *Harper's Weekly*, July 6, 1861.

16. *CG*, 37th Congress, 1st Session, 24, 32.

17. *CG*, 37th Congress, 1st Session, 222, 265; William E. Gienapp, *Abraham Lincoln and Civil War America* (New York, 2002), 88; James G. Blaine, *Twenty Years of Congress* (2 vols.; Norwich, Conn., 1884), 1: 341; Michael S. Green, *Freedom, Union, and Power: Lincoln and His Party during the Civil War* (New York, 2004), 145.

18. *Harper's Weekly*, August 17, 1861; *CG*, 37th Congress, 1st Session, 119, 141, 143, 186, 190; Garrett Davis to Lincoln, August 4, 1861, ALP.

19. Siddali, *From Property to Person*, 3; *New York Times*, June 1, 1861; *CG*, 37th Con-

gress, 1st Session, 217–19; Blaine, *Twenty Years*, 341–43; George P. Sanger, ed., *The Statutes at Large, Treaties, and Proclamations of the United States of America*, vol. 12 (Boston, 1863), 319. The Confederacy had already acted to confiscate debts due to northerners. In response to the Union's Confiscation Act, the Confederate Congress authorized the seizure of all property of enemy aliens, which included citizens of the United States and southerners loyal to the Union. Daniel W. Hamilton, *The Limits of Sovereignty: Property Confiscation in the Union and the Confederacy during the Civil War* (Chicago, 2007), 86–92.

20. *CG*, 37th Congress, 1st Session, 412; Siddali, *From Property to Person*, 78–81; Robert Fabrikant, "Emancipation and the Proclamation: Of Contrabands, Congress, and Lincoln," *Howard Law Review*, 49 (Winter 2006), 322–25; Edward McPherson, *The Political History of the United States during the Great Rebellion* (2nd ed.; Washington, D.C., 1865), 195; *New York Times*, September 16, 1861.

21. Benjamin P. Thomas and Harold M. Hyman, *Stanton: The Life and Times of Lincoln's Secretary of War* (New York, 1962), 231–32; *OR*, ser. 2, 1: 760–62; *Private and Official Correspondence*, 1: 185–87, 207, 215; *CW*, 4: 478; Chester G. Hearn, *When the Devil Came Down to Dixie: Ben Butler in New Orleans* (Baton Rouge, 1971), 35; John E. Wool, Special Order on Payment of Colored Contrabands, October 14, 1861; Charles Calvert to Lincoln, August 3, 1861, both in ALP; Edna Medford, "Abraham Lincoln and Black Wartime Washington," in Linda N. Suits and Timothy P. Townsend, eds., *Papers from the Eleventh and Twelfth Annual Lincoln Colloquia* (Springfield, Ill., n.d.), 120–22; Sarah J. Day, *The Man on a Hilltop* (Philadelphia, 1931), 254.

22. John C. Frémont to Lincoln, July 30, 1861, ALP; Frederick J. Blue, *No Taint of Compromise: Crusaders in Antislavery Politics* (Baton Rouge, 2005), 256; Paludan, *Presidency*, 86–88.

23. Carnahan, *Act of Justice*, 7–8, 12–13, 16–18; David Herbert Donald, *"We Are Lincoln Men": Abraham Lincoln and His Friends* (New York, 2003), 58; Joshua F. Speed to Lincoln, May 19, 1860, and September 1 and 3, 1861; Robert Anderson to Lincoln, September 13, 1861; J. F. Bullitt et al. to Lincoln, September 13, 1861, all in ALP; *CP*, 3: 92–93.

24. Paludan, *Presidency*, 125; *CW*, 4: 506, 518; Montgomery Blair to Lincoln, September 4, 1861, ALP; Pamela Herr and Mary Lee Spence, eds., *The Letters of Jessie Benton Frémont* (Urbana, Ill., 1993), 245–46. In her recollection of the meeting written in 1891, Frémont also claimed that Lincoln remarked that the war was for the Union and her husband "should never have dragged the negro" into it. Ibid., 264–67.

25. Charles A. Jellison, *Fessenden of Maine* (Syracuse, 1962), 138; John Bigelow, *Retrospections of an Active Life* (5 vols.; New York, 1909–13), 1: 362–63; William Salter, *The Life of James W. Grimes* (New York, 1876), 153; Brownson, *Works of Orestes A. Brownson*, 17: 173–74; Frank Freidel, ed., *Union Pamphlets of the Civil War, 1861–1865* (2 vols.; Cambridge, Mass., 1967), 1: 162–63.

26. James M. McPherson, *Tried by War: Abraham Lincoln as Commander in Chief* (New York, 2008), 52; *New York Herald*, October 6, 1861; *New York Times*, Septem-

ber 16, 1861; Henry Jones to Lincoln, September 24, 1861; Charles Reed to Lincoln, September 24, 1861; W. McCauly to Lincoln, September 20, 1861, all in ALP.

27. John L. Scripps to Lincoln, September 23, 1861, ALP.

28. Orville H. Browning to Lincoln, September 17, 1861, ALP; *CW*, 4: 531.

29. Michael Burlingame, ed., *Dispatches from Lincoln's White House: The Anonymous Civil War Journalism of Presidential Secretary William O. Stoddard* (Lincoln, Neb., 2002), 33–34.

30. *Springfield Weekly Republican*, September 21, 1861; Walter M. Merrill, ed., *The Letters of William Lloyd Garrison* (6 vols.; Cambridge, Mass., 1971–81), 5: 17, 35; *Liberator*, September 20, 1861; *Weekly Anglo-African*, September 22, 1861; Benjamin F. Wade to Zachariah Chandler, September 23, 1861, Zachariah Chandler Papers, LC.

31. James M. McPherson, *The Struggle for Equality: Abolitionists and the Negro in the Civil War and Reconstruction* (Princeton, 1964), 51–63, 75–80; Freidel, *Union Pamphlets*, 1: 102–4; William Dusinberre, *Civil War Issues in Philadelphia, 1856–1865* (Philadelphia, 1965), 131–33; David Donald, *Charles Sumner and the Rights of Man* (New York, 1970), 15–16, 29; *The Works of Charles Sumner* (15 vols.; Boston, 1870–83), 6: 12, 38–39, 56; Richard W. Thompson to Lincoln, October 6, 1861, ALP.

32. George Bancroft to Lincoln, November 15, 1861, ALP; *CW*, 5: 26.

33. J. Thomas Scharf, *History of Delaware, 1609–1888* (2 vols.; Philadelphia, 1888), 1: 329–30; William H. Williams, *Slavery and Freedom in Delaware, 1639–1865* (Wilmington, 1996), xiii–xvii, 88–89, 173; Patience Essah, *A House Divided: Slavery and Emancipation in Delaware, 1638–1865* (Charlottesville, 1996), 6, 105–11; *CG*, 36th Congress, 2nd Session, 1488.

34. Williams, *Slavery and Freedom*, 174–75; H. Clay Reed, "Lincoln's Compensated Emancipation Plan and Its Relation to Delaware," *Delaware Notes*, 7 (1931), 38–40; *CW*, 5: 29–30.

35. Margaret M. R. Kellow, "Conflicting Imperatives: Black and White American Abolitionists Debate Slave Redemption," in Kwame A. Appiah and Martin Bunzl, eds., *Buying Freedom: The Ethics and Economics of Slave Redemption* (Princeton, 2007), 200–12; *Baltimore Sun*, May 29, 1862.

36. Peter Tolis, *Elihu Burritt: Crusader for Brotherhood* (Hamden, Conn., 1968), 245–61; *Chicago Tribune*, August 27, 1857; Merle Curti, ed., *The Learned Blacksmith: The Letters and Journals of Elihu Burritt* (New York, 1937), 118–21.

37. Stanley Harrold, *The Abolitionists and the South, 1831–1861* (Lexington, Ky., 1995), 119, 129; Daniel R. Goodloe, *Emancipation and the War: Compensation Essential to Peace and Civilization* (Washington, D.C., 1861), 1–5; Autobiography, Daniel R. Goodloe Papers, Manuscripts Department, Wilson Library, University of North Carolina at Chapel Hill.

38. *BD*, 1: 512; Joshua F. Speed to Lincoln, September 3, 1861, ALP.

39. Reed, "Lincoln's Compensated Emancipation Plan," 38–55; *New York Tribune*, February 11, 1862; *Peninsular News and Advertiser* (Milford, Del.), January 31 and February 14, 1862; Essah, *House Divided*, 167–69; Williams, *Slavery and Freedom*, 175.

40. Albert Mordell, ed., *Lincoln's Administration: Selected Essays by Gideon Welles* (New York, 1960), 234, 250; *WD*, 1: 150; Charles A. Barker, ed., *Memoirs of Elisha Oscar Crosby* (San Marino, 1945), 76–90; Ambrose W. Thompson to Lincoln, April 11, 1861, ALP. The majority of Lincoln scholars have found it difficult to take seriously Lincoln's embrace of colonization; they either ignore the subject or simply deny that Lincoln actually meant what he said. For a discussion of the place of colonization in his career, see Eric Foner, "Lincoln and Colonization," in Eric Foner, ed., *Our Lincoln: New Perspectives on Lincoln and His World* (New York, 2008), 135–66.

41. *Chicago Tribune*, June 5, 1861; *Private and Official Correspondence*, 1: 130; *BD*, 1: 478; Thomas Schoonover, "Misconstrued Mission: Expansionism and Black Colonization in Mexico and Central America during the Civil War," *Pacific Historical Review*, 49 (November 1980), 611–12.

42. Mordell, *Lincoln's Administration*, 102–3; Ninian W. Edwards to Lincoln, August 9, 1861; Francis P. Blair Sr. to Lincoln, November 16, 1861, both in ALP; *CW*, 4: 547, 561; Roy F. Basler, ed., *The Collected Works of Abraham Lincoln: First Supplement, 1832–1865* (New Brunswick, N.J., 1974), 112; *WD*, 1: 150.

43. *CW*, 5: 39, 48; G. S. Boritt, "The Voyage to the Colony of Lincolnia: The Sixteenth President, Black Colonization, and the Defense Mechanism of Avoidance," *Historian*, 37 (August 1975), 619; Alfred N. Hunt, *Haiti's Influence on Antebellum America* (Baton Rouge, 1988), 186; *New York Herald*, December 4, 1861.

44. *New York Times*, December 4, 5, and 7, 1861; *Philadelphia North American and United States Gazette*, December 21, 1861; *African Repository*, 37 (December 1861), 12.

45. John J. Crittenden to Lincoln, November 26, 1861, ALP; *CW*, 5: 48–50; *Chicago Tribune*, December 9, 1861.

46. *New York Times*, December 4 and 5, 1861; Blaine, *Twenty Years*, 1: 352–53; Merrill, *Letters of William Lloyd Garrison*, 5: 47, 53; S. York to Lyman Trumbull, December 5, 1861; John H. Bryant to Trumbull, December 8, 1861, both in LTP.

47. C. H. Ray to Trumbull, December 6, 1861, LTP; Mary F. Berry, *Military Necessity and Civil Rights Policy* (Port Washington, N.Y., 1977), 29–30, 37; Levin Tilmon to Lincoln, April 8, 1861, ALP; Hahn, *Political Worlds*, 70.

48. Symonds, *Lincoln and His Admirals*, 165–66; *OR*, 2 ser., 1: 773; Arnold, *History of Abraham Lincoln*, 236; *Chicago Tribune*, December 7 and 9, 1861.

49. William B. Parker, *The Life and Public Services of Justin Smith Morrill* (Boston, 1924), 127; *New York Times*, December 4, 1861.

50. Michael Burlingame, ed., *Lincoln's Journalist: John Hay's Anonymous Writings for the Press, 1860–1864* (Carbondale, Ill., 1998), 176; McPherson, *Struggle for Equality*, 93; Allen T. Rice, ed., *Reminiscences of Abraham Lincoln by Distinguished Men of His Time* (New York, 1888), 60; *Washington Star*, January 4, 1862; James A. Cravens to Lincoln, January 5, 1862, ALP; Brownson, *Works of Orestes A. Brownson*, 17: 261.

51. Freidel, *Union Pamphlets*, 1: 295; James B. Stewart, *Wendell Phillips: Liberty's Hero* (Baton Rouge, 1986), 227–38; Burlingame, *Lincoln's Journalist*, 233–35; Wendell Phillips, *Speeches, Lectures, and Letters* (Boston, 1863), 419; McPherson, *Struggle for Equality*, 83–85.

52. *Harper's Weekly*, April 20, 1861; *CG*, 37th Congress, 2nd Session, 1266, 3132; William G. Sewell, *The Ordeal of Free Labor in the British West Indies* (New York, 1861), 324; *Chicago Tribune*, August 11, 1862; Sarah F. Hughes, ed., *Letters and Recollections of John Murray Forbes* (2 vols.; Boston, 1899), 1: 309–13.

53. Gideon Welles, *Lincoln and Seward* (New York, 1874), 132; James C. Conkling to Trumbull, December 16, 1861, LTP; Howard K. Beale, ed., *The Diary of Edward Bates, 1859–1866* (Washington, D.C., 1933), 220.

54. *Springfield Weekly Republican*, December 7, 1861; *New York Times*, December 3, 1861; *Chicago Tribune*, December 5, 1861; *CG*, 37th Congress, 2nd Session, 15, 36, 82.

55. *CG*, 37th Congress, 2nd Session, 5, 6, 26, 78; Edward Magdol, *Owen Lovejoy: Abolitionist in Congress* (New Brunswick, N.J., 1967), 299; *Chicago Tribune*, December 5, 1861; D. L. Linegar to Trumbull, December 7, 1861, LTP; *New York Herald*, December 31, 1861.

56. *OR*, ser. 2, 1: 783; *CG*, 37th Congress, 2nd Session, 10, 26, 264, 310, 762; *CW*, 5: 72; *Frank Leslie's Illustrated Weekly*, December 21, 1861.

57. Arnold, *History of Abraham Lincoln*, 251–53; John Bigelow, ed., *Letters and Literary Memorials of Samuel J. Tilden* (2 vols.; New York, 1908), 1: 164–65; *CG*, 37th Congress, 2nd Session, 182, 355; appendix, 28; Reverdy Johnson to Lincoln, January 16, 1862, ALP; Wagandt, *Mighty Revolution*, 36.

58. *New York Times*, December 17, 1861; *CG*, 37th Congress, 2nd Session, 2203, 3002; Leonard P. Curry, *Blueprint for Modern America: Nonmilitary Legislation of the First Civil War Congress* (Nashville, 1968), 58–59; Timothy O. Howe to James H. Howe, December 31, 1861, Timothy O. Howe Papers, State Historical Society of Wisconsin.

59. Henry J. Raymond, *The Life and Public Services of Abraham Lincoln* (New York, 1865), 773; Harold Holzer, *Lincoln President-Elect: Abraham Lincoln and the Great Secession Winter, 1860–1861* (New York, 2008), 121; William Slade to Lincoln, November 22, 1864, ALP; *CW*, 4: 494; Michael Burlingame, *Abraham Lincoln: A Life* (2 vols.; Baltimore, 2008), 2: 92; Magdol, *Owen Lovejoy*, 276–77.

60. Richard Carwardine, *Lincoln* (London, 2003), 196–97; James R. Gilmore, *Personal Recollections of Abraham Lincoln and the Civil War* (Boston, 1898), 99; M. A. De Wolfe Howe, *The Life and Letters of George Bancroft* (2 vols.; New York, 1908), 2: 147; Don E. Fehrenbacher and Virginia Fehrenbacher, eds., *Recollected Words of Abraham Lincoln* (Stanford, 1996), 118; Henry D. Bacon to Samuel L. M. Barlow, January 20, 1862, Samuel L. M. Barlow Papers, HL; Allan Nevins and Milton H. Thomas, eds., *The Diary of George Templeton Strong* (4 vols.; New York, 1952), 3: 204–5. In his autobiography, published in 1904, Conway considerably embellished his account of his meeting with Lincoln, writing that the president urged him to "go home and try to bring the people to your view, and you may say anything you like about me, if that will help." Moncure D. Conway, *Autobiography: Memories and Experiences* (2 vols.; Boston, 1904), 1: 345–46.

61. *Douglass' Monthly*, 4 (January 1862), 577; *Liberator*, January 3, 1862; *Independent*, January 23, 1862; Basler, *Collected Works of Abraham Lincoln: First Supplement*, 69; W. E. B. Du Bois, *The Suppression of the African Slave-Trade to the United*

States of America, 1638–1870 (New York, 1896), 109; William Lee Miller, *President Lincoln: The Duty of a Statesman* (New York, 2008), 244–52; Jenny Martinez, "Antislavery Courts and the Dawn of International Human Rights Law," *Yale Law Journal*, 117 (January 2008), 550–642; Karen F. Younger, "Liberia and the Last Slave Ships," *CWH*, 54 (December 2008), 424–42; *Weekly Anglo-African*, March 1, 1862.

62. Fehrenbacher and Fehrenbacher, *Recollected Words*, 123; *Harper's Weekly*, February 22, 1862; W. A. Gorman to Henry Wilson, December 22, 1861, Henry Wilson Papers, LC; Berlin, *Freedom*, ser. 1, 1: 17–18; Arnold, *History of Abraham Lincoln*, 261; *CG*, 37th Congress, 2nd Session, 76.

63. *CG*, 37th Congress, 2nd Session, 944, 955, 958–59, 1143; Fabrikant, "Emancipation," 403.

64. Beverly W. Palmer, ed., *The Selected Letters of Charles Sumner* (2 vols.; Boston, 1990), 2: 85–93; *CW*, 5: 144–46.

65. Donald, *Charles Sumner*, 346; *Liberator*, March 14, 1862; Carl Schurz, *The Reminiscences of Carl Schurz* (3 vols.; New York, 1907–8), 2: 320; *Weekly Anglo-African*, March 22, 1862.

66. *Harper's Weekly*, March 22, 1862; *Chicago Tribune*, March 20, 1862; *New York Tribune*, March 7, 1862; *Baltimore Sun*, March 8, 1862; Winfield Scott to William H. Seward, March 8, 1862, ALP; *CG*, 37th Congress, 2nd Session, 1149, 1179, 1198, 1496, 1815–18; *Frank Leslie's Illustrated Weekly*, March 22, 1862.

67. Irving H. Bartlett, ed., "New Light on Wendell Phillips: The Community of Reform," *Perspectives in American History*, 12 (1979), 8; Fehrenbacher and Fehrenbacher, *Recollected Words*, 356.

68. McPherson, *Political History*, 210–11; *New York Tribune*, July 14, 1862.

69. Philip S. Foner, *The Life and Writings of Frederick Douglass* (5 vols.; New York, 1950–75), 3: 123; *CG*, 37th Congress, 2nd Session, 1172, 1175, 2917; *Harper's Weekly*, April 12, 1862; Francis S. Corkran to Montgomery Blair, May 20, 1862, ALP; *New York Times*, April 3, 1862.

70. Montgomery Blair to Lincoln, March 5, [1862], ALP; Wagandt, *Mighty Revolution*, 62; *CG*, 37th Congress, 2nd Session, 1359.

71. *Liberator*, March 28, 1862.

72. Holzer, *Lincoln President-Elect*, 409; Robert Harrison, "An Experimental Station for Lawmaking: Congress and the District of Columbia, 1862–1878," *CWH*, 53 (March 2007), 32; *CG*, 37th Congress, 2nd Session, 1191, 1300, 1523, 1526.

73. *CG*, 37th Congress, 2nd Session, 1191, 1266, 1300–1301, 1333–34, 1359, 1492, 1520–23; Curry, *Blueprint*, 39–41.

74. *CG*, 37th Congress, 2nd Session, 1336; John W. Crisfield to Mary Crisfield, April 25, 1862, John W. Crisfield Papers, Maryland Historical Society; *BD*, 1: 541; *CW*, 5: 169, 192; Nevins and Thomas, *Diary of George Templeton Strong*, 3: 216–17.

75. Michael J. Kurtz, "Emancipation in the Federal City," *CWH*, 24 (September 1978), 256; *Independent*, June 26, 1862; Daniel R. Goodloe, "Emancipation in the District of Columbia," *South-Atlantic*, 6 (1880), 245–70; Noah Brooks, *Washington in Lincoln's Time* (New York, 1895), 201; *Washington Star* in *New York Times*, December 27, 1887.

76. *African Repository*, 38 (August 1862), 243; Harrison, "Experimental Station," 33; Burlingame, *Dispatches*, 78.

77. *Annapolis Gazette* in *Easton Gazette* (Maryland), May 10, 1862; Charles B. Calvert to Lincoln, May 6, 1862; John H. Bayne to Lincoln, July 3, 1862, both in ALP; Ward Hill Lamon, *Recollections of Abraham Lincoln, 1847–1865*, ed. Dorothy Lamon (Chicago, 1895), 249–54; Henry G. Pearson, *James Wadsworth of Genesco* (New York, 1913), 134–40; Wagandt, *Mighty Revolution*, 119–20.

78. *CG*, 37th Congress, 2nd Session, 2623, 2231.

79. Roger N. Buckley, *Slaves in Red Coats: The British West India Regiments, 1795–1815* (New Haven, 1979); Christopher L. Brown and Philip D. Morgan, eds., *Arming Slaves: From Classical Times to the Modern Age* (New Haven, 2006); Berry, *Military Necessity*, 29–33; Jonathan Brigham, *James Harlan* (Iowa City, 1913), 170; Salter, *Life of James W. Grimes*, 196; *CG*, 37th Congress, 2nd Session, 2971; James G. Smart, ed., *A Radical View: The "Agate" Dispatches of Whitelaw Reid, 1861–1865* (2 vols.; Memphis, 1976), 2: 71–72.

80. *New York Herald*, December 10, 1861; *New York Times*, February 24, 1862; *CG*, 37th Congress, 2nd Session, 18, 2243; appendix, 194; Hamilton, *Limits of Sovereignty*, 7–9; Siddali, *From Property to Person*, 139–41.

81. *CG*, 37th Congress, 2nd Session, 1137, 2917–20, 2929, 2999; Jason Marsh to Trumbull, May 26, 1862, LTP.

82. Arnold, *History of Abraham Lincoln*, 259–60; *CG*, 37th Congress, 2nd Session, 2042–44, 2068, 2618.

83. Joseph C. G. Kennedy, *Population of the United States in 1860* (Washington, D.C., 1864), 557, 575; John A. Clark to Elihu B. Washburne, December 8, 1861, Elihu B. Washburne Papers, LC; *CG*, 37th Congress, 2nd Session, 2527.

84. William Aikman, *The Future of the Colored Race in America* (New York, 1862), 10. This essay originally appeared in the *Presbyterian Quarterly Review* for July 1862, and subsequently in pamphlet form.

85. George B. McClellan to Samuel L. M. Barlow, November 8, 1861, Barlow Papers, HL; Gienapp, *Abraham Lincoln*, 97–98.

7 *"Forever Free"*

1. Edward A. Miller, *Lincoln's Abolitionist General: The Biography of David Hunter* (Columbia, S.C., 1997), 96–104; Mark Grimsley, *The Hard Hand of War: Union Military Policy toward Southern Civilians, 1861–1865* (New York, 1995), 127.

2. Grimsley, *Hard Hand of War*, 127; Salmon P. Chase to Lincoln, May 16, 1862, ALP; *CW*, 5: 219, 222–23.

3. Frederic Bancroft, ed., *Speeches, Correspondence and Political Papers of Carl Schurz* (6 vols.; New York, 1913), 1: 206; *CW*, 5: 222–23; Burrus M. Carnahan, *Act of Justice: Lincoln's Emancipation Proclamation and the Law of War* (Lexington, Ky., 2007), 101–2; George W. Smalley to Sydney Howard Gay, June 21, 1862, GP; *Chicago Tribune*, May 24, 1862.

4. Miller, *Lincoln's Abolitionist General*, 104–6.

5. Judkin Browning, "Visions of Freedom and Civilization Opening before Them: African Americans Search for Autonomy during Military Occupation in North Carolina," in Paul D. Escott, ed., *North Carolinians in the Era of the Civil War and Reconstruction* (Chapel Hill, 2008), 74–75; Leon F. Litwack, *Been in the Storm So Long: The Aftermath of Slavery* (New York, 1979), 52–57; Steven V. Ash, *Middle Tennessee Society Transformed, 1860–1870: War and Peace in the Upper South* (Baton Rouge, 1988), 106–9; C. Peter Ripley, *Slaves and Freedmen in Civil War Louisiana* (Baton Rouge, 1976), 13–23; J. Carlyle Sitterson, *Sugar Country* (Lexington, Ky., 1953), 207–11; *New York Times*, December 30, 1861; *OR*, ser. 1, 10, pt. 2: 162–63.

6. Donald Yacovone, ed., *A Voice of Thunder: The Civil War Letters of George E. Stephens* (Urbana, Ill., 1997), 17, 203–4; Adams S. Hill to Sydney Howard Gay, undated (mid-June 1862), GP; Theodore Clarke Smith, *The Life and Letters of James A. Garfield* (2 vols.; New Haven, 1925), 1: 211–12; Sarah F. Hughes, ed., *Letters (Supplementary) of John Murray Forbes* (3 vols.; Boston, 1905), 1–2; Chandra Manning, *What This Cruel War Was Over: Soldiers, Slavery, and the Civil War* (New York, 2007), 43–50; D. D. Phillips to Lyman Trumbull, July 5, 1862, LTP.

7. *Private and Official Correspondence of Gen. Benjamin F. Butler during the Period of the Civil War* (5 vols.; Norwood, Mass., 1917), 1: 516–18, 613–15; 2: 41; *OR*, ser. 1, 15: 485–90; Louis S. Gerteis, *From Contraband to Freedman: Federal Policy toward Southern Blacks, 1861–1865* (Westport, Conn., 1973), 65–71.

8. Joseph Logsdon, *Horace White, Nineteenth-Century Liberal* (Westport, Conn., 1971), 90; *New York Tribune*, June 13, 1862.

9. Duane Mowry, ed., "Reconstruction Documents," *Publications of the Southern History Association*, 8 (July 1904), 292; Silvana R. Siddali, *From Property to Person: Slavery and the Confiscation Acts, 1861–1862* (Baton Rouge, 2005), 147–49; *Boston Daily Advertiser*, August 20, 1862; *Independent*, July 10, 1862.

10. Irving Katz, *August Belmont: A Political Biography* (New York, 1968), 120; William C. Davis, *Lincoln's Men* (New York, 1999), 90–91; Carl Schurz to Lincoln, May 19, 1862, ALP.

11. *CW*, 5: 278–79; *Liberator*, July 4, 1862.

12. Bancroft, *Speeches, Correspondence and Political Papers*, 1: 209; James R. Gilmore, *Personal Recollections of Abraham Lincoln and the Civil War* (Boston, 1898), 80; J. W. Edmonds, "What Shall Be the End?" *Continental Monthly*, 2 (July 1862), 4.

13. William C. Harris, *With Charity for All: Lincoln and the Restoration of the Union* (Lexington, Ky., 1997), 20–23, 40–50, 83–84; *CW*, 5: 302–3; *New York Times*, June 4, 1862; Leroy P. Graf and Ralph W. Haskins, ed., *The Papers of Andrew Johnson* (16 vols.; Knoxville, 1967–2000), 5: 210–11, 231.

14. Vincent Colyer, *Report of the Services Rendered by the Freed People to the United States Army . . .* (New York, 1864), 43–47; *OR*, ser. 1, 9: 395–402; *New York Times*, May 31, 1862; *Harper's Weekly*, June 21, 1862; *New York Evening Post*, June 17, 1862.

15. Colyer, *Report*, 5, 51; Harris, *With Charity for All*, 60–66; Virginia J. Laas, ed., *Wartime Washington: The Civil War Correspondence of Elizabeth Blair Lee* (Urbana, Ill., 1991), 156; Graf and Haskins, *Papers of Andrew Johnson*, 5: 451–52.

16. *CW*, 5: 317–18.

17. *New York Tribune*, July 14, 1862; Adams S. Hill to Sydney Howard Gay, undated (July 15, 1862), GP; Edward McPherson, *The Political History of the United States during the Great Rebellion* (2nd ed.; Washington, D.C., 1865), 214–18.

18. Isaac N. Arnold, *The History of Abraham Lincoln and the Overthrow of Slavery* (Chicago, 1866), 287–88; *CW*, 5: 324; Adams S. Hill to Sydney Howard Gay, July 14, 1862, GP.

19. *Philadelphia Press* in *Chicago Tribune*, July 18, 1862; *New York Times*, July 22, 1862; Richard Yates and Catharine Yates Pickering, *Richard Yates: Civil War Governor* (Danville, Ill., 1966), 174; *CG*, 37th Congress, 2nd Session, 3199.

20. Mary F. Berry, *Military Necessity and Civil Rights Policy* (Port Washington, N.Y., 1977), 41–42; George P. Sanger, ed., *The Statutes at Large, Treaties, and Proclamations of the United States of America*, vol. 12 (Boston, 1863), 597–600; *CG*, 37th Congress, 2nd Session, 3198.

21. *CG*, 37th Congress, 2nd Session, 3200–3201; *Chicago Tribune*, July 14, 1862.

22. Arnold, *History of Abraham Lincoln*, 277; Sanger, *Statutes at Large*, 589–92.

23. Siddali, *From Property to Person*, 232; Patricia M. L. Lucie, "Confiscation: Constitutional Crossroads," *CWH*, 23 (December 1977), 307; George S. Merriam, *The Life and Times of Samuel Bowles* (2 vols.; New York, 1885), 1: 353; *CG*, 37th Congress, 2nd Session, 2898.

24. *BD*, 1: 558–60; Michael Burlingame, *Abraham Lincoln: A Life* (2 vols.; Baltimore, 2008), 2: 358–59; *CG*, 37th Congress, 2nd Session, 3006, 3267–68, 3383, 3400; *CW*, 5: 329–31.

25. George W. Julian, *Political Recollections, 1840–1872* (Chicago, 1884), 219–20; *Independent*, July 24, 1862; *CG*, 37th Congress, 2nd Session, 3382; *Harper's Weekly*, July 26, 1862.

26. H. Draper Hunt, *Hannibal Hamlin of Maine: Lincoln's First Vice-President* (Syracuse, 1969), 428–29; Hannibal Hamlin to Lincoln, September 25, 1862, ALP; Matthew Pinkser, "Lincoln's Summer of Emancipation," in Harold Holzer and Sarah V. Gabbard, eds., *Lincoln and Freedom: Slavery, Emancipation, and the Thirteenth Amendment* (Carbondale, Ill., 2007), 81; *BD*, 1: 555; Adams S. Hill to Sydney Howard Gay, undated (July 9, 1862), GP.

27. Stephen W. Sears, ed., *The Civil War Papers of George B. McClellan* (New York, 1989), 344–45; Grimsley, *Hard Hand of War*, 2–3.

28. *WD*, 1: 70; Albert Mordell, ed., *Civil War and Reconstruction: Selected Essays by Gideon Welles* (New York, 1959), 236–39; Gideon Welles to Mary Welles, July 13, 1862, Gideon Welles Papers, LC. Much of Welles's "diary" is not contemporaneous, but was written later.

29. *CP*, 1: 348–50.

30. *CW*, 5: 336–37.

31. *Milwaukee Morning Sentinel*, July 19, 1862.

32. "The Cabinet on Emancipation," July 22, 1862, Edwin M. Stanton Papers, LC; *CP*, 1: 350–52; 3: 236–37; F. B. Carpenter, *The Inner Life of Abraham Lincoln: Six Months at the White House* (New York, 1867), 20–22; Montgomery Blair to Lincoln, September 23, 1862, ALP.

33. *Papers Relating to the Foreign Relations of the United States, 1861–1862* (Washington, D.C., 1862), 713–14; Howard Jones, *Abraham Lincoln and a New Birth of Freedom: The Union and Slavery in the Diplomacy of the Civil War* (Lincoln, Neb., 1999), 9–10, 38–41, 48–53, 63–67, 70; Bancroft, *Speeches, Correspondence and Political Papers*, 1: 185; Glyndon G. Van Deusen, *William Henry Seward* (New York, 1967), 330–34; Carl Schurz, *The Reminiscences of Carl Schurz* (3 vols.; New York, 1907–8), 2: 282–83; Frederick W. Seward, *Seward at Washington* (2 vols.; New York, 1891), 2: 118; "Cabinet on Emancipation," July 22, 1862; Francis B. Cutting to Edwin M. Stanton, February 20, 1867, both in Stanton Papers, LC.

34. Lerone Bennett, *Forced into Glory: Abraham Lincoln's White Dream* (Chicago, 2000), 502–3; *New York Evening Post* in *Chicago Tribune*, July 26, 1862; *New York Tribune*, August 22, 1862; *Springfield Weekly Republican*, August 30, 1862.

35. *CW*, 5: 341; *OR*, ser. 1, 11, pt. 3: 359; ser. 3, 2: 397; Daniel E. Sutherland, "Abraham Lincoln, John Pope, and the Origins of Total War," *Journal of Military History*, 56 (October 1992), 577–82.

36. *CW*, 5: 344–46, 350.

37. Michael Burlingame, ed., *Lincoln's Journalist: John Hay's Anonymous Writings for the Press, 1860–1864* (Carbondale, Ill., 1998), 309; Adams S. Hill to Sydney Howard Gay, August 25, 1862, GP; *Chicago Tribune*, August 12, 1861.

38. Robert Patterson to James R. Doolittle, April 15, 1862, James R. Doolittle Papers, LC; *CG*, 37th Congress, 2nd Session, Appendix, 95.

39. James Mitchell, *Report on Colonization and Emigration* (Washington, D.C., 1862), 5; *CG*, 37th Congress, 2nd Session, 1815, 2536; Henry G. Pearson, *The Life of John A. Andrew* (2 vols.; Boston, 1904), 2: 8; Brenda G. Plummer, *Haiti and the United States: The Psychological Moment* (Athens, Ga., 1992), 45–46; Alfred N. Hunt, *Haiti's Influence on Antebellum America* (Baton Rouge, 1988), 186.

40. *CG*, 37th Congress, 2nd Session, 944–46, 1605–6; James C. Conkling to Lyman Trumbull, December 16, 1861; Amherst Miller to Trumbull, January 24, 1862; W. W. Wright to Trumbull, July 7, 1862, all in LTP.

41. *CG*, 37th Congress, 2nd Session, 348, 441, 1107, 1631–34, 2301; appendix, 322; *New York Times*, April 17, 1862.

42. Leonard P. Richards, *"Gentlemen of Property and Standing": Anti-Abolition Mobs in Jacksonian America* (New York, 1970), 27–29; James L. Crouthamel, *James Watson Webb* (Middletown, Conn., 1969), 173; *Papers Relating to the Foreign Relations of the United States*, 704; Mitchell, *Report on Colonization*, 8–9.

43. Ambrose Thompson to Lincoln, April 25, 1862, ALP; Caleb B. Smith to Robert Murray, April 25, 1862; Smith to Lincoln, May 9, 1862, both in Letters Sent, September 8, 1858–February 1, 1872, RG 48, NA; *WD*, 1: 150–51; *CW*, 4: 547; James Mitchell to J. P. Usher, January 21, 1864, Communication Relating to Rev. James Mitchell, RG 48, NA. On Mitchell, see Mark E. Neely Jr., "Colonization and the Myth That Lincoln Prepared the People for Emancipation," in William A. Blair and Karen F. Younger, eds., *Lincoln's Proclamation: Emancipation Reconsidered* (Chapel Hill, 2009), 58–60.

44. *Lowell Daily Citizen and News*, June 16, 1862; James Mitchell to Lincoln, July

1, 1862, ALP; *Pacific Appeal*, September 20, 1862; Mitchell, *Report on Colonization*, 5.

45. Daniel A. Payne, *Recollections of Seventy Years* (Nashville, 1888), 146–48; *African Repository*, 38 (August 1862), 243. This is one of those rare letters by Lincoln that has almost never been quoted or cited. As far as I can ascertain, it is not included in any edition of his writings and the only book to have quoted it is Gregory U. Rigsby, *Alexander Crummell: Pioneer in Nineteenth-Century Pan-African Thought* (New York, 1987), 117–18.

46. *CW*, 5: 370–75; *New York Times*, August 15, 1862. James Oakes calls the meeting "a low point in his presidency." James Oakes, *The Radical and the Republican: Frederick Douglass, Abraham Lincoln, and the Triumph of Antislavery Politics* (New York, 2007), 194.

47. Edward M. Thomas to Lincoln, August 12, 1862, ALP; John Bigelow, *Retrospections of an Active Life* (5 vols.; New York, 1909–13), 1: 546; *CP*, 1: 362; *Douglass' Monthly*, 5 (October 1862), 722–23; *Christian Recorder*, September 27, 1862; *New York Times*, October 3, 1862; C. Peter Ripley et al., eds., *The Black Abolitionist Papers* (5 vols.; Chapel Hill, 1985–93), 5: 152.

48. *Douglass' Monthly*, 5 (September 1862), 705–7; Philip S. Foner, ed., *The Life and Writings of Frederick Douglass* (5 vols.; New York, 1950–73), 4: 313.

49. *London Daily News* in *Christian Recorder*, November 1, 1862; *National Anti-Slavery Standard*, August 20, 1862; Neely, "Colonization," 49–51; V. Jacque Voegeli, *Free but Not Equal: The Midwest and the Negro during the Civil War* (Chicago, 1967), 34; *Chicago Tribune*, August 22, 1862.

50. *New York Tribune*, August 26 and September 15, 1862; Caleb B. Smith to Samuel C. Pomeroy, September 12, 1862, Letters Sent, September 8, 1858–February 1, 1872, RG 48, NA; *CG*, 37th Congress, 2nd Session, 945; *Boston Daily Advertiser*, August 26 and 27, 1862; *New York Times*, August 30, September 13, and October 9, 1862; *San Francisco Evening Bulletin*, September 26, 1862; 39th Congress, 1st Session, Senate Executive Document 55, 13–16; Duane Mowry, ed., "Negro Colonization: From Doolittle Correspondence," *Publications of the Southern Historical Association*, 9 (November 1905), 402; *Baltimore Sun*, November 5, 1862.

51. *CP*, 1: 358; *New York Evening Post*, September 7, 1862; *Chicago Tribune*, August 29, 1862; William Salter, *The Life of James W. Grimes* (New York, 1876), 215; Rachel S. Thorndike, ed., *The Sherman Letters* (New York, 1894), 156–57; Benjamin Bannan to Lincoln, July 24, 1862; James W. White et al. to Lincoln, July 24, 1862, both in ALP.

52. Leonard Bacon, *Conciliation* (New Haven, 1862), 18–19; J. K. W. Levane and A. M. Milligan to Lincoln (1862); Petition from Washington County, Pennsylvania, August 28, 1862; Indiana Methodist Convention to Lincoln, September 12, 1862, all in ALP; Richard Carwardine, "Whatever Shall Appear to Be God's Will I Will Do: The Chicago Initiative and Lincoln's Proclamation," in Blair and Younger, *Lincoln's Proclamation*, 75–101; *CW*, 5: 420–25.

53. *New York Tribune*, August 20, 1862; Douglas L. Wilson, *Lincoln's Sword: The Presidency and the Power of Words* (New York, 2006), 148; *CW*, 5: 388–89.

54. *Harper's Weekly*, August 20, 1862; Timothy O. Howe to Lincoln, August 25, 1862, ALP; Wendell Phillips to Sydney Howard Gay, September 2, 1862, GP; Gay to Lincoln (August 1862), ALP; David Herbert Donald, *Lincoln* (New York, 1995), 368; *Springfield Weekly Republican*, September 27, 1862.

55. James M. McPherson, *Battle Cry of Freedom: The Civil War Era* (New York, 1988), 492; *CW*, 5: 356–57, 423; Jonathan Brigham, *James Harlan* (Iowa City, 1913), 172; James G. Smart, ed., *A Radical View: The "Agate" Dispatches of Whitelaw Reid, 1861–1865* (2 vols.; Memphis, 1976), 2: 74–75.

56. Gary Zellar, "The First Indian Home Guard and the Civil War on the Border and the Indian Expedition of 1862" (unpub. paper, American Historical Association annual meeting, 2010).

57. Berry, *Military Necessity*, 39–47; *Private and Official Correspondence*, 2: 125–27, 131–35, 164, 192, 207, 270; Adams S. Hill to Sydney Howard Gay, July 24, 1862, GP; *CG*, 38th Congress, 1st Session, 672; *OR*, ser. 1, 14: 377; Henry Wilson, *History of the Rise and Fall of the Slave Power in America* (3 vols.; Boston, 1872–77), 3: 370.

58. *Chicago Tribune*, August 27, 1862; *CP*, 1: 393–94; *WD*, 1: 142–43.

59. *CW*, 5: 433–36; Bennett, *Forced into Glory*, 504.

60. Mordell, *Civil War and Reconstruction*, 248–49; T. J. Barnett to Samuel L. M. Barlow, September 15, and October 6, 1862, Samuel L. M. Barlow Papers, HL; *Harper's Weekly*, October 4, 1862; *Springfield Weekly Republican*, September 27, 1862.

61. *Pacific Appeal*, September 27, 1862; *New York Tribune*, September 24, 1862; *OR*, ser. 1, 16, pt. 2: 909–11; Herbert Mitgang, ed., *Abraham Lincoln: A Press Portrait* (Chicago, 1971), 313; Norma L. Peterson, *Freedom and Franchise: The Political Career of B. Gratz Brown* (Columbia, Mo., 1965), 109–19; Benjamin Gratz Brown to Lincoln, September 27, 1862, ALP.

62. William H. Egle, *Life and Times of Andrew Gregg Curtin* (Philadelphia, 1895), 50–51, 138–40; Ira Harris to Lincoln, October 2, 1862; Charles Parker to Lincoln, September 28, 1862, both in ALP; *Independent*, September 25, 1862; Milton Meltzer and Patricia G. Holland, eds., *Lydia Maria Child: Selected Letters, 1817–1880* (Amherst, Mass., 1982), 419; Benjamin F. Wade to George W. Julian, September 29, 1862, Giddings-Julian Papers, LC; *Chicago Tribune*, September 24, 1862; *Douglass' Monthly*, 5 (October 1862), 721–22; *CW*, 5: 444.

63. *Springfield Weekly Republican*, September 27, 1862; *WD*, 1: 150–52, 158–59; Howard K. Beale, ed., *The Diary of Edward Bates, 1859–1866* (Washington, D.C., 1933), 262–63; *CP*, 1: 399, 402.

64. *WD*, 1: 123; Beverly W. Palmer and Holly B. Ochoa, eds., *The Selected Papers of Thaddeus Stevens* (2 vols.; Pittsburgh, 1997), 1: 319–20; Stephen J. Randall, *Colombia and the United States: Hegemony and Interdependence* (Athens, Ga., 1992), 47–49; Joseph Henry to Frederick W. Seward, September 5, 1862; Unknown to Joseph Henry, September 5, 1862, both in ALP; *Papers Relating to the Foreign Relations of the United States*, 883–84, 889, 893, 904; *New York Times*, October 9, 1862.

65. Seward, *Seward at Washington*, 2: 227; *The Works of Charles Sumner* (15 vols.; Boston, 1870–83), 5: 498; *Christian Recorder*, September 14, 1861; Gaillard Hunt, *Israel, Elihu and Cadwallader Washburn: A Chapter in American Biography* (New York, 1925), 116.

66. *Papers Relating to the Foreign Relations of the United States*, 202–4, 909–10; Mitchell, *Report on Colonization*, 16–19; J. P. Usher to George Edwards, October 7, 1862; Caleb B. Smith to Samuel G. Howe, October 24, 1862, both in Letters Sent, September 8, 1858-February 1, 1872, RG 48, NA; Roy F. Basler, ed., *The Collected Works of Abraham Lincoln: First Supplement, 1832–1865* (New Brunswick, N.J., 1974), 112.

67. William Dusinberre, *Civil War Issues in Philadelphia, 1856–1865* (Philadelphia, 1965), 137–47; Mary K. George, *Zachariah Chandler: A Political Biography* (East Lansing, 1969), 94–95; *New York Times*, October 7, 1862; Voegeli, *Free but Not Equal*, 58; John Cochrane to Lincoln, November 5, 1862; David D. Field to Lincoln, November 8, 1862, both in ALP; Cornelius Cole, *Memoirs of Cornelius Cole* (New York, 1908), 158; Henry G. Pearson, *James Wadsworth of Genesco* (New York, 1913), 156; Joel H. Silbey, *A Respectable Minority: The Democratic Party in the Civil War Era, 1860–1868* (New York, 1977), 85–86; Bruce Tap, "Race, Rhetoric, and Emancipation: The Election of 1862 in Illinois," *CWH*, 39 (June 1993), 101–25; Patience Essah, *A House Divided: Slavery and Emancipation in Delaware, 1638–1865* (Charlottesville, 1996), 176.

68. *Washington Daily Morning Chronicle*, November 17, 1862; Allen C. Guelzo, *Lincoln's Emancipation Proclamation: The End of Slavery in America* (New York, 2004), 80–81; John Eaton, *Grant, Lincoln and the Freedmen* (New York, 1907), 1–15; *Private and Official Correspondence*, 2: 447–50, 475; *Methodist*, in *Easton Gazette* (Maryland), August 23, 1862.

69. Edward Bates to Francis Lieber, October 21 and November 22, 1862; Lieber to Bates, November 25, 1862, all in Francis Lieber Papers, HL; *Official Opinions of the Attorneys General of the United States* (12 vols.; Washington, D.C., 1852–70), 10: 382–413; James P. McClure et al., eds., "Circumventing the Dred Scott Decision: Edward Bates, Salmon P. Chase, and the Citizenship of African Americans," *CWH*, 43 (December 1997), 279–309; *CP*, 1: 387; Rebecca J. Scott, "Public Rights, Social Equality, and the Conceptual Roots of the *Plessy* Challenge," *Michigan Law Review*, 106 (March 2008), 791; *New York Times*, December 12, 1862; *New York Tribune*, December 26, 1862.

70. David Davis to Leonard Swett, November 26, 1862, David Davis Papers, ALPLM; *CG*, 37th Congress, 3rd Session, appendix, 39.

71. *CW*, 5: 518–37; "Editor's Table," *Continental Monthly*, 3 (January 1863), 126.

72. Henry F. Brownson, ed., *The Works of Orestes A. Brownson* (20 vols.; Detroit, 1882–87), 17: 404–5; Smart, *Radical View*, 2: 187; Smith, *Life and Letters of James A. Garfield*, 1: 262–63; *CP*, 3: 320; Adams S. Hill to Sydney Howard Gay, December 2, 1862, GP.

73. Robert F. Horowitz, *The Great Impeacher: A Political Biography of James M. Ashley* (New York, 1979), 84; *CW*, 5: 434, 462–63, 470–71, 500, 505.

74. *CG*, 37th Congress, 3rd Session, 1016; Herman Belz, *Reconstructing the Union: Theory and Policy during the Civil War* (Ithaca, 1969), 100–15; John Cimprich, *Slavery's End in Tennessee, 1861–1865* (Tuscaloosa, Ala., 1985), 100–101; Brooks D. Simpson, *Let Us Have Peace: Ulysses S. Grant and the Politics of War and Reconstruction, 1861–1868* (Chapel Hill, 1991), 30; Graf and Haskins, *Papers of Andrew Johnson*, 6: 85–86; *CW*, 6: 26, 186–87; Benjamin P. Thomas and Harold M. Hyman, *Stanton: The Life and Times of Lincoln's Secretary of War* (New York, 1962), 243.

75. Charles H. Ambler, *Francis H. Pierpont* (Chapel Hill, 1937), 162–202; Forrest Talbot, "Some Legislative and Legal Aspects of the Negro Question in West Virginia during the Civil War, Part I," *West Virginia History*, 23 (April 1963), 8; *CG*, 37th Congress, 2nd Session, 3308; 3rd Session, 59.

76. *CG*, 37th Congress, 3rd Session, 50; William H. Seward to Lincoln, December 26, 1862; Edwin M. Stanton to Lincoln, December 26, 1862; Edward Bates to Lincoln, December 27, 1862, all in ALP; *WD*, 1: 208–9; *CW*, 6: 27–28; Ambler, *Francis H. Pierpont*, 202.

77. *CW*, 6: 41; Benjamin Quarles, *Lincoln and the Negro* (New York, 1962), 112; Mitchell, *Report on Colonization*, 21–22; *To His Excellency, Abraham Lincoln, President of the United States*, broadside, October 1, 1862, ALP; Beale, *Diary of Edward Bates*, 268; Laas, *Wartime Washington*, 223.

78. Guelzo, *Lincoln's Emancipation Proclamation*, 182; Harold Holzer et al., *The Emancipation Proclamation: Three Views* (Baton Rouge, 2006), x; Carpenter, *Inner Life*, 269; Seward, *Seward at Washington*, 2: 151.

79. *CW*, 6: 24–31.

80. Bennett, *Forced into Glory*, 525–26. *Harper's New Monthly Magazine* provided estimates of the number of slaves freed by the proclamation. *Harper's New Monthly Magazine*, 26 (February 1863), 411.

81. Benjamin R. Curtis, *Executive Power* (Boston, 1862); William Whiting, *The War Powers of the President, and the Legislative Powers of Congress in Relation to Rebellion, Treason and Slavery* (2nd ed.; Boston, 1862), i–v, 30, 66–68, 82.

82. Burlingame, *Abraham Lincoln: A Life*, 2: 362; *Memoir of the Hon. William Whiting* (Boston, 1874), 6–7; John Murray Forbes to Charles Sumner, December 27, 1862, ALP; Brian Dirck, "Abraham Lincoln, Emancipation, and the Supreme Court," in Brian Dirck, ed., *Lincoln Emancipated: The President and the Politics of Race* (DeKalb, Ill., 2007), 99–116; *New York Times*, December 31, 1862; *CW*, 6: 429.

83. *CW*, 6: 25; Graf and Haskins, *Papers of Andrew Johnson*, 6: 85–86; Arnold, *History of Abraham Lincoln*, 303.

84. *Harper's Weekly*, January 10, 1862; *Baltimore Sun*, January 5, 1862; Harris, *With Charity for All*, 69–70; William C. Harris, *Lincoln's Last Months* (Cambridge, Mass., 2004), 126; John Murray Forbes to Charles Sumner, December 27, 1862, ALP.

85. *New York Times*, January 3, 1863.

86. Lester D. Langley, *The Americas in the Age of Revolution, 1750–1850* (New Haven, 1996), 122, 269.

87. *Liberator*, January 9, 1863; Whiting, *War Powers*, i–ii.

88. *New York Herald*, January 1, 1863; Carnahan, *Act of Justice*, 123; Foner, *Life and Writings of Frederick Douglass*, 3: 214; CW, 5: 49.

89. CW, 7: 282; *Springfield Weekly Republican*, January 10, 1863; *Washington Daily Morning Chronicle*, December 8, 1862; *Pacific Appeal*, October 4, 1862.

90. *Christian Recorder*, February 14, 1863; Bancroft, *Speeches, Correspondence and Political Papers*, 1: 206.

91. Steven Hahn, *A Nation under Our Feet: Black Political Struggles in the Rural South from Slavery to the Great Migration* (Cambridge, Mass., 2003), 114; Benjamin R. Plumly to Lincoln, January 1, 1863, ALP.

92. Giuseppe Garibaldi et al. to Lincoln, August 6, 1863, ALP; Richard Enmale, ed., *The Civil War in the United States by Karl Marx and Frederick Engels* (3rd ed.; New York, 1961), 200. Marx wrote these words in August 1862, after Lincoln's final appeal to the border states for gradual emancipation.

8 *"A New Birth of Freedom"*

1. Mark A. Plummer, *Lincoln's Rail Splitter: Governor Richard J. Oglesby* (Urbana, Ill., 2001), 85.

2. William D. Foulke, *Life of Oliver P. Morton* (2 vols.; Indianapolis, 1899), 1: 230; BD, 1: 612–17; John Bigelow, *Retrospections of an Active Life* (5 vols.; New York, 1909–13), 1: 632; Moncure D. Conway, *Autobiography: Memories and Experiences* (2 vols.; Boston, 1904), 1: 381.

3. *New York Times*, October 18, 1863; CW, 5: 537; 7: 93.

4. Allan G. Bogue, "William Parker Cutler's Congressional Diary of 1862–63," CWH, 33 (December 1987), 327; Beverly W. Palmer and Holly B. Ochoa, eds., *The Selected Papers of Thaddeus Stevens* (2 vols.; Pittsburgh, 1997), 1: 354–56; CG, 37th Congress, 3rd Session, 601, 626–28, 680, 684, 858–63, 924; appendix, 93.

5. CW, 6: 59, 191; Henry G. Pearson, *The Life of John A. Andrew* (2 vols.; Boston, 1904), 2: 73–82; *Douglass' Monthly*, 5 (March 1863), 801, and (April 1863), 819; *Weekly Anglo-African*, January 17, 1863.

6. Adams S. Hill to Sydney Howard Gay, January 19, 1863, GP; Thomas Richmond to Abraham Lincoln, March 2, 1863, ALP; Steven V. Ash, *Firebrand of Liberty: The Story of Two Black Regiments That Changed the Course of the Civil War* (New York, 2008), 200–201; CW, 6: 56, 149, 158.

7. *Washington Daily Morning Chronicle*, April 20, 1863; *Harper's Weekly*, August 8, 1863; Edwin M. Stanton to Lincoln, February 8, 1864, ALP; Donald Yacovone, ed., *A Voice of Thunder: The Civil War Letters of George E. Stephens* (Urbana, Ill., 1997), 240.

8. CW, 6: 374; Ulysses S. Grant to Lincoln, July 23, 1863, ALP; *Harper's Weekly*, February 21, 1863; John Y. Simon, ed., *The Papers of Ulysses S. Grant* (Carbondale, Ill., 1967–), 8, 94n.

9. Steven V. Ash, *Middle Tennessee Society Transformed, 1860–1870: War and Peace in the Upper South* (Baton Rouge, 1988), 111–13; James M. McPherson, *What*

They Fought For, 1861–1865 (Baton Rouge, 1994), 30, 57–67; Chandra Manning, *What This Cruel War Was Over: Soldiers, Slavery, and the Civil War* (New York, 2007), 12–13, 83–85, 95, 115–16; Frank L. Byrne and Jean P. Soman, eds., *Your True Marcus: The Civil War Letters of a Jewish Colonel* (Kent, Ohio, 1985), 315–16; *CG*, 38th Congress, 1st Session, 404.

10. Ira Berlin et al., eds., *Freedom: A Documentary History of Emancipation, 1861–1867* (New York, 1982–), ser. 1, 1: 96; ser. 2, 1–15, 116–26, 185, 191–97; *OR*, ser. 3, 3: 860–61; Benjamin Quarles, *Lincoln and the Negro* (New York, 1962), 161–66; Thomas E. Bramlette to Lincoln, February 1 and March 8, 1864, ALP; John David Smith, "The Recruitment of Negro Soldiers in Kentucky, 1863–1865," *Register of the Kentucky Historical Society*, 72 (October 1974), 364–90.

11. *Brownson's Quarterly Review*, National Series, 1 (January 1864), 105; Berlin et al., *Freedom*, ser. 2: 1, 40, 303–12, 483–87; Drew G. Faust, *This Republic of Suffering: Death and the American Civil War* (New York, 2007), 45; George S. Burkhardt, *Confederate Rage, Yankee Wrath: No Quarter in the Civil War* (Carbondale, Ill., 2007), 1–2; *OR*, ser. 2, 4: 954; 6: 21–22.

12. *Chicago Tribune*, February 26, 1864; Berlin et al., *Freedom*, ser. 2, 28–29, 362–68, 401–2, 433–42, 611–13; Pearson, *Life of John A. Andrew*, 2: 98–117; *Christian Recorder*, April 16, 1864; H. O. Wagoner to Elihu B. Washburne, November 29, 1863, Elihu B. Washburne Papers, LC; *Harper's Weekly*, September 5, 1863; *CG*, 38th Congress, 1st Session, 2851.

13. Francis G. Shaw to Lincoln, July 31, 1863, ALP; Berlin et al., *Freedom*, ser. 2: 582–83; *CW*, 6: 357.

14. James Oakes, *The Radical and the Republican: Frederick Douglass, Abraham Lincoln, and the Triumph of Antislavery Politics* (New York, 2007), 211–14; *Douglass' Monthly*, 5 (August 1863), 849. Douglass offered various accounts of the meeting: *Liberator*, August 10, 1863; *Proceedings of the American Antislavery Society at Its Third Decade* (New York, 1864), 116–17; Allen T. Rice, ed., *Reminiscences of Abraham Lincoln by Distinguished Men of His Time* (New York, 1888), 185–88; Frederick Douglass, *Life and Times of Frederick Douglass* (Hartford, 1882), 347–50.

15. Burkhardt, *Confederate Rage*, 78–79, 109–10, 119–27; *CW*, 7: 302–3; James M. McPherson, *Tried by War: Abraham Lincoln as Commander in Chief* (New York, 2008), 247–48; *CG*, 38th Congress, 2nd Session, 24; *Chicago Tribune*, February 26, 1865.

16. *CW*, 2: 10; 7: 281, 499; Roy F. Basler, ed., *The Collected Works of Abraham Lincoln: First Supplement, 1832–1865* (New Brunswick, N.J., 1974), 243; Michael Burlingame, ed., *Dispatches from Lincoln's White House: The Anonymous Civil War Journalism of Presidential Secretary William O. Stoddard* (Lincoln, Neb., 2002), 167.

17. Robert Dale Owen, *The Wrong of Slavery, the Right of Emancipation and the Future of the African Race in the United States* (Philadelphia, 1864), 196–97; Adrian Cook, *The Armies of the Streets: The New York City Draft Riots of 1863* (Lexington, Ky., 1974); *New York Times*, March 7, 1864; *Washington Daily Morning Chronicle*, September 2, 1863; Yacovone, *Voice of Thunder*, 160; Francis Lieber to Charles

Sumner, March 6, 1864, Charles Sumner Papers, Houghton Library, Harvard University.

18. Rice, *Reminiscences*, 193; John Eaton, *Grant, Lincoln and the Freedmen* (New York, 1907), 175–76.

19. Harold Holzer, *Lincoln President-Elect: Abraham Lincoln and the Great Secession Winter, 1860–1861* (New York, 2008), 118; *CW*, 7: 542–43; 8: 272; Edmund Kelly to Lincoln, August 21, 1863; American Baptist Missionary Convention to Lincoln, August 21, 1863; African Civilization Society to Lincoln, November 5, 1863, all in ALP; *National Anti-Slavery Standard*, December 17, 1864; *Weekly Anglo-African*, May 14, 1864; *Washington National Intelligencer*, August 6, 1864; Julie Roy Jeffrey, *The Great Silent Army of Abolitionism: Ordinary Women in the Antislavery Movement* (Chapel Hill, 1998), 218; Michael Vorenberg, "Slavery Reparations in Theory and Practice," in Brian Dirck, ed., *Lincoln Emancipated: The President and the Politics of Race* (DeKalb, Ill., 2007), 125–27.

20. *CW*, 7: 483, 506–8; John McMahon to Lincoln, August 5, 1864, ALP.

21. *CW*, 4: 277; James Oakes, "Natural Rights, Citizenship Rights, States' Rights, and Black Rights: Another Look at Lincoln and Race," in Eric Foner, ed., *Our Lincoln: New Perspectives on Lincoln and His World* (New York, 2008), 115–16.

22. *Douglass' Monthly*, 5 (February 1863), 786; Willis Boyd, "Negro Colonization in the National Crisis, 1860–1870" (unpub. diss., University of California, Los Angeles, 1953), 154–56; Bogue, "William Parker Cutler's Congressional Diary," 328.

23. Thomas S. Malcolm, Memorandum, February 4, 1863; J. P. Usher to William H. Seward, April 22, 1863; Usher to Edwin M. Stanton, April 28, 1863; Usher to John Hodge, May 11, 1863, all in Letters Sent, September 8, 1858–February 1, 1872; Hodge to Usher, May 6 and 14, 1863, Communications Relating to Colonization in British Honduras, RG 48, NA; *New York Times*, May 18, 1863.

24. J. P. Usher to Lincoln, May 18, 1863, Letters Sent, September 8, 1858–February 1, 1872, RG 48, NA; *St. Louis Daily Globe-Democrat*, August 28, 1894.

25. *CW*, 6: 178; 39th Congress, 1st Session, Senate Executive Document 55, 27–61; Charles K. Tuckerman to Lincoln, March 31, 1863, ALP; J. P. Usher to Leonard Jerome, December 12, 1863, Letters Sent, September 8, 1858–February 1, 1872, RG 48, NA.

26. J. P. Usher to Charles K. Tuckerman, April 17 and July 8, 1863, and April 5, 1864, Letters Sent, September 8, 1858–February 1, 1872, RG 48, NA; James DeLong to Henry Conrad, June 25, 1863, ALP; Eaton, *Grant, Lincoln and the Freedmen*, 91–92; *CW*, 7: 164.

27. *Chicago Tribune*, March 23, 1864; J. P. Usher to Lincoln, May 18, 1863, Letters Sent, September 8, 1858–February 1, 1872, RG 48, NA; Michael Vorenberg, "Abraham Lincoln and the Politics of Black Colonization," *JALA*, 14 (Summer 1993), 40–43; Michael Burlingame and John R. Ettlinger eds., *Inside Lincoln's White House: The Complete Civil War Diary of John Hay* (Carbondale, Ill., 1997), 217; Michael Burlingame, ed., *Lincoln's Journalist: John Hay's Anonymous Writings for the Press, 1860–1864* (Carbondale, Ill., 1998), 280.

28. 38th Congress, 2nd Session, House Executive Document 1, pt. 3, 310; *Washing-

ton Daily Morning Chronicle, March 21, 1864; *New York Herald*, March 22, 1864; Michael Vorenberg, *Final Freedom: The Civil War, the Abolition of Slavery, and the Thirteenth Amendment* (New York, 2001), 106; *CG*, 38th Congress, 1st Session, 1770.

29. Heather C. Richardson, *The Greatest Nation of the Earth: Republican Economic Policies during the Civil War* (Cambridge, Mass., 1997), 164–67; F. P. Stanton, "The Freedmen of the South," *Continental Monthly*, 2 (December 1862), 731–32; *African Repository*, 40 (February 1864), 47.

30. *Douglass' Monthly*, 5 (October 1862), 724–25.

31. David A. Nichols, *Lincoln and the Indians: Civil War Policy and Politics* (Columbia, Mo., 1978), 76–127, 175–83; *OR*, ser. 1, 13: 686; Alexander Ramsay to Lincoln, November 28, 1862, ALP; *CW*, 2: 217; 3: 511; 4: 61; 5: 493, 542–43; 6: 6–7.

32. *CW*, 5: 526; 6: 151–53; 7: 47–48; 8: 147; Nichols, *Lincoln and the Indians*, 27–41, 186–99.

33. James M. McPherson, *Battle Cry of Freedom: The Civil War Era* (New York, 1988), 636–37. Douglas Wilson emphasizes the careful drafting and wide impact of Lincoln's public letters. Douglas L. Wilson, *Lincoln's Sword: The Presidency and the Power of Words* (New York, 2006).

34. Erastus Corning et al. to Lincoln, May 19, 1863, ALP; Philip S. Paludan, *"A People's Contest": The Union and Civil War, 1861–1865* (New York, 1988), 240–44; Charles B. Flood, *1864: Lincoln at the Gates of History* (New York, 2009), 22; Nathaniel P. Tallmadge to William H. Seward, May 24, 1863, ALP; *WD*, 1: 322.

35. *CW*, 6: 248, 262–69, 303–5.

36. Mark E. Neely Jr., *The Fate of Liberty: Abraham Lincoln and Civil Liberties* (New York, 1991), 67–71; Frederick P. Stanton, "Union Not to Be Maintained by Force," *Continental Monthly*, 5 (January 1864), 75; Henry W. Bellows, *Unconditional Loyalty* (New York, 1863), 5; Nicholas B. Wainwright, ed., *A Philadelphia Perspective: The Diary of Sidney George Fisher Covering the Years 1834–1871* (Philadelphia, 1967), 462. On wartime patriotism, the best account is Melinda Lawson, *Patriot Fires: Forging a New American Nationalism in the Civil War North* (Lawrence, Kans., 2002).

37. *CW*, 6: 407–10, 414, 430.

38. David P. Brown to Lincoln, June 15, 1863; Hugh McCulloch to Lincoln, June 16, 1863; William A. Hall to Lincoln, June 15, 1863; Israel Washburn Jr. to Lincoln, September 15, 1863, all in ALP; *Boston Transcript* in *Liberator*, September 11, 1863; V. Jacque Voegeli, *Free but Not Equal: The Midwest and the Negro during the Civil War* (Chicago, 1967), 121–31; Flood, *1864*, 22.

39. Gabor Boritt, *The Gettysburg Gospel: The Lincoln Speech That Nobody Knows* (New York, 2008), 98–113; *CW*, 7: 23.

40. *Springfield Weekly Republican*, November 28, 1863; Edward Everett to Lincoln, November 20, 1863, ALP; *Chicago Times*, November 23, 1863.

41. *CW*, 1: 108; *CG*, 37th Congress, 1st Session, 4; Dorothy Ross, "Lincoln and the Ethics of Emancipation: Universalism, Nationalism, Exceptionalism," *JAH*, 96 (September 2009), 387; Boritt, *Gettysburg Gospel*, 118. Psalm 90:10 reads, "The days of our years are threescore and ten."

42. *CG*, 37th Congress, 2nd Session, 736–37; Herman Belz, *Reconstructing the Union: Theory and Policy during the Civil War* (Ithaca, 1969), 40–63, 75–79.

43. *CW*, 6: 440–41; 7: 2.

44. *CW*, 6: 48–49, 358; Don E. Fehrenbacher and Virginia Fehrenbacher, eds., *Recollected Words of Abraham Lincoln* (Stanford, 1996), 146.

45. *CP*, 4: 6; *Brownson's Quarterly Review*, National Series, 1 (January 1864), 93.

46. *New York Times*, August 13, 1863; *Speech of the Hon. Montgomery Blair (postmaster general) on the Revolutionary Schemes of the Ultra Abolitionists . . .* (n.p., 1863), 3–6; *The Works of Charles Sumner* (15 vols.; Boston, 1870–83), 7: 493–546.

47. Montgomery Blair, *Comments on the Policy Inaugurated by the President, in a Letter and Two Speeches* (New York, 1863); Francis P. Blair Sr. to Appoline Blair, October 25, 1863, Blair Family Papers, LC; Henry Wilson to Lincoln, August 21, 1863; Zachariah Chandler to Lincoln, November 15, 1863, both in ALP; Burlingame and Ettlinger, *Inside Lincoln's White House*, 105–6; *CW*, 7: 24.

48. Allan Peskin, *Garfield* (Kent, Ohio, 1978), 223; Eric Foner, *The Story of American Freedom* (New York, 1998), 93–94; William E. Chandler to Montgomery Blair, November 20, 1863, Blair Family Papers, LC.

49. *CW*, 7: 36–56.

50. Michael Burlingame, *Abraham Lincoln: A Life* (2 vols.; Baltimore, 2008), 2: 594–98; *Chicago Tribune*, December 15, 1863; *Philadelphia North American and United States Gazette*, December 11, 1863; *New York Times*, December 10, 1863; Virginia J. Laas, ed., *Wartime Washington: The Civil War Correspondence of Elizabeth Blair Lee* (Urbana, Ill., 1991), 325–26; *Brownson's Quarterly Review*, National Series, 1 (January 1864), 93; *New York Herald*, December 11, 1863.

51. James G. Smart, ed., *A Radical View: The "Agate" Dispatches of Whitelaw Reid 1861–1865* (2 vols.; Memphis, 1976), 2: 110; Beverly W. Palmer, ed., *The Selected Letters of Charles Sumner* (2 vols.; Boston, 1990), 2: 216; *Boston Commonwealth*, December 18, 1863; *CP*, 4: 202–3, 225, 246; Montgomery Blair to Lincoln, December 6, 1864, ALP.

52. Michael Burlingame, ed., *Lincoln Observed: Civil War Dispatches of Noah Brooks* (Baltimore, 1998), 94; *Philadelphia Inquirer*, December 19, 1863; William B. Hesseltine, *Lincoln's Plan of Reconstruction* (Tuscaloosa, Ala., 1960), 96–97; *CW*, 6: 440.

53. Henry J. Raymond, *The Administration and the War* (New York, 1863), 9; Victor B. Howard, *Black Liberation in Kentucky: Emancipation and Freedom, 1862–1884* (Lexington, Ky., 1983), 36–61; Jesse W. Fell to F. Price, February 18, 1863, ALP.

54. John A. Williams, "The New Dominion and the Old: Ante-Bellum and Statehood Politics as the Background of West Virginia's 'Bourbon Democracy,' " *West Virginia History*, 33 (July 1972), 342–52; Richard O. Curry, "Crisis Politics in West Virginia, 1861–1870," in Richard O. Curry, ed., *Radicalism, Racism, and Party Realignment: The Border States during Reconstruction* (Baltimore, 1969), 83–90.

55. Richard P. Fuke, "Hugh Lennox Bond and Radical Republican Ideology," *JSH*, 45 (November 1979), 583–84; Charles L. Wagandt, *The Mighty Revolution: Negro Emancipation in Maryland, 1862–1864* (Baltimore, 1964), 26, 77–85, 143; Henry Winter Davis, *Speeches and Addresses* (New York, 1867), 384–92.

56. Montgomery Blair to Samuel L. M. Barlow, May 14, 1864, Samuel L. M. Barlow Papers, HL; Montgomery Blair to Augustus Bradford, September 26, 1863, Blair Family Papers, LC.

57. *CW*, 7: 226, 301–2.

58. Wagandt, *Mighty Revolution*, 222–29; *Chicago Tribune*, October 14, 1864.

59. *CW*, 8, 41; Allan Nevins and Milton H. Thomas, eds., *The Diary of George Templeton Strong* (4 vols.; New York, 1952), 3: 501; Burlingame, *Lincoln Observed*, 141–42; Joseph Hall to Lincoln, January 11, 1865, ALP; Herbert G. Gutman, *The Black Family in Slavery and Freedom, 1750–1925* (New York, 1976), 402–10; *Philadelphia North American and United States Gazette*, November 21, 1864.

60. *CW*, 6: 218, 234; Truman Woodruff to Lincoln, April 9, 1863; Samuel T. Glover to Lincoln, April 13, 1863; Charles D. Drake to Lincoln, April 29, 1863; Joseph W. McClurg to Lincoln, May 22, 1863, all in ALP.

61. William E. Parrish, *Turbulent Partnership: Missouri and the Union, 1861–1865* (Columbia, Mo., 1963), 143, 223n.; John M. Schofield to Lincoln, June 20, 1863; James S. Rollins to Lincoln, September 8, 1863, both in ALP; *CW*, 6: 291; *Kansas City Journal of Commerce* in *Milwaukee Daily Sentinel*, April 29, 1863.

62. William E. Parrish, *Frank Blair: Lincoln's Conservative* (Columbia, Mo., 1998), 178–80; *CW*, 6: 358, 500–503; Michael Burlingame, ed., *At Lincoln's Side: John Hay's Civil War Correspondence and Selected Writings* (Carbondale, Ill., 2000), 101.

63. Richard H. Abbott, *The Republican Party and the South, 1855–1877: The First Southern Strategy* (Chapel Hill, 1986), 25–27; Norma L. Peterson, *Freedom and Franchise: The Political Career of B. Gratz Brown* (Columbia, Mo., 1965), 145–51; *Chicago Tribune*, February 26, 1864; David D. March, "Charles D. Drake and the Constitutional Convention of 1865," *Missouri Historical Review*, 44 (January 1954), 110–23.

64. Charles H. Ambler, *Francis H. Pierpont* (Chapel Hill, 1937), 221–31.

65. Ruth C. Cowan, "Reorganization of Federal Arkansas, 1862–1865," *Arkansas Historical Quarterly*, 18 (Summer, 1959), 255–70; Don E. Fehrenbacher, *Lincoln in Text and Context* (Stanford, 1987), 153–54; *CW*, 7: 108, 155, 161.

66. Andrew Johnson to Lincoln, September 17, 1863; Horace Maynard to Lincoln, February 2, 1864; John S. Brien to Lincoln, January 30, 1864, all in ALP; Eric Foner, *Reconstruction: America's Unfinished Revolution, 1863–1877* (New York, 1988), 44; *CW*, 7: 209; 8: 58.

67. Foner, *Reconstruction*, 176; John Cimprich, *Slavery's End in Tennessee, 1861–1865* (Tuscaloosa, Ala., 1985), 109–10; Leroy P. Graf and Ralph W. Haskins, eds., *The Papers of Andrew Johnson* (16 vols.; Knoxville, 1967–2000), 6: 171–72, 251–52, 344, 489–91, 581–82; William C. Harris, *With Charity for All: Lincoln and the Restoration of the Union* (Lexington, Ky., 1997), 223–27.

68. Peyton McCrary, *Abraham Lincoln and Reconstruction: The Louisiana Experiment* (Princeton, 1978), 22–25, 78, 100, 160; William Cheault and Robert C. Reinders, "The Northern-Born Community of New Orleans in the 1850s," *JAH*, 51 (September 1964), 232–47; Joe G. Taylor, *Louisiana Reconstructed, 1863–1877* (Baton Rouge, 1974), 410.

69. *CW*, 6: 364–65; 7: 1–2.

70. *CW*, 7: 66; LaWanda Cox, *Lincoln and Black Freedom* (Columbia, S.C., 1981), 59–69; Ted Tunnell, *Crucible of Reconstruction: War, Radicalism, and Race in Louisiana, 1862–1877* (Baton Rouge, 1984), 26–50.

71. Cox, *Lincoln and Black Freedom*, 77; *OR*, ser. 1, 26, pt. 1, 694–95; ser. 3, 3: 232, 771; *CP*, 4: 133–34, 229–30, 320–21, 331; Nathaniel P. Banks to Lincoln, December 30, 1863, ALP; Harris, *With Charity for All*, 175–76.

72. Foner, *Reconstruction*, 49; Cox, *Lincoln and Black Freedom*, 94–95; *Liberator*, April 1, 1864; Ted Tunnell, "Free Negroes and the Freedmen: Black Politics in New Orleans during the Civil War," *Southern Studies*, 19 (Spring 1980), 16–17; *CW*, 7: 243. Lincoln's letter to Governor Hahn did not become public until June 23, 1865, when the *New York Times* printed it at the request of Congressman William D. Kelley.

73. McCrary, *Abraham Lincoln and Reconstruction*, 245–53; Taylor, *Louisiana Reconstructed*, 46; Nathaniel P. Banks to John Hay, March 28, 1864; Banks to Lincoln, July 25, 1864, both in ALP.

74. *CW*, 7: 486; 8: 106–7.

75. *New York Times*, January 3, 1863.

76. William H. Kimball, "Our Government and the Blacks," *Continental Monthly*, 5 (April 1864), 433–44; *Philadelphia Inquirer*, February 10, 1864.

77. John G. Sproat, "Blueprint for Radical Reconstruction," *JSH*, 23 (February 1957), 34–40; *OR*, ser. 3, 4: 382; James McKaye, *The Mastership and Its Fruits: The Emancipated Slave Face to Face with His Old Master* (New York, 1864), 35–37.

78. *Works of Charles Sumner*, 8: 480–81.

79. Willie Lee Rose, *Rehearsal for Reconstruction: The Port Royal Experiment* (Indianapolis, 1964); Cecil B. Ely Jr., ed., *A Virginia Yankee in the Civil War* (Chapel Hill, 1961), 148–50; William F. Messner, *Freedmen and the Ideology of Free Labor: Louisiana, 1862–1865* (Lafayette, La., 1978), 21–39; James D. Schmidt, *Free to Work: Labor Law, Emancipation, and Reconstruction, 1815–1880* (Athens, Ga., 1998), 95–97; *CP*, 3: 416.

80. Steven J. Ross, "Freed Soil, Freed Labor, Freed Men: John Eaton and the Davis Bend Experiment," *JSH*, 44 (May 1978), 215–17; Louis S. Gerteis, *From Contraband to Freedman: Federal Policy toward Southern Blacks, 1861–1865* (Westport, Conn., 1973), 123–26.

81. Berlin et al., *Freedom*, ser. 1, 3: 492–510, 757–62; McKaye, *Mastership*, 24; Gerteis, *From Contraband to Freedman*, 127–32.

82. Schmidt, *Free to Work*, 103–4; *CW*, 7: 212; Ronald F. Davis, *Good and Faithful Labor: From Slavery to Sharecropping in the Natchez District, 1860–1890* (Westport, Conn., 1982), 64–73; Eaton, *Grant, Lincoln and the Freedmen*, 163.

83. Eaton, *Grant, Lincoln and the Freedmen*, 88–91; Simon, *Papers of Ulysses S. Grant*, 8: 343–44; Edward L. Pierce, *Emancipation and Citizenship* (Boston, 1898), 87; John Eaton to Lincoln, July 18, 1863, ALP.

84. *CW*, 6: 453–57; 7: 98–99; *CP*, 3: 352; 4: 227–28, 259–60, 292–93; *Washington Daily Morning Chronicle*, January 19, 1864; *Weekly Anglo-African*, August 27, 1864; Rose, *Rehearsal*, 272–96.

85. *New York Times*, February 23, 1864; *CW*, 7: 54.

86. *CW*, 7: 145.

87. *CW*, 7: 185, 218; *New York Times*, July 10, 1864, and July 10, 1891; Daniel E. Sickles to Lincoln, May 31, 1864, ALP; Edcumb Pinchon, *Dan Sickles* (Garden City, N.Y., 1945), 208; Eaton, *Grant, Lincoln and the Freedmen*, 172–73.

88. *New York Times*, February 25, 1864.

9 *"A Fitting, and Necessary Conclusion"*

1. *New York Times*, December 12, 1862; Leonard Marsh, *On the Relations of Slavery to the War* (n.p., 1861), 6.

2. Henry Everett Russell, "Reconstruction," *Continental Monthly*, 4 (December 1863), 684; Michael Burlingame and John R. Ettlinger, eds., *Inside Lincoln's White House: The Complete Civil War Diary of John Hay* (Carbondale, Ill., 1997), 124; *Weekly Anglo-African*, September 23, 1863; *Liberator*, January 1, 1864; Sarah F. Hughes, ed., *Letters (Supplementary) of John Murray Forbes* (3 vols.; Boston, 1905), 2: 195.

3. Walter M. Merrill, ed., *The Letters of William Lloyd Garrison* (6 vols.; Cambridge, Mass., 1971–81), 5: 170–71; Julie Roy Jeffrey, *The Great Silent Army of Abolitionism: Ordinary Women in the Antislavery Movement* (Chapel Hill, 1998), 214–16; David Herbert Donald, *Charles Sumner and the Rights of Man* (New York, 1970), 148; *CG*, 38th Congress, 1st Session, 536; Charles F. Fletcher to Lincoln, March 10, 1864, ALP.

4. Isaac N. Arnold to Lincoln, December 4, 1863, ALP; Donald, *Charles Sumner*, 149–50; *CG*, 38th Congress, 1st Session, 1483–89; David E. Kyvig, *Explicit and Authentic Acts: Amending the U.S. Constitution, 1776–1995* (Lawrence, Kans., 1996), 159.

5. Michael Vorenberg, *Final Freedom: The Civil War, the Abolition of Slavery, and the Thirteenth Amendment* (New York, 2001), 36–49, 91; *CG*, 38th Congress, 1st Session, 17, 513, 1313–14; John D. Defrees to Lincoln, February 7, 1864, ALP; *CW*, 7: 172–73.

6. *CG*, 38th Congress, 1st Session, 761, 1419–24; Vorenberg, *Final Freedom*, 74–77.

7. Vorenberg, *Final Freedom*, 99–100; *CG*, 38th Congress, 1st Session, 1484, 2962; Lea S. VanderVelde, "The Labor Vision of the Thirteenth Amendment," *University of Pennsylvania Law Review*, 138 (December 1989), 439.

8. *CG*, 38th Congress, 1st Session, 1439–40, 1465, 2989–90; VanderVelde, "Labor Vision of the Thirteenth Amendment," 473–74; Vorenberg, *Final Freedom*, 132.

9. Dorothy Ross, "Lincoln and the Ethics of Emancipation: Universalism, Nationalism, Exceptionalism," *JAH*, 96 (September 2009), 397; *CG*, 38th Congress, 1st Session, 523; *Chicago Tribune*, November 14, 1864; Alexander Tsesis, *The Thirteenth Amendment and American Freedom* (New York, 2004), 40–45; James D. Schmidt, *Free to Work: Labor Law, Emancipation, and Reconstruction, 1815–1880* (Athens, Ga., 1998), 114–17.

10. *CG*, 38th Congress, 1st Session, 1490, 2995; *New York Herald*, April 9, 1864; *New York Times*, June 17, 1864.

11. Patrick W. Riddleberger, *George Washington Julian: Radical Republican* (Indianapolis, 1966), 188–94; George W. Julian, *Speeches on Political Questions* (New York, 1872), 221–26; *CG*, 38th Congress, 1st Session, 513, 3327; *Chicago Tribune*, January 28, 1864; James M. McPherson, *The Struggle for Equality: Abolitionists and the Negro in the Civil War and Reconstruction* (Princeton, 1964), 247–56.

12. *CG*, 38th Congress, 1st Session, 19, 709, 740, 2972; Beverly W. Palmer, ed., *The Selected Letters of Charles Sumner* (2 vols.; Boston, 1990), 2: 238; Heather C. Richardson, *The Greatest Nation of the Earth: Republican Economic Policies during the Civil War* (Cambridge, Mass., 1997), 230–36.

13. Allan G. Bogue, *The Earnest Men: Republicans of the Civil War Senate* (Ithaca, 1981), 189; Edward McPherson, *The Political History of the United States during the Great Rebellion* (2nd ed.; Washington, D.C., 1865), 242–43; Donald, *Charles Sumner*, 153–61; Palmer, *Selected Letters of Charles Sumner*, 2: 247, 253.

14. *CG*, 38th Congress, 1st Session, 554, 1639, 1652, 1705, 1844, 2351, 2386; Henry J. Raymond to James R. Doolittle, April 30, 1864, James R. Doolittle Papers, LC.

15. Lyman Trumbull to H. G. McPike (draft), February 6, 1864, LTP; *CG*, 38th Congress, 1st Session, 439; appendix, 64.

16. Theodore Clarke Smith, *The Life and Letters of James A. Garfield* (2 vols.; New Haven, 1925), 1: 375; *New York Times*, December 23, 1863; *CG*, 38th Congress, 1st Session, 114, 1197; Hans L. Trefousse, "Owen Lovejoy and Abraham Lincoln during the Civil War," *JALA*, 22 (Winter 2001), 15–32; *Springfield Weekly Republican*, June 11, 1864.

17. Philip S. Paludan, *The Presidency of Abraham Lincoln* (Lawrence, Kans., 1994), 268–69.

18. *CW*, 7: 281–82.

19. Benjamin B. French to Lincoln, May 5, 1864, ALP; Vorenberg, *Final Freedom*, 116–19; Charles B. Flood, *1864: Lincoln at the Gates of History* (New York, 2009), 107; McPherson, *Political History*, 410–14.

20. McPherson, *Political History*, 412–13; *New York Tribune*, June 1, 1864; Irving H. Bartlett, ed., "New Light on Wendell Phillips: The Community of Reform," *Perspectives in American History*, 12 (1979), 175.

21. *Chicago Tribune*, June 1, 1864; *Harper's Weekly*, June 18, 1864; Donald, *Charles Sumner*, 163; David E. Long, *The Jewel of Liberty: Abraham Lincoln's Re-election and the End of Slavery* (Mechanicsburg, Pa., 1994), 182; Hans L. Trefousse, *Thaddeus Stevens: Nineteenth-Century Egalitarian* (Chapel Hill, 1997), 147.

22. Vorenberg, *Final Freedom*, 123–26; *Independent*, June 16, 1864; *Proceedings of the First Three Republican National Conventions* (Minneapolis, 1893), 176–77, 225–26; *CW*, 7: 380.

23. James G. Smart, ed., *A Radical View: The "Agate" Dispatches of Whitelaw Reid, 1861–1865* (2 vols.; Memphis, 1976), 2: 166; William E. Parrish, *Turbulent Partnership: Missouri and the Union, 1861–1865* (Columbia, Mo., 1963), 186; Charles Hamlin to Sally Hamlin, June 9, 1864, Hannibal Hamlin Papers, University of Maine; *Proceedings of the First Three Republican National Conventions*, 177–78, 191, 203–22.

24. David Herbert Donald, *Lincoln* (New York, 1995), 505–6; Lincoln endorsement on John G. Nicolay to John Hay, June 5, 1864, ALP; Michael Burlingame, ed., *An Oral History of Abraham Lincoln: John G. Nicolay's Interviews and Essays* (Carbondale, Ill., 1996), 68; H. Draper Hunt, *Hannibal Hamlin of Maine: Lincoln's First Vice-President* (Syracuse, 1969), 179–89; Smart, *Radical View*, 2: 171–72.

25. *Chicago Tribune*, February 24 and June 10, 1864; Douglas L. Wilson and Rodney O. Davis, eds., *Herndon's Informants* (Urbana, Ill., 1998), 315.

26. Merrill, *Letters of William Lloyd Garrison*, 5: 207–8, 212; CG, 38th Congress, 1st Session, 3368; CW, 7: 418.

27. CG, 38th Congress, 1st Session, 2108, 3449; Herman Belz, *Reconstructing the Union: Theory and Policy during the Civil War* (Ithaca, 1969), 198–221; Michael Les Benedict, *A Compromise of Principle: Congressional Republicans and Reconstruction, 1863–1869* (New York, 1974), 79–81.

28. Burlingame and Ettlinger, *Inside Lincoln's White House*, 217–18; Belz, *Reconstructing the Union*, 226–27; CW, 7: 433–34; Harold M. Hyman, ed., *The Radical Republicans and Reconstruction, 1861–1870* (Indianapolis, 1967), 144–46; *Harper's Weekly*, August 20, 1864; Hans L. Trefousse, *Benjamin Franklin Wade: Radical Republican from Ohio* (New York, 1963), 220–24; Benedict, *Compromise*, 74–76.

29. CG, 38th Congress, 1st Session, 2104; WD, 2: 98.

30. Flood, *1864*, 99–116, 247; William Lee Miller, *President Lincoln: The Duty of a Statesman* (New York, 2008), 373.

31. *Harper's Weekly*, May 28, 1864; Martin F. Conway to Lincoln, July 22, 1864, ALP.

32. William C. Harris, *Lincoln's Last Months* (Cambridge, Mass., 2004), 107; James F. Jaquess to James A. Garfield, May 19, 1863, ALP; CW, 6: 330–31.

33. Horace Greeley to Lincoln, July 7 and 13, 1864, ALP; CW, 7: 451; Edward C. Kirkland, *The Peacemakers of 1864* (New York, 1927), 65–84.

34. James R. Gilmore, *Personal Recollections of Abraham Lincoln and the Civil War* (Boston, 1898), 232–47, 261–73.

35. *Chicago Tribune*, August 10, 1864; James M. McPherson, *Tried by War: Abraham Lincoln as Commander in Chief* (New York, 2008), 238; *New York Times*, July 23, 1864; Horace Greeley to Lincoln, August 8 and 29, 1864; Greeley to John G. Nicolay, September 4, 1864, all in ALP.

36. Long, *Jewel of Liberty*, 193; Charles D. Robinson to Lincoln, August 7, 1864, ALP.

37. CW, 7: 499–500.

38. CW, 7: 506–8.

39. Philip S. Foner, ed., *The Life and Writings of Frederick Douglass* (5 vols.; New York, 1950–75), 3: 405–7, 422–24; Frederick Douglass, *Life and Times of Frederick Douglass* (Hartford, 1882), 434–35; James Oakes, *The Radical and the Republican: Frederick Douglass, Abraham Lincoln, and the Triumph of Antislavery Politics* (New York, 2007), 229–30.

40. Thurlow Weed to William H. Seward, August 22, 1864; Henry J. Raymond to Lincoln, August 22, 1864, both in ALP; Henry J. Raymond to Simon Cameron, August 21, 1864, Simon Cameron Papers, LC.

41. *CW*, 7: 514.

42. Harris, *Lincoln's Last Months*, 15–16; *CW*, 7: 517–18; Michael Burlingame, ed., *With Lincoln in the White House: Letters, Memoranda, and Other Writings of John G. Nicolay, 1860–1865* (Carbondale, Ill., 2000), 152–53; Glyndon G. Van Deusen, *William Henry Seward* (New York, 1967), 386–87.

43. *New York Times*, December 17, 1864; *CW*, 6: 410–11; 7: 51.

44. Noah Brooks to John G. Nicolay, September 2, 1864, ALP; Joel H. Silbey, *A Respectable Minority: The Democratic Party in the Civil War Era, 1860–1868* (New York, 1977), 119–67; Long, *Jewel of Liberty*, 276–83; *General McClellan's Letter of Acceptance, Together with His West Point Oration* (New York, 1864), 1–2.

45. Frank Freidel, *Francis Lieber: Nineteenth-Century Liberal* (Baton Rouge, 1947), 351; Solomon N. Pettis to Lincoln, September 4, 1864; Theodore Tilton to John G. Nicolay, September 6, 1864; Thurlow Weed to William H. Seward, September 10, 1864, all in ALP; William Cassidy to Samuel L. M. Barlow, September 5, 1864, Samuel L. M. Barlow Papers, HL.

46. *CW*, 8: 18; Joseph Medill to Lincoln, February 17, 1864, ALP; *Springfield Weekly Republican*, October 1, 1864; Winfred A. Harbison, "Zachariah Chandler's Part in the Reelection of Abraham Lincoln," *Mississippi Valley Historical Review*, 22 (September 1935), 267–76; Long, *Jewel of Liberty*, 240–42.

47. Irving Katz, *August Belmont: A Political Biography* (New York, 1968), 146; Miller, *President Lincoln*, 375; Long, *Jewel of Liberty*, 153–71; Vorenberg, *Final Freedom*, 160.

48. *Harper's Weekly*, September 10, 1864; "The Next General Election," *North American Review*, 99 (October 1864), 560–66; Peter Ufland, "The Politics of Race in the Midwest 1864–1890" (unpub. diss., University of Illinois, Chicago, 2006), 13–19; *Speeches of William D. Kelley* (Philadelphia, 1864), 28, 47–55; William Dusinberre, *Civil War Issues in Philadelphia, 1856–1865* (Philadelphia, 1865), 175; Foner, *Life and Writings of Frederick Douglass*, 3: 406–7, 422–24.

49. Benjamin Quarles, *Lincoln and the Negro* (New York, 1962), 224–29; *Proceedings of the National Convention of Colored Men Held in the City of Syracuse, N. Y.* (Boston, 1864), 4–5, 44–52; Larry E. Nelson, "Black Leaders and the Presidential Election of 1864," *Journal of Negro History*, 63 (January 1978), 42–54.

50. *CW*, 7: 505, 512, 528; 8: 83; "Abraham Lincoln," *North American Review*, 100 (January 1865), 11.

51. *CW*, 8: 46, 100–101; Paludan, *Presidency*, 290; William E. Gienapp, *Abraham Lincoln and Civil War America* (New York, 2002), 174; Chandra Manning, *What This Cruel War Was Over: Soldiers, Slavery, and the Civil War* (New York, 2007), 186; Allan Nevins and Milton H. Thomas, eds., *The Diary of George Templeton Strong* (4 vols.; New York, 1952), 3: 511.

52. Richard J. Oglesby to Lincoln, November 20, 1864, ALP; *CW*, 8: 149–52; *New Orleans Tribune*, December 21, 1864.

    Two supposed instances of continued commitment by Lincoln to colonization date from after 1864. In January 1865, Lincoln dispatched General Daniel E. Sickles on a diplomatic mission to Colombia, where the colonization plans of

1862 had been focused. A Panama City newspaper reported that Sickles had been authorized to promise the government of Colombia one million dollars to allow the establishment of a colony of 30,000 emancipated slaves. Some biographers of Sickles accept the truth of this report, but neither Sickles's instructions from Secretary of State Seward nor his own letters to Washington say anything about such a project, and Sickles explicitly contradicted the rumor, explaining to his hosts that the freedmen "were invaluable to us in a military as well as in an economical point of view." The main purpose of his trip was to establish the right of transit across the Isthmus of Panama for American soldiers on their way to and from California. *Mercantile Chronicle* (Panama City), February 13, 1865; Sickles to Seward, January 26, February 23, and April 17, 1865, all in Dispatches from U. S. Ministers to Colombia, 1820–1906, vol. 20, RG 59, NA; Seward to Sickles, January 6 and March 18, 1865, both in Diplomatic Instructions of the Department of State 1801–1906, Special Missions: Instructions, vol. 2, RG 59, NA; Thomas Keneally, *American Scoundrel: The Life of the Notorious Civil War General Dan Sickles* (New York, 2003), 310–14; W. A. Swanberg, *Sickles the Incredible* (New York, 1956), 269–71.

Writing in the 1880s and 1890s, Benjamin Butler claimed that shortly before Lincoln's death, Butler suggested sending demobilized black soldiers to the Isthmus of Panama to construct a canal and that Lincoln, hoping to revive the idea of colonization, promised to speak to Seward about the proposal. Most historians doubt the reliability of Butler's recollection. In February 1865, Butler had explicitly repudiated the idea of colonization in a speech in Boston and a letter to Charles Sumner. Allen T. Rice, ed., *Reminiscences of Abraham Lincoln by Distinguished Men of His Time* (New York, 1888), 150; Benjamin F. Butler, *Autobiography and Personal Reminiscences of Major-General Benjamin F. Butler: Butler's Book* (Boston, 1892), 903–4; *New York Tribune*, February 6, 1865; Butler to Charles Sumner, February 5, 1865, Charles Sumner Papers, Houghton Library, Harvard University; Mark E. Neely Jr., "Abraham Lincoln and Black Colonization: Benjamin Butler's Spurious Testimony," *CWH*, 25 (March 1979), 77–83; Philip W. Magness, "Benjamin Butler's Colonization Testimony Reevaluated," *JALA*, 29 (Winter 2008), 1–29.

53. James Speed to Lincoln, December 22, 1861; Charles Sumner to Lincoln, October 12 and 24, 1864; Joseph Medill to Lincoln, November 19, 1864; William Stone to Lincoln, November 2, 1864; Norman B. Judd to Lincoln, December 28, 1864, all in ALP; *Baltimore American* in *Chicago Tribune*, December 25, 1864; *CG*, 38th Congress, 2nd Session, appendix, 83.

54. Michael Burlingame, *Abraham Lincoln: A Life* (2 vols.; Baltimore, 2008), 2: 748–49; Michael S. Green, *Freedom, Union, and Power: Lincoln and His Party during the Civil War* (New York, 2004), 164–66; Don E. Fehrenbacher and Virginia Fehrenbacher, eds., *Recollected Words of Abraham Lincoln* (Stanford, 1996), 383; Robert F. Horowitz, *The Great Impeacher: A Political Biography of James M. Ashley* (New York, 1979), 103; *Chicago Tribune*, January 12, 1865.

55. Vorenberg, *Final Freedom*, 176–87, 203; LaWanda Cox and John H. Cox, *Poli-*

tics, Principle, and Prejudice, 1865–1866 (Glencoe, N.Y., 1963), 6–13; Montgomery Blair to Samuel L. M. Barlow, January 12, 1865, Samuel L. M. Barlow Papers, HL; David Lindsey, *"Sunset" Cox: Irrepressible Democrat* (Detroit, 1959), 93.

56. Vorenberg, *Final Freedom*, 206; *CG*, 38th Congress, 2nd Session, 122, 236, 258–60, 531; Cox and Cox, *Politics*, 25.

57. *CG*, 38th Congress, 2nd Session, 531; Eric Foner, *Reconstruction: America's Unfinished Revolution, 1863–1877* (New York, 1988), 66; *Washington Daily Morning Chronicle*, February 1, 1865; George S. Merriam, *The Life and Times of Samuel Bowles* (2 vols.; New York, 1885), 1: 415–16; *CW*, 8: 254.

58. *CW*, 8: 151–52, 220; John G. Nicolay and John Hay, "Blair's Mexican Project and the Hampton Roads Conference, the Thirteenth Amendment," *Century Magazine*, 16 (October 1889), 839–44.

59. Wilson and Davis, *Herndon's Informants*, 413–14; *CW*, 8: 248; E. W. Clarke to Henry Wilson, January 31, 1865, Henry Wilson Papers, LC.

60. *CW*, 8: 284–87; John A. Campbell, *Reminiscences and Documents Relating to the Civil War during the Year 1865* (Baltimore, 1887), 5–17; Alexander H. Stephens, *A Constitutional View of the Late War between the States* (2 vols.; Philadelphia, 1868–70), 2: 599–619; R. M. T. Hunter, "The Peace Commission of 1865," *Southern Historical Society Papers*, 3 (April 1877), 168–76.

61. Stephens, *Constitutional View*, 2: 613–14; *CW*, 8: 260–61, 284–85; Burlingame, *Oral History*, 66; *WD*, 2: 237.

62. Zachariah Chandler to Letitia Chandler, February 10, 1865, Zachariah Chandler Papers, LC; Harris, *Lincoln's Last Months*, 122.

63. *Washington Daily Morning Chronicle*, February 4, 1865; Patience Essah, *A House Divided: Slavery and Emancipation in Delaware, 1638–1865* (Charlottesville, 1996), 2–6, 18; Robert J. Breckinridge to Lincoln, November 16, 1864; Edwin M. Stanton to Lincoln, March 3, 1865, both in ALP; Harold D. Tallant, *Evil Necessity: Slavery and Political Culture in Antebellum Kentucky* (Lexington, Ky., 2003), 18; William H. Williams, *Slavery and Freedom in Delaware, 1639–1865* (Wilmington, 1996), 170; *Louisville Journal* in *Chicago Tribune*, November 24, 1864; Marion B. Lucas, *A History of Blacks in Kentucky*, vol. 1: *From Slavery to Segregation, 1760–1891* (Frankfort, 1992), 159–60.

64. Cornelius Cole, *Memoirs of Cornelius Cole* (New York, 1908), 220; *CG*, 38th Congress, 2nd Session, 138, 179, 199, 202, 236.

65. *Harper's Weekly*, February 11 and 25, 1865; *A Memorial Discourse by Rev. Henry Highland Garnet Delivered in the Hall of the House of Representatives* (Philadelphia, 1865), 89; *Washington Daily Morning Chronicle*, March 1, 1865; *Christian Recorder*, February 25, 1865; Vorenberg, *Final Freedom*, 166.

66. John Cochrane to Lincoln, January 28, 1865, ALP; Foner, *Reconstruction*, 62.

67. Foner, *Reconstruction*, 62–65; Jean-Charles Houzeau, *My Passage at the New Orleans "Tribune": A Memoir of the Civil War Era*, ed. David C. Rankin, trans. Gerard F. Denault (Baton Rouge, 1984), 2–5, 19–23; *New Orleans Tribune*, February 23, 1865.

68. *CW*, 8: 106–7, 148–49; *Washington Daily Morning Chronicle*, February 6, 1865.

69. Palmer, *Selected Letters of Charles Sumner*, 2: 258; Donald, *Charles Sumner*, 196.

70. Belz, *Reconstructing the Union*, 251–54; William C. Harris, *With Charity for All: Lincoln and the Restoration of the Union* (Lexington, Ky., 1997), 235; Burlingame, *Abraham Lincoln: A Life*, 2: 777; CG, 38th Congress, 2nd Session, 967–68, 1002.

71. Harris, *With Charity for All*, 237–44; CG, 38th Congress, 2nd Session, 582; *The Works of Charles Sumner* (15 vols.; Boston, 1870–83), 9: 322; *Springfield Weekly Republican*, April 8, 1865; CW, 8: 337.

72. Burlingame, *Abraham Lincoln: A Life*, 2: 773–75; Palmer, *Selected Letters of Charles Sumner*, 2: 273, 279.

73. McPherson, *Struggle for Equality*, 287–95; *Liberator*, November 11, 1864, January 13 and February 3 and 10, 1865; *National Anti-Slavery Standard*, May 20, 1865.

74. "Colloquy with Colored Ministers," *Journal of Negro History*, 16 (January 1931), 88–94; CP, 5: 6–7.

75. Foner, *Reconstruction*, 71.

76. John C. Robinson to Lincoln, February 1, 1865, ALP; John Eaton, *Grant, Lincoln and the Freedmen* (New York, 1907), 231; CW, 8: 325.

77. Foner, *Reconstruction*, 69–70, 159; Celia E. Naylor, *African Cherokees in Indian Territory: From Chattel to Citizens* (Chapel Hill, 2008), 222–23.

78. Nicholas B. Wainwright, ed., *A Philadelphia Perspective: The Diary of Sidney George Fisher Covering the Years 1834–1871* (Philadelphia, 1967), 499.

EPILOGUE *"Every Drop of Blood"*

1. Benjamin Quarles, *Lincoln and the Negro* (New York, 1962), 233–35; Gabor S. Boritt, *The Gettysburg Gospel: The Lincoln Speech That Nobody Knows* (New York, 2006), 121; Isaac N. Arnold, *The History of Abraham Lincoln and the Overthrow of Slavery* (Chicago, 1866), 628.

2. Eric Foner, *Reconstruction: America's Unfinished Revolution, 1863–1877* (New York, 1988), 71–72.

3. CW, 8: 332–33.

4. Thomas A. Bayard to Samuel L. M. Barlow, March 12, 1865, Samuel L. M. Barlow Papers, HL.

5. CW, 8: 282, 332–33.

6. Benjamin Barondess, *Three Lincoln Masterpieces* (Charleston, W. Va., 1954), 84; Philip S. Foner, ed., *The Life and Writings of Frederick Douglass* (5 vols.; New York, 1950–75), 2: 190; *Chicago Tribune*, March 6, 1865, quoting its editorial of August 12, 1862.

7. CW, 8: 333; Mark Neely Jr., "The Constitution and Civil Liberties under Lincoln," in Eric Foner, ed., *Our Lincoln: New Perspectives on Lincoln and His World* (New York, 2008), 54–57; CW, 8: 217, 308, 319–20; Beverly W. Palmer, ed., *The Selected Letters of Charles Sumner* (2 vols.; Boston, 1990), 2: 281.

8. William C. Harris, *Lincoln's Last Months* (Cambridge, Mass., 2004), 142; Barondess, *Three Lincoln Masterpieces*, 68; Ronald C. White, *Lincoln's Greatest*

Speech: The Second Inaugural (New York, 2002), 116–19; Nicholas Parillo, "Lincoln's Calvinist Transformation: Emancipation and War," *CWH*, 46 (September 2004), 227–54; Gary S. Smith, *Faith and the Presidency: From George Washington to George W. Bush* (New York, 2006), 91–99; *CW*, 5: 403–4.

9. *CW*, 4: 482; 6: 155–56, 332, 497, 535–36; 7: 533; 8: 55; Lucas E. Morel, *Lincoln's Sacred Effort: Defining Religion's Role in American Self-Government* (Lanham, Md., 2000); Richard Carwardine, "Lincoln's Religion," in Foner, ed., *Our Lincoln*, 223–48; Mark A. Noll, " 'Both . . . Pray to the Same God': The Singularity of Lincoln's Faith in the Era of the Civil War," *JALA*, 18 (Winter 1997), 1–26.

10. Frederick Douglass's *Life and Times of Frederick Douglass* (Hartford, 1882), 444–45, presents Douglass's later recollection of his meeting with Lincoln after the speech. Henry Clay Warmoth, an army officer from Illinois and later Reconstruction governor of Louisiana, who was present, took note in his diary of the encounter and of Lincoln's words. Henry Clay Warmoth Diary, March 4, 1865, Henry Clay Warmoth Papers, Southern Historical Collection, University of North Carolina at Chapel Hill.

11. Barondess, *Three Lincoln Masterpieces*, 89; Harris, *Lincoln's Last Months*, 149; White, *Lincoln's Greatest Speech*, 183–94; *New York Times*, April 17, 1865; Worthington C. Ford, ed., *A Cycle of Adams Letters, 1861–1865* (2 vols.; Boston, 1920), 2: 257; *CW*, 8: 356; Allan Nevins and Milton H. Thomas, eds., *The Diary of George Templeton Strong* (4 vols.; New York, 1952), 3: 561.

12. *CW*, 8: 360–61.

13. A. A. Hoehling and Mary Hoehling, *The Day Richmond Died* (San Diego, 1981), 202–7, 240–42; Edwin S. Redkey, ed., *A Grand Army of Black Men: Letters from African-American Soldiers in the Union Army, 1861–1865* (New York, 1992), 175–78; R. J. M. Blackett, ed., *Thomas Morris Chester: Black Civil War Correspondent* (Baton Rouge, 1989), 3, 294–97; Palmer, *Selected Letters of Charles Sumner*, 2: 282.

14. *CW*, 8: 386–89; Charles H. Ambler, *Francis H. Pierpont* (Chapel Hill, 1937), 254–58.

15. *CW*, 8: 405–6; Michael Burlingame, *Abraham Lincoln: A Life* (2 vols.; Baltimore, 2008), 2: 794; George W. Julian, *Political Recollections, 1840–1872* (Chicago, 1884), 254; *WD*, 2: 279.

16. *New York World*, April 13, 1865; Foner, *Reconstruction*, 182; Philip S. Paludan, *The Presidency of Abraham Lincoln* (Lawrence, Kans., 1994), 305.

17. *CW*, 399–405; Peyton McCrary, *Abraham Lincoln and Reconstruction: The Louisiana Experiment* (Princeton, 1978), 5–7; *CP*, 5: 17.

18. Jerome Mushkat, *The Reconstruction of the New York Democracy, 1861–1874* (Rutherford, N.J., 1981), 65; Palmer, *Selected Letters of Charles Sumner*, 2: 283–85; R. F. Fuller to Charles Sumner, April 13, 1865, Charles Sumner Papers, Houghton Library, Harvard University; *New York Times*, April 13, 1865.

19. *New York World*, April 13, 1865; *Independent*, April 13, 1865; *Chicago Tribune*, April 8 and 14, 1865; Burlingame, *Abraham Lincoln: A Life*, 2: 803.

20. *CP*, 1: 528–30; 5: 15–16; Benjamin P. Thomas and Harold M. Hyman, *Stanton:*

The Life and Times of Lincoln's Secretary of War (New York, 1962), 357–58; WD, 2: 281.

21. WD, 2: 298; Burlingame, *Abraham Lincoln: A Life*, 2: 819–25; *New York World*, April 17, 1865.

22. *Independent*, April 20, 1865; Boritt, *Gettysburg Gospel*, 173–87; David W. Blight, *Race and Reunion: The Civil War in American Memory* (Cambridge, Mass., 2001).

23. "Reconstruction," *North American Review*, 100 (April 1865), 556.

24. *New York Times*, April 17, 1865.

25. Foner, *Reconstruction*, 176–280.

26. Andrew Ward, *The Slaves' War* (Boston, 2008), 253; "Abraham Lincoln: A Speech," (ca. December 1865), Frederick Douglass Papers, LC.

27. *The Works of Charles Sumner* (15 vols.; Boston, 1870–83), 9: 427.

28. *CG*, 38th Congress, 1st Session, 2615; Lydia Maria Child to George W. Julian, April 8, 1865, Giddings-Julian Papers, LC.

29. Henry Cowles to John Pierpont, March 6, 1863, ALP.

Index

About the Author

ERIC FONER, DeWitt Clinton Professor of History at Columbia University, is one of this country's most prominent historians. He received his doctoral degree at Columbia under the supervision of Richard Hofstadter. He has served as president of the three major professional organizations: the Organization of American Historians, the American Historical Association, and the Society of American Historians.

Professor Foner's publications have concentrated on the intersections of intellectual, political, and social history, and the history of American race relations. His books include *Free Soil, Free Labor, Free Men: The Ideology of the Republican Party before the Civil War* (1970; reissued with new preface 1995); *Tom Paine and Revolutionary America* (1976); *Nothing but Freedom: Emancipation and Its Legacy* (1983); *Reconstruction: America's Unfinished Revolution, 1863-1877* (1988) (winner, among other awards, of the Bancroft Prize, Parkman Prize, and Los Angeles Times Book Award); *The Story of American Freedom* (1998); and *Who Owns History? Rethinking the Past in a Changing World* (2002). His survey textbook of American history, *Give Me Liberty! An American History* and a companion volume of documents, *Voices of Freedom*, appeared in 2004 and are revised regularly. His most recent books are *Forever Free: The Story of Emancipation and Reconstruction* (2005), and *Our Lincoln: New Perspectives on Lincoln and His World* (2008), an edited collection of original essays . His books have been translated into Chinese, Korean, Italian, Japanese, Portuguese, and Spanish.

Eric Foner has also been the co-curator, with Olivia Mahoney, of two prize-winning exhibitions on American history: *A House Divided: America in the Age of Lincoln*, which opened at the Chicago Historical Society in 1990, and *America's Reconstruction: People and Politics after the Civil War*, which opened at the Virginia Historical Society in 1995 and traveled to several other locations.

Eric Foner is a winner of the Great Teacher Award from the Society of Columbia Graduates (1991), and the Presidential Award for Outstanding Teaching from Columbia University (2006). He was named Scholar of the Year by the New York Council for the Humanities in 1995. He is an elected fellow of the American Academy of Arts and Sciences and the British Academy, and holds an honorary doctorate from Iona College. He has taught at Cambridge University as Pitt Professor of American History and Institutions, Oxford University as Harmsworth Professor of American History, Moscow State University as Fulbright Professor, and at Queen Mary, University of London as Leverhulme Visiting Scholar. He serves on the editorial boards of *Past and Present* and *The Nation*, and has written for the *New York Times*, *Washington Post*, *Los Angeles Times*, *London Review of Books*, and many other publications, and has appeared on numerous television and radio shows, including *Charlie Rose*, *Book Notes*, *The Daily Show with Jon Stewart*, *The Colbert Report*, *Bill Moyers Journal*, *Fresh Air*, and *All Things Considered*, and in historical documentaries on PBS and the History Channel. He has lectured extensively to both academic and nonacademic audiences.